Recommended by Teachers
Trusted by Toppers

AF814570

All in One

English Language & Literature

CBSE Class 9

Reading, Writing, Grammar & Literature ▪ Review Exercises ▪ Sample Papers

Authors
Parneet Kaur
Neha Vats

arihant
SUCCESS AND NOTHING LESS

arihant
SUCCESS AND NOTHING LESS

ARIHANT PRAKASHAN
(School Division Series)

卐 ADMINISTRATIVE & PRODUCTION OFFICES

Regd. Office

'Ramchhaya' 4577/15, Agarwal Road, Darya Ganj, New Delhi -110002
Tele: 011- 47630600, 43518550; Fax: 011- 23280316

卐 *Head Office*

Kalindi, TP Nagar, Meerut (UP) - 250002, Tel: 0121-7156203, 7156204

卐 SALES & SUPPORT OFFICES

Agra, Ahmedabad, Bengaluru, Bareilly, Chennai, Delhi, Guwahati, Hyderabad, Jaipur, Jhansi, Kolkata, Lucknow, Nagpur & Pune.

PO No : TXT-XX-XXXXXXX-X-XX

Published By Arihant Publications (India) Ltd.

For further information about the books published by Arihant, log on to www.arihantbooks.com or e-mail at info@arihantbooks.com

Follow us on

卐 PRICE ₹415.00

PRODUCTION TEAM

Publishing Managers
Mahendra Singh Rawat & Keshav Mohan

Cover Designer
Rakesh Rawat

Inner Designer
Ankit Tyagi

Project Head
Manju

Page Layouting
Lalit Chaprana

Proof Readers
Harsh Agarwal, Naina Rajya

Index *cum* Study Planner

SECTION C

Literature Textbook

Prose- Beehive

One Book- Endless Features
to Help you Succeed

Chapter Summary

In each chapter of the Prose, Poetry & Supplementary, Summary of the chapter & Explanation is given in simple and easy to understand language. It will help the students to understand theme of the chapter easily.

The Fun They Had

by Isaac Asimov

CHAPTER 1

CHAPTER SUMMARY The chapter 'The Fun They Had' has been written by Isaac Asimov. The story is a fictional account of how books and schools will be in the future. Asimov compares the educational systems of today with that of the year 2157 through the character of an eleven year old girl, Margie. The story compares the robotic teachers of 2157 with the human teachers of the past and highlights the lack of human interaction and fun.

Word Meaning

In each chapter of the Prose, Poetry and Supplementary, difficult words are given along with their meaning. This will help students to understand difficult words easily.

Word Meaning

Word	Meaning	Word	Meaning
crinkly	with many folds or lines	punch code	method of giving answers by punching holes in paper
attic	a space just below the roof	geared (to)	adjusted to a particular standard or level
stood still	were not moving	superior eyes	eyes showing his feeling of being better
gee	exclamation of surprise	loftily	in a superior way
you're through with	you have read	betcha	(used in informal conversation) (I) bet you (in fast speech); I'm sure.
scornful	hateful	dispute	disagreement
sent for	called	nonchalantly	not showing much of interest or enthusiasm; carelessly
county inspector	a local person whose job is to repair robots	tucked	kept safely
took the teacher apart	opened the inside of the robot	lit up	lighted
put it together	assemble it	with a sigh	unwillingly
slot	a given space, time or position		

Format of a Diary Entry

Today you went for a trip to the zoo which made you upset about the condition of the caged birds and animals. Write a Diary Entry in about 100-120 words expressing your feelings.

Day and Date / Time: Wednesday, 27th October, 20XX 10:00 pm

Greetings: Dear Diary

Content/Body: Today turned from excitement to disappointment for me. I went to my favourite place in the world. Yes! I went to the zoo with my family. It is not hidden from people who know me that I am very fond of birds and animals. However, contrary to my expectations, it turned out to be a sad experience. I did see many birds and animals in the zoo. However, they did not look happy at all in their confined spaces. Even though they were well-fed, they looked angry. I think that they were missing the blue skies and the freedom to run around in the vast forest land. Not to forget, the constant poking of humans must have irritated them. Sure, they are fed well and receive regular health check-ups, but I can't overlook how tired and angry they seemed. I guess that is a result of their inactive life.
I don't think zoos are bad as they protect many endangered species. Still, it hurts to see the animals and birds being kept that way. I don't think I can visit a zoo again.

Singnature/Name of the writer: XYZ

Formats in Writing Section

In Writing section standard format has been given. This will help students to learn proper format of each writing task.

One Book- Endless Features

to Help you Succeed

NCERT Folder

Here, we have covered questions of CBSE Textbook (Intext & Exercise) with their detailed answer in simple and easy language.

NCERT FOLDER

NCERT Intext and Exercise Questions

THINKING ABOUT THE TEXT (NCERT PAGE 10)

I. Answer these questions in a few words or a couple of sentences each.

Q.1 How old are Margie and Tommy?

Ans. Margie is eleven and Tommy is thirteen years old.

Q.2 What did Margie write in her diary?

Ans. Margie wrote a diary entry dated 17th May, 2157, titled 'Today Tommy found a real book.'

She wrote about Tommy finding an actual book in the attic.

Q.3 Had Margie ever seen a book before?

Ans. No, Margie had never seen a book before.

Q.4 What things about the book did Margie find strange?

Ans. Margie found many things about the book strange. The pages were yellow and wrinkled. The words were not moving and when one read it for the second time, everything was the same as earlier.

Ans. (i) 'They' refers to the people who lived hundreds of years ago and went to an actual school.

(ii) Here, 'regular' refers to the usual (mechanical) teachers that Tommy and Margie had.

(iii) The human teacher of earlier times is being contrasted with a mechanical teacher.

III. Answer each of these questions in a short paragraph (about 30 words).

Q.1 What kind of teachers did Margie and Tommy have?

Ans. Margie and Tommy had mechanical teachers in the form of a computer. The teacher had a big black screen on which all the lessons were flashed and questions were asked. The teacher also had a slot where students had to put their homework and test papers.

Q.2 Why did Margie's mother send for the County Inspector?

Ans The mechanical teacher had been testing Margie in

Assessment Exercise

At the end of the chapter, there are unsolved questions for practice and assessment of students. By practising these questions, students can assess their preparation level for the chapter.

Review Exercise

Each chapter cover all types of questions like Extract Based Questions, Short Answer & Long Answer Type Questions.

ASSESSMENT EXERCISE

Extract Based Questions

Read the following extracts carefully and answer the questions that follow.

1. They turned the pages, which were yellow and crinkly, and it was awfully funny to read words that stood still instead of moving the way they were supposed to–on a screen, you know. And then when they turned back to the page before, it had the same words on it that it had when they read it the first time.

   (i) What does the phrase 'yellow and crinkly' signify?
   (a) It is dirty. (b) It is old.
   (c) It is destroyed. (d) It is beautiful.

   (ii) Complete the sentence appropriately.
   The'screen' here refer to ....

   (iii) Why was the book funny to read for them?

   (iv) Where was the book found?

2. Margie was scornful. "School? What's there to write about school? I hate school."

   Margie always hated school but now she hated it more than ever. The mechanical teacher had been giving her test after test in geography and she had been doing worse and worse until her mother had shaken her head sorrowfully and sent for the County Inspector.

   (i) Margie had not been doing well in
   (a) Geography (b) Science
   (c) History (d) English

   (ii) Fill in the blank with one word only.
   .... in the extract is the opposite of 'appreciative'.

   (iii) Which word can replace the underlined word in the sentence.
   Mayank's situation is becoming gradually bad.

   (iv) Why was Margie scornful?

Short Answer (SA) Type Questions

1. What do the yellow and crinkly pages show?
2. How was the arrival of the County Inspector beneficial to Margie?
3. What 'fun' did Margie think about and wished for?
4. Describe the teachers that Margie and Tommy had.

Long Answer (LA) Type Questions

1. What was the fun available to the students of the past according to the story?
2. 'Machines can't replace human beings.' Explain this in reference to the lesson 'The Fun They had'.
3. Describe the kind of books that the grandfather of Margie's grandfather had studied.

REVIEW EXERCISE

Including Competency Based Questions

Multiple Choice Questions

1. How did Margie feel about the book? Competency Based
(a) Curious (b) Indifferent
(c) Ambiguous (d) Overwhelmed

Ans. (a) Curious

2. To which world does the story take the readers to?
(a) Future world where computers will play a major role.
(b) A world of robots with no humans.
(c) A world of humans with no robots.
(d) A world which is not on Earth.

Ans. (a) Future world where computers will play a major role.

3. How does Margie's attitude towards old style schools change? Competency Based
(a) Excitement to disappointment
(b) Prejudice to acceptance
(c) Curiosity to confusion
(d) Surprise to yearning

Ans. (d) Surprise to yearning

4. What prompts Margie's mother to send for the County Inspector?
(a) The mechanical teacher couldn't turn on.
(b) Repeated geography tests were too difficult for Margie's level.
(c) The mechanical teacher's maths tests were too difficult for Margie.
(d) Margie refused to interact with the mechanical teacher.

Ans. (b) Repeated geography tests were too difficult for Margie's level.

5. Margie was disappointed.
Margie was disappointed because..... . Competency Based
(a) the book was boring
(b) the teacher was repaired
(c) her geography marks were poor
(d) she had to wait till the next day to read the book

Ans. (d) she had to wait till the next day to read the book

6. Who said the following dialogue? - "Well, I don't know what kind of school they had all that time ago."
(a) Tommy (b) Margie
(c) Margie's grandfather (d) Margie's mother

Ans. (b) Margie

7. Why did Tommy laugh when Margie said, "I wouldn't want a strange man in my house to teach me"?
(a) Because Margie didn't know much about old schools.
(b) Because old schools did not take place at homes.
(c) Because Tommy was rude to Margie.
(d) Both (a) and (b)

Ans. (d) Both (a) and (b)

8. "........If you don't like it, you don't have to read the book"- Who said this?
(a) Tommy (b) Margie
(c) County Inspector (d) Mrs. Jones

Ans. (a) Tommy

9. Which word best describes Tommy's attitude towards Margie? Competency Based
(a) Indifferent (b) Patronising
(c) Thoughtless (d) Domineering

Ans. (d) Domineering

10. What distracts Margie as her lesson starts?
(a) The thought of the old schools centuries ago.
(b) The memory of Tommy's rudeness.
(c) A fly buzzing.
(d) The thought of her Maths homework.

Ans. (a) The thought of the old schools centuries ago.

11. Which arithmetic lesson was being taught to Margie?
(a) Addition of proper fractions
(b) Addition of rational numbers
(c) Addition and subtraction
(d) Addition of integers

Ans. (a) Addition of proper fractions

12. 'Margie even wrote about it that night in her diary' This sentence suggests that finding the book was .... Competency Based
(a) an unusual event
(b) a remarkable achievement
(c) an important milestone in her life
(d) a discovery of historic importance

Ans. (a) an unusual event

Latest Course *Structure*

Section			Total Weightage
A	Reading Skills	40 Periods	20
B	Writing Skills with Grammar	40 Periods	20
C	Language Through Literature	50 Periods	40
	Total		80

**This is a suggestive number.*

Section A

Reading Skills

Reading Comprehension through Unseen Passage **20 Marks**

I. Discursive passage of 400-450 words. *(10 marks)*

II. Case-based factual passage (with visual input- statistical data, chart etc.) of 200-250 words *(10 marks)*

(Total length of two passages to be 600-700 words)

Multiple Choice Questions / Objective Type Questions/Very Short Answer Questions will be asked to assess comprehension, interpretation, analysis, inference, evaluation and vocabulary.

Section B

II. Grammar *(10 marks)*

- i. Determiners
- i. Tenses
- ii. Modals
- iii. Subject – Verb Concord
- iv. Reported Speech
  - a. Commands and Requests
  - b. Statements
  - c. Questions

The courses at the secondary level seek to cement high professional grasp of grammatical items and levels of accuracy. Accurate use of spelling, punctuation and grammar will be assessed through Gap Filling/ Editing/Transformation exercises. Ten out of twelve questions will be attempted.

Writing Skills **10 Marks**

I. Writing a Descriptive Paragraph (word limit 100-120 words), describing a person / event / situation, based on visual or verbal cue/s. One out of two questions to be answered. *(5 marks)*

II. Writing a Story (on a given cue/title)/Diary Entry, in 100-120 words. One out of two questions is to be answered. *(5 marks)*

Section C

Language Through Literature **40 Marks**

Reference to the Context **5+5=10 Marks**

i. One extract out of two from Drama / Prose.

ii. One extract out of two from poetry.

Multiple Choice Questions / Objective Type Questions will be asked to assess interpretation, analysis, inference, evaluation, appreciation and vocabulary.

Short & Long Answer Questions

i. Four out of Five Short Answer Type Questions to be answered in 40-50 words from the book BEEHIVE to assess interpretation, analysis, inference and evaluation. *4x3=12 marks*

ii. Two out of Three Short Answer Type Questions to be answered in 40-50 words from the book MOMENTS to assess interpretation, analysis, inference and evaluation. *3x2=6 marks*

iii. One out of two Long Answer Type Questions from BEEHIVE to be answered in about 100-120 words to assess creativity, imagination and extrapolation beyond the text and across the text. This can also be a passage-based question taken from a situation/plot from the text. *6 marks*

iv. One out of two Long Answer Type Questions from MOMENTS, on theme or plot involving interpretation, extrapolation beyond the text and inference or character sketch to be answered in about 100-120 words. *6 marks*

Prescribed Books

Beehive

Prose

a. The Fun They Had
b. The Sound of Music
c. The Little Girl
d. A Truly Beautiful Mind
e. The Snake and the Mirror
f. My Childhood
g. Reach For The Top
h. Kathmandu
i. If I were You

Poems

1. The Road Not taken
2. Wind
3. Rain on The Roof
4. The Lake Isle of Innisfree
5. A Legend of The Northland
6. No Men Are Foreign
7. On killing a tree
8. A Slumber Did My Spirit Seal

Moments

1. The Lost Child
2. The Adventures of Toto
3. Iswaran the Storyteller
4. In the kingdom of Fools
5. The Happy Prince
6. The Last Leaf
7. A House is not a Home
8. The Beggar

CHAPTER 1

Reading Comprehension

Let's REVISE Reading comprehension is a language activity that involves a thorough understanding of a given passage. It tests the understanding powers and analytical skills of a student with questions that evaluate the reader's ability to comprehend and analyse the information given in the passage.

Types of Passages

In the examination, two types of passages have been included. They are discussed as follows

(i) **Discursive Passage** (400–450 words) A discursive passage may include the opinions of a person which are generally argumentative, persuasive and interpretative.
It allows students to arrive at a conclusion through reasoning and understanding rather than intuition. It presents a balanced and objective approach towards the subject being discussed.

(ii) **Case Based Factual Passage** (200–250 words) A case based factual passage is composed of information on a particular subject. It contains verbal and visual inputs such as graphs, charts, pie-charts, etc. These passages focus completely on details or facts. It may include instructions, a report or a description. It helps the reader to develop a complete idea of a specific person, place, object or being.

Types of Questions

In Discursive both Passage and Case Based Factual Passage, Multiple Choice Questions/Objective Type Questions are asked to test the inferential and understanding skills of students.

Points to be Kept in Mind While Answering Reading Comprehension

- Read the passage carefully and thoroughly to understand its contents.
- Read all the given questions.
- Now, read the passage for the second time and underline the words, phrases and sentences which can be answers to the questions asked.
- For Subjective Type Questions
  - (i) Write the answers in one or two sentences. Word count should not be more than 30-40 words.
  - (ii) Write your answers in the same tense in which the questions are asked.
  - (iii) Answer should be to-the-point and in your own words.
- For MCQs
  - (i) Read all the four options carefully.
  - (ii) Choose the answer that best connects with the question as per the passage.
- Underline the words you don't understand and try to guess their meaning from the meaning of the sentence. It will help you in answering vocabulary related questions.
- Read the passage again to counter check your answers and write your answers briefly and to-the-point.

SOLVED EXAMPLES

Discursive Passages

PASSAGE 1

Read the given passage carefully and answer the questions that follow.

1. What does the word 'Society' connote? To put it briefly, when we speak of 'Society' we conceive of it as one by its very nature. The qualities which accompany this unity are praiseworthy- community of purpose and desire for welfare, loyalty to public ends and mutuality of sympathy and co-operation.

2. Are these ideals to be found in Indian Society? The Indian Society does not consist of individuals. It consists of an innumerable collection of castes which are exclusive in their life and have no common experience to share and have no bond of sympathy. Given this fact, it is not necessary to argue the point. The existence of the Caste System is a standing denial of the existence of those ideals of society and therefore of democracy.

3. Indian Society is so embedded in the Caste System that everything is organised on the basis of caste. Enter Indian Society and you can see caste in its glaring form. An Indian cannot eat or marry with an Indian, cannot touch an Indian because he or she does not belong to his or her caste. Go and enter politics and you can see caste reflected therein. How does an Indian vote in an election? He votes for a candidate who belongs to his own caste and no other. Even the Indian Congress exploits the Caste System for election purpose as no other political party in India does.

   Examine the lists of its candidates in relation to the social composition of the constituencies and it will be found that the candidate belongs to the caste which is the largest one in that. The Congress, as a matter of fact, is upholding the Caste System against which it is outwardly raising an outcry.

4. Go into the field of industry. What will you find? You will find that all the topmost men drawing the highest salary belong to the caste of the particular industrialist who runs the industry. The rest hang on for life on the lowest rungs of the ladder of pittance. Go into the field of commerce and you will see the same picture. The whole commercial house is one camp of one caste, with no entry board on the door for others.

5. Go into the field of charity. With one or two exceptions all charity in India is communal. If a Parsi dies, he leaves his money for Parsis. If a Jain dies, he leaves his money for Jains. If a Marwadi dies, he leaves his money for Marwadis. If a Brahmin dies, he leaves his money for Brahmins. Thus, there is no room for the downtrodden and the outcastes in politics, in industry, in commerce and in education.

Questions

1. How does an Indian vote in an election?

2. Society means a praiseworthy community of ....

(a) equality and fraternity

(b) purpose and desire for welfare

3. List a few fields where Caste System pervades. Why is there no room for the downtrodden and the outcastes in politics, industry, etc.?

4. Indian society consists of men who have ....

(a) no practical knowledge

(b) no common bond of sympathy

5. State whether the given statement is True or False.

The political parties also exploit the Caste System for election purpose.

6. Complete the sentence given below.

The existence of the Caste System is against the ....

(a) values and ideals of society

(b) Preamble of the Constitution

(c) equality and human rights

(d) All of the above

7. What does the existence of Caste System indicate?

8. Choose the option that correctly states the two meanings of 'embedded', as used in the passage.

(i) Fixed firmly and deeply	(ii) Attached
(iii) Showing	(iv) Creating
(v) Joining	(vi) Implant

(a) (i) and (ii) (b) (iii) and (vi)

(c) (iv) and (v) (d) (i) and (vi)

Answers

1. In an election, an Indian votes for a candidate that is of the same caste as his.

2. (b) purpose and desire for welfare

3. The Caste System is prevalent in marriage, elections, job, charity, education and food. There is no room for the downtrodden and the outcastes in politics, industry, etc. because of the Caste System.

4. (b) no common bond of sympathy
5. True
6. (a) values and ideals of society
7. The existence of Caste System indicates the degradation of our society. It points out that our society does not value its morals and ideals as well as the democratic nature of our country.
8. (a) (i) and (ii)

PASSAGE 2

Read the given passage carefully and answer the questions that follow.

1. Creamy outlook with soft speech presentation is a prime facial attraction that brings joy on the withering faces with a mixture of sensational touch. A smile with grace is the ultimate boon to mankind, keeping any melancholy at bay. Old age is often miscalculated as a liability with little attention paid to the aged. Their talents and learned potential are buried alive with undue care by an oblivious approach due to their disfigured or deformed physical structure taken over by age. It happens to us all, however hard we may try to delay the process. We grow old. Cosmetic surgery may remove the wrinkles, skin which has sagged may be tightened by means of a facelift and a hairdresser may dye grey hair to a more youthful colour, but we cannot remain young forever.
2. However, what is important is the quality of life. Some people are lucky to be taken care of at home whereas others may have to move to old age residential homes.

   Most of the elders in old age homes are not very happy as they are confined and feel isolated. But there are some elders who feel comfortable in old age homes for the freedom and friendly atmosphere with other elders who keep their company, enjoying the time with TV, games and gossip. The worst part of ageing is that often the mind becomes less alert. As people grow older, they experience short-term memory loss. Later, some may suffer from dementia, often in the form of Alzheimer's disease. By no means are all elderly people in this category.
3. Many senior citizens are in possession of all their faculties and see retirement as a time of freedom. Not only that, if they have a generous retirement pension, they are likely to be quite well off with money to be spent on a holiday and other luxuries. Because of this, both businesses and government have a new respect for what is known as 'Grey Power'.
4. It is unfortunate that many people regard old people as geriatrics who have one foot in the grave. Someone should remind them that they too would be old one day! They are honoured with the senior citizen label granted by the authorities with due regard being paid to them by other people. One should always bear in mind the old saying 'tit for tat' which denotes its symbolic regulation of periodical sufferings. The aforesaid misdoings of emotional disparity, done by striding steps, is a curse to mankind.

Questions

1. What is the worst part of ageing?
2. What all can cosmetic surgery do for us?
   (a) It may produce wrinkles.
   (b) It tightens the sagging skin.
3. How do most elders feel in old age homes?
4. Complete the sentence appropriately.

   .... attention is paid to the aged and old age is often seen as a ....
5. State whether the following statement is True or False.

   Alzheimer's disease is a type of mental breakdown.
6. Which of the following will be the most appropriate title for the passage?
   (a) Wisdom and Age
   (b) Grey Power
   (c) Senior Citizens
   (d) Unfortunate Trend-Cosmetic Surgery
7. Why are some old people lucky?
8. Why, according to the passage, are some elders comfortable in old age homes?
   (a) Because there they have freedom.
   (b) Because there they have a friendly atmosphere.
   (c) Because there they can play games, watch TV and gossip.
   (d) All of the above

Answers

1. The worst part of ageing is that the mind becomes less alert.
2. (b) It tightens the sagging skin.
3. Most of the elderly people living in old age homes are not very happy as they are confined. As a result, they feel isolated and unloved.
4. Little, liability
5. False
6. (b) Grey Power

7. Some old people are lucky because they are taken care of by their children at home.
8. (d) All of the above

Case Based Factual Passages

PASSAGE 1

Read the given passage carefully and answer the questions that follow.

1. The present generation is well updated in the use of the internet and computers. The rapid development in computer technology and increase in accessibility of the internet for academic purposes has changed the face of education for everyone associated with it. Let's look at the data arising out of a recent survey that was done to ascertain the time spent on utilisation of the computer and internet.

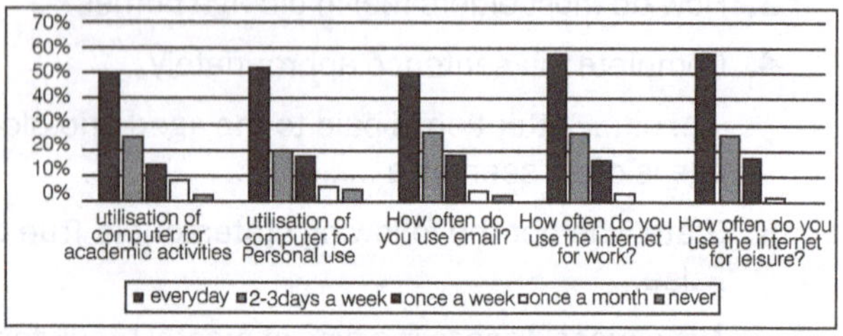

2. At present, many schools and universities have been implementing internet-based learning, as it supplements the conventional teaching methods. The internet provides a wide variety of references and information to academics as well as scientific researchers. Students often turn to it to do their academic assignments and projects.
3. However, research on the net is very different from traditional library research and the differences can cause problems. The net is a tremendous resource but it must be used carefully and critically.
4. According to a 2018 Academic Student e-book Experience Survey, conducted by LJ's research department and sponsored by EBSCO, when reading for pleasure almost 74% of respondents said they preferred print books for leisure whereas 45% of respondents chose e-books rather than the printed versions for research or assignments.
5. When asked what e-book features make them a favourite for research, the respondents were clear. Having page numbers to use in citations topped the list (75%); followed by the ability to resize text to fit a device's screen (67%); the ability to bookmark pages, highlight text, or take notes for later reference (60%); downloading the entire e-book (57%); and allowing content to be transferred between devices (43%) were the varied responses.

Questions

1. From which of the following is the research on the net different?
   (a) Academic research (b) Paper research
   (c) Field research (d) Traditional library research
2. Which of the following is a feature of an e-book which is not a favourite of researchers?
   (i) Citations (ii) Ability to resize text
   (iii) Copy images (iv) Highlight text
   (v) Take screenshots (vi) Bookmark pages
   (a) (i) and (v) (b) (ii) and (iv) (c) (iii) and (v) (d) Only (i)
3. Substitute the word 'enforce' in the following sentence with one word similar in meaning from Paragraph 2.
   The government will enforce new rules for internet usage.
4. According to the information presented in the passage, what is the percentage share of print books and e-books?
5. Infer one reason for the following based on information given in Paragraph 1.
   How has the internet changed the face of education?
6. How has educational institutions used internet based learning?
7. Complete the following analogy correctly with a word/phrase from Paragraph 2.
   Presently : Currently :: Traditional : ....
8. Complete the sentence appropriately.
   Many schools and universities have been implementing .... learning, as it supplements the conventional ....
9. What does the internet provide to academics and scientific researchers? How do the students use it?

Answers

1. (d) Traditional library research
2. (c) (iii) and (v)
3. implement
4. The percentage share of print books is 74% whereas e-books is 45%.
5. The internet has changed the face of education by the rapid development in computer technology and increase in accessibility of the internet for academic purposes.
6. Educational institutions have used internet based learning to supplement the conventional learning methods.
7. Conventional

8. internet-based, teaching methods
9. The internet provides a huge variety of references and information to academics and scientific researchers. Students often use it to do their academic assignments and projects.

PASSAGE 2

Read the following text, an excerpt from a case study titled 'Bridging the Gap: Enhancing Youth Access to the Olympic Games - A Case Study'.

1. The Olympic Games, hailed as the pinnacle of athletic excellence and international camaraderie, present an unparalleled platform for showcasing talent and promoting sportsmanship. However, ensuring equitable access to the Games, particularly among youth demographics, remains a pressing concern.
2. In recent years, efforts have been made to democratise access to the Olympic Games, particularly among youth cohorts, through various initiatives aimed at increasing participation and engagement. One such initiative is the Youth Olympic Games (YOG), introduced in 2010 by the International Olympic Committee (IOC). The YOG serves as a platform for young athletes aged 15 to 18 to compete in Olympic sports, providing them with invaluable experience and exposure on an international stage.

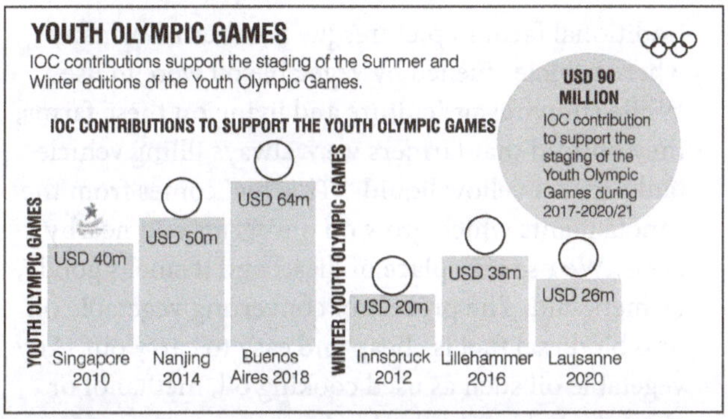

3. Furthermore, advancements in digital technology and media have played a pivotal role in expanding youth access to the Olympic Games. With the proliferation of livestreaming platforms and social media channels, youth audiences now have unprecedented opportunities to engage with Olympic events in real-time, regardless of geographical barriers. Moreover, the IOC's emphasis on youth-oriented content and interactive experiences has resonated with younger demographics, fostering a sense of ownership and belonging within the Olympic movement.
4. Despite these strides, challenges persist in ensuring comprehensive youth access to the Olympic Games, particularly in marginalised communities with limited resources and infrastructure. Addressing these challenges requires concerted efforts from stakeholders across the Olympic ecosystem, including policymakers, sports organisations, and community leaders, to implement targeted interventions and foster a culture of inclusivity and accessibility for future generations.

Questions

1. Which of the following best describes the role of digital technology in increasing youth participation in the Olympic Games?

(a) Reducing the cost of attending the Games in person.
(b) Replacing traditional sports with e-sports competitions.
(c) Increasing the number of youth athletes who can compete in the Games.
(d) Providing real-time access and engagement through livestreaming and social media.

2. Select the option that is true for the Assertion and Reason given below.

Assertion (A) Olympic Games is not inclusive in allowing the youth to participate in games.

Reason (R) The Olympic ecosystem includes policymakers, sports organisations, and community leaders.

(a) Both the Assertion and Reason are true, and the Reason is the correct explanation of the Assertion.
(b) Both the Assertion and Reason are true, but the Reason is not the correct explanation of the Assertion.
(c) The Assertion is true, but the Reason is false.
(d) The Assertion is false, but the Reason is true.

3. What is the writer referring to by the following phrase?

'Culture of inclusivity'

4. What inference can be made regarding youth participation in Olympic Games in India?

5. Fill in the blank by selecting the correct option.

The Olympic Games, hailed as the pinnacle of athletic excellence and .... (geopolitical unity/international camaraderie), present an unparalleled platform for showcasing talent and promoting sportsmanship.

6. List two functions of Youth Olympic Games (YOG).

(a) .... (b) ....

7. What can be inferred about the efforts to expose youth to Olympic Games mentioned in Paragraph 2? In recent years, efforts have been made to democratise access to the Olympic Games, particularly among youth cohorts, through various ....
8. Complete the following sentence with correct facts and figures from the table.

   IOC contributed .... to support the staging of Youth Olympic Games during 2017-2020/21.
9. What initiatives have been introduced to increase youth participation in the Olympic Games, and what challenges still hinder this participation in India?

Answers

1. (d) Providing real-time access and engagement through livestreaming and social media.
2. (d) The Assertion is false, but the Reason is true.
3. By the following phrase, the writer refers to creating an environment where all youth, regardless of background, have equal access to the Olympic Games.
4. Youth participation in the Olympic Games in India is improving, but resource and infrastructure challenges still limit comprehensive access.
5. international camaraderie
6. (a) Serves as a platform for young athletes aged 15 to 18 to compete in olympic sports.

   (b) Provides them with invaluable experience and exposure on an international stage.
7. initiatives aimed at increasing participation and engagement
8. USD 90 million
9. The Youth Olympic Games and digital media engagement initiatives have increased youth participation, but challenges like limited resources and infrastructure in marginalised communities still hinder comprehensive access in India.

REVIEW EXERCISE

Including Discursive and Case Based Factual Passages

Discursive Passages

PASSAGE 1

Read the given passage carefully and answer the questions that follow.

1. At a time when the use of fossil fuels to power vehicles is making environmentalists angry, an alternative source of fuel, biodiesel has emerged as a useful solution. Additionally, its use solves a disposable problem. The fuel is nothing but used vegetable oil which has been tested satisfactorily. It has made a vehicle called the Veggie Van (a motor home) run more than 16000 km across the United States. Also, it has visited 20 major cities causing absolutely no harm to the environment. Vegetable oils from various restaurants in America were used along the entire journey. The novel experiment was started as a college project by two students, Joshna and Kaia. It eventually ended in a Massive Public Awareness Programme.
2. The idea of using vegetable oil as fuel for a diesel engine first occurred to them when they visited a traditional farm in picturesque Southern Germany where vehicles fuelled by vegetable oil were in use. While studying agriculture and living on these farms, they noticed that farmers were always filling vehicle tanks with a yellow liquid. "This fuel comes from the canola plants which grow on our farms and nearby areas. We use it in place of diesel and it smells good", farmers said. The process of converting vegetable oil into biodiesel fuel is cheap and easy to carry out. Any vegetable oil such as used cooking oil, methanol or clear alcohol can be used as fuel.
3. The diesel engine which is being used can run on altered vegetable oil or biodiesel without any modification. Not only does biodiesel require zero modifications to the engine, this fuel works either by itself or blended with petroleum diesel. Biodiesel has since been recognised as an official alternative fuel in the US. Its use by the bus and truck fleet has soared by more than 100%.
4. Biodiesel does not disrupt the natural carbon cycle of the biosphere as fossil fuels do. Originating from contemporaneous plant sources, biodiesel effectively

takes in as much carbon dioxide as it ultimately releases upon burning, while fossil fuels, trapped deep in the ground for millions of years, increase the net carbon total in the atmosphere when extracted and burned. This increase in carbon dioxide in the atmosphere is linked to global warming. The carbon dioxide, when emitted from fossil fuels, travels up to the highest layers of the atmosphere where it traps reflected sunlight from escaping the planet, inevitably leading (some think) to global climate change. The real benefits of using biodiesel are in the long term, and measured not only at the tailpipe but also through an analysis of the life cycle of the fuel.

Questions

1. What changes are required in the vehicle that uses biodiesel as a fuel?
2. Complete the sentence appropriately.
   The phrase 'soared by more than 100%' means ....
   (a) its use has more than doubled
   (b) its use is exponentially on the fall
3. Give reasons why the writer says that 'the use of fossil fuels to power vehicles is making environmentalists angry'.
4. The passage includes some words that are opposed to each other. From the set given below, identify two sets of antonyms.
   (a) Absolutely and eventually
   (b) Ultimately and effectively
   (c) Traps and releases
   (d) Fuelled and disrupt
5. State whether the given statement is True or False.
   Unlike fossil fuels biodiesel does not disrupt the natural carbon cycle of the biosphere.
6. Select the option that displays what the writer feels about the usage of biodiesel.
   (a) Doubt (b) Caution
   (c) Denial (d) Conviction
7. What connection does the writer draw out between biodiesel and sustainability? (Paragraph 4)
   List two sources from which biodiesel can be obtained.
8. Which of the following will be the most appropriate title for the passage?
   (a) Unsustainable Oils
   (b) Biodiesel-An Alternate Oil
   (c) Veggie Van
   (d) Doing Away with Fuel

PASSAGE 2

Read the given passage carefully and answer the questions that follow.

1. Artificial Intelligence (AI) stands at the forefront of technological innovation, revolutionising industries, and reshaping societies worldwide. In this discursive passage, we delve into the multifaceted implications of AI, exploring its transformative potential, ethical considerations, and societal impacts.
2. AI encompasses a broad range of technologies that enable machines to simulate human-like intelligence, including machine learning, natural language processing, and computer vision. From virtual assistants and recommendation systems to autonomous vehicles and medical diagnostics, AI applications permeate various facets of our daily lives, streamlining processes, enhancing productivity, and driving innovation.
3. One of the most significant contributions of AI lies in its ability to augment human capabilities and solve complex problems at scale. Machine learning algorithms analyse vast datasets to uncover patterns and insights that would elude human cognition, revolutionising fields such as healthcare, finance, and transportation. For instance, AI-powered medical imaging systems can assist radiologists in diagnosing diseases with unprecedented accuracy, leading to earlier detection and better patient outcomes.
4. Moreover, AI holds the potential to address some of humanity's most pressing challenges, from climate change and resource scarcity to healthcare disparities and social inequality. By leveraging AI-driven predictive modeling and optimisation techniques, policymakers can make informed decisions and allocate resources more effectively, mitigating risks and maximising societal welfare.
5. However, alongside its transformative potential, AI raises ethical and societal concerns that must be addressed to ensure responsible development and deployment. The proliferation of AI raises questions about data privacy, algorithmic bias, and the concentration of power in the hands of tech giants. Moreover, the automation of jobs and the displacement of human workers by AI-driven technologies threaten to exacerbate socio-economic inequalities and widen the digital divide.
6. Furthermore, the ethical implications of AI extend to issues such as autonomous weapons systems, algorithmic accountability, and the preservation of human autonomy

and dignity. As AI becomes increasingly integrated into critical infrastructure and decision-making processes, ensuring transparency, accountability, and human oversight is paramount to safeguarding against unintended consequences and ethical lapses.

7. Despite these challenges, the potential benefits of AI far outweigh the risks, provided that we adopt a proactive and inclusive approach to its development and deployment. By fostering interdisciplinary collaboration, promoting ethical guidelines, and prioritising diversity and inclusion in AI research and development, we can harness the transformative power of AI to create a more equitable, sustainable, and prosperous future for all.

Questions

1. What technologies enable AI to stimulate human like intelligence?

2. What are some ethical concerns raised by the proliferation of Artificial Intelligence (AI), according to the passage?
(a) Data privacy, algorithmic bias, and concentration of power.
(b) Climate change, resource scarcity, and social inequality.

3. Analyse the tone of the writer in the given lines from Paragraph 2? Rationalise your response in about 40 words.
"AI raises ethical and societal concerns that must be addressed to ensure responsible development and deployment."

4. The passage mentions that AI raises ethical and societal concerns that must be addressed. Select two antonyms of 'concerns' as used in this context?
(a) Worried (b) Unhinged
(c) Detached (d) Bothered
(e) Apathetic

5. State whether the following statement is True or False.
According to the passage, the potential benefits outweigh the risks associated with AI.

6. Based on Paragraph 3, complete the following sentence approprlately.
Machine learning algorithms .... vast datasets to uncover patterns and insights that would elude human cognition, revolutionising fields such as healthcare, finance, and transportation.
(a) analyse (b) create (c) store (d) convert

7. How can society mitigate the risks posed by AI while maximising its benefits?

8. What is the primary focus of the passage on Artificial Intelligence (AI)?
(a) Discussing its transformative potential
(b) Highlighting its ethical implications
(c) Exploring its societal impacts
(d) All of the above

PASSAGE 3

Read the given passage carefully and answer the questions that follow.

1. The world we inhabit is abundant beyond our wildest imagination. There are trees, dreams, sunrises; there are thunderstorms, shadows, rivers; there are wars, flea bites, love affairs; there are the lives of people, Gods, entire galaxies. To focus on images alone is a form of hubris-and shortsighted. From the smallest variation in gesture to the vast expanses of space and time, human comprehension can encompass neither the endless particularity of the surface of things, nor the extreme variations in scale that define the physical world. The social fabric of the world we inhabit has been divided and categorised under many different headings but the division on the basis of material wealth is the most glaring and common across all the nations.

2. It is a stark reality that the world can be divided into two slots – the haves and the have-nots and also that all affluent cities are surrounded by slums. Just as a coin has two sides, every city has two faces –the bright, the well-lit and the illuminated world of the rich and the dark, dingy, depressing world of the poor. The poor people exist on the periphery, constantly yearning for the bright world and the rich are dependent on them to keep their world well-scrubbed and spruced up.

3. It is not surprising that Delhi is poised on the brink of disaster. With five lakh people migrating to this metropolis every year, it is not difficult to see why the quality of life has deteriorated at such an alarming rate. The newspapers are full of crimes committed because of the breakdown of basic facilities and the corrosion of human values.

4. This brings us to slums – the alleged breeding grounds of most of Delhi's problems. Over the years, the number of slums and unauthorised settlements has leapfrogged. There is hardly any residential colony in this city that is not hemmed in by them. Yet, they too serve a purpose – they provide cheap labour and captive vote banks.

The very people who turn up their noses at the dirt, disease and filth that festers in these areas, use these 'breeding grounds' as a pool for domestic servants who can be hired and fired at will and daily wage labourers who are grateful for any kind of employment. Even the children born in slums do not have a bright future. Their future becomes dark and they are forced to work in order to help their families meet their daily needs. They live in acute poverty. Isn't it about time that we examine our own role and acknowledge our responsibility for the proliferation of these slums?

Questions

1. Why are newspapers full of crimes?

2. According to the passage, what is the purpose served by the slums?
(a) They look after rich people's children.
(b) They provide cheap labour and captive vote banks.

3. What are the two sides of a coin that the writer is referring to?

4. How do the rich and the poor depend on each other?
(a) For their survival
(b) For a means of earning
(c) For their luxury
(d) Both (a) and (b)

5. Complete the sentence appropriately.
Delhi is poised on the brink of disaster as ....

6. What does human comprehension not encompass?
(a) The endless particularity of the surface of things.
(b) The extreme variations in scale that define the mental world.
(c) The extreme variations in scale that define the physical world.
(d) Both (a) and (c)

7. The division of the social fabric of the world on the basis of material wealth is the most common across all the nations. Justify.

8. Choose the option that correctly states the two meanings of 'affluent', as used in the passage.
(i) Substantial
(ii) Wealthy
(iii) Well-maintained
(iv) In great quantity
(v) Loaded
(a) (i) and (iv)
(b) (ii) and (iv)
(c) (ii) and (v)
(d) (ii) and (iii)

PASSAGE 4

Read the given passage carefully and answer the questions that follow.

1. Time management is the act of planning and managing time that is spent on various activities. It helps to increase the effectiveness and efficiency of the time utilised. It helps us to work smarter instead of harder and also enables us to get more work done in less amount of time. Planning the time may seem as a wastage of time in itself; however, the benefits of time management are enormous. It results in less stress, increased productivity, efficiency, professional and personal growth, etc.

2. Time is limited and hence, it is important that we plan our time wisely and make the best use of the limited hours in a day. Time is something that we cannot store or save for later use. We cannot retrieve the time that has been wasted hence, we need to learn to use it effectively. If we have to manage time effectively, we need to be organised and focused.

3. With the help of time management techniques, we can accomplish more with lesser efforts. Time management includes effective planning of activities, setting of goals, setting deadlines, delegating work, prioritising our activities, etc.

4. Most people feel that they always have too much to do within too little time. Managing time wisely will help to find the right balance between time and work. A few people resort to multi-tasking in order to get the work done within the specified time limit.

5. At times, this may result in poor performance in the various tasks assigned. The major mistake committed while working is when one is in a rush to meet the deadline without taking proper breaks for rest or relaxation. It is impossible for anyone to focus on work and to produce good results without considering any break in between.
It helps to perform better if one takes five minute to break every two hours of work. One can either take a walk, enjoy a cup of coffee or simply meditate. Proper time management is the cornerstone of a successful life and ensures achievement of one's goals in a healthy manner.

6. When it comes to harnessing your time, time management books are a must. They are a great way to learn from an expert and understand your time better than ever before. Many of the best lessons can be picked from these books. And it just so happens that many of those life-changing books are listed on the internet.

7. So, whether you are looking for time management for school/college students, stay-at-home parents, business executives or anyone else looking to better utilise their time, reading these books is a wise way to learn the skill of managing your time.

Questions

1. Complete the sentence appropriately.
   Time management includes ....
2. Time management helps us in ....
   (a) multi-tasking
   (b) increasing effectiveness and efficiency
3. Why is a short break helpful between hectic sessions of work?
   What major mistake is made when one is in a rush to meet the deadline?
4. Which of the following is a benefit of time management?
   (i) Less stress (ii) Increased productivity
   (iii) Growth (iv) Multi-tasking
   (v) Prioritising (vi) Meeting deadlines
   (a) (i), (ii) and (iii) (b) (iv), (v) and (vi)
   (c) (i), (iii) and (v) (d) (ii), (iv) and (vi)
5. Complete the sentence appropriately.
   If we have to manage time effectively we need to be .... and ....
6. Which one of the following results in poor performance?
   (a) Multi-tasking
   (b) Using time management techniques
   (c) Meeting deadlines
   (d) Not taking proper breaks in between work
7. Define time management as per the passage. What is the best way to learn time management?
8. Which of the following will be the most appropriate title for the passage?
   (a) Making Time (b) Time Management
   (c) More Time-Less Efforts (d) Let us Learn to Utilise Time

PASSAGE 5

Read the given passage carefully and answer the questions that follow.

1. Everybody wants to succeed in life. For some, success means achieving whatever they desire or dream. For many it is the name, fame and social position. Whatever be the meaning of success, it is success which makes a man popular.
2. All great men have been successful. They are remembered for their great achievements. But it is certain that success comes to those who are sincere, hard working, loyal and committed to their goals. Success has been man's greatest motivation. It is very important for all. Success has a great effect on life. It brings pleasure and pride. It gives a sense of fulfilment. It means all-around development. Everybody hopes to be successful in life but success smiles on those who have a proper approach, planning, vision and stamina. A proper and timely application of all these things is bound to bear fruit. One cannot be successful without cultivating these certain basic things in life. It is very difficult to set out on a journey without knowing one's goals and purposes. Clarity of the objective is a must to succeed in life. A focused approach with proper planning is certain to bring success. Indecision and insincerity are big obstacles on the path to success.
3. One should have the capability, capacity and resources to turn one's dreams into reality. Mere desire cannot bring you success. The desire should be weighed against factors like capability and resources. This is the basic requirement of success. The next important thing is the eagerness, seriousness and the urge to be successful. It is the driving force which decides the success. It is the first step on the ladder of success.
4. One needs to pursue one's goals with sincerity and passion. One should always be in high spirit. Lack of such spirit leads to an inferiority complex which is a big obstruction on the path to success. Time is also a deciding factor. Only the punctual and committed have succeeded in life. Lives of great men are examples of this. They had all these qualities in plenty which helped them rise to the peak of success.
5. Hard labour is also one of the basic requirements of success. There is no substitute for hard labour. It alone can take one to the peak of success. Every success has a ratio of five percent inspiration and ninety-five percent perspiration. It is patience, persistence and perseverance which play a decisive role in achieving success. Failures are the pillars of success as they are our stepping-stones and we must get up and start again and be motivated.

Questions

1. Explain "Failures are pillars of success."
2. According to the author, what, from the following, is the first and foremost step on the journey to achieve success?
   (a) Keenness and urge to be successful
   (b) Indecisive behaviour and sincerity
3. What did great men have in plenty to rise to the peak of success? To whom does success come certainly?
4. Choose the option that best conveys the message in

'It gives a sense of fulfillment.'

(a) Failure makes you understand success.

(b) Achieving success feels like a person's life's purpose is fulfilled.

5. State whether the given sentence is True or False.

A focused approach with proper planning will definitely bring success.

6. Which of the following shows the correct meaning of the phrase "Whatever be the meaning of success"?

(a) Success means to become powerful, rich and famous.

(b) Success can mean different things to different people.

(c) Success is the acquiring of money through whichever method possible.

(d) Success is the acquiring of knowledge through whichever method possible.

7. What does the writer advise in Paragraph 4?

8. According to the passage, what plays a decisive role in achieving success?

(a) Inferiority complex and big obstruction

(b) Five-percent inspiration and ninety-five percent perspiration

(c) Proper approach, planning, stamina

(d) Patience, persistence and perseverance

PASSAGE 6

Read the given passage carefully and answer the questions that follow.

Cybercrimes have emerged as a pervasive and insidious threat in the digital age, posing significant dangers to individuals, businesses, and societies worldwide. Firstly, cybercrimes encompass a wide range of illicit activities conducted through digital platforms, including hacking, identity theft, phishing scams, malware distribution, and online fraud. These crimes exploit vulnerabilities in computer systems and networks, compromising the confidentiality, integrity, and availability of sensitive information. From personal data breaches to financial fraud schemes, cybercrimes can wreak havoc on individuals' lives, leading to financial losses, reputational damage, and psychological distress.

Moreover, businesses and organisations are prime targets for cybercriminals seeking to steal valuable intellectual property, trade secrets, and financial assets. Sophisticated cyberattacks, such as ransomware and supply chain breaches, can disrupt operations, cause financial losses, and erode trust among stakeholders. The proliferation of interconnected devices in the Internet of Things (IoT) era has further amplified cyber risks, as insecure IoT devices can serve as entry points for malicious actors to infiltrate networks and launch coordinated attacks.

In addition to economic repercussions, cybercrimes pose significant threats to national security and public safety. State-sponsored cyber espionage, cyber terrorism, and cyber warfare tactics have the potential to destabilise governments, disrupt critical infrastructure, and compromise essential services, such as healthcare, energy, and transportation systems. The interconnected nature of cyberspace means that cyber threats transcend geographical boundaries, necessitating international cooperation and coordinated efforts to combat cybercrime effectively.

Furthermore, the proliferation of cybercrimes has profound implications for privacy and civil liberties in the digital age. Mass surveillance programs, data breaches, and unauthorised surveillance practices undermine individuals' right to privacy, exposing them to unwarranted scrutiny and surveillance. The collection and misuse of personal data by tech giants and government agencies raise concerns about surveillance capitalism and the erosion of digital freedoms, necessitating legislative reforms and regulatory frameworks to safeguard privacy rights. Moreover, the rapid evolution of cyber threats and the anonymity afforded by the dark web present significant challenges for law enforcement agencies and cybersecurity professionals tasked with combating cybercrimes. The asymmetric nature of cyber warfare, coupled with the global nature of cyberspace, makes attribution and prosecution of cybercriminals notoriously difficult, often resulting in impunity and a lack of accountability for their actions.

Questions

1. What are some sophisticated cyberattacks mentioned in the passage that target businesses and organisations?

2. What is a significant factor contributing to the increased risk of cyberattacks on businesses and organisations in the IoT era?

(a) Insecure IoT devices as entry points

(b) Increased use of mobile devices

3. Analyze the tone of the writer in the given lines from Paragraph 3. Rationalise your response in about 40 words.

"The interconnected nature of cyberspace means that cyber threats transcend geographical boundaries, necessitating international cooperation and coordinated efforts to combat cybercrime effectively."

4. The passage mentions that the impacts of cybercrimes are far-reaching and profound. Select two antonyms of 'profound' as used in this context.

(a) Reaching (b) Sophisticated
(c) Superficial (d) Implication
(e) Mild

5. Based on Paragraph 3, complete the following sentence appropriately.

From personal data breaches to financial fraud schemes, cybercrimes can .... on individuals' lives, leading to financial losses, reputational damage, and psychological distress.

(a) wreak havoc (b) bring hell
(c) not be justified (d) None of these

6. State whether the following statement is True or False.

Cybercrimes only affect individuals and have no significant impact on businesses or national security.

7. What are the implications of mass surveillance and data breaches for individuals' privacy? Why do these implications necessitate legislative reforms and regulatory frameworks?

8. How do cybercrimes impact national security and public safety according to the passage?

(a) By causing widespread panic through misinformation campaigns
(b) By undermining the legal system through data manipulation
(c) By destabilising governments and disrupting critical infrastructure
(d) By reducing economic growth through consistent cyber theft

PASSAGE 7

Read the given passage carefully and answer the questions that follow.

1. Archaeology as a profession faces two major problems. First, it is the poorest of the poor. Only paltry sums are available for excavating and even less is available for publishing the results and preserving the sites once excavated. Yet archaeologists deal with priceless objects every day. Second, there is the problem of illegal excavation, resulting in museum quality pieces being sold to the highest bidder.

2. I would like to make an outrageous suggestion that would at one stroke provide funds for archaeology and reduce the amount of illegal digging. I would propose that scientific archaeological expeditions and governmental authorities sell excavated artefacts in the open market. Such sales would provide substantial funds for the excavation and preservation of archaeological sites and the publication of results. At the same time, they would break the illegal excavator's grip on the market, thereby decreasing the inducement to engage in illegal activities.

3. You might object that professionals excavate to acquire knowledge, not money. Moreover, ancient artefacts are part of our global cultural heritage which should be available for all to appreciate, not sold to the highest bidder. I agree. Sell nothing that has unique artistic merit or scientific value. But, you might reply, everything that comes out of the ground has scientific value.

   Here, we part company. Theoretically, you may be correct in claiming that every artefact has potential scientific value. Practically, you are wrong.

4. I refer to the thousands of pottery vessels and ancient lamps that are essentially duplicates of one another. In one small excavation in Cyprus, archaeologists recently uncovered 2,000 virtually indistinguishable small jugs in a single courtyard, even precious royal seal impressions known as 'Melekh Handles' have been found in abundance—more than 4,000 examples so far.

5. The basement of museums is simply not large enough to store the artefacts that are likely to be discovered in the future. There is not enough money even to catalogue the funds. As a result, they cannot be found again and become as inaccessible as if they had never been discovered. Indeed, with the help of a computer, sold artefacts could be more accessible than are the pieces stored in bulging museum basements. Prior to sale, each could be photographed and the list of the purchasers could be maintained on the computer. A purchaser could even be required to agree to return the piece if it should become needed for scientific purposes. It would be unrealistic to suggest that illegal digging would stop if artefacts were sold in the open market. But the demand for the clandestine product would be substantially reduced. Who would want an unmarked pot when another was available whose provenance was known and that was dated in a stratigraphic manner by the professional archaeologist who excavated it?

Questions

1. Define archaeology on the basis of your understanding from the passage.

2. According to the author, what is the lesson taught by the process of excavation?

(a) Archaeology is the most important branch of studies.
(b) Finding and preserving artefacts is integral to knowing more about our cultural past.

3. In one sentence, present the author's view on sale of artefacts.

4. The passage includes some words that are opposites of each other. From the options given below, identify a pair of antonyms.

(a) constantly and stopping
(b) paltry and substantial
(c) valuable and worth
(d) excavate and dig

5. Fill in the blank.

Archaeologists deal with .... everyday.

6. Which of the following statements are true?

(i) Very large sums are available for excavating.
(ii) Very less funds are available for publishing the results and preserving the sites once excavated.
(iii) Ancient artefacts are part of our global cultural heritage.
(iv) There is enough money to catalogue the funds.

(a) (i) and (ii)
(b) (ii) and (iii)
(c) (iii) and (iv)
(d) (iv) and (i)

7. Substitute the underlined word/phrase with a nearest meaning word from the passage.

There had been some sort of <u>secretly conducted</u> liaison between the lady and Darrel for sometime.

8. Which of the following can be said about the people in the profession of archaeology?

(a) Collectors of artefacts
(b) Seekers of knowledge
(c) Smugglers of knowledge
(d) Acquires of knowledge for business purposes

PASSAGE 8

Read the given passage carefully and answer the questions that follow.

Exam stress is a pervasive issue among students, manifesting in various forms of anxiety, depression, and physical ailments. Managing this stress is crucial not only for academic success but also for overall well-being. Effective stress management involves a multifaceted approach that includes time management, mental health strategies, physical well-being, and supportive environments.

Time management is fundamental in alleviating exam stress. Procrastination often exacerbates anxiety, as last-minute cramming can be overwhelming. Students can benefit from creating a study schedule well in advance of their exams. Breaking down the material into manageable chunks and setting realistic goals can help make the task less daunting. By allocating specific times for study and ensuring these periods are free from distractions, students can increase their efficiency and reduce stress. Moreover, incorporating regular breaks and leisure activities within the study schedule can prevent burnout and maintain motivation.

Mental health strategies are equally important in managing exam stress. Techniques such as mindfulness, meditation, and deep-breathing exercises can help students stay calm and focused. Cognitive-behavioral strategies, such as challenging negative thoughts and maintaining a positive outlook, can mitigate feelings of hopelessness and fear of failure. Encouraging a growth mindset, where challenges are viewed as opportunities for learning rather than threats, can significantly reduce anxiety. Support from peers, teachers, and counselors also plays a critical role. Sharing concerns and receiving reassurance can provide emotional relief and practical advice.

Physical well-being is another critical aspect of managing exam stress. Adequate sleep, a balanced diet, and regular exercise are essential. Sleep deprivation can impair cognitive function, making it difficult to concentrate and retain information. A nutritious diet supports brain function and energy levels, while exercise can reduce stress hormones and increase endorphins, improving mood and reducing anxiety. Simple activities like walking, yoga, or even stretching can have a positive impact.

Creating a supportive environment at home and school is also vital. Parents and teachers should encourage a balanced approach to exams, emphasising effort and learning over grades. High expectations and pressure can heighten stress levels, whereas a supportive and understanding attitude can help students feel more secure and confident. Schools can offer workshops on stress management, time management, and study techniques, providing students with tools to handle their workload effectively.

In conclusion, managing exam stress requires a comprehensive approach that addresses time management, mental health, physical well-being, and supportive environments. By implementing these strategies, students can navigate the pressures of exams more effectively, leading to better academic performance and overall health. Recognising and addressing exam stress as a multifaceted issue is essential for fostering resilient, confident and successful students.

Questions

1. After a thorough reading of the passage, select the sentence which encapsulates the main focus of the passage.
   (a) The benefits of exercise and a balanced diet for students
   (b) Techniques for improving academic performance
   (c) Comprehensive strategies for managing exam stress in students
   (d) The importance of parental support during exams
2. Analyse the tone of the writer in the given lines from Paragraph 2? Rationalise your response in about 40 words.
   "Exam stress is a pervasive issue among students, manifesting in various forms of anxiety, depression, and physical ailments."
3. Based on the passage, complete the following sentence appropriately.
   Effective stress management involves a .... that includes time management, mental health strategies, physical well-being, and supportive environments.
4. The passage mentions that breaking down the material into manageable chunks and setting realistic goals can help make the task less daunting. Select two antonyms of 'daunting' as used in this context?
   (a) Applicable (b) Manageable
   (c) Deterioration (d) Delayed
   (e) Encouraging
5. How does time management help in reducing exam stress?
6. Describe how a supportive environment at home and school can alleviate exam stress.
7. Which mental health strategy is mentioned for managing exam stress?
   (a) Deep-breathing exercises
   (b) Regular exercise
8. State whether the given statement is True or False.
   According to the passage, sleep deprivation can impair cognitive function and increase exam stress.

Case Based Factual Passages

PASSAGE 1

Read the given passage carefully and answer the questions that follow.

The adoption of electric vehicles (EVs) in India is accelerating, driven by government initiatives and increasing environmental awareness. As of 2023, India has approximately 1.5 million EVs on the road, a significant increase from previous years. The market is expected to grow at a compound annual growth rate (CAGR) of 36% from 2021 to 2026.

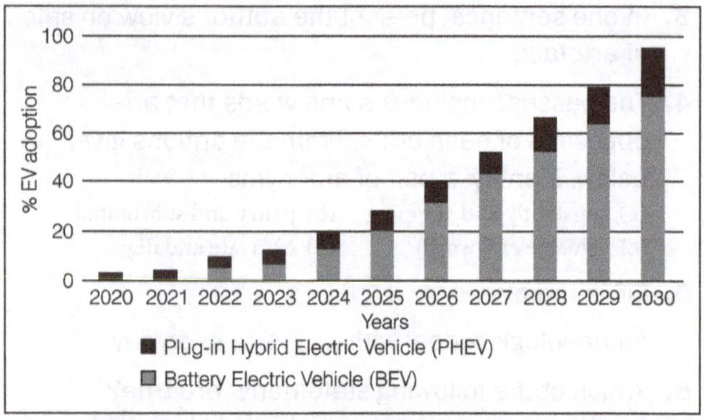

Government policies, such as the Faster Adoption and Manufacturing of Hybrid and Electric Vehicles (FAME) scheme, have been pivotal. FAME II, launched in 2019, allocates ?10,000 crores (around $1.3 billion) to promote EV adoption through subsidies and incentives for manufacturers and consumers. Additionally, the Goods and Services Tax (GST) on EVs has been reduced from 12% to 5%, making EVs more affordable.

Infrastructure development is also critical. As of 2023, India has around 1,700 public charging stations, with plans to install 69,000 more by 2025. Major cities like Delhi, Mumbai, and Bengaluru are leading in the deployment of charging infrastructure.

The two-wheeler segment dominates the Indian EV market, accounting for about 80% of total EV sales. Notable players include Hero Electric, Ola Electric, and Ather Energy. In the four-wheeler segment, Tata Motors leads with a 70% market share, primarily due to the success of models like the Tata Nexon EV and Tigor EV.

EV adoption is also contributing to environmental goals. By 2030, India aims to have 30% of all vehicles be electric, potentially reducing carbon emissions by up to 37% and saving about 474 million tonnes of oil equivalent.

Questions

1. Which segment dominates the Indian EV market?
   (a) Two-wheeler (b) Four-wheeler
   (c) Commercial vehicles (d) Public Transport
2. Select the option that is true for the Assertion and Reason given below.
   Assertion (A) FAME scheme provides subsidies and incentives for manufacturers and consumers.
   Reason (R) Because of the FAME scheme, India has around 1,700 public charging stations, with plans to install 69,000 more by 2025.

(a) Both the Assertion and Reason are true, and the Reason is the correct explanation of the Assertion.
(b) Both the Assertion and Reason are true, but the Reason is not the correct explanation of the Assertion.
(c) The Assertion is true, but the Reason is false.
(d) The Assertion is false, but the Reason is True.

3. Why is the adoption of EVs in India expected to grow rapidly in the coming years?

4. From "the market is expected to grow at a compound annual growth rate (CAGR) of 36% from 2021 to 2026", what can be inferred about the future of the EV market in India?

5. Complete the following sentence with the correct facts from the passage.

"As of 2023, India has approximately .... EVs on the road."

6. What does compound annual growth rate (CAGR) of 36% mean in the context of the EV market?

7. List two notable players in the Indian two-wheeler EV market.

(a) .... (b) ....

8. Fill in the blanks according to Paragraph 2.

Major cities like .... , Mumbai and .... are leading in the deployment of charging infrastructure.

9. How have government policies influenced EV adoption in India, and what role does infrastructure development play in this context?

PASSAGE 2

Read the given passage carefully and answer the questions that follow.

In 2024, the tech sector witnessed a significant phenomenon termed 'brain drain', where skilled professionals migrated from one region to another, predominantly from developing countries to developed ones.

The tech industry, known for its rapid advancements and lucrative opportunities, became a magnet for talented individuals worldwide. However, disparities in economic opportunities, political instability, and limited career growth prospects in their home countries prompted many skilled workers to seek greener pastures abroad. For instance, countries like India and Nigeria experienced a notable exodus of tech talent to tech hubs such as Silicon Valley and Singapore.

This migration of skilled workers had multifaceted repercussions. While destination countries benefited from a diverse talent pool and enhanced innovation, source countries faced a depletion of their intellectual capital, hindering their own technological advancement and economic growth. Additionally, the brain drain widened the global technology gap, exacerbating inequalities between developed and developing nations.

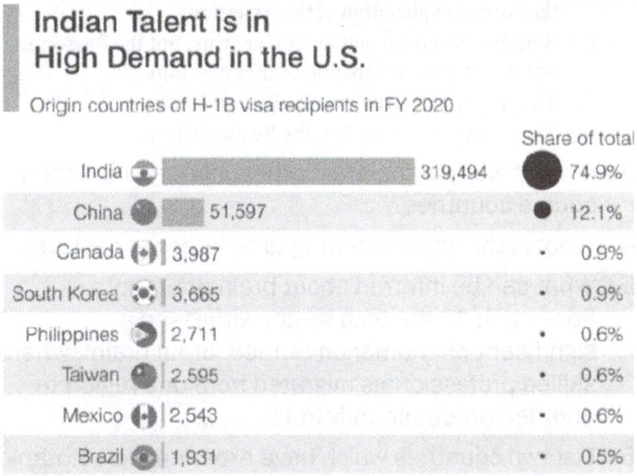

The H-18 is a non-immigrant, i.e., temporary visa that allows U.S. companies to employ foreign workers in high-skilled specialty occupations.

Furthermore, the departure of skilled workers often resulted in a loss of investment in education and training, as governments and private sectors struggled to retain talent and foster innovation domestically. 1.8 million Indians will be spending close to $85 billion on studying abroad by the year 2024. This perpetuated a cycle of underdevelopment in source countries, exacerbating socio-economic inequalities and impeding progress towards sustainable development goals.

In conclusion, the phenomenon of brain drain in the tech sector in 2024 underscored the urgent need for global cooperation and equitable policies to mitigate its adverse effects on both source and destination countries. Efforts to address the root causes of brain drain, such as improving economic opportunities and promoting inclusive growth, are essential for fostering a more balanced and sustainable global tech ecosystem.

Questions

1. What multifaceted repercussions did the migration of skilled workers have, according to the passage?

(a) Enhanced innovation in destination countries
(b) Depletion of intellectual capital in source countries
(c) Widened global technology gap
(d) All of the above

2. Select the option that is true for the Assertion and Reason given below.

Assertion (A) Governments and private sectors struggled to retain talent and foster innovation domestically.

Reason (R) Skilled professionals migrated from one region to another, predominantly from developing countries to developed ones.

(a) Both the Assertion and Reason are true, and the Reason is the correct explanation of the Assertion.
(b) Both the Assertion and Reason are true, but the Reason is not the correct explanation of the Assertion.
(c) The Assertion is true but, the Reason is false.
(d) The Assertion is false but, the Reason is true.

3. In what way did the brain drain phenomenon impact source countries?

4. What is the writer referring to by 'greener pastures'?

5. What can be inferred about brain drain from Paragraph 1? the tech sector witnessed a significant phenomenon termed 'brain drain', where skilled professionals migrated from one region to another, predominantly from ....

6. List two countries which have experienced a notable exodus of tech talent to tech hubs such as Silicon Valley and Singapore.

(a) .... (b) ....

7. Fill in the blanks with appropriate words..

Efforts to address the root causes of..............., such as improving economic opportunities and promoting inclusive growth, are essential for .... a more balanced and sustainable global tech ecosystem.

8. Complete the following sentence with correct facts and figures from the table.

US granted majority H1B visas to indian skilled workers, the number was as high as .... in FY 2020.

9. After reading the passage, give a brief explanation on how brain drain has impacted the education industry in India. Give statistics.

PASSAGE 3

Read the given passage carefully and answer the questions that follow.

Media and Entertainment (M&E) is a very wide industry and constitutes segments like television, online gaming, animation and VFX, music, digital advertising, films, print and radio. It is a sunrise sector of the Indian economy as each of its segment is making high growth strides and is expected to grow at a much faster rate than the global average and is bound to prove its resilience to the other developed economies.

M&E industry's growth is mainly driven by the digitalisation and immense usage of the internet over the last half decade backed by rising consumer demand and their changing lifestyles. The upcoming half decade is favourable to the industry's growth due to an increase in the use of digital technologies across the sector.

Share of major industry segments (FY 2018)

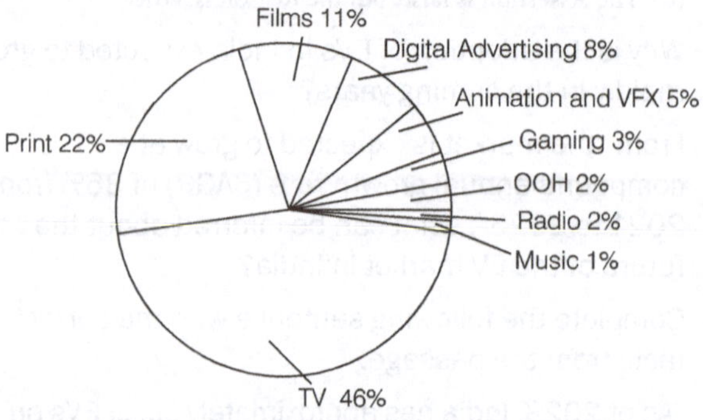

Television (TV), print and films combined together hold 80% of the market share of the M&E industry in India. The nation has the second largest television market in the Asia Pacific region in terms of subscribers and the largest contributing segment for the domestic M&E sector.

The launch of new regional language channels and digitalisation supported the segment and resulted in the growth of a number of television channels.

Though implementation of GST is likely to impact the advertising revenue, a strong viewership backed by TV digitalisation, Free to Air (FTA) and the free dish will support in continuation of the segment's supremacy in the M&E industry in India.

The second largest segment of the M&E in India is the print industry, which accounts for a share of 22% . Although the growth rate was and will remain the lowest among all the segments due to increasing pressure from digital platforms and a weak advertising demand owing to implementation of the GST, but unlike global markets, newspaper reading trend has increased in India across all age groups, demographics and mainly among the youths as it is necessary for students aspiring for government jobs to read such material.

The Indian film industry is now the third largest segment of the M&E in India and is the largest producer of films all across the globe, with 400 production and corporate houses involved in creating and production of films.

The digital advertising, animation and VFX (visual effects), gaming, OOH (Out Of Home) and radio are some of the emerging and fast-growing segments of the M&E industry in India. Although the share of the market size of all these five segments is only 20% of the total market size of the industry, all these are moving with tremendous growth strides, especially the digital advertising which has grown rapidly. The Indian digital advertising market has emerged as the 3rd largest advertising medium after TV and print advertising in India and is projected to grow more, backed by immense growth of the internet penetration and data use due to smartphone growth, with the launch of 4G services and declining tariffs.

Questions

1. Complete the sentence appropriately.
In the line '................ the ability of customised', the word 'customised' does not refer
(a) to be made in a new manner
(b) to be modified according to needs
(c) to be changed according to requirements
(d) to take a new approach

2. Which of the following statements is not true regarding the television industry?
(a) The Television industry alone accounts for 80% of the M&E industry.
(b) The launch of new regional language channels resulted in the growth of a number of television channels.
(c) India has the second largest television market in the Asia Pacific region in terms of subscribers.
(d) Free to Air (FTA) and the free dish supports the segment's supremacy in the M&E industry in India.

3. Why does the growth rate of the print industry remain low?

4. What will help in the growth of the Indian digital advertising market?

5. Based on your understanding of the passage, choose the option that lists the various parts of the M&E industry.

(i) Gaming	(ii) OOH	(iii) Radio
(iv) Film	(v) E-commerce	(vi) Sports

6. Why is the M&E industry called the Sunrise Industry?

7. Complete the following sentence appropriately.
The launch of .... supported the growth of the M&E industry.

8. Complete the sentence appropriately.
The growth of the M&E industry results from ....

9. Justify the following.
Newspapers will not go away from the Indian M&E industry.

PASSAGE 4

Read the given passage carefully and answer the questions that follow.

1. The Municipal Corporation of Gurugram recently admitted before the National Green Tribunal that untreated sewage from the city mixes with treated wastewater in the drains into the Yamuna. The putrid river that flows through New Delhi is only one of the many severely polluted surface water bodies in the country. Government agencies estimate that as much as 80% of India's surface water is contaminated and most of it comes from sewage.

2. The effects of this contamination are immediately felt with the onset of the monsoons. No sooner had the rains begun, the reports of water-borne diseases like diarrhoea and cholera breakouts trickled in from Delhi, Pune, Varanasi and Chennai as broken water pipes and flooding allowed faecal sludge mix (polluted water) into potable water.

3. The Central Pollution Control Board in 2009 calculated that major cities and towns together generate more than 38 billion litres of sewage every day, of which only 30% is collected. Less than 20% of this is treated because that's all the treatment capacity available. The rest is just emptied into rivers, lakes, seas and ponds.

4. A soon-to-be-released report by Water Aid India on faecal sludge management documents the gaps in India's sewage system. Seventeen million, or roughly 20% of urban households lack sanitation facilities, the report says.

   Among those that have access to sanitation, only 32% are connected to a sewage network, the rest depending on septic tanks and pit latrines. There are more numbers to raise a stink about. More than 5 lakh pit latrines are unsanitary, being nothing more than open pits. More than 9 lakh toilets empty directly into drains. Among the 18% of urban households that don't have access to individual toilets, more than 12% resort to open defecation.

5. The story gets murkier beyond the numbers. Where sewers exist, they often leak or overflow. Instead of being cleaned every few years, septic tanks are left to accumulate faecal sludge that percolates into groundwater. When the tanks are cleaned the black water is disposed of in fields and water bodies, once again contaminating open fresh water.

6. The Water Aid report looks at sanitation systems in six states and offers a snapshot of how much wastewater is dumped untreated. Delhi, for instance, uses 4,346 million litres of water per day of which 87% returns as waste.

   However, Delhi has the capacity to treat only 61% of the total wastewater it generates. The class I cities of Maharashtra together consume three times as much as Delhi does, turn 80% of that into sewage and treat less than half of their total wastewater. The statistics are far worse for class II cities.

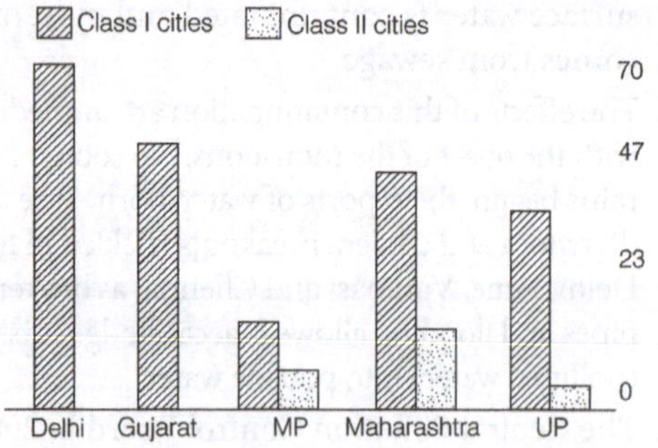

Perentage of total wastewater that is treated

7. Even with the creation of the National Urban Sanitation Policy in 2008 and several thousands of crores being spent by states on sewage networks, the problem has grown worse in the last five years.

Questions

1. What is true regarding the contaminated water?

(a) Less than 20% of the contaminated water is treated.

(b) Most of the contaminated water is dumped into the water bodies.

(c) Contaminated water is the reason for the lack of potable water.

(d) Both (a) and (b)

2. Why does the presence of septic tanks result in contamination of groundwater?

(a) They leak on the ground water due to overflow.

(b) They are not cleaned.

(c) They are an inefficient system of sewage management.

(d) Both (b) and (c)

3. In the line 'The putrid river that flows through....', 'putrid' means ....

4. What does the revelation made by the Municipal Corporation of India point to?

5. The class I cities of which state together consume water three times as much as Delhi?

6. The expression the story gets murkier beyond the numbers show .... (desperation/hopelessness).

7. Complete the following appropriately.

.... is the reason for Yamuna being one of the most polluted rivers in the country?

8. Complete the sentence appropriately.

.... is disposed of in fields and water bodies when the tanks are cleaned.

9. How much of India's surface water is contaminated? In front of whom did the Municipal Corporation of Gurugram admit that untreated sewage from the city mixes with treated wastewater?

PASSAGE 5

Read the given passage carefully and answer the questions that follow.

In the recent years the trend towards health, figure and fitness has increased. Energy imbalance between calories consumed on one hand, and calories expended on the other hand, due to urbanization, sedentary lifestyles and excessive consumption of sugary foods along with increased fat consumption, especially saturated fats is leading the Indian population to obesity.

Sugar substitutes in various food and beverages are very popular in most of the countries. Extensive scientific research has demonstrated the safety of the six low-calorie sweeteners currently approved for use in foods in the U.S. and Europe (stevia, acesulfame-K, aspartame, neotame, saccharin and sucralose) each with an acceptable daily intake.

A number of studies have been carried out to confirm the safety of artificial sweeteners. A number of studies have also shown the adverse effects of the same. But most of the studies have limitations such as effects shown only in animals not in human, small sample size, high doses, statistically non-significant or borderline significant, etc. The sugar substitutes are thoroughly investigated for safety with hundreds of scientific studies and then approved by different regulatory authorities like the U.S. FDA, JECFA and FSANZ. Some agents are approved with warning labels too.

Artificial sugar substitutes	Potency [Times sweeter than sucrose]	Approved by FDA	Acceptable daily intake (ADI) (mg/kg of body weight/day)
Acesulfame potassium	200	1988	15
Alitame	2000	Pending approval	—
Aspartame	160-200	1981	40
Salt of aspartame acesulfame	350	—	—
Cyclamate	30	Banned 1969, pending re-approval	—
Dulcin	250	Banned 1950	—
Glucin	300	—	—
Neohesperidin dihydrochalcone	1500	—	—
Neotame	8000	2002	18
Saccharin	300	1958	5
Sucralose	600	1998	Permitted for use under interim regulation

So further exploration is required with well-designed large-scale studies in the general population. On the anecdotal evidence, it has been concluded that based on analysis of the database of case histories, there are a number of symptoms that are recurrently reported by individuals who believe that they are caused by sugar substitute ingestion. The information gathered in this analysis can be useful in guiding the design and format of any investigative study that may be undertaken to determine individual sensitivity to sugar substitutes.

Questions

1. Which of the following best captures the writer's perspective on the safety of artificial sweeteners?
   (a) Completely safe, no further research needed.
   (b) Generally safe, but more large-scale studies needed.
   (c) Unsafe, should be avoided.
   (d) Only a concern for those with health issues.
2. Select the option that is true for the Assertion and Reason given below.

   Assertion (A) There are a number of symptoms that are recurrently reported by individuals who believe that they are caused by sugar substitute ingestion.

   Reason (R) Anecdotal evidence can be useful in guiding the design and format of any investigative study that may be undertaken to determine individual sensitivity to sugar substitutes.

   (a) Both the Assertion and Reason are true, and the Reason is the correct explanation of the Assertion.
   (b) Both the Assertion and Reason are true, but the Reason is not the correct explanation of the Assertion.
   (c) The Assertion is true, but the Reason is false.
   (d) The Assertion is false, but the Reason is true.
3. What inference can be made regarding the need for further research on sugar substitutes?
4. What is the writer referring to by 'anecdotal evidence'?
5. List the regulatory authorities mentioned in the passage that approve the use of artificial sweeteners.
   (a) .... (b) ....
6. Fill in the blank.

   The need for well-designed large-scale studies is emphasised because many existing studies on artificial sweeteners have shown .... (adverse/favourable) effects in animals that may not apply to humans.
7. What can be inferred about the current limitations of studies on artificial sweeteners mentioned in Paragraph 3? Many studies on artificial sweeteners are limited by factors such as ....
8. Complete the following sentence with correct facts and figures from the table.

   Aspartame is 160-200 times sweeter than sucrose with a daily acceptable intake of 40 mg/kg of body weight/day, it was approved by FDA in ....
9. After reading the passage, give a brief description of 'Energy Imbalance'. Give its causes and one disease caused by it.

PASSAGE 6

Read the given passage carefully and answer the questions that follow.

1. **Coverage and Significance**
   - Oceans cover 71% of Earth's surface and hold 97% of the planet's water.
   - Vital for regulating weather, climate, coastlines, food supply, and producing oxygen.
   - Historical importance in trade and cultural exchange.
2. **World Oceans Day**
   - **Date** 8th June, designated by the UN General Assembly (Resolution 63/111, 5th December, 2008).
   - **Purpose** Raise awareness about the ocean's role and promote its protection.
   - **2024 Theme** 'Awaken New Depths' aims to highlight the need for deeper commitment to ocean preservation.
3. **Challenges to Ocean Health**
   - **Climate Change and Global Warming** Ocean temperatures have risen by 1.45°C on average, with some areas exceeding 2°C. Leads to coral bleaching and negative impacts on marine ecosystems.
   - **Ocean Acidification** Ocean absorbs 25-30% of $CO2$ emissions, causing a 30% increase in acidity since pre-industrial times. Projected to rise by 170% by 2100, affecting marine species and coastal ecosystems.
   - **Rising Sea Levels** Contributing 40% of global sea level rise, with a 9 cm increase over the past three decades. Causes flooding, erosion, and contamination of agricultural lands.
   - **Plastics and Ocean Debris** Over 80% of marine pollution comes from land-based sources; 8 million tons of plastic enter the ocean annually. Creates large garbage patches, harming marine life.
   - **Other Pollutions** Includes oil spills, noise pollution, and runoff from agriculture and industry.
   - **Overfishing and Commercial Whaling** Drives species to extinction, affecting food security and ecological balance.
   - **Shipping and Transport** Contributes to pollution through waste disposal and emissions.
4. **Solutions and Actions**
   - **Marine Protected Areas (MPAs)** Protect endangered species and local ecosystems.
   - **Reducing Pollution** Adopt renewable energy, enforce waste disposal regulations, and ban single-use plastics.
   - **Changing Consumption Habits** Promote sustainable fishing and plant-based diets.
   - **Sustainable Energy** Invest in clean technologies and lower emissions in maritime transport.
   - **Research and Awareness** Enhance scientific research and public education on ocean issues.

Protecting the ocean requires global cooperation, sustainable practices, and increased awareness to ensure its health and vitality for future generations.

Questions

1. Which of the following options does not mean the same as 'erosion'?

(a) Corrosion (b) Disintegration
(c) Breakdown (d) Construction

2. Select the option that is true for the Assertion and Reason given below.

Assertion (A) Implementing Marine Protected Areas (MPAs) is crucial for the conservation of endangered species and ecosystems.

Reason (R) Establishing MPAs helps reduce human impact on marine environments, while adopting renewable energy and sustainable practices further protects ocean health and biodiversity.

(a) Both the Assertion and Reason are true, and the Reason is the correct explanation of the Assertion.
(b) Both the Assertion and Reason are true, but the Reason is not the correct explanation of the Assertion.
(c) The Assertion is true, but the Reason is false.
(d) The Assertion is false, but the Reason is true.

3. Identify the word that refers to 'an amount of a substance that is produced and sent out into the air that is harmful to the environment'.

4. What percentage of the Earth's surface is covered by oceans, and why are they significant?

5. What is the purpose of World Oceans Day, and when is it celebrated?

6. What challenges do oceans face due to climate change?

7. Complete the sentence suitably.

The ocean absorbs 25-30% of $CO2$ emissions, leading to a 30% increase ....

8. Complete the following with a suitable reason.

Rising sea levels contribute 40% of global sea level rise and have resulted in ....

9. What are some key solutions and actions to protect the ocean, and why is global cooperation important?

PASSAGE 7

Read the given passage carefully and answer the questions that follow.

Over the past decade, India has experienced significant infrastructural growth, with numerous projects aimed at improving transportation, energy, and urban development. One notable area of expansion is the transportation sector, where the government has invested heavily in building new roads, railways, and airports.

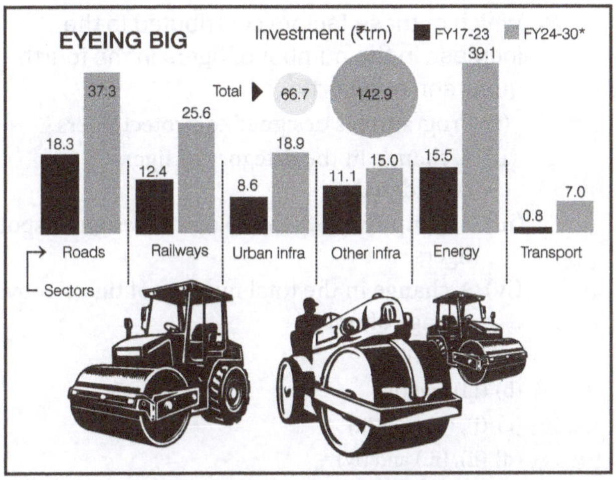

According to data from the Ministry of Road Transport and Highways, India's road network has expanded rapidly in the past decade, with the total length of national highways increasing from around 70,000 kilometers in 2010 to over 1,35,000 kilometers by 2020. This expansion has improved connectivity between cities and rural areas, facilitating trade and economic development.

In addition to roads, the Indian Railways has also undergone significant modernisation and expansion efforts. The introduction of high-speed trains, such as the Vande Bharat Express, has reduced travel times and improved passenger comfort. Furthermore, the government's ambitious Sagarmala project aims to develop ports and coastal infrastructure to enhance maritime trade and logistics.

India's energy infrastructure has also seen considerable growth, with a focus on renewable energy sources. According to the Ministry of New and Renewable Energy, the country's renewable energy capacity has more than doubled in the past decade, reaching over 90 gigawatts by 2020. This expansion of renewable energy infrastructure aligns with India's commitment to reducing carbon emissions and combating climate change.

Urban development has been another priority, with initiatives like the Smart Cities Mission aimed at creating sustainable and livable urban centers. Under this program, over 100 cities across India have been selected for various infrastructure projects, including improved public transportation, waste management systems, and digital connectivity.

In conclusion, India has made significant strides in infrastructural growth over the past decade, with investments in transportation, energy, and urban development. These efforts have not only improved connectivity and livability but also contributed to economic growth and sustainable development.

Questions

1. What is one of the main priorities of the Smart Cities Mission mentioned in the passage?
   (a) Improving agricultural productivity
   (b) Enhancing digital connectivity
   (c) Expanding military infrastructure
   (d) Investing in space exploration
2. Write the word that can replace 'strides' as used in the following context.
   India has made significant strides in infrastructural growth over the past decade, with investments in transportation, energy and urban development.
3. How has the expansion of India's road network impacted the country's economic development?
4. What can be inferred about the Indian government's commitment to environmental sustainability from its energy infrastructure projects?
5. What is the writer referring to by 'infrastructural growth'?
6. According to the Ministry of New and Renewable Energy, the country's renewable energy capacity has more than doubled in the past decade, reaching over 90 gigawatts by 2020. What is its implication?
7. Fill in the blank with the appropriate answer.
   This expansion of renewable energy infrastructure .... India's commitment to reducing carbon emissions and combating climate change.
8. Complete the following sentence with correct facts from Paragraph 2.
   According to data from the Ministry of Road Transport and Highways, India's road network has expanded the total length of national highways from around 70,000 kilometres in 2010 to over .... by 2020.
9. What modernisation efforts have been made in the Indian Railways in the past decade? How have these efforts improved passenger experiences?

PASSAGE 8

Read the given passage carefully and answer the questions that follow.

1. The fourth quadrennial report on the status of tigers released by the Government of India revealed that the number of tigers in India increased by 74% between 2010 and 2018, and by more than 33% between 2014 and 2018.
2. Certain methodological changes along with tiger conservation programmes have contributed to the increase. The tiger population has been estimated in three phases, wherein phase three made extensive use of camera traps. The 2018 data has been lauded since 83% of the tiger population was individually camera trapped. Additionally, in this data, all tigers above the age of one have been included while in all the previous surveys (in 2010 and 2006), only tigers above 1.5 years of age were included.
3. The estimate of tiger population may not be accurate owing to the limitations in counting the highly secretive carnivore. Hence, the survey provided not a specific number but the range of tiger numbers i.e., between 2,603 and 3,346.This data has a possible error of 14%. Currently, India is home to 75% of the global tiger population.
4. To estimate the tiger population pragmatically (since tigers keep moving within forests and are not restricted to any one state), India's states have been classified into five different regions—Shivalik Hills and Gangetic plains, North-East Hills and Brahmaputra Plains, Sunderbans, Central India and Eastern Ghats, and Western Ghats. The graph shows the region wise distribution of India's tiger population.

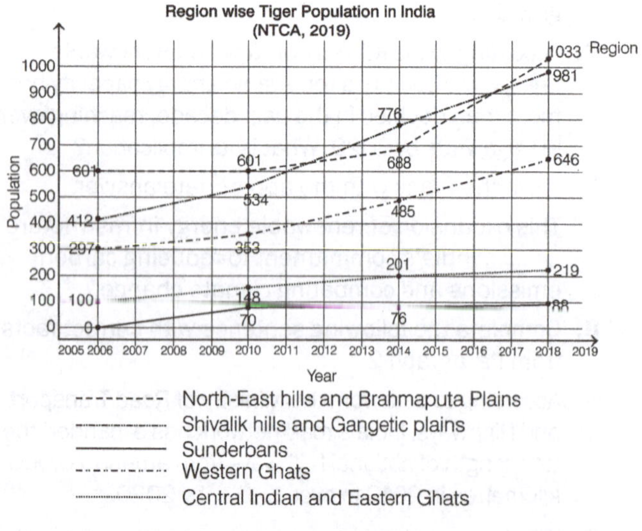

Questions

1. Why is it a challenge to accurately estimate the total number of tigers present?
   (a) People who are skilled at estimating without errors are few.
   (b) Tigers are difficult to be spotted since they are good at hiding.
   (c) Tigers are dangerous since they are prone to attacking humans.
   (d) People find it difficult to keep up with the fast growing number of tigers.
2. Which of these factors contributed to the increase in the number of tigers in the fourth quadrennial report?
   (i) Programmes designed to protect tigers.
   (ii) A change in the category of tigers considered.
   (iii) An improved methodological design to spot tigers.
   (iv) A change in the total number of tigers above the age of one.
   (a) (i) and (iii)
   (b) (iii) and (iv)
   (c) (i), (ii) and (iii)
   (d) (ii), (iii) and (iv)
3. What does the phrase 'wildlife trafficking' in Paragraph 5 refer to?
4. Fill in the blank.
   The data may not be .... (incorrect/precise) given the secretive nature of the tigers.
5. What does the given statement taken from Paragraph 2 mean? '83% of the tiger population was individually camera trapped'?
6. State ways in which each of us can contribute to the conservation of tigers.
7. Based on the graph given, ... and .... regions showed a trend different from other regions between 2006 and 2010.
8. Complete the following statement with an appropriate inference from the passage.
   It is appropriate to refer to India as the Land of Tigers because ....
9. Why does the author state that the increase in the tiger population between 2010-2018 is 'a step in the right direction'?

ANSWERS (REVIEW EXERCISE)

Discursive Passages

Passage 1

1. No changes are required to be made in the vehicle that uses biodiesel as a fuel.
2. (a) its use has more than doubled
3. The writer makes the given statement because fossil fuels disrupt the natural carbon cycle of the biosphere. They increase the net carbon total in the atmosphere when extracted and burned. This increase in CO_2 in the atmosphere is linked to global warming and climate change.
4. (c) and (d)
5. True
6. (d) Conviction
7. According to the writer, biodiesel is a sustainable fuel. This means that biodiesel furthers the idea of sustainability as it does not disrupt the natural carbon cycle of the biosphere. The two sources of biodiesel are
   (i) Canola plants (ii) Methanol
8. (b) Biodiesel-An Alternate Oil

Passage 2

1. The technology that enables AI to stimulate human like intelligence are machine learning, natural language processing and computer vision.
2. (a) Data privacy, algorithmic bias, and concentration of power
3. The tone of the writer in these lines is cautious and admonitory. They emphasise the importance of addressing ethical and societal concerns associated with AI, indicating a sense of urgency and responsibility in its development and deployment.
4. (c) and (e)
5. True
6. (a) analyse
7. Society can mitigate AI risks with ethical guidelines, transparency and human oversight, fostering collaboration while maximising AI benefits for societal welfare.
8. (d) All of the above

Passage 3

1. Newspapers are full of crimes because there is breakdown of basic facilities and corrosion of human values.
2. (b) They provide cheap labour and captive vote banks.
3. The two sides of a coin that the writer is referring to are
   (i) The bright, well-lit and illuminated world of the rich in the city.
   (ii) The dark, dingy and depressing world of the poor in the same city.
4. (d) Both (a) and (b)
5. the quality of life has deteriorated at an alarming rate due to the influx of lakhs of people every year
6. (d) Both (a) and (c)
7. According to the passage, it is apparent that although the poor and the rich live in the same city, they lead completely different lives. There is a stark contrast in their circumstances and way of life.
8. (d) (ii) and (iii)

Passage 4

1. goal setting and prioritising
2. (b) increasing effectiveness and efficiency
3. A short break between hectic sessions at work gives us time for rest and relaxation. This helps us to improve our performance. The major mistake of not taking proper breaks is made when one is in a rush to meet the deadline.
4. (a) (i), (ii) and (iii)
5. organised, focused
6. (a) Multi-tasking
7. Time management is the act of planning and managing time that is spent on various activities. Books are the best way of learning time management.
8. (b) Time Management

Passage 5

1. Failures are the stepping-stones to success. We must get up after each failure and start again. We must always stay motivated and learn from our failures and mistakes.
2. (a) Keenness and the urge to be successful
3. Great men had sincerity, passion, high spirits, punctuality, commitment and hard labour in plenty to rise to the peak of success. Success certainly comes to people who possess these qualities.
4. (b) Achieving success feels like a person's life's purpose is fulfilled.
5. True
6. (b) Success can mean different things to different people.
7. The writer advises to always be sincere and passionate about one's goals. He also adds that in order to be successful, it is essential to be punctual, committed and in high spirits.
8. (d) Patience, persistence and perseverance

Passage 6

1. Sophisticated cyberattacks mentioned include ransomware and supply chain breaches.
2. (a) Insecure IoT devices as entry points
3. The writer's tone in these lines is urgent and collaborative. By emphasising the global nature of cyber threats and the need for international cooperation, the writer underscores the critical importance of unified, coordinated efforts to effectively combat cybercrime.
4. (c) and (e)
5. (a) wreak havoc
6. False
7. Mass surveillance and data breaches undermine individuals' right to privacy, exposing them to unwarranted scrutiny and surveillance. These implications necessitate legislative reforms and regulatory frameworks to safeguard privacy rights and protect against the misuse of personal data by tech giants and government agencies.
8. (c) By destabilising governments and disrupting critical infrastructure

Passage 7

1. Archaeology is the study of human activity through recovery and analysis of material culture.
2. (b) Finding and preserving artefacts is integral to knowing more about our cultural past.
3. According to the author, the artefacts, which are a part of our global cultural heritage and have unique artistic merit or scientific value, should not be sold.
4. (b) paltry and substantial
5. priceless objects
6. (b) (ii) and (iii)
7. clandestine
8. (b) Seekers of knowledge

Passage 8

1. (c) Comprehensive strategies for managing exam stress in students
2. The tone of the writer in the given lines is serious and concerned, highlighting the widespread and multifaceted impact of exam stress on students' mental and physical health. The use of terms like 'pervasive', 'anxiety', 'depression' and 'physical ailments' underscores the urgency of addressing this issue.
3. multifaceted approach
4. (b) and (e)
5. Time management prevents last-minute cramming, making tasks more manageable and reducing anxiety.
6. A supportive environment encourages effort over grades, reduces high-pressure expectations and provides emotional reassurance. Workshops on stress and time management equip students with tools to handle workload effectively, fostering a secure and confident mindset.
7. (a) Deep-breathing exercises
8. True

Case Based Factual Passages

Passage 1

1. (a) Two-wheeler
2. (b) Both the Assertion and Reason are true, but the Reason is not the correct explanation of the Assertion.
3. The adoption of EVs in India is expceted to grow rapidly in the coming years due to supportive government policies and increasing environmental awareness.
4. From the given line we can infer that the EV market in India is projected to expand significantly over the next few years.
5. 1.5 million
6. It means that the EV market is expected to grow by 36% each year on average over the specified period.
7. (a) Hero electric (b) Ola electric
8. (a) Delhi, Bengaluru
9. Government policies like FAME II and reduced GST have incentivised EV adoption, while the expansion of charging infrastructure supports the practical use and convenience of EVs.

Passage 2

1. (d) All of the above
2. (a) Both the Assertion and Reason are true and the Reason is the correct explanation of the Assertion.
3. The brain drain phenomenon led to a depletion of intellectual capital, hindering technological advancement and economic growth in source countries.
4. The phrase 'greener pastures' typically refers to better opportunities or circumstances elsewhere, often implying a more favorable environment for personal or professional growth and success.
5. developing countries to developed ones
6. (a) India (b) Nigeria
7. brain drain, fostering
8. 74.9%
9. The departure of skilled workers often resulted in a loss of investment in education and training, as governments and private sectors struggled to retain talent and foster innovation domestically. 1.8 million Indians will be spending close to $85 billion on studying abroad by the year 2024.

Passage 3

1. (a) to be made in a new manner
2. (a) The television industry alone accounts for 80% of the M&E industry.
3. The growth rate of the print industry remains low globally and is bound to remain low due to the increasing pressure from the growth and popularity of digital platforms along with a weak advertising demand owing to the implementation of GST.

4. The Indian advertising industry is projected to grow more because of
 (i) smartphone usage growth
 (ii) launch of 4G services
 (iii) declining tariffs
5. (ii), (iii) and (iv)
6. The M&E industry is called the Sunrise Industry because its various parts are still growing to reach its full potential.
7. new regional language channels
8. digitalisation and internet
9. It is true that newspapers would never go away from the Indian M&E industry because while this print section is reducing globally with the dominance of digital platforms, newspaper reading has increased in India across all age groups and demographics. In addition, this section of media is crucial for students preparing for government exams.

Passage 4

1. (d) Both (a) and (b) 2. (d) Both (b) and (c)
3. decaying and smelly
4. The revelation made by the Municipal Corporation of India points to the problem of contamination of water bodies due to sewage.
5. The class I cities of Maharashtra consume water thrice as much as Delhi does.
6. hopelessness
7. Lack of proper sewage systems
8. Black water
9. As much as 80% of India's surface water is contaminated. In front of the National Green Tribunal, the Municipal Corporation of Gurugram admitted that untreated sewage from the city mixes with treated wastewater.

Passage 5

1. (b) Generally safe, but more large-scale studies needed.
2. (b) Both the Assertion and Reason are true, but the Reason is not the correct explanation of the Assertion.
3. The passage suggests that while sugar substitutes have undergone extensive scientific scrutiny, there is still a need for well-designed large-scale studies in the general population to fully understand their effects.
4. The writer refers to 'anecdotal evidence' as the collection of case histories where individuals have reported symptoms that they believe are caused by sugar substitute ingestion.
5. (a) U.S. FDA (Food and Drug Administration)
 (b) FSANZ (Food Standards Australia New Zealand)
6. adverse
7. small sample sizes, testing primarily on animals and borderline statistical significance
8. 1981
9. Energy imbalance is caused when the calories consumed and calories expended are disproportionate. It happens due to urbanization, sedentary lifestyles and excessive consumption of sugary foods along with increased fat consumption, especially saturated fats. This is leading the Indian population to obesity.

Passage 6

1. (d) Construction
2. (a) Both the Assertion and Reason are true, and the Reason is the correct explanation of the Assertion.
3. The word that refers to 'an amount of a substance that is produced and sent out into the air that is harmful to the environment' is emissions.
4. Oceans cover 71% of Earth's surface and hold 97% of the planet's water, playing a vital role in regulating weather, climate and food supply.
5. World Oceans Day, celebrated on 8th June, aims to raise awareness about the ocean's importance and promote its protection for future generations.
6. Climate change has raised ocean temperatures by an average of 1.45°C, causing coral bleaching and adversely affecting marine ecosystems by threatening biodiversity and fisheries.
7. in acidity since pre-industrial times
8. a 9 cm increase over the past three decades.
9. To protect the ocean, key solutions include establishing Marine Protected Areas (MPAs), reducing pollution through renewable energy and regulations, promoting sustainable fishing and plant-based diets, investing in clean technologies, and enhancing research and public awareness. Global cooperation is crucial to ensure these practices are effectively implemented, safeguarding ocean health for future generations.

Passage 7

1. (b) Enhancing digital connectivity
2. (c) Progress
3. The expansion of India's road network has improved connectivity between cities and rural areas, facilitating trade and economic development by enhancing transportation efficiency and accessibility.
4. The Indian Government's focus on renewable energy projects, which more than doubled the renewable energy capacity to over 90 gigawatts, reflects a strong commitment to reducing carbon emissions and combating climate change.
5. By 'infrastructural growth', the writer is referring to the expansion and development of transportation, energy and urban infrastructure projects in India over the past decade.

6. The implication of the given fact is that the expansion of renewable energy infrastructure is in accordance with India's commitment to reducing carbon emissions and combating climate change.
7. aligns with
8. 1,35,000 kilometers
9. The Indian Railways has introduced high-speed trains like the Vande Bharat Express, and launched the Sagarmala project to develop ports and coastal infrastructure. These efforts have reduced travel times, improved passenger comfort, and enhanced maritime trade and logistics, contributing to overall improved transportation experiences.

Passage 8

1. (b) Tigers are difficult to be spotted since they are good at hiding.
2. (c) I, II and III
3. The phrase 'wildlife trafficking' in paragraph 5 refers to illegal gathering, transportation and distribution of protected wildlife
4. precise
5. The statement that 83% of the tiger population was individually camera trapped means that 83% of the tigers were identified through special cameras that were set up in the tigers' natural habitats.
6. We can contribute to the conservation of tigers by not purchasing products that are made from tigers or their parts, by spreading awareness and sharing news about the tiger population, by volunteering for tiger conservation programmes, by donating for wildlife conservation projects and by carefully driving in the natural habitats of tigers.
7. Central India and Eastern Ghats
8. India is home to 75% of the tiger population in the world
9. The writer states that the increase in the tiger population between2010-2018 is 'a step in the right direction' because the outcome contributes towards the success of the Sustainable Development Goal 15 established by the United Nations. The goal focuses on the prevention of threatened species. Since tigers are an endangered species, the increase in the tiger population is aligned to this goal.

ASSESSMENT EXERCISE

Discursive Passages

Passage 1

Read the given passage carefully and answer the questions that follow.

Overpowering prey is a challenge for creatures that do not have limbs. Some species like Russell's viper inject poison. Some others opt for an alternative non-chemical method - rat snakes, for instance, catch and push their prey against the ground, while pythons use their muscle power to crush their prey to death. But snakes can't be neatly divided into poisonous and non-poisonous categories.

Even species I listed as non-poisonous aren't completely free of poison. The common Sand Boa, for instance, produces secretions particularly poisonous to birds. So the species doesn't take any chance - it crushes its prey and injects poison as an extra step. Do vipers need poison powerful enough to kill hundreds of rats with just one drop? After all, they eat only one or two at a time. While hunting animals try their worst to kill most efficiently, their prey use any trick to avoid becoming a meal, such as developing immunity to poison. For instance, Californian ground squirrels are resistant to Northern Pacific rattlesnake poison.

Competition with prey is not the only thing driving snakes to evolve more and more deadly poison. Snakes also struggle to avoid becoming prey themselves. Some snake killers have partial immunity to poison. Famously, mongooses are highly resistant to cobra poison, and with their speed and agility, kill snakes fearlessly. It would be the death of cobras as a species if they didn't evolve a more deadly poison to stop mongooses. Poison has another important role. It's an extreme meat softener; specific enzymes break up the insides of the prey. Normally, a reptile depends on the sun's warm rays to aid digestion.

But I wonder if we cannot use venom in our favour. In remote parts of India, local hospitality often involves leather-tough meat. I chew and chew until my jaws ache. If I spit it out or refuse, our hosts would be offended, I swallow like a python stuffing a deer down its throat and hope I don't choke. If only I had poison.

1. What dual strategy does the common Sand Boa use to ensure its prey is subdued?

2. Which of the following best explains why snakes continue to evolve more deadly poison, according to the passage?

(a) To develop immunity against their prey's defenses.

(b) To defend against predators like mongooses that have developed resistance to their poison.

3. Analyse the tone of the writer in the given lines from Paragraph 2? Rationalise your response in about 40 words.

"Do vipers need poison powerful enough to kill hundreds of rats with just one drop? After all, they eat only one or two at a time."

4. Based on Paragraph 3, complete the following sentence appropriately.

The writer notes that mongooses are highly resistant to cobra poison, forcing cobras to evolve more deadly poison to avoid becoming prey themselves.

5. State whether the following statement is True or False According to the passage, all species of snakes can be neatly divided into poisonous and non-poisonous categories.

6. The passage mentions that some snakes use their muscle power to crush their prey. Select two antonyms of 'crush' as used in this context?

(a) Release (b) Unhand

(c) Inject (d) Choke

(e) Swallow

7. How do the hunting strategies of rat snakes and pythons differ from those of vipers, according to the passage?

8. Which statement best captures the writer's skepticism about the necessity of potent viper poison?

(a) Vipers do not consume hundreds of rats at once.

(b) Rats are immune to viper poison.

(c) Poison is unnecessary for hunting.

(d) Vipers often struggle with digestion.

Passage 2

Read the given passage carefully and answer the questions that follow.

1. Corruption, terrorism, communalism, greed for power and wealth and the list of ailments that affect modern society continues. More than half the population of India is below the age group of 25 and the future of the country will only be bright if youngsters are equipped to deal with these ailments.
2. A child is a storehouse of potential and it is essential to nurture and develop these attributes from a very young age. Since they spend much of their time in school, the curriculum in school should be such that it enables children to understand, care and practise ethical values like respect, justice and civic sense. Education should aim to develop a sense of rights and duties as well as moral values like honesty, responsibility and respect for others.
3. Moral education should be directed towards enhancing a child's ability to critically analyse situations, make decisions, empathise with people and work in cooperation towards a common goal.
4. As a means of direct instruction to students, schools are very influential in the character development of a child and the methods of education affect the development of morally upright citizens who can bring about a much-needed change in the country.
5. The youth of today have to face many problems like drug abuse, violent behaviour and family issues. If they are not taught morals, they would fail to differentiate between good and bad values. Hence, they would be incapable of dealing with different types of issues.

   A sound moral base would help a child make the right decisions, especially in an era where the youth is increasingly coming under the negative influence of the media.

6. Schools in India have introduced moral education as part of their curriculum because they realise that morally sound citizens are the need of the hour. Since most children look up to their teachers as role models, it is most appropriate that they be the facilitators of moral values.

7. Thus, schools should focus more on the personality development of children since it is one of the most important responsibilities of a school. Schools should take the initiative to mould children into better human beings so that they can make the world a better place to live in.

1. Which moral values are important for children to learn?

2. Select the option that conveys the message "Morally sound citizens are the need of the hour."
   (a) Government should take major decisions about spreading moral education.
   (b) Better human beings can make the world a better place to live in.
   (c) Developing moral qualities is the only way to solve these social issues.
   (d) Moral citizens can only be possible by giving moral education to the mass population.

3. Why is it important to inculcate moral values since childhood? Answer in about 40 words.

4. Find the word in the passage which means the same as 'diseases'.

5. State True or False.
   Schools in India have understood that moral education is the need of the hour.

6. Complete the sentence appropriately.
   According to the passage, moral education helps children in ...., decision-making, cooperation and ....

7. What kind of problems are being faced by today's youth? Mention and elaborate in about 40 words.

8. Choose from the quotes given below which can represent the central idea of the passage.
   (a) "Education without morals is like a ship without a compass, merely wandering nowhere." - Martin Luther King Jr.
   (b) "People who try hard to do the right thing always seem mad." - Stephen King
   (c) "A quiet conscience makes one strong" - Anne Frank
   (d) "Our very lives depend on the ethics of strangers and most of us are always strangers to other people." - Bill Moyers

Passage 3

Read the given passage carefully and answer the questions that follow.

1. Through the Sustainable Development Goal (SDG), the countries of the world have resolved to achieve universal access to safe drinking water and adequate sanitation and hygiene for all by 2030. The aim is to ensure the consumption of safe drinking water and practice safe sanitation and hygiene, resulting in lower exposure to a contaminated environment, resulting in lower morbidity and mortality, especially amongst children.

2. The Swachh Bharat Mission was launched by the Government of India on 2nd October, 2014 to achieve the vision of 'Swachh Bharat' by 2nd October, 2019. The Swachh Bharat Mission Gramin-SBM (G) endeavours to accelerate rural sanitation coverage, reduce open defecation and improve the management of solid and liquid wastes in rural areas. The implementation of SBM (G) is the responsibility of the Ministry of Drinking Water and Sanitation (MDWS). The MDWS, while issuing guidelines for Open Defecation Free (ODF) verification, stressed on "safe technology option which aimed at no contamination of surface soil, groundwater or surface water; excreta management inaccessible to flies or animals; no human handling of fresh excreta and freedom from odour and unsightly condition". Over the past 4 years, over 92 million new households have received access to household toilets and by the end of the SBM (G) programme, all 16.5 million rural households will have such access. However, the issue is of usage and thus, the goal is to create ODF communities and villages, with no one defecating in the open.

3. The status of ODF villages published on the website of MDWS indicates that as of 01.04.2019, over 99% of rural HHs in India have toilet access. The declared ODF villages at all India levels accounted for 556,824 spreading over 2,47,723 Gram Panchayats, 6,031 Blocks and 616 Districts.

4. UNICEF in India accords high priority to the provision of safe sanitation and water services to people in rural areas and has over the past many years aided through catalytic technical support to MDWS, the Government of India and 15 State Governments in the implementation of the various sanitation programmes and since 2014, specifically to the SBM (G). With the progress of the SBM (G) and the declaration of ODF communities, there is an emerging question on whether the campaign to eliminate open defecation and create ODF communities is resulting in a decrease in faecal contamination in the environment.

1. Fill in the blank.
   The passage provides data that proves that ....

2. Complete the sentence with correct option.
   The government is successful in providing access to toilets to over 99% of rural households because of ....
   (a) awareness of hygiene
   (b) SBMG Programme

3. According to the passage, who is responsible for the progress of the Swachh Bharat Mission?

4. Suggest a suitable title for the passage. Give reason for your choice.

5. What happened with the progress of the SBM(G) and the declaration of ODF communities?

6. Complete the sentence appropriately.
   The purpose of the launch of Swachh Bharat Mission (G) was to ....

Choose the correct option.

(i) accelerate rural sanitation coverage
(ii) reduce open defecation
(iii) improve management of solid and liquid wastes in rural areas

(a) (i) and (ii) (b) (ii) and (iii) (c) (i), (ii) and (iii) (d) (i) and (iii)

7. Mention two benefits of the Swachh Bharat Mission.

8. Select the option that the given sentence refers to

"Over the past 4 years, over 92 million new households have received access to household toilets."

(a) There is an increase in the building of toilets inside households.
(b) There is an increase in the construction of community-shared toilets.
(c) There is an increase in the usage of toilets among rural households.
(d) There is an increase in access to toilets but are not being used by the villagers.

Passage 4

Read the given passage carefully and answer the questions that follow.

1. A rank outsider has no place in the assessment of beauty of either personality or person. That is why any elaborate beauty contest with judges fills me with wonderment. How can beauty be judged by means of tape and weighing machine? Perception of beauty seems to be an entirely personal matter, peculiar to each individual and even to each country. This is the reason why we remain unmoved when we see in our newspapers photographs of beauty queens of other lands. What is beautiful in one country or in one part of the country may be viewed differently in another. Among certain aborigines, piercing the upper lip and riveting on it several layers of metal discs is considered indispensable for any lady of social standing.
In our part of the country nose ornaments are very popular, and not so in the North; green eyes and red hair are probably considered masterly touches of nature in the West, while we think they handicap a girl's future.
2. It's not only in a perfectly measuring figure but also in features that real beauty is to be perceived; and this perception may turn out to be a highly individual view. For this reason a photo finish for deciding beauty is not feasible. The eye of the camera, though perfect in judging neck to neck of horses, is no better judge than the human eyes, where human beauty is concerned, for the simple reason that its data, once again will have to be verified and accepted only by us. The camera cannot be an absolute instrument of perception. Sometimes people look better than their photographs and sometimes photographs are better than the originals.
3. It is for this reason that any astute would-be-bridegroom refuses to be led away by photographs when he has to make up his mind, but insists upon holding over his decision till he has a chance to view the girl which becomes a turning point in any young man's life.
It is all, as anybody knows, elaborately staged and arranged. The girl is decked and dressed in her best. She is induced by her parents and sisters to come forward and show herself properly. The young man has to watch the curtain or the doorway through which she has to come with the greatest anxiety and curiosity and yet not seem to watch for the sake of propriety. The girl may come up and take a seat opposite but it does not help the young man. He is afraid to stare and judge. He is for the moment a beauty judge, but handicapped by proprieties which will not let him stare and assess.

1. Complete the sentence appropriately.
The beauty contests fill the author with ....

2. What makes the narrator wonder?

(a) Judging of beauty by means of tape and weighing machine.
(b) The judging of intelligence by conducting IQ tests.

3. Justify the following.
The perception of beauty by a camera is not absolute.

4. Choose the option that correctly states the two meanings of 'peculiar', as used in the passage.

(i) Bizarre (ii) Unique
(iii) Individual (iv) Weird
(v) Suspicious (vi) Specific

(a) (i) and (ii) (b) (ii) and (vi) (c) (iii) and (iv) (d) (i) and (v)

5. Complete the sentence appropriately.

A bridegroom who chooses his bride on seeing her photograph is ....

6. What is presented in the last paragraph of the passage?

(a) A prevailing tradition in the society.
(b) How a girl is judged in India with respect to beauty.
(c) Marriage is based on beauty.
(d) An arranged marriage.

7. As per the author, what is popular in our part of the country?

8. What are the words 'green' and 'red' in the passage used to describe?

(a) Vibrancy of nature (b) Mysteriousness
(c) Love for the West (d) Desire for something new

Passage 5

Read the given passage carefully and answer the questions that follow.

1. We have but one method of acquiring knowledge. From the lowest man to the highest yogi, all have to use the same method, and that method is called 'Concentration'. The chemist who works in his/her laboratory concentrates all the powers of his/her mind, brings them into one focus and throws them on the elements, and the elements stand analysed and thus his/her knowledge comes. The astronomer also concentrates the powers of his/her mind and brings them into one focus and then throws them on to objects through his/her telescope and stars and systems roll forward and give up their secrets to him. So, it is the same in every case—with the professor in his/her chair, the students and his/her books—with every man who is working to know.

2. The more this power of concentration is, the more is the knowledge acquired because this is the one and the only method of acquiring it. Even the lowest shoeblack,
if he/she pays more concentration, will polish shoes better, the cook with his/her concentration will focus all his/her attention on the work in hand and will cook a better meal. In making money or in worshipping God or in doing anything, the stronger the power of concentration, the better will be that work done.

3. Even though concentration is the key to acquiring knowledge—Concentration itself is not easy to attain. It is a skill that can be developed only through a lot of patience and practice. He/she who masters it is a real 'yogi'. To control our senses and to gather all our awareness into one focus is by no means an easy task. Life itself is complex and there are invariably several issues vying for our attention which makes it even more difficult to focus on only one thing. Even if we try to concentrate fully on the work in hand, our subconscious mind is scattered in varied directions and soon drags our conscious mind along without even our realising it.
It therefore requires a lot of discipline, will power and self-control to focus or concentrate.

4. However, the effort is worth it and pays rich dividends in the form of accomplishment of our goals. This is the one call, the one knock which opens the gate of nature and lets out floods of light.

1. Complete the sentence appropriately.
Concentration is difficult to attain because ....

2. Find the antonym of 'gathered' from the passage.

3. In your opinion, how does concentration help in acquiring knowledge?

4. What examples of professionals, who use their powers of concentration, are cited in the passage?

(i) Chemist (ii) Professor
(iii) Students (iv) Astronomer
(v) Physician

5. What is the prerequisite for acquiring knowledge?

6. Complete the sentence appropriately by choosing the correct option. The passage deals with methods of ....

(a) acquiring knowledge (b) being a yogi
(c) meditation (d) concentration

7. What is the key to acquiring knowledge? Why is it difficult to obtain?

8. List some qualities essential to attain concentration.

(i) A lot of patience and practice (ii) Discipline
(iii) Will power (iv) Self-control

(a) (i) and (ii) (b) (iii) and (iv)
(c) All of these (d) None of these

Case Based Factual Passages

Passage 1

Read the given passage carefully and answer the questions that follow.

Over the past decade, the Earth has experienced significant changes due to climate change, with rising global temperatures being one of the most alarming trends. NASA data shows a consistent increase in average global temperatures, with 2016, 2019, and 2020 being the hottest years on record. This rise is primarily attributed to the increase in greenhouse gas emissions from activities like burning fossil fuels. Atmospheric carbon dioxide rose by about 25 parts per million.

Keeling to the ceiling
Atmospheric carbon dioxide, parts per million

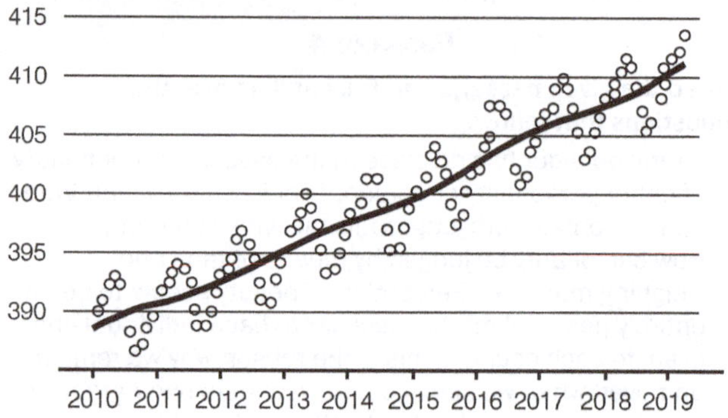

Another concerning consequence is the rapid melting of polar ice caps and glaciers. The Arctic, in particular, has seen record-breaking ice loss, with sea ice extent shrinking to just 3.41 million square kilometers in September 2012. This not only contributes to rising sea levels but also threatens species that rely on ice for habitat, such as polar bears and seals.

Climate change has also intensified extreme weather events worldwide. Hurricanes, typhoons, heatwaves, and wildfires have become more frequent and severe. For example, Hurricane Harvey caused unprecedented flooding in Houston in 2017, while Australia experienced its hottest and driest year on record in 2019, leading to devastating bushfires.

These environmental changes have far-reaching impacts on human health, food security, and economies. Climate change exacerbates air pollution, spreads diseases, and disrupts agriculture. Without urgent action to reduce emissions and build resilience, the World Bank warns that an additional 100 million people could be pushed into poverty by 2030.

In conclusion, the past decade has underscored the urgent need to address climate change. By reducing greenhouse gas emissions, transitioning to renewable energy sources, and adapting to a changing climate, we can work towards a sustainable future for all.

1. Fill in the blank by selecting the correct option.

Climate change exacerbates air pollution, spreads diseases, and disrupts agriculture. Without urgent action to reduce emissions and build resilience, the World Bank warns that an additional .... people could be pushed into poverty by 2030.

(a) 50 billion (b) 11 million (c) 100 million (d) 25 trillion

2. Select the option that is true for the Assertion and Reason given below.

Assertion (A) Hurricane Harvey caused unprecedented flooding in Houston in 2017.

Reason (R) By reducing greenhouse gas emissions, transitioning to renewable energy sources, and adapting to a changing climate, we can work towards a sustainable future for all.

(a) Both the Assertion and Reason are true, and the Reason is the correct explanation of the Assertion.
(b) Both the Assertion and Reason are true, but the Reason is not the correct explanation of the Assertion.
(c) The Assertion is true, but the Reason is false.
(d) The Assertion is false, but the Reason is true.

3. What can be inferred about the relationship between climate change and biodiversity from the passage?
4. Which year did the Arctic sea ice extent reach its lowest recorded level?
5. List two intensified extreme weather events in the past decade.
6. What is the writer referring to by the following phrase? "Over the past decade, the Earth has experienced significant changes due to climate change".
7. What can be inferred about the devastating effects of climate change mentioned in Paragraph 3? It can be inferred that climate change has also intensified .... worldwide.
8. Complete the following sentence with correct facts and figures from the table.

Atmospheric carbon dioxide was .... parts per million in 2019.

9. How has the rise in global temperatures over the past decade been quantified, and what are the implications of this trend for Arctic wildlife?

Passage 2

Read the given passage carefully and answer the questions that follow.

1. Whether it be Right to literacy, accessibility to schools and household expenditure on education, the rural-urban gap remains significant. There is a digital divide too, with just 4% of rural households having access to computers as compared to 23% in urban areas.

These and other trends on a rural-urban gap in education are revealed in the details of a survey conducted by the National Statistical Office (NSO).

2. The report on 'Household Social Consumption Education' surveyed 1.13 lakh households spread across over 8,000 villages and 6,000 urban blocks between July 2017 and June 2018. The study involved 1.52 lakh students across different levels of study.
3. On accessibility, while 92.7% of the rural households have a primary school within 1 km as compared to 87.2% in urban areas, the situation gets skewed as only 38% of the rural households have access to secondary school as compared to 70% in the urban areas on similar parameters.
4. While accessibility to a neighbourhood school at the primary level is not an issue in rural areas, the gross attendance ratio is also satisfactory with nearly 100% of boys and girls in rural as well as urban areas attending classes. However, in sync with reduced accessibility, there is a gap at the secondary level between rural and urban settings. The all-India literacy rate among persons aged 7 years and above is 77.7%. However, for the same age group, rural literacy is 73.5% and for urban areas it is 87.7%.
5. The digital divide between rural and urban households is stark with just 4% of the rural population having access to computers. The report highlighted that while only 15% surveyed population in the rural cluster has internet access, 42% of the students in the urban areas have access to the internet.
6. At the school level while the majority of the urban households had shown a preference for private schools, it's the opposite for rural households. The report highlights that 76.1% of the rural children are attending a primary and middle school run by the government while only 38% of the urban children attend government schools. However, for graduate and above studies, 49.7% of rural students are attending classes in government institutions as compared to 41% of their urban counterparts in government institutions.

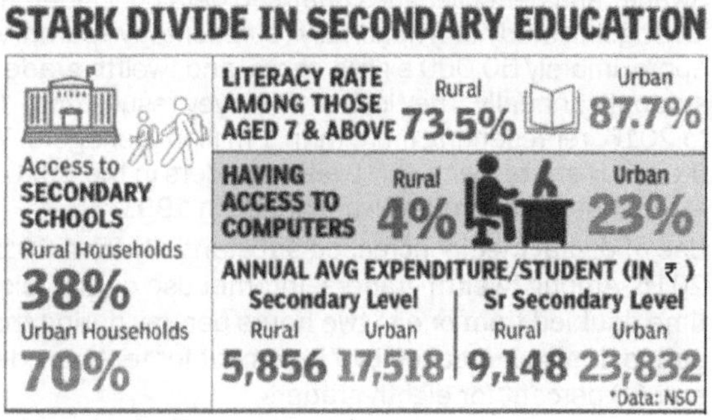

1. What does the Household Social Consumption: Education focus on?

(a) Rural-urban gap in education.
(b) Backtracking of online education. How the digital divide is more evident in education.
(c) Need for making technology more affordable. Rural-urban gap in education.
(d) How the digital divide is more evident in education.

2. Based on your understanding of the passage, choose the option that lists the factors that indicate the rural-urban gap.

(i) Right to literacy (ii) Accessibility to schools
(iii) Household expenditure (vi) Digital divide
(v) Employment opportunities
(vi) Infrastructure development

(a) (i) and (ii) (b) (iii) and (iv)
(c) (v) and (vi) (d) All of these

3. What did the survey conducted by the NSO cover?
4. In which aspect is the condition of education in the urban and rural households equal?

5. Fill in the blank.

The number of students (7 and above) educated in rural areas is .... (higher/lower) than that in urban areas.

6. Complete the sentence appropriately.

An appropriate title for the passage will be .... (Rich-Poor Divide/Rural-Urban Gap) in education.

7. Fill in the blank with the correct option.

The majority of urban households show preference to ....

8. What did the 'Household Social Consumption: Education' survey find out?

PASSAGE 3

Read the given passage carefully and answer the questions that follow.

1. News–if you can't remember the last time you saw a teenager reading a book, newspaper, or magazine, you're not alone. In recent years, less than 20 percent of teens report reading a book, magazine, or newspaper daily for pleasure. More than 80 percent say they use social media every day, according to research published by the World Psychological Association.
2. "Compared with previous generations, teens in the 2010s spent more time online and less time with traditional media such as books, magazines and television." said lead author of the book yGen and Professor of Psychology at ABC University. "Time on digital media has displaced time once spent enjoying a book or watching TV."
3. Swaner and her colleagues analysed data concluded from an ongoing study of a nationally representative sample of approximately 50,000 eighth, tenth, and twelfth-grade students annually. They looked at survey results from 1976 to 2016, representing more than 1 million teenagers. While the study started with only twelfth-graders in the 1970s, eighth and tenth-graders were added in 1991.
4. Use of digital media increased substantially from 2010 to 2016. Among twelfth-graders, internet use during leisure time doubled from one to two hours per day during that period. It also increased by 75 percent for tenth-graders and 68 percent for eighth-graders.
5. "In the mid-2010s, the average twelfth-grader reported spending approximately two hours a day texting, just over two hours a day on the internet – which included gaming – and just under two hours a day on social media." said Swaner. That's a total of about six hours per day on just three digital media activities during their leisure time.
6. In comparison, tenth-graders reported a total of five hours per day and eighth-graders reported four hours per day on those three digital activities. Consequently, the time spent in the digital world is seriously degrading the time they spend on more traditional media such as print books and newspapers.
7. The decline in reading print media was especially steep. In early 1984, 33 percent of tenth-graders said they read a newspaper almost every day. By 2016, that number was only 2 percent. In the 1970s, 60 percent of twelfth-graders said they read a book or a magazine almost every day; by 2016, only 16 percent did. Twelfth graders also reported reading fewer books each year in 2016 compared to how much they read in 1976, and approximately one-third did not read a book (including e-books) for pleasure in the year prior to the 2016 survey.
8. There's no lack of intelligence among young people. However, due to over-dependence on digital media they find it difficult to focus for long periods of time and to read long-form text. Subsequently, they find it challenging to understand complex issues and develop critical thinking skills.

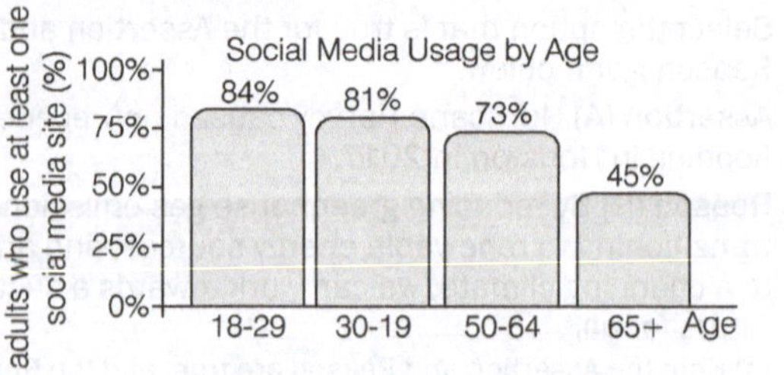

1. Select the option that displays the most likely reason for this research.

In order to find out ....

(a) reading choices of teenagers.
(b) digital competency of teenagers.
(c) speed of reading text.
(d) the decline of time spent on traditional media.

2. Select the option that is true for the Assertion and Reason given below.

Assertion (A) Concentration and focus of students is being lost at an exponentially high rate.

Reason (R) the trend of scrolling through anything has reduced the trend of reading newspapers.

(a) Both the Assertion and Reason are true, and the Reason is the correct explanation of the Assertion.
(b) Both the Assertion and Reason are true, but the Reason is not the correct explanation of the Assertion.
(c) The Assertion is true, but the Reason is false.
(d) The Assertion is false, but the Reason is true.

3. What does the author mean by 'degrading the time' in Paragraph 6?

4. Complete the given sentence by selecting the most appropriate option.

The digital activities that the twelfth-graders indulge in are ....

(a) texting, gaming and television
(b) texting, gaming and social media
(c) newspaper, books and magazine
(d) television, books and gaming

5. Complete the sentence appropriately with one/two words.

Teens today hardly read print media for ....

6. Do you think that the researchers of study added tenth and eighth-graders to the survey deliberately?

7. Complete the statement based on the passage.

Traditional media has been replaced by digital media, we can say this because ....

8. Complete the given sentence by selecting the most appropriate option.

The concluding sentence of the text makes a clear case for .... by listing it as a core competency for analysis and application.

(a) following social media
(b) reading long texts
(c) building focus and concentration
(d) developing constructive habits

9. Based on the reading of the text, state a point to challenge the given statement.

"Time on digital media has displaced time once spent enjoying a book or watching T.V."

PASSAGE 4

Read the given passage carefully and answer the questions that follow.

1. India is a country of many languages. The Constitution recognises 22 languages officially but over 121 unique languages have been identified in the country.
2. To preserve and encourage the literary function of language, the government introduced 'classical languages' in 2004. According to the Ministry of Culture, a classical language is one that is at least 1,500 years old and has ancient, valuable literature recorded in it. Further, such a language is original and not derived from another language. Based on these guidelines, six languages have been classified as classical languages. Tamil, Sanskrit, Kannada, Telugu, Malayalam and Odia.
3. The following graph shows the percentage of Indian people whose mother tongue is a classical language. This is as per data collected by the census of 2011. The census was not conducted in 2021 due to the pandemic.

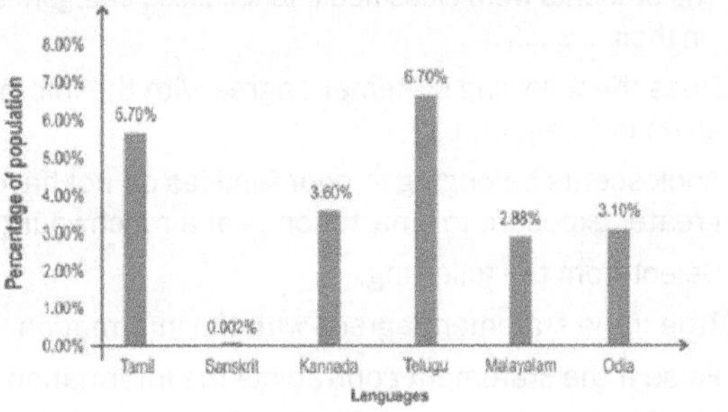

4. According to the graph, around 6.7% of the Indian population are native speakers of Telugu whereas Sanskrit has been identified as a mother tongue by only 0.002% of the population, which is around 24,821 people. Malayalam has the second lowest number of native speakers, making up about 2.9% of Indians.
5. The 2011 census data also noted that a majority of the native speakers reside in the area that their mother tongue originated from. For example, 93% of Kannada speakers live in Karnataka. Similarly, 93% of Malayalam speakers live in Kerala.
6. Balancing preservation of culture and inclusivity is a delicate equation for a heterogeneous country like India. With growing awareness, concepts like 'classical languages' may help us achieve harmony.

1. Which of these pieces of information can be confirmed by reading the passage?

(i) The number of people in India who speak Tamil.
(ii) Where the majority of native Sanskrit speakers live.
(iii) The reason Malayalam is considered a classical language.
(iv) The year when the idea of classical languages was introduced in India.

(a) Only (i)
(b) Only (iii)
(c) Only (i) and (ii)
(d) Only (iii) and (iv)

2. Select the option that is true for the Assertion and Reason given below.

Assertion (A) The government introduced classical languages to encourage the literary function of languages.

Reason (R) There are six classical languages.

(a) Both the Assertion and Reason are true, and the Reason is the correct explanation of the Assertion.
(b) Both the Assertion and Reason are true, but the Reason is not the correct explanation of the Assertion.
(c) The Assertion is true, but the Reason is false.
(d) The Assertion is false, but the Reason is true.

3. Imagine that a committee was formed to ensure that classical languages have more native speakers by the time the next census is conducted. In 40 words, answer the following questions to help the committee achieve its objective.

(a) Which classical language needs its attention most urgently and why?
(b) Which classical language would be third on its priority?

4. State an example from the passage that shows that India is a 'heterogeneous country'. Answer in one sentence.

5. Why has the writer stated the following line in the passage? Give a reason.

The census was not conducted in 2021 due to the pandemic.

6. Sanskrit can be called an almost dead language. Why?

7. Fill in the blanks with the appropriate option from those given in brackets.

Based on the passage, the .... (functional/historical) value of a language is of utmost importance while .... (preserving/categorising) it as a classical language.

8. Complete the sentence based on information from the passage.

If Tamil originated from Tamil Nadu, we can infer that .... of the native Tamil speakers would be living in Tamil Nadu.

9. Which of these hypothetical situations would help India achieve harmony? Justify your answer in about 40 words.

(a) If the majority of Indians who speak a classical language are settled abroad.
(b) If more languages from remote and tribal areas of India are identified as classical languages.
(c) If the percentage of Indians who are native Telugu speakers increases to more than 10 percent.

PASSAGE 5

Read the given passage carefully and answer the questions that follow.

1. Social media addiction is an emerging health problem in India, especially among the young population. Nowadays, irrespective of their socioeconomic background, adolescents have greater exposure to electronic gadgets like smartphones at a much younger age. The introduction of internet and the launch of low-cost data packages in 2016-2017 has put India on the global map for large-scale consumption of mobile data with active social media users going up to 197 million (14% of the population).
2. For adolescents, phone-based communication is an important way to maintain their social relationships. The use of social media websites then is one of the most common activities that has become an integral part of their day-to-day lives. Hence, making them more prone to social media overuse or addiction which may have a deleterious effect on the physical and psychological health. Hence, it became important to study the pattern of social media usage and associated physical and mental health issues among Pre-University (PU) college students as they are the vulnerable group.
3. A cross-sectional study was conducted in Government and Private PU colleges situated in Urban Bengaluru city, Karnataka, India during July to December 2016. The objectives of the study were to assess and compare the prevalence of social media addiction in different organisations, to assess the health problems related to social media usage, and to assess the various factors associated with social media addiction.
4. A total of 1870 study participants were recruited from both Government and Private PU colleges. Each participant was administered a pretest and semi-structured questionnaire as the study tool. They were asked to answer about the non-academic usage of social media. Scale comprised 10 questions, each given a score ranging from 0 to 4 (0-never, 1-seldom, 2-occasionally, 3-often, and 4-always), with a minimum score of 0 and a maximum score of 40. Participants were classified based on the scores as: Normal (<12), mild addiction (13–20), moderate addiction (21–32) and severe addiction (33).

Grading	Government	Private	Total
Mild	182 (80.3)	191 (66.3)	373 (72.7)
Moderate	39 (17.3)	93 (32.2)	132 (25.7)
Severe	4 (1.9)	4 (1.5)	8 (1.6)
Total	225 (100)	288 (100)	513 (100)

Figures in parenthesis indicate percentages

5. There was no difference in the prevalence of Social Media Addiction between Government and Private PU college study subjects contrary to the assumption that private college subjects will be more prone to social media addiction due to higher social status and purchasing capacity.

1. Which of the following was not an objective for the study?

(a) To assess the health problems associated with social media usage

(b) To assess and compare the prevalence of social media in a particular organisation

(c) To assess the various factors related to social media usage

(d) To assess and compare the prevalence of social media in different organisations

2. Select the option that is true for the Assertion and Reason given below.

Assertion (A) The study did not show much difference between government and PU colleges in Karnataka.

Reason (R) Private school students show to be much more addicted to social media.

(a) Both the Assertion and Reason are true, and the Reason is the correct explanation of the Assertion.

(b) Both the Assertion and Reason are true, but the Reason is not the correct explanation of the Assertion.

(c) The Assertion is true, but the Reason is false.

(d) The Assertion is false, but the Reason is true.

3. What, according to you, makes the adolescents susceptible to social media overuse?

4. Give one reason for the rise in active social media users in India?

5. Complete the sentence by selecting the most appropriate option.

The students were classified into .... categories based on their ....

6. Does the following statement agree with the information given in Paragraph 1?

Adolescents belonging to poor families do not have greater exposure to smartphones at a much younger age.

Select from the following.

True If the statement agrees with the information

False If the statement contradicts the information

Not Given If there is no information on this

7. Complete the sentence appropriately.

The study tool used in the survey comprised of ....

8. Complete the sentence based on the passage.

It was assumed that private college students will be more prone to social media addiction. This was because of their ....

9. Based on the reading of the text, state a point to challenge the given statement.

Higher social status and purchasing capacity is directly linked to Social Media Addiction.

CHAPTER 1

Descriptive Paragraph

A description is a detailed account of certain or salient aspects, characteristics or features of a person, place, thing or process, etc. It is a short and factual composition written in 100-120 words.

We write descriptions of many things but in Class IX syllabus, we focus on three types of descriptive paragraphs. They are

(i) Description of a person (ii) Description of an event (iii) Description of any situation

Points to be Kept in Mind

- It should give complete details about the person, place or thing being described in it.
- One should use simple language and short sentences in writing the paragraph.
- The word limit of 100-120 words should be adhered to strictly.
- The visual and verbal clues given in the question can be used in constructing the descriptive paragraph.
- It should not include the opinion of the writer, personal comments or recommendations about the person, place or event being described in the paragraph.

Description of a Person

Description of a person includes his/her physical appearance, habits, profession, intellectual and emotional qualities, special traits, social status or role in the society and his/her influence on the society (if he/she is a famous personality).
The description should begin with a biographical sketch mentioning the details of time, place and date of birth of a person. Their achievements should also be mentioned.

SOLVED EXAMPLES

1. Describe the young Indian Chess Grandmaster, Gukesh Dommaraju. You can use the following hints to form your answer.

Early Life

- Mention his birthplace and birth date (Gukesh Dommaraju, born in 2006 in Chennai, India).
- Include his early interest in chess and when he started playing the game.

Chess Career

- Highlight his rise in the chess world, particularly his rapid ascent in international tournaments.
- Mention his achievement of becoming the youngest Indian to achieve the title of Grandmaster in 2019 at the age of 12 years and 7 months.

Significant Achievements

- Include key milestones in his career, such as notable tournament wins and his performance in international competitions.
- Talk about his achievements in Chess Olympiads, rapid, and blitz formats.

Style and Strengths

- Discuss his playing style and strategies, known for his aggressive and tactical approach.
- Mention any notable games or victories that have made him stand out.

Ans. Gukesh Dommaraju, born on 29th November, 2006 in Chennai, India, is one of the brightest young talents in the world of chess. He developed an early interest in the game and quickly demonstrated remarkable skill. Gukesh's determination and strategic thinking led him to rise through the ranks at a rapid pace. At the age of 12 years and 7 months, Gukesh achieved the title of Grandmaster in 2019, making him the youngest Indian to do so at that time. This achievement marked a significant milestone in his chess career and catapulted him into the international chess spotlight. His rise in the chess world was fueled by his victories in various tournaments, including strong performances in international events. Known for his aggressive and tactical playing style, Gukesh has earned a reputation for his sharp and precise moves. His games often display a deep understanding of the game. Gukesh's future in chess looks promising, as he continues to compete at the highest levels. His dedication, talent, and ability to thrive under pressure suggest that he is destined for even greater accomplishments in the world of chess.

2. Write a descriptive paragraph about your favourite cartoon character based on the hints given below.

Name of the character - description - qualities - what you like the most about it

Ans. I like to watch cartoons and there are many cartoon characters I like. Some of them are Tom, Doraemon, He-Man, Mickey Mouse, etc. However, the cartoon character that I like the most is Jerry. Jerry is a mouse that appears in my favourite cartoon show, Tom and Jerry Show. I have been watching Jerry in the Show since I was a kid. He is portrayed in the cartoon series as a small mouse which is brown in colour. The other character in the show is Tom, the cat. Tom is much bigger than Jerry and is always after it. This is because Jerry is mischievious and has a habit of teasing Tom. Jerry plays a lot of pranks on Tom and is not fearful of the cat at all. It is a lot of fun watching both of them running after each other. It seems obvious to viewers that Tom would be able to catch Jerry but that doesn't happen. It is the prankster Jerry that wins in the end and steals the show. I enjoy this show very much and I am always in awe of Jerry.

3. Write a description of the great table master Zakhir Husaain. You can look at his image and other hints given below to form your answer.

Early Life

- Mention his birth date and place (Zakir Hussain was born on March 9, 1951, in Mumbai, India).
- Discuss his early exposure to music, especially his family's musical background.

Musical Training

- Include information about his training in tabla
- Talk about his early influences and how he developed his unique style of tabla playing.

Career Milestones

- Mention his international recognition and success as a tabla virtuoso.
- Highlight his collaborations with renowned musicians from various genres, including classical, jazz, and fusion music.

Notable Achievements

- Include his prestigious awards, such as the Padma Bhushan, Padma Shri, and Grammy Awards.

Contributions to Music

- Mention his contributions to film music and his work as a composer for Indian films.
- Discuss his role in founding institutions like the Zakir Hussain Foundation.

Ans. Zakir Hussain, born on 9th March, 1951, in Mumbai, India, is one of the world's most renowned tabla masters the world had ever seen. He hails from a family with a deep musical legacy, as his father was a legendary tabla maestro. Growing up in this environment, Zakir developed a passion for music at an early age and began his formal training. Zakir's unique playing style, which blends traditional Indian classical rhythms with innovative techniques, soon gained him recognition in India and abroad.

His collaborations with some of the greatest musicians helped him gain international fame. His fusion of Indian classical music with jazz, world music, and other genres set him apart as a versatile and innovative artist. Throughout his illustrious career, Zakir has received numerous accolades, including the Padma Shri (1988), Padma Bhushan (2002), and Grammy Awards, underscoring his global recognition and impact on the world of music. In addition to his performance career, Zakir Hussain is a dedicated educator and philanthropist. He established the Zakir Hussain Foundation, which supports various musical and cultural initiatives, and works to preserve and promote Indian classical music for future generations. Zakir's ability to bridge the gap between traditional Indian music and global sounds has made him a cultural ambassador for India.

4. Write a descriptive paragraph based on the visual clue given below.

Ans. Dr. APJ Abdul Kalam is a famous name in the whole world in several fields. He is among the greatest scientists of the 21st century. Even more, he was the 11th President of India and served his country to bring about great changes in it. His contribution as a scientist and as a President is beyond comparison. Dr. Kalam's contribution to the ISRO (Indian Space Research Organisation) is so remarkable that it will always be remembered by the nation. He headed many projects that contributed to the society. He was the one who helped in the development of Agni and Prithvi missiles. For his involvement in the Nuclear Power in India, he was known as 'Missile Man of India'. And due to his contribution to the country, the government awarded him with the highest civilian award.

5. Write a descriptive paragraph on Droupadi Murmu based on the information given below.

- former Cabinet Minister of Odisha and Governor of Jharkhand
- born into a humble family based in the remote village of Mayurbhanj, Odisha.
- assistant teacher and a junior assistant in the Odisha state irrigation department
- started her political journey with the BJP in 1997
- worked as a councilor in Rairangpur
- worked as the President of the Scheduled Tribe Morcha of the BJP Odisha unit
- elected twice to Odisha State Legislative Assembly
- felicitated with the best legislative member award.
- personal life full of struggle and tragedy
- lost her husband and two grown-up sons
- created history as she became the First Woman Governor of Jharkhand, the first Tribal Governor of a tribal state, and the first Odisha-born woman to be a governor.

Ans. Draupadi Murmu is the 15th and current President of India. She is also the former Cabinet Minister of Odisha and Governor of Jharkhand. She was born into a humble family based in the remote village of Mayurbhanj, a tribal district of Odisha. She had worked as an assistant teacher and a junior assistant in the Odisha state irrigation department. Murmu started her political journey with the BJP in 1997 and worked as a councilor in Rairangpur. She has also worked as the President of the Scheduled Tribe Morcha of the BJP Odisha unit before being elected twice to Odisha State Legislative Assembly on the BJP ticket where she was felicitated with the best legislative member award. Though her personal life remained full of struggle and tragedy, Murmu touched the pinnacle of public life and achieved monumental records in politics and social services. She lost her husband and two grown-up sons, but she stood strong on all occasions. Murmu created history as she became the First Woman Governor of Jharkhand, the First Tribal Governor of a tribal state, and the first Odisha-born woman to be a Governor.

Description of an Event

Description of an event is quite similar to writing a report. It should have factual details and is written using past tense. The following details can be included

- Time, Date and Venue
- Organising Authority
- Purpose of the Event
- People who Participated
- Details of Chief Guest

SOLVED EXAMPLES

1. A free health camp was organised by your school during autumn break. Well known health specialists were invited on this occasion. Write a description of the event.

The date - the venue - number of students and people who benefitted from this camp - purpose - Chief Guest

Ans. During the autumn break, a free health check-up camp was organised by our school in the school playground. The camp was organised for three days and various specialist doctors were called from different cities for this purpose. The free check-up for diabetes, blood pressure, obesity, joint pains, etc. was provided to the residents of neighbouring areas. Around 150 students and 200 people benefitted from this camp. The purpose of the camp was to spread awareness regarding the increasing health problems among growing children and middle aged people due to eating unhealthy food and leading an inactive lifestyle. Pamphlets containing diet charts for the patients of diabetes and blood pressure were distributed. The closing ceremony was graced by Mr. Pitambar Singh, the MLA of the area. He appreciated the efforts of the school and the doctors who gave their valuable time to make the camp a grand success.

2. Write a descriptive paragraph on a tree plantation drive organised in your school on World Environment Day based on the clues given below.

Tree plantation drive-organised in coordination with an NGO - inaugurated by a noted environmentalist every student planted sapling - teachers and principal also participated.

Ans. A tree plantation drive was organised by our school in collaboration with 'Green World', an NGO, on 5th June, 20XX on the occasion of World Environment Day. The motto of the drive was 'Each one-Plant at least one'. A number of saplings of plants like Neem, Peepal, Guava, Jamun and Mango were provided by the NGO. The drive was declared open when noted environmentalist Sh. Bittu Sahgal planted a sapling along with our respected Principal. He also gave a small speech encouraging us to take care of our environment and Mother Earth. All the students made a queue and planted at least one sapling each in our school ground. After planting the saplings, we watered them and vowed to take care of them in the future. Our teachers and administrative staff also took part in the drive. Some of the students took a selfie while planting the saplings and sent it to their friends and relatives, thereby motivating them to plant trees. The drive was declared a great success as over one thousand saplings were planted by our school.

3. You have recently attended a robotics workshop. Write a factual description of the same. You can take help of the given image.

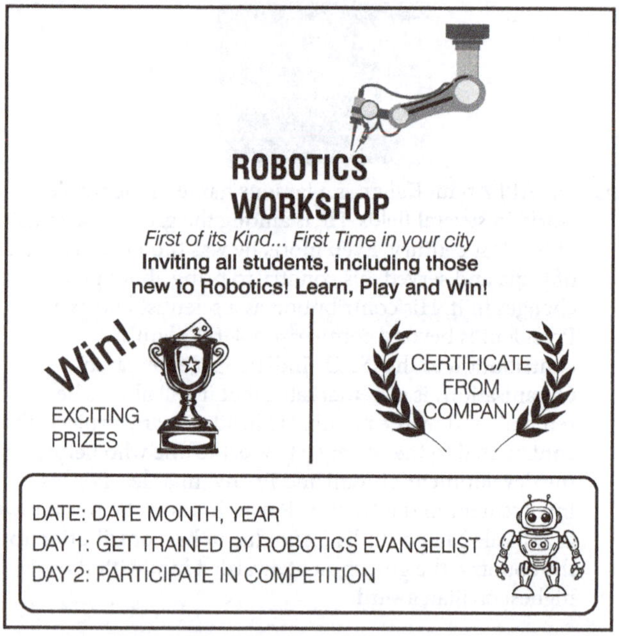

Ans. Our school, in association with the Science and Technology Department of the XYZ college, organised a robotics workshop in the school premises. The event was aimed at providing both educational insights and hands-on experiences to the young minds who will lead the industry in the future. The workshop started with an engaging introduction to the principles of robotics. The facilitator, an industry expert with years of experience, told us how robotics has evolved over the years, highlighting key milestones that have shaped the industry. Then, with the help of some engineers, we started with the hands-on activities. Our task was to design and build a simple robot using kits provided by the organisers. With basic components like motors, sensors and a microcontroller, we began brainstorming ideas in small groups and started building the robot. Under the facilitator's guidance, we learned to troubleshoot and modify our designs, fostering a problem-solving mindset that proved invaluable. After several hours of diligent work, our robots were ready for its first test run, which they did perfectly. The workshop also included inspirational talks from industry leaders who shared their experiences in robotics. The interactive and intriguing workshop was a great success as it inspired many of us to take up robotics as a career choice.

4. Write a factual description on an English extempore held at your school. Mention date, time, venue, participants, topics and overall atmosphere.

Ans. The English extempore held at PQR Public School, Delhi on 28th July, 20XX saw a large participation by students of standard IX – XII. The event was held at the Multi-purpose hall at 11:00 am. Numerous participants queued backstage awaiting their turn. The extempore was organised in a methodical manner, where participants were called onstage and asked to choose a folded sheet containing the topic. Whichever topic they chose was to be their theme for the extempore. The topics mainly involved environmental and societal issues. However, there were some really creative topics too like- If I get to know my future, A world without newspapers, etc. Each participant got five minutes to prepare and then, had to come back onstage to speak on the topic. The competition was tough as each candidate was quick in preparing and fine-tuning their thoughts on their subjects and were able to present any situation that cropped up onstage. The event was filled with excitement and was very memorable for the students.

5. A book fair was organised in your city in the month of August. Describe the fair using the following hints.
Time and place - purpose of the fair - arrangements - participants - number of people who attended the fair - what was special about it.

Ans. A book fair was organised at Pragati Maidan, Delhi in the month of August. The theme of the book fair was 'Role of Books in Revolutionising the World.' It was a rare opportunity for book lovers as there was a variety of books from different publishers all under one roof. Security arrangements were tight as people from Delhi and many other neighbouring cities came to attend the fair. To ensure safety of all, people had to pass through metal detectors to reach the different halls. Each hall was segmented into many stalls. There were local, national and international publishers offering books in various genres. There were also stalls that sold unique stationery items. Food stalls and ice-cream parlours were also set up to facilitate the visitors. The book fair was a grand success.

Description of a Situation

A description of a situation must include the following information

- Time and location of the situation
- A brief chronological description of what happened
- How did you feel
- Consequences
- What did you learn from it, if applicable

1. You are stuck in the lift of your residential apartment. Write a paragraph based on this in about 100-120 words.

Ans. I was returning home yesterday evening after attending my classes. It was about 7 pm. I took the lift to my 4th floor apartment from the ground floor of my residential colony. The lift had hardly reached the 2nd floor when it stopped with a jerk. The lights in the lift went off.
I panicked as there was no one in the lift and it was pitch dark. I screamed for help but no one came to my rescue. I felt suffocated inside and started sweating. I prayed to God to get me out of the lift. Suddenly, an idea come to my mind. Patiently, I located my mobile phone that was kept in my bag. I dialed my father's number and briefed him about the situation. Within minutes, my father came with the lift-man and the lift-man opened the gate of the lift using the key. I came out and gave a sigh of relief and hugged my father.

2. You are the monitor of your class. A new girl has joined your class. She is reserved in nature and is finding it difficult to adjust to the new environment. Write a descriptive paragraph in about 100-120 words describing how you helped her out.

Ans. When the school opened after the summer break, a new girl named Arisha joined our class. The teacher made her sit at the first bench. In the first few days of her joining, she hardly spoke to anyone in the class. In the sports period and recess too, she did not mix up with others and did not play with us. Noting her hesitancy and being the monitor of my class, I came forward to help her. I talked to her in the recess. She told me that she had come from Dehradun as her father had got posted to Delhi recently. I asked her about her family, her old school friends, teachers and city. The students in our class were eager to become her friends. Within a few days, Arisha started to open up and made ten friends in the class. I felt happy to see her come out of her shell and felt that my efforts paid off.

3. After giving the final exams of Class IXth, you are in a dilemma regarding which extracurricular activity to pick up for the holidays. Write a descriptive paragraph based on it in about 100-120 words.

Ans. After completing my final exams for Class IX, I find myself at a crossroads, unsure of which extracurricular activity to pursue during the holidays. The options seem endless, each offering its own unique appeal and opportunities for growth. Should I immerse myself in the world of painting, letting my creativity flow onto the canvas? Or perhaps I should join a local theater group, exploring different characters and honing my acting skills? Then, there's the option of learning a new musical instrument, filling the air with melodies that speak to the soul. As I weigh my choices, I feel a sense of excitement combined with uncertainty, knowing that whichever path I choose, it will be a journey filled with new experiences and discoveries.

4. Yesterday it rained heavily and your area was waterlogged. Your school van could not reach your home and your parents were out of the house for some urgent work. Write a description of the incidents which took place in this situation.

Ans. It had rained incessantly yesterday night. Today, at 7:30 in the morning, my school van failed to show up in front of my house. It was drizzling continuously, without any sign of stopping. All the roads were waterlogged and there was water everywhere as far as eyes could see. My parents were out of station and unreachable over phone. So, I was worried about missing school and with that my chances of getting the 100 % attendance award. I decided to brave it on my bicycle through the waterlogged roads, and succeeded in reaching school on time, albeit in soaking socks and trousers. Very few students were present and we enjoyed our close knit classes with our teachers. The sky had cleared by the time the school bell rang of dispersal and I reached home safely as the water had started dried up and vehicles could move freely once more.

5. You were on a school trip and were on your way back to the hotel late one night when your school bus, full of children, broke down in a lonely area. Describe what you saw and experienced as you looked around. How was the problem solved?

Ans. The seventh-grade school trip to Jaipur was an unforgettable adventure filled with excitement and unexpected challenges. We explored the majestic Amber Fort, marveled at the intricate designs of the Hawa Mahal, and learned about astronomy at Jantar Mantar. The grandeur of the City Palace left us in awe of Jaipur's rich history and culture. However as evening came, our journey took an unexpected turn when our bus broke down in a remote area. With darkness all around us, the surroundings seemed eerie and teachers as well as students grew nervous. Just when uncertainty filled the environment, a group of Banjaras on camels emerged from the shadows, offering assistance and guiding us safely through the night. Despite our initial fear, their kindness and good cheer turned the ordeal into a memorable adventure that will be cherished lifelong.

ASSESSMENT EXERCISE

1. Write a descriptive paragraph on your favourite singer you admire the most based on the clues given in the box (100-120 words).
   - Name of personality - physical features - birth place/ date - reason for being famous - his/ her struggles - major achievements - qualities that you admire most about him/her.
2. Write a descriptive paragraph on Mother Teresa based on the clues given in the box (100-120 words).

   Founder of Missionaries of Charity - Albanian - Indian Roman Catholic Nun - received several awards including Nobel Peace Prize - admired for her charitable work.
3. Write a descriptive paragraph on the celebration of Children's Day in your school based on the clues given below (100-120 words).
   - Combined assembly of all wings - Principal gave speech on importance of the day - followed by fancy dress competition - sweets distributed in lunch time - fun activities and games organised by teachers in class.
4. Write a descriptive paragraph on International Yoga Day based on the clues given below (100-120 words).
   - Celebrated on 21st June across the world - UNs promotion of good health, harmony and peace - aims to raise awareness worldwide of the many benefits of practising yoga.
5. You are Ankit/Ankita of Class IX. Your pocket has been picked while travelling in the metro. Write a descriptive paragraph on how you dealt with this situation (100-120 words).
6. You are Simran/Simarpreet of Class IX. You have been chosen to represent your school in the inter-school debating competition. This is the first time you will represent your school. Write a descriptive paragraph in 100-120 words.
7. You have an exam tomorrow. There is a power outage in your area as a transformer has stopped working. Write a descriptive paragraph in 100-120 words on how you tackled this situation.
8. Write a descriptive paragraph about your experience of reaching late for an examination.
9. A science fest was organised in your city to mark the birth anniversary of the famous anthropologist Charles Darwin. Describe the event using the following points
   - held at Parade Ground on 6th July
   - inaugurated by Dr. AK Sinha, a famous sociologist
   - five colleges and ten schools participated
   - career options in science stream displayed
   - achievements in science and technology highlighted through posters and power point presentations
   - role of science in growth of cultures
10. You recently participated in a sustainable living event in your shool. Participants from as many as 30 schools in the city took part in the event. Write about the event in 100-150 words describing the focus of the event, activities involved and any other key takeaways.
11. Describe the day of elections. Mention date, time, venue, participants and over atmosphere.
12. Write a descriptive paragraph on the person depicted in the photograph given below.

13. Write a composition.

    You walk home from school one afternoon to find the door unlocked and on entering you are shocked to see the house in total disarray. You call out but get no answer. Describe in detail what you saw, the reason behind your house being in total disarray and how you found your family. Also mention how the experience ended and what impact it had on your life.
14. Describe an early morning walk through your city or town in winter. Give details of the smells, sights, sounds and feelings you experienced.

CHAPTER 2

Diary Entry

A diary entry is an informal and a personal account of an event of significance that took place on a given day in the life of an individual. It is essentially a first person narrative wherein a person writes about his/her feelings, emotions, thoughts, ideas, memories, activities and daily life incidents. It is quite like talking to a close friend. It helps the writer to connect with his/her inner feelings and analyse them. Such a piece of writing allows free expression of feelings that the writer may be unwilling or unable to share with anyone else.

Keeping a diary has been a regular practice with many great people in the past. One of the most famous of diary entries was written by Anne Frank.

Points to be Kept in Mind while Writing a Diary

- A diary is intimate and personal in tone and style. It is generally written at night before bed.
- Use personal pronouns in your entry.
- Always write the day, date and time of the entry.
- Use clear and simple language.
- Always include your own feelings in your entry.
- Do not exceed the limit of 150 words.
- Remember to read your diary entry to make sure there are no grammatical or punctuation errors in it.

Format of a Diary Entry

Today you went for a trip to the zoo which made you upset about the condition of the caged birds and animals. Write a Diary Entry in about 100-120 words expressing your feelings.

Day and Date	Wednesday, 27th October, 20XX
Time	10:00 pm
Greetings	Dear Diary
Content/Body	Today turned from excitement to disappointment for me. I went to my favourite place in the world. Yes! I went to the zoo with my family. It is not hidden from people who know me that I am very fond of birds and animals. However, contrary to my expectations, it turned out to be a sad experience. I did see many birds and animals in the zoo. However, they did not look happy at all in their confined spaces. Even though they were well-fed, they looked angry. I think that they were missing the blue skies and the freedom to run around in the vast forest land. Not to forget, the constant poking of humans must have irritated them. Sure, they are fed well and receive regular health check-ups, but I can't overlook how tired and angry they seemed. I guess that is a result of their inactive life. I don't think zoos are bad as they protect many endangered species. Still, it hurts to see the animals and birds being kept that way. I don't think I can visit a zoo again.
Singnature/Name of the writer	XYZ

SOLVED EXAMPLES

1. You are Arpit of class IX. You were the anchor for the annual day function at your school today. Make a diary entry in 100-120 words sharing your experience and feelings.

Ans. Thursday, 11th September, 20XX 10:00 pm

Dear Diary

I am really happy today. It was the annual day function in my school and I was the anchor for the function. I was anxious in the morning as it was the first time that I was given a chance to be an anchor.

However, my teacher helped me in overcoming my nervousness. Fortunately, everything went really well. I started off confidently and maintained my confidence throughout. Everyone was pleased with the way I delivered the speech and vote of thanks. I was very excited to listen to the golden words of advice that our Chief Guest, the City Mayor gave us. As always, everyone was impressed by his speech.

I felt really lucky to experience the presence of such an influential person of our city.

It was a wonderful day at school.

Arpit

2. You went to see the India International Trade Fair held at Pragati Maidan, New Delhi. Using the hints given below together with your ideas on the subject, make a diary entry of what you saw and experienced there.

Hints - As usual IITF was held at Pragati Maidan - all leading countries participated - Chinese dominated the show - all states - separate pavilions - all states of India - cultural programmes - Food Courts - high prices dampened the spirit

Ans. Thursday, 16th October, 20XX 8:00 pm

Dear Diary

A visit to the Indian International Trade Fair has always been a rewarding experience for me. It was the same this year too. I went to this year's trade fair which was held at Pragati Maidan with my parents. It was a different world over there. To be precise, it was a fairyland. The sections of Germany, Canada, the USA, China and Great Britain attracted a large crowd, but Chinese dominated the event. India was represented by almost all states and establishments like the Indian Railways, Indian Tourism, LIC, Tatas and what not. The 'Food Courts' served all tastes from Pizzas to the Choley Bhaturey. The fair provided opportunities for a lot of fun and entertainment. Film show, folk dances and puppet shows drew huge crowds. Even though the prices were high, it was a very pleasant and rewarding experience as I bought many traditional things that I would never be able to find in Delhi.

PQR

3. You are Bali, a student of class IX. Inspite of being so young, you were given a chance to be a Radio Jockey for a day at a popular radio station of your city. Write a diary entry in 100-120 words sharing your experience.

Ans. Friday, 29th December, 20XX 10:00 pm

Dear Diary

I am so excited to tell you that I was given a chance to be a Radio Jockey for a day. It was a great experience. When I woke up in the morning, I was excited and nervous at the same time. Upon reaching the office of the local FM radio station, I was welcomed with warmth. I was curious to make use of the advanced music system, microphone and earphones. The moment we went on air, I was filled with confidence.

I was so cheerful that everyone applauded my happy-go-lucky attitude. We played songs, cracked jokes and interacted with the listeners. It was so much fun. My friends and family tuned into the station all day long as they did not want to miss anything. I was on top of the world. I wish the day had not ended so soon!

Bali

4. You had a student from a school in Australia living with you as part of a Student Exchange Programme and he/she has just returned to his/her own country. Make a diary entry in 100-120 words about his/her stay at your home and how you have benefitted from the experience. You are Madhav/Madhavi.

Ans. Saturday, 19th August, 20XX 9:00 pm

Dear Diary

I have already started missing Scarlet. We had a wonderful time together. There were tears in her eyes when we were parting at the airport.

Scarlet had come to India as a part of the student exchange programme. I did not think that I would ever become close to someone except my best friend. But, here I was, Scarlet had become a really good friend. We spent a wonderful time together in exchanging information, ideas and experiences. We compared our lives in school too, learning many new things, about our cultures and education system.

She told me about the schooling system in Australia was very different and much advanced in comparison to our system. Everybody in my family was quite impressed with the way she talked. When I showed her the photos of my childhood, she was overjoyed to see the old houses and compounds. She also shared her old memories with me. I hope she returns to her country safely.

I will always remember the time spent with her. I wish her the best for her future.

Madhavi

5. You are Nikita/Nitin. You are used to travelling in your school bus. Today you happened to go to Agra alone in a crowded bus on a hot summer day. Record your adventurous experience in the form of a diary entry.

Ans. Thursday, 3rd May, 20XX 10:00 pm

Dear Diary

You know that I am used to travelling in my comfortable school bus. However, today I had to go to Agra alone in a crowded bus. My mother and father had already reached Agra two days ago to attend my cousin's wedding.

I made my way through the bustling crowd at the bus stand and was shocked to enter the crowded bus. There was no place to sit and it seemed as if more and more people wanted to board the bus.

I overheard someone saying that a few buses operating on the Delhi-Agra route had been cancelled due to shortage of buses. Ignoring everyone, I made my way through the crowd at the door and stood in a corner of the bus. The scorching heat was making me uncomfortable. So, I sipped some lemonade and tried to pass my time. After four hours of the bus ride, we finally reached Agra where my parents were waiting to pick me up.

From this adventurous experience, I learnt how to travel independently in public transport. When I reached Agra as a brave little soldier bearing all the hardships, I finally hugged my mother.

Nikita

6. Write a diary entry entailing the short account of how you played a prank on your grand mother.

Ans. Saturday, 12 April, 20XX, 9:00 pm

Dear Diary

I had a lot of fun pulling a prank on my grandmother today. My grandma was boiling milk in the evening. While it was boiling, she went to the bedroom for a few minutes. When the milk was ready, I poured it into a container, placed it in the refrigerator and put the pan on the rack. When grandma arrived a short while later, she noticed the burner was empty. She was really puzzled.

She, then, started to boil a second pack of milk. This time she went to attend a telephone call when I played my trick again on her. After returning to the kitchen, she discovered that the milk was missing again. This time, she yelled in horror. She believed that the house was haunted. I yelled "pranked you" and laughed so hard.

I told dad the story when he got home. Even he laughed heartily. I'll be writing soon again. Now, its time for me to go to bed.

ABC

7. You saw a TV programme on the 'Himalayan Yeti' on Discovery Channel today. Yeti is a human-sized snowman with its entire body covered with hair. Express your thoughts on the same in your diary in 100-120 words.

Ans. Thursday, 3rd December, 20XX 11:45 pm

Dear Diary

I chanced upon something very interesting today. While surfing channels as usual, I came upon this programme on 'Himalayan Yeti' on Discovery Channel.

'Yeti' is a human-sized snowman whose entire body is covered with hair. At first, I was surprised. Could such a creature really exist? Huge human footmarks have been noticed in the Himalayas. Also, many mountaineers claim to have seen the 'Yeti' with their own eyes.

After watching the complete programme, I came to the conclusion that 'Yetis' are robots used by some evil minds to hide their illegal activities in the Himalayan snowlands. Till the scientists solve this mystery, I would like to believe this theory only. I am feeling very sleepy now as I have been watching TV for the last four hours continuously.

Raman

8. You are a girl of the new generation and owing to the generation gap, your grandmother is different from other people in various aspects. Make a diary entry expressing your feelings and state how your grandmother is so different.

Ans. Saturday, 8th May, 20XX 9:30 pm

Dear Diary

We are in our ancestral home right now. When we reached here this week, I was delighted to meet my grandmom and hugged her. She was also very happy to see me and showered many blessings on me. My grandmother has taken a lot of pains to maintain this house. Life would have been dull if she had not been with us. She is a lady with firm determination and a loving soul. She is very particular about proper behaviour, and concentrates on our hygiene and education. She even checks our shoes to see if they are polished properly or not. Father tells us that she has sacrificed a lot for keeping us all properly looked after.

In her behaviour, she is somewhat different from others because she is conservative. She doesn't allow us to wear modern clothes or keep our hair open. But again, she is so lovely that we don't mind it at all and do as she wishes. Love you Dadi!

Jyoti

9. You are Mahesh/Manasvi of class IX. Today you witnessed some students littering the corridors and field of your school. You were very disappointed at that sight. Make a diary entry about how you felt.

Ans. Tuesday, 31st March, 20XX 9:30 pm

Dear Diary

I am very sad today. During the recess time, I saw a group of students littering in the school premises. They littered the corridors with plastic bags, foils, wrappers, etc. It was a very disappointing sight. I told them repeatedly not to litter and use the dustbin but they did not listen to me.

Not just this, even the playing field behind the classrooms was not spared by them. I feel disgusted that our environment has to suffer because of our bad habits. I wish I could do something about it. I plan to drop a letter in the suggestion box for appointment of prefects to keep a check and ensure a clean environment at school. I hope things will get better due to my suggestions.

Manasvi

10. During the summer vacation, you (Vicky) and your friend enrolled in 'The School for Flying'. While training, you had an interesting and unforgettable experience. Share your experience in the form of a diary entry in 100-120 words, expressing what you have learnt till now.

Ans. Friday, 15th May, 20XX 9:00 pm

Dear Diary

As you know I had recently joined 'The School for Flying' with my friend Nick. It was an enjoyable as well as learning experience. I found all the aviation activities and tasks interesting. The school imparted good flight instruction values by conducting safe, professional flights in well-equipped, well-maintained aeroplanes. I felt as if I was in a miniature airport with an active and friendly atmosphere. I was excited to see the use of advanced aeroplanes and modern technologies like GPS to impart flying instructions. The school had a reality-based training approach. In some high level tasks, the pilots were even made to fly in challenging weather scenarios. I belive that this training will help me and my friend in developing good judgement, decision-making and proficiency skills. I feel that all of us should utilise our summer vacations in broadening our knowledge and skills in such activities.

Vicky

11. You got the topic 'The Mystery of the Bermuda Triangle' for your English project. You used Charles Berlitz's bestseller 'The Bermuda Triangle' as a reference book for your submission. Share your experience and personal opinion with your diary with the help of the clues given below in 100-120 words. You are Tanya.

Popularised belief - ships prone to disappearance - the theory you think is right - your take on the book

Ans. Wednesday, 11th November, 20XX 9:45 pm

Dear Diary

I am very happy today. I am one of the few students in the class who have bagged an A+ for 'The Bermuda Triangle' project. However, all credit for the success of my project goes to Dad. On noticing my interest, he bought me the famous book titled 'The Bermuda Triangle' written by Charles Berlitz in 1974.

It was an interesting book from the first page to the last. After reading it, I feel people are just spreading rumours about sea monsters and aliens. I feel the disappearance of aeroplanes and ships is due to a strong magnetic field present in the area. I hope scientists will unfold this mystery soon and then I will get all my answers. I am very tired now. See you tomorrow.

Tanya

12. You recently visited the Ranthambore Tiger Reserve and were enchanted with the wilderness and natural beauty of the place. You also had an encounter with the tigers roaming freely. Describe your experience in not more than 100-120 words through a diary entry.

Ans. Thursday, 14th July, 20XX 8:00 pm

Dear Diary

I had a wonderful experience during my recent visit to Ranthambore Tiger Reserve. Wildlife has always fascinated me. Up till now, I had seen wild animals either on TV or behind the cage in the zoo. However, this time I got the opportunity to see them roaming in the wild. I was thrilled to see the tigers roaming in their natural habitat. Some of them were playing with water while some were basking in the Sun. At one point, a tiger came really close to our jeep.

I was scared to death but the Guide assured us that the tiger would not cause any harm to us. We also visited the Ranthambore Fort and the famous temple of Lord Ganesha. It is the only temple in the country with a three-eyed idol of Lord Ganesha. This visit was a memorable one and I am never going to forget it.

Rishi

ASSESSMENT EXERCISE

1. You have recently visited the virtual reality workshop wherein you learnt its various use. Write a diary entry on the same in 100-120 words.
2. You experienced sea diving for the first time in your life. As Vaibhav/Vanshika, make a diary entry in about 100-120 words, expressing how you felt.
3. A competition of Kite Flying was organised in your school on the eve of Independence Day. Write a 100-120 words diary entry using the clues given below.

   Clues– Morning prayer– Principal addressed Chief Guest–Both of them flew kites– Participats flew kites– Colourful kites beautiful sky, nice day.
4. You are Raj. You performed a group activity where you invented your own TV channel and presented a programme on it. Make a diary entry in 100-120 words sharing your experience.
5. You recently visited the 24th Crafts and Cuisine Mela at Suraj Kund, Faridabad. It was Mini India assembled at one place. Make a diary entry of what you saw and experienced there. (100-120 words).
6. You paid a visit to an 'Orphanage' with your parents. Make a diary entry of what you saw and experienced there. (100-120 words).
7. You are Mehak. You participated in a play at the National School of Drama. It was recorded and will be telecast next week. Make a diary entry in 100-120 words sharing your experience.
8. You are Karan/Kiran. You saved a girl from drowning in the river which flows near your home, but it is a mystery to you how you got the courage to do so. Write your experience and feelings in the form of a diary entry in 100-120 words.
9. You are Ankit/Ankita, member of the Political Club of your school. A few weeks back your school celebrated Constitution Day. Various informative programmes were showcased in the morning assembly. Write a diary entry in 100-120 words expressing what you learnt through those activities based on your own ideas.
10. Impressed by your performance on your school's Annual Sports Day, the Chief Guest (the Minister of Youth Affairs and Sports) decided to offer you a sports scholarship. Write a diary entry in 100-120 words about your performance and the scholarship offered.

CHAPTER 3

Story Writing

A story is a record of an event which can be true or imaginary. It can impart a moral, or capture a moment, event or someone's life to inculcate values and be there just for entertainment. Story Writing is a language skill that tests the student's creativity and writing skills.

Main Elements of a Short Story

1. **Theme** It is the main idea or message of the story.
2. **Plot** It is the logical connection among all parts of the story. A proper beginning, a middle and an end are essential components of a good plot.
3. **Setting** It is the time, location and the background suitable to work out the theme.
4. **Characters** The people, animals or other living creatures of the story are its characters. A short story has one main character and very few minor characters to support the plot.

Steps to Write a Short Story

1. Read the cue/outline given in the question carefully.
2. Think about the possible plot and characters.
3. Start the story as instructed in the question.
4. Starting or beginning should be brief and interesting.
5. Build the plot by using dialogues and interesting points.
6. End the story appropriately by giving a climax.

Points to be Kept in Mind

- Always use past tense while writing a story.
- Consequences/Climax of the story should be clear and satisfying.
- Make simple and innovative use of language.
- Stick to the limit of 100-120 words.
- Make sure that the story has a moral/message, if it requires one.
- A title may be given to the story if the question requires it; otherwise it is optional.
- Reread the story to make sure you have not made any mistake in it.

Format of Short Story

1. Develop a story in 100-120 words which starts as given below.

"This is an unsolved mystery about a beggar I came to know very well through daily interaction with him on my way ....

Ans.

Title — **The Mystery of the Unusual Beggar**

An Interesting Start — This is an unsolved mystery about a beggar I came to know very well through daily interaction with him on my way to school. There is a footpath opposite my school beside a housing complex. In one of its unnoticed dark corners, there lived a beggar. I saw him every day when I went to school. He looked quite cultured unlike other beggars I had seen. On my birthday, my mother had told me to give some care boxes to beggars. That was the day when I talked to him for the very first time. Fortune had not been in his favour and he had been reduced to becoming a beggar even after having lived a comfortable life earlier.

Building the Plot — I tried to give him money many times but he always refused to take it. He repeatedly said that he was not a beggar by choice and if someone could employ him, he would love to work. Hence, I asked many people to give him some work but no one was ready.

Fortunately, a friend's father needed a car cleaner for their housing society. With some persuasion, they agreed to employ the beggar. I was happy and ran to the beggar to inform him about the good news.

A Justified Climax — Surprisingly, he was nowhere to be found. I searched the nearby area but could not trace him. Since that day, I have been eager and restless to know about his whereabouts.

SOLVED EXAMPLES

1. Develop a story in 100-120 words with the following beginning.

" Whenever John goes to Uncle Sam's house, he feels something different. He feels that Neil, Uncle Sam's son, has some supernatural powers. Whenever he is around ...."

Ans. **A Story about Spirits**

Whenever John goes to Uncle Sam's house, he feels something different. He feels that Neil, Uncle Sam's son, has some supernatural powers. Whenever he is around, unusual and paranormal things start happening. It sounds absurd but John told me that Neil can see spirits. John had once encountered him talking to someone in his room but when John stepped into his room, he found that Neil was all alone.

I did not believe what John was saying and told him that in today's modern scientific world, such things should not be believed. What happened next day was astonishing! I saw Neil doing the same thing, that is, talking alone but nobody was infront of him on a quiet street. I gathered all my courage and went straight up to him to make sure that everything was alright. I questioned him about it indirectly, as if out of concern.

To my surprise, he told me that he had been practising for his audition at school for a play. I told him about what John and I had been thinking about his behaviour recently. In response, he burst out laughing.

2. Write a story with the help of the given hints in 100-120 words. Also give a suitable title.

Seema – working as maid – eager to go to school – unable to do so – family responsibilities – I lent a hand to support – soon pass high school exams – can teach her own children now life changed

Ans. **A Good Deed**

Seema, our maid, is a very quiet lady but she is a diligent worker. One day, when I was completing my homework, I saw her looking keenly at my books. Curiously, I asked her if she had been to school before starting to work.

Seema replied that she had attended primary school but was subsequently unable to continue her studies due to her early marriage and family responsibilities. Upon asking if she would like to study now, she told me that she was still eager to learn and wished that she could read books like me. Thus, began her home-schooling. I taught her every evening from 6 to 7 pm.

She was a good student and always did her homework on time. In less than a year, she had memorised everything I had taught her. She later applied for high-school examinations through open school and secured good marks.

She says that she owes her success to me. Even her children are getting proper education as she is now able to help them with their studies.

She feels that her children's future is secure now and they would not have to work like her. It gives a very satisfying feeling when you understand that you have changed someone's life for the better.

3. Complete the story in 100-120 words, giving a suitable heading to it.

"It was a rainy day and I was all alone at home. It was pitch dark outside. Suddenly, I heard someone knocking at my door ...."

Ans. **The Worst Nightmare**

It was a rainy day and I was all alone at home. It was pitch dark outside. Suddenly, I heard someone knocking at my door continuously. I was scared at first but decided to see through the peep hole if it was someone I knew. I was shocked to find no one outside the door. I started walking towards my room but the knocking started again. My heart was in my mouth by that time. I did not know what to do. My parents were out of town. I was overcome with fear and was almost in tears, but I knew only I could do something about it.

I decided to lock myself in my room and hide under the bed. All I could think of doing at that time was to pray.

I was ashamed of myself as I had not imagined myself to be being such a coward ever. I immediately decided to get rid of my fear and face the situation. As I moved to get out, I hit my head on the bedside. That is when I realised it was just a dream. I sighed in relief and went back to sleep again, hoping to catch some sleep free from all worries.

4. Complete the story in 100-120 words with an appropriate title.

"Sunil is an over-ambitious boy. He wants to be a film hero. However, he doesn't get appropriate roles in films. He approached several production houses and met directors but couldn't succeed.

Depression and stress overpower him. One fine morning he meets a man who ...."

Ans. **Haste Makes Waste**

Sunil is an over-ambitious boy. He wants to be a film hero. However, he doesn't get appropriate roles in films. He approached several production houses and met directors but couldn't succeed.

Depression and stress started overpowering him. One fine morning, he met a man who was very impressed with his acting skills. He told Sunil that he could arrange for auditions at some very top-end production houses. Sunil was hoping for such an opportunity for a long time. However, he was also very worried to learn that the agent would charge him a lot of money.

Sunil had very little savings left. He had left his home two years ago to come to Mumbai to become an actor. He knew that asking for financial help from his father would be of no use. This was a desperate time. As his restlessness grew, Sunil decided to take a loan from his friends. Most of them agreed to help him and Sunil handed over the money to the agent.

However, he never heard from the agent again. He enquired about him and discovered a shocking truth. The agent was a cheat and had duped many people like Sunil before. In his haste, Sunil had never tried to confirm his identity. Now the cheat had run away with all the money and with it, Sunil's dream of becoming an actor shattered into pieces.

5. Look at the given image and write a short story titled 'The Helpful Girl'.

Ans. **The Helpful Girl**

In a small and quiet village nestled among lush green fields, there lived a young girl named Maya. She possessed a kind heart and a gentle spirit, always eager to lend a helping hand to those in need. One scorching summer day, Maya noticed an elderly farmer struggling to water his crops under the blazing Sun. Without hesitation, she fetched buckets of water from the nearby well and assisted him until the task was complete. Grateful for her selfless act, the farmer blessed Maya with a handful of seeds from his prized sunflower plant. Maya planted the seeds with care and watched as they blossomed into a stunning field of sunflowers, brightening the entire village. Through her kindness, Maya taught everyone that even the smallest acts of generosity can sow seeds of joy and beauty in the world.

6. Write the story based on the visual clue in about 120 words.

Ans. I have always had a knack for giving interesting and inspiring speeches. This is something I had loved since I was a child. During my holidays, I listened to and read many speeches by the great personalities of present times and of the past. I also attended a short course on Public Speaking to sharpen my skills for the perfect opportunity.

Then one day, in the morning assembly, it was announced that our school was going to participate in the zonal level speech competition. This was the kind of thing I had been waiting for. I submitted my name to the class teacher and she told me that she was expecting it and told me that she was confident that I would be the winner in the competition. This gave a boost to my confidence.

I was very excited and participated in the competition. However, I grew slightly nervous as it was a very tough competition. There was little chance for making any mistake. I was given the topic 'Science and Superstition' to speak on. Science had always been my favourite subject and I poured my heart out into the speech. My effort paid off and I was judged to be the best speaker at the competition. I will never forget the feeling of receiving a prestigious award, with my parents sitting among the audience and applauding my success.

7. Complete the story in 100-120 words which begins with the following sentence.

'Once in a bustling town, there lived a wealthy merchant named Ravi, who hoarded his riches ..... .'

Ans. Once in a bustling town, there lived a wealthy merchant named Ravi, who hoarded his riches and never shared with those in need. One stormy night, a beggar knocked on his door, seeking shelter from the rain. Annoyed, Ravi turned him away. The next morning, disaster struck—Ravi's warehouse caught fire, destroying all his wealth. Penniless and desperate, Ravi wandered the streets, seeking help. To his surprise, the beggar from the night before offered him food and shelter. Humbled by this act of kindness, Ravi promised to change his ways. He began helping the less fortunate, realising that true wealth lies in generosity and compassion.

The moral of the story Kindness and generosity enrich both the giver and the receiver, fostering a sense of community and happiness.

8. Write a story using the hints given below in 100-120 words.

Visit to your friend's house – take shortcut to home – path through jungle – palms were sweating – suddenly followed by a ghost – need help – story told by ghost about her accident – screamed – went back to friend's house – fever for three days – unforgettable experience

Ans. It was a fine summer evening when I had gone to see a friend of mine. I didn't realise that it was late. So, I rushed back home as I knew my mother would be worried.

As I was leaving, my friend told me a shorter way to home but it led through a deserted place. I decided to take the shortcut thinking that I would be able to reach home early.

It was through a small stretch of deserted jungle and was very quiet. It was a horrific feeling to be going through such a place all alone.

My palms started sweating when I saw the shadow of someone behind me. Without turning back, I started running. The shadow followed me till I stumbled and fell down after covering some distance.

A strange glass-like figure appeared in front of me. I was still screaming and crying for help. The figure stared at me for a while and then, started speaking to me. She told me about how she had met with an accident when she took the same route home as me.

The moment she looked away, I sneaked away quietly and ran towards my friend's house to ask for a ride home. He requested his father to help me reach home. So, his father dropped me home in his car. Afterwards, I was down with fever for three days. It was the most terrible experience of my life and from that day onwards, I never went out alone.

9. Write a story in 100-120 words beginning with the following line and give it a suitable title.

"At the annual town fair, Tom, known for his love of food, decided to enter the pie-eating contest..."

Ans. Pie Eating Champion

At the annual town fair, Tom, known for his love of food, decided to enter the pie-eating contest. With his stomach growling in anticipation, he eagerly took his place at the table alongside other enthusiastic competitors. The rules were simple: eat as many pies as possible within the allotted time. As the countdown began, Tom dove headfirst into the mountain of pies, his face covered in cherry filling and whipped cream. With each bite, the crowd cheered him on, impressed by his huge appetite. However, halfway through the contest, disaster struck – Tom's chair collapsed under his weight, sending him tumbling to the ground in a heap of pies and laughter. Despite the mishap, Tom emerged victorious, earning the title of "Pie-Eating Champion" and a belly full of memories that he would cherish for years to come.

10. Write a story in about 100-120 words on the basis of the given outline.

The illiterate boy......... caught for pick pocketing.......sent to juvenile prison.........forced to do lessons.........becomes sullen rebellious ....watches French comic film on T.V. during recreation hour........fascinated with the language..........requested coaching classes.........a French tourist guide today.

Ans. Man—The Master of His Own Destiny

Raju was a little boy who was born in a poor family. He wanted to get properly educated but his financial condition did not allow him to do so. He remained illiterate and so, would not get a decent job with stable earning. So, he took to pick-pocketing and small thievery. One day, he was caught red-handed for pick-pocketing. Since he was only thirteen, he was sent to juvenile prison where he was forced to do study. By this time, he had lost all interest in them and the strict behaviour of the prison-people made him sullen and rebellious. It was only during the recreation hour that he seemed to be his normal self.

One day, he watched a French comic film on T.V. He was fascinated with the French language and wanted to learn it. He requested the prison authorities for coaching classes in French. They agreed to his proposal as they were themselves interested to make him learn something so he could be self-dependent. Raju showed a keen interest in learning the language and in a very short period, had acquired mastery over it. Raju was set free after two years. Now, he was working as a French tourist guide and started leading an honourable life. He forgot all about his past and is happy these days for the sudden but positive turn in his life. He has set an example for others that man is a master of his own destiny.

11. A teacher asked her students to write a story for a competition organised by the Champak Magazine. Kartik could not complete the story. Help him complete the story in 100-120 words on the basis of the beginning of the story given below. Also give it a suitable title.

"Gaurav was delighted to know that he would be studying in the city in a new school. He was eager to meet his new teachers and classmates. He thought that his bad days were over. However, he was shocked..."

Ans. A Hasty Conclusion

Gaurav was delighted to know that he would be studying in the city in a new school. He was eager to meet his new teachers and classmates. He thought that his bad days were over. However, he was shocked when he entered the school for the first time.

He saw a group of boys beating a small student. He also saw a teacher standing there who was actually encouraging the bullies while the other students of the school were merrily laughing and clapping. "What kind of school is this?", he thought to himself. Being scared, he ran back home and narrated the whole incident to his parents.

His father was surprised but also felt doubtful about the reality of what Gaurav had seen, as it was one of the best schools of the city. He decided to go to the school with Gaurav immediately.

He went to the Principal's room and narrated the incident to him. There were a few teachers present in the room at that time. Everybody had a hearty laugh when it was revealed that the students were actually rehearsing a street play and the teacher was directing the students. Then, the teacher said that there was a character of the play that would perfectly suit Gaurav. The character also did things in haste and formed opinions without going into the details of the matter.

12. You've been having strange dreams for the last few months. You observe that your dream often comes true. Convert one such dream, in which you helped in saving a small child from getting kidnapped into a short and interesting story in 100-120 words. You can take help from the visual given below.

Ans. **Strange Dreams**

I woke up in the morning with the night's dream still fresh in my mind. I got ready for school, had my breakfast and picked up my school bag before leaving for school. When I reached the bus stop, I realised that I was late and the school bus must have already left. I decided to walk to school as it would take only 20 minutes if I took a shortcut via a road closed for repairs and felt a sense of familiarity I realised that my dream seemed to be coming true yet again.

Last night, I had dreamt that I was on a stretch of lonely road. As I was walking on the road, I saw a child's bicycle lying abandoned by the roadside. Some distance away, three men were carrying a small child. As I started going towards them, the trio took the child to an old abandoned building and threatened to kill him if he made any noise.

The entire dream scenario unfolded before my eyes again. I walked beyond the abandoned building and called the police from a PCO. When the police arrived, I guided them to the kidnappers' hideout. The police caught the kidnappers red-handed. The child was unharmed. I thanked God for enabling me to save the child's life and wondered whether my school principal would accept my reason for coming late to school.

ASSESSMENT EXERCISE

1. Sumit decided to write a story, but after some time he could not complete the story, as he had lost interest. Complete the story on the basis of the beginning given below in 100-120 words.

   "Once the fairies of the trees set out to choose their dwelling places ......"

2. Write a story in 100-120 words that begins as follows.

   "I didn't tell my dad about the red lizard I found at the bottom of the garden because..."

3. Given below is the outline of a story. Write it using this outline and your own ideas in 100-120 words.

   Train journey - found a lost child - tried to help - parents come searching - accused of kidnapping - child revealed the truth

4. What happened next? Complete the story in 100-120 words.

   "The afternoon was hot and so was the railway carriage. The next stop was Kajiguda. The old lady opposite me was fast asleep and I wondered whether she had missed her stop. But I didn't dare wake her up...."

5. Write a story using the given sentences: As I walked through the thick pine forest in Shimla, I sensed someone following me and...

6. Here is a story that is to be published in the school magazine. Unfortunately, it has been left unfinished. Complete the story by adding a few points of your own.

   "Pooja was coming out of her history class. She saw Ms. Mary, her English teacher, waiting in the corridor. Suddenly, two boys came running and pushed Ms. Mary ....".

7. Write a story with a suitable title using the following hints in 100-120 words.

   Holidaying on a beach - got far out to see on a boat- find secluded island- lighthouse- abandoned- ghost ship- reality something else.

8. Write a story titled 'Always be Patient' in 100-120 words beginning as follows.

   "I was shocked to know that my friend ...."

9. Write a story which illustrates the truth of the statement, "One lie leads to another".

10. Study the picture given below. Write a story on what the picture suggests to you. There must be a clear connection between the picture and the composition.

11. Write a story in about 150-200 words with the following beginning and give a suitable title to it.

    Rahul was alone at home. Suddenly the phone rang ....

Section B : Grammar

CHAPTER 1

Tenses

Tense is defined as the form of verb that tells the relation between time and action. It denotes the time when the action is completed or the state of being.

Tenses are classified into three main types

(i) Present Tense (ii) Past Tense (iii) Future Tense

These forms are further classified into the following subdivisions

TENSE

- **Present**
  - Indefinite
  - Continuous
  - Perfect
  - Perfect Continuous
- **Past**
  - Indefinite
  - Continuous
  - Perfect
  - Perfect Continuous
- **Future**
  - Indefinite
  - Continuous
  - Perfect
  - Perfect Continuous

Note that

V1 - First form of the verb/base form

V2 - Second form of the verb/past form

V3 - Third form of the verb/past participle

1.1 Present Tense

Present Indefinite (or Simple Present) Tense

Present Indefinite tense denotes an action that takes place in the present time.

Structure

Sentence Type	Structure	Example
Affirmative	Subject + V1(s/es) + object	John likes to paint.
Negative	Subject + do/does + not + V1 + object	John doesn't like to paint.
Interrogative	Do/Does + subject + V1+ object?	Does John like to paint?

This form of the present tense is used in the following ways

(i) To express habitual action, or custom.

e.g.
- My grandmother reads newspaper in the morning. (habitual action)
- She prays by offering flowers and incense sticks. (custom)

(ii) To talk about a universal truth.

e.g.
- Africa is a continent.

(iii) To indicate a future event which is part of a plan or arrangement.

e.g.
- The coffee shop reopens tomorrow.
- The election commences next month.

(iv) To introduce quotes with the reporting verb 'says'.

e.g.
- Robert Frost says, "We love the things we love for what they are."
- Nelson Mandela says, "Education is the most powerful weapon which you can use to change the world."

Present Continuous Tense

Present Continuous tense denotes an action that is taking place at the time of speaking.

Structure

Sentence Type	Structure	Example
Affirmative	Subject + be verb (is/am/are) + V1 + ing + object	You are coming with us.
Negative	Subject + be verb (is/am/are) + not + V1 + ing + object	You are not coming with us.
Interrogative	be verb (is/am/are) + subject + V1 + ing + object?	Are you coming with us?

This form of the present tense is used in the following ways.

(i) To indicate an action that is not happening at the time of speaking but is in progress.

e.g.
- She is pursuing a degree in electrical engineering.
- Mr. Khanna is teaching in a dance academy.

(ii) To denote an action that has been prearranged to take place in the near future.

e.g.
- I am watching a football match at XYZ stadium today.
- The wedding is taking place tomorrow.

(iii) To express possibility or determination.

e.g.
- I am going to buy a new car. (determination)
- She is going to catch cold. (possibility)

Present Perfect Tense

Present Perfect tense describes an action that has just been completed.

Structure

Sentence Type	Structure	Example
Affirmative	Subject + has/have + V3 + object	I have read the book.
Negative	Subject + has/have + not + V3 + object	I have not read the book.
Interrogative	Has/Have + subject + V3 + object?	Have I not read the book?

This form of the present tense is used in the following ways.

(i) To describe an action that started sometime in the past and have continued to the present.

e.g.
- Mrs. Swift has taught in this school for a decade now.
- They have tended to the garden as long as I can remember.

(ii) To describe past events, the effect of which still exists.

e.g.
- I have some free time now as I have completed my work for the day.
- She has finished exercising and now she's having breakfast.

(iii) To describe an action, the time of which is not given or definite.

e.g.
- I have been to Vietnam once.
- Khushi has purchased the book.

Present Perfect Continuous Tense

Present Perfect Continuous tense expresses an action that began at some time in the past and is still continuing in the present.

Structure

Sentence Type	Structure	Example
Affirmative	Subject + has/have + been + V1 + ing + object	She has been cleaning the house.
Negative	Subject + has/have + not + been + V1 + ing + object	She has not been cleaning the house.
Interrogative	Has/Have + subject + been + V1 + ing + object?	Has she been cleaning the house?

1.2 Past Tense

Past Indefinite (Simple Past) Tense

Simple Past tense indicates an action that was completed in the past.

Structure

Sentence Type	Structure	Example
Affirmative	Subject + V2 + object	They went to see the exhibition.
Negative	Subject + did + not + V1 + object	They did not go to see the exhibition.
Interrogative	Did + Subject + V1 + object?	Did they go to see the exhibition?

This form of the past tense is used in the following ways.

(i) It is often used in recounts and narratives.

e.g.
- I often laughed at my friend's silly jokes. (recount)
- The earthquake left a long lasting effect. (narrative)

(ii) To indicate past habits or repeated events that are over now.

e.g.
- She used to have tea in the afternoon. (past habit)
- He was always in a rush. (repeated event)

(iii) To indicate an action that was true for some time in the past.

e.g.
- He was a diligent student.
- That house was haunted.

Past Continuous Tense

Past Continuous tense indicates an action that was happening at some time in the past in which the time of action may or may not be indicated.

Structure

Sentence Type	Structure	Example
Affirmative	Subject + be verb (was/were) + V1 + ing + object	I was listening to music.
Negative	Subject + be verb (was,were) + not + V1 + ing + object	I was not listening to music.
Interrogative	Be verb (was,were) + subject + V1 + ing + object?	Was I listening to music?

This form of the past tense is used in the following ways.

(i) To denote persistent habits in the past. It is generally used with always, continually, often, etc.

e.g. • We were always supporting each other.
• I was continually feeling unwell.

Past Perfect Tense

Past Perfect tense denotes an action completed before another past event.

Structure

Sentence Type	Structure	Example
Affirmative	Subject + had + V3 + object	She had looked for her phone everywhere.
Negative	Subject + had + not + V3 + object	She had not looked for her phone everywhere.
Interrogative	Had + subject + V3 + object?	Had she looked for her phone everywhere?

Past Perfect Continuous Tense

Past Perfect Continuous tense indicates an action that began in the past and continued up to a certain point of time in the past.

Structure

Sentence Type	Structure	Example
Affirmative	Subject + had + been + V1 + ing + object	They had been searching for a place to stay since 2 O'Clock.
Negative	Subject + had + not + been + V1 + ing + object	They had not been searching for a place to stay since 2'o clock.
Interrogative	Had + subject + been + V1 + ing + object?	Had they been searching for a place to stay since 2'o clock?

1.3 Future Tense

Future Indefinite (or Simple Future) Tense

Simple Future tense expresses an action that will take place some time in the future.

Structure

Sentence Type	Structure	Example
Affirmative	Subject + will/shall + V1 + object	I shall wait for you.
Negative	Subject + will/shall + not + V1 + object	I shall not/shan't wait for you.
Interrogative	Will/Shall + subject + V1 + object?	Shall I wait for you?

This form of the future tense is used in the following ways

(i) To express a warning, order, request, advice or proposal.

e.g. • You will be punished if you break the rules. (warning)
• You will bring me the file. (order)
• Will you lend me your book? (request)
• You will take this vitamin daily. (advice)
• Will you go to the movie with me? (proposal)

Future Continuous Tense

Future Continuous tense denotes an action that will be in progress at a point of time in the future.

Structure

Sentence Type	Structure	Example
Affirmative	Subject + will/shall + be + V1 + ing + object	He will be responding to your mail soon.
Negative	Subject + will/shall + not + be + V1 + ing + object	He will not be responding to your mail soon.
Interrogative	Will/Shall + subject + be + V1 + ing + object?	Will he be responding to your mail soon?

This form of the future tense is used in the following ways.

(i) To indicate an action that will occur in a continuous course.

e.g. • I shall be practising my handwriting.
• Bella will be handling the project.

Future Perfect Tense

Future Perfect tense denotes an action that will be completed before another event in the future.

Structure

Sentence Type	Structure	Example
Affirmative	Subject + will/shall + have + V1 + object	We shall have sent the package by then.
Negative	Subject + will/shall + not + have + V3 + object.	We shall not have sent the package by then.
Interrogative	Will/Shall + subject + have + V3 + object?	Shall we have sent the package by then?

Future Perfect Continuous Tense

Future Perfect Continuous tense denotes an action that will be in progress over a period of time or that will be the cause of another event in the future.

Structure

Sentence Type	Structure	Example
Affirmative	Subject + will/shall + have + been + V1 + ing + object	Mother will have been teaching for twenty years in the college.
Negative	Subject + will/shall + not + have + been + V1 + ing + object	Mother will not have been teaching for twenty years in this college.
Interrogative	Will/Shall + subject + have + been + V1 + ing + object?	Will mother have been teaching for twenty years in this college?

Tenses at a Glance

The summarised tables of the Present, Past and Future tenses are given as follows

Types of Tense	Structure	Examples
Present Tense		
Indefinite or Simple	Subject + V1 (+ s/es) + object	(i) I play football. (ii) We play football.
Continuous	Subject + be verb (is, am, are) + V1 + ing + object	(i) I am playing football. (ii) We are playing football.
Perfect	Subject + has/have + V3 + object	(i) I have played football. (ii) We have played football.
Perfect Continuous	Subject + has/have + been + V1 + ing + object	(i) I have been playing football. (ii) We have been playing football.
Past Tense		
Indefinite or Simple	Subject + V2 + object	(i) I played football. (ii) We played football.
Continuous	Subject + be verb (was, were) + V1 + ing + object	(i) I was playing football. (ii) We were playing football.
Perfect	Subject + had + V3 + object	(i) I had played football. (ii) We had played football.
Perfect Continuous	Subject + had + been + V1 + ing + object	(i) I had been playing football. (ii) We had been playing football.

Future Tense		
Indefinite or Simple	Subject + will/shall + V1 + object	(i) I shall play football. (ii) We shall play football.
Continuous	Subject + will/shall + be + V1 + ing + object	(i) I shall be playing football. (ii) We shall be playing football.
Perfect	Subject + will/shall + have + V3 + object	(i) I shall have played football. (ii) We shall have played football.
Perfect Continuous	Subject + will/shall + have + been + V1 + ing + object	(i) I shall have been playing football. (ii) We shall have been playing football.

REVIEW EXERCISE

Objective and Subjective Questions

Objective Type Questions

I. Directions (Q. Nos. 1-15) Choose the correct option to fill the blanks in the following sentences.

1. Rashi .... working all afternoon and has just finished her assignment.
(a) has been (b) had been
(c) shall be (d) is

2. The Earth .... on its own axis.
(a) rotated (b) is rotating
(c) rotates (d) rotating

3. The next train .... this evening at 17.00.
(a) leaving (b) is leaving
(c) leave (d) leaves

4. I will talk to Drishti when I .... her.
(a) saw (b) will see (c) see (d) seeing

5. Please be quiet. The children ....
(a) had slept (b) were sleeping
(c) are sleeping (d) have slept

6. What .... next week?
(a) did you do (b) are you done
(c) have you done (d) are you doing

7. Prem .... three articles and he is working on another one.
(a) has written (b) had written
(c) had been writing (d) is writing

8. My last birthday was the worst day I ....
(a) had ever had (b) have ever had
(c) had (d) have

9. Mintoo .... with us since last week.
(a) had stayed (b) had been staying
(c) has stayed (d) has been staying

10. I have always .... Tendulkar.
(a) liked (b) been liking
(c) like (d) had liked

11. Who .... food in your family when your mother is not at home?
(a) cooks (b) is cooking
(c) has been cooking (d) cooked

12. Where is John? He .... his car in the garage.
(a) repairs (b) is repairing
(c) has repaired (d) repaired

13. She .... the living room when she heard a strange noise in the kitchen.
(a) has cleaned (b) has been cleaning
(c) was cleaning (d) have cleaned

14. I envy you. At five tomorrow you .... some suntan on a nice beach in Goa.
(a) will get (b) will be getting
(c) will have gotten (d) will have been getting

15. You arrived two days ago. You are going to leave next Sunday. By the time you leave, you .... nine days here.
(a) spend (b) have spent
(c) are spending (d) will have spent

II. Directions (Q. Nos. 1-15) Fill in the blanks with suitable form of verbs.

1. They .... (build) a new power station at the moment.
(a) built (b) are building
(c) will build (d) building

2. The Sun .... (rise) in the morning.
(a) will rise (b) rises
(c) rose (d) will be rising

3. I .... (visit) my grandfather in the nursing home every Friday.
(a) will be visiting (b) visited
(c) visit (d) visits

4. My favourite country is Canada. I .... (be) there four times.
(a) have been (b) was
(c) is (d) Both (a) and (b)

5. The grass is wet because it .... (rain) all day long.
(a) was raining (b) has been raining
(c) rained (d) had rained

6. Where .... (be) you yesterday?
(a) were (b) was (c) is (d) had

7. My friend .... (know) the answer to the question.
(a) knew (b) know
(c) has known (d) knows

8. We ...... (finish) our breakfast an hour ago.
(a) finished (b) will finish
(c) have been finishing (d) finishes

9. She jumped off the train while it .... (move).
(a) moved (b) was moving
(c) moving (d) moves

10. When I reached home yesterday, my dog .... (sit) at the door waiting for me.
(a) sat (b) was sitting
(c) had been sitting (d) has been sitting

11. When I .... (buy) the stamps somebody .... (call) my name.
(a) was buying, called (b) bought, called
(c) was buying, calls (d) will be buying, called

12. I .... (not go) to the cinema last night. I .... (be) too tired.
(a) did not go, was (b) did not go, is
(c) did not went, was (d) did not went, is

13. As you can .... (see). I .... (become) a real cricket fan already.
(a) see, have become (b) saw, became
(c) seen, become (d) seeing, becoming

14. Where .... (you go) on holiday? "I don't know. We .... (not decide) yet."
(a) are you going, have not decided
(b) went, not decided
(c) will go, not decided
(d) will you go, have not decided

15. Kavita .... (invite) us to the party but we .... (not go). We had other things to do.
(a) invited, did not go
(b) had invited, did not go
(c) had been inviting, did not went
(d) invites, did not go

III. Directions (Q. Nos. 1- 2) Complete the following passages by filling in the blanks with suitable form of verb.

1. If the officer (i) .... the bribe, he (ii) .... arrested. Now, his family will also (iii) .... suffer. He must (iv) .... careful about it.

(i) (a) would not have taken (b) has not taken
(c) did not take (d) had not taken

(ii) (a) wouldn't have been (b) is not
(c) will not be (d) wouldn't be

(iii) (a) had to (b) get to (c) Is to (d) have to

(iv) (a) has been (b) have been
(c) will have been (d) had been

2. Mount Abu (i) .... (be) the only hill station of Rajasthan, which is very popular in that region. According to the legend, it (ii) .... (be) the home of Saint Vashishtha who (iii) .... the four powerful Rajput tribes. Maharaja of Sirohi (iv) ....it on rent to the British Government who used it as the headquarters for the Resident of Rajputana situated at the Nakki Lake. It is known as a place that increases joy.

(i) (a) was (b) is
(c) were (d) has been

(ii) (a) is (b) were (c) was (d) had been

(iii) (a) creating (b) create (c) creates (d) created

(iv) (a) had given (b) gives
(c) give (d) gave

IV. Directions (Q. Nos. 1-5) Select the option that identifies the error and supplies the correction for the following line.

1. Since its beginning, artificial intelligence is come under scrutiny from scientists and the public alike.

Options	Error	Correction
(a)	its	It's
(b)	is	has
(c)	under	to
(d)	alike	altogether

2. Have you not been worked on this essay for more than a week?

Options	Error	Correction
(a)	Have	Had
(b)	been	be
(c)	worked	working
(d)	than	then

3. We will have finished all the water before we have been halfway through the trek.

Options	Error	Correction
(a)	will have	have
(b)	all	some
(c)	before	until
(d)	have been	are

4. Have you ever gone to Old Delhi since you move here?

Options	Error	Correction
(a)	Have	Had
(b)	ever	never
(c)	since	after
(d)	move	moved

5. One day, she is just walking down the street when suddenly a man came up to her and asked her to lend him some money.

Options	Error	Correction
(a)	is	had been
(b)	when	then
(c)	came	had come
(d)	asked	had asked

Subjective Type Questions

I. Directions (Q. Nos. 1-15) Fill in the blank with most suitable form of verb.

1. During the past few years, technology ....(grow) rapidly.
2. I ....(learn) Japanese language for 2 years now.
3. India .... (get) her independence in 1947.
4. A fire .... (break) out in the nearby locality as a result of cooking gas explosion.
5. .... (you reach) your destination?
6. The poet .... (create) vivid impressions of the snake in the poem.
7. One day, Miss Sullivan ....(attract) my attention to a strange object which she had captured basking in the shallow water.
8. As expected, the trip .... (be) rather smooth and enjoyable.
9. At this time next week, I .... (reach) Sikkim.
10. If I .... (study) harder, I would have passed the exam.
11. We shall wait for you here until you .... (come).
12. She .... (suffer) from fever since yesterday evening.
13. What .... (you do) about this situation?
14. She .... (think) that the cat might make a great companion.
15. The horseshoe crab .... (return) to the sea which was its home.

II. Directions (Q. Nos. 1-15) Fill in the blank with most suitable form of verb.

1. Bob was really unlucky that day as he .... (fire) from his job.
2. The year 2022 .... (bring) AI into the mainstream through widespread familiarity with applications of Generative Pre-Training Transformer.
3. The building .... (renovate) at a cost of 10 crore last month.
4. When he .... (reach) the platform, the metro had just left.
5. I am quite late. They say that they................ (wait) for me.
6. Unfortunately, the writer passed away before he............. (finish) the book.
7. Please maintain silence inside the hospital. The patients .... (sleep).
8. Nowadays, most people .... (use) e-mail instead of writing letters as it is more convenient.
9. Our class .... (organise) a trip to Kathmandu in January.
10. The cat .... (drink) all the milk that I had kept on the dining table.
11. Two and two .... (make) four.
12. It ....(start) raining at the beginning of the month.
13. If it rains, you .... (remain) inside the house.
14. Constipation is avoidable if we .... (consume) more fibre and do regular exercise.
15. He couldn't see her face as she .... (sit) with her back to him.

III. Directions (Q. Nos. 1- 2) Complete the following passages by filling in the blanks with suitable form of verb.

1. David P. Abbot was a US magician, who (i) .... (invent) the basis of ball trick back in 1907. He (ii) .... (use) to make a golden ball float around in his parlour. Abbot (iii) .... (will) absentmindedly leave the ball on a bookshelf. Guests would sneak over from the left and (iv) .... (find) it was much heavier than a thread could support.

2. An earthquake, perhaps one of the strongest in history (i) .... (strike) Japan in March, 2011. It (ii) .... (kill) around nineteen thousand people and (iii) .... (destroy) hundreds of buildings. Thousands of people (iv) .... (injure) or found missing.

IV. Directions (Q.Nos. 1-5) Identify the errors in the given sentences and supply the corrections.

1. Every atom of water was formed from two molecules of hydrogen and one molecule of oxygen.

Error	Correction

2. Disease became pandemic if it spreads in many regions or places.

Error	Correction

3. The boys were motivating when they heard their coach's speech.

Error	Correction

4. When I reached home yesterday, I would witnessed a heartwarming scene.

Error	Correction

5. The garbage truck was collective the trash from each and every household.

Error	Correction

ANSWERS

Objective Type Questions

I. 1. (b) had been 2. (c) rotates
3. (d) leaves 4. (c) see
5. (c) are sleeping 6. (d) are you doing
7. (a) has written 8. (a) had ever had
9. (d) has been staying 10. (a) liked
11. (a) cooks 12. (b) is repairing
13. (c) was cleaning 14. (b) will be getting
15. (d) will have spent

II. 1. (b) are building 2. (b) rises
3. (c) visit 4. (a) have been
5. (b) has been raining 6. (a) were
7. (d) knows 8. (a) finished
9. (b) was moving 10. (b) was sitting
11. (a) was buying, called 12. (a) did not go, was
13. (a) see, have become
14. (a) are you going, have not decided
15. (b) had invited, did not go

III. 1. (i) (d) had not taken (ii) (a) wouldn't have been
(iii) (d) have to (iv) (b) have been
2. (i) (b) is (ii) (c) was
(iii) (d) created (iv) (a) had given

IV. 1. (b) error – is, correction – has
2. (c) error – worked, correction – working
3. (d) error – have been, correction – are
4. (d) error – move, correction – moved
5. (a) error – is, correction –had been

Subjective Type Questions

I. 1. has been growing 2. have been learning
3. got 4. broke
5. Have you reached 6. created
7. attracted 8. was
9. shall have reached 10. had studied
11. come 12. has been suffering
13. will you do 14. thought
15. had returned

II. 1. was fired 2. brought
3. was renovated 4. reached
5. will be waiting 6. had finished
7. are sleeping 8. are using
9. is organising 10. drank
11. makes 12. had started
13. will remain 14. consume
15. was sitting

III. 1. (i) invented (ii) used
(iii) would (iv) find
2. (i) struck (ii) killed
(iii) destroyed (iv) were injured

IV. 1. Error – was, correction – is
2. Error – became, correction – becomes
3. Error – motivating, correction – motivated
4. Error – would, correction – had
5. Error – collective, correction – collecting

Modals

CHAPTER 2

2.1 Definition of Modals

Helping or auxiliary verbs that express the mode or manner of the actions denoted in the main verb are termed as Modal Auxiliaries or Modals. This class of helping verbs not only assists in forming questions and negatives, but also expresses a wide range of meanings.

These helping verbs are **can, could, will, would, shall, should, may, might and must.**

Functions of Modals

Will

(i) To show promise, intention, willingness, determination with the first person (I, we)

e.g.
- I *will* buy you a bicycle next month. (promise)
- We *will* assist you. (willingness)
- I *will* finish this project today. (determination)
- I *will* go there today. (intention)

(ii) To express request, invitation, insistence, assumption, characteristic or habit

e.g.
- *Will* you please lend me some money? (request)
- Mohan *will* be practising karate at this time. (assumption)
- *Will* you be interested in joining our bookclub? (invitation)
- We *will* go with you to the police station. (insistence)
- It *will* start raining around June. (characteristic)
- She *will* go to sleep at night at 10 pm. (habit)

Negative Form of Will (Will not/Won't)

e.g.
- She *will not* be coming today.
- They *won't* wait for me.

Would (Past Form of 'Will')

(i) To express past habit

e.g.
- She *would* run 5 kilometers every day.
- I *would* have a glass of warm milk before going to sleep.

(ii) For request

e.g.
- *Would* you please lend me your jacket?
- *Would* you let me see your physics notes?

(iii) To express wish

e.g.
- We wish our teachers *would* be always healthy.
- She *would* be an artist.

(iv) To express an imaginary condition

e.g.
- If I worked out every day, I *would* be fit.
- I *would* have been a billionaire if I had inherited a big company.

Negative Form of Would (Would not/Wouldn't)

e.g.
- *Wouldn't* she have already reached Dubai?
- I *wouldn't* be this careless if I were you.

Shall

(i) To ask for suggestion, request or advice with the first person (I, we) in the interrogative

e.g.
- *Shall* we write a book together? (suggestion)
- *Shall* I have a glass of water? (request)
- *Shall* I code it in this manner? (advice)

(ii) With the second and third person, to indicate threat, warning, command, promise, assurance and determination

e.g.
- He *shall* not be allowed to go outside if he doesn't finish his homework. (threat/warning)
- You *shall* come back at once. (command)
- Minnie *shall* receive her paycheck early. (promise)
- You *shall* do well, don't panic. (assurance)
- He *shall* win this match. (determination)

Negative Form of Shall (Shall not/Shan't)

e.g.
- I *shan't* eat dinner today.
- We *shall not* agree to take up this offer unless we discuss first.

Should (Past Form of 'Shall')

(i) To express duty or obligation

e.g.
- We *should* not litter public places. (obligation)
- He *should* always be there for his family. (duty)

(ii) To express opinion

e.g.
- They *should* be reaching in a few hours.
- He *should* be on night duty today.

(iii) To give or take advice or suggestion

e.g. • We *should* respect our elders.
• You *should* eat less at night.

(iv) After 'lest' when someone expresses fear

e.g. • Study well lest you *should* fail the exam.
• They woke up early lest they *should* miss the sunrise.

Negative Form of Should (Should not/Shouldn't)

e.g. • You *shouldn't* have said that.
• We *should not* be late today.

Can

(i) To express an ability, capability, capacity or power

e.g. • She *can* study for twelve hours in a day. (ability)
• Kalam *can* speak 13 languages. (capability)
• I *can* carry only this much. (capacity)
• She *can* take you there. (power)

(ii) To show possibility

e.g. • Hema *can* ask for some money.
• He *can* go trekking today.

(iii) To take or give permission

e.g. • *Can* I get some juice?
• You *can* have some juice from the fridge.

Negative Form of Can (Cannot/Can't)

e.g. • I *cannot* go to the aquarium.
• She *can't* play the guitar.

Could (Past Form of 'Can')

(i) To express ability/talent in the past

e.g. • She *could* hold her breath for 4 minutes under water.
• He *could* walk when he was just a year old.

(ii) To express polite request

e.g. • *Could* you please move aside?
• *Could* I borrow your bicycle?

Negative Form of Could (Could not/ Couldn't)

e.g. • I *couldn't* reach the venue on time.
• *Couldn't* you have shown some decency?

May

(i) To show possibility or probability

e.g. • I *may* buy that book next Sunday. (possibility)
• Neha *may* do well in the board exam. (probability)

(ii) To give or take permission

e.g. • *May* I take this pen?
• Yes, you *may* take it.

(iii) To wish or pray

e.g. • *May* you get a good job!
• *May* God bless you with a good future!

(iv) To show a purpose

e.g. • He is working hard so that he *may* buy a house next year.
• She is studying hard so that she *may* get a scholarship.

Negative Form of May (May not)

e.g. • She *may not* be at home.
• I *may not* have met him.

Might (Past Form of 'May')

(i) To express less possibility

e.g. • I *might* come but I'm not sure.
• Rahul *might* ask for your bike.

(ii) For permission

e.g. • *Might* we start the program?
• *Might* I begin my speech?

(iii) To express a guess

e.g. • She *might* have gone back home.
• That guitar *might* be hers.

Negative Form of Might (Might not/Mightn't)

e.g. • I *might not* be available this evening.
• It *mightn't* have been the best idea.

Note It 'May' and 'might' can be used interchangeably to express possibility. However, we usually use 'might' when something is less likely and 'may' when it is more likely.

Must

(i) To express necessity or obligation

e.g. • We *must* keep our surroundings neat and clean. (necessity)
• You *must* take care of your parents when you are older. (obligation)

(ii) To indicate assumption or conclusion

e.g. • He *must* have participated in the painting competition. (assumption)
• Mr. Khurana *must* be rich. (conclusion)

(iii) In case of prohibition

e.g. • You *must* obey the traffic rules.
• One *must* not smoke in an enclosed space.

Negative Form of Must Must not/ Mustn't

e.g. • The child *must not* be playing with water.
• You *mustn't* overexert yourself.

Use of 'Need', 'Need to', 'Dare', 'Used to' and 'Ought to'.

Need, dare, used to and **ought to** are considered semi-modals because they can be used either as modal auxiliaries or as main verbs.

Need/Need to

As a modal auxiliary verb in negative terms, it indicates absence of obligation. It expresses the speaker's authority or advice and is used for the present and the future.

e.g. I *needn't* use this machine.

The interrogative is formed by inversion.

e.g. • *Need* I speak to him?
• *Need* you go there?

Dare

As a modal auxiliary, **dare** refers to being bold and courageous. The negative is formed by **dare not** and the interrogative by inversion.

e.g. • *Dare* I insult her?
• We *dare* not talk to him.

Used to

(i) A discontinued habit or a past situation which is no more in the present.

e.g. • I *used* to go to the temple daily.
• She *used* to study for six hours everyday.

(ii) Something existing in the past.

e.g. • There *used to* be a park here.
• It *used to* be quite pleasant to stay at the farmhouse during summers.

Ought to

(i) To express moral obligation or duty

e.g. • You *ought to* respect your parents. (moral obligation)
• You *ought to* serve the nation. (duty)

(ii) To give advice

e.g. • You *ought to* be more polite to others.
• You *ought to* take proper care of yourself.

REVIEW EXERCISE

Objective and Subjective Questions

Objective Type Questions

I. Directions (Q. Nos. 1-15) Choose the correct modal to fill in the blanks.

1. This bill .... be right. 50$ for a cup of coffee!
(a) must not (b) should not
(c) cannot (d) could not

2. Is there any way I .... ride with you to work?
(a) must (b) could (c) would (d) had to

3. Leave on time lest you .... miss the train.
(a) should (b) would (c) could (d) must

4. After several hours of futile research, James decided to take a break before he .... his search for pertinent data once again.
(a) would resume (b) could resume
(c) will resumed (d) should resumed

5. .... I get something to drink, please? I am very thirsty.
(a) Should (b) Will
(c) Can (d) Dare

6. A newspaper editorial read, "The 2019-nCoV is a member of the beta coronaviruses and .... cause acute severe respiratory symptoms or possibly mild, cold-like symptoms."
(a) will (b) shall
(c) ought to (d) can

7. An internet article read, "Delay of implementation of protocols .... compromise the quality of healthcare."
(a) will (b) shall (c) ought to (d) can

8. A health report states that, "Many fear that they .... have contracted the disease in the facility."
(a) might (b) could (c) may (d) shall

9. A research journal states, "The clinical trials .... start in September with the goal to generate public interest."
(a) will (b) shall (c) ought to (d) could

10. The university website states, "All students of this institution .... abide by the rules and instructions provided."
(a) should (b) shall (c) ought to (d) will

11. He is working very hard so that he .... get an appraisal.
(a) might (b) could (c) must (d) may

12. If we had money, we .... bought a house.
(a) may have (b) could have
(c) should have (d) must have

13. How ..... you enter my room? Get out at once.
(a) need (b) may (c) dare (d) could

14. You ...... to take carbohydrates rich food.
(a) ought not (b) ought (c) must (d) need

15. I .... Arabic fluently when I was a child and we lived in Morocco.
(a) should speak (b) will speak
(c) can speak (d) could speak

II. Directions (Q. Nos. 1-15) Choose the correct modal to fill in the blanks.

1. A slogan on a wall read, "Electricity ...... kill."
(a) can (b) will (c) should (d) would
2. Students were asked to write on the proverb "The longest day .... have an end."
(a) could (b) must (c) shall (d) should
3. Fill in the blank to complete the proverb; All good things .... come to an end.
(a) should (b) must (c) can (d) ought to
4. Fill in the blank to complete the banner on the school notice board.
You .... work hard if you want to get good marks.
(a) could (b) should (c) can (d) must
5. .... I go to the market?
(a) May (b) Can (c) Shall (d) Would
6. Accidents can happen anywhere and .... result in injuries.
(a) should (b) will (c) need not (d) may
7. If you step on a dog, it .... bite you.
(a) could (b) will (c) ought to (d) should
8. It is dangerous to drive in the rain. You .... be very careful.
(a) would (b) might (c) could (d) should
9. You ....not eat here. It's prohibited.
(a) must (b) could (c) should (d) can
10. You need to work harder lest you .... fail to get admission in that college.
(a) should (b) might (c) may (d) could
11. .... you wait a little longer?
(a) Should (b) Need (c) Dare (d) Can
12. If Eiser left home at two, he .... be here soon.
(a) shall (b) will (c) could (d) should
13. You .... have waited for me. (cannot/need not/shall not/will not)
(a) need not (b) will not (c) can't (d) shan't
14. .... you pass this message to Emily on your way home?
(a) Could (b) Should (c) Will (d) Shall
15. How .... you talk back?
(a) ought (b) need
(c) dare (d) could

III. Directions (Q. Nos. 1- 2) Complete the following passages by filling in the blanks with suitable form of verbs.

1. Water is the elixir of life. A person .... (i) live for about a month without food, but only a week without water. Everyone .... (ii) drink at least eight glasses of water daily to stay hydrated. But all of it .... (iii) be in liquid form. Some of it .... (iv) be in the solid form.
(i) (a) may (b) can (c) will (d) might
(ii) (a) ought to (b) must (c) should (d) would
(iii) (a) should not (b) will not (c) need not (d) must not
(iv) (a) can (b) could (c) must (d) should
2. Artificial Intelligence (AI) is the software engine that drives the Fourth Industrial Revolution. Its impact .... (i) already be seen in homes, businesses and political processes. Artificial General Intelligence (AGI) is when a computer program .... (ii) perform any intellectual task that a human .... (iii). In its embodied form of robots, it .... (iv) soon be driving cars, stocking warehouses and caring for the young and elderly.
(i) (a) can (b) could (c) may (d) would
(ii) (a) must (b) may (c) might (d) can
(iii) (a) could (b) would (c) should (d) might
(iv) (a) shall (b) should (c) will (d) would

IV. Directions (Q. Nos. 1-5) Select the option that identifies the error and supplies the correction for the following line.

1. If no one thinks you may then you have to.

Options	Error	Correction
(a)	If	When
(b)	no one	none
(c)	may	can
(d)	have	need

2. In order to succeed, we must first believe that we could.

Options	Error	Correction
(a)	In	At
(b)	must	may
(c)	believe	belief
(d)	could	can

3. **Children might follow the path shown by their parents, teachers and mentors.**

Options	Error	Correction
(a)	might	should
(b)	follow	followed
(c)	shown	showed
(d)	by	to

4. **According to UN reports, half of the world's population should be living in areas facing water scarcity by as early as 2025.**

Options	Error	Correction
(a)	half	halves
(b)	should	could
(c)	facing	faced
(d)	by as	as

5. **Bare With Me Mineral Cushion and the latest Lip Cushion shall complete your natural look.**

Options	Error	Correction
(a)	Bare	Bear
(b)	shall	will
(c)	complete	be completed
(d)	look	looks

Subjective Type Questions

I. Directions (Q. Nos. 1-15) Fill in the blanks using appropriate modal.

1. We ....obey our teachers. (need to, must)
2. She .... pass this test of patience. (ought to, would)
3. There ....be a hockey ground right here. (used to, would)
4. He .... not buy a car. (dare, need)
5. I .... not ask further questions. (need, dare)
6. He walks carefully lest he ....fall down. (should, must)
7. Do you .... cook your own meal? (should, need to)
8. The villagers ....use kerosene lamps a few years ago. (must, would)
9. The old lady............take a bath every day before taking meals. (ought to, should)
10. She .... finish this work before I go. (could, must)
11. The class monitor said that she .... report to the principal on Monday. (should, ought to)
12. Students .... prepare their lessons well before examination. (ought to, must)
13. Miss Betty is ill today. She.........not come to school. (may, need)
14. .... I talk to Shivani, please? (Would, Could)
15. Since it is cloudy today, the flight to Delhi ....be delayed. (could, shall)

II. Directions (Q. Nos. 1-15) Fill in the blanks using appropriate modals.

1. Always believe in yourself that you .... definitely do anything.
2. .... I ask you for your name, Sir?
3. My hands are wet. .... you help me open the lid of this container?
4. When Anya called up, Ronan was not home. He .... have been at his friend's home.
5. Mr Raman, you can wait for the Headmaster in the lobby. He ....be here in 5 minutes.
6. Driving without putting on the seat belt......... really prove to be harmful.
7. She is a genius in Mathematics. She .... solve even complex problems in a jiffy.
8. We .... use our natural resources wisely.
9. Which of those shirts .... you pick? Help me choose one.
10. She .... reach home on time if the metro isn't delayed.
11. What languages .... you speak?
12. Since it's not allowed, you .... not enter without a proper ticket.
13. One .... serve one's country.
14. They would be here any moment. It .... not take them more than an hour to reach here.
15. I .... need the book today as I have exams tomorrow.

III. Directions (Q. Nos. 1- 2) Complete the following passages by filling in the blanks with suitable form of verbs.

1. If you ever approach the spot where a hummingbird has built its nest, you (i)............ (must/ought to) be careful. The mother bird (ii) .... (will) dart at you and try to peck your eyes. Its sharp beak (iii) ....(may) hurt your eyes severely and even destroy your eyesight. It is because the little thing doesn't know any other way of defending its young ones, and instinct teaches it that you (iv) ....(may) carry off its nest if you find it.

2. When wet waste is mixed with dry waste, it is called garbage. For zero garbage, the two ....(i) (must/should) be kept separately. Dry waste ....(ii) (can/may) be recycled and wet waste can be turned into compost and used for gardening in place of chemical fertilisers. To make compost at home, you ....(iii) (will, might) need a bin. Fill the bin with wet waste–vegetable peelings, fruit waste, tea bags and plant pruning. You ....(iv) (can/would) add offerings made at temples, such as fruits and flowers which commonly end up polluting water.

IV. Directions (Q. Nos. 1-5) Identify the errors in the given sentences and supply the corrections.

1. All children under the age of 14 would go to school. It is the law.

Error	Correction

2. You could leave sharp tools in places where children can't reach.

Error	Correction

3. I can walk for ten kilometers without feeling exhausted during my teenage years.

Error	Correction

4. It is hoped that the successful candidate could be able to take up the post no later than two weeks from now.

Error	Correction

5. At NTT DOCOMO, we're confident that blue-sky thinking will redefine the way we live our lives – for the better.

Error	Correction

ANSWERS

Objective Type Questions

I. 1. (c) cannot 2. (b) could
3. (a) should 4. (a) would resume
5. (c) Can 6. (d) can
7. (d) can 8. (a) might
9. (a) will 10. (c) ought to
11. (d) may 12. (b) could have
13. (c) dare 14. (a) ought not
15. (d) could speak

II. 1. (a) can 2. (b) must
3. (b) must 4. (b) should
5. (b) Can 6. (d) may
7. (b) will 8. (d) should
9. (a) must 10. (a) should
11. (d) Can 12. (d) should
13. (a) need not 14. (a) Could
15. (c) dare

III. 1. (i) (b) can (ii) (c) should
(iii) (c) need not (iv) (a) can
2. (i) (a) can (ii) (d) can
(iii) (a) could (iv) (c) will

IV. 1. (c) error – may, correction – can
2. (d) error – could, correction – can
3. (a) error – might, correction – should
4. (b) error – should, correction – could
5. (b) error – shall, correction –will

Subjective Type Questions

I. 1. must 2. ought to
3. used to 4. need
5. dare 6. should
7. need to 8. would
9. should 10. must
11. should 12. ought to
13. may 14. Could
15. could

II. 1. can 2. May 3. Can 4. might
5. should 6. can 7. can 8. should
9. would 10. may 11. can 12. must
13. cought to 14. should 15. will

III. 1. (i) must (ii) will
(iii) may (iv) might
2. (i) should (ii) can
(iii) will (iv) can

IV. 1. error – would, correction – should
2. error – could, correction – should
3. error – can, correction – could
4. error – could, correction – will
5. error – will, correction – can

CHAPTER 3

Determiners

3.1 Definition of Determiners

Determiners are words that can be used before nouns to determine or to modify their meaning. Determiners function like adjectives and are generally placed before nouns.

Classification of Determiners

Determiners can be classified into

1. **Articles** a, an, the
2. **Demonstrative Adjectives** this, that, these, those
3. **Quantifiers** Types of quantifiers are as follows
   (i) **Definite** one, two, hundred, ..., first, second, both, etc.
   (ii) **Indefinite** some, many, much, enough, few, a few, the few, all, little, a little, the little, several, most, etc.
   (iii) **Distributive** each, every, all, either, neither
   (iv) **Difference** another, other
   (v) **Comparative** more, less, fewer
4. **Possessives** my, your, his, her, its, our and their.

1. Articles – 'A', 'An', 'The'

An article is used to point out the noun that is referred to in a sentence. It also tells us whether we are referring to a noun in general or to a specific noun.

e.g.
- I would like to have **a** slice of cake.
- Do you have **an** umbrella?
- **The** dogs are fighting.

Types of Articles

There are only three articles- 'A', 'An' and 'The'. These three articles are further classified into two types– Definite and Indefinite articles.

Indefinite Articles

The words 'A' and 'An' are called Indefinite articles. They do not refer to any specific or unique noun. They make the noun general and are used only with singular noun.

e.g.
- They surprised her with **a** bouquet.
- I have **an** uncle who lives in Canada.

Use of Article 'A'

The article 'A' is used before singular countable noun that begin with a consonant sound.

e.g.
- I planted **a** tree last year.
- Rupa wanted to buy **a** bag.

Note In some cases, the article 'A' is used before words that begin with a vowel letter. This is so because the words start with a consonant sound.

e.g.
- Harry is **a European.** (European starts with the sound of 'y')
- This is **a one-word** substitution exercise. (One- word starts with the sound of 'w')
- She was fascinated with the idea of having **a unicorn.** (Unicorn starts with the sound of 'y')

Use of Article 'An'

The article 'An' is used before singular countable noun that start with a vowel sound.

e.g.
- I would need **an** egg and some sugar to make the dough.
- Could you pass me **an** orange from the table?

Note In some cases, the article 'An' is used before words that start with a consonant letter. This is so because the consonant letter is silent and the word starts with a vowel sound.

e.g.
- She needs **an hourglass** to conduct an experiment. (Hourglass starts with the sound of 'o')
- Although the boy looked lost, he was indeed **an heir** to the conglomerate. (heir starts with the sound of 'e')
- I heard that you have **an M.Sc.** degree in Chemistry. (M.Sc. starts with the sound of 'a')

Definite Article

The word 'The' is the only Definite article. It is used to refer to particular noun and is used with both countable and uncountable nouns.

e.g.
- Would you like to eat **the** cake from Wenger's?
- I don't like **the** sugar from Mr. Khanna's shop.

Use of Article 'The'

'The' is used

I. While talking about a particular person or thing or one already referred to (that is, when it is clear from the context which one do we mean).

e.g. **The** man whom you're looking for is not here today.

II. When a singular noun represents the whole class.

e.g. **The** cow produces milk.

III. Before some proper names that denote physical features.

(a) Oceans and Seas

e.g. **The** Indian Ocean, **The** Arabian Sea

(b) Rivers

e.g. **The** Ganges, **The** Amazon river

(c) Canals

e.g. **The** Panama Canal, **The** Great Canal

(d) Deserts

e.g. **The** Thar Desert, **The** Sahara Desert

(e) Group of islands

e.g. **The** West Indies, **The** Netherlands

(f) Mountain ranges

e.g. **The** Himalayas, **The** Andes

(g) A few names of countries, which include words like States, Republic or Kingdom

e.g. **The** People's Republic of China, **The** United Kingdom, **The** USA, **The** Republic of Korea, **The** Hague, etc.

IV. Before the names of religious or mythological books.

e.g. **The** Vedas, **The** Puranas, **The** Gita, **The** Quran (but we say Homer's Iliad, Valmiki's Ramayana).

V. Before the names of things which are unique or one of their kind.

e.g. **The** Sun, **The** Moon

VI. Before a proper noun, when it is qualified by an adjective or a defining adjectival clause.

e.g.
- **The** Great Caesar, **The** King of Rome.
- **The** Mrs. Sharma whom you met last night is my highschool teacher.

VII. With superlative degrees.

e.g. This is **the** best decision I have ever made.

VIII. With ordinals.

e.g. He was **the** first man to experience the phenomenon.

IX. Before musical instruments.

e.g. He is learning how to play **the** sitar.

X. Before an adjective when the noun is understood.

e.g. **The** rich never understand **the** poor. Here, the word 'people' is understood.

XI. As an adverb with comparatives.

e.g. **The** more time we have, **the** more we procrastinate.

Omission of Article 'The'

(i) Before material, abstract and proper nouns used in a general sense.

e.g.
- I prefer silver to gold.
- No one deserves to die of hunger.
- Varanasi is a magical city in India.

(ii) Before plural countable nouns used in a general sense.

e.g. Students like PE classes.

(iii) Before names of people

e.g. Sachin, Rabindranath, Ruskin Bond

(iv) Before names of continents, countries, cities, etc.

e.g. Asia, Malaysia, Imphal

(v) Before names of individual mountains

e.g. Mount K2, Mount Everest

(vi) Before names of meals used in a general sense.

e.g. Have dinner before you go.

(vii) Before languages and words like school, college, university, church, hospital, etc.

e.g.
- I can speak Bengali.
- The child despises hospitals.

(viii) Before names of relations, like father, mother, etc.

e.g. Brother and sister are fighting since the past five days.

(ix) In certain phrases consisting of preposition followed by its object.

e.g. At home, in hand, by night, in case, on foot, by train, on demand, etc.

2. Demonstrative Adjectives (This, That, These, Those)

I. **This** (in case of plural, these)

(a) It refers to person(s) or thing(s) near the speaker.

e.g.
- **This** painting is rather realistic.
- **These** children are very lively.

II. **That** (in case of plural, those)

(a) It refers to person(s) or thing(s) far from the speaker.

e.g.
- I want **that** flower.
- **Those** horses look healthy.

(b) It is used to differentiate two people or things in two different groups.

e.g. • **Those** colours don't mix well with these colours.
• I like this cat better than **that** cat.

3. Quantifiers

A quantifier is a word or phrase which is used before a noun to indicate the amount or quantity. Quantifiers can be used in affirmative sentences, questions, requests or commands with both countable and uncountable nouns.

e.g. • I have kept **some** money aside.
• How **many** people have you come with?

Some quantifiers can go only with countable nouns (e.g. friends, people, cups), some can go only with uncountable nouns (e.g. sugar, tea, money, advice), while some can be used with both countable and uncountable nouns.

Examples of quantifiers are given below

Only with Uncountable Nouns	With both Countable and Uncountable Nouns	Only with Countable Nouns
a little	no, none, not any	a few
a bit of	some, all	a number of
—	any	several
a great deal of	a lot of, lots of	a great number of
a large amount of	plenty of	a large number of

Usage of quantifiers are as follows

I. Use of **few/a few/the few** and **little/a little/the little**

(a) **Few, a few** and **the few**

Few emphasises the lack of something.

e.g. We only have **few** minutes left before we board the train.

A few emphasises that something still remains.

e.g. I have quite **a few** jackets. You can take one if you'd like.

The few signifies not many but all there is.

e.g. He used up **the few** chances that he had.

(b) **Little, a little** and **the little.**

Little emphasises the lack of something.

e.g. She has **little** chance of recovering from that chronic illness.

A little emphasises that something still remains.

e.g. Can you leave **a little** ice-cream for your brother?

The little signifies not much, but all there is

e.g. He gave **the little** money that he had to the injured man.

Note Few/a few/the few and little/a little/the little have similar meaning. However, few/a few/the few is used with countable nouns while little/a little/the little are used with uncountable nouns.

II. Use of **much** and **many**

(a) We use **much** with singular uncountable nouns and **many** with plural nouns.

e.g • She hasn't asked for **much** pocket-money ever since that day.
• I came across **many** squirrels while I was walking beside the trees on the roadside.

(b) We usually use **much** and **many** with interrogative sentences and negative sentences.

e.g. • There wasn't **much** sunlight although it wasn't cloudy.
• How **many** books have you read this year?

III. Use of **more, less** and **fewer** (comparative determiners)

(a) We use **more** or **less** before singular uncountable nouns by adding 'than' after it to indicate an additional or lesser quantity of something.

e.g. • Can I have some more cake?
• Rajesh handles less work than Ragini.

(b) We use **fewer** before plural countable nouns to refer to a group of things smaller than another.

e.g. • **Fewer** students had attended the meeting than last time.

IV. Use of **each** and **every** (distributive determiners)

(a) We use **each** when the number in the group is limited or definite, but **every** is used when the number is indefinite or unknown.

e.g. • **Each** of the two girls was given a prize.
• **Every** person in this world deserves peace and happiness.

V. Use of **most, several** and **all**

(a) We usually use most with plural Uncountable nouns.

e.g. • **Most** of the time, he doesn't stay at home as he travels all over the world.

(b) We usually use **several** with plural nouns to refer to a number which is not very large. (i.e. less than **most**)

e.g. • I have seen **several** people rush to the supermarket for the weekend sale.

(c) **All** requires a plural verb when used with a countable noun but requires a singular verb with an uncountable noun.

e.g. • **All** the kids are asked to write down their parents' names.
• I'll give him **all** the time that he needs.

VI. Use of **another** and **other**

We use **another** only with singular countable nouns, whereas **other** can be used with singular countable, plural countable or uncountable nouns.

e.g. • Can I get **another** slice of cake?
• I have asked the **other** members for their opinions as well.

VII. Use of **either** and **neither**

(a) We use **either** to refer to two things, people, situations, etc. It may mean one or the other of two or each of the two.

e.g. **Either** your mother or father has to come and collect the report card.

(b) We use **neither** with only singular countable nouns and a singular verb. **Neither** is the negative of **either**.

e.g. **Neither** of the two children took her advice seriously.

4. Possessives (My, Your, His, Her, Its, Our, Their, etc.)

Possessive determiners or possessive adjectives tell us who owns something. We use a possessive determiner before a noun to show who owns the noun we are talking about. They come in front of any other adjectives.

e.g. • I still haven't given **your** book back.
• The dog is wagging **its** tail.

Subject	Possessive Determiner	Used with Type of Noun
I	my	first person singular
We	our	first person plural
You	your	second person singular/plural
They	their	third person plural
He	his	third person singular masculine
She	her	third person singular feminine
It	its	third person singular neuter

Determiners and Kinds of Nouns with which they are Used

- **A, an, each, everyone, another** and **either** are used with singular countable nouns.
- **This** and **that** are used with uncountable nouns/singular countable nouns.
- **These** and **those** are used with uncountable nouns/plural countable nouns.
- **A little, a lot of, a great deal of, much** are used with uncountable nouns.
- **More, most, a lot of, enough, adequate, some** are used with uncountable nouns/plural countable nouns.
- **A few, several, many, both** are used with plural nouns.
- **The, some, any, my, her, your, our, their, its, which, whose, what** are used with any type of noun.

REVIEW EXERCISE

Objective and Subjective Questions

Objective Type Questions

I. Directions (Q. Nos. 1-15) Fill in the blanks with suitable determiners from the options given below.

1. Has she got .... friends?
(a) little (b) much (c) any (d) most

2. .... of the shops are closed on Sundays.
(a) Any (b) Little
(c) Much (d) Most

3. Janice earns the .... money in my family.
(a) more (b) much
(c) some (d) most

4. I didn't find .... in the classroom so I returned to the cafeteria.
(a) no one (b) anyone
(c) someone (d) one

5. .... politicians are honest and should be chosen as our representatives.
(a) Few (b) The few
(c) A few (d) A little

6. German indigo replaced .... traditional vat dyeing process.
(a) a (b) the
(c) an (d) No article

7. It will be .... sad day for many when Ronaldo retires from the field.
(a) a (b) the
(c) an (d) No article

8. .... most profitable business product in the area now is granite.
(a) A (b) The
(c) An (d) No article

9. .... jade hairpin is .... heirloom of the family.
(a) A, an (b) The, a
(c) A, the (d) The, an

10. Charles Babbage is known as .... father of computers.
(a) a (b) the
(c) an (d) No article

11. The old generation does not know how to use .... smartphones.
(a) the (b) an
(c) some (d) a

12. Raman is .... smarter than we know.
(a) some (b) many
(c) a lot (d) none

13. There is hardly .... work left for you to do.
(a) much (b) any
(c) all (d) enough

14. .... of them were selected as the President.
(a) Some (b) None
(c) Few (d) Little

15. Can I have .... bowl of noodles?
(a) more (b) another
(c) enough (d) little

II. Directions (Q. Nos. 1-15) Fill in the blanks with suitable determiners from the options given below.

1. 80 percent attendance is compulsory for .... students.
(a) several (b) many
(c) much (d) all

2. I don't like .... of them.
(a) neither (b) both
(c) either (d) much

3. .... Statue of Liberty is famous world-wide.
(a) A (b) Many
(c) The (d) All

4. .... businessman wants to be successful in his projects.
(a) Many (b) Most
(c) Every (d) Enough

5. .... event is scheduled according to the plan.
(a) Each (b) Several (c) Every (d) All

6. Is there .... I could help you with?
(a) everything (b) more
(c) anything (d) much

7. Though it was a cold day, there were .... people climbing the mountain.
(a) much (b) more
(c) many (d) very few

8. .... Cantonese is one of the most widely spoken languages in the world.
(a) The (b) An
(c) A (d) No article required

9. The rich should help .... poor.
(a) a (b) an
(c) the (d) No article required

10. There aren't .... peaches on the tree.
(a) many (b) most
(c) much (d) some

11. .... of our passengers have complained about the lack of adequate seating in our waiting area.
(a) The few (b) Little
(c) Few (d) A few

12. Mr. Kalam is a man of .... words.
(a) a few (b) few (c) little (d) the little

13. .... citizens must abide by the laws given in the Constitution.
(a) Whole (b) Every (c) Each (d) All

14. We don't have .... money to arrange a grandiose wedding ceremony.
(a) much (b) more (c) little (d) enough

15. Do you have .... information about the internship programme?
(a) much (b) some (c) any (d) all

III. Directions (Q. Nos. 1-2) Fill in the blanks by using suitable determiners and complete the passages.

1. (i) .... days later, Munshi Prem Chand resigned from (ii) .... job of inspector of schools after having worked in (iii) .... department for 10 years. He was one of the (iv) .... important story writers.

(i) (a) A few (b) Few
(c) The few (d) Some

(ii) (a) its (b) the
(c) a (d) his

(iii) (a) his (b) is
(c) their (d) the

(iv) (a) much (b) most
(c) more (d) more over

2. Throughout (i) .... greater part of Bertrand Russell's childhood, (ii) .... most important hours of his days were (iii) .... that he spent alone in (iv).......... garden full of different kinds of flowers.

(i) (a) the (b) to
(c) a (d) from

(ii) (a) in (b) the
(c) these (d) this

(iii) (a) which (b) when
(c) his (d) those

(iv) (a) the (b) a
(c) some (d) an

IV. Directions (Q. Nos. 1-5) Select the option that identifies the error and supplies the correction for the following statements.

1. Sachin Tendulkar is the Bradman of India. He used to play a game of cricket with ease.

Options	Error	Correction
(a)	the	a
(b)	of	in
(c)	a	the
(d)	with	in

2. The police are on the lookout for a thief who had not only looted jewellery but had also taken a motorbike of the owner.

Options	Error	Correction
(a)	the	a
(b)	taken	took
(c)	a	the
(d)	of	with

3. The entire political system needs to be changed from the top to bottom.

Options	Error	Correction
(a)	the	a
(b)	needs	need
(c)	from	by
(d)	to	to the

4. I bought a watch and a wallet as birthday gifts. Though an watch is working fine, the wallet's leather doesn't seem to be of good quality.

Options	Error	Correction
(a)	as	for
(b)	gifts	gift
(c)	an	the
(d)	the	a

5. He was holding a Gita in his hands.

Options	Error	Correction
(a)	holding	holds
(b)	a	the
(c)	a	an
(d)	in	with

Subjective Type Questions

I. Directions (Q. Nos. 1-15) Fill in the blanks with suitable determiners.

1. Do you need .... assistance?
2. What is the time by .... watch?
3. .... is your favourite Chinese dish?
4. .... is the most frightening horror storyever read by me.
5. Show me .... maps.
6. You are the only teacher who is .... MA.
7. It is .... lowest level of water.
8. You are living with .... parents.
9. He was efficient in .... profession.
10. How .... milk is left in the bowl?
11. In the container, I found .... items missing.
12. That he is .... honest boy is known to all.
13. Which is the highest grossing movie of .... director who has turned 80 today?
14. I have lost .... high school certificate.
15. See that white building; it is .... residence.

II. Directions (Q. Nos. 1-15) Fill in the blanks using appropriate modals.

1. .... (My/Mine) younger brother will reach Delhi today.
2. Copper is........... (a/an) useful metal.
3. It is a public holiday today, so........... (nothing/nowhere) is open.
4. This is .... (the/a) best book of Elementary Chemistry.
5. Honest men speak .... (a/the) truth.
6. .... (Few/The few) persons can keep a secret.
7. .... (A few/Few) words spoken in earnest will convince him.
8. .... (The few/Few) friends he has are all very poor.
9. It is .... (a/the) one-rupee note.
10. .... (The/A) poor are always with us.
11. .... (The/A) dinner we had at the tourist hotel was very nice.
12. I went to .... (a/the) hospital to see my uncle.
13. Mr. Roy was ...... (a/the) great orator and statesman.
14. .... (The/A) Secretary and Treasurer are absent.
15. .... (A little/The little) grain they had was damaged by sea water.

III. Directions (Q. Nos. 1-2) Fill in the blanks by using suitable determiners and complete the passages.

1. (i) .... (A/An) abbreviation is (ii).................. (a, the) shortened form of a word or a group of words. It is used to save time and space. (iii) .... (Some/Most) abbreviations are also used while speaking.
(iv) .... (Most, Much) of the dictionaries include a list of commonly used abbreviations.
2. India's maiden solar mission, Aditya-L1 undertook (i).................. (a/an/the) journey of around 1.5 million kilometers from Earth and 127 days to reach (ii)................... (its/their) final destination after the mission was launched by PLSV-C57 on September 2, 2023. The mission went through (iii).................. (several/most) maneuvers and course corrections before it reached the orbit around L1. It has (iv)...................... (a/an/the) lifespan of five years.

IV. Directions (Q. Nos. 1-5) Identify the errors in the given sentences and supply the corrections.

1. Development is understood as a social condition within a nation, in which a needs of its population are satisfied by the rational and sustainable use of natural resources and systems.

Error	Correction

2. Aditya-L1 is described as a satellite dedicated to the comprehensive study of an Sun.

Error	Correction

3. A poster on noise pollution:
To keep your health in order, keep a noise low.

Error	Correction

4. Every of the two students has received a letter of recommendation from the school.

Error	Correction

5. War is never the isolated act.

Error	Correction

ANSWERS

Objective Type Questions

I.
1. (c) any
2. (d) Most
3. (d) most
4. (b) anyone
5. (a) Few
6. (b) the
7. (a) a
8. (b) The
9. (d) The, an
10. (b) the
11. (c) some
12. (c) a lot
13. (b) any
14. (b) None
15. (b) another

II.
1. (d) all
2. (c) either
3. (c) The
4. (c) Every
5. (c) Every
6. (c) anything
7. (c) many
8. (d) No article required
9. (c) the
10. (a) many
11. (d) A few
12. (b) few
13. (d) All
14. (d) enough
15. (c) any

III.
1. (i) (a) A few
(ii) (d) his
(iii) (d) the
(iv) (b) most
2. (i) (a) the
(ii) (b) the
(iii) (d) those
(iv) (a) the

IV.
1. (c) error – a, correction – the
2. (c) error – a, correction – the
3. (d) error – to, correction – to the
4. (c) error – an, correction – the
5. (b) error – a, correction –the

Subjective Type Questions

I.
1. any
2. your
3. Which
4. This
5. those
6. an
7. the
8. your
9. his
10. much
11. some
12. an
13. the
14. my
15. my

II.
1. My
2. a
3. nothing
4. the
5. the
6. Few
7. A few
8. The few
9. a
10. The
11. The
12. the
13. a
14. The
15. The little

III.
1. (i) An
(ii) the
(iii) Some
(iv) Most
2. (i) a
(ii) its
(iii) several
(iv) a

IV.
1. error – a needs, correction – the needs
2. error – an, correction – the
3. error – a, correction – the
4. error – Every, correction – Each
5. error – the, correction – an

CHAPTER 4

Subject-Verb Concord

Subject-Verb Concord refers to a set of rules that implies that the subject and verb in a sentence must agree with each other in number and person.

The basic rule of Subject Verb Agreement is

- Singular Subject → Singular Verb
- Plural Subject → Plural Verb

This means that if the subject is singular, the verb should also be singular, if the subject is plural, the verb should also be plural.

e.g.
- **She goes** on a walk every evening.
- **We are** distributing blankets to the children there.

Rules

(i) When two or more singular subjects are joined together by 'and' plural verb is used.

e.g. Janu and Manju **are** working together for a project.

(ii) When two subjects together express one idea, singular verb is used.

e.g. Virtue and vice **is** a man's inherent quality.

(iii) Everybody, somebody, nobody, anybody and anyone take a singular verb.

e.g. **Is** anyone available to take the call?

(iv) If subjects are joined by 'either … or' and 'neither … nor'. the verb agrees with the subject nearest to it.

e.g.
- Either he or his brothers **are** coming to pick her up.
- Neither the children nor the teacher **was** amused at the principal's joke.

(v) The title of a book, play, story or a musical composition, even though plural, takes a singular verb.

e.g. 'Cinderella and the seven dwarfs' **is** a fairytale.

(vi) When a plural noun comes between a singular subject and its verb, the verb agrees with the singular subject.

e.g. Neither of the boys **was** playing football.

(vii) If subjects are joined by 'as well as', 'together with', 'with' or 'along with' the verb must agree with the first subject, irrespective of whether it **is** singular or plural.

e.g. The coach, together with the players, **has** entered the field.

(viii) Two nouns qualified by 'each' or 'every', even though connected by 'and', take a singular verb.

e.g. Each pencil and each book **is** arranged vertically.

(ix) None is singular but takes the verb according to the sense involved in the sentence.

e.g.
- None **were** selected for the final round.
- I wanted a black pen, but none **was** found.

(x) When the plural noun is a proper name for some single object or some collective unit, it must be followed by a singular verb.

e.g. The United Nations **is** the largest inter-governmental organisation.

(xi) Nouns like glasses (spectacles), **pants, trousers, shoes, people, police, scissors** always take a plural verb. Also, descriptive nouns like **the rich, the blind, the guilty** are always plural.

e.g.
- Nowadays, people **have** become more dependent on machine.
- The blind **are** sensitive towards sound.

(xii) Uncountable nouns like **advice, news, media, stationery, weather, progress** are singular and take a singular verb.

e.g. No news **is** good news.

(xiii) A collective noun takes a singular verb, when the collection is thought of as one whole. It takes a plural verb when the stress is on the individuals.

e.g.
- The class **has** agreed to set up a temporary stall at the upcoming school festival.
- The class **are** having disagreements on what type of food they are going to sell.

(xiv) A singular verb is used when subject denotes some specific quantity or amount.

e.g. Only two kilometres **is** left until we reach the destination.

(xv) If the words 'a lot of', 'plenty of', 'most of' or 'some of' refer to numbers instead of an amount, then plural verb is used.

e.g.
- Most of the participants **are** professional in music.
- Some of the rice **was** given to the dog.

(xvi) If two subjects are 'joined by the conjunction 'not only .... but also', then the verb agrees with the subject nearest to it.

e.g. Not only his friends, but also his sister **was** disappointed in him.

REVIEW EXERCISE

Objective and Subjective Questions

I. Directions (Q. Nos. 1-15) Fill in the blanks by choosing the most suitable words from the given options.

1. The level of intoxication .... from subject to subject.

(a) vary (b) varies
(c) have varied (d) None of these

2. Fifteen hundred miles .... a long distance to travel to visit one's family.

(a) is (b) are (c) was (d) were

3. Either you or he .... mistaken.

(a) is (b) are
(c) has (d) have

4. Few students .... present in the class today.

(a) is (b) are
(c) has been (d) Both (b) and (c)

5. He asked me whether either of the applicants .... suitable.

(a) were (b) are (c) was (d) has

6. The Chairperson or the CEO .... the proposal before proceeding.

(a) approves (b) approve
(c) approving (d) None of these

7. I will offer a ₹ 1,000 gift card to everybody who .... in the study.

(a) participate (b) participates
(c) are participating (d) is participate

8. The information obtained from the business owners .... to be included in the study.

(a) were relevant (b) was relevant
(c) has been relevant (d) have been relevant

9. Locally produced goods .... the advantage of shorter supply chains.

(a) has (b) is
(c) have (d) None of these

10. The proceeds from the sale .... to support the homeless population in the city.

(a) will goes (b) goes
(c) gone (d) go

11. One of my friends .... gone to France.

(a) has (b) have
(c) had (d) have been

12. Each of the boys .... given a present.

(a) were (b) was (c) had (d) has

13. Neither of the contestants .... able to win a decisive victory.

(a) were (b) was (c) is (d) has

14. Oil and water .... not mix.

(a) do (b) does
(c) did (d) None of these

15. He and I .... at Oxford together.

(a) were (b) was
(c) am (d) will

II. Directions (Q. Nos. 1-15) Fill in the blanks by choosing the most suitable words from the given options.

1. Your friend .... (talk) too much.

(a) talk (b) talks
(c) talked (d) will talk

2. The man with the roses .... (look) like your brother.

(a) look (b) looks
(c) looked (d) has looked

3. The woman in the pool ....(swim) well.

(a) swims (b) swam
(c) swim (d) will swim

4. Basant .... (drive) a cab daily.

(a) drives (b) drive
(c) drove (d) driving

5. The football players .... (run) five kilometres everyday.

(a) running (b) runs
(c) run (d) will run

6. Each of the girls .... (look) good on stage.

(a) look (b) looks
(c) looking (d) will look

7. Everybody .... (be) asked to remain quiet.

(a) was (b) were (c) will (d) has

8. Neither of the men .... (be) here yet.

(a) is (b) are (c) be (d) will

9. Several of the sheep .... (be) sick.

(a) is (b) are (c) be (d) will

10. Nobody in the class .... (be) the answer.

(a) have (b) has (c) was (d) will

11. Here, into the main ring of the circus .... (come) the trained elephants.

(a) comes (b) came (c) come (d) coming

12. **Either the workers or the boss .... (deliver) the merchandise.**
(a) deliver (b) have delivered
(c) delivering (d) delivers

13. **The committee .... (work) hard for better schools.**
(a) works (b) work (c) worked (d) working

14. **Some members of the faculty .... (be) present.**
(a) is (b) are (c) be (d) will

15. **Each of the girls .... (observe) all the regulations.**
(a) observing (b) observe
(c) observed (d) observes

III. Directions (Q. Nos. 1- 2) Fill in the blanks using appropriate verbs and complete the given passages.

1. Delhi (i) .... become the crime capital of the country. Cases of robbery and chain snatching (ii) .... increasing day by day. The criminals, it seems are not afraid of the police. Robberies in broad daylight (iii) .... very common these days. The citizens (iv) .... not feel safe in the city.

(i) (a) have (b) has
(c) having (d) had

(ii) (a) is (b) are
(c) have (d) has

(iii) (a) is (b) are
(c) was (d) be

(iv) (a) are (b) is
(c) does (d) do

2. Media (i) .... revolutionised the world because it allows individuals to connect with others at the push of a button, (ii) .... marketing platforms and (iii) .... a large source of entertainment. There (iv) .... many types of communication technologies, such as television, the internet, movies and the radio.

(i) (a) have (b) has (c) is (d) are
(ii) (a) creates (b) create (c) created (d) creating
(iii) (a) are (b) was (c) is (d) were
(iv) (a) are (b) is (c) has (d) have

IV. Directions (Q. Nos. 1-5) Select the option that identifies the error and supplies the correction for the following line.

1. **Five hundred rupees are a hefty amount for me.**

Options	Error	Correction
(a)	are	is
(b)	a	an
(c)	amount	amounts
(d)	for	to

2. **One-third of the city are experiencing a blackout tonight.**

Options	Error	Correction
(a)	city	cities
(b)	are	is
(c)	experiencing	experienced
(d)	tonight	that night

3. **When he talks, everyone listen.**

Options	Error	Correction
(a)	when	while
(b)	talks	talked
(c)	everyone	everybody
(d)	listen	listens

4. **Neither the farm workers nor the farmer are willing to settle the strike.**

Options	Error	Correction
(a)	neither	either
(b)	nor	or
(c)	are	is
(d)	willing	willed

5. **Gender equality mean providing equal opportunities to both men and women in every sector, be it the workplace, wages earned, or the opportunities provided.**

Options	Error	Correction
(a)	providing	provides
(b)	earned	earn
(c)	every	all
(d)	mean	means

Subjective Type Questions

I. Directions (Q. Nos. 1-15) Fill in the blanks using the most suitable verb.

1. Two thousand rupees .... my monthly transport expenditure.
2. A horse and a carriage .... waiting at the door.
3. None of the students .... done their homework.
4. Neither of the girls .... participating today.
5. Each student .... passed with flying colours.

6. Mr. Grover, together with his sons, ... a business in New Delhi.
7. My friends, as well as I .... going on a trip.
8. Snakes and mongoose .... supposed to be enemies.
9. The plate and the bowl .... kept in the cupboard.
10. The news ....getting more and more surprising every day.
11. Measles .... to affect children the most.
12. Four weeks .... a long vacation.
13. The team .... received their recommendation letters.
14. The police .... investigating the robbery case.
15. Nothing .... me well nowadays.

II. Directions (Q. Nos. 1-15) Fill in the blanks using appropriate modals.

1. None of these plants .... (grow/grows) well inside the house.
2. Neither of these two machines .... (work/works) properly.
3. Bread and eggs ...... (is/are) my favourite.
4. Don't you think petroleum in the middle east .... (cost/costs) lesser than in India?
5. Each of the children .... (has/have) his own desk.
6. Five kilometres .... (is/are) a short distance.
7. Many men .... (have/has) tried hard to climb the slippery mountain.
8. Few students ...... (is/are) coming to the coaching class this evening.
9. The level of patience .... (vary/varies) from person to person.
10. Either you or your sister .... (is/are) telling lies.
11. The government .... (was/were) criticised by the Supreme Court for their actions.
12. Here .... (is/are) the place where the accident took place.
13. Junk food, like chips and street food, ... (is/are) harmful to our health.
14. If anybody ....(asks/ask) for me, do let them in my chamber.
15. The people ....(have/had) lived without smartphones for many years.

III. Directions (Q. Nos. 1- 2) Fill in the blanks using appropriate verbs and complete the given passages.

1. India (i) ....(has/have) had a patriarchal system for ages, and it (ii) .... (be) high time that women stand up for themselves. Inequality between males and females (iii) .... (be) seen on a wide spectrum, even in today's modern era. Ancient traditions and customs (iv) .... (has/have be) so deeply embedded in our Indian society for such a long time that they curb the free will, independence, and personal views of women.
2. Keeping a pet (i) .... the best way to fight loneliness. But clean and comfortable housing for them (ii) .... essential. If they (iii) .... carnivores, a high protein diet is required. Veterinary appointments (iv) .... a must.

IV. Directions (Q. Nos. 1-5) Identify the errors in the given sentences and supply the corrections.

1. There is many advantages to this kind of teaching method.

Error	Correction

2. Neither the teacher nor the students wants to reschedule the final exam.

Error	Correction

3. Some of the research are conducted at the Indian Institute of Technology.

Error	Correction

4. Nobody like to fail their college entrance examinations.

Error	Correction

5. The arguments is well rounded and supported.

Error	Correction

ANSWERS

Objective Type Questions

I. 1. (b) varies 2. (a) is
3. (a) is 4. (b) are
5. (c) was 6. (a) approves
7. (b) participates 8. (b) was relevant
9. (c) have 10. (d) go
11. (a) has 12. (b) was
13. (b) was 14. (a) do
15. (a) were

II. 1. (b) talks 2. (b) looks
3. (a) swims 4. (a) drives
5. (c) run 6. (b) looks
7. (a) was 8. (a) is
9. (b) are 10. (b) has
11. (c) come 12. (d) delivers
13. (a) works 14. (b) are
15. (d) observes

III. 1. (i) (b) has (ii) (b) are
(iii) (b) are (iv) (d) do
2. (i) (b) has (ii) (a) creates
(iii) (c) is (iv) (a) are

IV. 1. (a) error – are, correction – is
2. (b) error – are, correction – is
3. (d) error – listen, correction – listens
4. (c) error – are, correction – is
5. (d) error – mean, correction – means

Subjective Type Questions

I. 1. is 2. is
3. have 4. is
5. has 6. runs
7. are 8. are
9. are 10. is
11. seems 12. is
13. have 14. are
15. fits

II. 1. grows 2. works
3. is 4. costs
5. has 6. is
7. have 8. are
9. varies 10. is
11. was 12. is
13. is 14. asks
15. had

III. 1. (i) has (ii) is
(iii) is (iv) have been
2. (i) is (ii) is
(iii) are (iv) are

IV. 1. error – is, correction – are
2. error – wants, correction – want
3. error – are, correction – is
4. error – like, correction – likes
5. error – is, correction – are

CHAPTER 5

Reported Speech

The act of reporting the words of a speaker is called **Narration**. There are basically two ways in which the words of the speaker can be conveyed in writing.

(a) **Direct Speech** (*Direct Narration*) The reporting of the exact words of the speaker is known as **Direct Speech**.

In a sentence in Direct Speech

- the exact words of the speaker are stated in double quotation marks (" ")
- the direct speech of the speaker is separated from the introductory phrase using a comma (,)
- the exact words of the speaker start with a capital letter
- the punctuation mark of the exact words of a speaker like question mark (?), full stop (.) and exclamation mark (!) come before the closing quotation mark.

(b) **Indirect Speech** (*Indirect Narration*) The act of reporting the words of the speaker by making necessary changes to it is called **Indirect Speech**. In indirect speech, changes are made in the original words of the person.

In a sentence in Indirect Speech,

- the comma (,) and the double quotation marks (" ") are removed
- the conjunction 'that' is used to join the introductory phrase and the speech
- the punctuation marks like the question mark (?) and exclamation mark (!) are replaced by a full stop (.).
- The tenses, pronouns and possessive adjectives along with words indicating nearness of time and position are also changed.

Look at the given example to understand these types for more clarity.

(i) My mother told me, "You have to work harder at school." (Direct speech)

(ii) My mother told me that I had to work harder at school. (Indirect speech)

In sentence (i) we can notice that this is the speaker's direct narration as it is shown inside double quotation marks, but in sentence (ii) tense and pronouns are changed and quotation marks are removed.

Reporting Verb and Reporting Speech

Reporting Verb

The verb that is not part of the speech which is given inside the quotation marks is called the Reporting Verb. It is the verb that is placed before the Statement given in the inverted commas.

Reported Speech

The words spoken by the speaker and written in quotation marks ("......") are collectively called the Reported Speech.

e.g. • He <u>said</u>, **"I go for a walk every evening."**

The underlined part is the reporting verb and the statement in bold is the reported speech.

Rules for Changing Direct Speech into Indirect Speech

The rules are discussed below

Change in Tense

When we convert a sentence from direct to indirect speech, the tense of the speech may or may not change depending on the reporting verb.

- If the reporting verb is in Present, the tense of the verbs in the introdctory phrase and exact words of the speaker do not change.

e.g. • Priyam says to me, "You can always count on me." (Direct)

• Priyam tells me that I can always count on him. (Indirect)

- If the reporting verb is in Past Tense, the tense of the speech in double quotation marks undergoes a change as given in the table.

Present Tense (Statement)

Rules of Conversion	Direct Speech	Indirect Speech
Simple Present to Simple Past	Hanika said, "I am not used to this."	Hanika said that she was not used to that.
Present Continuous to Past Continuous	He said, "She is leaving today."	He said that she was leaving that day.
Present Perfect to Past Perfect	Ruhi said, "Sabir has asked me to do homework together."	Ruhi said that Sabir had asked her to do homework together.
Present Perfect Continuous to Past Perfect Continuous	He said, "I have been singing since morning."	He said that he had been singing since morning.

Past Tense (Statement)

Rules of Conversion	Direct Speech	Indirect Speech
Simple Past to Past Perfect	Ravi said, "My mother wanted to go shopping."	Ravi said that his mother had wanted to go shopping.
Past Continuous to Past Perfect Continuous	She said, "I was suffering from fever."	She said that she had been suffering from fever.

Note It Statements in Past Perfect Tense and Perfect Continuous Tense forms do not undergo any change while transforming from direct speech into indirect speech.

Future Tense (Statement)

In future tense, the modal will/shall change to would/should in all cases.

Rules of Conversion	Direct Speech	Indirect Speech
Simple Future:	She said, "He will reach soon."	She said that he would reach soon.
Future Continuous:	He said, "I shall be playing video games."	He said that he should be playing video games.
Future Perfect:	Darsana said, "He will have brought the cat back."	Darsana said that he would have brought the cat back.
Future Perfect Continuous:	Karan said, "I shall have been eating by then."	Karan said that he should have been eating by then.

Changes in Pronoun

1. The pronoun in the indirect speech remains unchanged if the speaker is in first person.
   e.g. • I said, "I am not going today." (Direct speech)
   • I said that I was not going that day. (Indirect speech)
2. The pronoun in the indirect speech is changed to second person if the speaker is in second person.
   e.g. • You said, "I have a headache." (Direct speech)
   • You said that you had a headache. (Indirect speech)
3. The pronoun in the indirect speech is changed to third person in accordance with the gender of the speaker, if the speaker is in third person.
   e.g. • She said, "I wanted to eat sandwich and fries." (Direct speech)
   • She said that she had wanted to eat sandwich and fries. (Indirect speech)

Change in Modals

Modal verbs are changed in the following manner

- May - might
- Must - had to
- Can - could
- Ought to - ought to

Change in Time and Place Expressions

The words that indicate time or position also undergo a change when a direct speech is converted into indirect speech.

Time Indicators

Direct Speech	Indirect Speech
Now	Then
Ago	Before
Today	That day
Tonight	That night
Yesterday	The previous day/the day before
Tomorrow	The next day/ the following day
In an hour	An hour later
Hither	Thither

Place Indicators

Direct Speech	Indirect Speech
Here	There
This	That
These	Those

Rules for Changing Interrogative Sentences into Indirect Speech

Interrogative sentences are of two types (i) Yes-No type questions or verbal questions (ii) Wh-type questions

Yes-No Type Questions

When the reported speech is a yes-no type question

- the conjunction 'if' or 'whether' is used.
- the interrogative sentence (or question) is converted into an assertive sentence.
- the reporting verb is changed from 'says' and 'said' to 'asks' and 'asked' respectively.

Direct Speech	Indirect Speech
She said, "Has everybody submitted the paper?"	She asked whether everybody had submitted the paper.
He said to me, "Is there anything I can help you with?"	He asked me if there was anything he could help me with.

Wh-Type Questions

- No conjunction is used as the Wh-word itself works as a conjunction to join the reporting verb with the reported speech.
- All other changes are made in the same manner as the yes-no type questions.

Direct Speech	Indirect Speech
He said, "How do you feel now?"	He asked how I felt then.
Sonia said to me, "What were you doing?"	Sonia asked me what I had been doing.

Rules for Changing Imperative Sentences into Indirect Speech

If the direct speech contains a request or a command, the reporting verb changes to told, requested, ordered, commanded, suggested, advised, etc. according to the intent of the spoken words. Other changes are done according to the rules mentioned below.

Rules	Direct Speech	Indirect Speech
Use conjunction 'to' instead of 'that'.	• She said, "Do not speak loudly." • Mansi says to me, "Please give me a glass of water." • Our teacher said, to us "Solve these sums daily."	• She ordered not to speak loudly. • Mansi requests me to give her a glass of water. • Our teacher advised us to solve those sums daily.
In sentences beginning with 'Let', the reporting verb 'said' is changed to 'proposed' or 'suggested'.	• She said, "Let us go jogging in the morning."	• She suggested that we should go jogging in the morning.

Rules for Changing Exclamatory Sentences into Indirect Speech

Changing of exclamatory sentences into indirect speech takes place in following way

1. The reporting verb 'said/ said to' is changed to 'exclaimed'.
2. The exclamatory word (interjection) is replaced by 'exclaimed with joy/ sorrow/ regret/ surprise/ contempt, etc.', other changes are done according to the rules mentioned above.

Direct Speech	Indirect Speech
He said, "Hurrah! I have won the scholarship."	He exclaimed with joy that he had won the scholarship.
She said, "What a magnificent sight!"	She exclaimed with excitement that it was a magnificent sight.

REVIEW EXERCISE

Objective and Subjective Questions

Objective Type Questions

I. Directions (Q. Nos. 1-10) Choose the correct indirect form of the following sentences from the given options.

1. Rupak said, "I live in the City Centre."

(a) Rupak said that he lives in the City Centre.
(b) Rupak said that he had lived in the City Centre.
(c) Rupak said that he lived in the City Centre.
(d) Rupak said that he has lived in the City Centre.

2. She said, "I haven't seen them since last week."

(a) She said that she hadn't seen them since the previous week.
(b) She says that she hadn't seen them since the previous week.
(c) She said that she hadn't seen them since last week.
(d) She said that she has seen them since last week.

3. Nupur said to me, "Did you see my cat?"

(a) Nupur asked me if I have seen my cat.
(b) Nupur asked me if I had seen her cat.
(c) Nupur told me if I had seen her cat.
(d) Nupur said to me if I had seen her cat.

4. The old man said, "Please always speak the truth."

(a) The old man says to them to always speak the truth.
(b) The old man requests to always speak the truth.
(c) The old man requested to always speak the truth.
(d) The old man told them to always speak the truth.

5. Roopali said "Alas! My brother died of Covid."

(a) Roopali said that her brother had died of Covid.
(b) Roopali told me that her brother died of Covid.
(c) Roopali exclaimed with wonder that her brother had died of Covid.
(d) Roopali exclaimed with sorrow that her brother had died of Covid.

6. She said to me, "Can you type?"

(a) She asked me if I could type.
(b) She asked me if I can type.
(c) She said to ask me if I could type.
(d) She told me I could type.

7. "What time does the train arrive?" she asked.

(a) She said what time the train arrived.
(b) She asked what time the train had arrived.
(c) She asked what time the train arrived.
(d) She told what time the train does arrive.

8. The policeman said to the boy, "Where do you live?"

(a) The policeman asked the boy where he had lived.
(b) The policeman told the boy where he did lived.
(c) The policeman asked the boy where he lived.
(d) The policeman said to the boy where he do lived.

9. The teacher said to the pupil, "Have you done your work?"

(a) The teacher asked the pupil if he had done his work.
(b) The teacher asked the pupil if he has done his work.
(c) The teacher asked the pupil whether he did his work.
(d) The teacher said to the pupil whether he had done his work.

10. He said to me, "Why have you resigned from your job?"

(a) He said to me why had I resigned from my job.
(b) He asked me why I did resigned from my job.
(c) He asked me why I had resigned from my job.
(d) He told me why did I resigned from my job.

II. Directions (Q. Nos. 1-10) Choose the correct indirect form of the following sentences from the given options.

1. He said to me, "When did you buy these books?"

(a) He asked me when I had bought these books.
(b) He asked me when had I bought those books.
(c) He asked me when I did buy those books.
(d) He asked me when I had bought those books.

2. Akash said to Pari, "Can I borrow twenty rupees from you?"

(a) Akash asked Pari if he could borrow twenty rupees from her.
(b) Akash asked Pari whether he can borrow twenty rupees from him.
(c) Akash said to Pari if he could borrow twenty rupees from her.
(d) Akash told Pari whether he could borrow twenty rupees from her.

3. "Can you ride a bicycle?" I said to Sonia.

(a) I said to Sonia whether she could ride a bicycle.

(b) I told Sonia if she could ride a bicycle.

(c) I asked Sonia whether she could ride a bicycle.

(d) I asked Sonia if she rode a bicycle.

4. The stranger said to me, "Can you tell me the way to the post office?"

(a) The stranger said to me if I could tell him the way to the post office.

(b) The stranger asked me whether I could tell him the way to the post office.

(c) The stranger told me if I can tell me the way to the post office.

(d) The stranger said whetheryou could tell him the way to the post office.

5. Raman said to me, "Do you know Akshay?"

(a) Raman asked me if I knew Akshay.

(b) Raman told me whether I knew Akshay.

(c) Raman asked whether I know Akshay.

(d) Raman told me whether I knew Akshay.

6. The teacher said to us, "Don't neglect your studies".

(a) The teacher advised us not to neglect our studies.

(b) The teacher advised us to not neglect your studies.

(c) The teacher told us to neglect our studies.

(d) The teacher ordered us that we should not neglect our studies.

7. She said to him, "Please lend me your pen".

(a) She requested him to lend her his pen.

(b) She told him to please lend her his pen.

(c) She said to him to lend her his pen.

(d) Anita asked him to lend her his pen.

8. He said, "Let us go for a walk".

(a) He said to go for a walk.

(b) He suggested that we should go for a walk.

(c) He proposed that he should go for a walk.

(d) He asked to go for a walk.

9. She said to me, "Thank you for your help".

(a) She said to me thank you for your help.

(b) She thanked me for my help.

(c) She told me she thanked me for my help.

(d) She thanked that for my help.

10. The boy says, "How clever I am!"

(a) The boy says that he is clever.

(b) The boy exclaimed proudly that he was clever.

(c) The boy says with pride that he is very clever.

(d) The boy says proudly that he was very clever.

III. Directions (Q. Nos. 1-10) Fill in the blanks with most suitable option.

1. The man .... with surprise that it was a very big fish.

(a) told (b) tells

(c) exclaimed (d) exclaim

2. My mother said that honesty .... the best policy.

(a) is (b) was

(c) has (d) had

3. Nikita says that she .... the child.

(a) do not know (b) does not know

(c) did not know (d) had not know

4. Nikhil said that he had made some money ....

(a) yesterday (b) the previous day

(c) the next day (d) the following day

5. He wished that I .... live long.

(a) may (b) can (c) could (d) might

6. The girl said that it .... to be there that evening.

(a) gave her great pleasure (b) give her great pleasure

(c) gives her great pleasure (d) has given her great pleasure

7. The man said that he .... as soon as possible.

(a) must go (b) had gone

(c) should be gone (d) could be gone

8. She said that she .... to see any of them and asked them to go away.

(a) does not want (b) did not want

(c) had not wanted (d) has not wanted

9. The teacher says that if you work hard you ....

(a) would pass (b) will pass

(c) pass (d) passes

10. He said that he ....

(a) won (b) has won

(c) had won (d) wins

IV. Directions (Q. Nos. 1 – 3) Read the dialogues given below and fill in the blanks by choosing the correct option.

1. Ruby: Why are you walking so fast, Elena?
Elena: Don't you know about the cultural festival today?
Ruby: No, I didn't know about it. Let me go with you then.
Elena: We must hurry up. The school ground is already packed with people.

Ruby asked Elena (i) .... Elena asked in response if she didn't know about the cultural festival that day. Ruby replied in the negative and told her that she had not known about it and (ii) .... then. Elena told Ruby (iii) .... as the school ground was already packed with people.

(i) (a) why she was walking so fast
(b) why was she walking so fast
(c) why she had been walking fast
(d) if she was walking fast

(ii) (a) told her to go with her
(b) asked her if she could go with her
(c) suggested that she could go with her
(d) suggested that she should go with her

(iii) (a) that they would hurry up
(b) that they hurry up
(c) that they must hurry up
(d) that they might hurry up

2. Father: Have you packed everything you need?
Daughter: Yes father, it is almost done.
Father: Have you checked your ticket?
Daughter: Yes, I have checked it. My flight will take off at 8 pm.
Father: Okay, we will have to leave for the airport by 5 pm then.
Father asked daughter (i) .... The daughter replied in the affirmative and told him that it was almost done. Father then asked if she had checked her ticket. Daughter gave a positive response and told him that (ii) .... Father proceeded to tell her that (iii) .... for the airport by 5 pm then.

(i) (a) whether she has packed everything she needs
(b) if she had packed everything she need
(c) whether she has packed everything she needed
(d) if she had packed everything she needed

(ii) (a) my flight would take off at 8 pm
(b) her flight would take off at 8 pm
(c) her flight will take off at 8 pm
(d) my flight will take off at 8 pm

(iii) (a) we would have to leave
(b) they will have to leave
(c) they would have to leave
(d) we will have to leave

3. Guide: Sir, the left turn leads to your hotel room and that way is the lakeside.
Tourist: Oh! Amazing! I would like to take a look in the evening.
Guide: Sure, please let me know the timing.
Tourist: Does 5 o'clock work for you?
Guide: Yes, it does.
The guide told the tourist that the left turn (i) .... and the other way was the lakeside. The tourist exclaimed with (ii) .... and told him that he would like to take a look in the evening. The guide respectfully told him to let him know the timing. The tourist asked (iii) .... and the guide replied in the affirmative saying that it did.

(i) (a) led to his hotel room
(b) lead to his hotel room
(c) led to your hotel room
(d) lead to your hotel room

(ii) (a) surprise that that was amazing
(b) annoyance that it was amazing
(c) wonder that it was amazing
(d) surprise that it was amazing

(iii) (a) if 5 o'clock works for him
(b) whether 5 o'clock works for you
(c) whether 5 o'clock worked for him
(d) if 5 o'clock worked for you

Subjective Type Questions

I. Change the following into reported speech.

1. Rita says, "Kishore sang a song."
2. The saint said, "Man is mortal."
3. We said, "We are learning our lesson."
4. He said to me, "My father went to Mumbai last week."
5. I said to her, "Are you leaving tonight?"
6. He said to her, "Can you lend me your umbrella?"
7. She said, "I saw a tiger here."
8. The principal said, "Well done! my boys".
9. She said, "Let them play."
10. I said to Harsh, "Please help me."
11. He said to me, "Where has he gone?"
12. The Prime Minister said, "National Integrity will be preserved at all costs."
13. She said, "My uncle came yesterday."
14. Sheela said to us, "You must work hard."
15. They said, "We trust in God."

II. Complete the sentence in reported speech.

1. Ravi said, "I love this place".
Ravi said ....
2. "Do you like football?" he asked me.
He asked me ....
3. "I can't drive a lorry", he said.
He said ....
4. "Be nice to your brother", he said
He asked me ....
5. "Don't be nasty", he said
He urged me ....
6. "Don't waste your money", she said.
She told the boys ....

7. "What have you decided to do?"
   She asked him ....
8. "I always wake up early", he said.
   He said ....
9. "You should revise your lessons", he said.
   He advised the students ....
10. "Where have you been? "he asked me.
   He wanted to know ....

III. Read the dialogues and complete the reports.

1. **Doctor** How do you feel now?
   Patient Slightly better.
   Doctor Did you take the medicines regularly?
   Patient Yes
   The doctor asked the patient how (a) .... The patient replied that (b) .... better. When the doctor asked him if (c) .... the medicines regularly, he replied in affirmation.
2. **Teacher** Why are you crying, Radha?
   Radha Madam, Mansi has broken my pen.
   Teacher I'll arrange a new pen for you.
   Radha You said this yesterday also.
   Radha was crying in her classroom. The teacher saw her and asked (a) .... Radha replied (b) .... her pen. The teacher promised that she would arrange a new pen for her. Radha replied that (c) ....that the previous day also.
3. **Shubham** Didn't you see the football match?
   Vaibhav No, sorry, I did not. I hate games.
   Shubham Why do you think like this?
   Vaibhav The players are rough and they misbehave with the referee.
   Last night, the final football match was played between Germany and Holland. The match was very interesting. Shubham asked Vaibhav (a) .... the football match. Vaibhav replied in the negative and regrettably said that he had not seen the match because he hated games. Shubham enquired (b) .... like that. Vaibhav replied that the players (c)........with the referee.

ANSWERS

Objective Type Questions

I. 1. (c) Rupak said that he lived in the City Centre.
2. (a) She said that she hadn't seen them since the previous week.
3. (b) Nupur asked me if I had seen her cat.
4. (c) The old man requested to always speak the truth.
5. (d) Roopali exclaimed with sorrow that her brother had died of Covid.
6. (a) She asked me if I could type.
7. (c) She asked what time the train arrived.
8. (c) The policeman asked the boy where he lived.
9. (a) The teacher asked the pupil if he had done his work.
10. (c) He asked me why I had resigned from my job.

II. 1. (d) He asked me when I had bought those books.
2. (a) Akash asked Pari if he could borrow twenty rupees from her.
3. (c) I asked Sonia whether she could ride a bicycle.
4. (b) The stranger asked me whether I could tell him the way to the post office.
5. (a) Raman asked me if I knew Akshay.
6. (a) The teacher advised us not to neglect our studies.
7. (a) She requested him to lend her his pen.
8. (b) He suggested that we should go for a walk.
9. (b) She thanked me for my help.
10. (c) The boy says with pride that he is very clever.

III. 1. (c) exclaimed
2. (a) is
3. (b) does not know
4. (b) the previous day
5. (d) might
6. (a) gave her great pleasure
7. (a) must go
8. (b) did not want
9. (b) will pass
10. (c) had won

IV. 1. (i) (a) why she was walking so fast
(ii) (d) suggested that she should go with her
(iii) (c) that they must hurry up
2. (i) (d) if she had packed everything she needed
(ii) (b) her flight would take off at 8 pm
(iii) (c) they would have to leave
3. (i) (a) led to his hotel room
(ii) (d) surprise that it was amazing
(iii) (c) whether 5 o'clock worked for him

Subjective Type Questions

I. 1. Rita says that Kishore sang a song.
2. The saint said that man is mortal.
3. We said that we were learning our lesson.
4. He told me that his father had gone to Mumbai the previous week.
5. I asked her if she was leaving that night.
6. He asked her if she could lend him her umbrella.
7. She said that she had seen a tiger there.
8. The principal exclaimed with pride that the boys had done well.
9. She suggested that they should be allowed to play.
10. I requested Harsh to help me.
11. He asked me where he had gone.
12. The Prime Minister declared that National Integrity would be preserved at all costs.
13. She said that her uncle had come the previous day.
14. Sheela told us that we must work hard.
15. They said that they trusted in God.

II. 1. that he loved that place
2. whether I liked football
3. that he couldn't drive a lorry
4. to be nice to my brother
5. not to be nasty
6. not to waste their money
7. what he had decided to do
8. that he always wakes up early
9. to revise their lessons
10. where I had been

III. 1. (a) he felt
(b) he felt slightly
(c) he had taken
2. (a) why she was crying
(b) that Mansi had broken
(c) she had said
3. (a) if he had not seen
(b) why he thought
(c) were rough and they misbehaved

Integrated Exercise

Type I : Gap Filling

I. Directions (Q. Nos. 1–25) Fill in the blanks by choosing the correct options from the given sentences.

1. As long .... the rain continues, we must stay indoors.
(a) with (b) because
(c) between (d) as

2. As he is on the death bed, there is .... hope of his recovery.
(a) every (b) each
(c) little (d) few

3. I .... clarify the doubt with him.
(a) should (b) need to
(c) shall (d) might

4. I watched a movie yesterday .... was very interesting.
(a) who (b) whose
(c) which (d) whom

5. Shreya .... in England while her parents were .... in India.
(a) was staying/ staying (b) is staying/ stay
(c) will be staying/ stayed (d) stay/ staying

6. The Delhi Police ....busted a gang of robbers ....had robbed 20 crore from a bank.
(a) had/ whom
(b) has been/ which
(c) have/ who
(d) did/ whose

7. There is general belief of students that .... who write long sentences got .... marks.
(a) most/ least (b) those/ more
(c) that/ many (d) them/ much

8. Authorities settled .... keeping 32 pages in .... next answer book for the undergraduate courses.
(a) on/ the (b) in/ an
(c) behind/ a (d) beside/ the

9. The students accompanied by their teacher .... gone on a picnic.
(a) has (b) have (c) had (d) was

10. She didn't get .... job despite her brilliant qualifications.
(a) some (b) a (c) the (d) that

11. She has to catch the 4 o'clock train tomorrow. Thus, she .... go to bed late tonight.
(a) have to (b) needn't (c) may (d) mustn't

12. The victims .... to a nearby hospital.
(a) was taken (b) were taken
(c) taken (d) took

13. These days, majority of the news .... about violence and conflicts.
(a) are (b) is (c) has (d) have

14. There .... many attempts at developing a modern snowboard.
(a) have been (b) has been
(c) were being (d) was being

15. Machu Picchu was declared .... UNESCO world heritage site in 1983.
(a) a (b) an
(c) the (d) No article required

16. Our solar system .... to the Milky Way galaxy.
(a) belong (b) Is belonging
(c) belonged (d) belongs

17. The lady who is wearing a white shirt and brown pants .... my brother's friend.
(a) is (b) are
(c) were (d) has been

18. A computer virus is a programme that .... infect a computer without the knowledge of the owner.
(a) would (b) can (c) may (d) should

19. Martin Cooper, a Motorola researcher and executive, is widely known to be the inventor of .... first mobile phone in 1973.
(a) a (b) an
(c) the (d) No article required

20. Before her new semester started, Annie .... lots of books but now she just doesn't have the time.

(a) ought to be reading (b) had better read
(c) used to read (d) can read

21. As she watched Martina get in the car and drive away, Menon knew that his life .... be the same again.

(a) won't (b) wouldn't
(c) couldn't (d) shouldn't

22. Arpana failed her tests because she was always out with her friends when she ....

(a) should have been studying
(b) used to study
(c) could be studying
(d) will have studied

23. Mr. Dennis feels that the world today is not as safe as it was during .... childhood.

(a) their (b) her
(c) our (d) his

24. Jasmine, after working all day, ... to eat from outside rather than cook a meal for herself.

(a) prefer (b) prefers
(c) has preferred (d) is preferred

25. You have to take the full course of your antibiotics so that you feel better; otherwise your illness ....

(a) will return (b) will have returned
(c) will be returning (d) will have been returning

II. Directions (Q. Nos. 1–10) Fill in the blanks with appropriate words.

1. It looks nice, but it .... (may/might) be very expensive.
2. You .... (have to/has to) take off your shoes before you get inside the mosque.
3. .... (Both/Every) of you should attend the meeting tomorrow.
4. He should work .... (little/less) and take a break every now and then.
5. The gardener .... (work) in the garden trying to grow new flowers.
6. They .... (has) friends since childhood and now they are getting married.
7. You can pick .... (either/some) of the two toys.
8. He .... (draw) beautiful pictures last week at the competition.
9. David .... (could/would) speak fluent French when he was five.
10. There isn't .... (much/more) cash left with us at home.

III. Directions (Q. Nos. 1–4) Fill in the blanks by using the correct forms of the words in the brackets for the given portions of the letters.

1. **Subject**

   Complaint of misbehaviour

   Dear Sir,

   This is to bring to your kind notice that last week, an employee from the Sales Department .... (misbehave) with me. He was not only rude and impolite but also threatened to harm me.

2. **Subject**

   Requirement of new books for the store

   Dear Sir,

   I have received the books that you sent last week. The books are .... (with/in) perfect condition, and they were delivered on time.

3. **Subject**

   Repair of the road in Cheran Nagar

   Sir,

   I would like to bring to your notice that the people in and around Cheran Nagar .... (face) difficulties in travelling back and forth because of the bad condition of the roads there. We have appealed to the Municipality, but there has not been any response on the issue so far.

4. **Subject**

   Request for salary increase

   Dear Ma'am,

   I am writing to you to request a review of my salary. I have been working as a Technical Support Engineer .... (since/for) three years now at your company since the 20th of December, 2018.

IV. Directions (Q. Nos. 1–5) Choose the correct options to fill in the blanks to complete the note.

1. Information Technology (i).......... the way we access information. Since its introduction in the 1980's, the internet has become cheap and commonplace. Some people (ii).......... this as an opportunity to deal with problems like unemployment. They (iii).......... that the government should provide free internet access to people looking for a job.

   (i) (a) had changed (b) has changed
   (c) changes (d) will change

   (ii) (a) saw (b) will see
   (c) had seen (d) seeing

   (iii) (a) argue (b) argued
   (c) will argue (d) are arguing

2. Many animals mimic leaves. The most successful are insects, whose veined wings (i).......... to change into leaf-like shapes and surfaces. There are also excellent vertebrates which mimic leaves such as chameleons, toads, frogs and fish. But the most remarkable leaf mimic among the vertebrates is done by the South American leaf fish and the bat fish from Indo-Pacific coasts. The leaf fish (ii).......... mimic that lives in deep freshwater streams. On the other hand , the bat fish (iii).......... mangrove leaves and lives in the shallow water in which mangroves grow.

(i) (a) are ideally suited (b) suits
(c) will be ideally suited (d) has to be suited

(ii) (a) are a generalised form of leaf
(b) is a generalised leaf
(c) are general leafs
(d) will be generalised leaves

(iii) (a) resembles (b) will resemble
(c) specifically resembles (d) none of these

3. Our health-care program (i).......... medical care and quality you can count on. Your hospital coverage (ii).......... nursing and physicians' care, surgery, therapy, laboratory tests and medicines. We want to keep you well by preventing illness, so your benefits include regular checkups and vision and hearing examinations. Emergencies (iii).......... up for you in your hometown and when you travel anywhere in the world.

(i) (a) provided a complete
(b) provides complete
(c) will provide a complete
(d) has provided a complete

(ii) (a) includes (b) will include
(c) included (d) including

(iii) (a) covers (b) will cover
(c) covered (d) are covered

4. In the last hundred years, travelling (i)........... much easier and very comfortable. In the 19th century, it (ii)........... two or three days to cross North America by a covered wagon. The trip (iii)........... very rough and often dangerous. Things changed a great deal in the last hundred and fifty years. Now you can fly from New York to Los Angeles in a matter of hours.

(i) (a) has become (b) became
(c) becomes (d) will become

(ii) (a) took (b) takes
(c) take (d) will take

(iii) (a) is (b) was
(c) has been (d) would

5. An elephant (i) .... other animals in intelligence. Whenever it is (ii)............ with any difficulty, it (iii) .... a way out, becoming one of the most difficult animals in the world to tame.

(i) (a) excel (b) excels
(c) excelled (d) had excelled

(ii) (a) faced (b) face (c) faces (d) facing

(iii) (a) has found (b) finds
(c) will find (d) had found

V. Directions (Q. Nos. 1–5) Complete the following passages by filling in the blanks with suitable answers.

1. Think about it. Every time you use a mobile phone, you expose your head to electromagnetic emission. Manufacturers (i) .... (need/are needed) to prove there is no risk of brain cancer or memory loss . Some evidence, so far (ii) .... (suggests/suggest) that mobile phone emissions are likely to cause illnesses. (iii) .... (These/Those) health scares are based on press reports. So, people worry needlessly.

2. It (i) .... (was/is) a rainy day and there was heavy traffic jam on the road. (ii) .... (The/A) speeding bus accidentally hit a car which was making a turn in the market. Five commuters (iii) .... (was/were) injured while one person died on the spot.

3. One of (i) .... (the/a) most significant advantages of 5G technology (ii) ...... (was/is) its faster data transfer speed. 5G is expected to offer peak data transfer speeds of up to 20 gigabits per second (Gbps), which is over 100 times faster than the peak speeds of 4G. This means that 5G networks (iii) .... (will be able, should be able) to handle more data and provide a smoother and faster mobile experience for users.

4. Milk (i) .... (be) a complete food, full of vitamins and proteins. Children should drink it regularly otherwise they (ii) .... (suffer) from under- nourishment. Elders should also take it but those who (iii) .... (should/ can) not afford it should take pulses, fruits and vegetables as an alternative. We should purchase milk of good quality from milk booths opened by the government.

5. People have a tough time learning new languages as they (i) .... (grow) older, but infants have the ability to learn any language easily. For a long time, scientists (ii) .... (struggle) to explain how babies can learn the complicated grammatical rules and sounds required to communicate in words. New researches are giving them (iii) .... (a/the/no article required) better insights.

Type II : Transformation

I. Directions (Q. Nos. 1 – 5) Read the dialogue given below and fill in the blanks accordingly.

1. Meena: How did you like the play you saw last Saturday?

   Asha: I would say it was not the best.

   Meena: Why so?

   Asha: The storyline was ridiculous and the acting wasn't good either.

   Meena asked Asha (i) .... Asha replied that she would say (ii) .... To this, Asha further asked why she thought so. Asha responded that (iii) .... and the acting had not been good either.

2. Doctor: Apply this ointment for a week, and you'll begin to feel better on the back.

   Patient: But this ointment doesn't work on me.

   Doctor: Are you sure?

   Patient: Yes, I have already tried. Can you please prescribe a different one?

   Doctor advised the patient (i) .... and after that, he would begin to feel better on the back. The patient told the doctor ointment didn't work on him. The doctor was surprised and asked (ii) .... The patient replied in affirmative and told him that he had already tried it. He further requested the doctor (iii) ....

3. Student: Good morning sir, I wish to open a Savings Bank account.

   Banker: Good morning. Go through this application, please.

   Student: Application seeks information about my address, occupation and income details.

   Banker: Yes. Please fill it.

   A student wished the banker a good morning and expressed (i) .... The banker returned his greetings and (ii) .... The student confirmed with the banker and said that the application (iii) .... about his address, occupation and income details.

4. Son: Dad, there will be a food carnival in our school.

   Father: Oh, it is very nice. When will it be organized?

   Son: This weekend, Dad.

   Father: Alright, have fun with your friends.

   Son told father that (i) .... Father exclaimed with surprise that it was very nice and asked him (ii) .... Son replied that it was that weekend. Father gave his permission and (iii) ....

5. Remi: Did you visit the book fair at Max Street?

   Ankita: No. I haven't. Have you visited it?

   Remi: Yes. I had gone there yesterday.

   Ankita: I should definitely go today then.

   Remi asked Ankita (i) .... the book fair as Max Street. Ankita replied in negative and told her that she hadn't. She asked her if he had visited it. Remi replied in affirmative and told her that (ii) .... Ankita got excited hearing that and said to Ankita that (iii) .... then.

II. Directions (Q. Nos. 1–5) Choose the correct options to fill in the blanks to complete the given dialogue.

1. One day, Grandpa had a stupid idea. He told grandma (i)........... the cartoonist was spying on us for his comic strip ideas, then that person must be watching or listening to them right then. Grandma found him right and (ii)............ With his thought, Grandpa suggested that if they just sat down and do nothing funny then (iii)........... in his comic.

(i) (a) with awe whether it were true that (b) in awe if it was true that
(c) in awe whether it was true that (d) with awe if it were true that

(ii) (a) responded in affirmative (b) agreed
(c) approved with agreement (d) responded by accepting his thought

(iii) (a) that person will stop using them (b) the cartoonist will not use them
(c) the cartoonist would stop using them (d) that person would not use them

2. Rohan (i)................ by staying inside his house at all times. He told his father that he felt like he (ii)................ He missed going out to Movie Theater or the pizza parlour. He even missed his friends. Listening to Rohan's complaints, his father told him that Anne Frank (iii)................ for two years. Rohan was shocked and thus had a blank face as expected by his father.

(i) (a) is so irritated (b) was absolutely irritated (c) had been irritated (d) has been absolutely irritated

(ii) (a) has been inside forever (b) is inside forever
(c) had been inside since forever (d) have been inside forever

(iii) (a) were inside an attic (b) had to stay inside an attic
(c) were staying in an attic (d) stayed inside in an attic

3. When James, Nathan and Chris read the news they (i).............. . James informed his friends that climate change is a national security threat. Nathan is skeptical as he (ii).............. they are going to fight it if their spend more money on military than climate research. Just then they looked to the side and found people (iii)...............others to give their best in fighting climate change.

(i) (a) started to worry (b) are worries (c) were worried (d) have been worrying

(ii) (a) enquires about how (b) enquired how (c) asked about how (d) asks about how

(iii) (a) look in the atmosphere and giving encouragement (b) looking at the atmosphere and giving encouragement
(c) looking at the atmosphere and encouraging (d) look at the atmosphere and encouraging

4. Ravi (i).............. of the patio looking at his dog Hugo. When his grandfather found him sitting like that, he sat with him. Ravi suddenly asked his grandfather about why dogs don't live as long as people. His grandfather (ii).............. of a dog's life is equal to seven years for us. Ravi (iii) .... and so asked his grandfather if dogs cram seven years of life into one year of human life. To this, grandpa agreed.

(i) (a) was sitting sadly on the stairs
(b) sat sadly on the stairs
(c) is sitting sad on the stairs
(d) had been sitting sadly on the stairs

(ii) (a) replied that one year
(b) said to him that one year
(c) told him that one year
(d) answered that one year

(iii) (a) got confused
(b) was confused
(c) is confused
(d) confused

5. Mindy (i).............. munching on some tea and snack. Her mother was doubtful of her decision of not using her cellphone that day. To clear her mother's doubt, (ii).............. it was earth day and they all have to do their part by using as little energy as possible. Hearing this, her father (iii).............. that he was already on it.

(i) (a) sat along with her mother
(b) is sitting along with her mother
(c) was sitting with her mother
(d) will be sitting with her mother

(ii) (a) she told her mother
(b) she said to her mother that
(c) she replied that
(d) she informed her mother that

(iii) (a) who was reading a newspaper answered
(b) whom was reading a newspaper told
(c) who read the newspaper that time said
(d) whom was going to read a newspaper answered

III. Directions (Q. Nos. 1–5) Convert the following sentences into indirect speech.

1. Saurabh said to Priya, "Why are you sketching on the wall?"
(a) Saurabh asked Priya why was she sketching on the wall.
(b) Saurabh asked Priya why had she been sketching on the wall.
(c) Saurabh asked Priya that why is she sketching on the wall.
(d) Saurabh asked Priya why she was sketching on the wall.

2. "Sumit fell as he'd have wished", the father said.
(a) The father said that Sumit has fallen as he would have wished.
(b) The father said that Sumit had fallen as he would have wished.
(c) The father said that Sumit had fallen as he had wished.
(d) The father said that Sumit had been fallen as he would have been wished.

3. Harshit said to Tara, "Karan will leave for his mother's place tomorrow".
(a) Harshit told Tara that Karan will leave for his mother's place tomorrow.
(b) Harshit told Tara that Karan will leave for his mother's place the next day.
(c) Harshit told Tara that Karan would leave for his mother's place the next day.
(d) Harshit informed Tara that Karan would be leaving for his mother's place the next day.

4. She said to the interviewer, "Could you please repeat the question?"
(a) She asked the interviewer to repeat the question.
(b) She requested the interviewer to repeat the question.
(c) She said to the interviewer to repeat the question.
(d) She said that the interviewer could repeat the question.

5. The traffic police told the man, "Do not park your vehicle here."
(a) The traffic police ordered the man not to park his vehicle there.
(b) The traffic police requested the man not to park his vehicle there.
(c) The traffic police asked the man not to park his vehicle there.
(d) The traffic police said to the man that he cannot park his vehicle there.

IV. Directions (Q. Nos. 6-15) Transform the sentences as directed in each question.

6. Choose the correct option that gives the correct future continuous tense for the given sentence.
Sonu work as hard as he could.
(a) Sonu will be working as hard as he could.
(b) Sonu would be working as hard as he could.
(c) Sonu was working as hard as he could.
(d) Sonu has been working as hard as he could.

7. Choose the correct option that gives the correct simple present tense for the given sentence.
Sonia did not want to play.
(a) Sonia has not want to play.
(b) Sonia do not want to play.
(c) Sonia does not want to play.
(d) Sonia will not want to play.

8. Choose the correct option that gives the correct future continuous tense for the given sentence.
Ramesh is leaving for Mumbai tomorrow.
(a) Ramesh would be leaving for Mumbai tomorrow.
(b) Ramesh will be leaving for Mumbai tomorrow.
(c) Ramesh has been leaving for Mumbai tomorrow.
(d) Ramesh leaves for Mumbai tomorrow.

9. Choose the correct option that gives the correct simple past tense for the given sentence.
Simmi hadn't thought about Anuj's proposal.
(a) Simmi did not think about Anuj's proposal.
(b) Simmi does not think about Anuj's proposal.
(c) Simmi is not thinking about Anuj's proposal.
(d) Simmi was not thinking about Anuj's proposal.

10. Choose the correct option that gives the correct simple present tense for the given sentence.
I knew how to drive a car.
(a) I will know how to drive a car.
(b) I am knowing how to drive a car.
(c) I have known how to drive a car.
(d) I know how to drive a car.

11. She said,"How will they get here?" (into indirect speech)
(a) She said how will they get here.
(b) She said how would they get there.
(c) She asked how they would get there.
(d) She asked me how will they get here.

12. I will drive there. (into past perfect continuous tense)
(a) I will have been driving there.
(b) I would have driven there.
(c) I had been driving there.
(d) I will have been driving there.

13. "I met my friend yesterday", he said. (into indirect speech)
(a) He said that he would meet his friend the previous day.
(b) He said he had met his friend the previous day.
(c) He told that he met his friend the previous day.
(d) He said that he had met his friend the previous day.

14. She is coming this week to discuss this matter. (into future perfect tense)
(a) She shall be coming this week to discuss this matter.
(b) She will have come this week to discuss this matter.
(c) She has come this week to discuss this matter.
(d) She shall have coming this week to discuss this matter.

15. He said, "Alas! I have failed." (into indirect speech)
(a) He exclaimed sadly that he failed.
(b) He exclaimed sadly that I failed.
(c) He exclaimed that he failed.
(d) He exclaimed sadly that he had failed.

V. Directions (Q. Nos. 1-10) Transform the sentences as directed in each question.

1. Aman said, "What a beautiful rainbow it is". (into Indirect speech)
2. "This world", she said, "is full of sorrow. Wish that I were dead". (into Indirect speech)
3. The policeman said, "Where is the license?" (into Indirect speech)
4. Rahul said, "Ah! I am ruined." (into Indirect speech)
5. She said, "I have made a pie." (into Indirect speech)
6. People are cleaning their houses during the festival. (Change into past perfect continuous tense)
7. Simran wanted to know more about historical places. (Change into simple present tense)
8. Pankaj will not pass the exam. (Change into future perfect tense)
9. All my friends went to see the cricket match. (Change into past perfect tense)
10. Sandeep always wanted to be a pilot. (Change into present perfect tense)

VI. Directions (Q. Nos. 1-15) Fill in the blanks by choosing the most appropriate answers from the given options.

1. Most Indian exports and imports are carried out in New Delhi. (change into present continuous tense)
Most Indian exports and imports .... in New Delhi.
(a) are being carried out
(b) was carried out
(c) has been carried out
(d) are carried out

2. A fly is transferring toxic particles into the human system indirectly. (change into simple present tense)
A fly .... toxic particles into the human system indirectly.
(a) transfer (b) transfers
(c) had been transfer (d) was transferred

3. The child said that the Earth revolves around the sun. (change into simple past tense)

The child said that the Earth .... around the sun.

(a) revolve (b) revolved
(c) has been revolving (d) revolves

4. At a time, when private schools have seemed to grow similar in all aspects, the international school nearby the state library, strikes a distinctive note. (change into simple present tense).

At a time, when private schools .... in all aspects, the international school nearby the state library, strikes a distinctive note.

(a) seem to be growing similar
(b) seems to be growing similar
(c) seemed to be growing similar
(d) are seeming to grow similar

5. She stayed in the United States for two years. She went there to pursue her Bachelor degree. (change into past perfect tense)

She stayed in the United States for two years. She .... there to pursue her Bachelor degree.

(a) have been there (b) had gone
(c) had been gone (d) was gone

6. I asked him .... taken dinner.

(a) whether he has (b) why he has
(c) if he had (d) if he has

7. I told them that I .... living with my parents till last year.

(a) have been (b) was (c) had lived (d) am

8. Credit card facilities .... it easy to buy many things by paying the amount later or in EMI.

(a) has made (b) are made
(c) have made (d) had been made

9. The fire .... when the residents were sleeping.

(a) broke out (b) break out
(c) was breaking out (d) has broken out

10. She exclaimed with .... that she had lost her only son.

(a) excitement (b) joy (c) sorrow (d) wary

11. Grandmother .... to the flowers in our garden every morning.

(a) tends (b) is tending
(c) was tending (d) tended

12. He asked me ....

(a) why I had not contacted him?
(b) why had I not contacted him?
(c) whether I had not contacted him.
(d) if had I not contacted him.

13. Not all information which .... in the news is suitable for every age.

(a) have provided (b) is provided
(c) provided (d) Is provided

14. Some crumbs of bread fell down the ground and .... by the birds.

(a) were being eaten (b) are eating
(c) have eaten (d) is eaten

15. This winter vacation, we .... our grandparents in the village.

(a) will be visiting (b) shall be visiting
(c) should be visiting (d) would be visiting

Subjective Type

VII. Directions (Q. Nos. 1–15) Fill in the blanks with suitable forms of verb.

1. Miss Beam .... me when I was coming back to school.
2. Our teacher said, "Where will you like to go for an excursion?"

   Our teacher asked us where .... to go for the excursion.
3. The jury said, "Call the first convict."

   The jury .... to call the first convict.
4. The pied piper never ...... the truth. (tell)
5. I said, "Let's take matters seriously."

   I suggested that we .... matters seriously.
6. Make hay while the Sun .... (shine)
7. The man said, "Quick, call the ambulance."

   The man urged .... the ambulance.
8. Meena exclaimed sadly that her cat ....
9. Teacher prayed that God .... me. (bless)
10. Seeing a crow eating a piece of bread, the fox to .... trick that fellow.
11. Farmers .... fruits from the orchard.
12. Her uncle and aunt .... (visit) her today afternoon.
13. She .... (pass) the viva last month.
14. The children .... (playing) since morning.
15. The doctor advised the patient .... (do) exercise regularly.

Type III : Error Detection

I. Directions (Q. Nos. 1–20) Select the option that identifies the error and supplies the correction for the following line.

1. Riya has begun working for a local paper without even graduating from high school, and she is supporting herself through her journalism ever since.

Options	Error	Correction
(a)	is	was
(b)	herself	her
(c)	has	had
(d)	since	then

2. Every of the countries of Western Europe used to have its own currency, but now most of them use the euro.

Options	Error	Correction
(a)	Every	Each
(b)	its	their
(c)	most	all
(d)	the euro	euro

3. To be appreciated fully, Nandi hills have to be seen at sunrise.

Options	Error	Correction
(a)	fully	wholly
(b)	at	on
(c)	have to	should
(d)	Nandi hills	The Nandi hills

4. Much more opium was being grown in Afghanistan this year than last year.

Options	Error	Correction
(a)	Much more	Too many
(b)	was	is
(c)	being grown	grown
(d)	in	at

5. Protesters attempting to reform the World Bank and the International Monetary Fund has not had much success so far.

Options	Error	Correction
(a)	attempting	attempt
(b)	has	have
(c)	much	many
(d)	so	too

6. The Mayan civilisation had ceased to exist long before the first Europeans arrived in the America.

Options	Error	Correction
(a)	The Mayan	Mayan
(b)	the first	first
(c)	had ceased	ceased
(d)	the America	America

7. Much writers say that they never enjoy writing another book as much as they enjoyed writing their first one.

Options	Error	Correction
(a)	Much	Many
(b)	enjoy	enjoyed
(c)	as much as	more than
(d)	their	its

8. Sanskrit is the difficult language and is of too little practical use that only few people attempt to study it.

Options	Error	Correction
(a)	the	a
(b)	is of	is
(c)	too little	too few
(d)	attempt	attempted

9. You would have to study for years if you intend to stay in the research field.

Options	Error	Correction
(a)	if	unless
(b)	the research	research
(c)	would	will
(d)	to study	study

10. The minister has made so many mistakes that no one trust him anymore.

Options	Error	Correction
(a)	has made	has been making
(b)	so	too
(c)	trust	trusts
(d)	no one	nobody

11. Should you please repeat that? I wasn't able to hear it properly.

Options	Error	Correction
(a)	Should	Could
(b)	repeat	repeating
(c)	hear	heard
(d)	it	that

12. Hundreds of years ago, oil lamps was used by men.

Options	Error	Correction
(a)	Hundreds	Hundred
(b)	by	for
(c)	oil lamps	oils lamp
(d)	was	were

13. We have been condition to fear about reptiles such as snakes.

Options	Error	Correction
(a)	about	of
(b)	such as	like
(c)	have been	had been
(d)	condition	conditioned

14. He first saw the elephant when he is crossing the small stream.

Options	Error	Correction
(a)	He	Him
(b)	is	was
(c)	saw	had seen
(d)	the small	small

15. Discipline and punctuality shall be inculcated in everyone by practising it again and again.

Options	Error	Correction
(a)	shall	should
(b)	punctuality	punctuality
(c)	be	have been
(d)	again and again	then and now

16. The original constitution of India do not have preamble but it was later on added to the constitution.

Options	Error	Correction
(a)	do	does
(b)	the original	original
(c)	preamble	the preamble
(d)	was	is

17. The giant panda are the official symbol of World Wide Fund for Nature (WWF).

Options	Error	Correction
(a)	panda	pandas
(b)	of	for
(c)	the	-
(d)	are	is

18. The police came and took the injured man to an hospital.

Options	Error	Correction
(a)	came	came over
(b)	took	to take
(c)	the injured	injured
(d)	an	the

19. In the dead of the night, when she hears a loud sound, she ran towards the kitchen.

Options	Error	Correction
(a)	In	On
(b)	hears	heard
(c)	ran	have run
(d)	towards	over

20. Every chair and table in the classroom were kept in order.

Options	Error	Correction
(a)	each	every
(b)	in	at
(c)	the	-
(d)	were	was

II. Directions (Q. Nos. 1-20) Identify the error in the given sentence and supply the correction.

1. It is estimated that nearly 40,000 people succumb to air pollution each year in major cities of India.

Error	Correction

2. The new craze among teenagers is the inclination in fast food.

Error	Correction

3. It is ironic that we live with animals for years, yet we are to give them the status of fellow beings.

Error	Correction

4. Ganga is not merely a river for all the Indians and more particularly to the Hindus, but it is the lifeline of India and the physical and spiritual nourisher of crores of its people.

Error	Correction

5. Kailash Satyarthi brought laurels to the people of India for being awarded with Nobel Peace Prize in 2014 along with Malala for their battle for child safety.

Error	Correction

6. Freshly made tea is tasty and beneficial if some simple rules are observing.

Error	Correction

7. Facebook, with more than one billion users, is celebrated its 10th anniversary this year.

Error	Correction

8. Mangoes are juicy fruit which are available in much varieties.

Error	Correction

9. It is true that natural disaster was a natural process and we cannot stop it, but by making certain preparations, we can reduce the magnitude of the loss of life and property.

Error	Correction

10. We could conserve electricity so that we can conserve our natural resources.

Error	Correction

11. Environment change and constant usage of renewable energy has become a concern for all of us around the globe.

Error	Correction

12. A very common misconception regarding feminism is that only women will be feminists.

Error	Correction

13. It takes around 3 years to complete the draft of the Indian Constitution.

Error	Correction

14. According to a recent survey, people who pay more for his vehicles drive more responsibly than others.

Error	Correction

15. A computer is a complex piece of machinery made up of many parts, every of which can be considered a separate invention.

Error	Correction

16. The border dispute had resulted in spoiling a relations between the two nuclear neighbours.

Error	Correction

17. Gir National Park was one of the major wildlife sanctuaries in North India.

Error	Correction

18. I do not agreed with what you were saying.

Error	Correction

19. Neha exclaimed with sorrow that she had just won the lottery.

Error	Correction

20. The teacher said that moon was earth's only natural satellite.

Error	Correction

Answers

Type I : Gap Filling

I. 1. (d) as
2. (c) little
3. (b) need to
4. (c) which
5. (a) was staying, staying
6. (c) have, who
7. (b) those, more
8. (a) on, the
9. (b) have
10. (c) the
11. (d) mustn't
12. (b) were taken
13. (b) is
14. (a) have been
15. (a) a
16. (d) belongs
17. (a) is
18. (b) can
19. (c) the
20. (c) used to read
21. (b) wouldn't
22. (a) should have been studying
23. (d) his
24. (b) prefers
25. (a) will return

II. 1. might
2. have to
3. Both
4. less
5. is working
6. had been
7. either
8. drew
9. could
10. much

III. 1. misbehaved
2. in
3. have been facing
4. for

IV. 1. (i) (b) has changed
(ii) (a) saw
(iii) (a) argue

2. (i) (a) are ideally suited
(ii) (b) is a generalised leaf
(iii) (c) specifically resembles
3. (i) (b) provides complete (ii) (a) includes
(iii) (d) are covered
4. (i) (a) has become (ii) (a) took
(iii) (b) was
5. (i) (b) excels (ii) (a) faced
(iii) (c) will find

V. 1. (i) need (ii) suggests (iii) These
2. (i) was (ii) A (iii) were
3. (i) the (ii) is (iii) will be able
4. (i) is (ii) will suffer (iii) can
5. (i) grow (ii) have struggled
(iii) no article required

Type II : Transformation

I. 1. (i) how she had liked the play she had seen last Saturday
(ii) it had not been the best
(iii) the storyline had been ridiculous
2. (i) to apply that ointment for a week
(ii) if he was sure
(iii) to prescribe a different one
3. (i) his wish to open a Savings Bank account
(ii) requested him to go through that application
(iii) sought information
4. (i) there would be a food carnival in their school
(ii) when it would be organised
(iii) told him to have fun with his friends
5. (i) if she had visited
(ii) she had gone there the previous day
(iii) she should definitely go that day

II. 1. (i) (b) in awe if it was true that
(ii) (a) responded in affirmative
(iii) (c) the cartoonist would stop using them
2. (i) (b) was absolutely irritated
(ii) (a) has been inside forever
(iii) (d) stayed inside in an attic
3. (i) (c) were worried
(ii) (b) enquired how
(iii) (c) looking at the atmosphere and encouraging
4. (i) (a) was sitting sadly on the stairs
(ii) (c) told him that one year
(iii) (b) was confused
5. (i) (c) was sitting with her mother
(ii) (d) she informed her mother that
(iii) (a) who was reading a newspaper answered

III. 1. (d) Saurabh asked Priya why she was sketching on the wall.
2. (b) The father said that Sumit had fallen as he would have wished.
3. (c) Harshit told Tara that Karan would leave for his mother's place the next day.
4. (b) She requested the interviewer to repeat the question.
5. (a) The traffic police ordered the man not to park his vehicle there.

IV. 6. (a) Sonu will be working as hard as he could.
7. (c) Sonia does not want to play.
8. (b) Ramesh will be leaving for Mumbai tomorrow.
9. (a) Simmi did not think about Anuj's proposal.
10. (d) I know how to drive a car.
11. (c) She asked how they would get there.
12. (c) I had been driving there.
13. (d) He said that he had met his friend the previous day.
14. (b) She will have come this week to discuss this matter.
15. (d) He exclaimed sadly that he had failed.

V. 1. Aman exclaimed with wonder that the rainbow was very beautiful.
2. She observed that the world is full of sorrow. She wished to be dead.
3. The policeman enquired where the license was.
4. Rahul exclaimed with sorrow that he was ruined.
5. She said that she had made a pie.
6. People had been cleaning their houses during the festival.
7. Simran wants to know more about historical places.
8. Pankaj will not have passed the exam.
9. All my friends had gone to see the cricket match.
10. Sandeep has always wanted to be a pilot.

VI. 1. (a) are being carried out
2. (b) transfers 3. (b) revolved
4. (a) seem to be growing similar
5. (b) had gone 6. (c) if he had
7. (b) was 8. (c) have made
9. (a) broke out 10. (c) sorrow
11. (a) tends
12. (a) why I had not contacted him
13. (b) is provided 14. (a) were being eaten
15. (b) shall be visiting

VII. 1. asked 2. we would like
3. ordered 4. speaks
5. should take 6. shines
7. to call 8. died
9. might bless 10. thought
11. are picking 12. are visiting
13. had passed 14. have been playing
15. to do

Type III : Error Detection

I. 1. (c)

Error	Correction
has	had

2. (a)

Error	Correction
Every	Each

3. (c)

Error	Correction
have to	should

4. (b)

Error	Correction
was	is

5. (b)

Error	Correction
has	have

6. (d)

Error	Correction
the America	America

7. (a)

Error	Correction
Much	Many

8. (a)

Error	Correction
the	a

9. (c)

Error	Correction
would	will

10. (c)

Error	Correction
trust	trusts

11. (a)

Error	Correction
Should	Could

12. (d)

Error	Correction
was	were

13. (d)

Error	Correction
condition	conditioned

14. (b)

Error	Correction
is	was

15. (a)

Error	Correction
shall	should

16. (a)

Error	Correction
do	does

17. (d)

Error	Correction
are	is

18. (d)

Error	Correction
an	the

19. (b)

Error	Correction
hears	heard

20. (d)

Error	Correction
were	was

II. 1.

Error	Correction
each	every

2.

Error	Correction
in	towards

3.

Error	Correction
live	have lived

4.

Error	Correction
Ganga	The Ganga

5.

Error	Correction
Nobel	The Nobel

6.

Error	Correction
observing	observed

7.

Error	Correction
celebrated	celebrating

8.

Error	Correction
much	many

9.

Error	Correction
was	is

10.

Error	Correction
could	must

11.

Error	Correction
has	have

12.

Error	Correction
will	can

13.

Error	Correction
takes	took

14.

Error	Correction
his	their

15.

Error	Correction
every	each

16.

Error	Correction
a	the

17.

Error	Correction
was	is

18.

Error	Correction
agreed	agree

19.

Error	Correction
sorrow	excitement

20.

Error	Correction
was	is

Section C : Literature
Textbook : Beehive *(Prose)*

The Fun They Had

CHAPTER 1

by Isaac Asimov

CHAPTER SUMMARY The chapter 'The Fun They Had' has been written by Isaac Asimov. The story is a fictional account of how books and schools will be in the future. Asimov compares the educational systems of today with that of the year 2157 through the character of an eleven year old girl, Margie. The story compares the robotic teachers of 2157 with the human teachers of the past and highlights the lack of human interaction and fun.

Diary Entry by Margie and the Real Book

Margie, an eleven year old girl wrote a diary entry dated 17th May, 2157, titled "Today Tommy found a real book!." Once, Margie's grandfather had told her about the time when all stories were printed on paper.

Tommy found the book in the attic of his house. Margie and Tommy turned the pages of the book, which were yellow and crinkly (wrinkled). It was a very old book. Margie found it funny to read the book as the words in it were not moving like they moved on her telebook.

Opinion about the Book

Tommy, a thirteen year old boy, called the book a waste because after reading it once, it could be thrown away. Margie also felt the same way. They compared the book with their television screen which could have a million books on it and still had space for more. Moreover, it did not need to be thrown away after reading.

Margie's Hatred about her School

Tommy told Margie that the book he found was about the school but Margie showed no interest as she hated her school and mechanical teacher. Margie's mechanical teacher was large, black and ugly, and had a big screen. All the lessons were shown on the screen and the questions were asked.

Margie hated the slot where she had to put her homework and test papers daily. She had to write them in a punch code which she had learned when she was six years old.

Margie's Poor Performance

The mechanical teacher gave Margie tests in geography continuously. She had not been doing well in the tests. Margie's mother, Mrs. Jones, was worried about Margie's poor performance. So, she called the County Inspector to come and find out if there was something wrong with the mechanical teacher.

The Arrival of the County Inspector

The County Inspector was a round little man, with a red face. He carried a box of tools, dials and wires.

Margie hoped that the County Inspector would not be able to fix the mechanical teacher and would take it with him. She was hoping for this as Tommy's teacher was taken away by the Inspector for one month when there was a problem with the history sector.

The Geography Sector Set Right

The County Inspector repaired the mechanical teacher. He told Margie's mother that it was not Margie's fault. In fact, the geography sector was a little too quick for Margie to read and understand. He had fixed the geography sector by slowing down the speed according to the level of a 10 year-old child. He also stated that Margie's overall performance had been quite satisfactory.

Discussion about Old Schools

Tommy had a discussion with Margie after reading the book which described the schools of the past. The schools in the past were located in special buildings, away from the students' houses. The students were taught by human teachers and all the kids of the same age learnt the same thing.

Margie argued that humans were not smart enough to be teachers. To this, Tommy replied that his father was smarter than a teacher.

Margie didn't wish to argue so they continued learning about the schools of the past.

The teacher taught them lessons, asked questions and gave them homework. Margie wanted to know more about those funny schools but it was the time for both Tommy and Margie to go to their school. So, they decided to read the book later.

Margie's Schoolroom

Margie's schoolroom was located next to her bedroom in her house. Her mechanical teacher was turned on when her school time started. Her school was open everyday except on Saturday and Sunday because her mother believed that little girls learned better if they learned at regular hours.

The mechanical teacher was going to teach her a lesson on arithmetic about the addition of proper fractions but she was not interested in studying.

Margie Thinks of Old Schools

Margie put her home work in a slot as commanded by the mechanical teacher. She was thinking about the old schools where all the kids came laughing and shouting in the schoolyard, and sat together in the schoolroom.

They were taught by human teachers, learnt the same things and helped each other in their homework. The mechanical teacher was flashing a question of fractions on the screen but Margie was thinking of the fun kids had at the school in the past.

Word Meaning

Word	Meaning
crinkly	with many folds or lines
attic	a space just below the roof
stood still	were not moving
gee	exclamation of surprise
you're through with	you have read
scornful	hateful
sent for	called
county inspector	a local person whose job is to repair robots
took the teacher apart	opened the inside of the robot
put it together	assemble it
slot	a given space, time or position

Word	Meaning
punch code	method of giving answers by punching holes in paper
geared (to)	adjusted to a particular standard or level
superior eyes	eyes showing his feeling of being better
loftily	in a superior way
betcha	(used in informal conversation) (I) bet you (in fast speech); I'm sure.
dispute	disagreement
nonchalantly	not showing much of interest or enthusiasm; carelessly
tucked	kept safely
lit up	lighted
with a sigh	unwillingly

NCERT FOLDER

NCERT Intext and Exercise Questions

THINKING ABOUT THE TEXT (NCERT PAGE 10)

I. Answer these questions in a few words or a couple of sentences each.

Q.1 How old are Margie and Tommy?

Ans. Margie is eleven and Tommy is thirteen years old.

Q.2 What did Margie write in her diary?

Ans. Margie wrote a diary entry dated 17th May, 2157, titled 'Today Tommy found a real book.'

She wrote about Tommy finding an actual book in the attic.

Q.3 Had Margie ever seen a book before?

Ans. No, Margie had never seen a book before.

Q.4 What things about the book did Margie find strange?

Ans. Margie found many things about the book strange. The pages were yellow and wrinkled. The words were not moving and when one read it for the second time, everything was the same as earlier.

Q.5 What do you think a telebook is?

Ans. A telebook is a virtual or digital book that can be read on a screen. One doesn't have to turn pages because the words themselves move across the screen.

Q.6 Where was Margie's school? Did she have any classmates?

Ans. Margie's school was next to her bedroom.

No, she didn't have any classmates.

Q.7 What subjects did Margie and Tommy learn?

Ans. Margie and Tommy learned subjects such as geography, arithmetic and presumably other standard school subjects typically taught by mechanical teachers.

II. Answer the following with reference to the story.

Q.1 "I wouldn't throw it away".

(i) Who says these words?

(ii) What does 'it' refer to?

(iii) What is 'it' being compared with by the speaker?

Ans. (i) These words are said by Tommy.

(ii) Here, 'it' refers to television screen with telebooks on it.

(iii) The speaker is comparing the television screen containing telebooks with real books.

Q.2 "Sure *they* had a teacher, but it wasn't a *regular* teacher. It was a man."

(i) Who does 'they' refer to?

(ii) What does 'regular' mean here?

(iii) What is it contrasted with?

Ans. (i) 'They' refers to the people who lived hundreds of years ago and went to an actual school.

(ii) Here, 'regular' refers to the usual (mechanical) teachers that Tommy and Margie had.

(iii) The human teacher of earlier times is being contrasted with a mechanical teacher.

III. Answer each of these questions in a short paragraph (about 30 words).

Q.1 What kind of teachers did Margie and Tommy have?

Ans. Margie and Tommy had mechanical teachers in the form of a computer. The teacher had a big black screen on which all the lessons were flashed and questions were asked. The teacher also had a slot where students had to put their homework and test papers.

Q.2 Why did Margie's mother send for the County Inspector?

Ans. The mechanical teacher had been testing Margie in geography continuously due to which Margie had not been doing well in the tests. This worried Margie's mother so she called the County Inspector to check what was wrong with Margie's mechanical teacher.

Q.3 What did he do?

Ans. The County Inspector fixed the mechanical teacher and adjusted the geography sector to the level of a ten year old child (Margie's level).

Q.4 Why was Margie doing badly in geography? What did the County Inspector do to help her?

Ans. Margie was doing badly in geography because the geography sector of her mechanical teacher was set a little too quick. So, Margie was unable to understand it properly. The County Inspector helped Margie by slowing down the geography sector of her mechanical teacher so that she could understand it properly.

Q.5 What had once happened to Tommy's teacher?

Ans. Once, Tommy's teacher was taken away for nearly a month because the history sector of his mechanical teacher had a problem.

Q.6 Did Margie have regular days and hours for school? If so, why?

Ans. Yes, Margie had regular days and hours for school. Margie had to attend her school at the same time everyday except for Saturday and Sunday. Her mother ensured this because she believed that little girls learnt better if they learned at regular hours.

Q.7 How does Tommy describe the old kind of school?

Ans. Tommy described the old kind of school that existed centuries ago where the teacher was a 'man' instead of a mechanical teacher. All the students went to a special building where they all learned the same thing according to their respective ages.

Q.8 How does Tommy describe the old kind of teachers?

Ans. Tommy described the old kind of teachers as human beings who taught in a special building where all the kids went together. The teachers told the kids about several things, gave them homework and asked them questions.

IV. Answer each of these questions in two or three paragraphs (100-150 words).

Q.1 What are the main features of the mechanical teachers and the schoolrooms that Margie and Tommy have in the story?

Ans. Margie and Tommy had mechanical teachers which had the following features

(i) A mechanical teacher was a machine which had a big screen. It was large, black and ugly.

(ii) The lessons were shown on the screen and questions were asked. It also gave tests to the students.

(iii) It had a slot in it where students could put their homework and test papers.

(iv) The mechanical teacher was fast and calculated marks very quickly.

(v) Every mechanical teacher was adjusted according to the level of the student.

(vi) The mechanical teacher was kept in the schoolroom of the student's houses. It started flashing everyday at a certain time except on Saturday and Sunday.

(vii) It never fell ill, never forgot to ask questions and never forgot to conduct tests.

Q.2 Why did Margie hate school? Why did she think the old kind of school must have been fun?

Ans. Margie hated her school because it had a mechanical teacher which was impersonal and ineffective. The large and black, big screen of the mechanical teacher looked ugly to Margie. She had to sit alone in front of it everyday to learn. It kept on giving tests to Margie in geography even when she was performing poorly in them. It never gave Margie any feedback or tips to perform well in the tests.

Margie thought that the old schools must have been fun because of its more engaging and communal learning experience. In the old schools, all the kids from the whole neighbourhood went to the schools laughing and shouting. They sat together in the schoolroom and went home together at the end of the day. They learned the same things so they could help one another in their homework. Moreover, in the old schools, the teachers were humans.

Q.3 Do you agree with Margie that schools today are more fun than the school in the story? Give reasons for your answer.

Ans. I totally agree with Margie that schools today are more fun than the school in the story. In the story, Margie had a school in her house. Her school teacher was mechanical and she had no classmates. It was a boring and dull school.

Margie could not play with her friends in the school playground and they could not come home together. Moreover, the mechanical teacher gave tests continuously even if one wasn't performing well in it.

The schools today are located in a special building in the neighbourhood. The kids go to the school laughing and shouting. They play together, make friends and go home together. They are taught by a human teacher who makes teaching interesting and joyful to the students. He/She is able to understand the feelings and emotions of the students and helps in developing their overall personality.

Thus, in modern schools, we can access various interactive technologies, hands-on learning experiences, and extracurricular activities that make learning engaging and enjoyable. Modern schools often promote creativity, critical thinking, and student collaboration, encouraging a dynamic and stimulating learning environment.

THINKING ABOUT LANGUAGE (NCERT PAGE 11)

I. Adverbs

Read this sentence taken from the story

They had once taken Tommy's teacher away for nearly a month because the history sector had blanked out <u>completely</u>. The word <u>complete</u> is an adjective. When you add-ly to it, it becomes an adverb.

Q.1 Find the sentence in the lesson which have the adverbs given in the box below.

awfully	sorrowfully	completely	loftily
carefully	differently	quickly	nonchalantly

Ans. The sentences in the lesson which have the adverbs are

Awfully They turned the pages, which were yellow and crinkly and it was awfully funny to read words that stood still instead of moving the way they were supposed to-on a screen, you know.

Sorrowfully The mechanical teacher had been giving her test after test in geography and she had been doing worse and worse until her mother had shaken her head sorrowfully and sent for the County Inspector.

Completely They had once taken Tommy's teacher away for nearly a month because the history sector had blanked out completely.

Loftily and Carefully He added loftily, pronouncing the word carefully, 'centuries ago'.

Differently "But, my mother says a teacher has to be adjusted to fit the mind of each boy and girl it teaches and that each kid has to be taught differently."

Quickly "I didn't say I didn't like it," Margie said quickly.

Nonchalantly "May be," he said nonchalantly.

Q. 2 Now use these adverbs to fill in the blanks in the sentences below.

(i) The report must be read .... so that performance can be improved.

(ii) At the interview, Sameer answered our questions ...., shrugging his shoulders.

(iii) We all behave .... when we are tired or hungry.

(iv) The teacher shook her head ...... when Ravi lied to her.

(v) I .... forgot about it.

(vi) When I complimented Revathi on her success, she just smiled .... and turned away.

(vii) The President of the company is .... busy and will not be able to meet you.

(viii) I finished my work ...... so that I could go out to play.

Ans. (i) carefully (ii) nonchalantly
(iii) differently (iv) sorrowfully
(v) completely (vi) loftily
(vii) awfully (viii) quickly

Remember

An adverb describes action. You can form adverbs by adding -ly to adjectives.

Spelling Note When an adjective ends in -y, the y changes to i when you add -ly to form an adverb.

For example: angr-y → angr-i-ly

Q. 3 Make adverbs from these adjectives.

(i) Angry **(ii) Happy**
(iii) Merry **(iv) Sleepy**
(v) Easy **(vi) Noisy**
(vii) Tidy **(viii) Gloomy**

Ans. (i) Angrily (ii) Happily
(iii) Merrily (iv) Sleepily
(v) Easily (vi) Noisily
(vii) Tidily (viii) Gloomily

II. If Not and Unless

- Imagine that Margie's mother told her, "You'll feel awful if you don't finish your history lesson."
- She could also say "You'll feel awful unless you finish your history lesson."

Unless means if not. Sentences with unless or if not are negative conditional sentences.

Notice that these sentences have two parts. The part that begins with if not or unless tells us the condition. This part has a verb in the present tense (look at the verbs don't finish, finish in the sentences above).

The other part of the sentence tells us about a possible result. It tells us what will happen (if something else doesn't happen). The verb in this part of the sentence is in the future tense (you'll feel/you will feel).

Notice these two tenses again in the following examples.

Future Tense		Present Tense
There won't be any book left	unless	we preserve them
You won't learn your lessons	if	you don't study regularly
Tommy will have an accident	unless	he drives more slowly

Q.1 Complete the following conditional sentences. Use the correct form of the verb.

(i) If I don't go to Anu's party tonight, ...

(ii) If you don't telephone the hotel to order food, ...

(iii) Unless you promise to write back, I ....

(iv) If she doesn't play any games, ...

(v) Unless that little bird flies away quickly, the cat ....

Ans. (i) she will not speak to me
(ii) you will miss your meal
(iii) will not write to you
(iv) she will become lazy
(v) will pounce on it

WRITING (NCERT PAGE 12)

A new revised volume of Isaac Asimov's short stories has just been released. Order one set. Write a letter to the publisher, Mindfame Private Limited, 1632 Asaf Ali Road, New Delhi, requesting that a set be sent to you by Value Payable Post (VPP) and giving your address. Your letter will have' the following parts.

- Addresses of the sender and receiver
- The salutation
- The body of the letter
- The closing phrases and signature

Ans. E-1570,
RK Puram, Sector 12
New Delhi -110066

4th April, 20XX

Mindfame Private Limited
1632, Asaf Ali Road
New Delhi -110002

Dear Sir/Madam

This is to inform you that I have come to know that you have just released a new revised volume of Isaac Asimov's short stories. I am a big fan of his writing style and the revised volume is really hard to find. Therefore, I would like to place an order for one set of the same. Kindly send it to the above mentioned address by Value Payable Post (VPP) after deducting the ongoing discount.

Thanking you in advance.

Yours faithfully
Tushar

REVIEW EXERCISE

Including Competency Based Questions

Multiple Choice Questions

1. How did Margie feel about the book? Competency Based

(a) Curious (b) Indifferent
(c) Ambiguous (d) Overwhelmed

Ans. (a) Curious

2. To which world does the story take the readers to?

(a) Future world where computers will play a major role.
(b) A world of robots with no humans.
(c) A world of humans with no robots.
(d) A world which is not on Earth.

Ans. (a) Future world where computers will play a major role.

3. How does Margie's attitude towards old style schools change? Competency Based

(a) Excitement to disappointment
(b) Prejudice to acceptance
(c) Curiosity to confusion
(d) Surprise to yearning

Ans. (d) Surprise to yearning

4. What prompts Margie's mother to send for the County Inspector?

(a) The mechanical teacher couldn't turn on.
(b) Repeated geography tests were too difficult for Margie's level.
(c) The mechanical teacher's maths tests were too difficult for Margie.
(d) Margie refused to interact with the mechanical teacher.

Ans. (b) Repeated geography tests were too difficult for Margie's level.

5. Margie was disappointed.
Margie was disappointed because..... . Competency Based

(a) the book was boring
(b) the teacher was repaired
(c) her geography marks were poor
(d) she had to wait till the next day to read the book

Ans. (d) she had to wait till the next day to read the book

6. Who said the following dialogue? - "Well, I don't know what kind of school they had all that time ago."

(a) Tommy (b) Margie
(c) Margie's grandfather (d) Margie's mother

Ans. (b) Margie

7. Why did Tommy laugh when Margie said, "I wouldn't want a strange man in my house to teach me"?

(a) Because Margie didn't know much about old schools.
(b) Because old schools did not take place at homes.
(c) Because Tommy was rude to Margie.
(d) Both (a) and (b)

Ans. (d) Both (a) and (b)

8. "........If you don't like it, you don't have to read the book"- Who said this?

(a) Tommy (b) Margie
(c) County Inspector (d) Mrs. Jones

Ans. (a) Tommy

9. Which word best describes Tommy's attitude towards Margie? Competency Based

(a) Indifferent (b) Patronising
(c) Thoughtless (d) Domineering

Ans. (d) Domineering

10. What distracts Margie as her lesson starts?

(a) The thought of the old schools centuries ago.
(b) The memory of Tommy's rudeness.
(c) A fly buzzing.
(d) The thought of her Maths homework.

Ans. (a) The thought of the old schools centuries ago.

11. Which arithmetic lesson was being taught to Margie?

(a) Addition of proper fractions
(b) Addition of rational numbers
(c) Addition and subtraction
(d) Addition of integers

Ans. (a) Addition of proper fractions

12. 'Margie even wrote about it that night in her diary' This sentence suggests that finding the book was .... Competency Based

(a) an unusual event
(b) a remarkable achievement
(c) an important milestone in her life
(d) a discovery of historic importance

Ans. (a) an unusual event

Extract Based Questions

1. Read the following extract carefully and answer the questions that follow.

It was a very old book. Margie's grandfather once said that when he was a little boy his grandfather told him that there was a time when stories were printed on paper.

They turned the pages, which were yellow and crinkly and it was awfully funny to read words that stood still instead of moving the way they were supposed to–on a screen, you know.

(i) Fill in the blank with one word from the brackets. The pages of the book were yellow and crinkly because it was quite .... (destroyed/old).

Ans. old

(ii) Why was Margie surprised to see the book? What does it indicate about her reaction?

Ans. Margie was surprised to see the book because all the stories in it were printed on paper. Her reaction indicates that the books in her time were very different from the book that she was reading.

(iii) Select the option that correctly captures the application of the word 'awfully' as used in the extract.

(a) Awfully be went to the office to complete his task.

(b) He followed me awfully to the new school.

(c) The traffic was awfully bad today. It took me two hours to reach to work.

(d) Sumit is awfully my senior in the music class.

Ans. (c) Option (c) correctly captures the application of the word 'awfully'.

(iv) Why was the printed book 'awfully funny to read'?

Ans. The printed book was awfully funny to read because the printed words were static unlike words on a screen.

2. Read the following extract carefully and answer the questions that follow.

He was a round little man with a red face and a whole box of tools with dials and wires. He smiled at Margie and gave her an apple, then took the teacher apart. Margie had hoped he wouldn't know how to put it together again, but he knew how all right and after an hour or so, there it was again, large and black and ugly, with a big screen on which all the lessons were shown and the questions were asked.

(i) Complete the analogy by selecting the suitable word from the extract.

Apart : Together :: Part : ....

Ans. Whole

(ii) What does he mean when the writer says, "he wouldn't know how to put it together again"?

Ans. When the writer said "he wouldn't know how to put it together again", he meant that the County Inspector wouldn't know how to repair it.

(iii) What was Margie feeling at the end of the extract?

(a) Overwhelmed (b) Nostalgic

(c) Gloomy (d) Angry

Ans. (c) Gloomy

(iv) How did the teacher appear to Margie?

Ans. Since Margie hated the mechanical teacher, it appeared large, black and ugly to her.

3. Read the following extract and answer the questions that follow.

Margie did so with a sigh. She was thinking about the old schools they had when her grandfather's grandfather was a little boy. All the kids from the whole neighbourhood came, laughing and shouting in the schoolyard, sitting together in the schoolroom, going home together at the end of the day. They learned the same things, so they could help one another with the homework and talk about it. And the teachers were people ...

(i) What do you think could be the least possible reason for Margie's liking for old funny schools?

Ans. The least possible reason for Margie liking the "old funny schools" would be that children used to go home together.

(ii) Choose the statement which tells about Margie.

1. **Margie had a hatred for school and mechanical teacher.**
2. **She fell in love with old funny schools.**
3. **Margie was studying History lesson while thinking about old schools.**

(a) Only 1 is true (b) Both 1 and 3 are true

(c) Both 1 and 2 are true (d) None of these

Ans. (c) Both 1 and 2 are true

(iii) What features of the 'old school' does Margie seem to think about?

Ans. Margie seems to think about how all the kids went to and returned from school together. She also seems to think about how they were all taught the same things in a single room so they could help one another with homework.

(iv) **Fill in the blanks with the correct word from the bracket.**

Margie's sigh is of .... (disappointment/desire)

Ans. desire

4. Read the following extract and answer the questions that follow.

They weren't even half finished when Margie's mother called, 'Margie! School!' Margie looked up. 'Not yet, Mamma.''Now!' said Mrs. Jones. 'And it's probably time for Tommy, too.' Margie said to Tommy, "Can I read the book some more with you after school?'' 'May be,' he said nonchalantly. He walked away whistling, the dusty old book tucked beneath his arm.

(i) **How did Margie feel when she was called for school?**

Ans. Margie felt irritated when she was called for school.

(ii) **State True or False.**

None of the give statements are true according to the given extract.

1. **Tommy was kind and compassionate with Margie.**
2. **Margie loved going to her school.**
3. **The book that they were reading belonged to Margie's grandfather.**

Ans. True

(iii) **Pick the option that correctly classifies fact/s (F) and opinion/s (O) of the students below.**

1. **I think both Margie and Tommy like the idea of old schools.**
2. **I think Margie will hate going to the old kind of schools.**
3. **I think Tommy is not excited about reading.**
4. **I think Tommy is arrogant.**

Ans. F-4 and O-1,2,3

(iv) **Margie posed a request to Tommy. What was it?**

Ans. Margie requested Tommy to read the book some more with her after school.

5. Read the following extract and answer the questions that follow.

It was always on at the same time every day except Saturday and Sunday, because her mother said little girls learned better if they learned at regular hours. The screen was lit up, and it said: "Today's arithmetic lesson is on the addition of proper fractions. Please insert yesterday's homework in the proper slot."

(i) **Where was the screen located?**

Ans. The screen was located in a room in Margie's house.

(ii) **What is the screen doing?**

(a) Notifying (b) Instructing
(c) Giving information (d) Scolding

Ans. (b) Instructing

(iii) **Fill in the blank with one word only.**

Margie did not have any classes on .... (Sundays/Fridays).

Ans. Sundays

(iv) **Which word from the extract would substitute the underlined phrase.**

All the students <u>leaving out</u> Shamshu attended the function.

Ans. except

Short Answer Type Questions

1. What did Margie's grandfather say to her?

Ans. Margie's grandfather told her that when he was a little boy, his grandfather had told him that there was a time when all stories were printed on paper. There were no computers and only books were used to get information at that time.

2. Give one reason for Tommy calling the book 'a waste'.

Or What makes the children think that books are wasteful? Competency Based

Ans. Tommy called the book 'a waste' because the words in it did not move like that on a telebook. He thought that after reading it once, it had to be thrown away. As he was not habitual of a real book, he did not understand the value and utility of such books.

3. What was Margie's initial reaction to the book being about school? Competency Based

Ans. Margie expressed doubt at the idea of a book centred around school, reflecting her existing dislike to the educational system. Her doubt was a result of her negative experiences with the mechanical teacher, leading her to reject anything related to traditional schooling.

4. What hope did Margie have when her mechanical teacher was taken apart? Did it come true?

Ans. Margie had hoped that the County Inspector would not be able to fix the mechanical teacher and he would take away the mechanical teacher with him. No, it didn't come true because the Inspector fixed the issue with the mechanical teacher at Margie's home itself.

5. How did Margie feel about attending school after reading about the old schools? Competency Based

Ans. Margie's encounter with the depiction of traditional schools led to longing for a different educational experience. She desired the friendship and shared learning of the past, contrasting it with her current isolated mechanised education, which left her feeling disconnected and unfulfilled.

6. What was Margie thinking about as she sat before her mechanical teacher?

Ans. As Margie sat before her mechanical teacher, she couldn't help but remember the old-fashioned schools described in the book. She thought about the sense of community, collaboration and joyous learning that seemed absent from her current educational setup, leading to a desire for a more humanised approach to education.

7. How did Margie and Tommy react differently to discovering the old book?

Ans. Margie was captivated or interested by the novelty of finding a physical book and expressed curiosity about its contents. At the same time, Tommy initially dismissed it as a waste, preferring the efficiency of their digital learning tools.

8. How did the portrayal of traditional schools in the old book influence Margie's perception of education?

Ans. The portrayal of traditional schools in the old book increased Margie's curiosity and imagination, leading her to question the efficiency of her current education. It prompted her to reevaluate her understanding of learning and yearn for a more humanised and engaging educational experience.

Long Answer Type Questions

1. Suppose Margie gets a chance to visit the old school for one day. Write a diary entry in about 100-120 words deserting Margie's experience and how she felt.

Ans. 10th February, 20XX 9:30 pm

Dear Diary

I have something very exciting to share with you. I got a chance to visit an old school today. It was quite different from the one we have now. It has a huge building with playgrounds, science labs and a library. What impressed me the most was that it had real teachers and real students. Being taught by a real teacher was a unique experience for me. I think it is far better than being taught online. It helps the student to clear his/her doubts instantly. Moreover, the bond that a real student shares with a real teacher cannot be replicated through online learning. I really enjoyed playing with my classmates in the lunch time and sharing my experiences with them. It was a truly unforgettable experience!

Shivani

2. You had an experience of online learning during the lockdown two years ago. Compare and contrast your experience with the one described in the chapter 'The Fun They Had' in not more than 120 words.

Ans. I had an experience of online learning two years ago when nationwide lockdown was imposed and physical schooling was discontinued. It was somewhat similar to the one described in 'The Fun They Had'. Like Margie, I had to attend online classes at regular times during the weekdays. I had to sit infront of my laptop everyday and listen to my teachers' lectures online.

The difference between my experience and that of Margie was that unlike Margie, I had my teacher, teaching me online and the homework/tests had to be submitted by sending them via e-mail rather than putting it into a slot like Margie did.

During this time, I longed to go back to school and meet my classmates and teachers physically. I also realised the fact that the fun factor I had while attending a physical school was missing in this mode of teaching.

3. The school in the story was not lovable to the kids. What should be done in order to make it lovable?

Ans. The school in the story was not lovable to the kids as there was no place for joy, pleasure and playfulness. Every kid had his school in his house only and there were no other kids to give them company. They were taught by a mechanical teacher who lacked human touch. All these things made the school boring.

To make the schools lovable, there must be a common building where all the kids from the neighbourhood come and sit together. They must be able to help one another in their homework. They should enjoy the things that a school can provide. Moreover, they should be taught by a human teacher.

A human teacher will be able to appreciate things and surroundings better. They possess human consideration unlike a mechanical teacher. They would participate in the learning process with the students and listen to their concerns.

The schools can be made lovable if the interaction between a teacher and students is available and increased. There must be an environment of pleasure, joy and fun which the kids love to have.

4. Margie was thinking about the old schools they had when her grandfather's grandfather was a little boy. All the kids from the whole neighborhood came, laughing and shouting in the schoolyard, sitting together in the schoolroom, going home together at the end of the day. At that time the teachers were people. How would you assess a mechanical teacher in comparison to a human teacher?

Ans. A teacher should be assessed on the basis of the ability to interact well with the children and to handle their queries well. A teacher must be capable of reading the psyche of a student. The mechanical teacher is not able to interact well with the children and is not able to read the psyche of the students.

On the other hand, a human teacher is able to perform both the tasks well. A human teacher knows how to teach the kids while keeping in mind their interests so that they don't feel boredom in studying and learning. Also, a human teacher can explain and interpret things well which is desirable.

Hence, it can be said that a human teacher is far better than a mechanical teacher.

5. Margie is the main character who embodies curiosity, independence, vulnerability, resilience, and nostalgia in 'The Fun They Had.' Comment.

Ans. Margie is the main character who embodies curiosity, independence, vulnerability and resilience in "The Fun They Had." She is an eleven-year-old girl who serves to highlight how the futuristic education system may not be as great as we make it out to be.

Here is her character sketch

Curious and Imaginative Margie is curious about the past and intrigued by the idea of traditional schools, which contrasts with the mechanical education system she experiences. She shows interest in the old book and her desire to learn more about outdated educational practices.

Independent Thinker Margie demonstrates independence of thought by questioning the effectiveness of the mechanical teacher and expressing dissatisfaction with her education. She challenges the status quo and desires a more engaging and personal learning experience.

Emotionally Sensitive Margie's emotions fluctuate throughout the story, ranging from curiosity and excitement to disappointment and longing. She feels frustrated by her struggles with the mechanical teacher and desirous for the communal learning environment of the past.

Resilient Despite her frustrations with the mechanical teacher and the limitations of her futuristic education, Margie remains resilient. She continues to seek knowledge and connection, as evidenced by her interest in reading old books.

Symbol of Lost Childhood Margie symbolises the loss of childhood innocence and wonder in a highly mechanised society. Her yearning for the simple pleasures of traditional schooling reflects a longing for a time when education was more personal and meaningful.

6. Tommy is portrayed as a confident, pragmatic, and tech-savvy character who contrasts Margie's curiosity and emotional vulnerability. Do you agree? Answer with reference to Tommy's character.

Ans. Tommy is portrayed as a confident, pragmatic and tech-savvy character who contrasts Margie's curiosity and emotional vulnerability. His friendship with Margie adds depth to the story and highlights different attitudes towards technology and education in their futuristic society.

Tommy is Margie's thirteen-year-old friend. He is depicted as confident and assertive. He sometimes displays a sense of superiority, particularly when explaining concepts to Margie or teasing her about her lack of knowledge about the past. Tommy is familiar with the advanced technology of his time, including telebooks and mechanical teachers. He appears to grasp better how things work in their futuristic society than Margie, as evidenced by his nonchalant attitude towards their educational system.

Unlike Margie, Tommy seems more accepting of the status quo and less inclined to question the effectiveness of their education system. Tommy is knowledgeable about the technology and education system of their time. However, he dismisses Margie's curiosity about traditional schools and appears to view them as outdated relics of the past.

Despite their differences, Tommy is Margie's faithful friend. He spends time with her, shares his discoveries with her, and even agrees to read the old book after school, albeit casually. His friendship with Margie provides both characters with a sense of companionship and support.

ASSESSMENT EXERCISE

Extract Based Questions

Read the following extracts carefully and answer the questions that follow.

1. They turned the pages, which were yellow and crinkly, and it was awfully funny to read words that stood still instead of moving the way they were supposed to-on a screen, you know. And then when they turned back to the page before, it had the same words on it that it had when they read it the first time.

(i) What does the phrase 'yellow and crinkly' signify?

(a) It is dirty. (b) It is old.

(c) It is destroyed. (d) It is beautiful.

(ii) Complete the sentence appropriately.

The'screen' here refer to ....

(iii) Why was the book funny to read for them?

(iv) Where was the book found?

2. Margie was scornful. "School? What's there to write about school? I hate school."

Margie always hated school but now she hated it more than ever. The mechanical teacher had been giving her test after test in geography and she had been doing worse and worse until her mother had shaken her head sorrowfully and sent for the County Inspector.

(i) Margie had not been doing well in

(a) Geography (b) Science

(c) History (d) English

(ii) Fill in the blank with one word only.

.... in the extract is the opposite of 'appreciative'.

(iii) Which word can replace the underlined word in the sentence.

Mayank's situation is becoming <u>gradually bad</u>.

(iv) Why was Margie scornful?

Short Answer (SA) Type Questions

1. What do the yellow and crinkly pages show?

2. How was the arrival of the County Inspector beneficial to Margie?

3. What 'fun' did Margie think about and wished for?

4. Describe the teachers that Margie and Tommy had.

Long Answer (LA) Type Questions

1. What was the fun available to the students of the past according to the story?

2. 'Machines can't replace human beings.' Explain this in reference to the lesson 'The Fun They had'.

3. Describe the kind of books that the grandfather of Margie's grandfather had studied.

The Sound of Music

by Deborah Cowley

CHAPTER 2

The chapter is divided into two parts. Both deal with aspects of music and legendary musicians who achieved excellence in their respective fields.

I. Evelyn Glennie Listens to Sound Without Hearing it

CHAPTER SUMMARY

Part-I This part has been written by Deborah Cowley. It is about the famous multi-percussionist, Evelyn Glennie. Evelyn became deaf at a young age. However, she worked hard to learn music and became one of the world's most famous multi-percussionist. She has won many awards and is a role model for the handicapped people. She was honoured with the Royal Philharmonic Society's prestigious Soloist of the year Award.

Evelyn Lost her Hearing at a Young Age

On the way to the Royal Academy of Music in London for her first day, Evelyn felt nervous but excited. She was a seventeen year old deaf girl from a Scottish farm who aspired to be a musician. Evelyn lost her sense of hearing gradually at a young age. It was first noticed by her mother, Isabel Glennie, when Evelyn was eight years old. Evelyn managed to hide her growing deafness from her friends and teachers for a long time. However, when she was eleven years old, her performance in school became worse.

So, her headmistress advised her parents to take her to a specialist. The specialist confirmed that her deafness was due to a gradual nerve damage and asked her parents to get her fitted with hearing aids. He also told them to send her to the school for the deaf.

Evelyn didn't Give up Hope and Never Looked Back

Despite her deafness, Evelyn was determined to lead a normal life and pursue her interest in music. One day, she noticed a girl playing a xylophone and decided to learn to play it. Most of the teachers discouraged Evelyn but the percussionist Ron Forbes recognised her potential. He supported Evelyn in achieving her goal. He began by tuning two large drums to different notes. Then, he advised Evelyn not to hear music through her ears but try to sense the music in a different way. Suddenly, Evelyn realised that she could feel the higher drum from the waist up and the lower one from the waist down. Later, she discovered that she could sense the vibrations in different parts of her body. She had learnt to open her mind and body to sounds and vibrations.

Evelyn's Achievements

Evelyn joined a youth orchestra and toured the United Kingdom with them. When she was sixteen, she decided to make music her life. She auditioned for the Royal Academy of Music and scored one of the highest marks in the history of the academy. She gradually left the orchestral work and started giving solo performances.

At the end of her three year course, she had received most of the top awards. She became the world's most famous multi-percussionist with a mastery over some thousand instruments.

She could understand what people were saying by watching their lips and that's why men with bushy beards gave her trouble.

She speaks English with a Scottish accent flawlessly and also learned French and Japanese.

In 1991, she was honoured with the Royal Philharmonic Society's prestigious Soloist of the year Award.

Evelyn Senses Music

Evelyn says that music flows through every part of her body. It tingles in her skin, her cheekbones and even in her hair. When she plays the xylophone, she can sense the sound passing up the stick into her fingertips. By leaning against the drums, she can feel the resonances (sounds) flowing into her body. On a wooden platform, she removes her shoes so that the vibrations pass through her barefeet and up her legs.

Evelyn : An Inspiration for the Handicapped

Evelyn admitted that she was a workaholic and works harder than other classical musicians.

Apart from the regular concerts, she gives free concerts in prisons and hospitals, and takes classes for young musicians. She delights her audiences and has given great pleasure to millions.

She has promoted percussion to the front of the orchestra. She has given inspiration to the handicapped people. Ann Richlin from the Beethoven Fund for deaf children praises Evelyn for being a shining inspiration to deaf children.

Word Meaning

Word	Meaning
rush hour	the usual hours of going to office and returning from the office when there is a lot of traffic.
jostle	push roughly
daunting	challenging
aspiring musician	a person who wants to be a musician
profoundly	completely
deteriorated	started to become poorer
impaired	weakened
pursue	to carry on with one's interest in something
xylophone	a musical instrument with a row of wooden bars of different lengths.

Word	Meaning
percussionist	a person who plays the tabla or drum etc
potential	quality that can be developed
sheer	great
sought-after	one whom people like and want very much.
intriguing	fascinating and curious
flawlessly	without a fault or mistake
lilt	a way of speaking
tingles	causes a slight pricking or stinging sensation
resonances	echoes of sounds
workaholic	(informal) a person who finds it difficult to stop working
priority	great importance

NCERT FOLDER

NCERT Intext and Exercise Questions

THINKING ABOUT THE TEXT (NCERT PAGE 20)

I. Answer these questions in a few words or a couple of sentence each.

Q.1 How old was Evelyn when she went to the Royal Academy of Music?

Ans. Evelyn was about seventeen years old when she went to the Royal Academy of Music in London.

Q.2 When was her deafness first noticed? When was it confirmed?

Ans. Evelyn's deafness was first noticed by her mother when she was eight years old.

Her deafness was confirmed by a specialist when she was eleven years old.

II. Answer each of these questions in a short paragraph (30-40 words.)

Q.1 Who helped Evelyn to continue with music? What did he do and say?

Ans. The percussionist, Ron Forbes helped Evelyn to continue with music.

To teach Evelyn, he began by tuning two large drums to different notes. He told Evelyn not to listen through her ears but to try to sense the sound through different parts of her body.

Q.2 Name the various places and causes for which Evelyn performs.

Ans. Evelyn gives free concerts in prisons and hospitals, apart from the regular concerts. She also takes classes for young musicians.

III. Answer the questions in two or three paragraphs (100-150 words).

Q.1 How does Evelyn hear music?

Ans. Evelyn used to 'hear' music by sensing the notes in different parts of her body. Ron Forbes taught her to 'hear' like this. When he tuned two drums to different notes and asked her to sense the sound in some other way, Evelyn realised that she could feel the higher drum from the waist up and the lower drum from the waist down.

When she played the xylophone, she could sense the sound passing up the stick into her fingertips. By leaning against the drums, she could feel the sounds flowing into her body. On a wooden platform, she removed her shoes so that the vibrations could pass through her bare feet. She also told that music flowed through every part of her body. It tingled in her skin, her cheekbones and even in her hair.

REVIEW EXERCISE

Including Competency Based Questions

Part I

Multiple Choice Questions

1. Evelyn realised about the approaching train by feeling its ....

(a) sound (b) vibration (c) structure (d) crowd

Ans. (b) vibration

2. Why was the first day at the prestigious Royal Academy of Music in London daunting for Evelyn?

(a) Because she was an inexperienced Scottish musician.
(b) Because she was deaf.
(c) Because she was in London for the first time.
(d) Both (a) and (b)

Ans. (d) Both (a) and (b)

3. Who said the following dialogue, "They called her name and she didn't move. I suddenly realised she hadn't heard"?

(a) Evelyn Glennie (b) Isabel Glennie
(c) Interviewer (d) James Blades

Ans. (b) Isabel Glennie

4. When did Evelyn start performing alone? **Competency Based**

(a) When she graduated from the Royal Academy of Music
(b) When she toured the United Kingdom as a teenager
(c) When she was at the Royal Academy of Music
(d) When she was in school

Ans. (c) When she was at the Royal Academy of Music

5. Which statement is Evelyn most likely to agree with? **Competency Based**

(a) Talent is at least as important as hard work for success.
(b) Success cannot be achieved without the support of others.
(c) Perseverance is the most important trait for success.
(d) Success depends most on the right circumstances.

Ans. (c) Perseverance is the most important trait for success.

6. How long was the course at the Royal Academy of Music?

(a) Two years (b) Three years
(c) Four years (d) Five years

Ans. (b) Three years

7. "And for all this, Evelyn won't accept any hint of heroic achievement." What does this mean?

(a) Even after achieving so much in life, Evelyn does not take pride in herself.
(b) Even after achievements, Evelyn is dissatisfied with herself.
(c) Evelyn does not achieve anything extraordinary.
(d) Both (b) and (c)

Ans. (a) Even after achieving so much in life, Evelyn does not take pride in herself.

8. Why did bearded men give trouble to Evelyn?

(a) Evelyn couldn't read their eyes.
(b) Evelyn couldn't read their lips.
(c) Evelyn couldn't read their smile.
(d) They spoke very low.

Ans. (b) Evelyn couldn't read their lips.

9. Why does Evelyn remove shoes on wooden platforms?

(a) To let the vibrations pass through her barefeet and up her legs
(b) To listen to the music
(c) To make herself comfortable
(d) All of the above

Ans. (a) To let the vibrations pass through her barefeet and up her legs

10. Where does Ann Richclin work?

(a) In Evelyn's school
(b) Beethoven Fund for Deaf Children
(c) Royal Academy of Music
(d) None of the above

Ans. (b) Beethoven Fund for Deaf Children

11. What word best describes the attitude of the author towards Evelyn? **Competency Based**

(a) Balanced (b) Laudatory
(c) Reverential (d) Deferential

Ans. (c) Reverential

12. What did specially-abled people say when looking at Evelyn?

(a) 'I am better than Evelyn' (b) 'I cannot be like Evelyn'
(c) 'If she can do it, I can too' (d) 'She is not worth it'

Ans. (c) 'If she can do it, I can too'

13. Why does Evelyn give free concerts in prisons and hospitals? **Competency Based**

(a) She knows it offers enormous rewards.
(b) She is empathetic towards the people in prisons and hospitals.
(c) She knows it is hard work.
(d) She knows she is an inspiration.

Ans. (b) She is empathetic towards the people in prisons and hospitals.

14. What is the theme of the story of Evelyn Glennie?

(a) Earnest efforts and guidance can pave one's way to success.
(b) Percussionist is a very profitable profession.
(c) Free concerts should be given in prisons and hospitals.
(d) All of the above

Ans. (a) Earnest efforts and guidance can pave one's way to success.

Extract Based Questions

1. Read the following extract carefully and answer the questions that follow.

Rush hour crowds jostle for position on the underground train platform. A slight girl, looking younger than her seventeen years, was nervous yet excited as she felt the vibrations of the approaching train. It was her first day at the prestigious Royal Academy of Music in London and daunting enough for any teenager fresh from a Scottish farm.

(i) The girl referred to here is

(a) Evelyn Glennie (b) Isabel Glennie
(c) James Blades (d) Ann Richlin

Ans. (a) Evelyn Glennie

(ii) Where was she going?

Ans. She was going to attend her first day at Royal Academy of Music.

(iii) Why was it daunting for Evelyn Glennie to be at the Royal Academy of Music, London?

Ans. A change of landscape made the situation daunting for Glennie, a teenager who for the first time was travelling away from the environment she was used to.

(iv) The word 'daunting' in the extract means ..... .

Ans. frightening

2. Read the following extract carefully and answer the questions that follow.

Evelyn confesses that she is something of a workaholic. "I've just got to work ... often harder than classical musicians. But the rewards are enormous." Apart from the regular concerts, Evelyn also gives free concerts in prisons and hospitals. She also gives high priority to classes for young musicians.

Ann Richclin of the Beethoven Fund for Deaf Children says, "She is a shining inspiration for deaf children. They see that there is nowhere that they cannot go." Evelyn Glennie has already accomplished more than most people twice her age. She has brought percussion to the front of the orchestra and demonstrated that it can be very moving. She has given inspiration to those who are handicapped, people who look to her and say, 'If she can do it, I can.' And, not the least, she has given enormous pleasure to millions.

(i) Why did Evelyn say that she works harder than classical musicians?

This is because ....

(a) she is deaf.
(b) she wants to make a difference.
(c) she wants to prove something.
(d) she wants to be successful.

Ans. (a) she is deaf.

(ii) Who, in the extract, points out that Evelyn Glennie is an inspiration for deaf children?

Ans. Ann Richclin of the Beethoven Fund for Deaf Children highlights that Glennie has become a role model for deaf children.

(iii) 'Evelyn confesses that she is something of a workaholic'. What does the word workaholic mean as used in the above line?

Ans. The word 'workaholic' refers to a person who works compulsively.

(iv) Fill in the blank with one word only.
In the extract, Evelyn is talking to a/an .... (interviewer/doctor).

Ans. interviewer

3. Read the following extract carefully and answer the questions that follow.

And for all this, Evelyn won't accept any hint of heroic achievement. "If you work hard and know where you are going, you'll get there." And she got right to the top, the world's most sought-after multi percussionist with a mastery of some thousand instruments and hectic international schedule.

(i) 'All this' in the given extract refers to

(a) her career as a percussionist.
(b) her journey in the Royal Academy of Music.
(c) receiving the highest marks in the history of Royal Academy of Music.
(d) Both (b) and (c)

Ans. (d) Both (b) and (c)

(ii) State True or False.

The set of statements are not true according to the given extract.

1. Evelyn did not participate in international concerts.
2. Evelyn knew how to play only the xylophone.
3. Evelyn became a teacher at the Royal Academy of Music.

Ans. True

(iii) Complete the sentence appropriately.
The phrase 'most sought after' indicates ....

Ans. popularity and fan following

(iv) According to Glennie, what is the key to achieve what one wants to?

Ans. According to Evelyn Glennie, to achieve what one wants, one must work hard and keep his/her eyes set on the goal.

Part II

Short Answer Type Questions

1. State one likely reason for Evelyn being nervous while going to the Royal Academy of Music.

Or **"A slight girl, looking younger than her seventeen years, was nervous yet excited as she felt the vibrations of the approaching train." Why was Evelyn nervous and excited?** Competency Based

Ans. Evelyn was nervous while going to the Royal Academy of Music as it was her first day at the prestigious Academy. She was excited because she had won over all the obstacles that her lack of hearing ability posed for her music career. Now, she was going to join the biggest institution of music.

2. How did Evelyn become able to sense different notes?

Ans. Evelyn became able to sense different notes by making her body and mind receptive to sounds and vibrations. She could sense sounds of music flowing into her body. She used to stand barefeet on a wooden platform so that she could sense the vibrations easily.

3. What did Evelyn say about sensing the music?

Ans. Evelyn said that she could sense the music through every part of her body. It creates a tingling sensation in her skin, cheekbones and her hair. She could sense the xylophone's sound passing up the stick into her fingertips. Her legs could feel the vibrations of the drum.

4. What special achievement did Evelyn have in the history of Royal Academy?

Ans. The special achievement that Evelyn had in the history of Royal Academy was that she scored one of the highest marks in the history of the Academy. Furthermore, at the end of her course in the Academy, she had won most of the top awards.

5. Give the reason for Evelyn removing her shoes on a wooden platform.

Ans. On a wooden platform, Evelyn used to remove her shoes so that she could sense the vibrations passing through her barefeet. With shoes, she could not feel the vibrations properly and therefore she would not be able to feel the music.

6. How was Evelyn able to express music so beautifully?

Ans. Evelyn was able to express music so beautifully because she was able to feel it far more deeply than others. Others could only hear music by ears but Evelyn could sense music through her body.

7. Evelyn is a modest person. Do you agree with the statement? Justify your answer. Competency Based

Ans. Evelyn is definitely a modest person. This can be proved by the fact that although her achievements verge on the border of unbelievable, she is not prideful or egoistic about her status. Instead, she focuses her efforts on helping others achieve their own goals by giving music lessons. She also has a humanitarian soul because she empathises with the patients in hospitals and the inmates in prisons.

8. Why do men with bushy beards give Evelyn trouble? Competency Based

Ans. Men with bushy beards give Evelyn trouble because the bushy beards make it hard for her to read the lips of the speaker. Since she is deaf, reading the lips is one of the only ways in which she can understand what the other person is saying.

9. What perspective does Evelyn offer on her achievements and work ethic?

Ans. Evelyn attributes her success to hard work and clarity of purpose. Rejecting notions of heroism, she emphasises dedication and direction. Despite challenges, her relentless pursuit of excellence in music yields immense personal and professional fulfillment.

10. How does Evelyn's commitment to giving back to her community reflect her values?

Ans. Evelyn's dedication to providing free concerts in prisons and hospitals and mentoring young musicians reflects her deep-seated values of compassion and inclusivity. She recognises the transformative power of music and seeks to share it with diverse audiences.

11. What role does Evelyn's mentor, percussionist Ron Forbes, play in her musical development?

Ans. Ron Forbes' innovative teaching methods and encouragement were instrumental in Evelyn's musical journey. His guidance allowed her to discover her ability to sense sound through vibrations, laying the foundation for her remarkable music career.

12. In what ways has Evelyn Glennie's story inspired individuals facing similar challenges?

Ans. Evelyn's story inspires and empowers people confronting disabilities or adversity. By demonstrating resilience, determination and the ability to overcome obstacles, she offers hope and encouragement to others on their journeys.

13. How can feeling music instead of just listening to it, as Evelyn Glennie does, change people's perceptions of disabilities? Competency Based

Ans. Evelyn's approach of feeling music instead of just listening to it highlights the importance of embracing diverse modes of perception and expression. By showcasing the richness of sensory experiences beyond hearing, she challenges stereotypes and fosters greater acceptance and inclusion for individuals with disabilities.

Long Answer Type Questions

1. How did Evelyn Glennie's determination and hard work lead to her success as a musician?

Ans. Evelyn Glennie's success as a musician can be attributed to her unwavering determination and relentless hard work. Despite facing profound deafness from a young age, Glennie refused to let her disability hinder her passion for music. She exhibited exceptional perseverance, refusing to accept defeat or limitations imposed by her condition. Instead, she embraced challenges head-on, continually seeking innovative ways to overcome obstacles. Glennie's dedication to her craft drove her to push boundaries and strive for excellence in her musical pursuits.

Through countless hours of practice and unwavering commitment, she honed her skills and mastery of percussion instruments, eventually gaining recognition as one of the world's most sought-after multi percussionist. Glennie's relentless determination and work ethic propelled her to success and inspired countless individuals worldwide, demonstrating the power of resilience and perseverance in achieving one's dreams.

2. Evelyn Glennie is portrayed as a remarkable individual whose life story is defined by resilience, determination, and a passionate pursuit of her dreams despite facing profound deafness. Elucidate.

Ans. Evelyn Glennie is portrayed as a remarkable individual whose life story is defined by resilience, determination and a passionate pursuit of her dreams despite facing profound deafness. She exhibits extraordinary resilience and determination from a young age. Despite gradually losing her hearing, she refuses to be discouraged or defined by her disability. Instead, she remains steadfast in her resolve to lead an everyday life and pursue her love for music. She learns to sense vibrations and feel the music through different body parts, allowing her to connect with the sounds in unique ways.

Evelyn's passion for music is evident throughout the article. Even when faced with the daunting prospect of being deaf, she remains unwavering in her commitment to music. Evelyn's journey to success is marked by her relentless work ethic and dedication. Her high marks at the Royal Academy of Music and numerous awards reflect her dedication and talent.

Evelyn finds time to give back to her community despite her busy schedule. She demonstrates compassion and generosity towards others through free concerts in prisons and hospitals or by prioritising classes for young musicians.

Throughout the excerpt, Evelyn emerges as an inspiring role model for others, especially individuals with disabilities. Her refusal to let her deafness hold her back inspires countless people facing their challenges. By achieving success in the music industry and sharing her story, she becomes a beacon of hope and motivation for others.

3. Evelyn has given inspiration to those who are handicapped, people who look to her and say, 'If she can do it, I can.' And, not the least, she has given enormous pleasure to millions.

Write a diary entry in about 100-120 words on how you felt after reading Evelyn's story.

Ans. 26th January, 20XX 9:15 pm

Dear Diary

Today, I read about the famous musician, Evelyn Glennie. Her success story was moving for me as she did not let her deafness come in way of achieving her goals. She had become completely deaf by the age of 12 due to gradual nerves damage. Despite this disability, she was determined to lead a normal life and pursue her interest in music. With time, Evelyn discovered that she could sense different notes in the different parts of her body. She learned to open her mind and body to different sounds and vibrations.

You know, Evelyn has won many prestigious awards and has performed around the world. She is the most popular percussionist in the world. Reading about her success story has inspired me and filled me with zeal to achieve my goal.

Aman

ASSESSMENT EXERCISE

Extract Based Questions

Read the following extract and answer the questions that follow.

Not surprisingly, Evelyn delights her audiences. In 1991 she was presented with the Royal Philharmonic Society's prestigious Soloist of the Year Award. Says master percussionist James Blades, "God may have taken her hearing but he has given her back something extraordinary. What we hear, she feels — far more deeply than any of us. That is why she expresses music so beautifully."

(i) Why was it even more notable that Evelyn was presented with the Royal Philharmonic Society's Soloist of the Year Award?

(ii) Which word from the given extract is a synonym of 'honourable'?

(a) Percussion (b) Prestigious

(c) Extraordinary (d) Notable

(iii) According to master percussionist James Blades, why does Evelyn express music so beautifully?

(iv) What are the possible reasons due to which Evelyn delights her audiences?

Short Answer (SA) Type Questions

1. How did Evelyn feel the music?
2. How could Evelyn express the music more beautifully than others?
3. How was Evelyn's hearing loss detected?

Long Answer (LA) Type Questions

1. With evidence from the lesson, point out the values displayed by Evelyn Glennie.
2. Write a letter to Ron Forbes from Evelyn's mother thanking him for inspiring her daughter.
3. Evelyn supported various causes apart from giving performances. What were these?

II. The Shehnai of Bismillah Khan

CHAPTER SUMMARY **Part-II** This part is about the renowned shehnai player, Bismillah Khan. He belonged to a well-known family of musicians from Bihar. He played the Shehnai on the auspicious occasion of national freedom on 15th August, 1947. He was honoured with the highest civilian award the Bharat Ratna in 2001.

Ban on Pungi and Origin of Shehnai

Emperor Aurangzeb banned the playing of the pungi (a musical instrument) in the royal palace as it had a loud and unpleasant sound.

A barber who belonged to a family of professional musicians decided to improve the tonal quality of the pungi. He took a pipe with a natural hollow stem. It was longer and broader than the pungi. He made seven holes on its body. When it was played by closing and opening some of these holes, soft and melodious sounds were produced. Everyone was impressed when he played the instrument in the palace.

Naming of Shehnai and its Importance

As the instrument was first played in the Shah's (King's) chambers by a nai (a barber), it was named as 'shehnai'.

The sound of the shehnai gradually became popular and it started to be considered auspicious with time. It is still played in temples and at weddings in North India.

In the past, the shehnai was part of the naubat or the traditional group of nine instruments found at Royal Courts. However, it became a part of classical music due to Ustad Bismillah Khan.

Bismillah Khan's Birth and Family

Bismillah Khan was born on 21st March, 1916 in a well-known family of musicians in Dumraon, Bihar. His grandfather, Rasool Bux Khan, was the shehnai-nawaz of the Bhojpur king's Court. His father, Paigambar Bux and other ancestors were also great shehnai players.

Bismillah's Interest in Music

Bismillah developed an interest in music at a small age. His mother took him to his maternal uncle's house in Benaras (now Varanasi) when he was three years old. There, he was fascinated by his uncle, Ali Bux, playing the shehnai.

Soon, he started accompanying his uncle to the Vishnu temple of Benaras where he was employed to play shehnai. Gradually, he started getting lessons on playing the instrument. Bismillah practised playing it in the temples of Balaji and Mangala Maiya, and at the banks of the river Ganga. The flowing waters of the Ganga inspired him to invent new raagas. He accompanied his uncle to the Allahabad Music Conference at the age of fourteen. Ustad Faiyaz Khan was impressed by his performance and encouraged him to work hard to achieve his goal.

Bismillah's Rise to Fame

Bismillah Khan got the first big break with the opening of the All India Radio in Lucknow in 1938. Soon, he became a popular shehnai player on the radio.

Bismillah became the first Indian to greet the nation with his shehnai on 15th August, 1947 when India gained independence. He played Shehnai from the Red Fort in front of an audience including Pandit Jawaharlal Nehru. He gave many memorable performances in India and abroad. His first trip abroad was to Afghanistan where King Zahir Khan became impressed by his performance and gifted him his priceless Persian carpets and other things.

Bismillah's Contribution in the Film World

Film director Vijay Bhatt named a film Goonj Uthi Shehnai after he was fascinated on hearing Bismillah playing the shehnai at a festival.

One of Bismillah Khan's compositions in the film Dil Ka Khilona Hai Toot Gaya became a national chartbuster. Bismillah only gave music in two films–Goonj Uthi Shehnai and a Kannada film, Sanadhi Apanna. This was because he did not like the artificiality and glamour of the film world.

A Renowned Musician

Ustad Bismillah Khan was the first Indian to be invited to perform at the prestigious Lincoln Centre Hall in the USA. He also took part in The World Exposition in Montreal, Cannes Art Festival and the Osaka Trade Fair. He became so popular internationally that an auditorium in Tehran was named after him.

Bismillah's Awards

Bismillah received many awards including National awards like the Padma Shri, the Padma Bhushan and the Padma Vibhushan. In 2001, he was awarded India's highest civilian award, the Bharat Ratna. He recommended Indians to teach the music to their children as it is Hindustan's richest tradition.

Bismillah's Love for his Roots

Bismillah Khan travelled to many countries, but he was extremely fond of Benaras and Dumraon. These remained the most wonderful towns of the world for him. His love for his heritage and culture could be seen when he refused one of his student's offer to head a Shehnai school in the USA by saying that he could not find the Ganga there.

His life is a perfect example of the rich, cultural heritage of India where a devout Muslim can play Shehnai in front of the Kashi Vishwanatha temple.

Ustad Bismillah Khan passed away on 21st August, 2006 at the age of ninety after a prolonged illness. He was given a state funeral and the Government of India declared one day of national mourning.

Word Meaning

Word	Meaning
generic name	a name given to a class or group as a whole
reeded	wind instruments which have reeds
revived	to get back to life or use
auspicious	promising to bring good fortune
indispensable	something that is an important part of anything
ensemble	a group of things
paternal ancestors	ancestors of the father
haunts	places visited more often
improvise	to do a thing in a new and in a different way
souvenirs	things given in the memory of something

Word	Meaning
chartbuster	record breaker
celluloid	the world of cinema
ventures	a risky task
conferred	to give someone a degree or an award
coveted	much desired
glinting	shining
exceedingly	beyond the limits
yearning	longing/desire
devout	strong believer of a religion
prolonged	that lasts for a long time

NCERT FOLDER

NCERT Intext and Exercise Questions

THINKING ABOUT THE TEXT

(NCERT PAGE 25-26)

I. Tick the right answer.

Q.1 The (shehnai, pungi) was a 'reeded noisemaker.'

Ans. *pungi*

Q.2 (Bismillah Khan, a barber, Ali Bux) transformed the *pungi* into a *shehnai*.

Ans. A barber

Q.3 Bismillah Khan's paternal ancestors were (barbers, professional musicians).

Ans. professional musicians

Q.4 Bismillah Khan learnt to play the *shehnai* from (Ali Bux, Paigambar Bux, Ustad Faiyaaz Khan).

Ans. Ali Bux

Q.5 Bismillah Khan's first trip abroad was to (Afghanistan, USA, Canada).

Ans. Afghanistan

II. Find the words in the text which show Ustad Bismillah Khan's feelings about the items listed below.

Q.1 Then mark a, tick (✔) in the correct column. Discuss your answers in class.

Bismillah Khan's feelings about	Positive	Negative	Neutral
1. Teaching children music			
2. The film world			
3. Migrating to the USA			
4. Playing at temples			
5. Getting the Bharat Ratna			
6. The. banks of the Ganga			
7. Leaving Benaras and Dumraon			

Ans.

Bismillah Khan's feelings about	Positive	Negative	Neutral
1. Teaching children music	✔		
2. The film world		✔	
3. Migrating to the USA		✔	
4. Playing at temples	✔		
5. Getting the Bharat Ratna	✔		
6. The banks of the Ganga	✔		
7. Leaving Benaras and Dumraon		✔	

III. Answer these questions in 30-40 words.

Q.1 Why did Aurangzeb ban the playing of the *pungi*?

Ans. Aurangzeb banned the playing of the *pungi* because it had a loud and unpleasant sound.

Q.2 How is a shehnai different from a *pungi*?

Ans. As compared to a pungi, shehnai is a pipe with a natural hollow stem that is longer and broader. It has seven holes on its body. When it is played by the closing and opening of some of the holes, it produces soft and melodious sounds.

Q.3 Where was the shehnai played traditionally? How did Bismillah Khan change this?

Ans. The shehnai was traditionally played in royal courts, temples and weddings.

Bismillah Khan changed this tradition by bringing the instrument onto the classical stage expanding its usage beyond traditional settings.

Q.4 When and how did Bismillah Khan get his first big break?

Ans. Bismillah Khan got his first big break with the opening of the All India Radio in Lucknow in 1938. He soon became a popular shehnai player, gaining significant recognition and popularity.

Q.5 Where did Bismillah Khan play the shehnai on 15th August, 1947? Why was the event historic?

Ans. On 15th August, 1947, Bismillah Khan played the shehnai from the Red Fort.

It was a historic day as India gained independence. Thus, he became the first Indian to greet the independent nation with his shehnai.

Q.6 Why did Bismillah Khan refuse to start a shehnai school in the USA?

Ans. Bismillah Khan refused to start a shehnai school in the USA because he could not live outside India. The student promised that he would recreate the atmosphere of Benaras by duplicating the temples in the city. However, Bismillah Khan refused his offer by saying that he could not find the essence of Ganga there.

Q.7 Find at least two instances in the text which tell you that Bismillah Khan loves India and Benaras.

Ans. The first instance is when he turned down his student's offer to start a shehnai school in the USA.

The second instance is when he was asked why he had not shifted to Pakistan during partition. He said that he would never leave Benaras and Dumraon.

THINKING ABOUT LANGUAGE

(NCERT PAGE 26-27)

Look at these sentences.

- Evelyn was determined *to live a normal life.*
- Evelyn managed *to conceal her growing deafness from friends and teachers.*

The italicised parts answer the questions: "What was Evelyn determined to do?" and "What did Evelyn manage to do?" They begin with a to- verb *(to live, to conceal)*.

I. Complete the following sentences. Beginning with a to-verb, try to answer the questions in brackets.

Q.1 The school sports team hopes .... (What does it hope to do?)

Ans. to win the tournament.

Q.2 We all want ...... (What do we all want to do?).

Ans. to succeed.

Q.3 They advised the hearing-impaired child's mother .... (What did they advise her to do?)

Ans. to show her to a specialist.

Q.4 The authorities permitted us to .... (What did the authorities permit us to do?)

Ans. play.

Q.5 A musician decided to .... (What did the musician decide to do?)

Ans. play a new *raaga*.

II. From the text on Bismillah Khan, find the words and phrases that match these definitions and write them down. The number of the paragraph where you will find the words/phrases has been given for you in brackets.

Q.1 The home of royal people (1) ....

Ans. royal residence

Q.2 The state of being alone (5) ....

Ans. solitude

Q.3 A part which is absolutely necessary (2) ....

Ans. indispensable

Q.4 To do something not done before (5) ....

Ans. improvise

Q.5 Without much effort (13) ....

Ans. effortlessly

Q.6 quickly and in large quantities (9) .... and ....

Ans. thick, fast

III. Tick the right answer.

Q.1 When something is *revived*, it (remains dead/lives again).

Ans. lives again

Q.2 When a government *bans* something, it wants it (stopped/started).

Ans. stopped.

Q.3 When something is considered *auspicious*, (welcome it/avoid it).

Ans. welcome it

Q.4 When we *take to* something we find it (boring/interesting).

Ans. interesting

Q.5 When you *appreciate* something, you (find it good and useful/find it of no use).

Ans. find it good and useful

Q.6 When you *replicate* something, you do it (for the first time/for the second time).

Ans. for the second time

Q.7 When we *come to terms with* something, it is (still upsetting/no longer upsetting).

Ans. no longer upsetting

WRITING (NCERT PAGE 29)

Q.1 "If you work hard and know where you're going, you'll get there," says Evelyn Glennie.

You have now read about two musicians, Evelyn Glennie and Ustad Bismillah Khan. Do you think that they both worked hard? Where did they want to 'go'? Answer these questions in two paragraphs, one on each of the two musicians.

Ans. Both Evelyn Glennie and Ustad Bismillah Khan worked hard to achieve their goals.

Evelyn Glennie, renowned percussionist, and Ustad Bismillah Khan, legendary shehnai player, exemplify hard work and perseverance in their musical journeys. Evelyn Glennie's dedication to mastering percussion, despite her hearing impairment, demonstrates her commitment to her craft. She faced numerous challenges and barriers along the way but remained determined to pursue her passion for music. Her relentless work ethic and focus allowed her to break through societal barriers and establish herself as one of the most accomplished percussionists in the world. For Evelyn Glennie, 'getting there' meant not only achieving excellence in her musical endeavors but also challenging perceptions about disabilities and inspiring others to pursue their dreams regardless of obstacles.

Similarly, Ustad Bismillah Khan's life story is a testament to the power of hard work exemplified by a family of musicians; Khan displayed an innate talent for the shehnai from a young age. He devoted countless hours to practising and refining his skills, drawing inspiration from his surroundings, particularly the holy city of Benaras. Khan's aspiration was not just to master his instrument but to elevate the status of the shehnai and Indian classical music on the global stage. He achieved widespread acclaim through tireless efforts and became a cultural icon, earning accolades such as the Bharat Ratna, India's highest civilian award. For Khan, 'getting there' meant achieving personal success and preserving and promoting India's rich musical heritage for future generations to cherish.

REVIEW EXERCISE

Including Competency Based Questions

Part I

Multiple Choice Questions

1. Why did emperor Aurangzeb ban pungi?

(a) It had a shrill sound. (b) It was not good looking.
(c) Both (a) and (b) (d) None of these

Ans. (a) It had a shrill sound.

2. Pungi became the generic name for reeded ....

(a) noisemakers (b) musicians
(c) shehnai (d) All of these

Ans. (a) noisemakers

3. How did shehnai get its name?

(a) It was invented by a barber.
(b) It was played for the first time in king's court by a barber.
(c) It was played in the Royal Court.
(d) Both (a) and (b)

Ans. (b) It was played for the first time in king's court by a barber.

4. Shehnai is still played in .... and ....

(a) South, North Indian temples
(b) South, North Indian weddings
(c) temples, North Indian weddings
(d) inside, outside India

Ans. (c) temples, North Indian weddings

5. Bismillah would regularly go to the nearby .... to sing the Bhojpuri 'Chaita'.

(a) Vishnu temple (b) Mangal Maiya temple
(c) Bihariji temple (d) Balaji temple

Ans. (c) Bihariji temple

6. Who was Bismillah's grandfather?

(a) Great Islamic priest
(b) A famous barber in Dumraon
(c) King's courtier
(d) Shehnai Nawaz of the Bhojpur King's Court

Ans. (d) Shehnai Nawaz of the Bhojpur King's Court

7. Who was Ali Bux?

(i) Bismillah's maternal uncle.
(ii) Shehnai player at the Vishnu temple in Benares.
(iii) Accompany of Bismillah Khan.

(a) Only (i) is correct (b) (i) and (ii) are correct
(c) (ii) and (iii) are correct (d) All of these

Ans. (b) (i) and (ii) are correct

8. What was the source of inspiration for Bismillah for inventing new raagas?

(a) Red Fort (b) Royal Palaces
(c) Ganga Ghats (d) None of these

Ans. (c) Ganga Ghats

9. Who said the following to Bismillah – "Work hard and you shall make it."

(a) Ali Bux (b) Paigamber Bux
(c) Rasool Bux Khan (d) Ustad Faiyaz Khan

Ans. (d) Ustad Faiyaz Khan

10. On 15th August, 1947, which Raaga was played by Bismillah Khan from the Red Fort?

(a) Raaga Malhaar (b) Raaga Deepak
(c) Raaga Kafi (d) Raaga Megh

Ans. (c) Raaga Kafi

11. Who gave Bismillah precious Persian carpets and other gifts?

(a) King Aurangzeb (b) Bhojpur King
(c) King Zahir Shah (d) None of these

Ans. (c) King Zahir Shah

12. Which was the South Indian venture film of Bismillah Khan?

(a) Gunj Uthi Shehnai (b) Sanadhi Apanna
(c) Dil Ka Khilona Hai Toot Gaya
(d) None of the above

Ans. (b) Sanadhi Apanna

13. Bismillah Khan became the first Indian to be invited to perform at the prestigious .... in the United States of America.

(a) Lincoln Centre Hall (b) World Exposition
(c) Cannes Art Festival (d) Osaka Trade Fair

Ans. (a) Lincoln Centre Hall

14. Which of the following awards had been given to Bismillah Khan?

1. Padma Shri **2. Padma Bhushan**
3. Padma Vibhushan **4. Bharat Ratna**

(a) 1 and 3 (b) 2, 3 and 4
(c) 1, 2 and 4 (d) All of these

Ans. (d) All of these

15. Bismillah Khan was fondly called ....

(a) Ustad Sahab (b) Khansaab
(c) Bismillah saab (d) Ustad

Ans. (d) Ustad

Extract Based Questions

1. Read the following extract carefully and answer the questions that follow.

He chose a pipe with a natural hollow stem that was longer and broader than the *pungi*, and made seven holes on the body of the pipe. When he played on it, closing and opening some of these holes, soft and melodious sounds were produced. He played the instrument before royalty and everyone was impressed.

(i) Fill in the blank with one word only.
'He' in the given extract refers to a .... (singer/barber).

Ans. barber

(ii) What is the name of the new instrument?

Ans. The name of the new instrument was Shehnai.

(iii) Why was *pungi* banned from the court of Aurangzeb?

Ans. The *pungi* was banned from the court of Aurangzeb because it had a very unpleasant sound.

(iv) Select the option that correctly captures the application of the word 'impressed' as used in the extract.

(a) Impressed in his dreams , he went out doing his work.
(b) Impressed by his performance, the director fired him from his job.
(c) The minister impressed upon the need of building a new and modern India.
(d) Were you not impressed by his performance?

Ans. (d) Were you not impressed by his performance?

2. Read the following extract carefully and answer the questions that follow.

For years to come the temple of Balaji and Mangala Maiya and the banks of the Ganga became the young apprentice's favourite haunts where he could practise in solitude. The flowing waters of the Ganga inspired him to improvise and invent ragas that were earlier considered to be beyond the range of the Shehnai.

(i) Explain Ustad Bismillah Khan's relationship with the Ganga river.

Ans. For Ustad Bismillah Khan, the Ganga river was extremely important. As a young boy, he learned to play the shehnai at the banks of river Ganga. The flowing waters of the Ganga inspired him to invent many ragas. He found his mastery in Shehnai by Ganga's holy waters. He considers the holy Ganga an integral part of his home.

(ii) Which of the following statement is true?

(a) Bismillah is the young apprentice as he was learning to play Shehnai.
(b) Bismillah is very fond of the bank of river Ganges.
(c) Bismillah couldn't see himself away from the Indian landscape.
(d) All of the above

Ans. (d) All of the above

(iii) Where did Bismillah Khan practice as a young apprentice?

Ans. As a young apprentice, Bismillah Khan practiced at the temple of Balaji and Mangala Maiya and the bank of the Ganga.

(iv) Complete the sentence appropriately.
The given extract points out that Bismillah Khan was ....

Ans. passionate, skilled and creative

3. Read the following extract carefully and answer the questions that follow.

The sound of the shehnai began to be considered auspicious. And for this reason it is still played in temples and is an indispensable component of any North Indian wedding. In the past, the Shehnai was part of the naubat or traditional ensemble of nine instruments found at royal courts. Till recently it was used only in temples and weddings. The credit for bringing this instrument onto the classical stage goes to Ustad Bismillah Khan.

(i) Who invented the shehnai?

Ans. A barber of a family of professional musicians invented the shehnai.

(ii) Complete the analogy by selecting the suitable word from the text.
Traditional : Modern : : Ominous : ....

Ans. Auspicious

(iii) Select the option that correctly captures the usage of the word 'indispensable' as used in the extract.

(a) After the loss, Suman felt indispensable.
(b) Our freedom fighters played an indispensable role in making India independent.
(c) Pratick's indispensable attitude toward his seniors was not approved.
(d) What a indispensable shot!

Ans. (b) Our freedom fighters played on indispensable role in making India independent.

(iv) Why is Bismillah Khan credited for bringing shehnai onto the classical stage?

Ans. Bismillah Khan is credited for bringing shehnai onto the classical stage as he made the shehnai famous and invented *ragas* which were beyond the range of the shehnai.

4. Read the following extract carefully and answer the questions that follow.

A student of his once wanted him to head a Shehnai school in the U.S.A., and the student promised to recreate the atmosphere of Benaras by replicating the temples there. But Khansaab asked him if he would be able to transport river Ganga as well. Later, he is remembered to have said, "That is why whenever I am in a foreign country, I keep yearning to see Hindustan. While in Mumbai, I think of only Benaras and the holy Ganga. And while in Benaras, I miss the unique mattha of Dumraon."

(i) Complete the sentence appropriately.
The name given to Bismillah Khan is ....

Ans. Khansaab

(ii) State True or False.
None of the statements are true according to the given extract.

(a) Bismillah Khan's popularity had spread worldwide.
(b) Bismillah Khan grew up in Benaras.
(c) Bismillah Khan always had the river Ganga in his memory.

Ans. False

(iii) How did the students promise to recreate the atmosphere of Benaras?

(a) By recreating the Indian landscape with the flora and fauna artificially.
(b) By constructing temples like that in Benaras.
(c) By creating an artificial river to replicate Ganga.
(d) All of the above

Ans. (b) By constructing temples like that in Benaras.

(iv) How did Khansaab counter the request made by the student?

Ans. The student promised to recreate the temples of Benaras for Khansaab but the latter countered the request by asking the student if it would be possible for the student to recreate the flow of the Ganga as well.

Short Answer Type Questions

1. Where did the shehnai get its due place and why?

Ans. The shehnai got its due place in temples and in weddings, as its sound was considered auspicious.

In the past, it had a place in the traditional group of nine musical instruments at the royal courts.
It is an indispensable part of any North Indian wedding.

2. Describe Bismillah Khan's family members.

Ans. The family members of Bismillah Khan were well known musicians. His grandfather, Rasool Bux Khan, played the shehnai in the Bhojpur king's court. His father, Paigambar Bux and other paternal ancestors were also great shehnai players.

3. How did Bismillah get the first lesson in the playing of the shehnai?

Ans. Bismillah got the first lesson in playing the shehnai by accompanying his maternal uncle Ali Bux, who visited the Vishnu temple at Benaras to play the *shehnai*. In his company, young Bismillah was captivated and inspired to practice the instrument.

4. What did Ustad Faiyaz Khan say to Bismillah?

Ans. Ustad Faiyaz Khan patted Bismillah on his back and asked him to work hard. He encouraged Bismillah by saying that he had the ability to succeed in the field of music.

Part II

5. Where was Bismillah's first journey to abroad? What impact did it leave there?

Ans. Bismillah's first journey abroad was to Afghanistan. Bismillah's performance there impressed the king of Afghanistan so much that the king gifted him many of his priceless Persian carpets and other things.

6. What did Bismillah say after getting the Bharat Ratna award?

Ans. After getting the Bharat Ratna, Bismillah said that Indians should value their music and teach it to their kids. Indian music is so rich that the West is now learning this art. This was a word of encouragement for the youngsters.

7. Which were the most beautiful towns for Bismillah Khan? Why?

Ans. The most beautiful towns for Bismillah Khan were Benaras and Dumraon.

Bismillah grew up in these two towns and developed a life-long attachment towards them, particularly to the Ganga and the unique 'Mattha' of Dumraon. He learned music in these places, therefore these towns remained the most beautiful towns for him.

8. What does Bismillah Khan's life exemplify about India's cultural diversity?

Ans. Bismillah Khan's life epitomises India's cultural richness. It highlights how a devout Muslim seamlessly integrated into Hindu traditions by playing in the Vishwanath temple, showcasing India's inclusive ethos.

Long Answer Type Questions

1. Naming of the shehnai has a story behind it. What values are associated with this naming?

Ans. Emperor Aurangzeb banned the playing of the *pungi* in his royal court because it had a very loud and unpleasant sound. After some time, a barber from a family of professional musicians decided to revive the pungi.

He chose a longer and broader pipe and made a few holes on its body. When he played on this pipe by opening and closing the holes, it produced a very melodious sound. As it was invented in the court of the *shah* (king) by a *nai* (barber), it got the name *shehnai*. Therefore, the barber revived a musical instrument that was considered a noisemaker.

This reflects the idea that with a positive mindset even noisemakers can be turned into melodious instruments. It is all about the creativity, determination and understanding. The barber had all those values and therefore, we still have the pungi with us in the form of the shehnai.

2. Ustad Bismillah Khan emerges as a figure of immense talent, dedication, and humility through the biographical piece. Comment.

Ans. Ustad Bismillah Khan emerges as a figure of immense talent, dedication and humility through the biographical piece. The article displayed Bismillah's natural talent for music from a young age. His fascination with the shehnai, influenced by his family's musical background, led him to become a master of the instrument. His ability to evoke melodic tunes and improvise ragas showcased his innate musical prowess.

Bismillah Khan's contributions extended beyond his musical talents. He pivotally elevates the shehnai from its traditional settings in temples and weddings to the classical stage. His performances captivated audiences in India and garnered international acclaim.

Despite his fame and accolades, Bismillah Khan remained humble and deeply connected to his roots. His refusal to leave his beloved Benaras exemplifies his attachment to his homeland and traditional values.

Thus, Ustad Bismillah Khan emerges as a multifaceted character-a musical genius, dedicated apprentice, cultural ambassador, humble individual, spiritual devotee, and patriotic citizen-all woven together to create a remarkable legacy in the history of Indian classical music.

3. Despite coming from different cultural backgrounds and musical traditions, Evelyn Glennie and Ustad Bismillah Khan shared similarities in their lives and careers. Elucidate.

Ans. Despite coming from different cultural backgrounds and musical traditions, Evelyn Glennie and Ustad Bismillah Khan shared similarities in their lives and careers. First, both musicians faced significant challenges and obstacles on their respective paths to success. Evelyn Glennie, who has been deaf since the age of twelve, encountered doubts about her ability to pursue a music career. Similarly, Ustad Bismillah Khan, born into a modest family in Bihar, had to overcome financial constraints and societal expectations to establish himself as a renowned shehnai player.

Second, Evelyn Glennie and Ustad Bismillah Khan displayed remarkable dedication and commitment to their craft. They devoted countless hours to practising and refining their skills.

Despite facing setbacks and challenges, they remained focused on their goals, driven by a passion for music and a desire to excel in their art. Both musicians achieved international acclaim and recognition for their contributions to the music world. Evelyn Glennie's innovative approach to percussion and ability to transcend barriers of perception earned her widespread admiration and accolades on the global stage.

Similarly, Ustad Bismillah Khan's mastery of the shehnai and his unique improvisational style captivated audiences both in India and abroad, earning him prestigious awards and honours.

While Evelyn Glennie and Ustad Bismillah Khan hailed from different backgrounds and musical traditions, their lives were united by their unwavering dedication, perseverance in the face of adversity, and remarkable achievements in music.

ASSESSMENT EXERCISE

Extract Based Questions

Read the following extract and answer the questions that follow.

"The sound of the shehnai began to be considered auspicious. And for this reason it is still played in temples and is an indispensable component of any North Indian wedding. In the past, the shehnai was part of the '*naubat*' or traditional ensemble of nine instruments found at royal concerts. Till recently it was used only in temples and weddings. The credit for bringing this instrument onto the classical stage goes to Ustad Bismillah Khan."

(i) Fill in the blank with one word only.

.... is still played in temples in India.

(ii) The word 'ensemble' in the extract means

(a) a group of people who perform music together.

(b) a group of birds who sit together.

(c) a group of items in a museum.

(d) a group of things intended to be used together.

(iii) State True or False.

The set of statements is not true according to the given extract.

1. The sound of shehnai is considered inauspicious.
2. Shehnai was part of the 'naubat'.
3. Shehnai is still played in any North Indian wedding.

(iv) What is *'naubat'* as defined in the extract?

Short Answer (SA) Type Questions

1. How can it be said that Bismillah Khan's success was due to his hard work?
2. How and where did Bismillah get fascinated with the shehnai?

Long Answer (LA) Type Questions

1. How did Bismillah Khan raise the level of the shehnai? What does it show about his love for music?
2. Justify the title of the chapter 'The Sound of Music'.

CHAPTER 3

The Little Girl

by Katherine Mansfield

CHAPTER SUMMARY The chapter 'The Little Girl' written by Katherine Mansfield describes the relationship between a strict father and his sensitive daughter (Kezia). The father wants his daughter to be a good girl and beats her when she does something wrong. So, Kezia is very afraid of her father and avoids him. However, at the end of the story, Kezia's perception about her father changes when her mother gets hospitalised and she is left alone at home. At this time, her father takes care of Kezia with love and sympathy. She finds that her father loves her and hence, she develops affection for him.

Kezia is Afraid of her Father

The little girl, Kezia was afraid of her father. She always avoided meeting him. Before going to the office, his father would go to Kezia's room and give her a casual kiss. Kezia always felt a sense of relief when her father went out to work. In the evening, when Kezia's father would come home, her mother would call Kezia to take off father's shoes. While Kezia took off her father's shoes, he asked her if she had been a good girl that day. Kezia used to stammer in front of her father whereas with others she used to talk normally. Kezia thought that her father was like a giant. He had big hands and neck. His mouth appeared very big to her when he yawned.

Incident on Sunday Afternoon

On Sunday afternoons, Kezia's grandmother would send her to the drawing room to have a talk with her parents. Kezia would always find her mother reading and her father sleeping on the sofa.

Her father had a handkerchief on his face, he put his feet on the cushion and snored while he slept. Kezia kept waiting for her father to wake up. After waking up, Kezia's father asked her not to stare at him as she looked like a little brown owl while staring.

Kezia Makes a Birthday Gift for her Father

One day, Kezia had a cold and she was resting at home. Her grandmother told her that her father's birthday was coming the following week. She suggested Kezia to make a pin-cushion of yellow silk as a gift for her father.

Kezia made a pin-cushion by stitching three sides. Now, she needed something to fill in the pin-cushion. So, she went into her mother's bedroom and found some papers on the table. She tore those papers and stuffed them into the pin-cushion. The paper contained an important speech that her father had to deliver for the Port Authority the next day.

Kezia gets Punished and the Reactions

Kezia's father was very angry when he could not find the papers containing his speech. Everyone in the house was questioned about the papers. When Kezia was asked, she told that she had torn up the papers and stuffed them into the pin-cushion. So, Kezia's father punished her by hitting her palms with a ruler. He wanted to teach Kezia not to touch anything that did not belong to her.

Kezia cried a lot. After a few hours, her grandmother wrapped Kezia in a shawl. Kezia was very disturbed about the incident of getting punished by her father. Her grandmother calmed Kezia and sent her to sleep. However, Kezia never forgot the punishment and always hid her hands when she saw her father.

Kezia's Neighbours : The Macdonalds

The Macdonalds had five children and they lived in the house next to Kezia. Mr. Macdonalds always played with his children when he was free. They laughed and enjoyed each other's company. Seeing all this, Kezia realised that there were different kinds of fathers.

Kezia's Nightmare

One day, Kezia's mother fell ill and had to be hospitalised. Her grandmother went to the hospital with her mother. Kezia was alone in the house with the cook, Alice and her father who was sleeping in his room. Kezia was not comfortable sleeping alone at night as she used to have nightmares.

While sleeping, Kezia had a frightful nightmare. In the nightmare, she saw a butcher with a knife and a rope, smiling and coming nearer to her. She was unable to move and was crying calling her grandmother.

Kezia Changes her Opinion about her Father

Kezia screamed and woke her father up. Her father took Kezia in his arms to his bedroom. He lied down beside her to comfort her and asked Kezia to rub her feet against his legs to get warmth.

While he slept, Kezia felt comfortable and noticed that although father's body was harder than grandmother's, it was still nice. Then, Kezia realised that her father had to work very hard all day and would get too tired to play with her like Mr. Macdonalds. She felt sorry for tearing his papers. She told her father that he had a very big heart.

Word Meaning

Word	Meaning
pull off	remove
casual	without any feeling
fainter	lesser
slip down	move noiselessly
stutter	having difficulty in talking
wretched	miserable
on the brink of	about to commit
stretched out	lying down with hands and legs spread out
soundly	deeply
cushions	pillows
snoring	making a snorting sound while sleeping
gravely	seriously
kept indoors	not allowed to go outside the house.
pin-cushion	a small pad for holding pins
laboriously	with much time and effort
stuffed	filled
wandered	walked around aimlessly
hue and cry	angry protest
port authority	the office of the port
this instant	immediately
suggested	proposed
double cotton	thick cotton

Word	Meaning
fetch	to go and bring
pacing	moving fast
damned thing	refers to the pin-cushion here
shadowed	poorly lighted
sad little pattern	light and shade pattern making a person feel sad
sorts	types
hold out	bring out
once and for all	now and for the last time
wrapped	covered
sobbed	cried noisily
flew into	appeared on
hose	pipe
clung	held tightly
nightmare	a frightening dream
whispery	scary
still	silent
blew out	extinguished
stirred	moved slightly
butcher	a person who kills animals for their flesh
tucked up	covered up properly in bed
snuggled	moved into a comfortable position

NCERT FOLDER

NCERT Intext and Exercise Questions

THINKING ABOUT THE TEXT (NCERT PAGE 38)

I. Given below are some emotions that Kezia felt. Match the emotions in Column A with the items in Column B.

A	B
1. Fear or terror	(i) father comes into her room to give her a goodbye kiss
2. Glad sense of relief	(ii) noise of the carriage grows fainter
3. A 'funny' feeling, perhaps of understanding	(iii) father comes home
	(iv) speaking to father
	(v) going to bed when alone at home
	(vi) father comforts her and falls asleep
	(vii) father stretched out on the sofa, snoring

Ans.

A	B
1. Fear or terror	(i) father comes into her room to give her a goodbye kiss (iii) father comes home (iv) speaking to father (v) going to bed when alone at home (vii) father stretched out on the sofa, snoring
2. Glad sense of relief	(ii) noise of the carriage grows fainter
3. A 'funny' feeling, perhaps of understanding	(vi) father comforts her and falls asleep

II. Answer the following questions in one or two sentences.

Q.1 Why was Kezia afraid of her father?

Ans. Kezia was afraid of her father due to his authoritarian and intimidating behaviour. He used physical punishment, such as threatening to beat her with a ruler, and exhibited a harsh demeanour, causing fear and unease in their interactions.

Q.2 Who were the people in Kezia's family?

Ans. Kezia's family consisted of her mother, father, grandmother and herself.

Q.3 What was Kezia's father's routine
(i) before going to his office?
(ii) after coming back from his office?
(iii) on Sundays?

Ans. (i) Before going to his office, Kezia's father usually went into Kezia's room to give her a casual kiss.

(ii) After coming back from his office, he ordered for tea to be brought into the drawing-room. He also ordered to bring newspaper and his slippers.

(iii) On Sundays, Kezia's father would sleep on the sofa. He would cover his face with his handkerchief, put his feet on the cushion and snore while sleeping.

Q.4 In what ways did Kezia's grandmother encourage her to get to know her father better?

Ans. Kezia's grandmother encouraged her to get to know her father better by sending her to the drawing-room to talk to her parents on Sunday afternoons. She also suggested that Kezia should make a pin-cushion out of a beautiful piece of yellow silk as a gift for her father's birthday.

III. Discuss these questions in class with your teacher and then write down your answers in two or three paragraphs each.

Q.1 Kezia's efforts to please her father resulted in displeasing him very much. How did this happen?

Ans. Kezia's efforts to please her father always resulted in displeasing him very much.

The first effort Kezia made to please her father was on a Sunday afternoon when her grandmother sent her to the drawing-room to have a talk with her parents. However, Kezia's presence irritated her father because he found Kezia staring at him when he woke up.

The next effort that Kezia made to please her father was when her grandmother suggested her to make a pin-cushion as a birthday gift for her father. Kezia made the pin-cushion by stitching the three sides. However, she could not find anything to stuff it with. When she found some papers on her mother's bedroom-table, she tore them into pieces and filled the cushion with them.

She did not know that those papers had her father's speech that was to be delivered for the Port Authority the next day. Her father was very angry when he came to know that Kezia had torn up his speech. He punished her by hitting her palms with a ruler for touching things that did not belong to her.

Q.2 Kezia decides that there are "different kinds of fathers." What kind of father was Mr. Macdonald and how was he different from Kezia's father?

Ans. Kezia compared her father with Mr. Macdonald, who lived next door with their five children. Mr. Macdonald was a loving, gentle and forgiving father. Whenever she looked at their house, she saw that he was always smiling and playing with his children. He treated his children in a friendly manner. Unlike Kezia's father, he never punished his children. He played with them whenever he was free.

On the other hand, Kezia's father was very harsh. He was a strict disciplanarian. He was busy in his work and never had time for Kezia. He never expressed his concern or affection for Kezia and never played with her. He also punished her. Due to all this, Kezia was afraid of her father and avoided him.

By comparing her father with Mr. Macdonald, she realised that there were different kinds of fathers.

Q.3 How does Kezia begin to see her father as a human being who needs her sympathy?

Ans. When Kezia's mother fell ill, Kezia's grandmother accompanied her to the hospital. Kezia was left alone with the cook, Alice. At night, she had a nightmare, wherein she saw a butcher with a knife and rope. Her father was sleeping in his room. When Kezia screamed, her father woke up. He took Kezia into his room and lay beside her to give her comfort.

Her father asked Kezia to rub her feet against his legs to get warmth. Soon, her father fell asleep as he was tired. It was then that Kezia realised that her father had to work hard every day and would get too tired to play with her like Mr. Macdonald. Despite his intimidating demeanour during waking hours, seeing him asleep shifts her perception. She empathises with his fatigue and responsibilities, acknowledging his hardships and the burden of his role. This realisation fosters a sense of understanding and compassion towards her father, leading to a more nuanced and empathetic view of him as a person with his challenges and emotions.

In this way, Kezia began to see her father as a human being who needs her sympathy.

THINKING ABOUT LANGUAGE

(NCERT PAGE 38-39)

I. Look at the following sentence.

There was a *glad* sense of relief when she heard the noise of the carriage growing fainter...

Here, *glad* means happy about something. *Glad*, *happy*, *pleased*, *delighted*, *thrilled* and *overjoyed* are synonyms (words or expressions that have the same or nearly the same meaning). However, they express happiness in certain ways.

Read the sentences below.

- She was *glad* when the meeting was over.
- The chief guest was *pleased* to announce the name of the winner.

Q.1 Use an appropriate word from the synonyms given above in the following sentences. Clues are given in brackets.

(i) She was .... by the news of her brother's wedding. (very pleased)

(ii) I was .... to be invited to the party. (extremely pleased and excited about)

(iii) She was .... at the birth of her granddaughter. (extremely happy)

(iv) The coach was .... with his performance. (satisfied about)

(v) She was very .... with her results. (happy about something that has happened)

Ans. (i) thrilled (ii) delighted (iii) overjoyed (iv) pleased (v) happy

Q.2 Study the use of the word *big* in the following sentence.

He was so *big* — his hands and his neck, especially his mouth...

Here, *big* means *large in size*.

Now, consult a dictionary and find out the meaning of *big* in the following sentences. The first one has been done for you.

(i) You are a big girl now. (*older*)

(ii) Today you are going to take the biggest decision of your career.

(iii) Their project is full of big ideas.

(iv) Cricket is a big game in our country.

(v) I am a big fan of Lata Mangeshkar.

(vi) You have to cook a bit more as my friend is a big eater.

(vii) What a big heart you've got, father dear.

Ans. (ii) most important (iii) innovative (iv) popular (v) great (vi) great (vii) generous

II. Verbs of Reporting

Study the following sentences.

- "What!" *screamed* mother.
- "N-n-no", she *whispered*.
- "Sit up," he *ordered*.

The italicised words are verbs of reporting. We quote or report what someone has said or thought by using a reporting verb. Every reporting clause contains a reporting verb. e.g.

- He *promised* to help in my project.
- "How are you doing?" Seema *asked*.

We use verbs of reporting to advise, order, report statements, thoughts, intentions, questions, requests, apologies, manner of speaking and so on.

Q.1 Underline the verbs of reporting in the following sentences.

(i) He says he will enjoy the ride.
(ii) Father mentioned that he was going on a holiday.
(iii) No one told us that the shop was closed.
(iv) He answered that the price would go up.
(v) I wondered why he was screaming.
(vi) Ben told her to wake him up.
(vii) Ratan apologised for coming late to the party.

Ans. (i) says
(ii) mentioned
(iii) told
(iv) answered
(v) wondered
(vi) told
(vii) apologised

Q.2 Some verbs of reporting are given in the box. Choose the appropriate verbs and fill in the blanks in the following sentences.

were complaining	shouted	replied
ordered	suggested	remarked

(i) "I am not afraid," .... the woman.
(ii) "Leave me alone," my mother ....
(iii) The children ....that the roads were crowded and noisy.
(iv) "Perhaps he isn't a bad sort of a chap after all," .... the master.
(v) "Let's go and look at the school ground," .... the sports teacher.
(vi) The traffic police .... all the passers-by to keep off the road.

Ans. (i) replied
(ii) shouted
(iii) were complaining
(iv) remarked
(v) suggested
(vi) ordered

WRITING (NCERT PAGE 40)

Q.1 Has your life been different from or similar to that of Kezia when you were a child? Has your perception about your parents changed now? Do you find any change in your parents' behaviour vis-à-vis yours? Who has become more understanding? What steps would you like to take to build a relationship based on understanding? Write three or four paragraphs (150-200 words) discussing these issues from your own experience.

Ans. Do it yourself.

REVIEW EXERCISE

Including Competency Based Questions

Part I

Multiple Choice Questions

1. "To the little girl he was a figure to be feared and avoided" who is being referred as 'he' in the given line?

(a) Kezia's cook Alice
(b) Kezia's father
(c) Kezia's grandfather
(d) None of these

Ans. (b) Kezia's father

2. When did Kezia use to feel a sense of relief?

(a) When her father went out to work.
(b) When her father used to kiss her goodbye.
(c) When her father talked to her.
(d) All of the above

Ans. (a) When her father went out to work.

3. Who said the following line, "If you're a good girl you can come down and take off father's boots"?

(a) Kezia's grandmother
(b) Kezia's father
(c) Kezia's mother
(d) Kezia's maid

Ans. (c) Kezia's mother

4. Why does Kezia say she stutters in front of her father? Competency Based

(a) She wished to please her father
(b) She was not a confident person
(c) She was only learning how to speak
(d) She did not like doing chores for her father

Ans. (a) She wished to please her father

5. 'Mother, I wish you taught this child not to appear on the brink of suicide...' What is the father's tone in the line above? Competency Based

(a) Distressed (b) Mocking
(c) Haughty (d) Livid

Ans. (b) Mocking

6. Which word can best describe the relationship between Kezia and her parents? Competency Based

(a) Cold (b) Formal
(c) Passive (d) Strained

Ans. (b) Formal

7. Where was Kezia's grandmother when she went into mother's bedroom to find stuffing for her cushion?

(a) In the kitchen (b) In the garden
(c) She was sleeping (d) She was not at home

Ans. (b) In the garden

8. Grandmother's actions show that she probably.... Competency Based

(a) wanted Kezia to be more disciplined
(b) believed that Kezia needed a hobby
(c) believed that father did not like Kezia
(d) wanted Kezia to grow closer to her parents

Ans. (d) wanted Kezia to grow closer to her parents

9. For whom did father write that speech?

(a) For his office colleague (b) For the President
(c) For the Port Authority (d) None of the above

Ans. (c) For the Port Authority

10. The incident with Father's speech suggests that Kezia was Competency Based

(a) curious (b) indifferent
(c) ambiguous (d) overwhelmed

Ans. (a) curious

11. What feelings did the Macdonalds invoke in Kezia? Competency Based

(a) Resentment (b) Nostalgia (c) Longing (d) Disdain

Ans. (c) Longing

12. Why did Kezia decide that there were different sorts of fathers?

(a) Because her father was very strict.
(b) Because she saw jovial Mr. Macdonalds playing with his children.
(c) Because Mr. Macdonalds used to play with Kezia.
(d) None of the above

Ans. (b) Because she saw jovial Mr. Macdonalds playing with his children.

13. What did Kezia mean by saying 'it all gets 'whispery'...'?

(a) She used to hear scary voices while sleeping.
(b) She used to have nightmares while sleeping.
(c) She was just making excuses to stay awake till late.
(d) Both (a) and (b)

Ans. (d) Both (a) and (b)

14. What nightmare did Kezia have?

(a) A giant with a knife.
(b) A butcher with a knife and rope.
(c) An accident across the countryside.
(d) A dreadful smile of the Macdonalds.

Ans. (b) A butcher with a knife and rope.

15. In the end, Kezia felt that

(a) her father is a very strict person.
(b) her father had a big heart.
(c) her father was not like Mr. Macdonalds.
(d) her father did not love her

Ans. (b) her father had a big heart.

Extract Based Questions

1. Read the following extract carefully and answer the questions that follow.

"What's the matter? What are you looking so wretched about? Mother, I wish you taught this child not to appear on the brink of suicide... Here, Kezia, carry my teacup back to the table carefully." He was so big his hands and his neck, especially his mouth when he yawned. Thinking about him alone was 'like thinking' about a giant.

(i) Which word can replace the underlined word in the given sentence.

India was on the point of losing the match when Sachin came to bat.

Ans. 'brink'

(ii) The statement that is true regarding the person referred in the above extract as per Kezia is

(a) Kezia wasn't attached to that person.
(b) he gave her appropriate attention.
(c) he didn't pamper Kezia like her grandmother does.
(d) Both (a) and (c)

Ans. (d) Both (a) and (c)

(iii) What did the man instruct Kezia to do?

Ans. The man, (Kezia's father) instructed her to keep the tea cup carefully on the table.

(iv) How does the little girl perceive her father's presence in her life?

Ans. The little girl perceives her father as a figure to be feared and avoided, with his morning kisses signalling a departure she welcomes. His authoritative demands and stern demeanour create a sense of unease and apprehension for her, making his presence something to be endured rather than enjoyed.

2. Read the following extract carefully and answer the questions that follow.

Laboriously, with a double cotton, the little girl stitched three sides. But what to fill it with? That was the question. The grandmother was out in the garden and she wandered into mother's bedroom to look for scraps. On the bed-table she discovered a great many sheets of fine paper, gathered them up, tore them into tiny pieces and stuffed her case, then sewed up the fourth side.

(i) Why was Kezia searching for scraps?

Ans. Kezia was searching for scraps to fill the pin-up cushion.

(ii) What did the fine sheets of paper contain?

Ans. The fine sheets of paper contained her father's speech.

(iii) What did Kezia fill the cushion with and where did she find the said material for it? Why were her actions wrong?

Ans. Kezia filled the cushion with papers which she found on her mother's table. Her actions were wrong because she used something that belonged to someone else (her father). In her innocence, she destroyed something important.

(iv) How did Kezia's father react on finding his torn speech?

(a) Disappointed (b) Angry
(c) Sad (d) Regretful

Ans. (b) Angry

3. Read the following extract carefully and answer the questions that follow.

That night there was a hue and cry in the house. Father's great speech for the Port Authority had been lost. Rooms were searched; servants questioned. Finally Mother came into Kezia's room. "Kezia, I suppose you didn't see some papers on a table in our room?" "Oh yes," she said, "I tore them up for my surprise." "What!" screamed Mother. "Come straight down to the dining-room this instant." And she was dragged down to where Father was pacing to and fro, hands behind his back.

(i) Fill in the blank with one word only.

Kezia's father punished her by hitting her hands with a .... (stick/ruler).

Ans. ruler

(ii) What did grandmother do when Kezia was crying?

Ans. Kezia's grandmother wrapped the crying Kezia in a shawl and rocked her in a rocking chair.

(iii) State True or False.

The following statements are not true in accordance with the passage.

1. Kezia's wanted her father to be like Mr. Macdonalds.
2. Kezia was afraid of her father.
3. Kezia's grandmother used to console Kezia.

Ans. False

(iv) Why did Kezia tear her father's speech?

Ans. Kezia tore her father's speech because she wanted to fill it in the cushion which was a birthday surprise for her father.

4. Read the following extract carefully and answer the questions that follow.

And she was dragged down to where father was pacing to and fro, hands behind his back. 'Well'? He said sharply. Mother explained. He stopped and stared at the child. "Did you do that?" 'N-No,' she whispered.

(i) Why was 'she' dragged?

Ans. She was dragged because she had torn the important papers that had her father's speech.

(ii) The statement that is true about the incidence discussed in the above extract is.

(a) Kezia didn't tear the papers.
(b) Grandmother encouraged her to tear the papers.
(c) Father wanted to enquire if Kezia had torn the papers.
(d) Kezia was never afraid of her father.

Ans. (c) Father wanted to enquire if Kezia had torn the papers.

(iii) What was father doing when Kezia was brought to him?

Ans. He was pacing to and fro, angrily, when Kezia was brought before him.

(iv) What was the mother trying to explain to the father?

Ans. The mother was trying to explain to the father that Kezia tore the papers to fill in the pin cushion.

5. Read the following extract carefully and answer the questions that follow.

The Macdonalds lived next door. They had five children. Looking through a gap in the fence the little girl saw them playing 'tag' in the evening. The father with the baby, Mao, on his shoulders, two little girls hanging on his coat pockets ran around the flower-beds, shaking with laughter. Once she saw the boys turn the pose on him and he tried to catch them laughing all the time. Then she decided that there were different sorts of fathers.

(i) How was the relation of the little girl with her father?

Ans. The little girl was scared of her father.

(ii) How would you describe the scene that the little girl saw?

Ans. The scene that the little girl witnessed was a joyful one filled with laughter and smiles.

(iii) Choose the option that lists the set of statements that are not true according to the given extract.

1. Little girl was afraid of her father.
2. Little girl didn't want to stay with her father.
3. Little girl always admired her father for his good behaviour.
4. Little girl wanted her father to be like Macdonald's father.
5. Her father was a fun-loving person.
6. Both father and daughter had a strong bond as they shared everything.

(a) 2, 3, 4 (b) 1, 2, 4
(c) 3, 5, 6 (d) 4, 5, 6

Ans. (c) 3, 5, 6

(iv) What did Kezia infer after watching the Macdonalds play together?

Ans. Kezia inferred that there were different kinds of fathers when she saw the Macdonalds playing together.

Part II

Short Answer Type Questions

1. Describe Kezia's father as she sees him.

Or What kind of a person was Kezia's father?

Ans. Kezia saw her father as a hard-working but short-tempered man. He was a strict disciplinarian. He could not spend much time with Kezia as he had a busy schedule. However, he cared for his family and took care of Kezia when she needed it the most.

2. How does the father interact with the little girl?

Ans. The father interacts with the little girl authoritatively, assigning tasks and criticising her speech. His questioning of her behaviour and harsh response to her efforts to please him foster an atmosphere of fear and tension between them, with his presence becoming as a source of anxiety.

3. What is the little girl's relationship with her father like during childhood?

Ans. During her childhood, the little girl's relationship with her father is filled with tension and misunderstanding. She struggles to meet his expectations but is criticised and punished. Her father's imposing presence and strict demeanour create a sense of distance and fear rather than warmth and affection.

4. What orders were passed to Kezia in the evening when father returned home from office?

Ans. The orders passed to Kezia in the evening when father returned home from office were to go down in the drawing room, take off her father's shoes and put them outside. She was also ordered to put her father's tea cup on the tea table.

5. Give one likely reason why Kezia stammered only with her father?

Ans. Kezia stammered only with her father because she was afraid of her father and felt nervous in front of him. She tried very hard to say the words properly.

6. What suggests that Kezia's father was a large man? **Competency Based**

Ans. Kezia's descriptions of her father suggest that he was a large man. Kezia describes that his neck, hands and mouth were very big. Thinking about him alone in a room made her think about a giant.

7. Why did Kezia's grandmother send her to the drawing-room on Sunday afternoons? How did she find her parents there?

Or What did Kezia find whenever her grandmother sent her down to have a talk with her parents on Sunday afternoons?

Ans. On Sunday afternoons, Kezia's grandmother sent her down to the drawing-room to have a nice talk with father and mother so that Kezia would get to know them better. However, Kezia always found her mother reading and her father sleeping on the sofa.

8. Why was Kezia severely punished by her father?

Or What made Kezia's father punish her?

Or What was father's intent when he beat Kezia? **Competency Based**

Ans. Kezia was severely punished by her father because she had torn up his papers which contained an important speech written by him.

She tore those papers into small pieces and used them to fill the pin-cushion that she was making as a birthday gift for her father.

9. How does the little girl perceive other fathers compared to her own?

Ans. The little girl perceives other fathers, such as the McDonald's father, as more caring and affectionate than her own. Observing their playful interactions and evident love for their children, she contrasts her father's sternness and lack of emotional connection with other fathers. This leads her to recognise the different kinds of fatherhood.

10. Describe the nightmare that Kezia had seen.

Ans. Kezia saw a butcher carrying a knife and a rope in her nightmare. He had a frightening smile and was coming nearer to Kezia.
She got so scared of him that she was unable to move and cried for her grandmother to help.

11. Where was Grannie on the night that Kezia slept on father's bed? Competency Based

Ans. On the night that Kezia slept in her father's bed, her granny was in the hospital. She was staying with Kezia's mother who had fallen sick and had been admitted to the hospital.

12. How did the father comfort the little girl, Kezia, when she got scared in her sleep?

Ans. Her father comforted the little girl, Kezia, when she got scared in her sleep by taking Kezia with him to his room. He lay down beside her to comfort her and asked her to rub her feet against his legs to get warmth.

13. 'Kezia was fond of her grandmother.' Validate the given statement by giving suitable reasons.

Ans. Kezia was fond of her grandmother because her father and mother had no time for her. Grandmother loved Kezia and was always very warm towards her. She was the only companion of Kezia.

14. A funny feeling came over her. What was the funny feeling? Competency Based

Ans. The funny feeling that overcame Kezia was the empathy as she understood her father's true nature for the first time. She realised that her father was not a scary monster and that his presence could defeat her fear of the dark.

She realised that he loved her and that he would always protect her. She also understood that her father worked really hard everyday and therefore he could not play with her in the way that Mr. Macdonald did with his children.

15. How does the little girl reconcile her father's shortcomings with his acts of kindness?

Ans. The little girl learns to see beyond her father's faults and focus on his acts of kindness and protection. Despite his shortcomings and moments of harshness, she acknowledges his efforts to comfort and support her, fostering a sense of gratitude and connection towards him.

16. hy does the little girl feel intimidated by her father's size and mannerisms, particularly when he yawns? Competency Based

Ans. The little girl is intimidated by/ scared of her father's size and commanding presence. His yawning, a seemingly mundane action, magnifies his physical dominance and reinforces her sense of smallness and vulnerability in his presence. His large stature and authoritative demeanour make her perceive him as formidable, evoking feelings of unease and intimidation.

Long Answer Type Questions

1. Why was Kezia punished by her father? Do you think Kezia deserved this? What should her father have done instead?

Ans. Kezia was punished by her father as she had unknowingly torn his important papers. She was making a pin-cushion as a gift for her father on his birthday. As she did not have anything to fill in the pin-cushion, she tore the papers that she found on her mother's bedroom table and used them to fill the pin-cushion. Her father was very angry with Kezia when he came to know this.
This was because he had written an important speech on those papers which he had to deliver at the Port Authority. So, he punished Kezia by beating her with a ruler.
No, Kezia did not deserve this punishment. She did not have any bad intention. As she had torn the papers unknowingly, her father should not have been so harsh with her. He should have made her understand in a loving manner that she should not touch anything that does not belong to her. This would have done a lot of good instead of beating her for something she did unknowingly.

2. Is the title of the story 'The Little Girl' appropriate? Discuss.

Ans. The title of the story 'The Little Girl' is very much appropriate as the story revolves around Kezia. It is told from the point of view of the little girl, Kezia and she remains in focus throughout the story. All the characters in the story are seen from Kezia's eyes.
Kezia looks upon her father as a busy, strict, unkind and short-tempered person. She is scared of him and as a result avoids his company.
She even comes to the conclusion that her father is different from other fathers when one day she notices Mr. Macdonald (her neighbour) playing with his children. She finds her grandmother warm and caring and is never hesitant to convey her feelings to her. Later, Kezia herself realises that her father is loving and caring in reality. He behaved harshly and was not able to spend much time with her as he was always overburdened with work. The whole story describes the feelings of the little girl, Kezia, very aptly. Hence, we can say that the title of the story 'The Little Girl' is appropriate.

3. How does the little girl express her newfound appreciation for her father, and what observation does she make about his character and responsibilities?

Ans. The little girl expresses her newfound appreciation for her father by acknowledging his actions and character. She remarks on the enormity of his heart, symbolically recognising his capacity for love and care. Additionally, she observes his daily responsibilities and their toll on him, realising the sacrifices he makes for the family.

Despite his strictness, she acknowledges her father's efforts to provide and protect. She understands the weight of his role as a father. Through these observations, she demonstrates a deeper understanding and gratitude for her father's presence and contributions to their family, fostering a more mature and empathetic perspective on their relationship.

4. How does the little girl's perception of her father change from the beginning to the end of the story, and what factors contribute to this transformation?

Ans. At the story's beginning, the little girl perceives her father as a figure to be feared and avoided. She found her father's presence in the household as imposing and intimidating. His authoritative demeanour instills fear in her as she often feels hesitant and apprehensive when interacting with him. His departure from work relieves her, characterised by a glad sense of escape from his intimidating presence. The noise of his carriage fading into the distance signifies a freedom from his commanding figure.

However, as the story progresses, a comforting incident, wherein her father shows unexpected tenderness during her nightmare, leads to a significant shift in her perception. She begins to empathise with him, understanding his burdens and struggles. This newfound empathy encourages a deeper appreciation for his efforts and protection, removing her initial fear.

5. Give a character sketch of Kezia.

Ans. Kezia is the central character in the story, a young girl navigating the complexities of familial relationships and her understanding of the world. At the story's beginning, Kezia is depicted as timid and fearful, particularly in her interactions with her father. She demonstrates hesitation and anxiety, reflecting her discomfort with his strict nature. However, her efforts to please her father with a handmade gift demonstrate her desire for connection and approval.

As the story progresses, Kezia's character evolves, reflecting her growing understanding of the world around her. Through observations of neighbouring families and her own experiences, she begins to question and analyse her familial relationships.

Despite facing disappointment and fear, Kezia demonstrates a capacity for empathy and forgiveness. Rather than simply resenting her father's actions, she seeks to understand them, reflecting a mature and compassionate outlook. Kezia emerges as a character marked by sensitivity, introspection and an increasing sense of empathy. Her journey of self-discovery and understanding forms a central narrative arc, enriching the story's exploration of familial dynamics and human relationships.

6. Children need to be treated with love and affection. Based on the story 'The Little Girl' write a paragraph in about 100-120 words on the topic 'Importance of Love and Affection for Children'.

Ans. **Importance of Love and Affection for Children**

Love and affection play a significant role in the healthy development of children. Beyond providing basic necessities, a nurturing environment filled with love creates a strong foundation for a child's emotional, social and mental growth.

When children feel loved, secure and valued, they are more likely to form positive attachments and develop a healthy sense of self-esteem. Loving relationships with parents can enhance a child's emotional intelligence, while also promoting empathy and compassion.

Moreover, love and affection contribute significantly to a child's mental well-being. It creates a sense of safety, while making the children capable of facing challenges. Children who experience love are better equipped to deal with stress, build trusting relationships and excel academically.

In essence, the emotional support derived from love and affection forms the cornerstone of a child's overall development, shaping their character and influencing their future relationships and achievements.

7. Kezia from 'The Little Girl' and the narrator from 'The Snake and the Mirror' are both afraid of something. Compare and contrast their experiences with fear. Do they manage to overcome it?

Ans. Everyone is afraid of something. It may be rational or irrational, dangerous or childish. Kezia is a little girl who is afraid of her father. His huge size scares her and his strict disciplinarian ways cement that fear in her mind. But her fear is irrational because her father loves her dearly.

On the other hand, the narrator from 'The Snake and the Mirror' is afraid of something truly dangerous and fatal, i.e. a snake. When a snake lands on his shoulder, he is scared and is unable to move. Thus, both Kenia and the narrator from 'The Snake and the Mirror' have different experiences with fear.

Kezia recognises the true nature of her loving father and overcomes her fear. However, the narrator is justified in feeling afraid of a venomous snake that could easily kill him. He stays calm and thinks of a way out of the deadly situation. However, he doesn't manage to overcome his fear of snakes.

ASSESSMENT EXERCISE

Extract Based Questions

Read the following extract carefully and answer the questions that follow.

To the little girl he was a figure to be feared and avoided. Every morning before going to work he came into her room and gave her a casual kiss, to which she responded with 'Goodbye, Father'. And Oh, there was a glad sense of relief when she heard the noise of the carriage growing fainter and fainter down the long road.

(i) Name the writer of the story from which this extract has been taken.

(a) Issac Asimov (b) Vaikom Basheer
(c) Katherine Mansfield (d) Coates Kinney

(ii) Why was the little girl afraid of her father?

(iii) What would the little girl's father do before going to his office? What does it signify about his feelings for Kezia?

(iv) Which word in the extract means the same as 'obscure'?

Short Answer (SA) Type Questions

1. What were Kezia's duties in the evening when her father returned home from office?
2. What were Kezia's feelings towards her father at the end of the story?
3. Why did Kezia's father beat her palms with a ruler?
4. Why did Kezia like her grandmother more than anyone else in the family?

Long Answer (LA) Type Questions

1. Kezia's father was actually different from what he appeared to Kezia. Justify.
2. Write a character sketch of Kezia's father.

A Truly Beautiful Mind

CHAPTER 4

CHAPTER SUMMARY The chapter recounts the life of Albert Einstein, the greatest scientist of the 20th century. Einstein was considered unusual by his mother. He was highly skilled in mathematics and physics. He became world famous after he published his General Theory of Relativity in 1915. He was awarded the Nobel Prize for Physics in 1921. He worked for world peace and democracy in the later years of his life.

Early Life of Einstein

Albert Einstein was born on 14th March, 1879 in the city named Ulm in Germany. His mother thought that he was abnormal because unlike other children, he had a large head. He was unable to speak even at the age of two and a half years. When he started speaking, he spoke everything twice.

Einstein did not like the company of friends. His friends called him 'Brother Boring'. He played by himself with mechanical toys. At school, he did not do well. Once, a headmaster told Einstein's father that Einstein would never succeed in life. Einstein learnt to play the violin at the age of six and later became an amateur violinist.

Einstein's Education

Einstein went to high school in Munich where his family had moved. He was a good student and scored good marks in every subject. Einstein did not like the strict discipline of the school and often had arguments with his teachers. He left the school at the age of 15. His parents shifted to Milan but Einstein continued his schooling in German-speaking Switzerland. Einstein was extraordinary in Mathematics and had an interest in Physics. After finishing school, he decided to study at a University in Zurich. At the University in Zurich, Einstein fell in love with a Serbian girl named Mileva Maric.

Albert's Views on Mileva

Albert found Mileva to be a 'clever creature.' Mileva was a Serbian woman who had come to Switzerland because the University in Zurich was one of the few in Europe where women could get degrees. Einstein and Mileva became good friends because he found someone to talk about 'philistines'— those people in his family and at the university with whom he was constantly at odds. Albert and Mileva consequently fell in love.

Einstein's Special Theory of Relativity

Einstein graduated at the age of 21 in the year 1900. After graduation, Albert worked as a teaching assistant and gave private lessons. He got a job as a technical expert in the patent office in Bern in 1902. At the job, Albert assessed other people's inventions. At the same time, he developed his own ideas secretly. He jokingly named his desk drawer at work the 'bureau of theoretical physics'.

He published his Special Theory of Relativity in 1905, according to which time and distance are not absolute. From this theory, he derived the world's most famous formula which described the relationship between mass and energy, $E = mc^2$. (where E is energy, m is mass and c is the speed of the light in a vacuum)

Einstein's Marriage

Einstein wanted to marry Mileva after finishing his studies but his mother was against it. Einstein's mother found Mileva, who was three years older than her son, to be too old for him. She was also bothered by Mileva's intelligence. However, Einstein married her in 1903. They had two sons but their marriage failed and they finally got divorced in 1919. Einstein married his cousin Elsa in the same year.

Einstein's General Theory of Relativity and Nobel Prize

In 1915, he published his General Theory of Relativity. It gave a new interpretation of gravity. An eclipse of the sun in 1919 proved his theory correct. Einstein had correctly calculated in advance the extent to which the light from fixed stars would be deflected through the sun's gravitational field. As a result, he became famous as his work was considered a scientific revolution. He received the Nobel Prize for Physics in 1921.

Einstein Emigrates to US

Einstein emigrated (moved) to the United States when the Nazis came to power in 1933. The process of nuclear fission was discovered in Berlin in 1938. The American physicists feared that the Nazis would build an atomic bomb.

On 2nd August, 1939 Einstein wrote a letter to the American President, Franklin D. Roosevelt about the massive destruction that can be caused by a single atomic bomb.
However, the Americans developed the atomic bomb secretly and dropped it on the Japanese cities of Hiroshima and Nagasaki in August 1945 during the World War II.

Einstein Works for Peace and Democracy

Einstein was deeply shaken with the huge destruction caused by the atomic bomb. So, he wrote a long official letter to the United Nations in which he proposed the formation of a world government. However, this did not have any effect.

He continued to work for world peace and democracy and involved himself more in politics in the coming years. He campaigned to end the arms build up. He died in 1955 at the age of 76. He was admired for being a visionary, a world citizen and a scientific genius.

Word Meaning

Word	Meaning
civil servant	a government employee
took the world by storm	became a sudden success
ground-breaking	pioneering; completely new
electrodynamics	branch of science concerning with electricity and magnetism
journals	professional magazines
cosmos	universe
destined for greatness	likely to achieve greatness in the future
on the contrary	quite the reverse
freak	an abnormal person
uttered	spoke
brother boring	a person who is not interesting
make a success	be successful
gifted	having an exceptional ability in a particular subject
amateur	doing something for pleasure only rather than as a profession.
regimentation	extreme discipline
clashed	argued
stifled	suffocated
for good	forever
prolonged	extended
liberal	respecting all opinions
dashing	stylish
walrus moustache	a moustache that is long and hangs down at both sides of the mouth
special interest	liking
clever creature	smart person
Serb	a person from Serbia
ally	friend or supporter
philistines	people who don't like art or culture.
constantly at odds	always in conflict
tenderness	kindness; gentleness

Word	Meaning
victorious	successful
secured	found
patent office	a government office certifying new inventions
assessing	evaluating
bureau	office
absolute	fixed
unravelling	starting to fail
bothered	disturbed
book like you	a bookworm like you
put the wedding off	postponed the wedding
faltered	weakened
intellectual ambition	interest in scholarly work
coincided	matched
interpretation	understanding
deflected	changed direction on hitting something
proclaimed	praised
lauded	praised highly
the press	newspapers and journalists
Nazis	a ruling party in Germany led by Adolf Hitler which controlled Germany from 1933 to 1945
emigrated	settled permanently
fission	breaking up
in an uproar	very upset
fascism	an extreme system of government
urging	persuasion
did not fail to have an effect	had an impact
shaken	shocked
public missive	a long and official open letter
decade	a period of ten years
agitating	campaigning
buildup	an increase in something over time
visionary	a person who can think about the future in an original and intelligent way

NCERT FOLDER

NCERT Intext and Exercise Questions

THINKING ABOUT THE TEXT

(NCERT PAGE 50-51)

Q.1 Here are some headings for paragraphs in the text. Write the number(s) of the paragraph(s) for each title against the heading. The first one is done for you.

(i) Einstein's equation 9

(ii) Einstein meets his future wife

(iii) The making of a violinist

(iv) Mileva and Einstein's mother

(v) A letter that launched the arms race

(vi) A desk drawer full of ideas

(vii) Marriage and divorce

Ans. (ii) 7 (iii) 3 (iv) 10 (v) 15 (vi) 8 (vii) 11

Q.2 Who had these opinions about Einstein?

(i) He was boring.

(ii) He was stupid and would never succeed in life.

(iii) He was a freak.

Ans. (i) Einstein's playmates or companions in school found him boring.

(ii) A headmaster thought that he was stupid and would never succeed in life.

(iii) Einstein's mother thought that he was a freak.

Q.3 Explain what the reasons for the following are

(i) Einstein leaving the school in Munich for good.

Or Why did Einstein leave the school in Munich?

Competency Based

(ii) Einstein wanting to study in Switzerland rather than in Munich.

(iii) Einstein seeing in Mileva an ally.

(iv) What do these tell you about Einstein?

Ans. (i) Einstein hated the strict discipline of his school in Munich. He always argued with his teachers. That is why he left school in Munich for good.

(ii) Einstein wanted to study in Switzerland rather than in Munich because Switzerland was more liberal than Munich for his intellectual and personal growth.

(iii) Einstein saw an ally in Mileva because she had a mindset just like Einstein and was very intelligent.

(iv) These snippets from Einstein's life give an idea about the extraordinary thinking power which he had since his childhood. He always liked to take his own decisions which is evident from his insistence on leaving Munich for a better future. He had qualities which helped him become a visionary and world citizen.

Einstein prioritised intellectual freedom and autonomy in his pursuits. He was unafraid to challenge conventional norms and seek environments that allowed him to pursue his interests and ideas freely. His ability to recognise allies in Mileva Maric demonstrates his capacity for forming meaningful interpersonal connections based on shared values and interests. These aspects of Einstein's character highlight his resilience, determination, and commitment to intellectual exploration and innovation.

Q.4 What did Einstein call his desk drawer at the patent office? Why?

Ans. Einstein called his desk drawer at the patent office the 'bureau of theoretical physics.'

Although, he was supposed to be assessing other people's inventions, he was busy exploring the possibilities of theoretical physics in secrecy and kept his theories in the drawer. This is why, he called his desk drawer the 'bureau of theoretical physics.'

Q.5 Why did Einstein write a letter to Franklin Roosevelt?

Ans. The Nazis had acquired the knowledge of developing the atomic bomb after the discovery of nuclear fission in Berlin. Einstein feared that the Nazis could build and use an atomic bomb against the United States. So, he wrote a letter to Franklin D. Roosevelt to warn him against the approaching threat.

Q.6 How did Einstein react to the bombing of Hiroshima and Nagasaki?

Ans. Einstein was deeply shocked by the destruction caused in the cities of Hiroshima and Nagasaki due to the atomic bombing. He wrote a letter to the United Nations and proposed the formation of a world government. He travelled all over the world agitating for an end to the arms buildup, using his popularity to campaign for peace and democracy.

Q.7 Why does the world remember Einstein as a 'world citizen'?

Ans. The world remembers Einstein as a 'world citizen' because of the responsibility he showed towards humanity irrespective of national borders. After the atomic bombing of Japan, he wrote to the United Nations proposing the formation of a world government that would work for global peace. Moreover, he also worked to put an end to the arms buildup and used his popularity to campaign for peace and democracy.

Q.8 Here are some facts from Einstein's life. Arrange them in chronological order.

[ ] Einstein publishes his special theory of relativity.

[ ] He is awarded the Nobel Prize in Physics.

[ ] Einstein writes a letter to U.S. President, Franklin D. Roosevelt and warns against Germany's building of an atomic bomb.

[ ] Einstein attends a high school in Munich.

[ ] Einstein's family moves to Milan.

[ ] Einstein is born in the German city of Ulm.

[ ] Einstein joins a university in Zurich, where he meets Mileva.

[ ] Einstein dies.

[ ] He provides a new interpretation of gravity.

[ ] Tired of the school's regimentation, Einstein withdraws from school.

[ ] He works in a patent office as a technical expert.

[ ] When Hitler comes to power, Einstein leaves Germany for the United States.

Ans. [1] Einstein is born in the German city of Ulm.

[2] Einstein attends a high school in Munich.

[3] Einstein's family moves to Milan.

[4] Tired of the school's regimentation, Einstein withdraws from school.

[5] Einstein joins a university in Zurich, where he meets Mileva.

[6] He works in a patent office as a technical expert.

[7] Einstein publishes his special theory of relatively.

[8] He provides a new interpretation of gravity.

[9] He is awarded the Nobel Prize in Physics.

[10] When Hitler comes to power, Einstein leaves Germany for the United States.

[11] Einstein writes a letter to US President, Franklin D. Roosevelt, and warns against Germany's building of an atomic bomb.

[12] Einstein dies.

THINKING ABOUT LANGUAGE

(NCERT PAGE 51-52)

I. Here are some sentences from the story. Choose the word from the brackets which can be substituted for the italicised words in the sentences.

Q.1 A few years later, the marriage *faltered*. (failed, broke, became weak).

Q.2 Einstein was constantly *at odds* with people at the university. (on bad terms, in disagreement, unhappy)

Q.3 The newspapers *proclaimed* his work as "a scientific revolution." (declared, praised, showed)

Q.4 Einstein got ever more involved in politics, *agitating* for an end to the arms buildup. (campaigning, fighting, supporting)

Q.5 At the age of 15, Einstein felt so stifled that he left the school *for good*. (permanently, for his benefit, for a short time)

Q.6 Five years later, the discovery of nuclear fission in Berlin had American physicists *in an uproar*. (in a state of commotion, full of criticism, in a desperate state)

Q.7 Science wasn't the only thing that *appealed to* the dashing young man with the walrus moustache. (interested, challenged, worried)

Ans. 1. became weak 2. in disagreement
3. declared 4. campaigning
5. permanently 6. in a state of commotion
7. interested

II. Study the following sentences.

- Einstein became a gifted amateur violinist, *maintaining this skill throughout* his life.
- Letters survive in which they put their affection into words, *mixing science with tenderness*.

The parts in italics in the above sentences begin with-ing verbs, and are called participial phrases. Participial phrases say something more about the person or thing talked about or the idea expressed by the sentence as a whole. For example

Einstein became a gifted amateur violinist. He maintained this skill throughout his life.

Complete the sentences below by filling in the blanks with suitable participial clauses. The information that has to be used in the phrases is provided as a sentence in brackets.

1. ...., the firefighters finally put out the fire. (They worked round the clock).
2. She watched the sunset above the mountain, ... (She noticed the colours blending softly into one another).
3. The excited horse pawed the ground rapidly, ... (While it neighed continually).
4. ...., I found myself in Bangalore, instead of Benaras. (I had taken the wrong train).
5. ...., I was desperate to get to the bathroom. (I had not bathed for two days).
6. The stone steps, ... needed to be replaced. (They were worn down).
7. The actor received hundreds of letters from his fans, ... (They asked him to send them his photograph).

Ans. 1. Working round the clock.
2. noticing the colours blending softly into one another.
3. neighing continually
4. Having taken the wrong train
5. Having not bathed for two days
6. being worn down
7. asking him to send his photograph

WRITING NEWSPAPER REPORTS
(NCERT PAGE 53)

Here are some notes which you could use to write a report.

21st August, 2005 — original handwritten manuscript of Albert Einstein unearthed — by student Rowdy Boeynik in the University of the Netherlands — Boeynik researching papers — papers belonging to an old friend of Einstein — fingerprints of Einstein on these papers — 16-page document dated 1924 — Einstein's work on this last theory — behaviour of atoms at low temperature — now known as the Bose-Einstein condensation — the manuscript to be kept at Leyden University where Einstein got the Nobel Prize.

Write a report which has four paragraphs, one each on:

- What was unearthed.
- Who unearthed it and when.
- What the document contained.
- Where it will be kept.

Your report could begin like this

Student Unearths Einstein Manuscript

21st August, 2005 An original handwritten Albert Einstein manuscript has been unearthed at a university in the Netherlands ....

Ans. **Student Unearths Einstein Manuscript**

21st August, 2005. An original handwritten manuscript of Albert Einstein has been unearthed at a university in the Netherlands. This belonged to an old friend of Einstein.

This manuscript was unearthed by a student named Rowdy Boeynik. Though Boeynik is still going through all the papers he had found, this particular one has created a sensation.

The reason why this document is important is that it contains Einstein's work on his last theory before his death. It is about the behaviour of atoms at very low temperatures. This is now known as the Bose-Einstein condensation. It has been proved that this document was written by Einstein because it has his fingerprints on it.

The manuscript would be kept at Leyden University where Einstein got the Nobel Prize.

REVIEW EXERCISE

Including Competency Based Questions

Part I

Multiple Choice Questions

1. What main point does the writer make about Einstein's childhood? Competency Based

(a) He stood out a lot from the other children.
(b) He was not treated kindly by other children in his school.
(c) His parents were very worried about his poor performance.
(d) His later achievements could not be predicted from his childhood.

Ans. (d) His later achievements could not be predicted from his childhood.

2. Why did Einstein's playmates call him 'Brother Boring'?

(a) Because he did not know how to play with other children.
(b) Because he liked to play alone with mechanical toys.
(c) Because he was a freak.
(d) Both (a) and (b)

Ans. (d) Both (a) and (b)

3. Why did Einstein hate the school?

(a) Because of too much crowd
(b) Because of its regimentation
(c) Teachers unable to understand students
(d) Too much load of studies

Ans. (b) Because of its regimentation

4. But science wasn't the only thing that appealed to the dashing young man with the walrus moustache.
In the sentence above, the writer is mainly trying to .... **Competency Based**

(a) establish a new argument
(b) elaborate a point made earlier
(c) highlight an important part of the text
(d) provide a transition to a different topic

Ans. (d) provide a transition to a different topic

5. Why did Einstein wish to continue his education in German-speaking Switzerland?

(a) It was more liberal than Munich.
(b) It had greater opportunities.
(c) It was much advanced city.
(d) All of the above

Ans. (a) It was more liberal than Munich.

6. Einstein and Mileva used to write letters to each other, in which they put their affection to words, mixing science with ....

(a) love
(b) tenderness
(c) comfort
(d) soft words

Ans. (a) love

7. Why did Einstein call his desk drawer 'Bureau of Theoretical Physics' at the patent office?

(a) He was developing his own ideas in secret.
(b) He used to assess other people's inventions secretly.
(c) He had some important and confidential information about nuclear fission.
(d) None of the above

Ans. (a) He was developing his own ideas in secret.

8. What does the expression 'marriage faltered' mean?

(a) Marriage was solemnised
(b) Marriage came to an end
(c) Led a happy married life
(d) Marriage could not be continued

Ans. (b) Marriage came to an end

9. When was Einstein's Special Theory of Relativity published?

(a) 1905 (b) 1919
(c) 1903 (d) 1915

Ans. (a) 1905

10. When did newspapers proclaim Einstein's work as 'a scientific revolution'?

(a) When he gave the famous formula $E = mc^2$.
(b) When nuclear fission was discovered in Berlin.
(c) When his General Theory of Relativity was proved accurate by the solar eclipse of 1919.
(d) When atomic bombs were dropped on Hiroshima and Nagasaki.

Ans. (c) When his General Theory of Relativity was proved accurate by the solar eclipse of 1919.

11. The physicists in America went into an uproar ....

(a) on the discovery of nuclear fission
(b) because they envious afraid that Nazis could build and use atomic bomb
(c) they were envious of Einstein and his intelligence
(d) Both (a) and (b)

Ans. (d) Both (a) and (b)

12. Einstein's reaction to America using the nuclear bomb shows that .... **Competency Based**

(a) he changed his mind about war
(b) he was humanitarian at heart
(c) he did not fully understand the impact of his own work
(d) he felt guilty about causing the atomic bomb to be built

Ans. (d) he felt guilty about causing the atomic bomb to be built

13. What is the tone of the text? **Competency Based**

(a) Factual (b) Admiring
(c) Nostalgic (d) Sympathetic

Ans. (a) Factual

14. What is the main purpose of the text? **Competency Based**

(a) To provide an overview of Einstein's life
(b) To highlight the significance of Einstein's work
(c) To argue that Einstein was not a typical scientist
(d) To describe the influences that led to Einstein's success

Ans. (a) To provide an overview of Einstein's life

15. What is Fascism as mentioned in the line "Many of them had fled from Fascism, just as Einstein had"?

(a) Centralised autocratic government headed by a dictatorial leader.
(b) A government that promotes communalism.
(c) A government ruled by the king or queen.
(d) A government ruled by the aristocrats of the society.

Ans. (a) Centralised autocratic government headed by a dictatorial leader.

16. Why did Einstein write a public missive to the United Nations?

1. **To prevent future incidents like that of Hiroshima and Nagasaki.**
2. **To promote world peace.**
3. **To get involved in politics.**

(a) Only 1 is true (b) Only 2 is true
(c) Only 3 is true (d) Both 1 and 2 are true

Ans. (d) Both 1 and 2 are true

17. What do you understand by the term 'missive'?

(a) A letter, especially a long or official one
(b) An important government document
(c) A short letter
(d) None of the above

Ans. (a) A letter, especially a long or official one

18. What did Einstein use his popularity for?

(i) For an end to the arms buildup.

(ii) For peace and democracy.

(a) Only (i) is correct
(b) Only (ii) is correct
(c) Both (i) and (ii) are correct
(d) Neither (i) nor (ii) is correct

Ans. (c) Both (i) and (ii) are correct

Extract Based Questions

1. Read the following extract carefully and answer the questions that follow.

Albert Einstein was born on 14th March, 1879 in the German city of Ulm, without any indication that he was destined for greatness. On the contrary, his mother thought Albert was a freak. To her, his head seemed much too large.
At the age of two-and-a-half, Einstein still wasn't talking. When he finally did learn to speak, he uttered everything twice. Einstein did not know what to do with other children, and his playmates called him "Brother Boring." So the youngster played by himself much of the time. He especially loved mechanical toys. Looking at his newborn sister, Maja, he is said to have said: "Fine, but where are her wheels?"

Competency Based

(i) What did Albert Einstein's mother think about him?

(a) Prodigy (b) Perfect
(c) Freak (d) Teacher

Ans. (c) Freak

(ii) "Fine, but where are her wheels?" Why did Einstein ask the above question about his newborn sister?

Ans. Einstein asked the above question about his newborn sister because he thought that she was a mechanical toy.

(iii) Why did young Einstein's playmates call him 'Brother Boring'?

Ans. Young Einstein's playmates called him 'Brother Boring' because Einstein was not interested in the usual games of their age. Therefore, he could not play with his playmates.

(iv) "Albert Einstein was born .... without any indication that he was destined for greatness." What is the intention of the author behind starting the passage with the line given above?

Ans. The author intended the reader to be focussed on the fact that despite being born like a normal child, Albert Einstein grew up to be one of the most genius men in the entire world. The peculiarities of Einstein that later assisted him in manifesting the incredible breakthroughs in astrophysics were present in him from his childhood.

2. Read the following extract carefully and answer the questions that follow.

To her, his head seemed too large? At the age of two-and-a-half, Einstein still wasn't talking. When he finally did learn to speak, he uttered everything twice. Einstein did not know what to do with other children, and his playmates called him 'Brother Boring'.

(i) To whom does 'her' refer to?

Ans. Einstein's mother

(ii) What did Einstein do instead of playing with other children?

Ans. Einstein played with mechanical toys instead of playing with other children.

(iii) Complete the analogy by selecting the suitable word from the text.

Lastly : Finally :: Spoke : ....

Ans. Uttered

(iv) Select the option that displays the reason why all other children called Einstein 'Brother Boring'.

(a) He did not stay with them
(b) He did not like to play with them
(c) He was always sleeping
(d) He was fighting with them

Ans. (b) He did not like to play with them

3. Read the following extract carefully and answer the questions that follow.

A headmaster once told his father that what Einstein chose as a profession wouldn't matter, because "he'll never be a success at anything." Einstein began learning to play the violin at the age of six, because his mother wanted him to; he later became a gifted amateur violinist, maintaining this skill throughout his life.

(i) What was the headmaster's opinion about Einstein?

(a) He will be a failure.
(b) He will not succeed in any profession.
(c) He will be able to perform much later.
(d) His hard work will not pay him.

Ans. (b) He will not succeed in any profession.

(ii) Why did Einstein begin learning to play the violin?

Ans. Einstein began learning to play the violin because his mother wanted him to do so.

(iii) State True or False.

The statements a, b and c are true for Einstein.

(a) He was a slow child during his childhood.
(b) He was overfriendly.
(c) He was intelligent but his headmaster didn't realise this fact.

Ans. True

(iv) How can we say that headmaster was not correct in his opinion of Einstein?

Ans. The headmaster was not correct in his opinion of Einstein as Einstein was a gifted child.

4. Read the following extract carefully and answer the questions that follow.

While Einstein was solving the most difficult problems in physics, his private life was unravelling. Albert had wanted to marry Mileva right after finishing his studies, but his mother was against it. She thought Mileva,who was three years older than her son, was too old for him. She was also bothered by Mileva's intelligence. "She is a book like you", his mother said. Einstein put the wedding off.

(i) Why did Einstein's mother oppose his marriage to Mileva?

Ans. Einstein's mother opposed his marriage to Mileva because she was three years older than him and was also very intelligent.

(ii) Which line from the passage indicates that his mother had a big impact on Einstein's life.

Ans. "Albert had wanted to marry Mileva right after finishing his studies, but his mother was against it."

(iii) Which word in the extract is the opposite of 'stupidity'?

(a) unravelling (b) intelligence
(c) difficult (d) studies

Ans. (b) intelligence

(iv) Why did Einstein put the wedding off ?

Ans. Einstein put the wedding off because his mother was against his marriage with Mileva.

5. Read the following extract carefully and answer the questions that follow.

Einstein was deeply shaken by the extent of the destruction. This time he wrote a public missive to the United Nations. In it he proposed the formation of a world government. Unlike the letter to Roosevelt, this one made no impact. But over the next decade, Einstein got ever more involved in politics—agitating for an end to the arms build-up and using his popularity to campaign for peace and democracy.

(i) Here, the extent of destruction refers to ....

Ans. Japan

(ii) .... from the extract means a long and official letter.

Ans. 'Missive'

(iii) What did Einstein write to the United Nations?

(a) He wrote regarding the formation of a world government.
(b) He wrote regarding the action against who were involved in the destruction.
(c) He wrote regarding the effects of this destruction on the world.
(d) He wrote regarding the formation of relief camps for the destruction caused area.

Ans. (a) He wrote regarding the formation of a world government.

(iv) Why did he write a letter to Roosevelt?

Ans. He wrote a letter to Roosevelt because he wanted to warn America that Germany had the ability to build and use the atomic bomb which if exploded in a port, would destroy the whole port with some of the surrounding territory.

Part II

Short Answer Type Questions

1. When and where was Albert Einstein born? What did his mother think during and after his birth? Why?

Ans. Albert Einstein was born in the city of Ulm in Germany on 14th March, 1879.

Einstein's mother thought that he was a freak because he did not look, behave or think like others. His head was larger than other children of his age and he was unable to speak even when he was two and a half years old.

2. How did Einstein's early childhood differ from conventional expectations?

Ans. Einstein's early childhood was marked by odd behaviour. He didn't speak until the age of two-and-a-half and often played alone, earning the nickname 'Brother Boring' from his playmates. His love for mechanical toys hinted at his future scientific interests.

3. What was Einstein's initial reception in school, and how did he react?

Ans. Despite clashes with teachers, Einstein scored well in almost every subject. However, he despised the school's strictness and left at 15. His father was told he'd never succeed, yet Einstein's resilience and unconventional thinking propelled him toward greatness.

4. Who was Mileva Maric? Why did she come to Switzerland?

Or **Why did Mileva Maric go to the University of Zurich?** Competency Based

Ans. Mileva Maric was a young Serbian girl. She came to Switzerland to study because University in Zurich was one of the few universities in Europe where women were allowed to pursue graduation.

5. How was Einstein's private life unravelling after he finished his studies?

Ans. Einstein's private life was unravelling after he finished his studies because he wanted to marry Mileva just after completing his studies. However, his mother was against it as she thought that Mileva was too old for Einstein and too intelligent to become a housewife. So, Einstein had to postpone his wedding.

6. What is Einstein's 'Special Theory of Relativity' about?

Ans. Einstein's 'Special Theory of Relativity' was published in 1905. According to this theory, time and distance are not absolute. Two perfectly accurate clocks will not continue to show the same time if they come together after a same journey. The formula of the relationship between mass and energy ($E = mc^2$) was derived from this theory.

7. What remarkable incident happened in the life of Einstein in 1921?

Ans. The remarkable incident that happened in the life of Einstein in 1921 was that he was awarded the Nobel Prize for Physics. He was honoured and invited all around the world. The press praised his work and the newspapers called it as 'a scientific revolution'.

8. Provide two instances from the text that show that Einstein's mother influenced his life. Competency Based

Ans. The following two instances show that Einstein's mother influenced his life

(i) He only learnt violin because his mother asked him to.

(ii) When his mother didn't agree, he postponed his marriage to Mileva Maric.

9. How did Einstein's involvement in politics reflect his worldview?

Ans. Einstein's experiences with Nazi persecution and the horrors of nuclear weapons deeply impacted him. He wrote to President Roosevelt, warning of the potential for atomic bombs and later, advocated for world government and peace. His actions demonstrated a commitment to global welfare beyond scientific achievements.

10. What legacy did Einstein leave behind upon his death in 1955?

Ans. Einstein's legacy extends beyond scientific achievements to encompass his advocacy for peace and humanitarian causes. Celebrated as a visionary and global citizen, he inspired generations with his intellect and moral compass. His contributions to both science and humanity continue to reverberate worldwide.

Long Answer Type Questions

1. Einstein was an unusual child with no indication of his potential greatness. Comment.

Ans. Einstein was an unusual child. He had a larger head than the children of his age. His mother thought him to be a freak. He wasn't able to speak even at the age of two and a half years. When he finally started to speak, he said everything twice. He did not like the company of his friends and played by himself with his mechanical toys. So, his playmates called him 'Brother Boring'.

There was no indication of his potential greatness when he was a child. One of his headmasters called Einstein's father and told him that he would never succeed at anything in life.

Therefore, we can say that although Einstein was an unusual child, his family and teachers never saw in him any potential of his future greatness.

2. Why did Albert Einstein leave school at the age of 15? Do you think a liberal environment in the school helps in learning in a better way?

Ans. Albert Einstein went to a high school in Munich. He was good at studies and scored good marks in all the subjects. However, he did not like the strict discipline or the regimented environment in the school. He often had arguments with his teachers. He was unable to adjust himself in the school environment properly and felt suffocated. So, he left school at the age of 15.

I think that a liberal environment in the school helps in learning in a better way.

A liberal environment allows free thinking. In such an environment, one can think and work according to one's own wish. It also helps in developing new and creative ideas as one is not bound by rules.
One learns more when one is allowed to learn according to one's capacity. So, better learning takes place when the environment in the school is liberal and student–friendly.

3. Discuss Einstein's employment at the patent office in Bern and how it contributed to his scientific pursuits.

Ans. Einstein's employment at the patent office in Bern played a crucial role in his scientific pursuits. Although tasked with assessing other people's inventions, Einstein found ample time to develop his ideas secretly. He humorously referred to his desk drawer at work as the 'bureau of theoretical physics'. This job provided him with a steady income and a conducive environment for thought, away from the pressures of academia.

Further, it allowed him the mental space to ponder complex scientific problems, leading to his groundbreaking insights into theoretical physics. Einstein's experiences at the patent office cultivated his intellectual curiosity and provided the stability necessary to pursue his revolutionary ideas, ultimately shaping the trajectory of his scientific career.

4. How did Einstein's relationships, particularly with Mileva Maric, influence his life and work?

Ans. Einstein's relationships, notably with Mileva Maric, significantly influenced his life and work. Maric, a fellow student with whom Einstein felt, was an intellectual companion and emotional support. Their relationship provided Einstein with someone who shared his passion for science and served as an ally against societal norms and academic pressures. Despite the eventual strain on their marriage, Maric's influence is evident in their collaboration and correspondence on scientific matters, including Einstein's work on relativity. The complexity of their relationship and subsequent divorce contributed to Einstein's personal growth and shaped his views on love, commitment and the human experience, influencing his work and world view.

5. When Einstein died, he was celebrated as a visionary and world citizen as much as a scientific genius.

Write a descriptive paragraph titled 'Einstein - A Scientific Genius' describing his achievements and commenting on his genius. (100-120 words)

Ans. **Einstein - A Scientific Genius**

Albert Einstein, widely regarded as one of the greatest scientific minds in history, revolutionised our understanding of the universe. Born in 1879, this German-born physicist developed the theory of relativity, challenging traditional notions of space and time. His equation, $E=mc^2$, encapsulates the profound relationship between energy and mass. Einstein's insights also laid the groundwork for quantum theory. Awarded the Nobel Prize in Physics in 1921, his contributions extended beyond scientific breakthroughs to philosophical reflections on life, knowledge and the universe. Einstein's enduring legacy continues to inspire scientists, educators and curious minds globally, leaving an indelible mark on the landscape of modern physics and our comprehension of the cosmos.

6. How do you think Albert Einstein from the chapter 'A Truly Beautiful Mind' would have fared in the school environment of Margie from the chapter 'The Fun They Had'?

Ans. Albert Einstein was a brilliant student in his school days. However, he did not like the strict discipline of the school and often had arguments with his teachers. If he was put in the same school as Margie, his experience could go either way. On one hand, he would have a better school experience because like Margie, his own schooling would be customised to his pace and interests.

On the other hand, the heightened rigidity of a robotic teacher would make him hate the experience that much more. In the end, since he was a prodigy in physics, we could expect him to take the robotic teacher apart and begin experimenting on it to suit Einstein's needs.

ASSESSMENT EXERCISE

Extract Based Questions

Read the following extract carefully and answer the questions that follow.

In 1900, at the age of 21, Albert Einstein was a university graduate and unemployed. He worked as a teaching assistant, gave private lessons and finally secured a job in 1902 as a technical expert in the patent office in Bern. While he was supposed to be assessing other people's inventions, Einstein was actually developing his own ideas in secret. He is said to have jokingly called his desk drawer at work the 'bureau of theoretical physics'.

(i) What odd jobs did Einstein do after his graduation?

(a) Worked as a teaching assistant

(b) Worked as a delivery boy

(c) Gave private lessons

(d) Both (a) and (c)

(ii) What name did Einstein give to his drawer?

(iii) Why did he name the drawer so?

(iv) Which word in the extract means the same as 'evaluating'?

Short Answer (SA) Type Questions

1. Why was Albert Einstein's mother against her son marrying Mileva?
2. Why was Einstein called 'Brother Boring' by his playmates?
3. What made Einstein leave school at Munich?
4. What were the American scientists afraid of?
5. Did Einstein's letter to American President, Franklin D. Roosevelt, have any effect? What was the result?

Long Answer (LA) Type Questions

1. Write down the details of the education of Albert Einstein.
2. Einstein succeeded in his professional life but failed miserably in his personal life. According to you which is more important—family or profession?
3. Einstein thought differently and succeeded in life. Do you believe that all those who think differently succeed in their life like him? Comment.

The Snake and the Mirror

CHAPTER 5

by Vaikom Muhammad Basheer

CHAPTER SUMMARY This chapter 'The Snake and The Mirror' has been written by Vaikam Muhammad Basheer. The chapter has been translated from the original Malayalam text by V. Abdulla. In this story, the narrator is a young homoeopathic doctor who has a frightening encounter with a cobra. In a comic turn of events, his life is saved by a mirror because the snake turns out to be taken with its own beauty!

The Narrator Shares a Story

The narrator questioned his audience whether a snake had ever coiled itself around their body. Then, he began narrating his tale. The narrator was a homeopath doctor. He lived in a small rented room which did not have an electricity connection. He had just started his medical practice and his earning was small. The narrator describes his experience with a snake to his friends.

It was a hot summer night. The doctor had returned to his room at about ten o'clock after having his meal at the restaurant. When he opened the door, he heard a noise from above. As his room had a lot of rats in it, he ignored the noise. He lived in a cheap rented room without electricity. Since he had just set up his medical practice, he was poor. He only owned sixty rupees, some shirts and dhotis as well as a single black coat. He took off his black coat, white shirt and dirty vest.

He lit the Kerosene lamp and hung up his clothes. He, then, opened the two windows and lay down on his bed. However, he was unable to sleep as it was very hot. He got up and went to the veranda to get some fresh air.

The Doctor and the Mirror

After coming back into his room, the doctor sat on a chair. He took out a medical book, *Materia. Medica* and opened it on the table. A lamp and a large mirror were kept on the table. A small comb also lay beside the mirror. The doctor was a bachelor and believed in making himself look handsome.

The doctor again heard the same sound but ignored it. He looked closely at his face in the mirror and made some important decisions–he would shave daily and grow a thin moustache. Further, he would always keep an attractive smile on his face. Suddenly, he heard the same noise again.

The doctor also thought that he would marry a female doctor who had a lot of money and a good medical practice. She had to be fat because if he made some silly mistake and needed to run away, she would not be able to catch him.

A Snake Falls on the Doctor

The doctor sat back down on the chair in front of the table with the mirror. For sometime, the doctor did not hear any sound from above. Suddenly, there was a dull thud (sound of something heavy falling) and a fat snake landed on his shoulder. The snake coiled around the doctor's left arm above the elbow. Its head was only 3-4 inches away from the doctor's face. The doctor did not move as if he had turned into stone. He felt pain in his left arm as the snake began to squeeze him.

Doctor's Escape From the Snake

The doctor prayed to God for help and then, realised that he was a foolish and stupid doctor as he did not have any medicine for snakebite with him. He forgot his danger and smiled at himself.

Just then, the snake turned his head. It looked into the mirror and saw its reflection. Then, it uncoiled itself from the doctor's arm and slowly moved towards his lap. From there, the snake crawled over to the table and moved towards the mirror as if it wished to see its reflection more closely.

The doctor, thus, got an opportunity to escape from the house. He got up from the chair and quietly went out through the door into the veranda. Then, he ran as fast as he could into the yard.

Doctor Decides to Shift to a Different Place

The doctor ran till he reached his friend's house. He covered his body in oil, took a bath and changed his clothes there. He decided to shift to a different place. So, the next morning at about eight thirty the doctor went to his room with his friend to shift his belongings. However, the doctor and his friends found that some thief had taken most of his things. From that day, the doctor never saw that snake again. Some one from his audience asked whether his wife was very fat. The narrator replied that his wife was a very thin person who could run really fast.

Word Meaning

Word	Meaning
electrified	having an electricity connection
meagre	small in quantity
not-so-white	dirty
gables	upper parts of walls below a sloping roof
traffic	movement
wind god seemed to have taken time off	there was no breeze
tempted	to want to do something
make my presence felt	to have a strong effect on other people.
parting	line on the head made by combing hair sideways
earth-shaking	important
paced	walked
resumed	went back to
wriggled	twisted and turned quickly
landed	dropped
slithered	moved with a twisting motion
merely	just
holding my breath	to deliberately not breathe out for a short time.
turned to stone	to become completely still

Word	Meaning
the creator of this world and this universe	God
leaden	made up of heavy metal
made of molten fire	burning hot
drained of all strength	feeling weak
lurked	waited in hiding
it struck	the snake bit
vermillion spot	orange spot put on centre of forehead by women
at closer quarters	from near
no mere image cut in granite	no longer still
willed otherwise	wanted something different
life companion	wife
reedy	tall
the gift of a sprinter	having the ability of running quickly
smeared	spreaded
cleaned out	all belongings were sloten
rascal	mischievous person

NCERT FOLDER

NCERT Intext and Exercise Questions

THINKING ABOUT THE TEXT

(NCERT PAGE 60-61)

I. Discuss in pairs and answer each question below in a short paragraph (30–40 words).

Q.1 "The sound was a familiar one." What sound did the doctor hear? What did he think it was? How many times did he hear it? (Find the places in the text) When and why did the sounds stop?

Ans. The doctor heard the familiar sound on the roof of his room. He thought that the sound was made by the rats that lived in the house. The doctor heard the sound thrice. The places in the text where the sound is mentioned are as follows

'The sound was a familiar one.'

'Again I heard the sound from above.'

'Again came the noise from above.'

The sounds stopped just before the snake landed on the doctor's shoulder. The snake moving around on the roof might have scared away the rats, which is why their sounds stopped.

Q.2 What two 'important' and 'earth-shaking' decisions did the doctor take while he was looking into the mirror?

Ans. The first important and earth-shaking (significant) decision taken by the doctor was to shave daily and grow a thin moustache to look handsome.

The second decision was to always keep an attractive smile on his face in order to look more handsome.

Q.3 "I looked into the mirror and smiled", says the doctor. A little later he says, "I forgot my danger and smiled feebly at myself." What is the doctor's opinion about himself when: (i) he first smiles, and (ii) he smiles again? In what way do his thoughts change in between, and why?

Ans. When the doctor first smiles, he is in a happy mood and is proud of being a handsome, bachelor doctor. When the doctor smiles again, he is full of nervousness and self pity.

In between these two moments, the doctor's thoughts shift as he becomes preoccupied with the danger posed by the snake. The sudden appearance of the snake interrupts his initial self-assuredness, leading to a change in his perception of himself and his surroundings.

II. This story about a frightening incident is narrated in a humorous way. What makes it humorous? (Think of the contrasts it presents between dreams and reality. Some of them are listed below).
Write short paragraphs on each of these to get your answer.

Q.1 (i) The kind of person the doctor is (money, possessions)

(ii) The kind of person he wants to be (appearance, ambition)

Ans. The story shows a contrast between dreams and reality in a humorous manner. The doctor's earnings were very less because he had just started his career. He was living in a small rented room without electricity. He had few clothes. Even his room was full of rats.

However, his dreams and ambition were totally in contrast to his situation. He was a great admirer of beauty and believed in looking handsome. That's why he decided to grow a thin moustache and shave daily. He also decided to always keep smiling to look more handsome. The doctor also wanted to be rich as he planned to marry a woman doctor who had plenty of money.

Q.2 (i) The person he wants to marry

(ii) The person he actually marries

Ans. The doctor had thought that he would get married to a woman doctor who had plenty of money and a good medical practice. She would be fat, so that if he made a silly mistake and needed to run away, she should not be able to run after him and catch him.

However, the woman he actually married was slender (thin) and she could run very fast like a sprinter (athlete).

Q.3 (i) His thoughts when he looks into the mirror.

(ii) His thoughts when the snake is coiled around his arm.

Ans. When the doctor looked into the mirror, he appreciated his good looks and wanted to look even more handsome by shaving daily and growing a thin moustache. He also decided to keep smiling so that he could look more handsome. However, when the snake was coiled around his arm, he turned into a stone. He felt that God was very close to him at that time. He realised that if the snake bit him, he did not have any medicines in his house to save himself. He thought that he was a poor, foolish and stupid doctor.

THINKING ABOUT LANGUAGE

(NCERT PAGE 61)

I. Here are some sentences from the text. Say which of them tell you, that the author :

(i) (a) was afraid of the snake, (b) was proud of his appearance (c) had a sense of humour (d) was no longer afraid of the snake.

1. I was turned to stone.
2. I was no mere image cut in granite.
3. The arm was beginning to be drained of strength.
4. I tried in my imagination to write in bright letters outside my little heart the words, 'O God'.
5. I didn't tremble. I didn't cry out.
6. I looked into the mirror and smiled. It was an attractive smile.
7. I was suddenly a man of flesh and blood.
8. I was after all a bachelor and a doctor too on top of it!
9. The fellow had such a sense of cleanlines...! The rascal could have taken it and used it after washing it with soap and water.
10. Was it trying to make an important decision about growing a moustache or using eye shadow and mascara or wearing a vermilion spot on its forehead.

Ans. (i) The following sentences tell that the author (a) was afraid of the snake.

(1), (3), (4), (5)

The following sentences tell that he (b) was proud of his appearance

(6), (8)

The following sentences tell that he (c) had a sense of humour

(9), (10)

The following sentences tell that he (d) was no longer afraid of the snake

(2), (7)

II. Expressions used to show fear

Can you find the expressions in the story that tell you that the author was frightened? Read the story and complete the following sentences.

(i) I was turned ....

(ii) I sat there holding ....

(iii) In the light of the lamp I sat there like ....

Ans. (i) to stone,

(ii) my breath

(iii) a stone image in the flesh

III. In the sentences given below some words and expressions are italicised. They variously mean that one

- is very frightened.
- is too scared to move.
- is frightened by something that happens suddenly.
- makes another feel frightened.

Match the meanings with the words/expressions in italics and write the appropriate meaning next to the sentence. The first one has been done for you.

(i) I knew a man was following me, I was *scared out of my wits*. (very frightened)

(ii) I got a fright when I realised how close I was to the cliff edge.

(iii) He nearly jumped out of his skin when he saw the bull coming towards him.

(iv) You really gave me a fright when you crept up behind me like that.

(v) Wait until I tell his story — it will make your hair stand on end.

(vi) Paralysed with fear, the boy faced his abductors.

(vii) The boy hid behind the door, not moving a muscle.

Ans. (ii) frightened by something that happens suddenly

(iii) very frightened

(iv) frightened by something that happens suddenly

(v) makes another feel frightened

(vi) too scared to move

(vii) too scared to move

IV. Reported questions

Study these sentences

- His friend asked, "Did you see the snake the next day, doctor?"

  His friend asked the doctor *whether/if* he had seen the snake the next day.

- The little girl wondered, "Will I be home before the TV show begins?"

  The little girl wondered *if/whether* she would be home before the TV show began.

- Someone asked, "Why has the thief left the vest behind?"

  Someone asked *why* the thief had left the vest behind.

  The words *if/whether* are used to report questions which begin with: *do, will, can, have, are* etc. these questions can be answered 'yes' or 'no'.

  Questions beginning with *why/when/where/ how/ which/what* are reported using these same words.

  The reporting verbs we use in questions with if/ whether/why/when etc are: *ask, inquire and wonder.*

Remember that in reported speech

- the present tense changes to past tense
- *here, today, tomorrow, yesterday* etc. change to *there, that day, the next day,* the *day before*, etc.
- *I/you* change to *me/him/he*, etc., as necessary.
- Example, He said to me, 'I don't believe you."
- He said he did not believe me.
- She said to him, 'I don't believe you'.
- She told him that she did not believe him.

Report these questions using *if/whether or why/when/where/how/which/what*. Remember the italicised verbs change into the past tense.

1. Meena asked her friend, "Do you *think* your teacher will come today?"
2. David asked his colleague, "Where *will* you go this summer?"
3. He asked the little boy, "Why *are* you studying English?"
4. She asked me, "When *are* we going to leave?"
5. Pran asked me, *"Have* you finished reading the newspaper?"
6. Seema asked her, "How long *have* you lived here?"
7. Sheila asked the children. *"Are* you ready to do the work"?

Ans. 1. Meena asked her friend if she thought her teacher would come that day.

2. David asked his colleague where he would go that summer.
3. He asked the little boy why he was studying English.
4. She asked me when we were going to leave.
5. Pran asked me if I had finished reading the newspaper.
6. Seema asked her how long she had lived there.
7. Sheila asked the children if they were ready to do the work.

WRITING (NCERT PAGE 63)

I. Try to rewrite the story without its humour, merely as a frightening incident. What details or parts of the story would you leave out?

Ans. I would leave out the following parts of the story while rewriting the narrator's frightening account without humour

- The doctor's admiration of himself while staring in the mirror.
- The doctor's appreciation of his 'handsome smile'.
- His reason for wanting to marry a fat lady.
- His imaginary conversation with God when confronted with death.
- When the doctor ran out of his home.
- The doctor's wife who is a 'thin, reedy sprinter'.
- The robbery of his meagre belongings except the dirty vest.
- The conclusion about the snake being mesmerised by its own beauty.

II. Read the description given alongside this sketch from a photograph in a newspaper (Times of India, 4th September, 1999). Make up a story about what the monkey is thinking, or why it is looking into a mirror.
Write a paragraph about it.

The Fairest Of Them All

A monkey preens itself using a piece of mirror, in the Delhi ridge.
('To preen oneself ' means to spend a lot of time making oneself look attractive, and then admiring one's appearance. The word is used in disapproval.)

Ans. In the heart of the busy Delhi ridge, a mischievous monkey found a strange form of amusement. Clutched in its tiny hands was a makeshift mirror he picked from the chaotic surroundings. The furry creature, sat atop a tree branch, engaged in a strange session of self-admiration, gazing intently into its reflection. As the sunlight filtered through the leaves, casting a warm glow, the monkey seemed absorbed in the act of preening, carefully adjusting its fur and striking poses as if participating in a primate beauty contest. Observing the onlookers with a sly grin, the monkey celebrated its newfound source of entertainment, transforming the ordinary Delhi ridge into its very own enchanted forest where it could declare itself the fairest of them all. The unconventional display of pride amidst the urban jungle left passersby both amused and bewildered, as the monkey continued to redefine the meaning of self-love with each playful gesture.

TRANSLATION (NCERT PAGE 64)

The text you read is a translation of a story by a well-known Malayalam writer, Vaikom Muhammad Basheer.

In translating a story from one language to another, a translator must keep the content intact. However, the language and the style differ in different translations of the same text.

Here are two translations of the opening paragraphs of a novel by the Japanese writer, Haruki Murakami. Read them and answer the questions given below.

Translation A	Translation B
When the phone rang I was in the kitchen, boiling a potful of spaghetti and whistling along with an FM broadcast of the overture to Rossini's *The Thieving Magpie*, which has to be the perfect music for cooking pasta.	I'm in the kitchen cooking spaghetti when the woman calls. Another moment until the spaghetti is done; there I am, whistling the prelude to Rossini's *La Gazza Ladra* along with the FM radio. Perfect spaghetti-cooking music!

Translation A	Translation B
I wanted to ignore the phone, not only because the spaghetti was nearly done, but because Claudio Abbado was bringing the London Symphony to its musical climax.	I hear the telephone ring but tell myself, ignore it. Let the spaghetti finish cooking. It's almost done, and besides, Claudio Abbado and the London Symphony Orchestra are coming to a crescendo.

Compare the two translations on the basis of the following points

(i) the tense of narration (past and present tense)
(ii) short, incomplete sentences
(iii) sentence length

Which of these translations do you like? Give reasons for your choice.

Ans. (i) Translation A is in the past tense while translation B is in the present tense.

(ii) Translation A has complete sentences while translation B has short, incomplete sentences.

(iii) Translation A has long sentences while translation B has short sentences.

I prefer translation A because it is more direct and uses powerful language with a lot of imagery. It uses more personal language which is the way it should be in stories and novels.

REVIEW EXERCISE

Including Competency Based Questions

Part I

Multiple Choice Questions

1. 'Has a snake ever coiled itself around any part of your body? A full-blooded cobra?' Why did the doctor ask these questions? Competency Based

(a) To ensure he had everyone's attention
(b) To learn about his listener's experiences
(c) To suggest that he was braver than the others
(d) To change the topic to one he wanted to discuss

Ans. (a) To ensure he had everyone's attention

2. What is the main idea of the second paragraph of the chapter? Competency Based

(a) The narrator needed a better place to live.
(b) The narrator was an inexperienced doctor.
(c) The narrator was leading a very simple life.
(d) The narrator's financial situation was not great.

Ans. (d) The narrator's financial situation was not great.

3. What does the narrator do in paragraph 4 and 5? Competency Based

(a) Make fun of his own vanity.
(b) Describe his appearance in detail.
(c) Express pride in the way he looked.
(d) Convey satisfaction at his success in life.

Ans. (a) Make fun of his own vanity.

4. Again I heard that sound from above. Why is the sound mentioned multiple times? Competency Based

(a) To distract the reader from what was really happening
(b) To emphasise the poor state of the house
(c) To show how anxious the narrator was
(d) To create a sense of suspense

Ans. (d) To create a sense of suspense

5. What is true about the narrator's encounter with the snake? Competency Based

(a) He saw himself much more clearly than before.
(b) It made him realise that he had a lot more to accomplish.
(c) It gave him a chance to recognise his absolute faith in God.
(d) He understood that he was not as brave as he thought he was.

Ans. (a) He saw himself much more clearly than before.

6. I was no mere image cut in granite. I was suddenly a man of flesh and blood. What do these lines mean? Competency Based

(a) The narrator felt all of his terror at once.
(b) The narrator found himself able to move again.
(c) The narrator was injured by the actions of the snake.
(d) The narrator caught himself admiring the beauty of the snake.

Ans. (b) The narrator found himself able to move again.

7. What word best describes the style of the author's writing in the text? Competency Based

(a) Plain (b) Vague (c) Lyrical (d) Formal

Ans. (c) Lyrical

8. What did the thief leave behind?

(a) The doctor's black coat
(b) The doctor's dirty vest
(c) The doctor's medical book
(d) The snake

Ans. (b) The doctor's dirty vest

9. Why could the doctor not sleep in the room?

(a) The room was very hot.
(b) The rats were making a lot of noise.
(c) Both (a) and (b)
(d) Neither (a) nor (b)

Ans. (c) Both (a) and (b)

10. Why did the narrator feel insulted when he found his dirty vest?

(a) Because he realised how unhygienic he was.
(b) Because the thieves had made his vest dirty.
(c) Because the thieves had burned his vest.
(d) Because the thieves had stolen everything except his dirty vest.

Ans. (d) Because the thieves had stolen everything except his dirty vest.

11. What kind of woman did the narrator want to have as his wife?

(a) A beautiful woman (b) A buxom woman
(c) A fat woman (d) A thin woman

Ans. (c) A fat woman

12. How did the narrator feel when the snake coiled around his left arm?

(a) He felt as if a leaden rod was piercing his heart.
(b) He felt as if he was going to die.
(c) He felt as if god had come there to save him.
(d) He felt as if a rod of fire was crushing his arm.

Ans. (d) He felt as if a rod of fire was crushing his arm.

Extract Based Questions

1. Read the following extract carefully and answer the questions that follow.

I had my meal at a restaurant and returned to my room. I heard a noise from above as I opened the door. The sound was a familiar one.

(i) Who is 'I' in these lines?

Ans. 'I' refers to the Doctor who is the narrator in the given lines.

(ii) The tone of the given lines is

(a) dramatic (b) factual
(c) nostalgic (d) argumentative

Ans. (b) factual

(iii) Which sound was heard when the door was opened? Why was it a 'familiar' sound?

Ans. The sound of rats moving around could be heard when the door was opened. It was a familiar sound because the narrator's room had many rats.

(iv) What will be the antonym of the word 'unknown' in the passage?

Ans. Familiar is the antonym of the word 'unknown'.

2. Read the following extract carefully and answer the questions that follow.

I didn't jump. I didn't tremble. I didn't cry out. There was no time to do any such thing. The snake slithered along my shoulder and coiled around my left arm above the elbow. The hood was spread out and its head was hardly three or four inches from my face!

(i) The given lines show that the narrator is

(a) terrified (b) awed (c) surprised (d) nervous

Ans. (a) terrified

(ii) State True or False.

The set of statements are not true according to the given extract.

1. The snake is harmless.
2. The snake is an admirer of beauty.
3. The narrator is recounting this incidence.

Ans. False

(iii) What happened to the narrator as the snake coiled around his left arm?

Ans. The narrator was unable to act and became speechless as the snake coiled around his left arm.

(iv) **Fill in the blank.**

The phrase .... from the extract means to slide.

Ans. slithered along

3. Read the following extract carefully and answer the questions that follow.

At my slightest movement the snake would strike me! Death lurked four inches away. Suppose it struck, what was the medicine I had to take? There were no medicines in the room. I was but a poor, foolish and stupid doctor. I forgot my danger and smiled feebly at myself. It seemed as if God appreciated that.

(i) **What has happened to the narrator in the passage?**

(a) Met with an accident
(b) Snake had curled around his arm
(c) A robber had entered
(d) Police caught him

Ans. (b) Snake had curled around his arm

(ii) **State True or False.**

The given options correctly answer the question .....

What was going on in the mind of the narrator while seeing the snake?

(a) What will happen if he will bite?
(b) What medicine I'll take if he will bite?
(c) Are there medicines in the house?

Ans. True

(iii) **Why did the doctor call himself poor and foolish?**

Ans. The doctor called himself poor and foolish because he didn't know the medicine to cure snake bite.

(iv) **Fill in the blank with one word only.**

The word .... from the extract means 'waited in hiding'.

Ans. 'lurked'

4. Read the following extract carefully and answer the questions that follow.

I forgot my danger and smiled feebly at myself. It seemed as if God appreciated that. The snake turned its head. It looked into the mirror and saw its reflection. I do not claim that it was the first snake that had ever looked into a mirror. But it was certain that the snake was looking into the mirror.

(i) **The tone of the narrator in the given extract is ..... .**

Ans. relieved

(ii) **From the given extract it seems that the snake is**

(a) trying to copy the narrator
(b) a narcissist
(c) attracted to the mirror
(d) not hungry

Ans. (b) a narcissist

(iii) **What did the snake do after it turned its head?**

Ans. The snake looked into the mirror and saw its reflection after he turned his head away.

(iv) **The word 'feebly' means ....**

Ans. without strength

Part II

Short Answer Type Questions

1. Describe the room in which the narrator lived.

Ans. The room in which the narrator lived was a small rented room without electricity. It was an outer room with two windows and one wall facing the yard.

The room had a tiled roof with long supporting gables that rested on the beam over the wall.

2. "......the wind god seemed to have taken off". What does the narrator mean by these words? Competency Based

Ans. When the narrator said that the wind God seemed to have taken off, he meant that there was no wind blowing when he went out to the balcony and it was quite a hot night.

3. How did the doctor show presence of mind when he encountered the snake?

Or How did the narrator react when the snake fell on him? Competency Based

Ans. The doctor showed great presence of mind on encountering the snake. He neither jumped nor cried out. He sat still on the chair like a stone, holding his breath. His body was still but his mind remained very active.

4. What made the doctor think "Death lurked four inches away"?

Ans. The doctor thought that death lurked four inches away because the snake had coiled around his left arm and its head was hardly three or four inches away from his face. The snake could bite him at any moment and he would surely die if it bit him.

5. Why did the snake leave the doctor's arm?

Ans. The snake left the doctor's arm because it saw its reflection in the mirror and was fascinated (attracted) by it . The snake moved closer to the mirror to enjoy its reflection and freed the arm of the doctor.

6. After the encounter with the snake, why did the narrator want to remove his things from his room? Why did he find that he had little to carry?

Ans. After the encounter with the snake, the narrator was afraid of the snake coming there again. So, he wanted to remove his things from his room to shift to some other place. He found that he had little to carry because a thief had stolen most of his things on the night he ran away to the house of his friend.

7. How did the snake change the doctor's opinion about himself?

Ans. Before the encounter with the snake, the narrator was very proud of himself as he was a bachelor and a doctor. The encounter with the snake made him realise that he was only a poor, stupid and foolish doctor. This was because although he was doctor, he did not have the medicine for snakebite with him.

8. Why does the narrator say that leaving behind the vest was an insult? **Competency Based**

Ans. The narrator says that leaving the vest behind was an insult to him because the thief had stolen everything else except the vest. The thief's actions thus implied that the dirty vest was not good enough for him.

9. How does the doctor describe his sensation when the snake coils around his arm?

Ans. The doctor describes a sensation of intense pain in his left arm, akin to a thick leaden rod or molten fire slowly crushing it. He feels his arm draining of strength, leaving him helpless in the face of impending danger.

10. What does the doctor's laughter suggest about his attitude towards the snake incident?

Ans. The doctor's laughter indicates a sense of amusement or perhaps relief. Despite the situation's initial terror, he now finds humour in the absurdity of the thief's actions and the snake's fascination with its reflection, showing resilience and acceptance of life's quirks.

11. What symbolism is suggested when the doctor reflects on the presence of God during his encounter with the snake? Does it have a humorous tone? **Competency Based**

Ans. During the doctor's encounter with a snake, he reflects on God's presence, which suggests themes of faith, mortality and the human condition. The doctor's contemplation/reflection of God's presence reflects a search for spiritual guidance and comfort during a moment of danger. Although the situation is critical and dangerous, the doctor's reflection is not meant to be humorous. Instead, it adds depth to the story by highlighting the doctor's introspection and recognition of something greater than himself amidst the surreal and potentially life-threatening encounter with the snake.

Long Answer Type Questions

1. According to the doctor's observations, how does the snake's behaviour change when it sees its reflection in the mirror?

Ans. According to the doctor's observations, when the snake sees its reflection in the mirror, its behaviour changes. Initially coiled around the doctor's arm, the snake's attention is diverted towards its reflection in the mirror. It appears intrigued or captivated by the sight, suggesting self-awareness or curiosity.

The doctor speculates/guesses whether the snake is admiring its beauty or thinking about its appearance, humorously pondering if it is deciding on matters like growing a moustache or applying cosmetics. This change in behaviour adds a surreal and somewhat humorous touch to the encounter, highlighting the unexpected and unpredictable nature of the snake's response to its reflection in the mirror.

2. Give a character sketch of the narrator.

Ans. The main character of 'The Snake and The Mirror' is a young doctor who serves as the story's central focus. The doctor has recently established his medical practice and so, is poor. He lives in a small rented room with meagre belongings. As a person, the doctor is described as someone who cares about his looks, as evidenced by his efforts to groom himself and maintain a neat appearance.

Throughout the story, the doctor's humorous outlook and lighthearted approach to adversity shine through. Despite facing a potentially dangerous situation, he maintains a sense of humour and finds amusement in the absurdity of his situation. His humorous inner monologue and absurd thoughts, such as considering marrying a wealthy, overweight woman for an escape plan, add a comedic element to the narrative.

However, when confronted with the unexpected presence of a snake coiled around him, the doctor demonstrates resilience and quick thinking. Despite the initial shock, he remains calm and rationally assesses the situation. His ability to react swiftly and make decisions under pressure reflects a resourceful and adaptable nature.

3. Justify the title of the story 'The Snake and the Mirror'.

Ans. The title of the story 'The Snake and the Mirror' is fully justified as the story centres around the snake and the mirror.

The doctor was sitting in front of a table that had a large mirror on it when a snake landed on him. The snake coiled itself around his left arm and stayed there for a long time. The doctor felt helpless in that situation. He could not move or cry as he feared that the snake would bite him if he did so.

He could not even think of any way to escape from this situation and stayed as still as if he had turned into a stone. He even prayed to God for helping him. The turning point in the story comes only when the snake turned its head and looked into the mirror and saw its reflection. After seeing its reflection in the mirror, the snake slowly uncoiled itself from the narrator's arm and moved into his lap. Then it creeped onto the table and moved towards the mirror. The narrator thus got a chance to escape from the snake and ran to his friend's house. Thus, we can say that the title of the story is very apt and justified.

4. Imagine yourself as the narrator of the story 'The Snake and the Mirror'. Write a diary entry in about 100-120 words describing how you felt after escaping from the snake biting you.

Ans. 20th December, 20XX 9 : 45 pm

Dear diary

Hey! I just escaped from a snake biting me! Do you know how? This is what happened. I was in my room when a snake dropped from the roof and coiled around my left arm. I was terrified and thought that my end was near. Somehow, I told myself to stay calm. I didn't tremble or cry. I knew if I did so the snake would surely bite me. I prayed to God to save me. After sometime, the snake moved its head and saw its reflection in the mirror. Then it slowly uncoiled itself from my arms and moved towards the mirror.

This gave me a chance to run away to my friend's house. I thanked God for saving my life! Wasn't my miraculous escape interesting to hear?

Prisha

ASSESSMENT EXERCISE

Extract Based Questions

Read the following extract carefully and answer the questions that follow.

Immediately I smeared oil all over myself and took a bath. I changed into fresh clothes. The next morning I took my friend to my room to move my things from there. But, we found we had little to carry. Some thief had removed most of my things.

(i) Where did the doctor stay in the night?

(ii) Trace the word from the extract that means 'spread'.

(a) Changed (b) Moved

(c) Smeared (d) Removed

(iii) Why did the doctor take his friend along with him?

(iv) Why did the doctor take bath and change his clothes?

Short Answer (SA) Type Questions

1. What did the doctor do on seeing the snake?
2. Why did the author of 'The Snake and the Mirror' fantasise a fat woman as his wife?
3. While looking into the mirror, what important and earth-shaking decisions did the doctor make?
4. What did the doctor think when the snake was looking into the mirror?
5. When the doctor returned to his room after having his meal, what did he do that shows that it was a hot summer night?

Long Answer (LA) Type Questions

1. 'Birds of a feather flock together' goes the saying. Does the encounter between the snake and the doctor in the story 'The Snake and the Mirror' support the saying? Why or why not?
2. The story 'The Snake and the Mirror' is humorous. Give examples in support of your answer.

CHAPTER 6

My Childhood

by APJ Abdul Kalam

CHAPTER SUMMARY This chapter is an extract taken from the autobiography of APJ Abdul Kalam, 'Wings of Fire'. In this chapter, he describes his house, family, friends and teachers. It also mentions how he earned his first wages. During his childhood, he faced religious discrimination but was able to overcome it with the support of some progressive people. The motivation given to him by his father and science teacher to pursue his goals made him a great scientist in the future.

Kalam's Birth and Family

Abdul Kalam was born in 1931 into a middle-class Tamil family in the island town of Rameswaram in Madras. His father's name was Jainulabdeen and his mother's name was Ashiamma. He had three brothers and one sister. Kalam's father was not much educated but he had great wisdom and generosity. He was not rich but he provided Kalam a very secure childhood. His mother fed many poor people and outsiders everyday.

The family lived in their ancestral house. It was a large *pucca* house, made during mid-nineteenth century. It was made of limestone and brick on the Mosque Street in Rameswaram. Kalam inherited honesty and self-discipline from his father and faith in goodness and deep kindness from his mother.

Kalam's First Earning

Kalam was eight years old when the Second World War started in 1939. There was a great demand for tamarind seeds at that time. Kalam used to collect these seeds and got one anna daily by selling them at a provision store on Mosque street. Kalam's brother-in-law, Jallaluddin told him stories about the war which Kalam later read in the newspaper, *Dinamani*. When India was forced to join the Allied Forces, several changes happened. The train which brought newspapers to Rameswaram was no longer allowed to stop there. So, the newspaper bundles had to be thrown from the moving train on the Rameswaram road between Rameswaram and Dhanushkodi. Kalam earned his first wages by working as a helper to his cousin, Samsuddin, who distributed newspapers in Rameswaram.

Kalam's Childhood Friends

Kalam had three close friends in his childhood. They were Ramanadha Sastry, Aravindan and Sivaprakasan. All of them belonged to orthodox Hindu Brahmin Families. Ramanadha was the son of the high priest of the Rameswaram temple. He later took over the priesthood of the Rameswaram temple from his father. Aravindan joined the business of arranging transport for visiting pilgrims. Sivaprakasan became a catering contractor for the Southern Railways.

Shri Sita Rama Kalyan Ceremony

During the annual ceremony, Kalam's family would arrange special boats for carrying the idols from the temple to the marriage site in the middle of a pond called Rama Tirtha. Kalam grew up listening to bedtime stories from Ramayana and the life of the Prophet.

Discriminatory Attitude of New Teacher in Kalam's School

Kalam sat in the front row in the class when he was studying in fifth standard at the Rameswaram Elementary School. His friend, Ramanadha Sastry, sat next to him.

One day, a new teacher came to the class. He recognised that Kalam was Muslim because he wore a cap and Ramanadha was Hindu because he wore a sacred thread. The teacher could not tolerate a Muslim boy (Kalam) sitting with a Hindu priest's son (Ramanadha). So, he asked Kalam to go and sit on the back bench. Both Kalam and Ramanadha felt very sad about this. When Kalam went to the last row, Ramanadha started crying.

It had a deep and lasting impression on Kalam's mind. Later, Ramanadha's father Lakshmana Sastry called the teacher and warned him against spreading social separation among the children. He was told to either apologise or quit the school and the island. The teacher felt sorry for his behaviour.

Kalam's Science Teacher

Kalam's science teacher, Sivasubramania Iyer, was a high-caste Brahmin. However, he was a rebel and did his best to break social barriers. He wanted Kalam to be a highly educated person in the future.

One day, he invited Kalam to his house for a meal. His wife refused to serve a Muslim boy (Kalam) in her kitchen as she was a conservative women. So, the teacher served Kalam with his own hands and sat next to him to eat.

He again invited Kalam for dinner next weekend. Upon Kalam's hesitation, the teacher told him that one must confront these problems if one wishes to change the system. When Kalam went to his house the next time, Sivasubramania's wife took him inside her kitchen and served him food with her own hands.

Kalam Seeks Permission to Leave Rameswaram

After the Second World War was over, India's freedom was certain. Gandhiji urged Indians to build their own country. Kalam took his father's permission to leave Rameswaram as he wanted to continue his studies at the district headquarters in Ramanathapuram.

His father allowed him to leave but his mother did not like it. So, his father comforted his wife by quoting Kahlil Gibran. He told her that her children are not her's but of life's longing for itself. They came through her and not from her. She could only give her love to them and should not impose her will on them because they have their own thoughts.

Word Meaning

Word	Meaning
erstwhile	former
innate	an inborn quality or feeling in one's nature
helpmate	wife
undistinguished	ordinary
austere	simple, strict and severe
inessential	those which are not necessary
tamarind	a small soft fruit with sticky brown skin (imli)
princely sum	a large amount of money (actually he means the reverse)
anna	an old Indian coin, worth about six paise
Dinamani	a local Tamil newspaper
Allied Forces	the armies of UK, USA and USSR during the Second World War
suspension	temporary cancellation
slot	vacancy
Surge	A sudden increase in the strength of a feeling.
figures of authority	persons who have the power to give orders or make decisions.
orthodox	traditional
priesthood	the work and responsibility of being a priest
pilgrims	pesons visiting holy places

Word	Meaning
catering	supplying of provisions
contractor	entrepreneur
idols	a picture or object that people pray to as part of their religion
Prophet	a person who speaks for God
marked	showed
sacred thread	religious thread worn by the Hindus
could not stomach	could not tolerate
downcast	sad or depressed
communal intolerance	refusal to accept behaviour, beliefs, or opinion of another community or religion.
bluntly	directly
segregation	separation
mingle	mix with each other
on par with	equal to
perturbed	disturbed
confronted	faced
imminent	about to take place
unprecedented	something that has never happened before.

NCERT FOLDER

NCERT Intext and Exercise Questions

THINKING ABOUT THE TEXT ACTIVITY

(NCERT PAGE 75)

I. Answer these questions in one or two sentences each.

Q.1 Where was Abdul Kalam's house?

Ans. Abdul Kalam's house was on the Mosque Street in Rameswaram.

Q.2 What do you think *Dinamani* is the name of? Give a reason for your answer.

Ans. *Dinamani* is the name of a local newspaper. The fact that Abdul Kalam used to read headlines in *Dinamani* to know about the World War indicates that it was the name of a newspaper.

Q.3 Who were Abdul Kalam's school friends? What did they later become?

Ans. Abdul Kalam's school friends were Ramanadha Sastry, Aravindan and Sivaprakasan.

Ramanadha Sastry became a priest in Rameswaram. Aravindan went into the business of arranging transport for visiting pilgrims. Sivaprakasan became a catering contractor for the Southern Railways.

Q.4 How did Abdul Kalam earn his first wages?

Ans. Abdul Kalam earned his first wages by helping his cousin Samsuddin in collecting newspaper bundles which were thrown out from the moving train during the Second World War.

Q.5 Had he earned any money before that? In what way?

Ans. Yes, Kalam had earned money before that. He did so by collecting the tamarind seeds and selling them to a provision store during the Second World War.

II. Answer each of these questions in a short paragraph (about 30 words).

Q.1 How does the author describe: (i) his father, (ii) his mother, (iii) himself?

Ans. (i) Abdul Kalam has described his father as a strict and serious man who possessed great wisdom and gave due care to all the needs of his family.

(ii) Abdul Kalam has described his mother as a large-hearted and generous woman who used to feed everyone visiting the house.

(iii) Abdul Kalam has described himself as a short and thin boy descended from tall and handsome parents.

Q.2 What characteristics does he say he inherited from his parents?

Ans. Abdul Kalam inherited honesty and self-discipline from his father, and a sense of kindness and faith in goodness from his mother.

III. Discuss these questions in class with your teacher and then write down your answers in two or three paragraphs each.

Q.1 "On the whole, the small society of Rameswaram was very rigid in terms of the segregation of different social groups," says the author.

(i) Which social groups does he mention? Were these groups easily identifiable (for example, by the way they dressed)?

(ii) Were they aware only of their differences or did they also naturally share friendships and experiences? (Think of the bedtime stories in Kalam's house; of who his friends were; and of what used to take place in the pond near his house.)

(iii) The author speaks both of people who were very aware of the differences among different people and those who tried to bridge these differences. Can you identify such people in the text?

(iv) Narrate two incidents that show how differences can be created and also how they can be resolved. How can people change their attitudes?

Ans. (i) Kalam has mentioned Hindus and Muslims as two distinct social groups living in Rameswaram.

These two groups were easily identifiable in the way they dressed. For example, Kalam being a Muslim wore a cap and his friend, Ramanadha, being a Hindu Brahmin wore a sacred thread.

(ii) They were aware of their differences but they also naturally shared friendship and experiences.

Kalam's mother and grandmother used to tell the children in his family the bedtime stories from the Ramayana and the life of the prophet.

Apart from this, Kalam's family used to arrange boats with a special platform during the annual Shri Sita Rama Kalyanam ceremony. They were used to carry the Idols of the Lord from the temple to the marriage site which was situated in the middle of a pond.

(iii) The people who were aware of the differences among them were Kalam's new teacher and the wife of his science teacher, Sivasubramania Iyer.

The people who tried to bridge the gap were Lakshmana Sastry, the father of Kalam's friend,

Ramanadha Sastry and Kalam's science teacher, Sivasubramania Iyer.

(iv) Two incidents from the text illustrate the creation and resolution of differences. First, a new teacher enforces segregation in the classroom based on religious identities, showcasing how discrimination can create divisions. However, Lakshmana Sastry confronts the teacher, advocating for equality and fostering inclusivity within the community.

Another example is where the author's science teacher faces resistance from his wife when inviting the author, a Muslim boy, to dine in their home. This incident demonstrates how societal norms can create barriers between people from different backgrounds. Yet, through his actions, Sivasubramania Iyer challenges stereotypes, fosters understanding, and promotes acceptance. Individuals must engage in self-reflection, empathy, and education to change attitudes. By questioning biases and fostering empathy through exposure to diverse experiences, people can recognise and appreciate the humanity in others. Education is crucial in challenging stereotypes and promoting inclusivity, providing opportunities for dialogue and critical thinking. Individuals can gradually change their attitudes and contribute to a more harmonious society through these efforts.

Q.2 **(i) Why did Abdul Kalam want to leave Rameswaram?**

(ii) What did his father say to this?

(iii) What do you think his words mean? Why do you think he spoke those words?

Ans. (i) Abdul Kalam wanted to leave Rameswaram to continue his studies (higher education) at the district headquarters in Ramanathapuram.

(ii) His father told Abdul that he had to go out to grow. He quoted the example of the seagull flying across the sun alone and without a nest to Abdul.

(iii) His words mean that one day one has to leave one's parents.

He spoke these words to encourage and inspire Abdul to leave the house for higher studies.

THINKING ABOUT LANGUAGE

(NCERT PAGE 75-77)

I. Find the sentence in the text where these words occur:

erupt surge trace undistinguished casualty

Look these words up in a dictionary which gives examples of how they are used.

Now answer the following questions

1. What are the things that can *erupt*? Use examples to explain the various meanings of erupt. Now do the same for the word *surge*. What things can *surge*?
2. What are the meanings of the word *trace* and which of the meanings is closest to the word in the text?
3. Can you find the word *undistinguished* in your dictionary? (If not, look up the word *distinguished* and say what *undistinguished* must mean.)

Ans. The sentences in the text where these words occur are as follows

(i) For reasons I have never been able to understand, a sudden demand for tamarind seeds *erupted* in the market.

(ii) Half a century later, I can still feel the *surge* of pride in earning my own money for the first time.

(iii) My brother-in-law Jallaluddin would tell me stories about the war which I would later attempt to *trace* in the headlines in *Dinamani*.

(iv) I was one of many children – a short boy with rather *undistinguished* looks, born to tall and handsome parents.

(v) The first *casualty* came in the form of the suspens- ion of the train halt at Rameswaram station.

Ans. 1, 2 and 3. Do it yourself.

II. THINKING ABOUT LANGUAGE

(NCERT PAGE 75-77)

Q.1 **Match the phrases in Column A with their meanings in Column B.**

	A		B
(i)	broke out	(a)	an attitude of kindness, a readiness to give freely
(ii)	in accordance with	(b)	was not able to tolerate
(iii)	a helping hand	(c)	began suddenly in a violent way
(iv)	could not stomach	(d)	assistance
(v)	generosity of spirit	(e)	persons with power to make decisions
(vi)	figures of authority	(f)	according to a particular rule, principle or system

Ans. (i) – (c), (ii) – (f), (iii) – (d), (iv) – (b), (v) – (a), (vi) – (e)

Q.2 **Study the words in italics in the sentences below. They are formed by prefixing *un* - or *in* - to their antonyms (words opposite in meaning).**

- I was a short boy with rather undistinguished looks. (un + distinguished)
- My austere father used to avoid all inessential comforts. (in + essential)
- The area was completely unaffected by the war. (un + affected)
- He should not spread the poison of social inequality and communal intolerance. (in + equality, in + tolerance)

Now form the opposites of the words below by prefixing un- or in-. The prefix in- can also have the forms il-, ir-, or im- (for example: illiterate -il + literate, impractical -im + practical, irrational - ir +rational). You may consult a dictionary if you wish.

--adequate	--acceptable	--regular	--tolerant
--demanding	--active	--true	--permanent
---patriotic	--disputed	--accessible	--coherent
--logical	--legal	--responsible	--possible

Ans.

inadequate	unacceptable	irregular	intolerant
undemanding	inactive	untrue	impermanent
unpatriotic	undisputed	inaccessible	incoherent
illogical	illegal	irresponsible	impossible

III. Rewrite the sentences below, changing the verbs in brackets into the passive form.

Q.1 In yesterday's competition, the prizes (give away) by the Principal.

Ans. In yesterday's competition, the prizes were given away by the Principal.

Q.2 In spite of financial difficulties, the labourers (pay) on time.

Ans. In spite of financial difficulties, the labourers were paid on time.

Q.3 On Republic Day, vehicles (not allow) beyond this point.

Ans. On Republic Day, vehicles are not allowed beyond this point.

Q.4 Second-hand books (buy and sell) on the pavement every Saturday.

Ans. Second-hand books are bought and sold on the pavement every Saturday.

Q.5 Elections to the Lok Sabha (hold) every five years.

Ans. Elections to the Lok Sabha are held every five years.

Q.6 Our National Anthem (compose) Rabindranath Tagore.

Ans. Our National Anthem was composed by Rabindranath Tagore.

IV. Rewrite the paragraphs below, using the correct form of the verb given in brackets.

Q.1 How Helmets Came To Be Used in Cricket?

Nari Contractor was the Captain and an opening batsman for India in the 1960s. The Indian cricket team went on a tour to the West Indies in 1962. In a match against Barbados in Bridgetown, Nari Contractor (seriously injure and collapse).

In those days helmets (not wear). Contractor (hit) on the head by a bouncer from Charlie Griffith. Contractor's skull (fracture). The entire team (deeply concern). The West Indies players (worry). Contractor (rush) to hospital. He (accompany) by Frank Worrell, the Captain of the West Indies Team. Blood (donate) by the West Indies players. Thanks to the timely help, Contractor (save). Nowadays, helmets (routinely use) against bowlers.

Ans. Nari Contractor was the Captain and an opening batsman for India in the 1960s. The Indian cricket team went on a tour to the West Indies in 1962. In a match against Barbados in Bridgetown, Nari Contractor was seriously injured and collapsed. In those days helmets were not worn. Contractor was hit on the head by a bouncer from Charlie Griffith. Contractor's skull had fractured. The entire team was deeply concerned. The West Indies players were worried. Contractor was rushed to hospital. He was accompanied by Frank Worrell, the Captain of the West Indies Team. Blood was donated by the West Indies players. Thanks to the timely help, Contractor was saved. Nowadays, helmets are routinely used against bowlers.

Q.2 Oil from Seeds

Vegetable oils (make) from seeds and fruits of many plants growing all over the world from tiny sesame seeds to big, juicy coconuts. Oil (produce) from cotton seeds, groundnuts, soya beans and sunflower seeds. Olive oil (use) for cooking, salad dressing etc. Olives (shake) from the trees and (gather) up, usually by hand. The olives (ground) to a thick paste which is spread onto special mats. Then the mats (layer) up on the pressing machine which will gently squeeze them to produce olive oil.

Ans. Vegetable oils are made from seeds and fruits of many plants growing all over the world from tiny sesame seeds to big, juicy coconuts. Oil is produced from cotton seeds, groundnuts, soya beans and sunflower seeds. Olive oil is used for cooking, salad dressing etc. Olives are shaken from the trees and gathered up, usually by hand. The olives are ground to a thick paste which is spread onto special mats. Then the mats are layered up on the pressing machine which will gently squeeze them to produce olive oil.

WRITING (NCERT PAGE 79)

Q.1 Think and write a short account of what life in Rameswaram in the 1940s must have been like.

Ans. In the 1940s, life in Rameswaram, a small island town in Tamil Nadu, was marked by simplicity, tradition and a close-knit community. The majority of residents were economically modest, engaged in fishing, agriculture and small businesses. The fishing community faced the challenges of the unpredictable sea, requiring courage and hard work for sustenance. Social dynamics were influenced by traditional values and the caste system played a significant role.

As India underwent significant political and social changes with the struggle for independence, residents likely held a mix of aspirations. Some embraced the winds of change, while others clung to familiar traditions. Life in Rameswaram during the 1940s reflected a delicate balance between the desire for modernisation and the preservation of cultural heritage, with the community navigating this nuanced landscape amidst the broader transformations in the country.

REVIEW EXERCISE

Including Competency Based Questions

Part I

Multiple Choice Questions

1. Where was Kalam born?

(a) In an island town of Dhanuskodi
(b) In an island town of Rameswaram
(c) In a city called Mosque Street
(d) In Andhra Pradesh

Ans. (b) In an island town of Rameswaram

2. How does the writer describe his mother? Competency Based

(a) A good cook (b) An honest lady
(c) A generous person (d) An authoritative figure

Ans. (c) A generous person

3. Who were the three close friends of Kalam?

(a) Ramanadha Sastry, Aravindan, Sivaprakasan
(b) Pakshi Lakshmana Sastry, Samsuddin, Sivasubramania Iyer
(c) Aravindan, Sivaprakasan, Jallaluddin
(d) Ramanadha Sastry, Aravindan, Sivasubramania Iyer

Ans. (a) Ramanadha Sastry, Aravindan, Sivaprakasan

4. What is the main idea of the third paragraph? Competency Based

(a) Why the writer had to work during his childhood?
(b) How the World War affected his childhood?
(c) How much the writer enjoyed his childhood adventures?
(d) Who was the main influence on the author during his childhood?

Ans. (b) How the World War affected his childhood?

5. How did the Kalam's family help in Shri Sita Rama Kalyanam Ceremony?

(a) By arranging boats with a special platform for carrying idols.
(b) By catering for the kalyanam ceremony.
(c) By singing songs for the ceremony.
(d) By performing events from Ramayana.

Ans. (a) By arranging boats with a special platform for carrying idols.

6. What kind of person is Lakshmana Sastry? Competency Based

(a) Authoritative but fair (b) Passionate but flexible
(c) Stubborn but courageous (d) Traditional yet open to ideas

Ans. (a) Authoritative but fair

7. Events from .... and from the .... were the bedtime stories for Kalam and his siblings.

(a) the Ramayana, life of the Prophet
(b) the Bhagvad Geeta, Ramayana
(c) the Ramayana, Bhagvad Geeta
(d) the Prophet's life, Hanuman's life

Ans. (a) the Ramayana, life of the Prophet

8. What was Sivasubramanian Iyer's attitude towards social change? Competency Based

(a) Passive but intelligent. (b) Resigned but optimistic
(c) Patient and determined (d) Belligerent and hypocritical

Ans. (c) Patient and determined

9. How did the teacher in fifth standard make out the difference in Kalam's and Ramanadha Sastry's religious beliefs?

(a) By hearing their languages (b) By seeing their clothes
(c) By seeing their writings (d) None of these

Ans. (b) By seeing their clothes

10. What did the writer try to accomplish with this text? Competency Based

(a) Argue against religious discrimination
(b) Describe various attitudes towards religion
(c) Provide a comprehensive picture of his early life.
(d) Defend the attitudes he inherited from his patients.

Ans. (c) Provide a comprehensive picture of his early life.

11. Which problems are talked about in the line "Once you decide to change the system, such problems have to be confronted."

(a) Communal differences (b) Differences in faith
(c) Biased behaviour (d) All of these

Ans. (d) All of these

12. Why did Sivasubramina's wife take Kalam into her kitchen and serve him with her own hands?

(a) She did not find him any different than them when he visited them for the second time.
(b) She liked his way of eating, drinking and cleaning.
(c) She found him to be just like a Brahmin.
(d) Both (a) and (c)

Ans. (a) She did not find him any different than them when he visited them for the second time.

13. What is the theme of the story 'My Childhood'?

1. **Children are precious.**
2. **Society, environment and childhood experiences shape one's life.**
3. **Childhood is a treasure.**

(a) Only 1 is true (b) Only 2 is true
(c) 1 and 3 are true (d) 2 and 3 are true

Ans. (b) Only 2 is true

14. Why did Kalam refer to his Science teacher Sivasubramnaia Iyer as a 'rebel'? Choose the one which is true.

(i) He did not believe in social rankings.
(ii) He did his best to break social barriers.

(a) Only (i) is true (b) Only (ii) is true
(c) Both (i) and (ii) are true (d) Neither (i) nor (ii) is true

Ans. (c) Both (i) and (ii) are true

15. Sivasubramania served Kalam himself and sat with him to eat ....

(a) to show equal respect for everybody.
(b) because he wanted to prove himself great.
(c) to demoralise his wife.
(d) None of the above

Ans. (a) to show equal respect for everybody.

Extract Based Questions

1. Read the following extract carefully and answer the questions that follow.

That forced my cousin Samsuddin, who distributed newspapers in Rameswaram, to look for a helping hand to catch the bundles and, as if naturally, I filled the slot. Samsuddin helped me earn my first wages. Half a century later, I can still feel the surge of pride in earning my own money for the first time.

(i) The tone of the given lines is

(a) argumentative (b) personal and emotional
(c) didactive (d) factual

Ans. (d) factual

(ii) What made Samsuddin look for a helping hand?

Ans. Samsuddin looked for a helping hand because the train that supplied the newspapers he sold would not stop at the Rameswaram station due to World War II. So, Samsuddin needed a helping hand in catching the bundles of newspaper that were thrown from the train.

(iii) Which word can replace the underlined word.

The recent <u>surge</u> in the cooking oil prices is due to the shortage in the production of soyabean and sunflower crops.

Ans. The word 'hike' can replace the underlined word.

(iv) What characteristics of the speaker is pointed out in the given lines?

Ans. Enterprising and hardworking are two characteristics of the speaker are pointed out in the given lines.

2. Read the following extract carefully and answer the questions that follow.

In accordance with our social ranking as the new teacher saw it, I was asked to go and sit on the back bench. I felt very sad, and so did Ramanadha Sastry. He looked utterly downcast as I shifted to my seat in the last row. The image of him weeping when I shifted to the last row left a lasting impression on me.

(i) Who is 'I' in the above extract?

(a) Ramanadha Sastry (b) Sivasubramania Iyer
(c) APJ Abdul Kalam (d) Lakshmana Sastry

Ans. (c) APJ Abdul Kalam

(ii) State True or False.

The statements that is True about the new teacher are a and c

(a) he had an orthodox personality.
(b) he was a broad-minded person with liberal thoughts.
(c) he had his own notion of social ranking.

Ans. True

(iii) Why did Ramanadha Sastry feel utterly downcast?

Ans. Ramanadha Sastry felt utterly downcast because he was separated from his dear friend.

(iv) Why was Kalam asked to sit on back bench?

Ans. The teacher asked Kalam to sit on the back bench owing to his 'social ranking'.

3. Read the following extract carefully and answer the questions that follow.

For reasons I have never been able to understand, a sudden demand for tamarind seeds erupted in the market. I used to collect the seeds and sell them to a provision shop on Mosque street. A day's collection would fetch me the princely sum of one Anna. My brother-in-law Jallaluddin would tell me stories about the war which I would later attempt to trace in the headlines in Dinamani.

(i) Which war is referred to in the above extract?

(a) First World War (b) Second World War
(c) India-China War (d) India-Pakistan War

Ans. (b) Second World War

(ii) State whether the following statement is True or False.

Kalam was hardworking and had faith in the dignity of labour.

Ans. True

(iii) Why were tamarind seeds collected by Kalam? How much was he paid for it?

Ans. Kalam collected tamarind seeds so that he could earn some money. He was paid one anna every day for the tamarind seeds that he managed to collect.

(iv) How did the Second World War affect Kalam's early life?

Ans. The Second World War, which began when Kalam was eight, created a demand for tamarind seeds, enabling him to earn money by selling them. The war also led to changes in newspaper delivery, prompting his cousin Samsuddin to employ Kalam, marking his first experience of earning a wage.

4. Read the following extract carefully and answer the questions that follow.

His wife watched us from behind the kitchen door. I wondered whether she had observed any difference in the way I ate rice, drank water or cleaned the floor after the meal. When I was leaving his house, Sivasubramania Iyer invited me to join him for dinner again the next weekend. Observing my hesitation, he told me not to get upset, saying, "Once you decide to change the system, such problems have to be confronted." When I visited his house the next week, Sivasubramania Iyer's wife took me inside her kitchen and served me food with her own hands.

(i) Why did the teacher's wife watch them from behind the kitchen door?

(a) She believed in segregation of different people.
(b) She didn't want Kalam to enter the kitchen area.
(c) She was observing the behaviour of Kalam.
(d) Both (a) and (b)

Ans. (d) Both (a) and (b)

(ii) What did Mr. Iyer's wife do when Kalam visited the following week?

Ans. The following week, when Kalam visited their house, Mrs. Iyer served him food with her own hands.

(iii) In the phrase 'change the system', the system is

Ans. caste system

(iv) Why was Kalam hesitant to eat food with the Hindu family?

Ans. Kalam was hesitant to eat food with the Hindu family because he felt that he was not welcomed in the family.

Part II

Short Answer Type Questions

1. Why does the author describe his father as austere? **Competency Based**

Ans. APJ Abdul Kalam has described his father as austere because he was a simple man. His father had a policy of never indulging in unnecessary luxuries. However, he did provide every necessary comfort to his family.

2. How did Abdul come to know about the progress of the World War?

Ans. Abdul came to know about the progress of the World War from the stories narrated to him by his brother-in-law Jallaluddin. Later on, he tried to find these events in the headlines in the local Tamil newspaper *Dinamani*. These were the ways in which Kalam used to get the news of the War.

3. How did the Second World War give an opportunity to Kalam to earn his first wages?

Ans. During the Second World War, a state of emergency was declared and hence, the stoppage of trains at Rameswaram station was suspended. So, Kalam helped his cousin, Samsuddin, in catching the bundles of newspapers that were thrown on the road from the running train. In this way, the Second World War gave an opportunity to Kalam to earn his first wages.

4. Kalam had a secure childhood. Do you agree/ disagree? Give reasons.

Or Kalam's childhood was a secure one, both materially and emotionally. Illustrate this fact.

Ans. I agree that Kalam had a secure childhood. This can be said because he lived in a large pucca house and all his basic needs like food, medicine or clothes were taken care by his father.

Thus, he had a materially and emotionally secure childhood.

5. What did Abdul Kalam's family do during the annual Shri Sita Rama Kalayanam ceremony?

Ans. During the annual Shri Sita Rama Kalayanam ceremony, Kalam's family would arrange for boats with a special platform for carrying the Idols of the Lord from the temple to the marriage site situated in the middle of the pond called as Rama Tirtha.

6. Do you think the new teacher deserved the treatment meted out to him? Why/ why not?

Ans. Yes, the new teacher deserved the treatment meted out to him because he tried to separate Abdul from his Hindu friend, Ramanadha. In this way, he was spreading the wrong message of communal intolerance in the minds of the children in the class.

7. Did Ramanadha Sastry genuinely like Abdul Kalam? Justify your response. Competency Based

Ans. Ramanandha Sastry genuinely liked Abdul Kalam. This can be proved by the fact that he even cried when Kalam was told to sit in the back row. He further complained about the prejudiced teacher to his father to make sure that his friend Kalam would be treated fairly at school.

8. What was the difference in the attitudes of the science teacher and his wife towards APJ Abdul Kalam?

Ans. The science teacher was an orthodox Brahmin but he did his best to break social barriers and mixed with other religions and communities. He invited Abdul to his home and served him food. He also sat beside Abdul to have his meal. On the other hand, his wife was very conservative and refused to serve Abdul as he was a Muslim.

9. Why is Sivasubramania Iyer referred to as 'something of a rebel'? Competency Based

Ans. Sivasubramaniam Iyer is referred to as something of a rebel because he did his best to break social barriers so that people from varying backgrounds could mingle easily. He even invited Kalam to dine with him at his home despite the reservations of his orthodox wife.

10. How did Abdul's father console his wife when Abdul left Rameswaram for higher studies?

Ans. Abdul's father consoled his wife by quoting Kahlil Gibran when Abdul left Rameswaram for higher studies. He told her that her children are not her children but are the sons and daughter's for life's longing for itself. He, further, told her that she can give them her love but not her thoughts.

11. How did the teacher's discriminatory actions emotionally affect Kalam and his friend Ramanadha Sastry?

Ans. The teacher's discriminatory actions made Kalam and Ramanadha Sastrysad and upset. Kalam was moved to the back of the class, separating him from his friend based on religious differences. This act of segregation deeply affected both boys emotionally, highlighting the injustice and inequality they experienced.

12. What role did Sivasubramania Iyer play in Kalam's life?

Ans. Sivasubramania Iyer, Kalam's science teacher, defied social barriers and encouraged Kalam's academic growth. Despite his conservative background, he mentored Kalam, aiming to elevate him to a highly educated individual. His support and guidance were instrumental in shaping Kalam's aspirations and breaking societal norms.

13. How did Kalam's friendship with Ramanadha Sastry demonstrate religious harmony?

Ans. Kalam's friendship with Ramanadha Sastry, a Hindu Brahmin, showcased religious harmony. Despite their different backgrounds, they shared a deep bond and mutual respect, transcending religious divides. Their friendship exemplified tolerance, understanding and acceptance, showing that unity and friendship can thrive despite religious differences.

14. What did Kalam's father mean by quoting Khalil Gibran to his mother about their children? Competency Based

Ans. By quoting Khalil Gibran, Kalam's father meant that children are independent individuals with thoughts and destinies. Parents can provide love and support but not impose their thoughts on their children. This emphasised the importance of allowing Kalam to pursue his path and personal growth.

Long Answer Type Questions

1. What happened in Abdul's school when a new teacher asked Abdul to sit at the back of the class? What values was the teacher lacking? What values did Lakshmana Sastry display at the conclusion of this incident?

Ans. Abdul sat in the front row in the class when he was studying in fifth standard at the Rameswaram Elementary school. His close friend, Ramanadha Sastry used to sit next to him. One day, a new teacher came to the class. Being communal-minded, he could not tolerate a Hindu priest's son sitting beside a Muslim boy in the class and ordered Abdul to sit on the back bench.

Both Abdul and Ramanadha felt very sad about it. Ramanadha started crying when Abdul went to the last row.

After school, both these boys informed their families about this matter. Ramanadha Sastry's father, Lakshmana Sastry, summoned the teacher and in the presence of the boys, scolded the teacher for spreading the thoughts of social inequality and communal intolerance in the minds of the innocent children.

The teacher lacked the value of considering all humans equal. Lakshmana Sastry displayed the values of considering people of all religions as equal, besides showing a strong sense of conviction which ultimately reformed the young teacher.

2. How could the science teacher Sivasubramania Iyer, though an orthodox Brahmin with a very conservative wife, be a friend of Abdul Kalam? Give incidents to support your answer.

Ans. The science teacher Sivasubramania Iyer was an orthodox Brahmin with a very conservative wife. Yet he could become friends with Abdul Kalam because of his scientific outlook and rational thinking.

The first incident of their friendship was when he urged Kalam to be highly educated, as he recognised the intelligence of the child. His friendly advice gave inspiration to Kalam for further studies, as later on Kalam asked his father's permission to go to the district headquarters in Ramanathapuram for higher studies.

The other incident which showed that the teacher was Kalam's friend was when he invited Kalam to his house for a meal. His orthodox wife was shocked when a Muslim boy was invited for dining in her kitchen but his wish prevailed ultimately. These two incidents show that the science teacher was a rebel and was determined to break these social barriers.

Therefore, he could become a friend of Kalam, even though they came from different religious communities.

3. "Once you decide to change the system, such problems have to be confronted." What system is being referred to in this sentence from the chapter 'My Childhood'? What are such problems?

Ans. The system referred to here is the system of discrimination on the basis of religion. It is due to the narrow mindedness of people who think that their religion is better or superior than the other religions. Hence, such people avoid mixing with the people of other religions and are intolerant towards them.

In the chapter, the Brahmin lady (the science teacher's wife) did not serve food to the Muslim boy (Abdul) because she felt that the purity of her kitchen would get spoilt if Abdul Kalam entered her kitchen.

Such problems refer to the problems related to changing the people's fixed mindsets. The science teacher's wife had a fixed mindset that her kitchen would get impure if a Muslim boy ate food in it. She was not ready to accept a Muslim guest in her house and hence was intolerant towards him.

4. What role did APJ Abdul Kalam's parents play in shaping his childhood experiences and values?

Ans. APJ Abdul Kalam's parents played a pivotal role in shaping his childhood experiences and values. Despite their modest means, they instilled in him invaluable qualities such as honesty, self-discipline, faith in goodness and kindness. His father, Jainulabdeen, possessed wisdom and generosity despite his limited formal education while his mother, Ashiamma, was known for her kindness and hospitality. Their ancestral home provided a secure and nurturing environment, emphasising essential needs over luxuries.

Through their actions and teachings, Kalam learned the importance of integrity, hard work and compassion. Their influence laid the foundation for his strong moral compass and guided his character throughout his life's journey.

5. Albert Einstein and Abdul Kalam were both great scientists.

Assume they meet each other and have a conversation about climate change.

Write this conversation in about 100-120 words.

Ans. **Albert** Hi Abdul, How are you?

Abdul Hi Albert, I am fine, How about you?

Albert I am also good. It's quite hot here at this time of the year. It didn't use to be so earlier.

Abdul Hmm... The winters are getting warmer here too! And the pollution is rising day by day.

Albert Yes. The situation is really grim. It's high time we did something about it.

Abdul Let's call a meeting of the world leaders, scientists and policy makers.

Albert That will be a good idea! It will help us in chalking out a plan to deal with this menace of climate change.

Abdul I will send the draft for the invitation of the meeting. Please go through it before we meet next. Till then, Bye!

Albert Will do that. Bye!

6. APJ Abdul Kalam from the chapter 'My Childhood' and Albert Einstein from 'A Truly Beautiful Mind' were both historical figures that were regarded as geniuses. Examine in 120 words.

Ans. Both APJ Abdul Kalam and Albert Einstein were geniuses in their own right, each leaving a permanent mark on the world. Kalam, known as the 'Missile Man of India' was a visionary scientist and former President of India. He was celebrated for his contributions to aerospace engineering and defense technology. He advocated for innovation and education, inspiring countless individuals with his generosity and dedication to serving humanity.

On the other hand, Albert Einstein revolutionised our understanding of the universe with his groundbreakingtheories in physics, notably the theory of relativity. His intellect reshaped modern science, laying the foundation for countless advancements in technology and space exploration. While their fields differed, both Kalam and Einstein are examples of unparalleled brilliance, leaving legacies that continue to inspire generations globally.

7. Kezia says there are different kinds of fathers. Do you think Kalam's father is different from Kezia's father? How?

Ans. Yes, Kalam's father is indeed different from Kezia's father, and this can be understood by looking at the contrasting characteristics and relationships each child shares with their father.

In the story 'The Little Girl', Kezia's father is portrayed as strict, distant and emotionally unapproachable. He is a man of authority, and Kezia views him with fear and anxiety. His coldness is seen in the way he scolds Kezia for small mistakes, and he seems to have little understanding or patience for her needs. For example, when Kezia tries to do something special for him by making a birthday gift, her efforts are misunderstood, and her father reacts sharply. Kezia's perception of her father is that of a stern figure, someone who lacks warmth and compassion, which causes her to feel isolated and disconnected from him.

In contrast, Kalam's father, as described in 'My Childhood', is a kind, compassionate and supportive figure. Kalam speaks highly of his father, describing him as a man with deep spiritual values and wisdom. Unlike Kezia's father, who creates emotional distance, Kalam's father fosters a close and nurturing relationship with him. He encourages Kalam to pursue his dreams and imbues him with strong moral principles. Kalam recalls how his father he provided emotional and intellectual guidance, helping him grow into a thoughtful and ambitious individual. Even when Kalam faced challenges, his father was there to offer reassurance and wisdom.

In short, Kalam's father is different from Kezia's father in terms of emotional warmth, parenting approach, and their influence on their children's development. These contrasting relationships highlight how different parenting styles can shape a child's perception of their father and influence their emotional development.

ASSESSMENT EXERCISE

Extract Based Questions

Read the following extract carefully and answer the questions that follow.

On the whole, the small society of Rameswaram was very rigid in terms of segregation of different social groups. However, my science teacher Sivasubramania Iyer, though an orthodox Brahmin with very conservative wife, was something of a rebel. He did his best to break social barriers so that people from varying backgrounds could mingle easily. He used to spend hours with me and would say, "Kalam, I want you to develop so that you are on par with the highly educated people of the big cities."

(i) How was the society of Rameswaram as a whole?

(ii) Sivasubramania Iyer belonged to

(a) Kshatriya class

(b) Shudra class

(c) Orthodox Brahmin

(d) Vaishyas class

(iii) How was Kalam's teacher different from others?

(iv) Though an orthodox Brahmin, why did Mr Iyer rebel?

Short Answer (SA) Type Questions

1. What did Abdul tell about his days during the World War?
2. What lesson did the priest Lakshmana Sastry teach the new teacher?
3. How was Abdul treated by the science teacher's wife when he was invited to have a meal the first time? What was different in her behaviour the second time?
4. Why was the science teacher called a rebel?
5. What did Abdul do after the Second World War was over?

Long Answer (LA) Type Questions

1. What does Kalam tell about his parents, his house and comforts he had in his childhood?
2. Abdul Kalam's science teacher and the 'new teacher' were different in each and every respect. Explain this statement in context of the lesson, 'My Childhood'.
3. "Once you decide to change the system, such problems have to be confronted." What system in this sentence is Mr Iyer referring to? What value did Iyer want to teach Abdul by saying this?

CHAPTER 7

Reach for the Top

Part-I Santosh Yadav

CHAPTER SUMMARY This chapter presents the journey of two successful women, Santosh Yadav and Maria Sharapova. Both women show that with determination and hard work, one can overcome all obstacles and achieve success.

Part-I It is about Santosh Yadav, a record holding mountaineer. Santosh was born in a very conservative society in Haryana where daughters had no freedom. However, Santosh, with her will and dedication, took control of her life. As a result, she became the first woman to climb Mt. Everest twice.

Santosh's Birth and Family Background

Santosh Yadav is the first woman in the world who has climbed Mt. Everest twice. She was born in a society where a son was considered as a blessing and a daughter was not welcomed. Once, a holy man visited the family to bless Santosh's mother with a son but Santosh's grandmother told him that they wanted a daughter. Santosh, a sister of five elder brothers, was born in a small village in Joniyawas of Rewari district in Haryana.

Non-Traditional Santosh

Santosh's name means contentment or satisfaction but she was never satisfied with the traditional life of her society. So, she started to live her life according to her own terms. The other girls of the society wore traditional dresses while Santosh wore shorts. Santosh believed that if she followed the right and a rational path, then the other people around her would have to change.

Early Education

Santosh's parents were rich landowners. They had the capacity to send Santosh to the best schools of Delhi. However, while her brothers were educated properly in good schools, she was sent to the local village school because of family custom. Santosh decided to fight this system.

Education in Delhi and Jaipur

Santosh's parents wanted to marry her off at the age of 16 because in her village, most of the girls got married at this age. Santosh refused to marry and threatened her parents that she would not get married until she gets proper education.

Santosh left her home and got admission in a school in Delhi. Her parents initially refused to pay the fees. However, when she told them that she would work part time to pay the fees, they agreed to pay for her education.

Santosh's Interest in Climbing

Santosh passed her high school and got admission in Maharani college in Jaipur. She got a room in Kasturba Hostel which faced the Aravalli Hills. She used to see some villagers going up the hills and then disappearing after some time. One day, Santosh checked herself to know where the climbers were disappearing. She found that those people were mountaineers. They motivated Santosh to take interest in climbing.

Admission in a Mountaineering Institute

Santosh was a determined girl. She took admission in Nehru Institute of Mountaineering located in Uttarkashi. After completing her course in Jaipur, she directly left for Uttarkashi. Her college semester in Jaipur was to end in April but it ended on 19th May. She was supposed to be in Uttarkashi on the 21st May. So, Santosh wrote a letter to her father and apologised for taking admission in Uttarkashi without his permission.

Santosh as a Mountaineer

In Uttarkashi, Santosh went on an expedition every year. She developed climbing skills and an amazing immunity to cold and high altitude. She as a mountaineer had an iron will, physical endurance (capacity to tolerate) and mental toughness.

Climbing Mt. Everest

Santosh's hard work and determination led her to climb Mt. Everest, the highest peak in the world in 1992. She had climbed Mt. Everest at just 20 years of age. She became the youngest female to climb Mt. Everest.

Santosh's Humanity

Apart from her mountaineering skills, Santosh also impressed her seniors with her humanity. Her concern for others and her desire to work together as a team, made her a special person.

During Everest mission in 1992, she provided special care to her teammate in South Col. Unfortunately, she could not save him. However, she saved another climber, Mohan Singh by sharing her oxygen with him.

The Second Climb to Mt. Everest

After a year of her first expedition, Santosh, joined an Indo-Nepalese Women's Expedition and again climbed Mt. Everest within a year. She became the first and only woman to climb Mt. Everest twice. Her achievements brought glory to her and also gave India a unique place in mountaineering. The Indian government recognised Santosh's achievements and awarded her with the Padma Shri.

The Happiest Moment of Santosh's Life

Santosh felt the happiest moment of her life when she climbed Mt. Everest. She describes the feeling as unreal. She felt proud when she unfurled the Indian flag.

Santosh Yadav is not only a mountaineer but she is also an environmentalist. She collected and brought down 500 kgs of garbage from the Himalayas.

Word Meaning

Word	Meaning
idolise	admire greatly
scaled	climbed
curse	a cause of trouble or bad luck
expecting	(herein) pregnant with
holy man	sage/saint
destiny	fate
contentment	satisfaction
preferred	like one thing or person better than others
rational	logical or based on reason
affluent	rich
afford	have enough money to pay for
prevailing	existing at a particular time
enrolled	registered
urge	persuade
vanishing	disappearing
affirmative	showing agreement or saying 'yes'.
semester	an academic session
headed	went
expedition	an organised journey for a specific purpose

Word	Meaning
resistance	opposition, the capacity to withstand something
equipped with	having
iron-will	strong desire
endurance	capacity to bear
culmination	summit, climax
barely	hardly
feat	a notable act
col	a pass between two mountain peaks or a gap in a ridge
annals	historical records
bestowed	present an award, title, etc
enormity	greatness
sink in	be understood
unfurled	spread or opened (a flag), hoisted
aloft	in the air
spiritual	sacred, concerned with the soul
fervent	having strong and sincere feelings
environmentalist	one who takes care of the environment

NCERT FOLDER

NCERT Intext and Exercise Questions

THINKING ABOUT THE TEXT

(NCERT PAGE 87-88)

I. Answer these questions in one or two sentences each.

Q.1 Why was the 'holy man', who gave Santosh's mother his blessing, surprised?

Ans. The 'holy man' was surprised because Santosh's grandmother told him that they did not want a son. Her family wanted a daughter which was against the nature of a traditional society.

Q.2 Give an example to show that even as a young girl Santosh was not ready to accept anything unreasonable.

Ans. Even as a young girl, Santosh was not ready to accept anything unreasonable. For example, other girls in the village wore traditional Indian dresses, but Santosh wore shorts.

Q.3 Why was Santosh sent to the local village school?

Ans. Santosh was sent to the local village school due to the existing traditional custom in the family.

Q.4 When did she leave home for Delhi and why?

Ans. When Santosh turned sixteen, her parents wanted her to get married. Santosh threatened her parents that she would never marry if she did not get proper education and left her home to study at a school in Delhi.

Q.5 Why did Santosh's parents agree to pay for her schooling in Delhi? What mental qualities of Santosh are brought into light by this incident?

Ans. Santosh's parents agreed to pay for her education when she informed them that she would earn money by working part time and pay her school fees. This shows that Santosh was determined and a strong-willed girl who would do anything to achieve her goals.

II. Answer each of these questions in a short paragraph (about 30 words).

Q.1 How did Santosh begin to climb mountains?

Ans. When Santosh was in Jaipur for her higher studies, she watched people from her room in Kasturba Hostel going up the Aravalli Hills and disappearing after sometime. One day, she decided to go there and found that those people were mountaineers.

They encouraged her to take up climbing and then, she began to climb mountains.

Q.2 What incidents during the Everest expedition show Santosh's concern for her teammates?

Ans. During the Everest mission, Santosh helped a dying climber but she was not able to save him. However, she saved another climber Mohan Singh by sharing her oxygen with him. These incidents show her concern for her teammates.

Q.3 What shows her concern for the environment?

Ans. Santosh was a sincere environmentalist. While on the Everest mission, she collected and brought down 500 kilograms of garbage from the Himalayas.

Q.4 How does she describe her feelings at the summit of the Everest?

Ans. Santosh said that the feeling at the summit of the Everest was indescribable and unreal. Hoisting the Indian flag was a spiritual moment for her and she felt proud as an Indian.

Q.5 Santosh Yadav got into the record books both times she scaled Mt. Everest. What were the reasons for this?

Ans. Santosh Yadav got into the record books both times she scaled Mt. Everest. For the first time, she became the youngest woman in the world to achieve the record. For the second time, she became the only woman to climb Mt. Everest twice.

III. Complete the following statements.

Q.1 From her room in Kasturba Hostel, Santosh used to ....

Ans. watch villagers going up the Aravalli hills and suddenly disappearing after a while.

Q.2 When she finished college, Santosh had to write a letter of apology to her father because ....

Ans. she got admission in Uttarkashi's Nehru Institute of Mountaineering without his permission.

Q.3 During the Everest expedition, her seniors in the team admired her .... while .... endeared her to fellow climbers.

Ans. climbing skills, physical fitness and mental strength; her concern for others and desire to work together with them

IV. Pick out words from the text that mean the same as the following words or expressions.

Q.1 Took to be true without proof ....

Ans. Assumed

Q.2 **Based on reason; sensible; reasonable ......**

Ans. Rational

Q.3 **The usual way of doing things ....**

Ans. Custom

Q.4 **A strong desire arising from within ....**

Ans. Urge

Q.5 **The power to endure without falling ill ....**

Ans. Resistance

REVIEW EXERCISE

Including Competency Based Questions

Part I

Multiple Choice Questions

1. Santosh's attitude towards the traditional way of life was **Competency Based**

(a) Indifferent
(b) Rebellious
(c) Submissive
(d) Contemptuous

Ans. (b) Rebellious

2. So she decided to fight the system in her own quiet way when the right moment arrived. What was the issue with the system? **Competency Based**

(a) Discouraging girl's education
(b) Providing children with low quality education
(c) Unwillingness to spend money on school education
(d) Not letting children go to distant schools for education

Ans. (a) Discouraging girl's education

3. How many siblings does Santosh have? **Competency Based**

(a) Five elder brothers
(b) Four elder brothers and one elder sister
(c) Three elder brothers and two younger sisters
(d) Five younger brothers

Ans. (a) Santosh has five elder brothers.

4. What was different about Santosh?

1. She always lived a life on her own terms.

2. She used to wear shorts unlike other girls of her village.

(a) Only 1 is correct
(b) Only 2 is correct
(c) Both 1 and 2 are correct
(d) Both 1 and 2 are incorrect

Ans. (c) Both 1 and 2 are correct

5. What encouraged Santosh to climb mountains? **Competency Based**

(a) Meeting with mountaineers in Jaipur.
(b) The sight of the beautiful Aravalli hills.
(c) The training at Uttarkashi Nehru Institute.
(d) Desire to visit the villages in the Aravalli Hills.

Ans. (b) The sight of the beautiful Aravalli Hills.

6. What action shows Santosh's concern for the environment?

(a) Collecting 500 kgs of garbage from the Himalayas.
(b) Giving emergency medical care to fellow climbers
(c) Becoming a beacon of hope for Haryanvi girls.
(d) Receiving the Padma shri from the Government of India.

Ans. (a) Collecting 500 kgs of garbage from the Himalayas.

7. What has always been the belief of Santosh Yadav?

(a) "If I choose a correct and a rational path, the others around me don't have to change, nor me."
(b) "I have to choose a correct and a rational path so that the others around me don't have to change."
(c) "I have to change myself so that the others around me don't have to change."
(d) "If I choose a correct and a rational path, the others around me have to change, not me."

Ans. (d) "If I choose a correct and a rational path, the others around me have to change, not me."

8. What did Santosh threaten her parents with, for her early marriage?

(a) She would run away from her home.
(b) She would never marry if she did not get a proper education.
(c) She would go to Delhi and live there.
(d) She would attempt suicide.

Ans. (b) She would never marry if she did not get a proper education.

9. What was Santosh fully equipped with when she climbed to the top of the world?

(a) Iron will
(b) Physical endurance
(c) Mental toughness
(d) All of the above

Ans. (d) All of the above

10. Why did the senior climbers praise Santosh during her first expedition to the top of Everest?

(a) For her physical endurance
(b) For her empathetic attitude
(c) For her climbing skills
(d) All of the above

Ans. (d) All of the above

Extract Based Questions

1. Read the following extract carefully and answer the questions that follow.

Santosh's parents were affluent landowners who could afford to send their children to the best schools, even to the country's capital, New Delhi, which was quite close by. But, in line with the prevailing custom in the family, Santosh had to make do with the local village school. So, she decided to fight the system in her own quiet way when the right moment arrived. And the right moment came when she turned sixteen. At sixteen, most of the girls in her village used to get married. Santosh was also under pressure from her parents to do the same.

(i) What happened to girls in her village regardless of their economic status?

Ans. Regardless of their economic status, girls in her village would be kept away from quality education and would be married around the age of sixteen.

(ii) Choose the option that lists the set of statements that are not true according to the given extract.

1. **Santosh's parents were conservative in nature.**
2. **Santosh was against the prevailing customs in her village.**
3. **Santosh went to a private school in Mumbai.**
4. **Santosh's brothers always supported her.**
5. **Santosh was never under the pressure of getting married early.**

(a) 2, 3 and 4 (b) 5, 3 and 4
(c) 1, 4 and 5 (d) 1, 2 and 3

Ans. (b) 5, 3 and 4

(iii) Why was she not sent to a good school?

Ans. Santosh was not sent to a good school because they were following the tradition of the family.

(iv) When did the right time come in her life to fight against the system?

Ans. The right time in her life to fight against the system came when she was sixteen.

2. Read the following extract carefully and answer the questions that follow.

Within twelve months, Santosh found herself a member of an Indo-Nepalese Women's Expedition that invited her to join them. She then scaled the Everest a second time, thus setting a record as the only woman to have scaled the Everest twice, and securing for herself and India a unique place in the annals of mountaineering.

(i) When did Santosh conquer Mount Everest the second time?

Ans. Santosh conquered Mt Everest the second time in 1993.

(ii) Choose the option that lists the set of statements that are not true according to the given extract.

1. **Santosh was a member of an Indo-Nepalese Women's Expedition.**
2. **Santosh's parents were affluent landowners.**
3. **Santosh's parents wanted her to become a sportsperson since her childhood.**
4. **Santosh was always supported by her family to pursue her studies.**
5. **Santosh was never pressurised for early marriage.**
6. **Santosh was honoured with the Padma Shri by the Government of India.**

(a) 1, 2 and 3
(b) 3, 4 and 5
(c) 4, 5 and 6
(d) 1, 5 and 6

Ans. (b) 3, 4 and 5

(iii) A word that means 'journey for a purpose' is ....

Ans. expedition

(iv) What made Santosh scale Mt Everest the second time?

Ans. Santosh was invited by an Indo-Nepalese Women's Expedition to scale Mt Everest again.

3. Read the following extract carefully and answer the questions that follow.

A marriage as early as that was the last thing on her mind. She threatened her parents that she would never marry if she did not get a proper education. She left home and got herself enrolled in a school in Delhi. When her parents refused to pay for her education, she politely informed them of her plans to earn money by working part time to pay her school fees. Her parents then agreed to pay for her education.

(i) From the given extract, we can say that santosh was

(a) bold (c) angry
(c) hopeful (d) Harsh

Ans. (a) bold

(ii) Based on the extract, do you think Santosh's family believed in the equal rights of the girl child or were they orthodox?

Ans. Based on the extract, it is clear that Santosh's family did not believe in the equal rights of the girl child. Santosh belonged to an orthodox family who didn't want her to have a good education or a career. In fact, they wanted to marry her off when she was just 16 years old.

(iii) Complete the sentence appropriately. The phrase 'last thing on her mind' means

Ans. not thought about or considered

(iv) How did she rebel against her parents?

Ans. Santosh refused to marry and got herself enrolled in a school in New Delhi. When her parents threatened to not pay for her fees, she offered to work part-time and pay the school fee herself.

4. Read the following extract carefully and answer the questions that follow.

"I used to watch villagers from my room, going up the hill and suddenly vanishing after a while. One day I decided to check it out myself. I found nobody except a few mountaineers. I asked if I could join them. To my pleasant surprise, they answered in the affirmative and motivated me to take to climbing."

(i) Complete the sentence appropriately. The hills refered to here are ....

Ans. Aravalli Hills

(ii) Santosh possessed a curious mind and adventurous spirit. Justify the statement based on evidence from the passage.

Ans. Santosh would watch the villagers disappearing up the hill and the image made her very curious. Therefore, she decided to solve the mystery. Later, she joined a group of unknown mountaineers without hesitance due to her adventurous spirit.

(iii) What did the mountaineers do when she asked to join them?

Ans. The mountaineers agreed to Santosh's request and encouraged her to take up climbing.

(iv) State whether the following statement is True or False.
The mountaineers discouraged Santosh from learning climbing.

Ans. False

Part II

Short Answer Type Questions

1. The 'holy man' who visited Santosh's mother shared the attitude of the society towards girls. Justify the statement. Competency Based

Ans. The holy man who visited Santosh's mother shared the attitude of the society towards girls because he had the presumption that Santosh's family would consider having a son as a blessing and having a daughter as a curse.

2. In what kind of society was Santosh Yadav born? How was her grandmother different from others?

Ans. Santosh Yadav was born in a society where the birth of a son was regarded as a blessing and a daughter was generally not welcomed. Her grandmother was different from others as she wanted a girl instead of a boy.

3. Why did Santosh want to fight the system?

Ans. Santosh's parents were rich landlords. They could have sent her to the best schools but as per the tradition, she was sent to the local village school. As a result, she felt dissatisfied and decided to fight the system.

4. How did Santosh fulfil her wish to study in Delhi?

Or What persuaded Santosh's parents to support her education in Delhi? Competency Based

Ans. Santosh's wish to study in a good school in Delhi was fulfilled after she warned her parents of never getting married if she did not get proper education. Then, she left home and got admission in Delhi.

5. What happened when Santosh's parents refused to pay for her fees?

Ans. When Santosh's parents refused to pay for her fees, she politely informed them of her plans to earn money by working part time to pay her school fees. Then, they agreed to pay for it.

6. What made Santosh scale Mt. Everest the second time? How was it important?

Ans. Santosh scaled Mt. Everest the second time as she was invited to be a member of an Indo-Nepalese Women's Expedition. It was important as she became the only woman in the world to climb Mt. Everest twice.

7. What is the secret of Santosh's success?

Ans. The secret of Santosh's success was her strong will power, great physical endurance and an amazing mental toughness. Her single-minded determination and dedication helped her overcome all hurdles to become a winner. She had qualities of hard work and sincerity, which led to her success.

Long Answer Type Questions

1. Santosh Yadav had the qualities that helped her get into the record books both times she conquered Mt. Everest. Write a descriptive paragraph highlighting the qualities of Santosh Yadav in 100-120 words.

Ans. Success needs qualities like dedication, hard work, focus and will power. Santosh Yadav, a record holding mountaineer has all these qualities. She was born in an orthodox society where a girl child was not welcomed and a woman did not have much freedom. However, she was determined to live her life on her own terms. Even as a child she was a rebel. Not only did she wear shorts instead of traditional dresses but she also went to study in Delhi despite her parents' unwillingness.

As a mountaineer, Santosh's will power, mental toughness, single-minded determination and sincerity led her to get into record books both times she conquered Mt. Everest. Her humanity, desire to work with the team and hard work led her into the path of success, and made her a source of inspiration for everyone, especially girls. Santosh's journeys of life teaches us that nothing is impossible. With passion, hard work and determination, one can always cross all problems and obstacles in one's path. One should never lose hope and give one's best.

2. "If I choose a correct and rational path, the others around me had to change, not me", said Santosh Yadav. How does her life justify her words?

Ans. Santosh Yadav was born in a conservative society where a son was a blessing and a daughter was not welcomed. In this society, women did not have much freedom and had to follow the illogical orthodox customs. In such a society, Santosh was a determined rebel. She did not let the social rules dictate her life and lived on her own terms. As a child, she wore shorts unlike all other girls who wore traditional Indian dresses.

She believed that if she choose the correct path, others would have to change according to her. She not only refused to marry without proper education but also left home to get her education in Delhi. She even convinced her parents to pay for her education.

Furthermore, taking up climbing was also her independent choice. She did not take permission for it from her father and apologised for the same. Thus, whatever she chose was absolutely unheard of for girls in her society. She chose a path for herself and the society accepted her with the identity she created for herself. Thus, her life justifies her belief.

3. Santosh Yadav possesses a deep feeling for others. What did she do on her expedition to Mt. Everest to make a special place in the hearts of fellow climbers? What does her deep feeling for others teach us?

Ans. A human being is identified by the compassion, love, care, sympathy and other virtues.

If anyone possess these humane values, he/she makes a special place in the heart of others. Santosh Yadav possessed these values for which she was admired by her seniors.

Apart from being an excellent mountaineer, Santosh possessed the qualities of being a true team-member and companion. Her concern for others and desire to work with others as a team makes her special.

Her humanity was seen when in the 1992 Everest expedition, she took special care of a dying fellow teammate. She could not save him. However, she helped and saved another teammate, Mohan Singh, by sharing her oxygen with him.

With such qualities, Santosh becomes a role model for all of us. Her concern teaches us to be helpful. We should help our classmates, friends, family members or anyone who is in need or facing trouble. We must remember that humanity is always bigger than any personal achievements. It makes a person a real hero.

4. Indians have taken leads in various fields and brought honour to the nation since its very independence. Comment on this statement with respect to the chapter 'The Sound of Music' and 'Reach for the Top'.

Ans. It is true to say that Indians taking leads in various fields and bringing honour to the nation since independence. The chapters 'The Sound of Music' and 'Reach for the Top' highlight the achievements of Indians who have excelled in their respective fields and made a significant impact, both nationally and internationally.

'The Sound of Music' focuses on the life of Ustad Bismillah Khan, a legendary Indian musician, and his remarkable contribution to Indian classical music. His musical genius and dedication elevated the shehnai to the global stage, showcasing India's rich cultural heritage to the world. Bismillah Khan's performances, including those at prestigious events like India's first

Independence Day ceremony in 1947, not only captured the essence of India's spiritual and cultural traditions but also symbolised the pride and unity of a newly independent nation. Bismillah Khan's international acclaim, particularly his performances abroad, made him an ambassador for Indian classical music and contributed to the global recognition of India's rich cultural heritage.

'Reach For the Top' introduces us to Santosh Yadav, an Indian mountaineer, who became the first woman in the world to climb Mount Everest twice. Her story is one of perseverance, courage and resilience. Santosh's determination to reach the top, despite the numerous challenges, symbolises the relentless spirit of Indians who strive to achieve greatness. Through her success, she brought global recognition to India in the field of mountaineering, inspiring countless individuals to pursue their dreams.

Both chapters reflect the broader theme of Indian excellence and leadership in various fields. Ustad Bismillah Khan's contributions to music and Santosh Yadav's achievements in mountaineering are just two examples of how Indians have brought honour to the nation, both in cultural and sporting arenas.

ASSESSMENT EXERCISE

Extract Based Questions

Read the following extract carefully and answer the questions that follow.

"It took some time for the enormity of the moment to sink in .... Then I unfurled the Indian tricolour and held it aloft on the roof of the world. The feeling is indescribable. The Indian flag was flying on top of the world. It was truly a spiritual moment. I felt proud as an Indian."

(i) What is 'I's' profession?
- (a) An environmentalist
- (b) A motivational speaker
- (c) A mountaineer
- (d) A professor

(ii) I is at .... in the given lines.

(iii) How is 'I' feeling at the place?

(iv) What does her achievement tell us about her?

Short Answer (SA) Type Questions

1. How was Santosh unlike other girls of her village?
2. What was the right moment? What did Santosh do at the moment?
3. Why and how did Santosh get enrolled in Nehru Institute of Mountaineering, Uttarkashi?
4. How did Santosh feel when she was literally 'On Top of the World'?

Long Answer (LA) Type Questions

1. Santosh decided to fight the system in her own "quiet way", says the author. How did Santosh rebel but quietly?
2. How did Santosh Yadav make her parents agree to pay for her school fees in Delhi? Do you think she had rebelled for the right reasons? What qualities in Santosh made her do so? What do we learn from her rebellious attitude?
3. Santosh Yadav collected and brought down 500 kg of garbage from the Himalayas. What traits of her personality are highlighted here? How can you help keep your environment clean?

Part II Maria Sharapova

CHAPTER SUMMARY

Chapter Overview

Part-II This part is about Maria Sharapova, a teenager, who achieved number one position in World's Women Tennis. In her journey, Maria had made many sacrifices and also suffered insults. However, all these only made her more determined and tough. Her hard work and her mental toughness finally led her to achieve her goal.

Number One Position in World Tennis

On 22nd August, 2005, Maria Sharapova gained number one position in world's women tennis. Maria was born in Siberia, Russia. She is a calm, confident and friendly teenager who reached the top position in only four years.

Maria's Journey and her Sacrifice

Maria's journey towards becoming the biggest women tennis player started when she was ten years old. She went to America to get formal training. In her journey to Florida, US, only her father, Yuri went with her. Maria's mother, Yelena could not go with Maria due to her visa restrictions. Maria lived without her mother for two years. During that time, Maria realised that she had to sacrifice a lot to gain excellence in Tennis.

Maria's Stay and Training in the US

In US, Maria stayed alone and missed her mother very badly. Maria could not even spend much time with her father as he was working hard to earn money for Maria's training.

Maria was the youngest child at her training center so she used to sleep at 8 pm. However, the senior players used to wake her up by 11 pm and ordered her to clean the room.

Maria's Determination and Toughness

Maria's experience of her training period made her more determined and tough. She struggled hard and learned to take care of herself. She was determined to reach her goal so she never thought about quitting. Due to her determination and toughness, Maria won the women's singles crown at Wimbledon in 2004. She became number one women tennis player in the world in 2005.

Maria's Success Mantra

Maria's journey inspired many youngsters. She believes that all the sacrifices that she had made were worth it. Maria's way of answering clearly indicated her confidence. She says that she is very competitive. She always works hard at what she does. For her, hardwork is her mantra for success.

Maria Proud of her Russian Roots

Maria speaks with an American accent but she is very proud of her Russian nationality. She says US is a big part of her life but her blood is Russian. She also has Russian citizenship and wishes to play in Olympics for Russia.

Maria's Hobbies

Maria's hobbies include fashion, singing and dancing. She loves reading the Novels of Arthur Conan Doyle and is very fond of evening gowns. She also loves to eat pancakes with chocolate spread and drink fizzy orange drinks.

Maria's View on Tennis

Maria's talent, determination and readiness to sacrifice led her to the path of success and fame. For Maria, apart from money, the dream of becoming number one in the world is her main motivation.

Word Meaning

Word	Meaning
summit	the highest level; top
disarming	tending to remove feelings of unfriendliness
at odds	in contrast to
glamorous	very exciting and attractive
poised	calm and confident
pinnacle	top; the highest point of success
ascent	the act of climbing or going up
fiercely	powerful
endure	tolerate; suffer
packed off	to send someone away to a different place
stardom	the state of being very famous
heart wrenching	causing great sadness
compelled	forced
restrictions	limitations
recalls	remembers; recollects
depress	make gloomy; deject
put up	faced
humiliation	insult

Word	Meaning
steadfastly	firm in purpose
bagging	winning
meteoric	very sudden or fast
sentiment	emotion, feeling
amply	more than enough
pronounced	to say something in a particular way
accent	way of speaking
parades	shows
sensations	greatly successful personalities
sophisticated	refined and cultured
pigeon-holed	categorise
unwavering	not shaking; resolute
readiness	willingness to do something
grudge	to dislike or feel angry towards someone for something
reaping	obtaining
monetary	related to money
kept me going	encouraging somebody to continue the work

NCERT FOLDER

NCERT Intext and Exercise Questions

BEFORE YOU READ (NCERT PAGE 89)

Q.1 Match the following.

Something disarming	Quickly, almost immediately
At odds with	More calm, confident and in control than people of her age usually are
Glamorous attire	In contrast to ; not agreeing with
In almost no time	Something that makes you feel friendly, taking away your suspiciousness
Poised beyond her years	Sent off
Packed off	Attractive and exciting clothes
Launched	Causing strong feelings of sadness
Heart wrenching	Started

Ans.

Something disarming	Something that makes you feel friendly, taking away your suspiciousness
At odds with	In contrast to ; not agreeing with
Glamorous attire	Attractive and exciting clothes
In almost no time	Quickly, almost immediately
Poised beyond her years	More calm, confident and in control than people of her age usually are
Packed off	Sent off
Launched	Started
Heart wrenching	Causing strong feelings of sadness

Q.2 **As you read, look for the answers to these questions**

(i) Why was Maria sent to the United States?

(ii) Why didn't her mother go with her?

(iii) What are her hobbies? What does she like?

(iv) What motivates her to keep going?

Ans. (i) Maria was sent to the United States for her tennis training.

(ii) Her mother could not go with her because of visa restrictions.

(iii) Her hobbies are fashion, singing and dancing. She likes reading the novels of Arthur Conan Doyle. She is also fond of sophisticated evening gowns, pancakes with chocolate spread and fizzy orange drinks.

(iv) The motivation to become number one in tennis in the world keeps her going.

THINKING ABOUT THE TEXT (NCERT PAGE 92)

Working in small groups of 4-5 students, go back over the two passages on Santosh Yadav and Maria Sharapova and complete the table given below with relevant phrases or sentences.

	Points of Comparison /Contrast	Santosh Yadav	Maria Sharapova
1.	Their humble beginning	"She was born in the small village of Joniyawas of Rewari District in Haryana."	"Siberian born teenager" "When you come from nothing and you have nothing....'
2.	Their parents' approach	"Santosh was also under pressure from her parents to do the same"	"Trip to Florida with her father Yuri launched her on the path to success and stardom."
		"When her parents refused to pay for her education"	"My father was working as much as he could to keep my tennis-training going."
3.	Their will power and strong desire to succeed	"She began living life on her own terms"	"Instead of letting that depress me, I became more quietly determined and mentally tough"
		"Equipped with iron will, physical endurance and an amazing mental toughness"	Her talent unwavering desire to succeed and readiness to sacrifice have lifted her to the top of the world.
4.	Evidence of their mental toughness	"So, I did not go back home, instead. I headed straight for the training"	"I would have put up with much more humiliation and insults than that to steadfastly pursue my dreams.

THINKING ABOUT LANGUAGE

(NCERT PAGE 92-93)

I. Look at the following sentences. They each have two clauses, or two parts each with their own subject and verb or verb phrase. Often, one part (italicised) tells us when or why something happened.

- **I reached the market when most of the shops had closed. (Tells us when I reached.)**
- **When Rahul Dravid walked back towards the pavilion, everyone stood up. (Tells us when everyone stood up.)**
- **The telephone rang and Ganga picked it up. (Tells us what happened next.)**
- **Gunjan has been with us ever since the school began. (Tells us for how long he has been with us.)**

Identify the two parts in the sentences below by underlining the part that gives us the information in brackets.

Q.1 **Where other girls wore traditional Indian dresses, Santosh preferred shorts. (Contrasts her dress with that of others)**

Ans. <u>Where other girls wore traditional Indian dresses,</u> Santosh preferred shorts.

Q.2 **She left home and got herself enrolled in a school in Delhi. (Tells us what happened after the first action.)**

Ans. She left home and <u>got herself enrolled in a school in Delhi.</u>

Q.3 **She decided to fight the system when the right moment arrived. (Tells us when she was going to fight the system.)**

Ans. She decided to fight the system <u>when the right moment arrived.</u>

Q.4 **Little Maria had not yet celebrated her tenth birthday when she was packed off to train in the United States. (Tells us when Maria was sent to the US).**

Ans. <u>Little Maria had not yet celebrated her tenth birthday</u> when she was packed off to train in the United States.

II. Now rewrite the pairs of sentences given below as one sentence.

Q.1 **Grandfather told me about the old days. All books were printed on paper then.**

Ans. Grandfather told me about the old days when all books were printed on paper.

Q.2 What do you do after you finish the book? Perhaps you just throw it away.

Ans. After finishing the book, perhaps you just throw it away.

Q.3 He gave the little girl an apple. He took the computer apart.

Ans. After giving the little girl an apple, he took the computer apart.

Q.4 You have nothing. That makes you very determined.

Ans. Having nothing makes you very determined.

Q.5 I never thought of quitting. I knew what I wanted.

Ans. I never thought of quitting as I knew what I wanted.

WRITING (NCERT PAGE 94)

I. Working in pairs, go through the table below that gives you information about the top women tennis players since 1975. Write a short article for your school magazine comparing and contrasting the players in terms of their duration at the top. Mention some qualities that you think may be responsible for their brief or long stay at the top spot.

Top-Ranked Women Players

The roll of honour of women who enjoyed life at the summit since everybody's favourite player, Chris Evert, took her place in 1975.

Name	Ranked on	Weeks as No. 1
Maria Sharapova (Russia)	22nd August, 2005	1
Lindsay Devenport (U.S.)	October 2004	82
Amelie Mauresmo (France)	13th September, 2004	5
Justine Henin-Hardenne (Belgium)	20th October, 2003	45
Kim clijusters (Belgium)	11th August, 2003	12
Serena Williams (U.S.)	8th July, 2002	57
Venus Williams (U.S.)	25th February, 2002	11
Jennifer Capriati (U.S.)	15th October, 2001	17
Lindsay Davenport (U.S.)	12th October, 1998	82
Martina Hingis (Switzerland)	31st March, 1997	209
Arantxa Sanchez-Vicario (Spain)	6th February, 1995	12
Monica Seles (U.S.)	11th March, 1991	178
Steffi Graf (Germany)	17th August, 1987	377
Tracy Austin (U.S.)	7th April, 1980	22
Martina Navratilova	10th July, 1978	331
Chris Evert (U.S.)	3rd November, 1975	362

Ans. **Tennis Titans- A Tale of Endurance and Flair**

by XYZ

Examining the table outlining top women tennis players since 1975, a fascinating narrative emerges regarding the duration of their reigns at the pinnacle of the sport. Steffi Graf and Martina Navratilova, stalwarts of the game, boast extended stays, a testament to their enduring excellence and unmatched skill. In contrast, Arantxa Sanchez-Vicario and Amelie Mauresmo, while formidable, experienced shorter tenures.

Endurance, both physical and mental, emerges as a key determinant of the total time a player spends at the top. Graf and Navratilova's unwavering commitment to the sport allowed them to navigate challenges consistently. In contrast, external factors, injuries and intense competition may have contributed to the shorter stays of Sanchez-Vicario and Mauresmo.

The dynamic nature of tennis, marked by evolving playing styles and technological advancements, also plays a role. Adaptable players tend to enjoy more extended stays, illustrating the importance of staying abreast of the game's transformations. As we celebrate these tennis titans, their journeys provide invaluable insights into the qualities influencing their enduring or brief reigns.

II. Which of these words would you use to describe Santosh Yadav? Find reasons in the text to support your choices, and write a couple of paragraphs describing Santosh's character.

contented	determined	resourceful
polite	adventurous	considerate
weak-willed	fearful	independent
pessimistic	patient	persevering

Ans. Santosh was determined, resourceful, adventurous, independent, persevering and considerate.

Santosh Yadav, a great Indian mountaineer, marked her name in history as the youngest woman to conquer the grand Mount Everest. Born in Haryana in 1969, Yadav achieved this remarkable feat at the age of 21, ascending the world's highest peak for the first time in 1992. Undeterred by the challenges that often accompany high-altitude expeditions, she displayed exceptional determination and courage. Notably, Santosh Yadav went on to conquer Mount Everest again in 1993, solidifying her reputation as a pioneering figure in mountaineering. Her extraordinary achievements have not only broken barriers but also inspired generations of women to pursue their dreams fearlessly in the face of adversity.

REVIEW EXERCISE

Including Competency Based Questions

Part I

Multiple Choice Questions

1. When did Maria Sharapova get the world's number one position in women's tennis?

(a) 22nd August, 2004
(b) 22nd August, 2005
(c) 22nd August, 2006
(d) 22nd August, 2007

Ans. (b) 22nd August, 2005

2. The writer says "Maria had a level of sacrifice few children would be prepared to endure." Choose the example of sacrifices being talked about.

(i) Separation from mother
(ii) Unable to spend time with father
(iii) Not celebrating birthdays
(iv) Taking care of herself on her own

(a) (i), (ii) and (iii)
(b) (ii), (iii) and (iv)
(c) (i), (ii) and (iv)
(d) (i), (ii), (iii) and (iv)

Ans. (d) (i), (ii), (iii) and (iv)

3. What best describes the behaviour of Maria Sharapova's fellow tennis pupils? Competency Based

(a) Disciplined
(b) Persuasive
(c) Intimidating
(d) Hardworking

Ans. (c) Intimidating

4. According to the writer, what is Maria Sharapova's attitude towards her own struggles? Competency Based

(a) Cynical
(b) Realistic
(c) Passive
(d) Frustrated

Ans. (b) Realistic

5. Based on the two texts, what is true? Competency Based

(a) Social norms were a hurdle for Santosh, not Sharapova.
(b) Both the players started pursuing their passions in childhood.
(c) Families played a major role in the success of both the players.
(d) Sharapova believes that business is a part of sports but Santosh does not.

Ans. (a) Social norms were a hurdle for Santosh, not Sharapova.

6. What novels did Maria Sharapova love to read?

(a) Novels of J K Rowling
(b) Novels of A C Doyle
(c) Novels of Sydney Sheldon
(d) Novels of Marquez

Ans. (b) Novels of A C Doyle

7. For how many weeks did Maria Sharapova stay as the women's no. 1 tennis player in the world?

(a) 7 weeks
(b) 1 week
(c) 8 weeks
(d) 20 weeks

Ans. (b) 1 week

8. Maria put up all the humiliations and insults during her training period to

(a) pursue her education
(b) pursue her music
(c) pursue her dream for tennis
(d) be the richest tennis player in world

Ans. (c) pursue her dream for tennis

9. The phrase 'meteoric rise' means

(a) going up in the air
(b) false success
(c) achieved success very quickly
(d) None of the above

Ans. (c) achieved success very quickly

10. Sharapova has expressed her wish to play .... for Russia if allowed.

(a) Wimbledon
(b) Olympics
(c) National League
(d) Australia's Open

Ans. (b) Olympics

Extract Based Questions

1. Read the following extract carefully and answer the questions that follow.

However, the rapid ascent in a fiercely competitive world began nine years before with a level of sacrifice few children would be prepared to endure. Little Maria had not yet celebrated her tenth birthday when she was packed off to train in the United States. That trip to Florida with her father Yuri launched her on the path to success and stardom. But it also required a heart-wrenching two-years separation from her mother Yelena. The latter was compelled to stay back in Siberia.

(i) Fill in the blank with one word only.

Maria was .... (ten/nine) years old when she went to Florida with her father.

Ans. nine

(ii) What were the sacrifices made by ten year old Maria Sharapova? What does this indicate about her?

Ans. Maria Sharapova was only ten years old when she left her country to get professional training in tennis. She gave up her home, her country, her childhood and even her mother to pursue her dream. Her sacrifices indicate that she is hard working, determined and strong-willed.

(iii) How did staying in the USA change her life?

Ans. Staying in USA pushed Maria towards the path to success and stardom.

(iv) Which word means the same as the underlined word.

Suryansh was <u>forced</u> to live on the streets due to utter poverty.

Ans. compelled

2. Read the following extract carefully and answer the questions that follow.

And that something in her lifted her on Monday, 22nd August, 2005 to the world number one position in women's tennis. All this happened in almost no time. Poised beyond her years, the Siberian born teenager took just four years as a professional to reach the pinnacle.

(i) What happened on 22nd August, 2005?

Ans. Maria Sharapova reached the first spot in Women's Tennis on 22nd August, 2005.

(ii) The sentence 'All this happened in almost no time' indicates

(a) slowness
(b) suddenness
(c) inevitability
(d) gradual process

Ans. (b) suddenness

(III) Complete the sentence appropriately.

The phrase 'poised beyond her years' indicates the person's ....

Ans. maturity

(iv) The word 'Pinnacle' means ....

Ans. top

3. Read the following extract carefully and answer the questions that follow.

The straight looks and the answers she gives when asked about her ambition make it amply clear that she considers the sacrifices were worth it. "I am very, very competitive. I work hard at what I do. It's my job." This is her mantra for success.

Though Maria Sharapova speaks with a pronounced American accent, she proudly parades her Russian nationality.

(i) What are the sacrifices referred to in the extract?

Ans. The sacrifices referred to the extract are staying away from parents and training all alone while being bullied.

(ii) Which of the following statements is not True about Maria Sharapova?

(a) Maria is very ambitious.
(b) Maria would like to play for Russia as well.
(c) Maria speaks in an American accent.
(d) None of the above

Ans. (d) None of the above

(iii) What is Maria's mantra for success?

Ans. Maria's mantra to success is 'letting her competetiveness fuel her hard work'.

(iv) Complete the sentence appropriately.

The phrase 'proudly parades' means

Ans. to display publicly

Part II

Short Answer Type Questions

1. Why did Maria Sharapova move to the United States? Comptency Based

Ans. Maria Sharapova moved to the United States to begin her training in tennis and to later become the top tennis player in the world.

2. Why did Maria have to stay away from her mother? How did she feel about that?

Ans. Maria had to stay away from her mother because she had to go to the United States for her professional training and her mother could not accompany her due to her visa restrictions.

She felt very lonely and depressed without her mother. She had to bear this separation just for her dream.

3. Why did Maria not retaliate against the humiliation at the hands of the other athletes?

Ans. Maria did not retaliate against the humiliation at the hands of the other athletes because she was working hard to become the world's number one tennis player. She took it as a challenge and worked harder to achieve success.

4. Why does Maria call herself totally Russian?

Ans. Although Maria lives in the USA, at heart she is a Russian. She says that her blood is totally Russian, and she wants to represent Russia in the Olympics. This is just an indication of her patriotism and her true love for her country.

5. What does Maria declare to be her 'Mantra' for success?

Ans. Maria's Mantra for success is that she considers herself to be very competitive. She works hard to be the best in whatever she does. She does not allow herself to be emotional and sentimental.

6. Detail some of the hobbies of Maria Sharapova.

Ans. Maria Sharapova's hobbies are just like any other teenager. She lists fashion, singing and dancing as her hobbies. In addition, she also loves reading novels of Arthur Conan Doyle and is very fond of evening gowns.

7. How are Maria's achievements significant?

Ans. Maria's achievements were significant because she achieved the top position in the world in women's tennis as a teenager. Her achievement was her dream for which she worked very hard. Not only did she train but she also made many sacrifices.

She suffered from separation from her mother and had to go through insults. Even Maria's father worked as much as he could to keep her training continued.

8. Maria's father played an important role in her success. How?

Ans. Maria's father, Yuri played an important role in her success. Maria would have not been able to get professionally trained without her father.

Her father worked day and night to make sure that Maria continued her training.

Long Answer Type Questions

1. "The nine-year-old girl had already learnt an important lesson in life-that tennis excellence would only come at a price." Do you agree with the 'lesson' that the girl had learned. What do you think motivated her to pay the price?

Ans. Yes, I agree with the important lesson learned by the little Maria Sharapova. Success always comes at a price. One pays for it with either hard work, determination, iron-will, etc., or by making sacrifices. Without paying the price one can never achieve good things. Maria Sharapova and her success is its example.

Maria achieved tennis excellence at a very young age. Her journey towards success shows that at a very young age, she made a sacrifice. She was only nine years old when she, along with her father, left for US to get her formally trained. She was separated from her mother for two years. Even in US, Maria was all alone. While her mother was in Siberia, her father worked hard to make sure that she continued her training. Maria sacrificed her childhood to train professionally. If she had not done so, she would not have achieved her goal of reaching the number one position that she achieved in 2005.

Maria's desire to achieve her goal, i.e. to become the top player in the world in women's tennis along with the monetary benefits motivated Maria to pay the price.

2. Mental toughness and determination became a key to Maria's success. Elaborate. What does one learn from Maria's journey to success?

Ans. Mental toughness and determination is a key to success as success demands the best of one's efforts. One must remember that during the journey to success, there are certain incidents or people who can depress anyone. In such cases, one can surely be deprived of success.

However, the little Maria was not the one to lose hope. Even when she was seperated from her parents as a child, she trained hard.

During her stay in the US, she was bullied by her senior players. It did not upset her but encouraged her. She became more determined and mentally tough.

According to her, she would have gone through much more humiliations and insults, just because it made her go towards her dream. Finally, she achieved her goal of becoming world's number one in women's tennis. Thus, it can be said that her mental toughness and determination helped her reach the top at the mere age of eighteen.

Maria's journey to success teaches us that success comes after hard work, dedication and sacrifices. So, to achieve one's goal, one has to be ready to work hard and sacrifice. One who hesitates from doing hard work can't achieve their goals. Since Maria was devoted to her sport, she achieved what she wished for.

3. You are Maria Sharapova. You are moving to the US with your father to get formal training in tennis. Your mother would not be able to accompany you on this trip. Write a diary entry in about 100-120 words describing your feelings?

Ans. 21st September, 20XX 10 p.m.

Dear Diary

I am very upset today. You know, I am leaving for the United States with my father to get formally trained in tennis. I should be happy but that's not the case. My mother is not accompanying me on this trip as she did not get a visa. This makes me feel very sad. I would have to stay without my mother. It is going to be very hard for me as I haven't lived even for a single day without her. My father told me that I have to make this sacrifice for becoming a professional tennis player. He motivated me to look on the brighter side of things and urged me to work harder to achieve my goal. I pray to God to give me the strength to bear this separation. That's all for now.

Maria

ASSESSMENT EXERCISE

Extract Based Questions

Read the following extract carefully and answer the questions that follow.

Maria Sharapova cannot be pigeon-holed or categorised. Her talent, unwavering desire to succeed and readiness to sacrifice have lifted her to the top of the world. Few would grudge her the riches she is now reaping. This is what she has to say about her monetary gains from tennis: "Of course, money is a motivation."

(i) What qualities have lifted Maria to the top of the world?

(ii) How does she look at money?

(a) As motivation

(b) As a priority

(c) As her main goal

(d) As something unnecessary

(iii) What did Maria dream about?

(iv) Why would people hold a grudge against Maria Sharapova?

Short Answer (SA) Type Questions

1. How does Yuri help Maria on the path of success and stardom?
2. Describe Maria's struggle to reach the top of the world in the field of the women tennis.
3. What is at odds with Maria's ready smile and glamorous attire?
4. How does Maria describe her journey from Siberia to United States?

Long Answer (LA) Type Questions

1. How did adversity stand Maria in a good stead in the long run?
2. Few people felt jealous of Maria because of the riches she reaped. In showing this attitude, what qualities of Maria were they unaware of? Would you feel the same if your friend is performing better than you at school? If no then why?

Kathmandu

CHAPTER 8

CHAPTER SUMMARY The chapter 'Kathmandu' is taken from the book 'Heaven Lake' by Vikram Seth. This chapter is a description of the two famous temples in Kathmandu i.e. Pashupatinath temple and Baudhnath Stupa. The author describes his visit to Kathmandu where he went to Pashupatinath temple and the Baudhnath Stupa. He describes the surroundings of these two shrines and the markets in the town. He also gives a vivid picture of a flute seller and its music that he encountered in the market.

The Chaos of Pashupatinath Temple, Kathmandu

After arriving in the town of Kathmandu, the author along with Mr. Shah's son and nephew decided to visit the two holy temples i.e. Pashupatinath temple of Hindus and the Baudhnath Stupa of the Buddhist located in the town.

The author visited the Pashupatinath temple and saw a sign at the entrance that proclaims 'Entrance for the Hindus only'. There was a huge crowd near the entrance of the temple. Animals were roaming around the ground. There was a lot of confusion. People were rushing towards the entrance and had gathered around it to get the priest's attention. When a Nepalese princess came to the temple, everyone bowed and made way for her to show respect.

A group of Westerners were trying to enter the temple by the main gate. They were wearing saffron coloured clothes. However, they couldn't convince the police that they were Hindus. Two monkeys were fighting and chasing each other around the temple which amused the author.

The Holy River Bagmati

The holy river Bagmati flows near the temple. A corpse was being cremated on the bank of the river. Washerwomen were washing clothes and the children were bathing in the river. There is a small temple on the river bank. The small shrine is half inside the river. The people believe that when the shrine completely comes out of the river, the goddess inside will escape and the evil period of Kaliyug will end on Earth.

The Calmness of the Baudhnath Stupa

After visiting the Pashupatinath temple, the author visited the Baudhnath Stupa. It was completely different from the Pashupatinath temple as there was peace or stillness around the Stupa. The Stupa had a white dome like structure and was surrounded by roads. On the outer edges of the roads, there were some small shops owned by Tibetan immigrants. One could get Tibetan prints, silver jewellery and felt bags from them. The surrounding was very quiet and peaceful and there were no crowds.

Kathmandu Bazaar

Kathmandu was a very lively place with small shrines along the narrowest and the busiest streets. In these streets, there were shops of fruit sellers, flute sellers, hawkers selling post cards, shops selling cosmetics, film rolls, chocolates, copper utensils, Nepalese antiques, etc. There was continuous blaring of songs, car horns and bicycle bells. Cows were lowing at motorcycles and vendors were shouting.

From the Kathmandu bazaar, the author purchased a bar of marzipan, a corn-on-the-cob, some comics, etc. While considering the topic of returning home, the author considers the long way to Delhi. He could take a bus and a train to patna, then sail up the Ganges from Benaras to Allahabad, and then, sail up the Yamuna past Agra to Delhi. However, he was tired and homesick. After leaving the bazaar, he went to Nepal Airlines office to buy a ticket for Delhi as he was feeling homesick.

The Flute Seller

In Kathmandu, the author came across a flute seller, standing in the corner of the square near his hotel. This seller was different from other sellers. He would occasionally select a flute from his pole and play a tune. He was not shouting to sell his flute. The melodious tune of the flute played by the seller attracted the author.

The Flute, its Music and Effects on the Author

The author believes that a flute is a universal instrument. Almost every culture has its flute like the reed *neh*, the recorder, the Japanese *shakuhachi*, the Hindustani classical *bansuri*, the breathy flutes of South America and the high pitched Chinese flutes. Each flute is different but all of them are played using the breath and thus, unites all human beings together. The author is surprised and mesmerised by the melodious flutes and now he started noticing small things that he never paid any attention to.

Word Meaning

Word	Meaning
sacred	holy; worthy of respect
proclaim	announce publicly; declare
febrile (confusion)	hurried activity; complete chaos
hawker	someone who sells goods in public places
devotee	a strong believer in a particular religion or God.
elbowed	push or strike someone with one's elbow
saffron-clad	covered in yellowish clothes
corpse	dead body
cremate	disposing of a dead body by burning it to ashes
offerings	something that is given to God as a part of religious worship
wilted	dried
shrine	a religious place
protrude	extend above a surface
emerges	comes out
stillness	quietness
immense	huge; big
dome	a large rounded roof that is shaped like half of a ball
immigrant	a person who comes to live permanently in a foreign country.
felt	a soft, heavy cloth made by pressing together fibers of wool, cotton etc.
haven	a safe place
vivid	lively
mercenary	working for money or other reward
flower-adorned	decorated by flowers
deities	Gods or Godesses
antique	a collectable object such as a piece of furniture or work of art that has a high value because of its age and quantity.
blare out	(here) played loudly

Word	Meaning
stray	(an animal) who is lost or has no home
vendors	sellers
wares	items that are offered for sale
mindlessly	requiring very little attention or thought
marzipan	a sweet made with grated almond
brazier	open stove
pavement	footpath
nauseating	sickening
propelled	(here) to go
homesick	longing for one's family or home
attachment	(here) hook or rope
quills	the hollow sharp spines of a porcupine
porcupine	a large rodent with defensive quills on the body and tail
meditatively	thoughtfully
offhanded	too casual
incidental	less important
enterprise	a business
reed	a thin strip of wood, metal or plastic inside some musical instruments that makes a sound when you blow over it
breathy	(here) played with the sound of a person's breath
compass	(here) range
weaves	(here) creates
associations	contacts; links
drawn into	attracted
commonality	common points
motive force	the force responsible to play the flute
invested	observed

NCERT FOLDER

NCERT Intext and Exercise Questions

THINKING ABOUT THE TEXT (NCERT PAGE 103)

I. Answer these questions in one or two words or in short phrases.

Q.1 Name the two temples the author visited in Kathmandu.

Ans. The author visited the Pashupatinath temple and the Baudhnath Stupa in Kathmandu.

Q.2 The writer says, "All this I wash down with Coca Cola." What does 'all this' refer to?

Ans. 'All this' refers to the food items that the author had bought in the Bazaar. They are a bar of marzipan and a corn-on-the-cob.

Q.3 What does Vikram Seth compare to the quills of a porcupine?

Ans. The author of the chapter, Vikram Seth compares the fifty or sixty flutes, tied to the pole of the flute seller, to the quills of a porcupine.

Q.4 Name five kinds of flutes.

Ans. The reed *neh*, the recorder, the Japanese *shakuhachi*, the deep *bansuri* of Hindustani classical music and the breathy flutes of South America are some kinds of flutes.

II. Answer each question in a short paragraph.

Q.1 What difference does the author note between the flute seller and the other hawkers?

Ans. When the author saw the flute seller, he noticed a difference between him and the other hawkers. The other hawkers shouted to call people to buy their products but the flute seller was not shouting to sell his flutes. Instead, he played the flutes occasionally in a slow and meditative manner to make people notice its melodious sound and get tempted to buy it.

Q.2 What is the belief at Pashupatinath about the end of Kaliyug?

Ans. At Pashupatinath, there is a small shrine on the bank of Bagmati river which is half inside the river. The belief is that when the complete temple would come out of the river, the Goddess inside the temple will escape and the evil period of *Kaliyug* will end on Earth.

Q.3 The author has drawn powerful images and pictures. Pick out three examples each of

(i) the atmosphere of 'febrile confusion' outside the temple of Pashupatinath (for example, some people trying to get the priest's attention are elbowed aside...)

(ii) the things he sees

(iii) the sounds he hears

Ans. (*i*) Many worshippers trying to get the priest's attention were pushing their way to the front. On the main gate, some Westerners were struggling for permission to enter as only Hindus were allowed to enter the temple.

A fight broke out between two monkeys. One was chasing the other who jumped onto a *Shivalinga*, then ran screaming around the temples and down to the holy Bagmati river.

(ii) He saw that the Baudhnath Stupa had an immense white dome, which was ringed by a road. Small shops were there on the outer edge where felt bags, Tibetan prints and silver jewellery could be bought. There were no crowds. On the busiest streets of Kathmandu, he saw fruit sellers, flute sellers, hawkers of postcards, shops selling Western cosmetics, film rolls, chocolates, copper utensils, Nepalese antiques, etc.

(iii) The sounds he heard were film songs that were played in the radios, car horns, bicycle bells and vendors shouting out their wares. He also listened to flute music.

III. Answer the following questions in not more than 100-150 words each.

Q.1 Compare and contrast the atmosphere in and around the Baudhnath shrine with the Pashupatinath temple.

Ans. When the author visited the Baudhnath shrine and the Pashupatinath temple, he found a difference in and around both the temples. While the Pashupatinath temple was noisy and confusing, the atmosphere around the Baudhnath Stupa was quiet and peaceful.

At the Pashupatinath temple, there was a large crowd rushing towards the entrance of the temple. People were pushing each other to get the priest's attention. At the same time, Westerners dressed in saffron clothes were trying to enter the temple and some monkeys were fighting with each other. Around the temple, there was the holy river Bagmati where a corpse was being cremated. A washerwoman was washing clothes and children were bathing.

In contrast, the Baudhnath Stupa was completely quiet. There was no crowd around it. There was a sense of stillness and serenity around the Buddhist shrine.

Q.2 How does the author describe Kathmandu's busiest streets?

Ans. The author has described Kathmandu in a very clear and detailed way. He has described the commercial centres, the temples and all that which is a part of the holy town. Along Kathmandu's narrowest and busiest streets, there were small shrines and flower-adorned deities. Apart from these, there were fruit sellers, flute sellers, hawkers of postcards, shops selling Western cosmetics, film rolls, chocolates, copper utensils, Nepalese antiques, etc.

The author heard film songs that were played in the radios, sounds of car horns and bicycle bells and vendors shouting out their products. He also saw a flute seller with many flutes. He was playing a flute meditatively and was not shouting out his wares. He contrasts the melodious music produced by the flute seller with the shouting of the hawkers.

Q.3 "To hear any flute is to be drawn into the commonality of all mankind." Why does the author say this?

Ans. For the author, to hear any flute is to be drawn into the commonality of all mankind. Music is a commonality for the mankind. Music draws everyone's attention and it is where all the things are considered equal. The one who knows and understands music knows the way it brings everyone together. It doesn't matter how this music is produced but every instrument has the same way of commonality.

The author considers flute music to be the most universal and most particular of all music. There is no culture that does not have its flute. The Japanese have their *Shakuhachi*, the Indians have the *bansuri*, the South Americans have the breathy flute and the Chinese have the high-pitched flutes.

Each kind of flute has a specific difference. In spite of their differences, every flute produces music with the help of the human breath. Similarly, in spite of the differences in caste, culture, religion and region, all human beings are the same, with the same living breath running through all of them.

THINKING ABOUT LANGUAGE

(NCERT PAGE 103-106)

Q.1 Read the following sentences carefully to understand the meaning of the italicised phrases. Then match the phrasal verbs in Column A with their meanings in Column B.

(i) **A communal war *broke out* when the princess was abducted by the neighbouring prince.**

(ii) **The cockpit *broke off* from the plane during the plane crash.**

(iii) **The car *broke down* on the way and we were left stranded in the jungle.**

(iv) **The dacoit *broke away* from the police as they took him to court.**

(v) **The brothers *broke up* after the death of the father.**

(vi) **The thief *broke into* our house when we were away.**

	A		B
(i)	break out	(a)	to come apart due to force
(ii)	break off	(b)	end a relationship
(iii)	break down	(c)	break and enter illegally; unlawful trespassing
(iv)	break away (from someone)	(d)	to start suddenly, (usually a fight, a war or a disease)
(v)	break up	(e)	to escape from someone's grip
(vi)	break into	(f)	stop working

Ans. (i) (d), (ii) (a), (iii) (f), (iv) (e), (v) (b), (vi) (c)

THINKING ABOUT LANGUAGE

Q.1 Use the suffixes _ion or _tion to form nouns from the following verbs. Make the necessary changes in the spellings of the words.

Example proclaim–proclamation

cremate .... act .... exhaust ....
invent .... tempt .... immigrate ....
direct .... meditate .... imagine ....
dislocate .... associate .... dedicate ....

Ans. cremate : cremation, act : action, exhaust : exhaustion, invent : invention, tempt : temptation, immigrate : immigration, direct : direction, meditate : meditation, imagine : imagination, dislocate : dislocation, associate : association, dedicate : dedication

Q.2 Now fill in the blanks with suitable words from the ones that you have formed.

(i) Mass literacy was possible only after the .... of the printing machine.

(ii) Ramesh is unable to tackle the situation as he lacks ....

(iii) I could not resist the .... to open the letter.

(iv) Hardwork and .... are the main keys to success.

(v) The children were almost fainting with .... after being made to stand in the Sun.

Ans. (i) invention (ii) imagination (iii) temptation (iv) dedication (v) exhaustion

III. Punctuation

Use capital letter, full stops, question marks, commas and inverted commas wherever necessary in the following paragraph.

An arrogant lion was wandering through the jungle one day he asked the tiger who is stronger than you you O lion replied the tiger who is more fierce than a leopard asked the lion you sir replied the leopard he marched upto an elephant and asked the same question the elephant picked him up in his trunk swung him in the air and threw him down look said the lion there is no need to get mad just because you don't know the answer.

Ans. An arrogant lion was wandering through the jungle one day. He asked the tiger, "Who is stronger than you?" "You, O lion!" replied the tiger. "Who is more fierce than a leopard?" asked the lion. "You, sir," replied the leopard.

He marched upto an elephant and asked the same question. The elephant picked him up in his trunk, swung him in the air and threw him down. "Look," said the lion, "There is no need to get mad just because you don't know the answer."

IV. Simple Present Tense

Q.1 Fill in the blanks with the correct form of the verb in brackets.

(i) The heart is a pump that .... (send) the blood circulating through our body. The pumping action .... (take place) when the left ventricle of the heart .... (contract). This .... (force) the blood out into the arteries, which .... (expand) to receive the oncoming blood.

(ii) The African lungfish can live without water for up to four years. During a drought it ....(dig) a pit and .... (enclose) itself in a capsule of slime and earth, leaving a tiny opening for air. The capsule ...... (dry) and ...... (harden), but when rain.......... (come), the mud .... (dissolve) and the lungfish .... (swim) away.

(iii) **MAHESH** We have to organise a class party for our teacher.
.... (Do) anyone play an instrument?

VIPUL Rohit ....(play) the flute.

MAHESH ....(Do) he also act?

VIPUL No, he ....(compose) music.

MAHESH That's wonderful!

Ans. (i) sends; takes place; contracts; forces; expands

(ii) digs; encloses; dries; hardens; comes; dissolves; swims

(iii) Does; plays; Does; composes

REVIEW EXERCISE

Including Competency Based Questions

Part I

Multiple Choice Questions

1. What does the first paragraph do? Competency Based

(a) It introduces the main characters in the text.
(b) It attracts the reader with interesting facts.
(c) It explains the motivations of the writer.
(d) It summarises the entire text.

Ans. (d) It summarises the entire text.

2. What does the writer mainly do in the second paragraph? Competency Based

(a) He tries to help the reader visualise the chaos.
(b) He warns visitors to be prepared for the chaos.
(c) He conveys his sense of confusion at the chaos.
(d) He highlights how differently some people are treated.

Ans. (a) He tries to help the reader visualise the chaos.

3. What is the last sentence in paragraph second? Competency Based

(a) An illustration of the chaos around.
(b) An attempt at sarcastic humour.
(c) The writer's religious conviction.
(d) An example of local belief.

Ans. (d) An example of local belief.

4. Why were the Westerners quarrelling at the Pashupatinath temple with the police?

(a) Because they wanted to get express darshan by paying the policeman.
(b) Because they were not allowed to go inside the temple.
(c) Because they were not wearing proper clothes for a temple visit.
(d) Because they wanted the pandit to do the aarti in English.

Ans. (b) Because they were not allowed to go inside the temple.

5. How does the writer describe the orange drink he had? Competency Based

(a) Sweet (b) Unusual (c) Delicious (d) Disgusting

Ans. (d) Disgusting

6. What impresses the writer about the flute seller? Competency Based

(a) His amazing musical skill. (b) His detached manner.
(c) His sales technique. (d) His friendly nature.

Ans. (b) His detached manner.

7. What is the main idea of paragraph seven? Competency Based

(a) Flute music is very similar to the human voice.
(b) Music is integral to human culture.
(c) Flute music has universal appeal.
(d) Music is universal.

Ans. (c) Flute music has universal appeal.

8. What does the opposite atmosphere at the two temples in Kathmandu signify?

(a) The different practices of worship in the two religions.
(b) The mismanagement at some religious sites.
(c) The importance of religious places as the cultural hub in Indian societies.
(d) All of the above

Ans. (d) All of the above

9. What is the point the writer is making in the last paragraph? Competency Based

(a) He has changed over the years.
(b) He has not travelled much in recent years.
(c) His home has become very important to him.
(d) Flute music has become very important to him.

Ans. (a) He has changed over the years.

10. What is the main purpose of the text? Competency Based

(a) To describe the writer's feelings while travelling through Kathmandu.
(b) To describe how music can remind you of home wherever you are.
(c) To describe the writer's love of things associated with his home.
(d) To describe the city of Kathmandu for new travellers.

Ans. (a) To describe the writer's feelings while travelling through Kathmandu.

Extract Based Questions

1. Read the following extract carefully and answer the questions that follow.

I consider what route I should take back home. If I were propelled by enthusiasm for travel per se, I would go by bus and train to Patna, then sail up the Ganges past Banaras to Allahabad, then up the Yamuna, past Agra to Delhi. But I am too exhausted and homesick; today is the last day of August. Go home, I tell myself: move directly towards home. I enter a Nepal Airlines office and buy a ticket for tomorrow's flight.
I look at the flute seller standing in a corner of the square near the hotel.

(i) What was the passage that the author would have taken had he not been tired and homesick?

Ans. The author loved travelling and visiting different places. He had planned an elaborate route from kathmandu to Delhi. He would go by bus and train to Patna. From there, he would sail up the Ganges past Benaras to Allahabad, then he would sail up the Yamuna past Agra to Delhi.

(ii) State whether the following statement is True or False.
The author loves to travel but is very exhausted and homesick at the moment.

Ans. True

(iii) The phrase 'sail up the Ganges' means ....

Ans. to sail upstream through a river.

(iv) Which word can replace the underlined word.
Shweta felt <u>tired</u> after working non-stop for 8 hours.

Ans. exhausted

2. Read the following extract carefully and answer the questions that follow.

Kathmandu is vivid, mercenary, religious, with small shrines to flower-adorned deities along the narrowest and busiest streets; with fruit sellers, flute sellers, hawkers of postcards; shops selling Western cosmetics, film rolls and chocolate; or copper utensils and Nepalese antiques. Film songs blare out from the radios, car horns sound, bicycle bells ring, stray cows low questioningly at motorcycles, vendors shout out their wares.

(i) The statement that is TRUE as per the above extract about Kathmandu is

(a) a religious place.
(b) a peaceful place to attain self-enlightenment.
(c) is famous as per the commercial sense.
(d) Both (a) and (c)

Ans. (d) Both (a) and (c)

(ii) The tone of the speaker in the above extract is

(a) Nostalgic
(b) Amusement
(c) Sarcastic
(d) Intense

Ans. (a) Nostalgic

(iii) State at least three adjectives that the author uses to describe Kathmandu.

Ans. 'Vivid', 'mercenary' and 'religious' are three adjectives that the author uses to describe Kathmandu.

(iv) Complete the sentence appropriately.
The phrase 'shout out their ware' means

Ans. advertising

3. Read the following extract carefully and answer the questions that follow.

A small shrine half protrudes from the stone platform on the river bank. When it emerges fully, the Goddess inside will escape, and the evil period of the Kaliyug will end on Earth.

(i) Where is the small shrine situated?

(a) Inside the temple
(b) Near temple
(c) On the bank of river Bagmati
(d) None of the above

Ans. (c) On the bank of river Bagmati

(ii) According to the legend, when will Kaliyug end?

Ans. According to the legend, Kaliyug will end when the stone platform emerges from the river bank and the Goddess inside it escapes.

(iii) Where does holy Bagmati river flow?

Ans. The holy river Bagmati flows just below the Pashupatinath temple.

(iv) Which word in the extract is an antonym for 'capture'?

Ans. 'Escape' in the extract is an antonym for 'capture'.

4. Read the following extract carefully and answer the questions that follow.

But I am too exhausted and homesick; today is the last day of August. Go home. I tell myself: move directly towards home. I enter a Nepal Airlines office and buy a ticket for tomorrow's flight.

(i) Who is 'I' in this extract?

(a) A priest
(b) A tourist
(c) Author
(d) A Tibetan shopkeeper

Ans. (c) Author

(ii) Why does the author want to return home?

Ans. The author wants to return home because he has been feeling homesick.

(iii) When did the author return to India from Nepal?

Ans. The author returned to India on 1st September.

(iv) What will be the antonym of 'Exhausted'?

Ans. Energetic

Part II

Short Answer Type Questions

1. Why are the devotees so eager to enter the Pashupatinath temple?

Ans. The devotees were so eager to enter Pashupatinath temple in order to get the priest's attention. They wanted the priest to give their offerings to the God and hence, were pushing, elbowing and shoving each other.

2. Why did the policeman stop the Westerners from entering the temple?

Ans. Only Hindu worshippers were allowed to enter the Pashupatinath temple. A group of Westerners wanted to enter the temple. They wore saffron clothes to get permission to enter the temple, but the policeman was not convinced and stopped the Westerners from entering the temple.

3. What does the author see near the Pashupatinath temple?

Ans. The author saw the holy river Bagmati flowing near the Pashupatinath temple. By the riverside, people were indulged in various activities. A corpse was being cremated while a washerwoman was washing clothes and the children were bathing. The old offerings of dried flowers was also being dropped in the river.

4. What did the Tibetan immigrants do near the Baudhnath Stupa? Did their activity disturb the atmosphere?

Ans. The Tibetan immigrants had set up small shops on the outer road around the Baudhnath Stupa. They were selling felt bags, Tibetan prints and silver jewellery in their shops. Their activity did not disturb the quiet and peaceful atmosphere of the Buddhist shrine.

5. Explain the statement "Kathmandu is vivid, mercenary, religious ...."

Ans. For the author Kathmandu was lively, commercial as well as religious. People from all over the world visited the tourist destination. Apart from the two most holy Hindu and Buddhist temples, there were small temples with flower-adorned gods for people to pray. In addition, the busy streets were full of street hawkers shouting to sell their products.

6. What alternative route does the author think of taking to go back home?

Ans. The author liked to travel. So initially, he thought of taking a longer route to go back home. For this alternative route, the author would have had to take the bus and then, a train to Patna. He would then have to sail up the Ganges to Allahabad and at last, sail up the Yamuna to Delhi.

7. In the chapter 'Kathmandu' what do you mean by "The flute seller occasionally makes a sale, but in a curiously offhanded way as if it were incidental to his enterprise"?

Ans. Music has been described as serene and sober by the author. He knows that music is much important than the sale of a flute for the flute seller. The flute seller keeps on playing his flute and he is so engrossed in it that when he makes a sale, it appears to be a minor thing to him.

8. What was the author's reaction to the flute seller? **Competency Based**

Ans. When the author heard the flute seller playing the flute, he was mesmerised by its sound. He was so enchanted by the melodious tune of the flute that he could not move from the square. It made him notice the small things that he had previously not seen or noticed.

9. How does the author pass his time in Kathmandu? **Competency Based**

Ans. The author spent his time in Kathmandu by visiting the famous temples and market places of Kathmandu. He observed his surroundings and the lives of the people in the town. He also ate the local street food, read some comics and magazines. He was completely mesmerised by the music of the flute in the town.

Long Answer Type Questions

1. What idea do you get about the author from the extract 'Kathmandu'? Write a descriptive paragraph on him in 100-120 words.

Ans. The extract 'Kathmandu', taken from Vikram Seth's travelogue, '*Heavenly Lake*', brings forth certain traits of his personality. As a traveller, Seth displays a keen sense of observation, and as a person with a fine aesthetic sense, his ability to capture the vivid details is commendable. The pictures of the temples of Kathmandu and its crowded streets came alive with his vivid descriptions. Though indirectly, he also appears to be a lover of serenity and tranquility when he terms the stupa as a 'haven of quietness'. He also shows his concern as an environmentalist who does not approve of the polluting activities carried on the banks of the Bagmati river. Vikram Seth's fondness for travelling is obvious by the fact that although being tired, he still contemplates taking a longer route back home to Delhi.

His fondness for music is brought forth when we find him so enchanted by the music of the flute that he has to force himself to leave the square where the flute is being played by the seller. Like a typical traveller, he indulges himself with the eatables he finds available in the bazaar of Kathmandu. Thus, the author emerges as a man with a profound fondness for travelling, love for music, a keen sense of observation, reflective mind and an ability to portray places and people realistically.

2. What is the main point of difference between the Hindu temple and the Buddhist temple, according to the text? **Competency Based**

Ans. During his visit to Kathmandu, writer Vikram Seth explored two contrasting places of faith - the Hindu Pashupatinath Temple and the Buddhist Baudhnath Stupa. Seth observed stark differences between the two. Pashupatinath was marked by chaos and distractions, with monkeys on the Shivling, crowded devotees, and market hustle. In contrast, an air of tranquillity enveloped Baudhnath Stupa. Minimal activity surrounded the marketplace, and the white dome created a beautiful serenity. These disparities reflect the unique atmospheres shaped by Hindu and Buddhist practices, emphasising the vibrant spiritual diversity within Kathmandu.

3. Suppose Vikram Seth went to Rameshwaram, Kalam's home town. He writes a blog on his visit to the holy town and compares it to his visit to the two temples in Kathmandu. Frame the blog for him.

You can start like this

Visit to the holy world is always a great experience.

Ans. Visit to the holy world is always a great experience. Every sacred place offers something unique-its own rhythm, its own aura. Recently, I had the privilege of visiting Rameshwaram, the revered town in Tamil Nadu that holds immense significance in both religious and historical contexts. This journey took me through the sacred streets of this coastal town, and I couldn't help but draw comparisons with my previous visits to two magnificent temples in Kathmandu, Nepal.

Rameshwaram is not just a town; it is a soul-stirring journey into the heart of spirituality. The Temple, dedicated to Lord Shiva, is a masterpiece of architecture and devotion. As I walked through the grand corridors, I was awed by the intricate carvings. What struck me most was the peacefulness that covered the place. The town, surrounded by the shimmering waters of the Bay of Bengal, filled me with a deep sense of connection with the divine, enhanced by the gentle sea breeze.

In contrast, my visits to the temple in Kathmandu, namely the Pashupatinath Temple offered a different yet equally profound spiritual experience. The air around the temple is thick with incense, the rhythmic chants of priests, and the sound of the holy river flowing by. The sacred cremation ghats add an element of introspection, as the Hindu ritual of cremation here connects life to death, reinforcing the eternal cycle of existence.

Both Rameshwaram and Kathmandu are treasures of spiritual heritage, each offering a distinct yet profound experience. Rameshwaram, with its sacredness tied deeply to the epic of Ramayana, evokes a sense of timeless devotion. Kathmandu, with its rich blend of Hindu and Buddhist traditions, showcases a more diverse spiritual landscape.

ASSESSMENT EXERCISE

Extract Based Questions

Read the following extract carefully and answer the questions that follow.

I find it difficult to tear myself away from the square. Flute music always does this to me: it is at once the most universal and most particular of sounds. There is no culture that does not have its flute.

(i) Why does the author find it difficult to move from the square? Because of
(a) Shopping
(b) Praying
(c) Impact of flute music
(d) Enjoying the nature

(ii) What does the author comment about flute?

(iii) Which is the motive force behind the music of a flute?

(iv) What does flute music do to the author?

Short Answer (SA) Type Questions

1. Why do the Westerners quarrel with the policeman at the Pashupatinath temple?
2. Give a short description of Kathmandu according to the author.
3. What are the things that the author bought from the local market of Kathmandu?
4. Name the flutes as described by the author in the chapter 'Kathmandu'.

Long Answer (LA) Type Questions

1. Temples or holy shrines are over crowded and poorly maintained nowadays which leads to great confusion and accidents. What should the authorities do to maintain and control the crowd at religious shrines?
2. Do you think music unites everyone? Answer with reference to the text.

If I Were You

by Douglas James

CHAPTER 9

CHAPTER SUMMARY The chapter 'If I Were You' is a one-act play written by Douglas James. It presents a dialogue between two people, Gerrard, a playwright and an intruder, a criminal. The intruder entered Gerrard's house with the plan of killing him and taking on his identity to live peacefully because they resemble each other.

When Gerrard got to know of the intruder's plan, he engaged the intruder in a conversation and told him a false story that he has killed a man. He also informed him that the police is about to catch them. With his cleverness, he convinced the intruder regarding the truth of the story and trapped him in the cupboard.

Gerrard, the Protagonist

The play opens with Gerrard talking on the phone. He was a man of medium height and lived in a lonely cottage in the forests of Essex. He was wearing his glasses, a lounge suit and a long coat. He was expecting a phone call in ten minutes time. After he put down the phone, he started packing a travelling bag. It appeared that he was going somewhere.

The Intruder Entered the House

While Gerrard was busy packing, a man with a revolver in his hand quietly entered the house. He looked similar to Gerrard. He was wearing a long coat and a soft hat. The intruder ordered Gerrard to put his hands up and to answer some questions. Gerrard remained calm and talked to the intruder politely.

Gerrard told the intruder that he was feeling uncomfortable while standing with his hands lifted up. So, the intruder allows Gerrard to sit on the chair and he himself sat on the diwan. He, then, started to ask questions. The intruder wanted to know some basic information, like full name, habits, talking style, etc, about Gerrard.

The Intruder's Motive

The intruder told Gerrard that he was a jewel robber. He had killed a policeman and was running away from the police. He further informed Gerrard that he had planned to kill him and take his identity. He wanted to live a peaceful and carefree life as Vincent Charles Gerrard. The intruder explained that he was in Aylesbury when he heard some people talking about Gerrard. He knew that Gerrard always phones his orders in and that his sudden travels are a mystery to everyone. He intruder added that Gerrard's personality was perfect for him to escape from the police.

Gerrard's False Story

After listening to the intruder, Gerrard cleverly made up a false story and informed the intruder that he himself was a criminal. He further stated that he must not shoot otherwise he would be hanged if not as himself, then as Gerrard.

Gerrard told the intruder that he had murdered someone and had run away. However, one of his men had been caught with things that could incriminate Gerrard and should have been burned. He (Gerrard) was also running away from the police and had already packed his bag to run. He convinced the intruder by showing his disguise outfits including false moustache, etc.

Intruder's Reaction

Gerrard's story almost convinced the intruder. The intruder began to think after this. This was an opportunity for Gerrard to work on his plan. Gerrard asked the intruder to hurry and run with him in his car as the police was about to reach there soon.

Since he was already expecting a call, he cleverly told the intruder that he had posted a man at the main road who would warn them if the police came by calling on the telephone. Coincidently, the telephone rang at that point.

Then, Gerrard opened the door to exit the house, which was actually the door of a cupboard. The intruder looked inside to make sure that it was actually a door to the garage.

The Intruder is Trapped

While the intruder looked inside, Gerrard gave him a push and locked him in the cupboard. The gun fell down from the intruder's hand. Gerrard picked the gun and called up the sergeant to arrest the intruder.

The true identity of Gerrard, who was actually a playwright, got revealed when he said that he got something for his next play from this experience.

Word Meaning

Word	Meaning
intruder	someone who breaks into a place
intends	plans
cultured	having or showing good education, tastes and manners
count on	rely
flashily	in a way that looks too bright and expensive.
bumps	to hit something or someone
paws	hands
melodramatic	something that involves drama
nonchalant	feeling or appearing casually calm and relaxed
sympathetic	showing concern about someone who is in a bad situation
gypsies	nomadic persons
inflection	a rise or fall in the sound of a person's voice
imitation	to copy something
assist	to help someone
tradespeople	businessmen
considerable	large
modest	humble
embrace	belong to
dandy	good or impressive
cops	police
retire	to relax
trifle	slightly
grave step	serious act
hunted	being chased

Word	Meaning
gratuitous	(of something such as bad behaviour) not necessary or with no cause
posh	elegant
pantomime	a way of expressing, using body movements and facial expressions.
tribute	a respect to someone/something
elude	to avoid or escape someone by being quick, skilful or clever
dodging	avoiding
queer	strange and odd
apparently	as far as one knows or can see
invested in	taken to
cloak	blanket
crook	a dishonest person
game's up	the plan/secret has been discovered.
disguise outfit	things to hide one's identity
clear off	go/ run away
musingly	in a manner that appears as though someone is thinking.
muddled	confused
frame	a trap to catch someone/something
leans	bows down
inspect	to check
props	support material
bother	trouble

NCERT FOLDER

NCERT Intext and Exercise Questions

THINKING ABOUT THE TEXT

(NCERT PAGE 115-116)

I. Answer these questions.

Q.1 'At last a sympathetic audience.'

(i) Who says this?

(ii) Why does he say it?

(iii) Is he sarcastic or serious?

Ans. (i) Gerrard says this.

(ii) He says it because the intruder had asked him to talk about himself.

(iii) He was being sarcastic. The intruder was in no way sympathetic. Infact, he told Gerrard, at gunpoint, to tell about himself so that he could use the information for his benefit.

Q.12 Why does the intruder choose Gerrard as the man whose identity he wants to take on?

Ans. The intruder chose Gerrard as the man whose identity he wanted to take on because the intruder looked similar to Gerrard. Also, Gerrard lived alone and did not meet a lot of people. Thus, no one would doubt the intruder and he would easily get away from the police.

Q.3 'I said it with bullets'.

(i) Who says this?

(ii) What does it mean?

(iii) Is it the truth? What is the speaker's reason for saying this?

Ans. (i) Gerrard says this.

(ii) It means that when things had gone wrong with him, he shot someone.

(iii) No, it was not the truth.
Gerrard said so because he wanted the intruder to believe that he was also a criminal. The intruder would have killed him if he had not lied about his identity.

Q.4 What is Gerrard's profession? Quote the parts of the play that support your answer.

Ans. Gerrard was a playwright.

There are several parts in the play which show the connection between him and theatre. When Gerrard saw the intruder, he said, "This is all very melodramatic, not very original, perhaps, but…" When the intruder asked Gerrard to talk about himself, he said, 'At last a sympathetic audience!'.

Gerrard also asked the intruder, "Are you American or is that merely a clever imitation?".

When the intruder told Gerrard about his plan of killing him and taking over his identity, he said, "In most melodramas the villain is foolish enough to delay his killing long enough to be frustrated."

Further, when Gerrard told the intruder about his false identity, he told him "That's a disguise outfit; false moustaches and what not." Finally, after locking up the intruder, Gerrard answered the phone and informed the caller that he can't send the props in time for rehearsal. He also said that he was in a tough situation and added that he had got something for his next play from the experience.

Q.5 'You'll soon stop being smart.'

(i) Who says this?

(ii) Why does the speaker say it?

(iii) What, according to the speaker, will stop Gerrard from being smart?

Ans. (i) The intruder says this.

(ii) The speaker (intruder) said this because Gerrard was not anxious or upset when the intruder entered into his house.

(iii) According to the intruder, Gerrard would stop being smart when he would get to know what was going to happen to him. The intruder's plan was to kill Gerrard and take on his identity.

Q.6 'They can't hang me twice.'

(i) Who says this?

(ii) Why does that speaker say it?

Ans. (i) The intruder says this.

(ii) The intruder had been telling Gerrard that he had murdered one man and he can murder Gerrard also. This is because the police could not hang him twice for two murders.

Q.7 'A mystery I propose to explain.' What is the mystery the speaker proposes to explain?

Ans. The mystery that Gerrard proposed to explain was the false story that he had made in order to trick the intruder. Gerrard tells him that he himself was a criminal like the intruder. When things went wrong with him, he had committed a murder and gotten away.

Unfortunately, one of his men had been arrested. Due to this, he was expecting some trouble from the police that night and therefore, he was packing his bag to escape.

Q.8 **'This is your big surprise.'**

(i) Where has this been said in the play?

(ii) What is the surprise?

Ans. (i) The given line was spoken twice in the play. First, it was spoken by the intruder when he revealed to Gerrard why he was there and what he was going to do with him.

On the second occasion, it was spoken by Gerrard when he was about to reveal his false story to the intruder.

(ii) When the intruder said this line, the surprise was that he was going to kill Gerrard and take on his identity.

When Gerrard said this line, the surprise was that he too was a criminal like the intruder.

THINKING ABOUT LANGUAGE (NCERT PAGE 116-117)

I. *Consult your dictionary and choose the correct word from the pairs given in brackets.*

Q.1 **The (site, cite) of the accident was (ghastly/ghostly).**

Ans. The **site** of the accident was **ghastly**.

Q.2 **Our college (principle/principal) is very strict.**

Ans. Our college **principal** is very strict.

Q.3 **I studied (continuously/continually) for eight hours.**

Ans. I studied **continuously** for eight hours.

Q.4 **The fog had an adverse (affect/effect) on the traffic.**

Ans. The fog had an adverse **effect** on the traffic.

Q.5 **Cezanne, the famous French painter, was a brilliant (artist/artiste).**

Ans. Cezanne, the famous French painter, was a brilliant **artist**.

Q.6 **The book that you gave me yesterday is an extraordinary (collage/college) of science fiction and mystery.**

Ans. The book that you gave me yesterday is an extraordinary **collage** of science fiction and mystery.

Q.7 **Our school will (host/hoist) an exhibition on cruelty to animals and wildlife conservation.**

Ans. Our school will **host** an exhibition on cruelty to animals and wildlife conservation.

Q.8 **Screw the lid tightly onto the top of the bottle and (shake/shape) well before using the contents.**

Ans. Screw the lid tightly onto the top of the bottle and **shake** well before using the contents.

II. Irony is when we say one thing but mean another, usually the opposite of what we say. When someone makes a mistake and you say, 'Oh! That was clever!' that is irony. You're saying 'clever' to mean 'not clever.'

Expression we often use in an ironic fashion are

Oh, wasn't that clever!/Oh that was clever!

You have been a great help, I must say!

You've got yourself into a lovely mess, haven't you?

Oh, very funny!How funny!

We use a slightly different tone of voice when we use these words ironically.

Read the play carefully and find the words and expressions Gerrard uses in an ironic way. Then say what these expressions really mean. Two examples have been given below. Write down three such expressions along with what they really mean.

What the author says	What he means
Why, this is a surprise, Mr—er—	He pretends that the intruder is a social visitor whom he is welcoming. In this way, he hides his fear.
At last a sympathetic audience!	He pretends that the intruder wants to listen to him whereas the intruder wants to find out information for his own use.

Ans.

What the author says	What he means
You won't kill me for a very good reason.	Gerrard was just pretending to have a very good reason. However, there was no such reason.
In most melodramas the villain is foolish enough to delay his killing long enough to be frustrated. You are much luckier.	Gerrard said that the 'villain' takes too long a time to make the killing and ends up being at the wrong end. As we know, Gerrard then tells him a cooked up story and the intruder turns out to be like the foolish villain of most melodramas.
Sorry I can't let you have props in time for rehearsal, I've had a spot of bother—quite amusing.	The 'spot of bother' that Gerrard found 'quite amusing' was actually a life-threatening situation. He was being held at gunpoint by a murderer who wanted to kill him and take his identity.

DICTIONARY USE (NCERT PAGE 117-118)

Look up the dictionary entries for the words sympathy, familiarity, comfort, care, and surprise. Use the information given in the dictionary and complete the table.

Ans.

Noun	Adjective	Adverb	Verb	Meaning
sympathy	Sympathetic	Sympathetically	Sympathise	Feel pity for others
familiarity	Familiar	Familiarly	Familiarise	To get to know about things
comfort	Comfortable	Comfortably	Comfort	Feeling of ease
care	Caring	Carefully	Care	Concern
surprise	Surprising	Surprisingly	Surprise	Shocked, amazed, astonished

I. Which of the words below describe Gerrard and which describe the Intruder?

smart humorous clever beautiful cool confident flashy witty nonchalant

Ans. **Gerrard** Smart, humorous, clever, cool, confident, nonchalant

Intruder Smart, flashy, clever, confident, witty.

II. Write a paragraph each about Gerrard and the Intruder to show what qualities they have. (You can use some of the words given above).

Ans. 'If I Were You' is a play written by Douglas James. In the play, Gerrard and the Intruder are two central characters with distinct qualities.

Gerrard, a seemingly ordinary man, initially appears as a victim of a home invasion. However, as the plot unfolds, his resourcefulness and quick thinking reveal a courage that surprises both the audience and the intruder. Gerrard exhibits qualities of adaptability and strategic intelligence, turning the table on the situation.

The Intruder, on the other hand, is cunning. His intrusion disrupts Gerrard's ordinary life, and he attempts to assert control through intimidation. The character of the Intruder is layered with a mix of desperation and aggressiveness, making him an almost perfect adversary for Gerrard.

III. Convert the play into a story (150–200 words). Your story should be as exciting and as witty as the play. Provide a suitable title to it.

Ans. **Title** 'The Intricate Gambit'

In the quaint town of Brookville, Gerrard, a common man of routine, found himself in an unexpected game of intellect. One fateful evening, an Intruder boldly invaded his home, setting the stage for a thrilling narrative.

Gerrard, initially caught off guard, quickly became the unsuspecting hero of his own story. With a quick mind and a great level of intelligence, he cleverly turned the tide against the Intruder. Gerrard told the intruder that he himslef was a criminal and wanted by the police.

The Intruder, thinking he had an easy mark, found himself stuck in a web of surprises. Gerrard's story left the Intruder shocked and confused, and he started questioning his own assumptions about the so-called victim.

As the night unfolded, the tables turned in a series of suspenseful twists. Gerrard's finally managed to capture the fugitive in a cupboard and called the police, thus saving his life. 'The Intricate Gambit' became a tale of unexpected heroes and unforeseen strategies, proving that even the most ordinary people can shine in extraordinary circumstances.

REVIEW EXERCISE

Including Competency Based Questions

Part I

Multiple Choice Questions

1. The beginning of the play suggests that .... Competency Based

(a) Gerrard is expecting a visitor
(b) Gerrard is planning to travel
(c) Gerrard is a rich man
(d) Gerrard is a criminal

Ans. (b) Gerrard is planning to travel

2. What did the intruder try to do as soon as he came in? Competency Based

(a) Try to rob Gerrard
(b) Intimidate Gerrard
(c) Make sure no one sees him
(d) Show off his knowledge about Gerrard

Ans. (b) Intimidate Gerrard

3. Why does Gerrard want to share his history? **Competency Based**

(a) He is a very lonely man.
(b) He is a very friendly man.
(c) He wants to distract the intruder.
(d) He wants to show that he is harmless.

Ans. (c) He wants to distract the intruder.

4. The intruder's repeated statements about his own intelligence suggests that he is **Competency Based**

(a) frank (b) clever
(c) nervous (d) arrogant

Ans. (d) arrogant

5. With you figuring so largely in it, that is understandable. What does the line above suggest about Gerrard? **Competency Based**

(a) He was getting frustrated
(b) He had an ironic sense of humour.
(c) He wanted to be polite to the intruder.
(d) He was getting worried about the intruder.

Ans. (b) He had an ironic sense of humour.

6. What does Gerrard most likely do for a living? **Competency Based**

(a) He is an actor
(b) He is a criminal
(c) He is a travel writer
(d) He is involved with the police

Ans. (a) He is an actor

7. How did Gerrard defend himself?

(a) By harming the intruder (b) By fabricating a lie
(c) By driving him out (d) By calling the sheriff

Ans. (b) By fabricating a lie

8. 'A little harsh isn't it?' Who poses this question?

(a) The intruder (b) The narrator
(c) The Sheriff (d) Gerrard

Ans. (d) Gerrard

9. Select the option that correctly captures the application of the underlined word in the given phrase

"To be ready to beat it at the sight of a cop"

(a) He beat the dust out of the rug with ease.
(b) She used a hammer to beat the metal into shape.
(c) She used a hammer to beat a nail into the wall.
(d) The thief beat the patrolling police and took off with ease.

Ans. (d) The thief beat the patrolling police and took off with ease.

10. Which option given below is not the right option to fill in the blank.

Gerrard's .... comes through clearly when he says , "but no one is interesting as yourself".

(a) wit and humour (b) presence of mind
(c) relaxed demeanour (d) fear and desperation

Ans. (d) fear and desperation

Extract Based Questions

1. Read the following extract carefully and answer the questions that follow.

Gerrard This is your big surprise. I said you wouldn't kill me and I was right. Why do you think I am here today and gone tomorrow, never see tradespeople? You say my habits would suit you. You are a crook. Do you think I am a Sunday-school teacher?

The game's up as far as I'm concerned. Things went wrong with me. I said it with bullets and got away. Unfortunately they got one of my men, and found things the fool should have burnt. Tonight I'm expecting trouble. My bag's packed ready to clear off. There it is.

(i) What does Gerrard boast to be right about?

Ans. Gerrard boasts to be right about not getting murdered by the intruder.

(ii) Choose the options that lists the set of statements that are not true according to the given extract.

1. Gerrard is a criminal.
2. Gerrard is trying to befool the listener.
3. The listener is an intruder who wants to take Gerrard's identity.
4. The police are waiting outside for Gerrard while he is talking.
5. Gerrard is a Sunday-school teacher.
6. The intruder does not believe Gerrard.

(a) 1,3 and 5 (b) 2,4 and 6
(c) 1,4 and 6 (d) 2,3 and 5

Ans. (c) 1, 4 and 6

(iii) According to Gerrard, why did things go wrong with him?

Ans. According to Gerrard, things went wrong with him because his crime was found out as one of his men was caught with evidence.

(iv) Complete the sentence appropriately.

The phrase 'said it with bullets' means ....

Ans. killed someone

2. Read the following extract carefully and answer the questions that follow.

Intruder My speciality's jewel robbery. Your car will do me a treat. It's certainly a dandy bus.

Gerrard I'm afraid jewels are few and far between in the wilds of Essex.

Intruder So are the cops. I can retire here nicely for a little while.

(i) What did the intruder want from Gerrard?

Ans. The intruder wanted to kill Gerrard and take his identity.

(ii) Why does the intruder choose Gerrard's house?

Ans. The intruder close Gerrard's house because it was located in the forests of Essex away from cities. Here, he could live a safe and peaceful life while hiding from the police.

(iii) Fill in the blank with one word only.

In the given lines, Gerrard is taking his time to come up with a .... to trap the intruder.

Ans. plan

(iv) What is the intruder's speciality?

(a) Jewel Robbery (b) Assassination
(c) Secret Agent (d) Forensics

Ans. (a) Jewel Robbery

3. Read the following extract carefully and answer the questions that follow.

Gerrard This is your big surprise. I said you wouldn't kill me and I was right. Why do you think I am here today and gone tomorrow, never see tradespeople? You say my habits would suit you. You are a crook. Do you think I am a Sunday-school teacher? The game's up as far as I'm concerned.

(i) Why was the listener going to kill Gerrard?

Ans. The listener was going to kill Gerrard in order to take his identity.

(ii) State whether the following statement is True or False.

The given lines reveal that Gerrard is gullible.

Ans. False

(iii) What characteristic of Gerrard is highlighted in the given line. "Do you think I'm a sunday-school teacher?"

Ans. Gerrard's sarcastic nature and cunningness is being highlighted in the given line.

(iv) How does Gerrard justify his surprise?

Ans. Gerrard justifies his surprise by listing out his habits and pointing out that they were mysterious because he was a criminal himself.

4. Read the following extract carefully and answer the questions that follow.

The game's up as far as I'm concerned. Things went wrong with me. I said it with bullets and got away. Unfortunately they got one of my men, and found things the fool should have burnt. Tonight I'm expecting trouble. My bag's packed ready to clear off. There it is.

(i) Who is the speaker in the above extract?

(a) Policeman
(b) Gerrard
(c) Intruder
(d) Tradesman

Ans. (b) Gerrard

(ii) What is the purpose of the given lines?

Ans. The purpose of the given lines is to convince the intruder not to kill the speaker and to distract him.

(iii) What had he done?

Ans. He had murdered someone

(iv) Complete the sentence appropriately. The phrase 'expecting trouble' means ....

Ans. going to get caught

Part II

Short Answer Type Questions

1. Explain the context involved in '......... and no funny business'?

Ans. The intruder said those words when Gerrard wanted to be seated as he was not comfortable while standing with his hands lifted up. The intruder said so because he thought that Gerrard might do anything to come out of the trouble.

2. Why did Gerrard call the intruder 'a sympathetic audience'?

Ans. When the intruder informed Gerrard that they were going to talk about him and get to know him, Gerrard called the intruder to be a sympathetic audience as he was willingly trying to listen to Gerrard.

The main purpose of the words was to divert the intruder's attention so that he (Gerrard) could plan something to come out of the situation.

3. What does Gerrard's reaction to the intruder suggest about Gerrard's characte Competency Based

Ans. When Gerrard's room was invaded by the intruder, he did not panic. He stayed calm and laid a trap for the intruder. He was even threatened at gunpoint but he remained collected. His reaction to the intruder suggests that he was a cool, calm, level-headed, and smart individual.

4. Why was Gerrard dodging the questions of the intruder that he could have answered easily?

Ans. Gerrard was dodging the intruder's questions so that he could come up with an idea to escape the situation. If he kept on talking longer with the intruder, then he would have the time required to think and he might also get some information about the intruder.

5. What happens when Gerrard tries to lie about the car? Competency Based

Ans. When the intruder asked whether Gerrard drove a car, Gerrard tried to lie and say that he couldn't drive. However, the tactic didn't succeed because the intruder had gained a lot of information. Therefore, he already knew that Gerrard owned and drove a car.

6. What was the special area of crime for the intruder? Why did he come there to Essex?

Ans. The intruder had a special area of crime. He was a jewel robber who was running away from the police. He came to Essex as according to him, it did not have as many cops as in the city. Consequently, he would be able to live calmly and peacefully.

7. What surprise did the intruder give to Gerrard? Why was it threatening?

***Or* What was the intruder's plan?** Competency Based

Ans. The surprise that the intruder gave to Gerrard was the information that he had planned to kill him.

The surprise was threatening because the intruder wanted to take on his identity and live as Gerrard.

8. The intruder has done some research on Gerrard. Do you agree with this statement? Justify your response. Competency Based

Ans. The intruder had certainly done a lot of research on Gerrard. This is why he knew a lot of things about him. For instance, he knew Gerrard's eating habits, his travelling habits, his loner lifestyle, and even knew that people generally perceived Gerrard to be a strange and mysterious man.

9. Why did Gerrard say that the intruder was luckier?

Ans. Gerrard says that the intruder was luckier than any other villains of melodrama because unlike other villains, the intruder's delay in murder would not frustrate him but is lucky for him.

If the intruder would have killed him, the police would still chase him as Gerrard himself was a criminal.

10. How did the intruder become a criminal?

Ans. The intruder was a jewel robber who had committed many robberies. He became a criminal when he had killed a cop during a robbery.

Since then, he had been running away from the police.

11. What mystery did Gerrard explain to the intruder?

Ans. Gerrard explained a mystery regarding himself to the intruder. He told him that he was also a criminal and if the intruder killed him to take his identity, it wouldn't do any good to him because he would still be hanged. So, there was no benefit in killing Gerrard.

12. What is the intruder's plan? Competency Based

Ans. The intruder was tired of living the life of a convict on the run from the law. Therefore, he decided to kill Gerrard and take over his life. He planned to wear Gerrard's clothes and speak like him as well.

This way he would be able to live a normal life without living in fear of the police.

13. How did Gerrard justify himself to be a criminal?

Ans. Gerrard, to justify himself as a criminal, used the same information that the intruder had used to come up with his plan. He asked the intruder to think about why he never met any tradespeople. He also asked the intruder to think why people thought he was mysterious.

14. How did Gerrard convince the intruder that he was not lying?

Ans. Gerrard told the intruder that he was also a criminal and convinced him by showing him his disguise outfits including moustache, etc. He also told him that his bag was packed as he was expecting trouble that night. Gerrard had taken the intruder in his confidence with his elaborate arguments that further convinced the intruder.

15. How did Gerrard get rid of the intruder?

Ans. Gerrard told the intruder that they both should escape because trouble was expected that night. He asked the intruder to hurry and run with him in his car. As the intruder moved towards the door which was actually a door to the cupboard, Gerrard pushed him and locked him in the cupboard. Further, he called for the Sergeant to get rid of the intruder.

Long Answer Type Questions

1. 'When the going gets tough, the tough get going'. Validate the given statement with reference to the character of Gerrard in 'If I Were You'.

Ans. Presence of mind and a never surrendering attitude are some of the qualities that help an individual during a time of crisis. If one stays cool, calm and composed, then any task could be done easily. In the play 'If I Were You', it is courage and Gerrard's presence of mind that helped him. Gerrard, the protagonist, was troubled with a problem that came in the form of an intruder. The intruder not only wanted to kill Gerrard but also wanted to take on his identity.

He would have been successful in his plan but Gerrard's steadfast attitude and his cleverness saved him. Using his presence of mind, Gerrard diverted the intruder into a conversation and gained time to make up a false story. He even made sure to add elements that would convince the intruder about the truth. As a result, Gerrard locked him in a cupboard and freed himself from the trouble.

Therefore, one can say that the character of Gerrard validates the statement 'When the going gets tough, the tough get going'.

2. Consider the statement "In most melodramas the villain is foolish enough to delay his killing long enough to be frustrated." On the basis of this statement justify the idea lying behind doing the right thing at the right moment.

Ans. The statement that doing the right thing at the right moment is justified. If a thing is done at the moment when it should be, then the net result is appreciable. If an act is delayed then, there are chances that the result might differ from the expectations often leading to frustrations.

Therefore, clever people do what is due at that moment and don't delay that act purposely.

This fact is proved in the play 'If I Were You'. The intruder might have succeeded in his plan of killing Gerrard and taking his identity before Gerrard came up with a false story. If the intruder had killed Gerrard immediately when he had all the information about him, then he might have been living a peaceful life.

However, he frustrated himself by constantly delaying the killing. Consequently, Gerrard got the time to think of a way to trap the intruder. The false story of Gerrard convinced the intruder and thus, failed his plans.

Hence, the statements hold true and is enough to justify that actions done on time leads to good results.

3. Talking about consideration of the situation that Gerrard faced, what safety measures will you suggest to Gerrard?

Ans. Safety and security always comes first. One's life is more precious than anything else. If one cannot ensure one's safety, then one could not do one's work well. An insecure person is always afraid of all the unwanted things.

In the play, 'If I Were You', Gerrard faced a similar situation. An unknown and unwanted person entered his house with a gun in his hand. He obviously had bad intentions. He wanted to kill Gerrard and take on his identity.

The fact that an intruder was easily able to break into Gerrard's house shows that his house was not secure enough. Hence, there exists a need of increasing security at his house to ensure his safety.

The thing that Gerrard needs to do is meet people who live near his house or come to his house. If possible, he should also employ a watchman to look after his cottage and install cameras in his house. He should also install locks in his cottage. Gerrard must not compromise with his safety at all.

4. The intruder was a meticulous planner and he planned everything in detail. Discuss the importance of a better planning for an efficient result in the same context and considering your opponent stronger than you generally think.

Ans. Planning is the most needed thing to do a task efficiently. If one doesn't plan well then, there are chances of failure. Planning gives an individual freedom to execute the plans efficiently and reach the aim. However, sometimes even the well-planned things collapse in the end.

In the story 'If I Were You', a similar thing happened with the intruder. He failed in executing his plan. Even though he had worked out everything in detail and knew almost all the facts about Gerrard, he could not be successful in killing Gerrard.

The main cause of intruder's failure was the lack of his presence of mind. Even though he was confident in his plan, he did not think about Gerrard's smartness. If he had understood that Gerrard was just trying to trick him, he would have been living a peaceful life. He also underestimated his opponent and thus was caught in his opponent's trap. Hence, it can be said that not just careful planning but many other factors are responsible in successful plans.

5. Gerrard, the protagonist of 'If I Were You' and the narrator from 'The Snake and the Mirror' both find themselves in fatal situations during the narrative. What can you learn from their responses to dangerous situations? Explain on the basis of the respective chapters in 120-150 words.

Ans. Whenever humans find themselves in dangers, they can have two reactions- they can panic and worsen the situation, or they can think calmly and save themselves. Both the doctor and Gerrard remain calm when danger finds them. The doctor finds his life in danger, when a venomous snake lands on his shoulder. He quickly realises that since he doesn't have the anti-venom in the room, the best thing for him would be to stay still. So, he stays still and as soon as the snake slides off of him, he runs away.

Gerrard, similarly finds himself in mortal danger when the intruder holds him at gunpoint and informs him that he is going to kill him and take his identity. Gerrard utilises his creativity and creates a story that he is a criminal himself and the police were after him. He manipulates the situation and succeeds in trapping the intruder inside a cabinet, thus saving his life. By their example, we learn that it is important to aways remain calm and think logically during dangerous situations as that is the only way of getting ourselves out of danger.

ASSESSMENT EXERCISE

Extract Based Questions

Read the following extract carefully and answer the questions that follow.

Gerrard Don't be a fool. If you shoot, you'll hang for sure. If not as yourself, then as Vincent Charles Gerrard.

Intruder What is this?

Gerrard This is your big surprise. I said you wouldn't kill me and I was right. Why do you think I am here today and gone tomorrow, never see tradespeople? You say my habits would suit you. You are a crook. Do you think I am a Sunday-school teacher?

(i) What does the expression 'Sunday-school teacher' mean?

(a) Part time teacher (b) Teacher in a Church
(c) Very religious person (d) Very honest person

(ii) What did Gerrard reveal about himself?

(a) Does not stay at one place
(b) Meets very few people
(c) Has committed a crime
(d) All of the above

(iii) Find the word from the extract similar in meaning to the word 'rogue'.

(iv) Why does Gerrard tell the intruder that he can be hanged as Vincent Charles Gerrard also?

Short Answer (SA) Type Questions

1. With what preparation did the intruder go to Gerrard's cottage.
2. What things were known to the intruder about Gerrard?
3. How did the intruder come up with his plan?
4. What does Gerrard tell about his life when the intruder asked him to sit down and have a nice talk?

Long Answer (LA) Type Questions

1. One's profession adds to one's enlightenment. In the light of the chapter, describe how Gerrard used the skills learnt from his profession to trap the intruder?
2. Brave people don't panic at the moment of crisis and use their presence of mind. How did Gerrard show his presence of mind in the play?

Section C : Literature
Textbook : Beehive *(Poetry)*

The Road Not Taken

CHAPTER 1

by Robert Frost

Introduction In the poem 'The Road Not Taken', the poet describes a very common experience of making a choice. He recalls one such choice he made in the past while travelling from the forest. From the two paths that diverged in the forest, the poet chose the one that seemed to him to be less travelled. He states that his choice has had a significant impact in his life. Through this choice, the poet highlights that the choice that we make have a huge impact on our future. So, we must be wise while making choices.

Explanation of the Poem

Stanza 1

Two roads diverged in a yellow wood,
And sorry I could not travel both
And be one traveller, long I stood
And looked down one as far as I could
To where it bent in the undergrowth.

Explanation The poet has come to a forest in the autumn season when the leaves have turned yellow. He reaches a point where the two roads separated into two directions. The roads symbolise the two ways of life. The poet, as a traveller, knew that he had to make a choice as he cannot travel both the roads at the same time. So, he stood there for a long time and looked down on both the roads. The poet looked at the first road and found that it has a bend which was covered with small plants and bushes.

Stanza 2

Then took the other, just as fair,
And having perhaps the better claim,
Because it was grassy and wanted wear;
Though as for that the passing there
Had worn them really about the same.

Explanation The poet looked at the other road. According to him, this road seemed better and more impressive as it was covered with grass. It was not walked over by many people. However as the poet walked on the road for some distance, he realised that both the roads have been walked over equally.

Stanza 3

And both that morning equally lay
In leaves no step had trodden black.
Oh, I kept the first for another day!
Yet knowing how way leads on to way,
I doubted if I should ever come back.

Explanation The poet now says that both the roads were similar on that morning as no one had travelled on either of them. The leaves were still green and fresh as they have not been crushed by anyone while walking. The poet decides to travel the second road and kept the first one for some other days. However, the poet had a doubt if he could ever come back again to walk on the first road. The poet knew that once he made a choice, he would not be able to come back to change his choice.

Stanza 4

I shall be telling this with a sigh
Somewhere ages and ages hence;
Two roads diverged in a wood and
I took the one less travelled by,
And that has made all the difference.

Explanation In these lines, the poet talks about the consequences of the choice. The poet states that sometime in future, he will remember the day he made the choice.
He would be telling about his decision with a sigh either with relief or regret (relief of making the right choice or regret of making the wrong choice). He would tell that from the two roads that went into the forest, he took the less travelled one and the choice had made a significant impact on his life.

Poetic Devices Used in the Poem

Assonance It is the repetition of same sounds in the beginning of the nearby words.

- Two roads diverged in a yellow wood.

Personification It is used to make an inanimate object or animals/birds look or feel human.

- Because it was grassy and wanted wear.

Imagery It is used to represent objects, actions and ideas in such a way that it appeals to our physical senses.

- Two roads diverged in a yellow wood.
- And both that morning equally lay/in leaves no step had trodden black.

Metaphor It is used to compare two things or qualities which are unlike.
The poem as a whole is a metaphor, because the poet is comparing the paths in the wood to the choices one must make in life.

Symbolism In this device, symbols are used to represent ideas or qualities.

- **"Undergrowth"**

Word Meaning

Word	Meaning
Stanza 1	
Diverged	separated
Yellow wood	the leaves on the trees are yellow, suggesting it is the autumn season
Undergrowth	dense growth of plants and bushes
Stanza 2	
Fair	good/beautiful
Better claim	it seemed better and more impressive
Grassy	full of grass
Wanted wear	looked less worn out or used
Passing	on walking down
Stanza 3	
Equally lay	were equally covered
Trodden black	turned the path black by crushing the leaves
Way leads on to way	one thing leads to another
Stanza 4	
Sigh	a long deep breath here either of relief/satisfaction or regret
Ages and ages hence	many years in the future

NCERT FOLDER | NCERT Exercise Questions

I. THINKING ABOUT THE POEM (NCERT PAGE 16)

Q.1 Where does the traveller find himself? What problem does he face?

Ans. The traveller finds himself at a place where two roads diverge into two directions. He faces a problem of making a choice. He cannot decide which road to take to continue his journey because it is not possible for him to travel in both directions at the same time.

Q.2 Discuss what these phrases mean to you.

(i) a yellow wood
(ii) it was grassy and wanted wear
(iii) the passing there
(iv) leaves no step had trodden black
(v) how way leads on to way

Ans. (i) A yellow wood refers to the forest in the autumn season. Symbolically, the yellow wood represents a period of transition and change, suggesting a moment in life when decisions and choices are to be made.

(ii) The expression conveys that the road was full of grass and nobody had used it or it was used by less people. It could also symbolise the unconventional or less popular choice/path.

(iii) The use of the road by people passing through the forest.

(iv) The leaves had not become black because no one has walked on them.

(v) This means how one road (symbolic of choice) leads to another road. In other words, once a path is chosen, it leads to further opportunities, experiences and decisions. Thus, each choice leads to a new set of possibilities.

Q.3 Is there any difference between the two roads as the poet describes them

(i) in stanzas two and three?
(ii) in the last two lines of the poem?

Ans. (i) In stanza two, the poet explains that the only difference between the two roads was that the road that he took had a better claim or looked more impressive because it was covered with grass and looked as if it had not been much walked over. However, at the end of the stanza, he says that both roads had been almost equally worn down by people walking on them.

In stanza three, the poet says that on that morning, both the roads were equally covered with leaves and that no person had stepped on them.

(ii) In the last two lines of the poem, the poet says that probably many years later in future that there would be a difference between the two roads because he took the road that was less travelled and that made all the difference to his journey and in his life.

Q.4 What do you think the last two lines of the poem mean? (Looking back, does the poet regret his choice or accept it?)

Ans. The last two lines of 'The Road Not Taken' brings out the theme of the poem. The lines convey that the poet had made a choice and his choice had a significant impact on his life. He had accepted his choice and had moved on in his life.

II. THINKING ABOUT THE POEM (NCERT PAGE 16)

Q.1 Have you ever had to make a difficult choice (or do you think you will have difficult choices to make)? How will you make the choice (for what reasons)?

Ans. No, till now I have never been in a situation in which I had to make a difficult choice. Perhaps, I am still too young to make an independent choice.

Yes, I think soon I will have difficult choices to make. After completing my general education, I will have to choose a profession. I will have many options before me. Then, it will be difficult to make a choice among them. However, I will make my choice according to my capabilities and interest.

I will choose a path that gives me satisfaction and mental peace. I will not just join the rat race for money. During such a situation, I will weigh the pros and cons of all the choices before making a decision. I may even consult my elders for my decision as I know that my choice will have a huge impact on my life.

Q.2 After you have made a choice, do you always think about what might have been, or do you accept the reality?

Ans. After I have made a choice, I would accept the reality. Taking a decision makes our future. Reconsidering a decision or contemplating over it is not a positive approach towards life. Such thoughts never allow us to be happy with what we have gained from our decision. Therefore, I believe in sticking to my decisions.

REVIEW EXERCISE
Including Competency Based Questions

Part – I

Multiple Choice Questions

1. What does poet's long stare at the path signify?

(a) The time taken by people to decide and make a choice
(b) Poet loves nature
(c) Idling away of time
(d) Relaxation hours

Ans. (a) The time taken by people to decide and make a choice

2. What is the dilemma of the poet?

(a) Whether he will get time for himself
(b) Whether he will be successful
(c) Whether he will be able to come back to the second road or not
(d) Whether he will be able to walk

Ans. (c) Whether he will be able to come back to the second road or not

3. What does the phrase 'wanted wear' mean?

(a) That the road is difficult and worthy of trying.
(b) That the road is not taken by many people.
(c) That the road is very common.
(d) That the road needs repairs.

Ans. (b) That the road is not taken by many people.

4. Consider the following statements and choose which of them are true.

1. **The poet made his decision about which road to take very quickly.**
2. **The season was autumn.**
3. **The poet wished he could travel along both the roads.**
4. **He took the road which had been used more.**

(a) 1 and 4
(b) 2 and 3
(c) All of them
(d) None of these

Ans. (b) 2 and 3

5. What is the rhyming scheme of the poem?

(a) Abcdb (b) Abbab
(c) Abcab (d) Abaab

Ans. (d) Abaab

6. Which figure of speech is used in the line 'Though as for that the passing there'?

(a) Metaphor (b) Alliteration
(c) Simile (d) Personification

Ans. (b) Alliteration

7. What does the poet's decision of taking less travelled road signify?

(a) Too many things
(b) He took the same decision as others
(c) He took a difficult and rare decision
(d) None of the above

Ans. (c) He took a difficult and rare decision

8. Why is the poet asking to be wise while choosing a pathway?

(a) Because it is the only one road
(b) Because there is no option of going back
(c) Because it is one sided road
(d) None of the above

Ans. (b) Because there is no option of going back

9. 'Just as fair' refers to

(a) the second road (b) the first road
(c) the dilemma (d) Both the roads

Ans. (a) the second road

10. Which road did the narrator choose?

(a) He chose the first road.
(b) He chose the road that was grassy and less travelled.
(c) He chose none of the roads.
(d) He chose the road that was worn out.

Ans. (b) He chose the road that was grassy and less travelled.

11. What is the poet not likely to say?

A. 'I do not regret my choice.'
B. 'Only if I had taken the other option.'
C. 'I don't know why I chose this path.'
D. 'This is the best time of my life.'

Codes

(a) A and B (b) Only C
(c) B and D (d) Only D

Ans. (d) Only D

Extract Based Questions

1. Read the following extract carefully and answer the questions that follow.

The roads diverged into a yellow wood,
And sorry I could not travel both
And be one traveller, long I stood
And looked down one as far as I could
To where it bent in the undergrowth;

(i) Select the appropriate option to complete the sentence, according to the extract.

The poet has used road as a metaphor for ....

Ans. the journey of life

(ii) Select the option that applies the same rhyme scheme as the lines of the given extract.

(a) This bird so small and sweet,
Sings aloud in the morn,
Perched on a branch green,
Chirp, chirp, tweet, tweet.
As the sun rises high.

(b) Perched on a branch green,
This bird so sweet and lean,
Sings aloud in a voice sweet,
Chirp, chirp, tweet, tweet.
Dancing in the morning scene.

(c) This bird so small without a care,
Sweet Perched on a branch green,
A song with the world to share,
With its feelings so keen.
Spreading joy where it's seen.

(d) This bird so small and
Sings aloud in the morn
Perched on a green branch
Singing its own melody
Bringing joy to all who see.

Ans. (b)

(iii) Comment on the symbolism of the 'undergrowth' in the poem.

Ans. The undergrowth symbolises the unknown, the potential challenges and obstacles of each choice. It suggests that the speaker can only see far into the future and must decide with complete knowledge.

(iv) Why did the traveller take so long to decide which road to take?

Ans. Since he wanted to make the right choice, the traveller took a long time to decide which road to take.

2. Read the following extract carefully and answer the questions that follow.

Then took the other, just as fair,
And having perhaps the better claim,
Because it was grassy and wanted wear;
Though as for passing there
Had worn them really about the same

(i) The poet has used a poetic device in the line 1 and line 3 of the extract. Identify the poetic device used.

Ans. Alliteration

(ii) State whether the following statement is True or False.

The narrator chose the road that was grassy and less travelled.

Ans. True

(iii) 'Just as fair' in the extract means

(a) the second road was as beautiful as the first one.
(b) the second road was less beautiful than the first one.
(c) the second road was more beautiful than the first one.
(d) the second road was longer than the first one.

Ans. (a) the second road was as beautiful as the first one.

(iv) Why did the second road present a better claim than the first one?

Ans. The second road presented a better claim than the first one because it was still grassy and had not been used by many travellers.

3. Read the following extract carefully and answer the questions that follow.

And both that morning equally lay
In leaves no step had trodden black.
Oh, I kept the first for another day!
Yet knowing how way leads on to way,
I doubted if I should ever come back.

(i) How does the speaker feel about the two paths in the poem?

Ans. The speaker expresses a sense of uncertainty and contemplation regarding the two paths, acknowledging that both have their own appeal.

(ii) What is the condition of the thing that the poem is talking about?

(a) Both of them are same. (b) Both of them are used.
(c) Both of them are clean. (d) Both of them are dirty.

Ans. (a) Both of them are same.

(iii) Comment on the tone of the poet in the given lines.

Ans. The tone of the poet in the given lines is contemplative and reflective. The poet engages in deep thought and introspection, contemplating a significant decision in his life.

(iv) Why was the poet made to choose?

Ans. The poet was made to choose because he could only travel by one road.

4. Read the following extract carefully and answer the questions that follow.

I shall be telling this with a sigh
Somewhere ages and ages hence;
Two roads diverged in a wood, and
I took the one less travelled by,
And that has made all the difference.

(i) Why does the poet say, "And that has made all the difference"?

(a) As the choice he had made has shaped his life accordingly.
(b) As the choice he had made caused him many problems.
(c) As the choice he had made turned him into a celebrity.
(d) As the choice he had made caused him to succeed.

Ans. (a) As the choice he had made has shaped his life accordingly.

(ii) Complete the sentence appropriately.
The phrase 'Somewhere ages and ages' indicates ....

Ans. an unknown future

(iii) What was the result of his going on the less travelled road?

Ans. His life had become what it is today as a result of his going on the less travelled road.

(iv) Why do you think the poet will sigh?

Ans. He was wondering what would have happened if he had travelled by the first road and that makes him sigh.

Part – II

Short Answer Type Questions

1. Describe the two roads that the poet finds. Which road did he choose?

Ans. The poet comes across a place at which two roads separated into two directions. One road is well used whereas the other one did not appear to have been walked over. The poet chose the second road as it looked much more promising to him.

2. What is the significance of the fact that the road 'bent in the undergrowth'? Competency Based

Ans. The bent in the undergrowth obstructs the vision of the traveller and he can't see where the road leads. This image expresses the significance that the future is unknown, mysterious and surprising; one can't know what it will bring.

3. The poet took a long time to make his decision. What was he thinking about?

Ans. The poet took a long time to make his decision because he wanted to choose the road that is best for him. However, he was not sure which road would suit him the best as he couldn't see the road beyond a particular point. Thus, the poet stood there for a long time to make a choice.

4. Why did the poet think that the other road had a better claim? What trait of his personality is revealed by his choice?

Ans. The poet thought that the other road had a better claim because it was not much used. He is reluctant to follow the tradition of using the same road that other people have previously used. This reveals him to be an adventurous person.

5. What does the poet promise himself, although he knows he can't keep his promise?

Ans. The poet promises himself that he would come back after some time and then, take the first road, even though he knew that he won't be able to keep his promise.
It is because once a choice is made and a decision is taken, he will move on and take many more decisions. As a result, he would not be able to come back and undo his choice.

6. Why does the speaker say "he will be telling this with a sigh/somewhere ages and ages hence"?

Ans. The speaker said these words over the thought that when he looks back at his life and the decisions he made, he may be sorry or happy about his decisions or about the roads he took. These might be sighs of satisfaction or regret. He is thinking back and it reflects on his decisions in life.

7. "I took the one less travelled by, and that has made all the difference." What is the poet saying here?

Ans. In the given lines, the poet highlights the essential theme he wants to bring out through the poem. The poet here says that in future, he will remember that he took the less travelled road. His decision and choice to do so has had a significant impact in his life/journey. In other words, our choices influence and shape our lives.

8. What do the two roads represent?

Ans. The two roads represent the dilemma a person faces when having to make a decision. The results of taking a decision one way or the other usually are different. The decision affects further events related to it.

9. 'The Road Not Taken' is a metaphor of life. Justify this statement.

Ans. In the poem 'The Road Not Taken', the poet Robert Frost presents a situation that each individual faces in life. In the poem, the roads represent all those situations when we need to make a difficult choice. The two divergences represent the multiple options. Furthermore, the poet's choice and his thoughts about the future tell us that in life when a choice is made, it leads to many other choices. These choices cannot be undone and have a significant impact on one's life. Hence, it is true that 'The Road Not Taken' is a metaphor of life.

10. Do you think Frost is celebrating individualism in the poem? Justify your position.

Ans. Yes, I think that Frost celebrates individualism as the speaker opts for the less-travelled path, showcasing a willingness to deviate from the norm and make independent choices. The poem emphasises personal agency and the significance of paving the path for one's unique journey.

Long Answer Type Questions

1. Do you agree that decision making is an important factor in people's lives? Support your answer in the context of the poem 'The Road Not Taken'.

Ans. Yes, I agree that decision making is an important factor in people's lives. We need to take decisions and make choices even in the simplest of situations like buying a product. Each one of our decisions/choices has far reaching consequences. It shapes our lives and makes us what we become in the future.

The poem 'The Road Not Taken' highlights exactly this point through a situation faced by the poet. The poet, while travelling in the forest, came across a point where the path divided into two roads going in different directions. He faces a dilemma of making a choice. After much thought, he chose the road that was less travelled. He knew that his choice will show its results in the future. Therefore, he states that in future he would either be relieved or regretful because of his choice as it will have a significant impact on his life. Hence, when making a decision, it is very crucial to make the right choice.

2. Bring out the contrast and similarities between the two roads mentioned in the poem.

Ans. In the poem 'The Road Not Taken', the poet comes across two roads going in different directions in the forest. He cannot see much into the roads but finds that they have many similarities as well as contrasts.
To the poet, both roads in the autumn season look equally inviting and puts the poet in a dilemma.
He stands and observes both the roads to decide which road to take.

He first observes the first road. He finds that it bends after some distance and is covered with dense growth of plants and bushes. The other road, according to the poet, is as beautiful as the first road. It is grassy and it seems that it has rarely been used.

However, on that morning, both the roads had not been used as they were covered with leaves. For the poet, these roads symbolise two different choices that an individual has to make in life. Once a road/choice is taken/made, it must be stuck to as both lead to two different journeys.

ASSESSMENT EXERCISE

Extract Based Questions

Read the following extract carefully and answer the questions that follow.

I shall be telling this with a sigh.
Somewhere ages and ages hence.
Two roads diverged in a wood and I
took the one less travelled by,
And that has made all the difference.

(i) Who is 'I' in the above lines? Why was 'I' feeling?

(ii) What does the given lines tell us about the speaker perception of his choice?

(iii) Complete the sentence appropriately.
The word 'sigh' in the extract means to ....

(iv) What is the rhyme scheme of the extract?

(a) abbaa (b) ababc
(c) abaab (d) abcab

Short Answer (SA) Type Questions

1. 'And looked down one as far as I could'. Where was the poet standing? Why did he look 'down one'?
2. Why did the poet think he will not return?
3. What does the poet mean by 'leaves no step had trodden black'?
4. Justify the tittle of the poem 'The Road Not taken'.
5. What is the significance of the two roads in real life?

Long Answer (LA) Type Questions

1. Give the properties of the two roads as described by the poet and explain how this made the poet decide to go down one.
2. When you face a difficult choice between two alternatives, how do you decide on one or the other?

Wind

by Subramania Bharati

CHAPTER 2

Introduction The poem depicts the power of wind and how it is destructive. The wind, as described in the poem, blows violently and breaks everything around. The poet has linked this powerful wind with the difficulties, obstacles and struggles of life. Just like the wind that destroys everything that is weak, these difficulties can also easily break down weak people. Only strong people can withstand them. The poem then, encourages us to have courage and firm determination. It gives a message that we must have strong hearts as well as will power to face any troubles or hardships of life.

Explanation of the Poem

Stanza 1

Wind, come softly.
Don't break the shutters of the windows.
Don't scatter the papers.
Don't throw down the books on the shelf.

Explanation In these lines, the poet requests the wind to blow gently and not destroy anything with its force. He asks the wind not to break the shutters of the windows and scatter the papers here and there. He also asks the wind not to throw down the books from the shelf. The repetition of the word 'don't' in these lines highlights the requests of mercy.

Stanza 2

There, look what you did–
you threw them all down.
You tore the pages of the books.
You brought rain again.

Explanation In these lines, as the wind had not paid any attention to the poet's request, the poet tone changes to anger. He says that the wind has thrown down the books from the shelf and torn the pages of the books. The poet also accuses that the wind has brought rain with it.

Stanza 3

You're very clever at poking fun at weaklings.
Frail crumbling houses, crumbling doors,
crumbling rafters, crumbling wood,
crumbling bodies, crumbling lives,
crumbling hearts
– the wind God winnows and crushes them all.

Explanation In these lines, the poet seems to be a little sad as well as accusatory (critical tone). The poet calls the wind clever as it makes fun of all weak things. The poet says that the wind destroys all weak things such as houses, doors, rafters and wood. It even destroys people, their lives and their hearts with its mighty power. The Wind God continues destroying or separating weak until only the strong people remain.

Here, the strong wind represents all the difficulties and struggles that an individual faces in life. Then, strong people are those who can go through hardships successfully.

Stanza 4

He won't do what you tell him.
So, come, let's build strong homes,
Let's join the doors firmly.
Practise to firm the body.

Make the heart steadfast.
Do this and the wind will be friends with us.

Explanation In these lines, the poet addresses the readers and asks them to make themselves strong as the wind will not listen to them. The poet asks the readers to build strong houses and to close/fix the doors tightly so that the wind cannot harm them. He encourages his readers to become bold and strong so as to face all the troubles in life. The poet asks the readers to practise hard to get a firm mind as well as a strong body so that they can face the wind and any challenge in life. If they are able to do so, the wind will become their friend and will not harm them.

Stanza 5

The wind blows out weak fires.
He makes strong fires roar and flourish.
His friendship is good.
We praise him every day.

Explanation In these lines, the poet describes wind as both a destroyer and a creator.
As a destroyer, the wind blows out the weak fires.
As a creator, it encourages and nurture strong fires.
In other words, wind can destroy all weak things and can also flourish a thing which is already strong.
The poet states that if we are strong, then the wind is a good friend to us and nothing can harm us.
We will praise the Wind God everyday for building our strength. Thus, we should make ourselves physically and mentally ready to accept all challenges.
Once we are strong, we will easily overcome the challenges and live our lives comfortably.

Poetic Devices Used in the Poem

Personification A figure of speech which is used to make an inanimate object or animals/birds look or feel human. The wind is personified throughout the poem. The poet is talking to the wind, scolding it and praising it.

- There, look what you did — you threw them all down. / You tore the pages of the books. / You brought rain again. / You're very clever at poking fun at weaklings.
- The wind God winnows (separates) and crushes them all. / He won't do what you tell him.
- Do this and the wind will be friends with us.
- He makes strong fires roar and flourish.
- We praise him every day.

Metaphor It is used to compare two things or qualities which are unlike.

- The wind God winnows ......

Anaphora This means repetition of the same word in successive lines. The instances are

- Lines 2, 3 and 4 — Repetition of 'Don't'
- Lines 6, 7 and 8 — Repetition of 'You'
- Lines 9, 10 and 11 — Repetition of 'crumbling'
- Lines 14 and 15 — Repetition of 'Let's'

Word Meaning

Word	Meaning
Stanza 1	
Shutters	hinged panels used to close/open windows
Scatter	throw in different directions
Stanza 2	
Tore	shred or break into pieces
Stanza 3	
Poking fun at	making fun of
Weaklings	weak bodies/ persons/ things
Frail	weak
Crumbling	destroying, breaking
Rafters	sloping beams supporting a roof
Winnows	a separating process, herein used to separate weak from strong
Stanza 4	
Firm	make strong
Steadfast	firm and determined
Stanza 5	
Blow out	to stop a fire
Flourish	grow healthy

NCERT FOLDER

NCERT Exercise Questions

I. THINKING ABOUT THE POEM (NCERT PAGE 31)

Q.1 What are the things the wind does in the first stanza ?

Ans. In the first stanza, the wind blows so strongly that it breaks the shutters of the windows. It scatters the papers and even throws down the books from the shelf.

Q.2 Have you seen anybody winnow grain at home or in a paddy field? What is the word in your language for winnowing? What do people use for winnowing? (Give the words in your language, if you know them.)

Ans. Yes, I have seen agricultural labourers (usually women) winnowing grain, i.e. separating the heavier grains from the lighter chaff by letting it fall gently while a strong wind is blown.

The word for winnowing used in our language Hindi is *'Phatakana'* (responses will vary in different languages).

For winnowing, usually a cane container with grain and a fan to blow air are used.

In Hindi, the winnowing fan called '*chhaaj*' is used by the village people.

Q.3 What does the poet say the Wind God winnows?

Ans. The poet says that the Wind God continues destroying or separating the weak until only the strong remains. He separates the weak from the strong so that only the strong and courageous exist in the world.

Q.4 What should we do to make friends with the wind?

Ans. To make friends with the wind, we should make ourselves physically as well as mentally strong. We should make our bodies firm and heart strong. We should also build homes that are stronger so that the wind favours us.

By reinforcing physical structures, strengthening the body and developing emotional resilience, humans can coexist harmoniously with the wind, turning it into an ally rather than a destructive force. The poet emphasises the importance of preparedness and resilience in the face of the wind's power.

Q.5 What do the last four lines of the poem mean to you?

Ans. The last four lines of the poem emphasise the essential theme that the poem wants to convey. It emphasises the need to be physically as well as mentally strong. It tells us that the wind will destroy the weak things but it flourishes the strong ones.

Just like the wind, difficulties and struggles also destroy everyone who is weak. It strengthens those people who are courageous and bold.

Q.6 How does the poet speak to the wind — in anger or with humour? You must also have seen or heard of the wind 'crumbling lives'. What is your response to this? Is it like the poet's?

Ans. Initially, the poet speaks to the wind with anger, saying that it has thrown down his books from the shelves and torn their pages. However, later the poet's tone changes and he speaks to the wind with humour, inviting it to attack him, as he intends to prepare himself as if waiting for a 'friend'.

Yes, I have heard of the wind 'crumbling lives'.
My response is similar to the poet's. I will prepare myself by becoming stronger and ready for any attack.

II. THINKING ABOUT THE POEM (NCERT PAGE 31)

Q.1 The poem you have just read is originally in Tamil. Do you know any such poems in your language?

Ans. Yes, there are many similar poems in my language. (Do it yourself)

Hint PB Shelley's – Ode to the West wind

Naresh Aggarwal – Toofan

REVIEW EXERCISE
Including Competency Based Questions

Part – I

Multiple Choice Questions

1. At the beginning of the poem, why does the poet ask the wind to come softly?

(a) To protect the weaklings.
(b) To maintain peace and order.
(c) To protect his house.
(d) To protect books from being thrown down.

Ans. (b) To maintain peace and order.

2. At the beginning of the poem, the wind is compared to ....

(a) a youth (b) an old person
(c) a child (d) a middle-aged person

Ans. (c) a child

3. Who are negatively affected by the wind?

(a) Weaklings (b) Strong people
(c) Both (a) and (b) (d) None of these

Ans. (a) Weaklings

4. Which of the following damages done by wind are mentioned in the poem?

1. Crumbling doors
2. Crumbling rafters
3. Breaking window shutters
4. Bringing storms
5. Uprooting trees
6. Bringing rain

(a) 1, 2, 3 and 5 (b) 2, 3 and 4
(c) 1, 2, 3 and 6 (d) 3, 4, 5 and 6

Ans. (c) 1, 2, 3 and 6

5. The destructive power of the wind is a symbol of ....

(a) anger (b) adversities
(c) solutions (d) All of these

Ans. (b) adversities

6. What is the effect of the wind on strong fires?

(a) It blows them out as usual.
(b) It lets them burn.
(c) It makes them roar and flourish.
(d) All of the above

Ans. (c) It makes them roar and flourish.

7. What does 'crumbling hearts' refer to?

(a) Old people (b) Weak people
(c) Rich and strong people (d) Despondent people

Ans. (b) Weak people

8. How can we make friends with the wind?

1. By building strong homes.
2. By building strong body and heart.

(a) Only 1 is correct
(b) Neither 1 nor 2 is correct
(c) Both 1 and 2 are correct
(d) Only 2 is correct

Ans. (c) Both 1 and 2 are correct

9. What are the 'weak fires' and 'strong fires' symbolic of?

(a) Weak and courageous people
(b) Strong and weak people
(c) Weak and shy people
(d) Strong and angry people

Ans. (a) Weak and courageous people

10. Who has translated this poem from Tamil to English?

(a) Subramania Bharati (b) A.K. Ramanujan
(c) Subramania Siva (d) M. Govinda Pal

Ans. (b) A.K. Ramanujan

11. Given below are some of the adjectives. Choose the ones which can be associated with 'wind' in context of the poem.

Furious, soft, constructive, obedient, diligent, destructive, strong, helping, subtle, mocking

(a) Furious, soft, constructive, obedient
(b) Diligent, destructive, strong, helping
(c) Strong, helping, subtle, mocking
(d) Furious, constructive, destructive, strong, mocking

Ans. (d) Furious, constructive, destructive, strong, mocking

12. What is the theme of the poem?

1. Potential of difficulties being both a destroyer and creator.
2. Weak and meager cannot withstand the fury of the strong wind.

3. Being strong is the only option in this world to face the challenges.

4. There is no need to fear the wind and its power.

(a) 1 and 2 (b) 3 and 4
(c) 1, 2 and 3 (d) 2, 3 and 4

Ans. (c) 1, 2 and 3

Extract Based Questions

1. Read the following extract carefully and answer the questions that follow.

Wind, come softly.
Don't break the shutters of the windows.
Don't scatter the papers.
Don't throw down the books on the shelf.

(i) From the given lines, the tone of the poet can be said to be

(a) friendly (b) order
(c) angry (d) requesting

Ans. (d) requesting

(ii) In the poem, what is the wind symbolic of?

Ans. In the poem, the wind is symbolic of trials and tribulations.

(iii) Complete the sentence appropriately.

The given lines tell us that the wind is blowing (gently/forcefully).

Ans. forcefully

(iv) State whether the following statement is True or False.

The literary device used in the lines 2, 3 and 4 of the extract is anaphora.

Ans. True

2. Read the following extract carefully and answer the questions that follow.

There, look what you did-you threw them all down.
You tore the pages of the books.
You brought rain again.
You're very clever at poking fun at weaklings.

(i) Whom does the poet address as 'you'?

Ans. The wind is being addressed as 'you'.

(ii) Complete the sentence appropriately.

The given lines indicate that the poet is ....

Ans. angry at the wind.

(iii) The literary device used in the given lines is

(a) repetition (b) anaphora
(c) oxymoron (d) metaphor

Ans. (b) anaphora

(iv) How does it deal with the 'weaklings'?

Ans. It terrifies them with its fierce power.

3. Read the following extract carefully and answer the questions that follow.

Frail crumbling houses,
crumbling doors, crumbling rafters,
Crumbling wood,
crumbling bodies,
crumbling lives
Crumbling hearts–
The wind God winnows and crushes them all.

(i) Complete the analogy by selecting the suitable word from the text.

Weak : Frail : : Destroys : ....

Ans. Crushes

(ii) Complete the sentence appropriately.

"The wind God winnows and crushes them all" indicates that ....

Ans. only the strong remain in the world.

(iii) The poet has used a poetic device in the given lines by repeating the word 'crumbling'. What effect does he wish to create by its use?

(a) Emphasis (b) Comparison
(c) Rhyme (d) Humour

Ans. (a) Emphasis

(iv) Why does the wind first winnow and then crush?

Ans. To separate the weak from the strong, the wind first winnows and then crushes.

4. Read the following extract carefully and answer the questions that follow.

He won't do what you tell him.
So, come, let's build strong homes.
Let's join the doors firmly.
Practise to firm the body.
Make the heart steadfast.

(i) Who is 'He' in the extract?

(a) The fire (b) The moon
(c) The wind (d) The sun

Ans. (c) The wind

(ii) Complete the sentence appropriately.

Through the given lines the poet is trying to ......

Ans. tell us the importance of being strong.

(iii) 'You' in the first line refers to ....

(a) the poet (b) the strong people
(c) the poet's friend (d) the listener

Ans. (d) the listener

(iv) Why will 'he' not listen?

Ans. He will not listen as it is his nature to exploit the weak.

5. Read the following extract carefully and answer the questions that follow.

The wind blows out weak fires
He makes strong fires roar and flourish
His friendship is good
We praise him everyday

(i) What does 'He' do to weak fires?

Ans. 'He' extinguishes the weak fires.

(ii) "The wind blows out weak fires/he makes strong fires roar and flourish" indicates which qualities of wind.

1. Constructive **2. Destructive**

3. Natural

(a) 1 and 2 (b) 2 and 3
(c) 1 and 3 (d) Only 3

Ans. (a) 1 and 2

(iii) Why does the poet say his friendship is good?

(a) Because it teaches us not to commit the same mistake twice.
(b) Because it teaches us how to live life.
(c) Because it fills us with confidence and courage.
(d) Because it ensures that we are successful in all our endeavors.

Ans. (c) Because it fills us with confidence and courage.

(iv) How can we make friends with the wind?

Ans. By being strong and courageous, we can make friends with the wind.

Part – II

Short Answer Type Questions

1. Why does the poet ask the wind to come softly in the beginning of the poem?

Ans. The poet asks the wind to come softly in the beginning of the poem so that peace and order may be maintained. When the wind blows fiercely, it creates a mess all around. It disturbs everything and everyone in the society. Therefore, the poet asks the wind to be soft so that it is harmless as well as enjoyable.

2. How does the wind cause rain?

Ans. When the wind blows violently, it appears as if a storm is coming. This storm brings dark rainy clouds from distant places and then causes them to make rain. Hence, the poet says that wind causes rain.

3. How does the wind make fun of the weaklings?

Ans. The strong wind, according to the poet, makes fun of weaklings. Its destructive power harms weak people and delicate things without showing any mercy. It crushes all the weak and fragile things including houses, doors and even human hearts and lives.

4. What does 'crumbling' suggest in the poem 'Wind'?

Ans. The word 'crumbling' as used in the poem means breaking of things. In the poem 'Wind', the word refers to the destruction caused by the strong winds. Its repetition signifies that the wind will destroy everything weak around it. The weak people will be 'crumbled' by the difficulties that they face.

5. Why does the poet want people to have firm bodies and strong hearts?

Ans. The poet wants the people to have firm bodies and strong hearts to fight the wind and all the difficulties, struggles and obstacles of life. According to him, if people are unhealthy and weak, they will be defeated by these difficulties. However, if they are physically strong and mentally confident, they can resist all the hardships boldly and successfully.

6. Who all are disturbed by the blowing of the wind and who are not?

Ans. According to the poet, all people who are physically weak and mentally not determined are disturbed by the blowing of the wind. Self-confident and strong people do not get disturbed by the wind. Infact, they come out as stronger and more confident than before.

7. What does the wind symbolise? **Competency Based**

Ans. The wind, in the poem, is a symbol of all difficulties, struggles and obstacles of life. Just like how our houses have to face the strong winds, we humans also face many hardships in life. We must face these hardships with confidence and boldness, otherwise they will destroy us.

8. How does the poet characterise the Wind God in the poem? **Competency Based**

Ans. The poet characterises the Wind God as clever at poking fun at weaklings. The Wind God winnows and crushes frail and crumbling things, refusing to obey human commands.

9. The poem is allegorical and symbolic in nature. Assess. **Competency Based**

Ans. The poem is allegorical and symbolic in nature. It uses the wind to represent life's challenges and adversities, making it an allegory for the complexities and dualities of human experiences. The allegorical elements in the poem contribute to its more profound layers of meaning and interpretation.

Long Answer Type Questions

1. What destructive events are caused by the wind? How can we prevent these destructive events from happening?

Ans. In the poem, the violent winds cause many destructive events. It breaks the shutters of the windows, scatters the papers, throws down books from its shelves and even tears their pages. The wind, through its fierce force holds the capacity to cause a lot of destruction. Its power can destroy rafters, houses, doors as well as people's hearts and lives.

We can prevent these destructive events by being firm and steadfast. We need to be positive and strong, both physically as well as mentally, besides making our houses stronger.

By being strong, we will become friends with the wind. As a result, we will be able to tackle the wind as well as the difficulties we face in life easily. It then helps us in achieving success and flourishes our lives.

2. The tone of the poem is contemplative, instructive and defiant. Comment.

Ans. It is true to say that the tone of the poem is contemplative, instructive and defiant.

Contemplative Tone The poet reflects on the nature of the wind and its impact on various aspects of life, such as physical structures, literature and human resilience. There is a thoughtful examination of the destructive and constructive aspects of the wind.

Instructive Tone The poet gives practical advice and instructions to counter the destructive force of the wind. There's a sense of guidance, urging the reader to build strong homes, secure doors and cultivate inner strength.

Defiant Tone There is a defiance against the destructive nature of the wind. The call to build strong homes and make the heart steadfast implies a refusal to succumb to external pressures.

Despite the challenges the wind poses, there is an appreciation for its positive attributes, such as extinguishing and nurturing strong fires. The poet acknowledges the wind's role in testing and strengthening, suggesting a nuanced view that includes adversity and growth.

3. The poet had used many symbols of destruction and renewal. Do you agree? Justify your stance.

Competency Based

Ans. I agree that the poet had used many symbols of destruction and renewal. The various symbols are

Wind It symbolises the forces of change, challenges and disruptions in life. It represents both the destructive and transformative aspects of nature.

Shutters of the Windows It symbolise the protective barriers or boundaries that individuals build to shield themselves from external influences or challenges. The wind's impact on the shutters reflects the inevitability of strugles and its ability to penetrate even the most guarded spaces.

Rain Symbolises cleansing and renewal. The wind's ability to bring rain signifies the potential for growth and purification through challenges.

Crumbling Houses, Doors, Rafters, Wood, Bodies, Lives, And Hearts They symbolise the fragility of human existence and societal structures. The wind's actions highlight the transient nature of life, and the need to make oneself strong both physically and emotionally against life's storms.

Building Strong Homes, Joint Doors Firmly, Firming The Body, Making The Heart Steadfast They Represents the poet's call to strengthen oneself physically, emotionally and spiritually to face life's challenges. It suggests resilience, self-improvement and the importance of inner strength.

Blowing Out Weak Fires, Making Strong Fires Roar And Flourish They symbolises the wind's role in testing and refining individuals. Weak fires may represent weak efforts or ambitions, while strong fires signify determination and resilience. The wind's friendship is beneficial, as it helps strengthen resolve and purpose.

4. Poets use the symbol of nature to teach many lessons to people. Using 'Wind' and 'The Road Not Taken', assess the validity of the statement.

Ans. It is true to say that poets use the symbol of nature to teach many lessons to people'. The poems 'Wind' by Subramania Bharati and 'The Road Not Taken' by Robert Frost use elements of nature-wind and the road-as powerful symbols to convey profound life lessons, emphasising strength, resilience, choices, and the importance of individuality.

In 'Wind', the poet uses wind as a central symbol, portraying it as a powerful, uncontrollable force of nature. The wind here symbolises challenges and adversity in life. The wind is seen as something that is both destructive and nurturing. The wind's power represents the difficulties and hardships people face in their lives. However, the poet emphasises that rather than fearing these challenges, one should learn to face them with strength and resilience.

In 'The Road Not Taken', the road is the central symbol used by Frost to explore the themes of choices, individuality, and the consequences of decisions.

The poem presents a moment in life when the speaker must choose between two paths, each leading to different outcomes. The two roads symbolise the decisions we face in life. Frost also teaches that every choice, no matter how small, shapes our future. The speaker reflects on the path he chose and wonders how it might have made all the difference in his life.

These poems show how nature, in its various forms, is a powerful metaphor for the human condition. Poets often use nature to reflect on complex life lessons, making these poems timeless and universally relevant.

ASSESSMENT EXERCISE

Extract Based Questions

1. Read the following extract carefully and answer the questions that follow.

Wind, come softly.
Don't break the shutters of the windows.
Don't scatter the papers.
Don't throw down the books on the shelf.

(i) In what tone the poet is addressing the wind in the given passage?
(a) Commanding tone (b) Requesting tone
(c) Scolding tone (d) None of the above

(ii) Which quality of wind is highlighted in the poem?

(iii) What does the wind do?

(iv) Which figure of speech is used in the given lines?

2. Read the following extract carefully and answer the questions that follow.

The wind blows out weak fires.
He makes strong fires roar and flourish.
His friendship is good.
We praise him everyday.

(i) What does the wind do to the strong?
(a) It befriends them.
(b) It helps them.
(c) It makes them strong.
(d) It destroys them.

(ii) What does the poet advice us to do?

(iii) Which figure of speech is used in the above lines?

(iv) How does the wind affect the weaklings?

Short Answer (SA) Type Questions

1. What does the wind God winnow?
2. 'He won't do what you tell him'. Who is 'he' and why will he not do as told?
3. 'Make the heart steadfast'. Why does the poet say this?
4. What is the significance of 'strong fires' near the end of the poem?
5. 'The wind blows out weak fires.' What do 'weak fires' signify?
6. Why does the poet want us to praise the wind every day?

Long Answer (LA) Type Questions

1. The wind deals very cruelly with all weak things. Justify this by mentioning what has been written at various places in the poem.
2. The wind is both creative as well as destructive. Justify.

CHAPTER 3

Rain on the Roof

by Coates Kinney

Introduction The poem describes the poet's thoughts when he hears the sound of rain falling on the tiled roof of his cottage. The sound produced by the rain reminds the poet of a memory of his mother. This memory stays in his mind and calms him. Through rain, the poet highlights the healing power of nature. According to him, the music produced by the simple act of falling of rain holds the power to bring back some of our fondest memories. These memories, then, provide us with comfort and calm us.

Explanation of the Poem

Stanza 1

When the humid shadows hover
Over all the starry spheres,
And the melancholy darkness
Gently weeps in rainy tears,
What a bliss to press the pillow
Of a cottage-chamber bed,
And lie listening to the patter
Of the soft rain overhead!

Explanation In these lines, the poet describes a rainy night. The poet says that the stars in the sky are not visible as they are covered by the dark rainy clouds. The sky looks sad and the rain looks like tears. This weather represents the poet's sorrowful mood. In such a mood, the only thing that can bring joy in the poet's heart is to lay his head down on the pillow of his bed in his cottage and listen to the soft sound of the rain falling on the roof.

Stanza 2

Every tinkle on the shingles
Has an echo in the heart;
And a thousand dreamy fancies
Into busy being start,
And a thousand recollections
Weave their air-threads into woof,
As I listen to the patter
Of the rain upon the roof.

Explanation In these lines, the poet now describes how the raindrops make a tinkling sound as they fall on the tiled rooftop of his cottage. According to the poet, each sound made by the rain affects the poet's heart deeply. As he is listening to the sound, many images (dreamy fancies) come into his mind. He starts recollecting memories of his childhood. These memories appear to be interwoven together to form a beautiful picture.

Stanza 3

Now in memory comes my mother,
As she used in years agone,
To regard the darling dreamers,
Ere she left them till the dawn:
O! I feel her fond look on me
As I list to this refrain
Which is played upon the shingles
By the patter of the rain.

Explanation In these lines, the poet says that out of the many memories the poet recollects, he identifies one fond memory of his mother. He remembers how, many years ago, his mother used to look at him and his siblings lovingly while they slept and used to dream.

She would look at her sleeping children every night because she knew she won't see them till the next morning. The poet can still feel the look of his mother while he lays on his bed and listens to the soft musical sound of the rain falling on the roof.

Poetic Devices Used in the Poem

Transferred Epithet It is a poetic device wherein an epithet (or adjective) grammatically qualifies a noun other than the person or thing it is actually describing.

- **Stanza 1** In this stanza, the poet transfers his melancholic mood from himself to the darkness of the night in which the poem is set.

Personification It is used for an inanimate object or animal/birds look or feel human.

- And the melancholy darkness/gently weeps in the form of rainy tears.

Refrain It is a poetic device in which a phrase is repeated at intervals throughout poem, especially at the end of each stanza.

- Patter of the rain

Metaphor A device which compares two things or qualities which are unlike.

- When the humid shadows hover.
- And a thousand recollections/ weave their air-threads into woof.
- Darling dreamers.

Onomatopoeia Using a word which suggests the meaning by its sound.

- 'Patter' is used that imitates the real sound of the rain falling.
- 'Tinkle' is used that imitates the real sound of the rain falling on the shingles of the roof.

Alliteration Repetition of initial consonant sounds in the same line.

- When the humid shadows hover.

Word Meaning

Word	Meaning
Stanza 1	
Humid shadows	clouds
Hover	hang
Starry spheres	stars
Melancholy	sad
Bliss	utmost joy
Cottage-chamber	room in a cottage
Patter	sound of rain falling on the roof
Overhead	above
Stanza 2	
Tinkle	ringing sound
Shingles	rectangular tiles used on sloping roofs
Echo	reverberation (a sound that repeats after the original sound stops)
Dreamy	having a magical or unreal quality; dreamlike
Recollections	memories/remembrances
Into woof	weaved into woven picture
Stanza 3	
Agone	gone by
Regard	observe
Darling dreamers	her sleeping children
Ere	before
Dawn	morning
List	listen
Refrain	part of song that is repeated
Played upon	the sound coming due to rain falling on

NCERT FOLDER

NCERT Exercise Questions

I. THINKING ABOUT THE POEM (NCERT PAGE 42)

Q.1 What do the following phrases mean to you? Discuss in class.

(i) Humid shadows

Ans. Dark clouds laden with (full of) droplets of rainwater.

(ii) Starry spheres

Ans. Stars in the sky.

(iii) What a bliss

Ans. Utmost joy experienced by the poet.

(iv) A thousand dreamy fancies into busy being start

Ans. This refers to the various imaginary thoughts and fantasies that are aroused in the poet's mind.

(v) A thousand recollections weave their air-threads into woof

Ans. This means that the poet recollects numerous (many) memories that intermingle (connect together) to form a beautiful picture.

Q.2 What does the poet like to do when it rains?

Ans. When it rains, the poet feels delighted to lie with his head pressed against the pillow of his bed in his cottage and listen to the patter (sound) of the soft rain on the tiles of the cottage roof.

Q.3 What is the single major memory that comes to the poet? Who are the 'darling dreamers' he refers to?

Ans. The single major memory that comes to the poet is that of his mother and her fond looks when she put the poet into the bed to sleep.

The 'darling dreamers' refer to the poet and his siblings in their childhood.

Q.4 Is the poet now a child? Is his mother still alive?

Ans. No, the poet is not a child now. He is a grown man.

His mother is probably not alive as he says in lines 17–18 that she comes in his memories just like she used to put him in his bed to sleep in the past.

II. THINKING ABOUT THE POEM (NCERT PAGE 42)

Q.1 When you were a young child, did your mother tuck you in, as the poet's did?

Ans. Yes, my mother used to tuck (put) me in when I was a young child, just like the poet's mother did.

Q.2 Do you like rain? What do you do when it rains steadily or heavily as described in the poem?

Ans. Yes, I like rain.

When it rains steadily, I go outside and enjoy the weather by dancing in the rain. It is a wonderful experience. I also enjoy eating some tasty snacks.

Q.3 Does everybody have a cosy bed to lie in when it rains? Look around you and describe how different kinds of people or animals spend time, seek shelter etc, during rain.

Ans. No, everybody is not fortunate enough to have a cosy bed to lie in when it rains. Not everybody gets to enjoy the comfort of cosy homes during rain.

I have seen animals seeking shelter under trees and under the tin roofs of small roadside stalls.

The people passing by chase away these animals so, these helpless creatures try to fit themselves under the limited space of these shops. The poor animals are left to get drenched in the open. The shopkeepers of such stalls are delighted as the people waiting for the rain ask for tea and whatever snacks are available with them.

REVIEW EXERCISE

Including Competency Based Questions

Part – I

Multiple Choice Questions

1. What are the humid shadows doing in the sphere?

(a) Steeping (b) Resting
(c) Floating in the air (d) Doing nothing

Ans. (c) Floating in the air

2. What does 'starry spheres' mean?

(a) Places where stars are born
(b) Sky filled with stars
(c) Star groups in the sky
(d) All of the above

Ans. (d) All of the above

3. What is 'bliss' for the poet?

(a) Bathing in the rain
(b) Getting a lot of money
(c) Going to an office in rain
(d) Lying on the bed in a joyful mood

Ans. (d) Lying on the bed in a joyful mood

4. What do you understand by the term 'darling dreamers'?

(a) The poet and his siblings when they were children and had sweet dreams.
(b) The poet having sweet dreams.
(c) The poet along with his mother having sweet dreams.
(d) None of the above

Ans. (a) The poet and his siblings when they were children and had sweet dreams.

5. What kind of refrain is the poet referring to when he says, 'As I list to this refrain'?

(a) He wants to avoid the sound of the rain on the tiled roof of the cottage.
(b) He wanted to hear more and more the sound of rain on the roof.
(c) The repeated pattering sound of the rain on the tiled roof of the cottage.
(d) All of the above

Ans. (c) The repeated pattering sound of the rain on the tiled roof of the cottage.

6. The poetic device used in 'starry spheres' and 'darling dreamers' is ....

(a) metaphor (b) alliteration
(c) personification (d) All of these

Ans. (b) alliteration

7. What revives the sweet memories in the poet's mind?

(a) Busy schedule (b) Daily routine
(c) Raindrops falling on the roof
(d) None of the above

Ans. (c) Raindrops falling on the roof

8. What is the meaning of the line "a thousand recollections weave their air-threads into woof"?

(a) Thousands of memories have come together to weave a beautiful picture in poet's mind.
(b) There are thousands of memories attached with the thread.
(c) The poet is remembering his childhood memories.
(d) None of the above

Ans. (a) Thousands of memories have come together to weave a beautiful picture in poet's mind.

9. What does the word 'refrain' indicate in the poem?

(a) Repetitiveness (b) Keeping away
(c) Selling off (d) Indicates staying apart

Ans. (a) Repetitiveness

10. What is/are the central idea/ideas of the poem?

1. The rain has power of healing the mind and the heart of humans.
2. The rain is healing the Earth.
3. The rain is reminding the poet of his childhood memories.

Codes
(a) 1 and 2 (b) 2 and 3
(c) 1 and 3 (d) All of these

Ans. (d) All of these

Extract Based Questions

1. Read the following extract carefully and answer the questions that follow.

When the humid shadows hover
Over all the starry spheres,
And the melancholy darkness
Gently weeps in rainy tears,

(i) The time of the day discussed in the given passage is .... (dawn/night)

Ans. night

(ii) **Select the option that applies the same rhyme scheme as the first four lines of the given extract.**

(a) I was a cottage maiden
Hardened by sun and air,
Contented with my cottage mates,
Not mindful I was fair.

(b) As long as it takes to pass
A ship keeps raising its hull;
The wetter ground like glass
Reflects a standing gull

(c) They cannot look out far.
They cannot look in deep.
But when was that ever a bar
To any watch they keep?

(d) Two golden-agers in a room
complained about mate's habits.
"It irritates and drives me mad,
I need to find relief".

Ans. (d) Two golden-agers in a room
complained about mate's habits.
"It irritates and drives me mad,
I need to find relief".

(iii) **Where is the poet when it is raining?**

Ans. When it is raining, the poet is in his cottage.

(iv) **Why is the 'melancholy darkness' weeping?**

Ans. The 'melancholy darkness' is weeping because it is dark all around and because it is raining.

2. Read the following extract carefully and answer the questions that follow.

Every tinkle on the shingles
Has an echo in the heart;
And a thousand dreamy fancies
Into busy being start,

(i) **The word 'tinkle' indicates ....**

Ans. the sound of rain falling

(ii) **How does the heart echo?**

(a) With sound sleep
(b) With the rain
(c) With peace and happiness
(d) All of the above

Ans. (b) With the rain

(iii) **Which 'dreamy fancy' is dearest to the poet?**

Ans. The 'dreamy fancy' of his mother is dearest to the poet.

(iv) **What does 'dreamy fancies' mean?**

Ans. The phrase 'dreamy fancies' means old memories.

3. Read the following extract carefully and answer the questions that follow.

As she used in years agone,
To regard the darling dreamers
Ere she left them till the dawn:
O! I feel her fond look on me
As I list to this refrain

(i) **Complete the sentence appropriately.**
The poetic device used in the line 2 of the given extract is ....

Ans. alliteration

(ii) **Complete the sentence appropriately.**
'Darling dreamers' in the extract refers to ....

Ans. the poet and his siblings

(iii) **In the given lines, the poet is feeling**

(a) sorrowful (b) relaxed (c) nostalgic (d) regretful

Ans. (c) nostalgic

(iv) **Which sound is the poet listening to?**

Ans. The poet is listening to the sound of the rain.

Part – II

Short Answer Type Questions

1. How does the poet describe the movement before rain?

Ans. Before the rain, the dark wet shadows of clouds can be seen in the sky. The stars become spheres as they are covered by these clouds. There is darkness all around and the atmosphere becomes very gloomy and sad.

2. What does the poet want to convey when he says 'when the humid shadows hover over all the starry spheres'?

Ans. The poet wants to convey that when the dark rain clouds (humid shadows) cover the whole sky such that the stars (starry spheres) are not visible, it is a sign that rain is going to fall. The poet compares darkness with sadness which sets the tone of the poem.

3. What does 'melancholy darkness', (in the poem 'Rain on the Roof') mean and what does it do?

Ans. In the phrase 'melancholy darkness', the poet has associated the feelings of sadness and gloom to the darkness that results due to the clouds. Just like the feeling of sorrow that leads to tears, the dark rain clouds cause rain. The lack of sunshine or hope leads to rain or sadness.

4. What does the poet consider 'a bliss'?

Ans. The poet considers listening to the sound of the falling of rain as a bliss. When it rains, the poet lies in his cosy bed in a cottage, listening to the melody of nature.

He listens to the pleasant pattering sound of the rain on the roof of the cottage.

5. When do the 'thousand dreamy fancies' begin in the poet's heart?

Ans. The 'thousand dreamy fancies' begin in the poet's heart when the sound of the rain falling on the roof echoes in his heart. He responds to this echo by dreaming fanciful dreams and recollecting memories of the past.

6. What does the poet dream of?

Ans. While listening to the soft sound of rain falling on the roof, the poet thought of many images and memories. From these, the poet dreamt of the memory of his mother. He recollects his childhood when his mother used to lovingly look at him and his siblings while they used to sleep and dream.

7. What is the significance of repeating the phrase "patter of the rain upon the roof" throughout the poem? Competency Based

Ans. The repetition of the phrase 'patter of the rain upon the roof' in the poem serves as a rhythmic refrain that captures the sensory essence of rain and carries profound symbolic weight. This repetition acts like a lullaby that leads the reader into the contemplative mood of the speaker.

8. What is the significance of the rain in the poem 'Rain on the Roof'? Competency Based

Ans. The rain in the poem catalyses nostalgic reflections and reflective moments. It creates a soothing and comforting atmosphere that brings forth memories, dreams and emotions, connecting the present moment to the past.

9. How does the poem explore the theme of the passage of time and the continuity of memories? Comptency Based

Ans. 'Rain on the Roof' delves into the theme of time and memory, highlighting the enduring nature of specific experiences. The speaker recalls the past, particularly the image of their mother watching over them as they slept. The patter of rain serves as a connective thread between past and present, as memories are woven into the speaker's consciousness. The poem suggests that the speaker is transported back in time through the auditory and sensory experience of rain, emphasising memories' timeless and cyclical nature.

10. 'Rain on the Roof' by Coates Kinney is a lyric poem with narrative elements. Substantiate.

Ans. 'Rain on the Roof' by Coates Kinney is a lyric poem with narrative elements. The poem focuses on expressing personal emotions, reflections and memories associated with the sound of rain, aligning with the characteristics of lyric poetry.

At the same it, the poem turns narrative in the third stanza is as the speaker recalls memories of their mother.

11. The overarching theme of 'Rain on the Roof' by Coates Kinney is rain's emotional and nostalgic impact, particularly the sound of raindrops on the roof, on the speaker's thoughts and memories. Assess. Competency Based

Ans. The overarching theme of 'Rain on the Roof' by Coates Kinney is rain's emotional and nostalgic impact, particularly the sound of raindrops on the roof, on the speaker's thoughts and memories.

The poem's revolves around the sound of rain which takes us to the speaker's recollections. This highlights the enduring emotional connection between the present experience of rain and memories. While there are subthemes such as comfort and the sensory experience of rain, the theme of nostalgia and memory dominates as the speaker reflects on the comforting and emotional associations the rain brings, especially concerning the presence of their mother.

Long Answer Type Questions

1. The 'Rain on the Roof' brings out how rain soothes everyone by its phenomenon. Elaborate.

Ans. It is true to say that the 'Rain on the Roof' brings out the soothing effect of rain. Rain is always a source of happiness and pleasure. Before rain, the weather is hot and humid. However, when it rains, it heals not only the humans who suffer from the hot climate but also the plants and animals.

In the poem 'Rain on the Roof', the poet highlights this soothing and healing quality of nature. The poet is relaxing on his bed in his room in a cottage when the rain starts falling. The sound of the rain falling on the cottage appeals to the poet. The music creates echoes in his heart. It fills the poet with many fond memories that come into his mind. Out of these 'dreamy fancies', the poet can identify a memory of his childhood that is associated with his mother. He can remember the loving looks of his mother when he and his siblings used to sleep. Rain is a healing phenomenon of the nature. Thus, the coming of rain is always blissful and pleasant.

2. The poet of 'Rain on the Roof' was a home loving, family loving and nature loving person who shows a deep attachment to his mother. Justify with examples from the poem. Competency Based

Ans. The poet of 'Rain on the Roof' was indeed a home loving, family loving and a nature loving person who showed a deep attachment to his mother.
In the poem, the poet is lying on his bed in his room of the cottage while it's raining.

The musical sound of the rain falling on the tiled roof along with his relaxing posture is a bliss for him. This shows that the poet was a home loving person.

Furthermore, cottages are generally found in countryside or rural region wherein nature is at its best, with few concrete buildings. Such areas are close to nature. Hence, the poet relaxing in such a region shows him to be a nature loving person.

The poet, while listening to the rain, recollects some of his fondest memories. Out of these, he remembers his mother who used to look at him while he and his siblings used to sleep. Even today, he remembers that look of love of his mother. This shows that the poet was a family loving man who loved his mother very much.

3. Comment on the symbolism and imagery used in the poem 'The Rain on the Roof'.

Ans. 'Rain on the Roof' by Coates Kinney, celebrates rain's soothing and nostalgic effects by using various symbols and imagery. They are

Symbols

Rain The rain in the poem symbolises more than just a natural phenomenon. It serves as a metaphor for emotional release, introspection and the passage of time. The sound of rain brings forwards memories and deep feelings, connecting the external weather to the internal emotional landscape of the speaker.

Mother The mention of the speaker's mother adds a layer of symbolism. The mother represents a figure of comfort, care and nurturing. The memories of the mother symbolise a longing for the security and warmth associated with maternal love.

Imagery

Humid Shadows The opening line introduces the imagery of dark rainy clouds. This creates a sensory image of the dampness and darkness associated with a rainy night.

Starry Spheres The poem mentions the 'starry spheres,' contributing to the celestial imagery. This phrase evokes a sense of the vast night sky and adds a cosmic dimension to the scene.

Melancholy Darkness The darkness is described as 'melancholy,' infusing an emotional quality into the visual imagery. It suggests a sad and reflective mood associated with the night.

Gently Weeps in Rainy Tears This symbolic imagery personifies the darkness, suggesting a sorrowful or tearful quality. The rain is portrayed as the cause of the weeping, creating a vivid emotional image.

Patter of the Soft Rain Overhead This phrase creates auditory imagery. The reader can almost hear the gentle patter of raindrops and feel the softness of the rain.

Tinkle on the Shingles The tinkle on the shingles contributes to the auditory imagery. It enhances the reader's ability to imagine the sound of raindrops on the roof.

ASSESSMENT EXERCISE

Extract Based Questions

Read the following extract carefully and answer the questions that follow.

Every tinkle on the shingles
Has an echo in the heart;
And a thousand recollections
And a thousand dream fancies
Into busy being start,
Weave their air-threads into woof,
As I listen to the patter
Of the rain upon the roof.

(i) How does the poet describe the falling rain?
   (a) Rain creates peace in his heart.
   (b) Rain creates immense pain in his heart.
   (c) Rain creates immense pleasure in his heart.
   (d) Rain creates echo in his heart.

(ii) How does the rain affect the poet?

(iii) Complete the sentence appropriately.
   The poet draws a comparison in the poem. It is ....

(iv) What does the mind of the poet fancy?

Short Answer (SA) Type Questions

1. How does the poet feel when the clouds blot out the stars?
2. How does the poet know when it is a sign for the rain to start?
3. How does the poet describe the rain when it starts falling?
4. What are the 'thousand dreamy fancies' in the poet's heart?

Long Answer (LA) Type Questions

1. Give the substance of what the poet is wanting to say in the poem.
2. Dreams hold importance in the poet's life. Is it true? Elaborate.

The Lake Isle of Innisfree

by William Butler Yeats

CHAPTER 4

Introduction The poem 'The Lake Isle of Innisfree' is about the beauty and charm associated with the countryside as compared to the dull, grey and boring life of the city. The poem reveals the poet's desire to escape from the noisy hustle and bustle of the city life and lead a simple life in the natural landscape of Innisfree, a lake island. For the poet, a simple and peaceful life with only a few simple needs is more delightful than the restless life of the city.

Explanation of the Poem

Stanza 1

I will arise and go now and go to Innisfree,
And a small cabin build there, of clay and wattles made:
Nine bean-rows will I have there, a hive for the honeybee,
And live alone in the bee-loud glade.

Explanation The poem begins with the poet saying that he will wake up and go to the island of Innisfree. On the island , he would build a small house from clay and wattles (fences). He would grow nine rows of bean and would also have a hive for honey bee. The honeybees residing (living in the hive) will fill the place with a buzzing sound. The poet here intends to live alone on the island full of natural beauty.

Stanza 2

And I shall have some peace there, for peace comes dropping slow
Dropping from the veils of the morning to where the cricket sings;
There midnight's all a glimmer and noon a purple glow,
And evening full of the linnet's wings.

Explanation The poet states that in the countryside, peace can be found at every location. It comes as naturally as the morning sun comes in the sky. It comes slowly just like how the morning removes the veil of darkness. In the morning, the poet would hear the crickets singing. At noon, he would see the purple sky and at midnight, he would look at the shining sky. In the evening, the poet would hear the sound of linnet flapping its wings.

Stanza 3

I will arise and go now, for always night and day
I hear the lake water lapping with low sounds by the shore;
While I stand on the roadway, or on the pavements grey,
I hear it in the deep heart's core.

Explanation In these lines, the poet takes a resolution to wake up and go to Innisfree right now. He decides so because, in his mind, he hears all day and night, the low and soft sound of the water reaching the shore of the island. He hears this sound even when he is standing on a road or a pavement in the city. The poet can hear the sound of the lake which leaves a deep effect on his heart.

Poetic Devices Used in the Poem

Alliteration Repetition of initial consonant sounds in the same line.

- Lake water lapping with low sounds.

Visual Imagery Use of words that creates a visual representation of ideas, pictures or scenes.

- Veils of the morning.
- Midnight a glimmer.
- An evening full of linnet's song.
- And noon a purple glow.

Auditory Imagery Use of words that represent a sound and pleases the sense of hearing

- Bee-loud glade.
- Cricket sings.
- Lake water lapping.

Metaphor A device which compares two things or qualities which are unlike.

- Peace comes dropping slow
- Veils of the morning
- Bee-loud glade

Onomatopoeia Using a word which suggests the meaning by its sound.

- I hear lake water lapping.

Repetition Repetition of words/phrases in the same line to emphasise something.

- And I shall have some peace there, for peace comes dropping slow, Dropping from the veils...:
- I will arise and go now.

Word Meaning

Word	Meaning
Stanza 1	
Arise	stand up
Innisfree	an island in a lake
Cabin	a small wooden shelter
Wattles	material consisting of rods interlaced with twigs or branches used for building walls or fences
Bean-rows	rows of bean plants
Hive	honey comb
Bee-loud	a place having the loud sound of bees buzzing
Glade	open space in a forest
Stanza 2	
Dropping	falling
Veils	covering, here misty atmosphere in morning
Cricket	an insect
All a glimmer	shining
Linnet	a small bird of brown and grey colour
Stanza 3	
Lapping	sound of water striking the shore
Low	soft
Pavements grey	dull and drab paths
Deep heart's core	deep in my heart

NCERT FOLDER

NCERT Exercise Questions

I. THINKING ABOUT THE POEM (NCERT PAGE 52)

Q.1 What kind of place is Innisfree? Think about

(i) the three things the poet wants to do when he goes back there (stanza I);

Ans. Innisfree is a calm and peaceful place where nature is beautiful, alive and full of life. It is an uninhabited island.

(i) The three things the poet wants to do in Innisfree are

(a) Build a small cabin of clay and wattles (fences) to live.

(b) Plant nine rows of beans.

(c) Install a beehive to breed bees.

(ii) what he hears and sees there and its effect on him (stanza II);

Ans. At Innisfree, the poet will see the peaceful mornings where peace comes dropping. He will hear the crickets singing in the morning. He will also see the midnight shine and purple glow in the sky. He will hear the flight of the linnet birds in the evening. All these things makes him peaceful and joyous.

(iii) what he hears in his 'heart's core' even when he is far away from Innisfree (stanza III).

Ans. The poet's longing for the beautiful landscape of Innisfree is so strong that even in the city, he can hear the lapping sound of the water in the lake. The poet's heart aches for going back to Innisfree, away from the concrete jungle of the city.

Q.2 By now you may have concluded that Innisfree is a simple, natural place, full of beauty and peace. How does the poet contrast it with where he now stands? (Read stanza III.)

Ans. The poet thinks that Innisfree is a simple, natural, calm and quiet place, very close to nature, as he mentions the insects, birds, bees, light of the stars and so on.

In contrast, the place where he now stands is noisy, far from nature and full of hustle and bustle (the place is the pavement of a highway in the city of London).

Q.3 Do you think Innisfree is only a place, or a state of mind? Does the poet actually miss the place of his boyhood days?

Ans. Although Innisfree is the poet's boyhood visiting place, it also represents his desired state of mind.

The poet wishes to escape to Innisfree as it is more peaceful than where he is now, i.e. in the city. Innisfree is representative of what the poet considers an ideal place to live in, which is devoid of the restless humdrum (routine) of his life. Yes, the poet actually misses the place of his boyhood days. Even when he is away from Innisfree, he recalls the sound of the lake water washing the shore.

II. THINKING ABOUT THE POEM (NCERT PAGE 55)

Q.1 Look at the words the poet uses to describe what he sees and hears at Innisfree.

(i) Bee-loud glade

(ii) Evening full of the linnet's wings

(iii) Lake water lapping with low sounds

What pictures do these words create in your mind?

Ans. (i) These words bring to our minds the image of buzzing bees in an open area which is full of greenery.

(ii) These words bring up the image of linnets flying across an evening sky.

(iii) These words evoke not only the image, but also the soft sound of a lake's water washing the shore.

Q.2 Look at these words.

... peace comes dropping slow

Dropping from the veils of the morning to where the cricket sings

What do these words mean to you? What do you think "comes dropping slow...from the veils of the morning"? What does "to where the cricket sings" mean?

Ans. The chosen lines evoke vivid and sensory descriptions of the arrival of peace on Innisfree. 'Peace comes dropping slow' suggests peace descends gradually and gently, like dewdrops or soft rain. The word 'dropping' implies a slow and deliberate descent, emphasising peace's unhurried and calming nature. 'From the veils of the morning' describes the source of this peace as the veils of the morning. This imagery suggests that tranquillity is associated with the early hours of the day, possibly the dawn when the world is quiet and nature is awakening. 'To where the cricket sings' signifies the destination of the peace. The cricket's song symbolises the serene and natural ambience of Innisfree. The arrival of peace is linked to the place where the cricket sings, emphasising the connection between the calming presence of nature and the auditory beauty of the cricket's song.

REVIEW EXERCISE

Including Competency Based Questions

Part – I

Multiple Choice Questions

1. What type of shelter does the poet want to build on the island?

(a) A well-furnished house

(b) A small wooden cabin

(c) A house made of twigs or branches and clay

(d) None as he wants to live in an open space

Ans. (c) A house made of twigs or branches and clay

2. Which of the following activity is not one among the many that the poet plans to do in Innisfree?

(a) To go and live in Innisfree all alone.

(b) Build a small shelter on the island.

(c) To plant bean in rows of nine.

(d) To be surrounded by hives of honeybees.

Ans. (d) To be surrounded by hives of honeybees.

3. "Dropping from the veils of the morning ......" What drops from the veils as mentioned in the above line?

(a) Cricket's singing (b) Peace

(c) Darkness (d) Morning

Ans. (b) Peace

4. What is the scene at Innisfree during midnight?

(a) There is a purple glow during midnight.

(b) The island shines at midnight.

(c) Innisfree would be filled with linnets flapping their wings.
(d) Crickets' singing surrounds the place.

Ans. (b) The island shines at midnight.

5. "....... and noon a purple glow."
What is the poetic device used in the above line?
(a) Visual imagery
(b) Audio imagery
(c) Alliteration
(d) Metaphor

Ans. (a) Visual imagery

6. What does the poet hear during his stay in Innisfree?
(a) The sound of bees buzzing loud
(b) The linnets' flapping in the evening
(c) The sound of the water striking the shore
(d) All of the above

Ans. (d) All of the above

7. Where is the poet standing at the end of the poem?
(a) Road or pavement in the city
(b) Besides the lake where the water is lapping
(c) In Innisfree, at his small cabin
(d) By the shore in Innisfree

Ans. (a) Road or pavement in the city

Extract Based Questions

1. Read the following extract carefully and answer the questions that follow.

I will arise and go now, and go to Innisfree,
And a small cabin build there, of clay and wattles made:
Nine bean-rows will I have there, a hive for the honeybee,
And live alone in the bee-loud glade.

(i) What do the given lines show?

Ans. The fact that the poet of the given lines wants to go to Innisfree shows that he wants peace and quiet.

(ii) State whether the following statement is True or False.
The last line of the stanza/extract shows that the poet wants to live in his town.

Ans. False

(iii) Complete the sentence appropriately.
The kind of house that the poet wants to live in reflects .... (simplicity/activity)

Ans. simplicity

(iv) From the given description of the place, Innisfree is a place
(a) with tranquility
(b) of natural beauty
(c) where his family lives
(d) Both (a) and (b)

Ans. (d) Both (a) and (b)

2. Read the following extract carefully and answer the questions that follow.

And I shall have some peace there, for peace comes dropping slow
Dropping from the veils of the morning to where the cricket sings;
There midnight's all a glimmer, and noon a purple glow,
And evening full of the linnet's wings.

(i) Select the option that applies the same rhyme scheme as the first four lines of the given extract.

(a) I was a cottage maiden
Hardened by sun and air,
Contented with my cottage mates,
Not mindful I was fair.

(b) As long as it takes to pass
A ship keeps raising its feet;
The wetter ground like glass
Reflects a standing gull

(c) They cannot look out far.
They cannot look in deep.
But when was that ever a bar
To any watch they keep?"

(d) Two golden-agers in a room
Complained about mate's habits.
"It irritates and drives me mad,
I need to find relief"

Ans. (c)

(ii) In this stanza, what does the speaker expect to find in Innisfree?

Ans. The speaker expects to find peace on Innisfree, described as coming 'dropping slow' from the veils of the morning. The stanza paints a tranquil picture of the island with references to the beauty of nature, including the glow of noon and the linnet's wings.

(iii) How does the speaker describe the sounds of Innisfree in the second stanza?

Ans. The speaker describes the sounds on Innisfree as the cricket singing, midnight being a glimmer, and the evening filled with the linnet's wings.

(iv) How will you describe the night 'there'?

Ans. The night 'there' can be described as charming and glimmering.

3. Read the following extract carefully and answer the questions that follow.

I will arise and go now, for always night and day
I hear the lake water lapping with low sounds by the shore;
While I stand on the roadway, or on the pavements grey,
I hear it in the deep heart's core.

(i) Why did the poet want to go to Innisfree?
(a) He wanted to relive his past.
(b) To enrich his spirit and feel light away from the noise of the city.

(c) To have a change of mood.
(d) To explore something new.

Ans. (b) To enrich his spirit and feel light away from the noise of the city.

(ii) What does the poet show in the given lines?

Ans. Through the given lines, the poet shows a desire to go back to Innisfree.

(iii) Through the words 'Lake water lapping with low sounds', what image is drawn in the mind?

(a) Flowing stream
(b) Sound of flowing stream
(c) Low soft sound of lake's water washing the shore
(d) None of the above

Ans. (c) Low soft sound of lake's water washing the shore

(iv) What sound does the poet hear even when he is away from Innisfree?

Ans. The poet, even when he is away from Innisfree, hears the sound of lake water.

Part – II

Short Answer Type Questions

1. What is the speaker's desire to leave urban life and go to Innisfree?

Ans. The speaker's desire to leave urban life and go to Innisfree is driven by a yearning for a peaceful and harmonious connection with nature. The speaker seeks existence away from the hustle and bustle of urban settings. Innisfree represents a safe sapce where the speaker can build a simple cabin, cultivate nature with bean-rows and live in solitude.

The constant, soothing sounds of lake water lapping by the shore contrast the urban noises, providing the speaker with a serene escape. The desire for this natural retreat reflects the human need for a quieter environment in harmony with the natural world's rhythms.

2. Why does the speaker use natural materials like clay and wattles to build the cabin on Innisfree? **Competency Based**

Ans. The speaker uses natural materials like clay and wattles to build the cabin on Innisfree to emphasise a connection with the environment and a desire for a simple, sustainable existence. The speaker seeks a harmonious integration with Innisfree's surroundings by opting for natural materials.

3. Why does the poet repeat 'I will arise and go now'?

Ans. The repetition of 'I will arise and go now' emphasises that the poet is extremely keen on abandoning the city and leave for the Lake Isle.
The use of 'arise' and 'go' reveal the intensity of his longing to escape from the restlessness and noise of the cities and reach the quiet, idyllic harmony and serenity of the world of nature available on the Lake Isle of Innisfree.

4. How would the poet enjoy his time in Innisfree?

Ans. The poet would enjoy his time in Innisfree by spending his time in nature.

He would wake up in the peaceful morning where he would only hear the cricket singing. In the evenings, he would see the linnet flapping its wings. At midnight, he would watch the stars shining in the sky. All these are enjoyable to him.

5. How is the roadway in the city different from the Isle of Innisfree?

Ans. In the poem, the poet compares and contrasts country life to the city life. In city and its roadways, life is dull and grey. However, there is nature's beauty all around in Innisfree. The poet hears the soft lapping of lake water, the singing of the cricket and sees linnet flapping its wings in the countryside.

6. Why does the colour purple describe the noon at Innisfree? **Competency Based**

Ans. In the poem 'The Lake Isle of Innisfree,' the line 'noon a purple glow' describes the serene atmosphere at midday. Using colour purple, Yeats captures the visual impact of heather's reflection (a type of flower native to the island) on the water. This creates a vivid and tranquil image that contributes to the overall sense of peace and beauty in the speaker's envisioned retreat to Innisfree. The choice of purple adds a specific and meaningful element to the portrayal of the landscape and enhances the reader's sensory experience.

7. Explain the words, 'lake water lapping with low sounds'?

Ans. These words describe the beautiful natural environment in Innisfree where the lake water strikes the island with a soft sound on its shore.

As there is no noise around, one can hear this soft sound. The poet says that he can hear this soft sound even in the hustle-bustle of the city life.

8. Why does the poet miss the Isle of Innisfree?

Ans. The poet lives in a busy city, most probably of London wherein he desires peace and calm. However, he is unable to find it in the restless city life. In such a situation, he remembers and misses the Lake Isle of Innisfree.

He keeps on hearing the soft sounds that he had heard at that place and feels that it is calling to him. Thus, he wants to escape from the city and go there.

9. 'The Lake Isle of Innisfree' by William Butler Yeats is a poem that falls into the categories of lyric and pastoral poetry. Assess.

Ans. 'The Lake Isle of Innisfree' by William Butler Yeats is a poem that falls into the categories of lyric and pastoral poetry. As a lyric poem, it is characterised by its expression of personal thoughts, emotions and reflections. The poem serves as a lyrical expression of the speaker's deep longing for a peaceful and idyllic life on the island of Innisfree. Simultaneously, the poem exhibits pastoral elements. The speaker envisions creating a rustic dwelling, cultivating bean-rows and living in a bee-loud glade. These pastoral themes evoke a romanticised vision of rural life and reflect the desire to escape the complexities of urban existence.

Long Answer Type Question

1. The poet presents an idyllic picture of the lake Isle of Innisfree as compared to the dull-grey life of the city. Justify using illustrations from the poem.

Ans. It is true that the poet in the poem 'Lake Isle of Innisfree', presents an idyllic picture of the lake Isle as compared to the dull and grey life of the city.

The poet had spent some part of his life in the rural island of Innisfree and finds his present city life to be boring. Thus, he compares and contrasts his present condition to the life he lived at the Island.

According to the poet, the Lake Isle of Innisfree is most suitable to lead a carefree, serene and a self-dependent life. Therefore, he desires to go to Innisfree, and lead a life of simplicity and peace. He feels that he will be fully contented if he lives there alone listening to the nature's music and admiring its beauty.

Furthermore, he would live in peace in Innisfree as peace comes naturally at every place on the island.
In contrast to this serene land is the city life where the roadways and pavements are grey and dull, life goes on in hustle and bustle. However, even in this scenario, he can hear the sound of nature of the Lake Isle of Innisfree.

2. The Tone of the poem shift from determined to reflective. Do you agree? Justify your answer.

Ans. I agree with the statement that the tone of the poem shift from determined to reflective. In the first stanza the poet seems determined to fulfill his desire for a peaceful life. The poet resolves to leave his life and build a simple cabin on Innisfree. The tone is driven by a strong desire for change and a more simple existence. The mention of materials like 'clay and wattles' suggests a return to basics.

As we move to the second stanza, the poem becomes tranquil and reflective. He describes the peace he expects to find in Innisfree. The tone becomes more contemplative as the imagery shifts to the slow descent of peace and the tranquil scenes of different times of the day. Nature, with its sounds of the cricket and visuals of noon and evening, is depicted as a source of serenity.

In the last stanza, the poet reaffirms his intention to go to Innisfree, emphasising the persistent allure of the island. The tone becomes more reflective as the speaker hears the sounds of the lake water lapping, creating a sense of connection with the natural world.

3. Critically comment on the themes of the poem.

Ans. The themes of the poem are

Escapism and Nature Yeats's poem is deeply filled with themes of nature, emphasising the poet's desire to escape urban life and connect with the natural world. The serene setting of Innisfree, with its reference to the small cabin, bean row, and the bee-loud glade, reflects a longing for a harmonious existence in a tranquil, natural environment.

Solitude and Spirituality The poem explores spiritual themes, particularly seeking inner peace and fulfilment. Innisfree is portrayed as a place where the speaker can attain spiritual peace away from the hustle and bustle of the outside world. The peace that 'comes dropping slow' suggests a deeper, more contemplative state of being.

Labour and Fulfillment Building a small cabin and cultivating nine bean rows indicates a desire for a simple and self-sustaining life. The mention of a hive for the honeybee suggests a connection to labour and productivity. The poem implies that engaging in purposeful, meaningful work, such as building and tending to one's surroundings, can lead to fulfilment and contentment.

Thus, the poem 'The Lake Isle of Innisfree' intertwines themes of nature, spirituality, and the connection between labour and fulfilment, vividly portraying the poet's yearning for a harmonious and meaningful existence in a natural haven.

4. Nature often brings back many memories which are stored deep in our mind. Substantiate with reference to 'Rain on the Roof' and 'The Lake Isle of Innisfree'.

Ans. It is true to say that 'Nature often brings back many memories which are stored deep in our mind'. The poems 'Rain on the Roof' by Coates Kinney and 'The Lake Isle of Innisfree' by W.B. Yeats beautifully illustrate how nature can evoke memories and emotions that are stored deep within the human mind, often offering a sense of solace, peace, and reflection.

In 'Rain on the Roof', the poet uses the sound of rain on the roof as a symbol of reminiscence and reflection. The gentle sound of rain falling on the roof at night awakens deep memories and emotions in the speaker.

The poet reflects that when the rain falls, it evokes memories of his lost loved ones, particularly a mother or a cherished figure. The rain also provides a moment of peace and introspection, where the speaker can reflect on past experiences. This soothing effect of nature helps in reconnecting with memories, making them feel fresh and vivid once again.

In 'The Lake Isle of Innisfree', W.B. Yeats expresses a longing for the peace and serenity he experienced in his childhood at Innisfree, a place where he felt at peace with nature and the world. The lake, the bees and the simple cabin all represent a past that the poet wishes to return to, evoking a sense of calm and inner peace that he feels is missing from his current life. The beauty of nature in the poem is not just about the physical place, but about the mental space it creates in the poet's mind. Yeats' memory of Innisfree provides him with comfort and inspiration, giving him strength to cope with the challenges of his present life.

In both poems, nature serves as a powerful trigger, accessing hidden emotions and memories, offering the speaker a sense of reflection, comfort, and emotional connection to the past. Thus, nature has a remarkable ability to revive memories and provide a deep, emotional connection to the experiences and emotions stored in the mind.

ASSESSMENT EXERCISE

Extract Based Questions

Read the following extract carefully and answer the questions that follow.

And I shall have some peace there, for peace comes dropping slow
Dropping from the veils of the morning to where the cricket sings;
There midnight's all a glimmer, and noon a purple glow.
And evening full of the linnet's wings.

(i) Where, according to you, is the poet while saying the above lines?

(ii) In the given lines, 'peace' has been compared to
(a) the morning sun (b) the dew drops
(c) cricket (d) colour of the sky

(iii) What is the poet most likely to do 'There'?

(iv) What kind of colours are used to describe Innisfree during noon time?

Short Answer (SA) Type Questions

1. What kind of living environment does the poet desire at Innisfree?
2. What does 'peace come dropping low' at Innisfree mean?
3. What picture does the poet portray of the lake water at Innisfree?
4. What quality does it display in the poet when he says 'I hear it in the deep heart's core'?
5. How significant is Innisfree for the poet?

Long Answer (LA) Type Questions

1. The poet gives many reasons for going to Innisfree. Give his reasoning for each of them.
2. How does the poet visualise the morning, noon, evening and midnight at Innisfree? How are they different from where he now stands?

A Legend of the Northland

by Phoebe Cary

CHAPTER 5

Introduction The poem 'A legend of the Northland' is a folktale (ballad) that is passed from one generation to another in Northland. In the tale, Saint Peter once reached the place after travelling the whole day. He was hungry and asked a woman, who was baking cakes, to give him a single piece. However, the woman did not give him even the smallest and thinnest cake. Thus, the angry saint cursed her and changed her into a woodpecker, a bird who would have to work hard to get food.

Through the story of the woman who was punished for her greed and selfishness, the legend teaches us not to be greedy and that we should acquire the qualities of kindness and empathy.

Explanation of the Poem

Stanza 1 & 2

Away, away in the Northland,
Where the hours of the day are few,
And the nights are so long in winter
That they cannot sleep them through;
Where they harness the swift reindeer
To the sledges, when it snows;
And the children look like bear's cubs
In their funny, furry clothes:

Explanation In the first two stanzas, the poet describes the place from where the story had originated. The story originated in the cold region of Northland where the days are short and nights are very long. The people of the Northland can't sleep due to extreme cold conditions in the night at this place.

When the snow falls in Northland, the people living there tie their reindeers to sledges to travel (reindeer pull the sledges). The children wear warm furry clothes which make them look like bear cubs.

Stanza 3 & 4

They tell them a curious story —
I don't believe, tis true;
And yet you may learn a lesson
If I tell the tale to you.
Once, when the good Saint Peter
Lived in the world below,
And walked about it, preaching,
Just as he did, you know.

Explanation In Northland, parents tell their children a story. The poet does not think that the story is true but still tells the tale. The poet believes that it contains an important lesson which we all must learn.

The poet, then, begins the tale. Once, Saint Peter lived on Earth as a human. He travelled the world teaching about God.

Stanza 5 & 6

He came to the door of a cottage,
In travelling round the earth,
Where a little woman was making cakes,
And baking them on the hearth;
And being faint with fasting,
For the day was almost done,
He asked her, from her store of cakes,
To give him a single one.

Explanation While travelling round the Earth, Saint Peter came to a cottage door. In the cottage, a little woman was baking cakes in the fireplace. Saint Peter had been fasting for the whole day and was hungry as well as weak. The day was now almost over. So, Saint Peter asked the woman to give him a cake from her store of cakes.

Stanza 7 & 8

So she made a very little cake,
But as it baking lay,
She looked at it and thought it seemed
Too large to give away.
Therefore she kneaded another,
And still a smaller one;
But it looked, when she turned it over,
As large as the first had done.

Explanation The woman started baking a small cake for Saint Peter. However, before she could give it to him, she felt that it was too big to give away. So, the woman went to make another small cake but when she turned it over, the cake looked as big as the first one.

Stanza 9 & 10

Then she took a tiny scrap of dough,
And rolled and rolled it flat;
And baked it thin as a wafer —
But she couldn't part with that.
For she said, "My cakes that seem too small
When I eat of them myself
Are yet too large to give away."
So she put them on the shelf.

Explanation Then, the woman took a small piece of dough and rolled it as thin as she could. The cake baked from it was as thin as wafer but the woman could not give that one to Saint Peter as well. She said that her cakes seemed too small when she would eat them. However, those cakes became too large to give away for free. Consequently, she put all the cakes on the shelf and did not give any cake to Saint Peter.

Stanza 11 & 12

Then good Saint Peter grew angry,
For he was hungry and faint;
And surely such a woman
Was enough to provoke a saint.
And he said, "You are far too selfish
To dwell in a human form,
To have both food and shelter,
And fire to keep you warm.

Explanation The selfish behaviour of the woman made Saint Peter angry. He was very weak and hungry. It was not easy for a compassionate and kind saint like Saint Peter to become angry, but the actions of the woman had been able to do so.

Hence, Saint Peter told her that she was very selfish. She did not deserve to be a human being and live a comfortable life with good food to eat and a house to live in with fire to keep her warm.

Stanza 13 & 14

Now, you shall build as the birds do,
And shall get your scanty food
By boring and boring and boring,
All day in the hard, dry wood.
Then up she went through the chimney,
Never speaking a word,
And out of the top flew a woodpecker,
For she was changed to a bird.

Explanation Saint Peter cursed the woman and transformed her into a bird. As a bird, the woman would now have to build her own nest and get her own food. To get food, she must dig holes into the hard dry wood. As a result, the woman went out through the chimney of her house without speaking a word. She, then, changed into a woodpecker.

Stanza 15 & 16

She had a scarlet cap on her head,
And that was left the same;
But all the rest of her clothes were burned
Black as a coal in the flame.
And every country schoolboy
Has seen her in the wood,
Where she lives in the trees till this very
day,
Boring and boring for food.

Explanation As a human, the little woman wore a red cap. When she was converted into a woodpecker, only her red cap remained and all her clothes had burned. In other words, the woodpecker had a red head but the rest of its body was black. The poet, then, says that since then every school boy has seen the woodpecker (the little woman) in the forest. She still lives there digging into the dry and hard wood (bark of trees) to look for her food.

Poetic Devices Used in the Poem

Assonance Repetition of vowel sounds.

- 'Away, away...'

Simile A device which compares two different things by using the words 'as' or 'like'.

- The children look like bears' cubs.

Consonance Repetition of consonant sounds.

- Swift, sledges, snows

Allusion A reference to a statement, person, place, etc. from history, religion, literature or any other field.

- Onwards Saint Peter

Repetition Repetition of words/phrases in the same line to emphasise an idea.

- Boring, and boring, and boring

Imagery Use of words to represent objects, ideas or actions.

- Black as a coal in the flame.
- Boring and boring for food.

Word Meaning

Word	Meaning
Stanza 1 and 2	
Legend (in title)	old traditional story
Away, away	very far away ('away' is repeated for emphasis)
Northland	a place located in the far North of Europe
Harness	tie
Reindeer	animal residing in North America or cold regions
Sledges	animal-drawn carriage used for transportation over snow
Furry	made of fur
Stanza 3 and 4	
Curious	strange
Tis	short form of 'it is'
Saint Peter	an apostle or prime disciple of Christ
Lived in the world below	was alive as a Human
Preaching	giving sermons of what God had said
Stanza 5 and 6	
Cottage	small house
Hearth	fireplace
Being faint	feeling like fainting due to weakness
Store	what she is already having
Single one	'one' is emphasised for showing that it is a small amount
Stanza 7 and 8	
Baking lay	was being baked
Give away	donate for free
Kneaded	moulded the dough of
Turned it over	reversed while baking
Stanza 9 and 10	
Tiny scrap	very small piece
Dough	cake mixture
Rolled and rolled	moulded the dough of
Wafer	thin slice
Part with	give away
Eat of them	eat them
Stanza 11 and 12	
For	because
Provoke	irritate or anger
Selfish	greedy or not considerate
Dwell	live
Stanza 13 and 14	
Build	make your nest
Scanty	very little
Boring	making holes in tree trunks with the beak to find food like insects
Chimney	shaft to draw away the smoke from a fireplace
Woodpecker	a bird with a reddish crown on the head which bores trees for food
Stanza 15 and 16	
Scarlet	bright red
Country schoolboy	schoolboys who live in rural areas

NCERT FOLDER

NCERT Exercise Questions

I. THINKING ABOUT THE POEM

(NCERT PAGE 67)

Q.1 Which country or countries do you think 'the Northland' refers to?

Ans. The name and description suggest that 'the Northland' is the North polar region of the world, probably countries like Norway, Sweden, Finland, Canada, etc.

Q.2 What did Saint Peter ask the old lady for? What was the lady's reaction?

Ans. Saint Peter asked the old lady for one of her baked cakes to satisfy his hunger as he had been fasting all day. The lady baked three cakes in succession, each smaller than the others, but did not give any of them away.

Q.3 How did he punish her?

Ans. He punished her by changing her into a woodpecker who would build her nest 'as birds do' and gather food by digging in the 'hard, dry wood' for the whole day.

Q.4 How does the woodpecker get her food?

Ans. The woodpecker gets her food (worms and insects) by boring holes into trees. They are known for tapping on tree trunks in order to find insects living in holes of a tree.

Q.5 Do you think that the old lady would have been so ungenerous if she had known who Saint Peter really was? What would she have done then?

Ans. No, probably the old lady would not have been so ungenerous if she had known who Saint Peter really was. Instead, she would have tried to please him and most probably, would have offered him her entire store of cakes for the fulfillment of desires.

Q.6 Is this a true story? Which part of this poem do you feel is the most important?

Ans. No, this is not a true story; it is a legend because people can't be changed into woodpeckers. I feel that the point in the story where the little woman is changed into a woodpecker is the most important. This is because the punishment given to the woman teaches us the value of generosity and charity.

Q.7 What is a legend? Why is this poem called a legend?

Ans. A legend is an old traditional story, usually with a moral. It is passed from one generation to another generation. Here, it is meant to be narrated to children. This poem is called a 'legend' because it preaches generosity towards fellow beings.

Q.8 Write the story of 'A Legend of the Northland' in about ten sentences.

Ans. Once Saint Peter stopped by an old lady's cottage because he was feeling hungry and weak after the day's fasting. The lady was baking cakes on the hearth. As he was weak with fasting, he asked her for a cake from her store of cakes. The selfish lady tried to bake small cakes but each time they seemed too big for her to give away.

Finally, she baked one that was as thin as a wafer. Unable to part with it too, she put it on a shelf and did not give any cake to the Saint. So, Saint Peter became very angry. He found her to be too selfish to live as a human. So, he punished her by changing her into a woodpecker that would have to build a nest to live in and dig into trees for food. The woodpecker has been seen by people even today in the forests, where she seems to be working hard to get food.

II. THINKING ABOUT THE POEM (NCERT PAGE 67)

Q.1 Let's look at the words at the end of the second and fourth lines, viz., 'snows' and 'clothes', 'true' and 'you', 'below' and 'know.' We find that 'snows' rhymes with 'clothes', 'true' rhymes with 'you' and 'below' rhymes with 'know'. Find more such rhyming words.

Ans. The rhyming words in the poem are given below

Stanza	Line	Word	Line	Word
1	2	few	4	through
2	2	snows	4	clothes
3	2	true	4	you
4	2	below	4	know
5	2	earth	4	hearth
6	2	done	4	one
7	2	lay	4	away
8	2	one	4	done
9	2	flat	4	that
10	2	myself	4	shelf
11	2	faint	4	saint
12	2	form	4	warm
13	2	food	4	wood
14	2	word	4	bird
15	2	same	4	flame
16	2	wood	4	food

Q.2 Go to the local library or talk to older persons in your locality and find legends in your own language. Tell the class these legends.

Ans. Yes, there are many legends in my language. (Do it yourself)

REVIEW EXERCISE
Including Competency Based Questions

Part – I

Multiple Choice Questions

1. How will you compare the winter days and nights in Northland?

(a) The days are too long and the nights are too short.
(b) The days are too short and the nights are too long.
(c) The days and nights are of twelve hours each.
(d) There are no days; it is always night there.

Ans. (b) The days are too short and the nights are too long.

2. How do the children wearing furry clothes look?

(a) They look like little pups. (b) They look like foxes.
(c) They look like fawns. (d) They look like bear's cubs.

Ans. (b) They look like bear's cubs.

3. What did Saint Peter do during his travels around the world?

(a) He looked after the poor and rich.
(b) He met little women.
(c) He preached the people about God.
(d) He begged for food.

Ans. (c) He preached the people about God.

4. How was Saint Peter feeling when he reached the little woman's cottage?

(a) Tired and hungry
(b) Hale and hearty
(c) Happy and refreshed
(d) Trembling with cold and fever

Ans. (a) Tired and hungry

5. What time of the day did Saint Peter reach the little woman's cottage?

(a) In the morning (b) At noon
(c) At the close of the day (d) At night

Ans. (c) At the close of the day

6. How many attempts did the little woman make to bake a cake for Saint Peter?

(a) One (b) Three (c) Four (d) Two

Ans. (b) Three

7. What made Saint Peter angry?

(a) The woman's greed. (b) The woman's selfishness.
(c) The woman's pride. (d) The woman's kindness.

Ans. (b) The woman's selfishness.

8. What happened to the old woman's clothes?

(a) They were burnt black as she went up through the chimney.
(b) They were lost in the wood.
(c) They were taken away by the thieves.
(d) They were torn by the wild animals.

Ans. (a) They were burnt black as she went up through the chimney.

9. Quote examples of alliteration used in the poem.

(a) Tell the tales to you.
(b) Faint with fasting.
(c) Cakes that seem too small
(d) All of the above

Ans. (d) All of the above

10. What message does this poem convey?

(a) Be greedy.
(b) Don't help the poor.
(c) Don't be greedy and help the poor and hungry people.
(d) All of the above

Ans. (c) Don't be greedy and help the poor and hungry people.

11. Why have the words like away, boring and rolled have been repeated ?

(a) To make it lyrical
(b) To enhance their impact
(c) To add rhythm
(d) None of the above

Ans. (c) To add rhythm

12. Choose the statement(s) which are not true according to the poem.

1. Saint Peter is an apostle of the Christ.
2. Saint Peter was an impatient soul.
3. The little woman was a baker.
4. The little woman was not selfish.
5. There was neither Saint Peter nor a little woman.

(a) 1, 2 and 3 (b) 2, 3, 4 and 5
(c) 2, 4 and 5 (d) None of these

Ans. (c) 2, 4 and 5

Extract Based Questions

1. Read the following extract carefully and answer the questions that follow.

Where they harness the swift reindeer
To the sledges, when it snows;
And the children look like bear's cubs
In their funny, furry clothes:
They tell them a curious story –
I don't believe' tis true;
And yet you may learn a lesson
If I tell the tale to you.

(i) Select the appropriate option to complete the sentence.

The poetic device used in the 4th line of the extract is ....

(a) personification (b) imagery
(c) simile (d) alliteration

Ans. (d) alliteration

(ii) Which tale is being referred to in the extract?

Ans. The tale of how the woodpecker came into being is referred to in the poem.

(iii) Complete the sentence appropriately.

The poet calls the tale curious because ....

Ans. he does not believe in it

(iv) What is the setting of the poem 'A Legend of the Northland'?

Ans. The poem's setting is in the Northland, where the days are short and the nights are long in winter. It describes a cold and remote region where reindeer are harnessed to sledges, and the inhabitants wear funny, furry clothes.

2. Read the following extract carefully and answer the questions that follow.

So, she made a very little cake,
But as it baking lay,
She looked at it and thought it seemed
Too large to give away.
Therefore, she kneaded another,
And still a smaller one;
But it looked, when she turned it over,
As large as the first had done.

(i) Select the option that applies the same rhyme scheme as the given extract.

(a) The tree that never had to fight
For sun and sky and air and light,
But stood out in the open plain
And always got its share of rain,

(b) Row, row, row the boat
Gently down the stream.
Merrily, merrily, merrily, merrily,
Life is but a dream.

(c) O my Luve is like a red, red rose
That's newly sprung in June;
O my Luve is like the melody
That's sweetly played in tune.

(d) "Heed not the folk who sing or say
In sonnet sad or sermon chill,
"Alas, alack, and well-a-day,
This round world's but a bitter pill."

Ans. (a) The tree that never had to fight
For sun and sky and air and light,
But stood out in the open plain
And always got its share of rain,

(ii) The poetic device used in the given lines is .... (Metaphor/Simile)

Ans. Simile

(iii) What aspect of her character is highlighted in the above stanza?

Ans. Greed

(iv) What did she think about as she saw it being baked?

Ans. As she saw it being baked, she thought that the cake was too big to be given away in charity.

3. Read the following extract carefully and answer the questions that follow.

Then good Saint Peter grew angry,
for he was hungry and faint,
and surely such a woman
was enough to provoke a saint!

(i) Complete the sentence appropriately.

The action of the woman showed her to be ....

Ans. greedy

(ii) The word 'provoke' in the extract means ....

(a) to make someone angry
(b) to make someone comfortable
(c) to make someone happy
(d) to make someone hungry

Ans. (a) to make someone angry

(iii) Why was Saint Peter about to faint?

Ans. Saint Peter was about to faint because he had preached and fasted the whole day.

(iv) Why was Saint Peter angry?

Ans. Saint Peter was angry because the little woman did not give him anything to eat.

4. Read the following extract carefully and answer the questions that follow.

And he said, "You are far too selfish
To dwell in a human form,
To have both food and shelter,
And fire to keep your warm.

Now, you shall build as the birds do,
and shall get your scanty food
By boring, and boring, and boring,
All day in the hard, dry wood."

(i) The given lines are taken from a ballad whose purpose seems to

(a) teach children how to be kind and not selfish.
(b) entertain the children.
(c) tell the story of the bird that they had seen.
(d) teach them about the story regarding their town.

Ans. (a) teach children how to be kind and not selfish.

(ii) The poet has used a poetic device in the line 'By boring and boring and boring' What effect does she wish to create by its use?

Ans. By repeating the word 'boring', the poet seeks to put emphasis on the action.

(iii) Why does he call the woman selfish?

Ans. He calls the woman selfish because she did not give him even the smallest of cakes.

(iv) Complete the sentence appropriately.
The word .... in the extract means 'to live'.

Ans. dwell

Part – II

Short Answer Type Questions

1. How has Northland been described in the poem?

Ans. In the poem, Northland has been described as a cold polar region. Here, the days are shorter and the nights are longer. Because of the extremely long nights and bitter cold, people cannot sleep all night. At the place, people use sledges pulled by reindeers whenever the land is covered in snow. Furthermore, people wear furry warm clothes to protect themselves from the cold.

2. Why and to what have the children in the Northland been compared?

Ans. The children in the Northland have been compared to little bear cubs. The reason for the comparison is the funny furry warm clothes that they wear to keep themselves warm in the extreme cold climate. Because of their clothes, they looks like small bear cubs.

3. The poet says, 'I don't believe,' tis true'; what then does the poet believe?

Ans. The poet of the poem 'A Legend of the Northland' believes that the story that parents tell their children is not true. Still she believes that the poem teaches an important lesson to everyone, particularly children. So, it must be told.

4. Who was Saint Peter? How did he reach the little woman's cottage?

Ans. Saint Peter was one of the most honourable disciples or apostles of Jesus Christ. He travelled from place to place to preach what God had said.

He reached the little woman's cottage after travelling for a whole day while fasting.

5. The little woman's refusal to part with the cake is a mirror of her character. How?

Ans. The little woman's refusal to part with even the thinnest of wafer-like cake gives us a clear picture of the selfish and greedy nature of the woman. It shows her to be a miserly (someone who cannot part away even with a small thing) and a stingy (mean) woman who does not have the heart to do even a smallest act of kindness and charity.

6. Why was Saint Peter angry at the little woman?

Ans. Saint Peter was angry at the little woman because of her selfish and greedy nature. Because of her greed, she had refused to give him a cake to eat. He believed that such a behaviour should not be characteristic of a human who lives a luxurious life.

7. 'For she was changed to a bird.' Who was she and why was she changed to a bird?

Ans. She was the little woman who did not give any cake to Saint Peter to eat when he visited her house. Because of her selfishness, she was punished by Saint Peter and was changed into a woodpecker bird so that she could work hard to build her nest and find food.

8. Do you think that the poem is a ballad? Justify.

Ans. Yes, I think that the poem is a ballad. A ballad is a poem or a song that narrates a story in short stanzas. It is passed orally from one generation to another. The poem 'A Legend of the Northland' is a ballad as it is a story revolving around Saint Peter and the little woman who was punished for her selfishness.

9. How does the poem use elements of fantasy and transformation to convey its message?

Ans. The poem uses elements of fantasy, such as the visit of Saint Peter and the magical transformation of the woman into a woodpecker. These fantastical elements illustrate the consequences of the woman's selfishness and add a mystical quality to the conveyed moral lesson.

10. What is the significance of the woodpecker's behaviour at the poem's end?

Ans. The woodpecker's boring behaviour for food in the hard, dry wood symbolises the woman's new life and the consequences of her actions. It reinforces the idea that selfishness can lead to a challenging and laborious existence, contrasting with the ease of having both food and shelter as a human.

Long Answer Type Questions

1. The poet, Phoebe Cary, introduces Saint Peter in the poem as 'Good Saint Peter'. What characteristic of Saint Peter justify this introduction?

Ans. Saint Peter, an apostle of Christianity, in the legend has been presented as the messenger of God whose mission was to teach the humans, the age old traditional values of kindness and charity. He is presented as a dedicated and a devoted saint living on the Earth with the purpose of imparting good values to humanity. His dedication is visible when he travels whole day on an empty stomach. Even when tired, he only asks for a single cake and waits patiently for his one small cake to bake.

Saint Peter also does not tolerate greed and selfishness. He believes that human beings are blessed with food, shelter and warmth, and that they should be ready to share these comforts with the needy. If they lack the will to share, then they have no right to stay as a human.

As a result, he is upset as well as angry at the little woman for her greed and selfishness. Thus, he punishes her to teach humanity a lesson.

It can be concluded that Saint Peter is a dedicated Christian who wants human beings to have positive values of generosity and empathy.

2. What moral lesson does the poem 'A Legend of the Northland' teach?

Ans. The poem 'A Legend of the Northland' teaches us a very important moral lesson that we must not be selfish or greedy. Instead, it teaches us to be generous and to help the needy if we are capable of doing so. The poem is a folklore told to the children to instil this moral lesson. In order to do so, the poem tells a story of a little woman who was punished by Saint Peter for refusing to give him any one of the cakes that she had baked.

In the story, Saint Peter reaches the cottage of the little woman and asks her to give him one cake because he is hungry and tired. But the little woman's greed and selfishness does not allow her to do so.

While baking the smallest and thinnest of cakes, she feels that the cake is too big to give away for free. The behaviour of the woman angers Saint Peter who curses her and changes her into a wood pecker. Thus, teaching a lesson to all humans that we must not be miserly and stingy.

3. The poem 'A Legend of the Northland' by Phoebe Cary explores several themes. Elucidate.

Ans. The poem 'A Legend of the Northland' by Phoebe Cary explores several themes.

Selfishness and Generosity The poem's first part presents a story of a woman unwilling to share her cakes, highlighting the theme of selfishness. This theme is emphasised when Saint Peter, in response to her hesitance, imposes a punishment that involves a transformation and a new way of obtaining food. The story is a cautionary tale about selfishness's consequences and generosity's importance.

Transformation and Consequences The poem introduces a supernatural element when Saint Peter transforms the selfish woman into a woodpecker due to her behaviour. This theme explores the idea that our actions, particularly those driven by selfishness, can lead to unexpected and sometimes irreversible consequences.

Humility and Gratitude Saint Peter's request for a simple cake reflects the themes of humility and gratitude. Despite his divine status, he is portrayed as humble and needing assistance. The woman's unwillingness to provide a simple act of kindness leads to her transformation, emphasising the importance of humility and gratitude for what she has.

Satire and Morality The poem incorporates elements of satire, using humour and exaggeration to criticise human flaws and moral shortcomings. Through the fictional story, the poet conveys a moral lesson about the consequences of selfishness and the virtues of generosity.

ASSESSMENT EXERCISE

Extract Based Questions

1. Read the following extract carefully and answer the questions that follow.

She had a scarlet cap on her head,
And that was left the same
But all the rest of her clothes were burned
Black as a coal in the flame

(i) The poetic device used in the given lines is
(a) Metaphor (b) Simile
(c) Alliteration (d) Personification

(ii) Complete the sentence appropriately.
The given extract shows ....

(iii) Complete the sentence appropriately.
By now, 'her clothes' had got turned into ....

(iv) The lady had transformed into ....

2. Read the following extract carefully and answer the questions that follow.

Where they harness the swift reindeer
To the sledges, when it snows;
And the children look like bear's cubs
In their funny, furry clothes:

(i) Which of the following is not true for Northland?
(a) Northland is the home to Saint Peter.
(b) It has short days and long nights.
(c) People travel in Northland with the help of reindeers.
(d) Northland is a cold country where it snows.

(ii) Who does 'they' refer to?

(iii) Complete the sentence appropriately.
Children look like bear cubs because of ....

(iv) What do the given lines tell us about the season?

Short Answer (SA) Type Questions

1. How did Saint Peter reach the little woman's cottage? What did he request her?
2. Describe the bird, the little woman was changed into?
3. What were the feelings of the little woman about the cakes she baked?
4. Why was the little woman changed into a bird?
5. Justify whether the punishment given by Saint Peter to the woman was too harsh or not.

Long Answer (LA) Type Questions

1. What is the message and moral of the poem?
2. What character traits of the little woman are revealed by her actions and thinking? Illustrate with examples.
3. What do we come to know of the life, culture, climate and other aspects of the Northland after reading this poem?

No Men are Foreign

CHAPTER 6

by James Kirkup

Introduction The poem 'No Men are Foreign' is about the concept of universal brotherhood and equality. The poet says that the whole world is one.

All of us have a common feeling of love and a common resource of our lives inspite of the different nationalities, religion or colour. We must unite to make everyone's life better. When we hate one another, we betray humanity. By indulging in wars against each other, we spoil the purity of this Earth which belongs to all of us. We all are human beings and we should remember that no man is foreign and no countries are strange.

Explanation of the Poem

Stanza 1

Remember, no men are strange, no countries foreign
Beneath all uniforms, a single body breathes
Like ours: the land our brothers walk upon
Is earth like this, in which we all shall lie.

Explanation In the given lines, the poet promotes global brotherhood and states that no person living on the planet is strange and no land is foreign. According to him, we all are brothers and sisters. There may exist a difference between the uniforms worn by soldiers of different countries. There may also exist a difference between our cultures, religions, etc. and we may be separated by man made boundaries but we all are human beings. God has made us in a similar way. Each and every land in the world is same. We all live upon the same Mother Earth and upon death shall be buried in the same Earth.

Stanza 2

They, too, aware of Sun and air and water,
Are fed by peaceful harvests, by war's long winter starv'd.
Their hands are ours and in their lines we read,
A labour not different from our own.

Explanation Herein, the poet states that those people who we call strangers use the same resources that we do. They are aware of the same Sun, air and water. They breathe the same air, enjoy the warmth of the same Sun and drink the same water. They get their food in the same manner as we get our food from the field.

They have also faced many hardships during wars, suffered the cold winter and starved with hunger. Further, just like us, the strangers also work hard to earn their livelihood. Thus, we all are similar to each other. According to the poet, if all of the things are common between all of us, then there is nothing strange or foreign.

Stanza 3

Remember they have eyes like ours that wake
Or sleep and strength that can be won
By love. In every land is common life
That all can recognise and understand.

Explanation The poet says that even the physical characteristics of the strangers are similar to ours. They have eyes that wake up or sleep just like us. They too have the same strength which can be won by love and sympathy. Our lives and their lives have no difference. Every country has the same type of life that can be easily noticed and appreciated.

Stanza 4

Let us remember, whenever we are told
To hate our brother, it is ourselves
That we shall dispossess, betray, condemn.
Remember, we who take arms against each
other

Explanation In these lines, the poet points out that in our world, there are some people who spread hatred and create differences. Such people give way to wars and make us kill other humans. In such a situation, we must remember that if we hate our brothers, we hate ourselves; we are only cheating and attacking ourselves. We must remember that we are equals and similar to each other before taking arms against each other.

Stanza 5

It is the human earth that we defile.
Our hells of fire and dust outrage the
innocence
Of air that is everywhere our own,
Remember, no men are foreign and no
countries strange.

Explanation In wars, we pollute and destroy the Earth that should be full of unity and peace. Our hatred and anger destroys the innocence as well as the positive qualities that we are born with. War leads to a lot of bloodshed and death which makes Mother Earth impure. The smoke full of dangerous chemicals during wars fills the air that we breathein. We are degrading ourselves with such inhumane acts. So, we must not commit such anti-human acts and remember that no one is strange and no country is foreign.

Poetic Devices Used in the Poem

Alliteration It is the repetition of the same sound in the beginning of the nearby words.

- Body breathes
- Or sleep, and strength
- Land is common life

Metaphor It is used to compare two things or qualities that are unlike

- Beneath all uniforms
- War's long winter starv'd

Repetition Repetition of words or phrases for emphasis.

- Remember, no men are strange, no countries foreign

Transferred epithet It is a device wherein when an epithet or adjective actually describing a noun is used for another object.

- Peaceful harvests

Symbolism It is a device wherein symbols are used to represent different ideas

- Fire—Symbol of anger, hatred and enmity

Word Meaning

Word	Meaning
Stanza 2	
Harvest	the produce from the fields
Starv'd	shortened form of starved that means died due to hunger
Stanza 4	
Dispossess	deprive
Betray	to cheat or to bluff
Condemn	attack
Stanza 5	
Defile	to pollute
Outrage	to overcome, to surpass

NCERT FOLDER

NCERT Exercise Questions

I. THINKING ABOUT THE POEM (NCERT PAGE 81)

Q.1 **(a) "Beneath all uniforms ..." . What uniforms do you think the poet is speaking about?**

(b) How does the poet suggest that all people on Earth are the same?

Ans. (a) The poet is speaking about 'uniforms' of different colours, castes, creeds, religions and nationalities of the people. The uniforms could represent the external differences and divisions that people create, whether through national or professional affiliations. The idea is that despite these outward differences, there is a shared humanity underneath.

(b) The poet says that though people of different nationalities look different from outside, we all are human beings. We have the same body, the same needs and we use the same resources.

Q.2 **In stanza 1, find five ways in which we all are alike. Pick out the words.**

Ans. In the following ways, we all are alike in stanza 1 :

(i) No men are strange.

(ii) No countries are foreign.

(iii) A single body breathes beneath all uniforms.

(iv) The land is same everywhere.

(v) The land where we all shall lie is also the same.

Q.3 How many common features can you find in stanza 2? Pick out the words.

Ans. Following common features can be found in stanza 2 :

(i) They, too, are aware of the Sun, air and water.

(ii) They, too, are fed by peaceful harvests.

(iii) Their hands are like ours.

(iv) A labour is not different from our own.

Q.4 "…. whenever we are told to hate our brothers …" . When do you think this happens? Why? Who 'tells' us? Should we do as we are told at such times? What does the poet say?

Ans. The line 'whenever we are told to hate our brothers' suggests instances where external influences, such as political or ideological agendas, may manipulate people into harbouring hatred or animosity towards others. This could occur during conflict, war or political tension, where divisive narratives are propagated to serve particular interests.

No, we should resist succumbing to such messages of hatred. An individual should always question the legitimacy and morality of such directives. Individuals should not unthinkingly follow instructions to hate their fellow human beings.

The poet's stance is clear: he advises against mindlessly following instructions to hate. Instead, he encourages readers to remember the shared humanity, common experiences, and interconnectedness of all people on Earth. The poet advocates for understanding, empathy, and unity in the face of attempts to sow discord and hatred.

REVIEW EXERCISE

Including Competency Based Questions

Part – I

Multiple Choice Questions

1. What does the title of the poem convey?

(a) All the people belong to the same Earth.

(b) People belong to one country.

(c) All people should live in one country.

(d) None of the above.

Ans. (a) All the people belong to the same Earth.

2. What is the rhyming scheme of this poem?

(a) aabd (b) abcd

(c) aabc (d) No rhyming scheme

Ans. (d) No rhyming scheme

3. What is this poem emphasising?

(a) All people are equal.

(b) All people are different.

(c) Different people live in different countries.

(d) None of the above

Ans. (a) All people are equal.

4. Who have created border, discriminations and countries according to the poet?

(a) Nature (b) God

(c) Human beings (d) All of these

Ans. (c) Human beings

5. How do we pollute the Earth according to the poet?

(a) By throwing waste

(b) By hating and killing others

(c) By cutting plants

(d) All of the above

Ans. (b) By hating and killing others

6. What things are common in all the people?

(i) All are born and brought up in the same way.

(ii) All sleep to take rest.

(iii) All breathe and eat to live and die in the same way.

(a) (i) and (ii) (b) (i), (ii) and (iii)

(c) (ii) and (iii) (d) (i) and (iii)

Ans. (b) (i), (ii) and (iii)

7. How can we understand common life on every land?

(a) By hating

(b) By proving ourselves powerful

(c) By leaving narrow thinking and hatred

(d) By researching on other people's lives

Ans. (c) By leaving narrow thinking and hatred

8. What does the poet ask the people to keep in mind in the last stanza?

(a) To hate more other people

(b) Not to be powerful

(c) Not to pay attention to the words of hate by selfish people

(d) To consider other people and countries as foreign

Ans. (c) Not to pay attention to the words of hate by selfish people

9. The poet proves that there are no foreign countries ....

(a) with the help of people
(b) as every human has same way of living and dying
(c) with the help of nature
(d) None of the above

Ans. (b) as every human has same way of living and dying.

10. "...in which we all shall lie", the phrase denotes

(a) lying down after success (b) lying on the land
(c) life after death (d) embracing life

Ans. (c) life after death

11. In the poem, the poet emphasises that we should not consider anyone our ....

(a) brother (b) enemy
(c) soldier (d) beloved

Ans. (b) enemy

12. "Remember, we who take arms against each other", here 'each other' means ....

(a) among different countrymen
(b) among the allies of North and South
(c) among West and East
(d) between poet and the reader

Ans. (a) among different countrymen

Extract Based Questions

1. Read the following extract carefully and answer the questions that follow.

Remember, no men are strange, no countries foreign
Beneath all uniforms, a single body breathes
Like ours: the land our brothers walk upon
Is Earth like this, in which we all shall lie.

(i) Through the given lines, what does the poet propose?

(a) Peace
(b) Secularism
(c) Fraternity
(d) Innocence

Ans. (c) Fraternity

(ii) Complete the given sentence appropriately.
The line 'single body breathes' indicates the relationship of .... (similarity/humanity)

Ans. similarity

(iii) Describe the poet's assumption about human being's reality.

Ans. The poet assumes all human beings to be indifferent or discriminatory.

(iv) What does the poet want to convey in the given lines?

Ans. The poet wants to convey that the life cycle of all humans is the same.

2. Read the following extract carefully and answer the questions that follow.

They, too, aware of Sun, air and water,
Are fed by peaceful harvests,
by war's long winter starv'd
Their hands are ours, and in their lines we read
A labour not different from our own.

(i) State whether the following statement is True or False.
All of us get the same gifts of nature in the same amount.

Ans. True

(ii) Complete the given sentence appropriately.
'Peaceful harvests' in the extract means ....

Ans. the crops grown during times of peace.

(iii) What is the significance of the word 'too'?

(a) It emphasises that 'they' are our enemies.
(b) It emphasises that 'they' are greedy.
(c) It emphasises that 'they' are just like us in their need of Sun, air and water.
(d) It emphasises that 'they' are wealthy.

Ans. (c) It emphasises that 'they' are just like us in their need of Sun, air and water.

(iv) What does "By war's long winter starv'd" indicate?

Ans. The given phrase indicates that all humans suffer through the same problems.

3. Read the following extract carefully and answer the questions that follow.

Remember they have eyes like ours that wake
Or sleep, and strength that can be won
By love. In every land is common life
That all can recognise and understand

(i) 'They' in the extract refers to

Ans. The people from other countries.

(ii) What does the poet suggest about commonalities between people in different countries?

Ans. The poet means that beneath external differences, such as uniforms and nationalities, there is a shared humanity among people in different countries.
All humans experience the same essential elements of emphasising sun, air, water and the need for sustenance. The poem emphasises the similarities in the human experience and the commonality that unites all people.

(iii) What is the poet's message in this stanza?

(a) Physical strength cannot be won.
(b) Physical strength can be won by hatred.
(c) Mental strength can be won by love.
(d) Physical strength can be won by love.

Ans. (d) Physical strength can be won by love.

(iv) What is it that can be recognised or understood?

Ans. The fact that life is common everywhere can be understood and recognised.

4. Read the following extract carefully and answer the questions that follow.

Let us remember, whenever we are told
To hate our brothers, it is ourselves
That we shall dispossess, betray, condemn
Remember, we who take arms against each other
It is the human Earth that we defile.
Our hells of fire and dust outrage the innocence
Of air that is everywhere our own,
Remember no men are foreign, and no
countries strange.

(i) How does the poem address the consequences of war and hatred?

Ans. The poem addresses the consequences of war and hatred, suffering and humanity of those in different countries. It points out that people in other nations also face the impact of war, experiencing hunger during prolonged conflicts. The poem condemns the idea of hating one's brothers and emphasises that such hatred ultimately harms ourselves and defiles the collective human existence.

(ii) How did the poet prove 'no men are foreign, and no countries strange'?

(a) With the help of physical features of humans.
(b) With the same patterns of life and death.
(c) With the help of natural produces.
(d) All of the above

Ans. (d) All of the above

(iii) The poet says "Whenever we are told to hate our brothers." Who do you think tells us to do so?

Ans. Selfish people tell us to do so.

(iv) What is the poet's message regarding the responsibility of individuals in times of conflict?

Ans. The poet's message is a call for individuals to resist hatred and the dehumanisation of others during times of conflict. It urges readers to remember that taking arms against each other harms those considered enemies and damages the shared human Earth. The poem emphasises personal responsibility in promoting understanding, empathy and peace, discouraging actions that lead to dispossessing and betraying one's humanity.

Part – II

Short Answer Type Questions

1. Does the Earth unite us in a sense? If yes, explain in the context of the poem.

Ans. Yes, the Earth does unite us in one of the most beautiful senses. It is the Earth that we walk upon and live our lives. Even after our deaths, we all shall lie inside the same Earth.

2. What is the irony in the use of the word 'uniform'?

Ans. Uniform is a dress that is meant to give an individual, a unique identity and a sense of belonging. However, ironically, uniform divides all humans and gives rise to differences based on culture and nation.

Instead of uniting, the uniform of each nation functions to divide the world.

3. In which context have the words 'harvests' and 'war' been used by the poet?

Ans. 'Harvest' is symbolic of the times of peace, when one does agricultural work in order to feed oneself.
In contrast, 'war' has been used to show an intensity that is similar to starvation and destruction.

4. How is the labour not different for us and for the so-called strangers?

Ans. The labour is not different for us and for the so-called strangers because all of us have to do it for survival on a regular basis. Also, the hands and the mechanism that we use are the same.

5. What meaning does the poet imply by saying 'strength that can be won by love'?

Ans. By saying this, the poet wants to imply the meaning that even the mightiest one can be conquered (won over) by the invincible (unbeatable) power of love. Love has the capability to soften anyone and unite the whole world.

6. How do we hate our brothers? Is it right?

Ans. We hate our brothers by taking arms against them, by judging them wrong and by seeing them as our enemy. This is not right as when we hate others, we hate ourselves. By harming them and blaming them, we only hurt our spirit and character.

7. How does the poet challenge the concept of 'foreignness'? Competency Based

Ans. The poet challenges the concept of 'foreignness' by repeatedly asserting that no men are strange and no countries are foreign. Through this, he destroys the notion of inherent differences between all human beings based on nationality or geography. The poem encourages readers to overcome prejudices and view individuals from other lands as fellow human beings, promoting a perspective recognising the shared humanity that transcends national boundaries.

8. James Kirkup's poem 'No Men Are Foreign' central theme revolves around universal humanity. Substantiate.

Ans. James Kirkup's poem 'No Men Are Foreign' central theme revolves around universal humanity. The poet emphasises the commonality that binds all individuals, going beyond boundaries of nationality, race and uniforms. Kirkup highlights the shared human experiences of life, love and suffering through vivid imagery and poignant language. The poem serves as a powerful call to reject prejudice, hatred and the dehumanisation of others. It advocates for a collective understanding of our interconnectedness, portraying nature as a unifying force.

Long Answer Type Questions

1. The poet has used various ways to establish the fact that we all are same. Explain these ways in accordance with the poem.

Ans. This poem is a revelation of the fact that the whole world is a union. Nothing is strange or foreign. No person or country can be categorised to be strange. We are the people who share this common land and hence, we can affirm that we are the same.

Despite being from different countries, speaking different languages, believing in different religions, we all are same. We feel pain and pleasure equally. We put our best and devoted efforts in the form of labour to procure the harvest. We are afraid of the war and rejoice at love. We share similar resources over the Earth and our hatred is harmful for the Earth. Keeping all these in mind, the poet has tried his best to establish the fact that we all are same.

2. Explain how does our hatred, jealousy and misdeed pollute our own Earth.

Ans. The world is a union, i.e. a singular entity. We may belong to different nations, may speak different languages or may believe in different religions, but still we are same. Every person on this Earth is our brother. In brotherhood, we share the joys of being together and enjoy the peace.

However, if we stand against our fellow men, who are our brothers and start a war with them, then we are polluting our own Earth. We not only lack our strength of character but also criticise our own values. Our misdeeds, hatred and jealousy are a blow to humanity. Because of them, we initiate wars which pollute the land as well as the air and water. It further spreads death and hunger. As a result, the Earth loses its purity. Its innocence is filled with the dirt and smoke which becomes unsuitable for human survival. Therefore, we must stick firmly to our values, ethics and dignity. Only these things can keep our Earth from being polluted so that it can continue being a beautiful place to live.

3. 'No Men Are Foreign' is a compelling call for empathy, understanding, and recognising our common humanity in the face of cultural, national, and ideological differences. Comment.

Ans. It is true to say that the poem 'No Men Are Foreign' is a compelling call for empathy, understanding, and recognising our common humanity in the face of cultural, national and ideological differences. The poem presents the idea that all humans share a common existence beneath the superficial differences of nationality and uniforms. The poet highlights the shared experiences of people worldwide, such as the awareness of nature (sun, air, and water) and the commonality of labour. The poet suggests that everyone undergoes similar struggles and joys regardless of background. The use of phrases like 'a single body breathes' and 'earth like this, in which we all shall lie' emphasises the interconnectedness of humanity.

The poem strongly argues against war and its dehumanising effects. The mention of the impacts of war on harvests, and the shared hands and lines in the third stanza suggests that the consequences of conflict are universal and affect all people. The poet, then, urges readers to empathise with others by reminding them that people in other countries have the exact basic needs, feelings and aspirations. This appeal for compassion extends to the call for understanding and tolerance instead of hatred or condemnation.

4. Critically evaluate the tone of the given poem.

Ans. 'No Men Are Foreign' by James Kirkup is a didactic or moralistic poem that conveys a specific message or moral lesson. The poet employs the lines to advocate for universal brotherhood, peace and understanding among people, regardless of national or cultural differences. The didactic nature of the poem is evident in its tone which calls for recognition of the shared humanity that unites all individuals.

The poet expresses a sincere and heartfelt plea for understanding and unity. The repetition of the word 'Remember' throughout the poem underscores the sincere desire to convey a crucial message about the shared humanity of all people.The poem encourages readers to reflect on the similarities among human beings and the consequences of hatred and war. The reflective nature of the poem prompts reflection on the interconnectedness of humanity.

Despite addressing the negative aspects of hatred and war, the overall tone carries an optimistic undertone.

The poet believes in the possibility of fostering understanding and peace among people by emphasising their shared humanity.

5. The poem uses many symbols to present its message. Do you agree? Justify.

Ans. I agree with the statement that the poem uses many symbols to present its message. These symbols are

Uniforms The mention of uniforms in the first stanza can be seen as a symbol of national identity and divisions. Beneath the uniforms, however, the poem suggests a shared humanity.

Land and Earth The repetition of the idea that the land others walk upon is "Earth like this, in which we all shall lie" symbolises the commonality of the human experience. It represents the shared destiny of all people, regardless of their nationality or origin.

Sun, Air and Water The second stanza's references to Sun, air and water symbolise the fundamental elements that sustain life. These elements are universal and shared by people in all countries, emphasising the commonality of the human experience.

Hands and Lines The hands mentioned in the second stanza symbolise labour and work. The lines on the hands are likely a symbol of the shared experiences and challenges faced by people in different lands, highlighting the commonality of human struggles.

Eyes, Sleep, and Strength The third stanza mentions eyes that wake or sleep, and strength that can be won by love, symbolising the shared human experiences of consciousness, rest and the transformative power of love.

Air The air in the fourth stanza symbolises the shared atmosphere that belongs to everyone. The poem suggests that the consequences of war, such as 'hells of fire and dust,' outrage the innocence of the air, emphasising the interconnectedness of humanity and the environment.

Foreign and Strange The repeated use of 'foreign' and 'strange' symbolises prejudices and biases based on nationality. The poem challenges these notions, urging readers to see beyond perceived differences and recognise the shared humanity.

Human Earth The phrase 'It is the human earth that we defile' symbolises humanity's collective responsibility for the planet's well-being. It suggests that the Earth belongs to all humans, and actions that harm it are ultimately self-destructive.

6. National identities, often made to unite people of the nation, creates division. Do you agree? Answer with reference to the lesson 'My Childhood' and the poem 'No Men are Foreign'.

Ans. Yes, the statement 'National identities, often made to unite people of the nation, creates division' is a valid observation. The story 'My Childhood' by A.P.J. Abdul Kalam and the poem 'No Men Are Foreign' by James Kirkup reflect on how national identities, while meant to unify people, can also create divisions, either within a nation or between nations.

In 'My Childhood', A.P.J. Abdul Kalam reflects on his early experiences growing up in the town of Rameswaram. As a young boy, he was deeply influenced by the diverse cultural and religious backgrounds in his community, where Hindus, Muslims, and people from different castes lived together peacefully. Kalam's realisation as a child was that national identities, though meant to unite, often lead to divisions-especially along religious lines.

In 'No Men Are Foreign', James Kirkup advocates for a broader, more inclusive concept of human identity, urging readers to see beyond national identities. The poem suggests that people from different nations, ethnicities and religions are fundamentally the same and that there should be no divisions based on nationality. Kirkup points out that wars, hostility and conflicts arise when people view those from other countries as 'foreign' or 'other'. The notion of national identity, as the poem argues, leads to the harmful idea of dividing people into 'us' and 'them'. The poet, then, calls for a universal perspective where no one is considered a foreigner, suggesting that national identities create artificial boundaries between people who are, at their core, the same.

Both works emphasise that true unity and peace lie in going beyond national identities and recognising the shared humanity that binds us all. Thus, while national identities can unite a nation, they also have the potential to create deep divisions, both within and across nations. The focus should be on human solidarity and a sense of belonging that goes beyond the constraints of national borders.

ASSESSMENT EXERCISE

Extract Based Questions

1. Read the following extract carefully and answer the questions that follow.

Remember they have eyes like ours that wake
Or sleep, and strength that can be won
By love. In every land is common life
That all can recognise and understand.

(i) Who are 'they' in the given lines?

(ii) How can we win others?

(a) With love
(b) With friendship
(c) With equality
(d) With fair treatment

(iii) What does 'strength that can be won by love' means?

(iv) What is the essence of these lines?

2. Read the following extract carefully and answer the questions that follow.

It is the human earth that we defile.
Our hells of fire and dust outrage the innocence
Of air that is everywhere our own,
Remember, no men are foreign, and no
countries strange.

(i) How do we pollute the air?

(ii) What does 'hell of fire' mean?

(a) Greed
(b) Jealousy
(c) Racism
(d) All of these

(iii) The word which means the same as 'damage' is ....

(iv) What is the theme of the given lines?

Short Answer (SA) Type Questions

1. How can strength be won according to the poem?

2. What does the poet ask us to remember?

3. What message does the poet convey through the poem?

Long Answer (LA) Type Question

1. This poem suggests the need of universal brotherhood. How is brotherhood important for peace and prosperity of the world?

On Killing a Tree

CHAPTER 7

by Gieve Patel

Introduction The poem 'On Killing a Tree' is like an instruction manual of killing a tree. It tells its reader that trees are like living beings. They are not cut but killed properly by uprooting the roots that are stuck deeply in the soil. Through the poem, the poet teaches us many lessons. First, it depicts the courage and strength of trees, through which it teaches us to be strong and determined. Second, it points out that vices are just like roots. They exist deep within us and even when we feel we have gotten rid of it, it suddenly appears. Therefore, to kill a bad habit we must put on our best efforts and uproot it. Third, it teaches us that we must bring all our work to a proper end. Lastly, it appeals (requests) us to not kill/cut trees that sustain our lives.

Explanation of the Poem

Stanza 1

It takes much time to kill a tree,
Not a simple jab of the knife
Will do it. It has grown
Slowly consuming the earth,
Rising out of it, feeding
Upon its crust, absorbing
Years of sunlight, air, water,
And out of its leprous hide
Sprouting leaves.

Explanation The poem starts by pointing out that it takes a lot of time to cut a tree. The simple act of stabbing it with a knife is not enough to kill a tree. It is not an easy job to kill a tree as it has grown strong by absorbing many elements for many years. It has taken nutrients from the soil and absorbed sunlight, air and water for a long time such that many leaves had grown on it.

Stanza 2

So hack and chop
But this alone wont do it.
Not so much pain will do it.
The bleeding bark will heal
And from close to the ground
Will rise curled green twigs,
Miniature boughs
Which if unchecked will expand again
To former size.

Explanation Herein, the poet states that we need to put a lot of effort to kill a tree. According to him, a simple stab and chop won't kill the tree completely. It would only injure the tree which would suffer the pain with its strength. With time, the injury (bleeding bark) will heal and the tree would grow again. Green twigs and small branches will grow again on the tree. Consequently, the tree will grow to its full size and strength.

Stanza 3

No,
The root is to be pulled out—
Out of the anchoring earth;
It is to be roped, tied,
And pulled out—snapped out
Or pulled out entirely,
Out from the earth-cave,
And the strength of the tree exposed
The source, white and wet,
The most sensitive, hidden
For years inside the earth.

Explanation In this stanza, the poet points out the exact manner through which a tree can be killed. He states that to kill a tree completely, its roots needs to be taken out of the deep soil where it is hiding inside the Earth. This root is the strength of the tree. It gives support to the tree and is the most vulnerable as well as sensitive part. It needs to be snapped out entirely from deep inside the Earth.

Stanza 4

Then the matter
Of scorching and choking
In sun and air,
Browning, hardening,
Twisting, withering,
And then it is done.

Explanation Once the roots are uprooted, it will get exposed to the sun and the air. As a result, the roots start dying due to the heat. The roots become brown and the soft surface becomes hard and dry. After some time, it loses its own shape and starts twisting. Finally, the tree will die.

Poetic Devices Used in the Poem

Alliteration It is the repetition of the same sound in the beginning of the nearby words.

- The bleeding bark will heal.
- The source, white and wet.

Word Meaning

Word	Meaning
Stanza 1	
Jab	to hit something forcefully or stab
Consuming	using the resources
Crust	the top layer of the soil
Leprous hide	discoloured bark of the tree
Sprouting	giving rise/birth to
Stanza 2	
Hack	cutting with heavy blows
Chop	cut in piece
Bleeding bark	the secretion of the liquid from the bark when it is cut with a sharp object
Heal	recovering from a wound
Curled	with twists and graceful moves
Twigs	tenderly leaves
Miniature	tiny and small
Boughs	branches
Unchecked	not being stopped
Expand	to grow in an enormous way
Former	belonging to the earlier
Stanza 3	
Pull out	to take out from somewhere by force
Anchoring Earth	trees are held securely with the help of roots in the Earth
Snapped out	chopped out
Earth-cave	the inside of the Earth
Exposed	subjected to one's limitations.
Stanza 4	
Scorching and choking	the drying up of the tree after being uprooted
Browning	the colour gradually getting brown
Hardening	the process of becoming hard and dry
Twisting	getting bent and moved
Withering	the process of decaying

NCERT FOLDER

NCERT Exercise Questions

THINKING ABOUT THE POEM

(NCERT PAGE 96)

Q.1 Can a "simple jab of the knife" kill a tree? Why not?

Ans. No, a simple jab of the knife wouldn't be enough to kill a tree. A simple jab of the knife will only injure it and in due course of time, it will heal itself.

Q.2 How has the tree grown to its full size? List the words suggestive of its life and activity.

Ans. The tree has grown to its full size by absorbing nutrients from the soil. It had absorbed the sun, air and water for a long time. The words are consuming, rising, feeding and absorbing.

Q.3 What is the meaning of 'bleeding bark'? What makes it bleed?

Ans. The phrase 'bleeding bark' refers to the bark of the tree which gives out a liquid after it is cut or hurt. Hacking and chopping the tree make its bark bleed.

Q.4 The poet says "No" in the beginning of the third stanza. What does he mean by this?

Ans. The poet says 'No' in the beginning of the third stanza to highlight the fact that a tree cannot be killed merely with a jab of a knife or by hacking and chopping.

Q.5 What is the meaning of 'anchoring Earth' and 'Earth- cave'?

Ans. 'Anchoring Earth' refers to the strong, stabilising connection between the tree's roots and the soil. The roots anchor the tree to the Earth, providing stability and support. The use of 'anchoring' suggests that the tree is firmly secured in the ground, emphasising the depth and strength of its root system.

The term 'Earth cave' is another metaphor for the soil or the ground in which the tree's roots are embedded. The word 'cave' implies an enclosed, hidden space beneath the surface. It highlights the idea that the roots are not only in contact with the Earth but are almost sheltered or concealed within it. Using 'cave' also adds a sense of mystery and depth to the underground environment where the tree sustains its sustenance.

Q.6 What does the poet mean by 'the strength of the tree exposed'?

Ans. The strength of the tree are its roots. They keep it anchored to the Earth.

They are the provider of nutrients for the tree. When the tree is pulled out of the Earth's soil, its roots, the source of resilience, are revealed, pointing out the tree's vulnerability. By advocating for uprooting, the poet emphasises the profound impact of disrupting the tree's anchoring connection to the Earth, symbolising the tree's ultimate defeat and destruction.

Q.7 What finally kills the tree?

Ans. The tree is killed when its roots are exposed to the outside. The burning heat of the sun and air chokes it. It loses all its leaves and gets brown. It twists, hardens and dries to finally die.

REVIEW EXERCISE

Including Competency Based Questions

Part – I

Multiple Choice Questions

1. The tree symbolises .... in this poem.

(a) prosperity
(b) greenery
(c) deep rooted evil
(d) None of the above

Ans. (c) deep rooted evil

2. Which figure of speech is used in the poem?

(a) Simile
(b) Personification
(c) Assonance
(d) Synecdoche

Ans. (b) Personification

3. 'The strength of the tree is exposed'. What do these words convey?

These words convey that

(a) Roots of the tree are taken out of the Earth
(b) Roots are withered
(c) Tree is withered
(d) All of the above

Ans. (a) Roots of the tree are taken out of the Earth

4. What is the rhyming scheme of this poem?

(a) aabc
(b) abcd
(c) abcb
(d) No rhyming scheme

Ans. (d) No rhyming scheme

5. What will again expand to a tree's full size?

(a) Roots
(b) Green twigs
(c) Fruit
(d) Flowers

Ans. (b) Green twigs

6. What is related to the death of roots?

(a) Pulling out (b) Scorching
(c) Choking (d) All of these

Ans. (d) All of these

7. Is hacking and chopping enough to kill a tree?

(a) No, twigs and branches will reappear
(b) Yes, the sprouting leaves will fall off
(c) Yes, the bark will get torn
(d) No, the poet finds it an impossible task to achieve

Ans. (a) No, twigs and branches will reappear

8. In the poem, 'miniature boughs' mean

(a) small and round things
(b) small bouquet of flowers
(c) tiny leaves falling off the tree
(d) tiny branches of the tree

Ans. (d) tiny branches of the tree

9. How do the roots need to be pulled out to kill a tree?

(a) Hacking and chopping
(b) Cutting the bark
(c) Jabbing the tree with knife
(d) Tying with ropes

Ans. (d) Tying with ropes

10. Which figure of speech is used in the line "Rising out of it, feeding upon its crust, absorbing"?

(a) Alliteration (b) Personification
(c) Simile (d) Enjambment

Ans. (d) Enjambment

Extract Based Questions

1. Read the following extract carefully and answer the questions that follow.

It takes much time to kill a tree,
Not a simple jab of the knife
Will do it. It has grown
slowly consuming the earth
Rising out of it feeding
Upon its crust, absorbing
Years of sunlight, air, water,
And out if its leprous hide
Sprouting leaves

(i) Complete the given sentence appropriately.

The poet is taking the tree to be symbolic of .... (human life/deep rooted evil)

Ans. deep rooted evil

(ii) Select the appropriate option to complete the sentence.

The poetic device used in line 1 of the extract is ....

(a) personification (b) alliteration
(c) simile (d) transferred epithet

Ans. (b) alliteration

(iii) Complete the given sentence appropriately.

The word 'jab' in the extract means ....

Ans. to push or hit something forcefully and quickly often with a sharp object

(iv) Describe the tone used by the poet in the given lines.

Ans. The poet's tone is sarcastic.

Or

(i) Complete the given sentence appropriately.

The poetic device used in the line 2 of the extract is ....

(a) personification (b) alliteration
(c) metaphor (d) simile

Ans. (a) personification

(ii) What is the extract about?

Ans. The given extract describes the cutting of a tree.

(iii) State whether the following statement is True or False.

'Consuming the Earth' in the extract means securing food and nourishment from the Earth.

Ans. True

(iv) 'It' in the fifth line of the extract refers to ....

Ans. the interiors of the Earth

2. Read the following extract carefully and answer the questions that follow.

So hack and chop
But this alone won't do it.
Not so much pain will do it.
The bleeding bark will heal
And from close to the ground
Will rise curled green twigs,
Miniature boughs
Which if unchecked will expand again
To former size.

(i) Complete the given sentence appropriately.

The process described in the given lines is of ....

Ans. killing a tree

(ii) If 'hack and chop' won't do it, what would be able to do it?

(a) Burning the tree (b) Relocating the tree
(c) Killings its roots (d) Infesting it with pests

Ans. (c) Killings its roots

(iii) Which characteristic of the trees is mentioned in the given lines?

Ans. Rejuvenation is the characteristic feature of trees mentioned in the lines.

(iv) What do these given lines tell us about humans?

Ans. It can be inferred that humans are merciless, thoughtless and callous.

3. Read the following extract carefully and answer the questions that follow.

Then the matter
Of scorching and choking
In sun and air
Browning, hardening
Twisting, withering
And then it is done.

(i) Whose 'scorching' and 'choking' is the poet talking about?

(a) The leaves of the tree
(b) The stem of the tree
(c) The flowers of the tree
(d) The roots of the tree

Ans. (d) The roots of the tree

(ii) Complete the given sentence appropriately.

In the poem, the process is symbolic of ....

Ans. removal of a bad habit

(iii) How does the tree get killed?

Ans. The tree gets killed when its roots are burnt by the Sun.

(iv) Describe the process the speaker mentions in stanza 4 to complete the act of killing a tree.

Ans. In stanza 4, the speaker describes the process of scorching and choking the tree in the Sun and air. This leads to the tree browning, hardening, twisting, and withering. The final result is the death of the tree.

Part – II

Short Answer Type Questions

1. Why does it take much time to kill a tree?

Ans. A tree will take much time to be killed because it has got strength till its roots are safe under the Earth and simple blows from any tool won't do any harm to it.

2. How has the tree grown to its present size?

Ans. The tree has grown to its present size by absorbing the resources from Earth.

It draws nourishment from the soil and from its surroundings like air, water and sunlight.

3. What has been compared with 'Leprous hide'?

Ans. 'Leprous hide' has been compared with the bark of the tree which has got discoloured over a period of time. It looks like someone who has leprosy (a disease) and the skin of the body has got discoloured. The comparison contributes to the imagery of the tree as a living entity with a textured, imperfect exterior. It suggests that even a seemingly robust and healthy exterior can conceal vulnerabilities and sensitivities. Green Twigs/Miniature Boughs.

4. In stanza 2, why does the speaker emphasise that hacking and chopping alone won't kill the tree?

Ans. The speaker emphasises that hacking and chopping alone won't kill the tree because the bleeding bark will heal, and the tree will continue to grow. The poem suggests that more drastic measures are required to kill the tree effectively.

5. How can the tree get back to its former size?

Ans. After the tree's bleeding bark is healed, small branches and bushes will rise from the stump of the tree which is close to the ground. With time, these tiny delicate branches of the trees will expand and grow to its original size.

6. Why did the poet want the tree to be snapped out?

Ans. As the earlier methods of killing a tree were not successful, the poet suggests another method to kill a tree completely.

He states that to kill a tree, its roots must be pulled out and snapped from deep inside the Earth.

7. What does the phrase 'white and wet' refer to in stanza 3?

Ans. The phrase 'white and wet' in stanza 3 refers to the exposed root of the tree. It is described as the source hidden for years inside the earth, and pulling it out exposes the sensitive and vulnerable part of the tree that needs to be destroyed to kill the tree.

8. How is the tree killed finally?

Ans. When the strength of a tree, that is, its roots are exposed to its surroundings, it starts decaying. A continuous exposure to sunlight and air will harden it. It will dry up and choke to finally kill a tree.

9. The poet has used irony in the poem to give a message. Elaborate. Competency Based

Ans. In the poem 'On Killing a Tree', the poet describes a method that will most effectively kill a tree. By stating the method, the poem conveys a message that Mother nature has regenerative powers and cannot be destroyed easily.

Furthermore, trees sustain our lives and hence, must be preserved.

10. The tree serves as the central and multifaceted symbol in the poem. Assess. Competency Based

Ans. The tree serves as the central and multifaceted symbol in the poem. It represents nature, strength and life. The various stages of attempting to kill the tree symbolise broader themes such as the resilience of nature, the destructive impact of human actions and the need for drastic measures to address deep-rooted issues.

Long Answer Type Questions

1. What is the underlying message of the poem?

Ans. The poem 'On Killing a Tree' describes the process of cutting a tree completely. Ironically, through the description of the process, the poet presents a severe criticism of human creulty and insensitive nature in chopping down trees for material benefit. The poet appeals its readers not to cut trees that gives us the basic necessities of life and sustain it. Therefore, one must not cut trees but plant more and more trees. Apart from this, the poet gives the readers a number of lessons.

First, it points out the sturdiness and resilience (toughness) of trees such that they take all kinds of attacks and wounds but refuse to die. Just like the trees, we must also be strong and determined to face any challenges in life. Second, the tree in the poem can be a symbol of evil habits. We may think that we have gotten rid of our wrong habits but they may suddenly appear until and unless we put in our best efforts. Lastly, the poem points out that we must complete our work efficiently and whole heartedly.

2. 'On Killing a Tree' is essentially a metaphorical exploration of the resilience of nature and the challenging process one must undertake to destroy it. However, it also covers other themes. Comment.

Ans. 'On Killing a Tree' is essentially a metaphorical exploration of the resilience of nature and the challenging process one must undertake to destroy it. However, it also covers other themes. These themes are

Resilience and Perseverance The poem vividly illustrates the tree's ability to withstand superficial attacks. Its slow growth and capacity to regenerate, even from bleeding bark, symbolise the resilience and perseverance of nature.Destructive Power of

Man The poem can be seen as a commentary on human intervention and the catastrophic impact of our actions on the environment. The tree represents nature, and the poet emphasises the difficulty in undoing the effects of human interference.

Vulnerability and Hidden Strength The exposure of the tree's root, described as 'white and wet' and 'most sensitive, hidden,' adds a layer of vulnerability to the seemingly strong tree. This vulnerability contrasts with the outward strength and hints at hidden, inner strengths that may be overlooked.

Environmental Awareness The poem can be interpreted as a plea for environmental consciousness. It prompts readers to consider the consequences of human actions, particularly those that harm the natural world.

3. 'A Legend of the Northland' and 'On Killing a Tree' both teach us moral lesson which impact our personality. Assess.

Ans. The poems 'A Legend of the Northland' by Phoebe Cary and 'On Killing a Tree' by Gieve Patel both offer moral lessons that deeply impact the way we view nature, compassion, and life in general. 'A Legend of the Northland' is a poem that tells the story of a woman from the North who is punished for her greed and selfishness. The woman's refusal to share her food, despite having plenty, leads to her transformation. This serves as a warning against selfishness and teaches the reader that greed and a lack of empathy can have long-lasting and sometimes irreversible consequences. It also highlights the value of empathy, suggesting that we should be considerate of others and their needs. This lesson promotes an attitude of compassion and kindness, which are integral to shaping a positive personality.

'On Killing a Tree' is a powerful poem that describes the slow and deliberate process of killing a tree. However, it is not just about the act of cutting down a tree; the poem goes deeper to explore that killing a bad habit is not a simple process. Further, it also teaches that the act of destruction-whether of nature or life-is not a simple, immediate process. By showing the violence and pain involved in killing a tree, the poem teaches that thoughtless actions can lead to irreversible harm and that we should act with care, compassion, and respect for all life.

Both poems leave a lasting impact on our personalities by encouraging ethical behaviour, responsibility, and a deeper understanding of the interconnectedness of all life. They make us more aware of the moral consequences of our actions, teaching us to cultivate kindness, empathy, and respect for nature and others. These lessons, when internalised, help shape a personality that values both human relationships and the environment.

ASSESSMENT EXERCISE

Extract Based Questions

1. Read the following extract carefully and answer the questions that follow.

So hack and chop
But this alone won't do it.
Not so much pain will do it.
The bleeding bark will heal

(i) Which activity does 'it' refer to?

(ii) Which figure of speech is used in the given lines?
(a) Alliteration (b) Simile
(c) Metaphor (d) Personification

(iii) Assess the use of 'bleeding bark'?

(iv) What characteristic of a tree is mentioned in the given lines?

2. Read the following extract carefully and answer the questions that follow.

No,
The root is to be pulled out—
Out of the anchoring Earth;
It is to be roped, tied,
And pulled out–snapped out
Or pulled out entirely,
Out from the earth-cave,
And the strength of the tree exposed
The source, white and wet,
The most sensitive, hidden
For years inside the earth.

(i) What does 'earth-cave' refer to?

(ii) What is the strength of a tree?
(a) Its branches (b) Its soil
(c) Its roots (d) Its stem

(iii) How can the strength of a tree be exposed?

(iv) Why is the strength of a tree sensitive?

Short Answer (SA) Type Questions

1. What has the bark been compared to?
2. When do the small boughs grow to its former size?
3. How does the Earth protect the tree?

Long Answer (LA) Type Question

1. The poet ironically says and mentions the ways to kill a tree. How do you think the poet reminds us of our duties related to the trees? Which values does he show in doing this?

A Slumber Did My Spirit Seal

by William Wordsworth

CHAPTER 8

Introduction In this poem, the poet has expressed his grief over the death of his loved one. The poet is deeply grieved and troubled over this. He says that the death has affected his soul deeply. His loved one, who is dead now, has become a part of nature. She can not sense anything and has no fears. She is now above the worldly affairs and is now resting peacefully within the Earth.

Explanation of the Poem

Stanza 1

A slumber did my spirit seal
I had no human fears.
She seemed a thing that could not feel
The touch of earthly years.

Explanation In this stanza, the poet expresses his grief over the death of a loved one. He says that he is so shocked with the death that he feels that his soul has gone into sleep. He has become numb and now does not have any human fears like loss, death, etc. After her death, his loved one seems to him like a thing who cannot feel anything. She is not affected by the physical existence of humans including human fears and time. She has peacefully left the human world behind.

Stanza 2

No motion has she now, no force
She neither hears nor sees
Rolled round in earth's diurnal course
With rocks and stones and trees.

Explanation Herein, the poet says that as the loved one is dead, she cannot move or has any force left in her body. She cannot hear or see anything. She is buried inside Earth and now is a part of nature. She is rotating along with the Earth as it rotates around the Sun everyday. She is now a part of the tree, rocks and stones that also move along with the Earth.

Poetic Devices Used in the Poem

Alliteration It is the repetition of the same sounds in the beginning of the nearby words.

- A slumber did my spirit seal.
- Rolled round in Earth's diurnal course.

Repetition It is the repetition of words/phrases in the same line.

- No motion has she now, no force.
- With rocks and stones and trees.

Metaphor A device which compares two things or qualities which are unlike.

- Earth's diurnal course

Word Meaning

Word	Meaning
Stanza 1	
Slumber	deep sleep/death
Spirit	soul/conscience
Seal	fill with
Seemed	appeared
Stanza 2	
Motion	activity
Force	strength
Rolled round	rotating around with
Diurnal course	daily activity of something as that of Earth's day and night

NCERT FOLDER

NCERT Exercise Questions

THINKING ABOUT THE POEM

(NCERT PAGE 107)

Q.1 'A slumber did my spirit seal', says the poet. That is, a deep sleep 'closed off' his soul (or mind). How does the poet react to his loved one's death? Does he feel bitter grief? Or does he feel a great peace?

Ans. The poet initially was shocked on the death of his beloved. He was so deeply grieved and troubled by the death that he was numb.

However, later he accepts the death and consoles himself with the fact that his loved one will be alive as a part of nature. In the end of the poem, he feels a great peace of mind.

Q.2 The passing of time will no longer affect her, says the poet. Which lines of the poem say this?

Ans. The lines that suggest that the passing of the time will no longer affect the poet's eloved one are "She seemed a thing that could not feel, The touch of earthly years." These lines (lines 3-4) suggest that during the state of slumber, the spirit (referred to as 'she') is portrayed as unaffected by the passage of time ('the touch of earthly years'). This implies a timeless or eternal quality to the spirit during this tranquil state, emphasising its immunity to the effects of ageing or the temporal nature of human existence.

Q.3 How does the poet imagine her to be after death? Does he think of her as a person living in a very happy state ('heaven')? Or does he see her now as a part of nature? In which lines of the poem do you find your answer?

Ans. The poet imagines the poem's subject as part of nature after death, integrated into the natural world. This perception is evident in the following lines: "No motion has she now, no force- She neither hears nor sees, Rolled round in Earth's diurnal course With rocks and stones and trees."

In these lines (lines 5-8), the poet describes the spirit as lacking motion, force, hearing and sight. The mention of being "rolled round in Earth's diurnal course" indicates a merging of the spirit with the cyclical processes of the Earth. The spirit is portrayed as a part of nature, existing harmoniously with rocks, stones and trees, emphasising an integration into the natural elements. The poet does not depict her as residing in a traditional heaven but rather as becoming one with the Earthly environment.

REVIEW EXERCISE

Including Competency Based Questions

Part – I

Multiple Choice Questions

1. What is the tone of the poem?

(a) Sad (b) Happy (c) Regretful (d) Nostalgic

Ans. (a) Sad

2. What is the poet coming to terms with?

(a) Separation from the beloved

(b) Death of a loved one

(c) Peace and tranquility

(d) Both (a) and (b)

Ans. (b) Death of a loved one

3. 'Human Fears' refer to ....

(a) pain (b) suffering (c) loss (d) All of these

Ans. (d) All of these

4. The term 'earthly years' indicates ....

(a) life (b) immortality (c) death (d) beauty

Ans. (a) life

5. What was the poet's loved one doing after her death?

(a) Coming to poet's dreams
(b) Was disturbing
(c) Moving here and there in the Earth's course of rotation
(d) Sleeping

Ans. (c) Moving here and there in the Earth's course of rotation

6. The poetic device used in 'A Slumber Did My Spirit Seal'.

(a) Alliteration
(b) Personification
(c) Metaphor
(d) Both (a) and (b)

Ans. (d) Both (a) and (b)

Extract Based Questions

1. Read the following extract carefully and answer the questions that follow.

A slumber did my spirit seal—
I had no human fears.
She seemed a thing that could not feel
The touch of earthly years.

(i) Complete the sentence appropriately.
The poetic device used in line 1 of the extract is .... (alliteration/assonance)

Ans. alliteration

(ii) What does the phrase 'I had no human fears' indicate?

Ans. It indicates that the poet had become numb in his grief and did not acknowledge or worry about things that most humans do.

(iii) The phrase 'the touch of earthly years' means

(a) active and living
(b) life on Earth
(c) the touch of beauty of the Earth
(d) None of the above

Ans. (a) active and living

(iv) How does the poet describe the initial state of the spirit in the poem?

Ans. The poet describes the initial state of the spirit as being in a deep slumber, free from human fears and seemingly unaffected by the touch of earthly years.

2. Read the following extract carefully and answer the questions that follow.

No motion has she now, no force—
She neither hears nor sees,
Rolled round in earth's diurnal course
With rocks and stones and trees.

(i) What is the beloved deprived of?

Ans. The poet's loved one is deprived of senses, life and all human qualities.

(ii) Why does 'she' has no motion?

Ans. 'She' has no motion because she is dead and is now a part of the Earth's soil.

(iii) The given lines point out that 'she' is

(a) now a part of nature (b) now just an imagination
(c) now a forceful entity (d) None of the above

Ans. (a) now a part of nature

(iv) Complete the sentence appropriately.
The phrase 'diurnal course' means ....

Ans. rotations

Part – II

Short Answer Type Questions

1. What has been referred to as 'slumber'? Why did the poet do so?

Ans. The word 'slumber' literally means a deep sleep. In the poem, 'slumber' refers to death of sensations or a numbness that fills the poet after the death of his beloved. The poet has used the word to represent the shock and grief which he was suffering from.

2. What effect did the slumber have upon the poet?

Ans. The death of a loved one fills the poet with slumber. The poet becomes shocked at the death of a loved one. He feels grieved and becomes numb. He becomes numb to all sensations and devoid of any human fears.

3. Explain: 'The touch of earthly years.'

Ans. 'Earthly years' has been used to show the feeling of pain and pleasure, the state of disease and being disease-free, the state of sorrow and happiness, etc. that come in the life of a person when he is alive.

4. What effect did a slumber have on the beloved of the poet after her death?

Ans. After death, the poet's loved one lost all her human characteristics. She now has no sense of emotions or feelings. She cannot move or has any force or strength in her body. She cannot hear or see. She has become a part of nature.

5. Explain: 'Earth's diurnal course'.

Ans. 'Earth's diurnal course' refers to the daily rotation of the Earth on its axis which causes day and night to come into existence. This is a universal phenomenon which never stops.

6. In what context rocks, stones and trees have been used in the poem?

Ans. Rocks, trees and stones have been used in the context to show the diurnal course of the Earth. They are an integral part of the Earth's daily rotation and are not affected by anything.

7. How does the poet blend personal experience with universal themes in the poem? **Competency Based**

Ans. The poet blends personal experience with universal themes by using the speaker's reflections on the loved one's death to explore broader concepts such as the transience of life, the acceptance of mortality, and the connection between the human spirit and the natural world.

8. Wordsworth, a key figure in the Romantic movement, often celebrated the connection between humans and nature. How is this reflected in the poem? **Competency Based**

Ans. Wordsworth, a key figure in the Romantic movement, often celebrated the connection between humans and nature. In this poem, nature is a backdrop for the exploration of the transience of life. The cyclic imagery, with the spirit being 'rolled round in Earth's diurnal course,' emphasises the inevitability of life's journey and the integration of the human spirit into the natural world.

Long Answer Type Question

1. Death is inevitable. Everyone has to die one day. People show different kinds of attitude towards death. But, in the poem, the poet has a completely different attitude. Elaborate

Ans. It is true that death is inevitable. It is the ultimate end and everyone has to die one day. We, as living beings, are aware of this truth but still no one wants to die.

We all fear death and try to avoid it as much as we can. Even when someone around us dies, we are deeply shocked and grieved.

In the poem 'A Slumber Did My Spirit Seal', the poet expresses his views after the death of the loved one. Initially, the poet is shocked. He is deeply grieved and troubled by the death of his beloved. He has gone numb. However, he realises that he needs to move on and accept fate. He develops a different attitude to death. He realises that death is inevitable and he needs to accept the fact that his beloved is no more. He shows the readers that even after death, his beloved or all our beloved dead people are alive as a part of nature. They are free from the worldly affairs and are immortal.

ASSESSMENT EXERCISE

Extract Based Questions

1. Read the following extract carefully and answer the questions that follow.

A slumber did my spirit seal—
I had no human fears.
She seemed a thing that could not feel
The touch of earthly years.

(i) In the given lines, the poet is ....
(ii) Whose slumber is referred to here?
(iii) Why could she not feel anything?
(iv) Complete the sentence appropriately.
The phrase 'I had no human fears' indicates that ..... .

Short Answer (SA) Type Questions

1. What sealed the spirit of the poet?
2. Why could she not feel anything?
3. What happened to the loved one of the poet after her death?

Long Answer (LA) Type Question

1. How did the poet console himself during the period of his beloved's death? What values did he depict then?

Section C : Literature
Textbook : Moments *(Supplementary)*

The Lost Child

CHAPTER 1

by Mulk Raj Anand

CHAPTER SUMMARY The following story 'The Lost Child' has been written by Mulk Raj Anand. In the story, the author highlights a child's love for his parents. It is a story about a young child who gets attracted by things around him on the way to the fair. However, he knows that his parents would refuse and so, he moves ahead. When he gets separated from his parents, all those things do not tempt him anymore.

Child Goes to Spring Fair with his Parents

It was the festival of spring and everyone was going to the spring fair. The child was going to the fair with his parents. He was very happy and excited. He was attracted by many things around him, especially, the toys. He told his parents that he wanted a toy. However, his parents refused. While his father looked at him angrily, his mother distracted him by showing him the flowering mustard fields.

The child was then attracted by the purple dragon flies, a black bee and a butterfly fluttering over the mustard flowers. He wanted to catch one of them but his mother called him. He was also attracted by small insects and worms along the footpath. Then, when his parents were sitting under a tree, he collected flower petals as they showered on him in the grove. Later, he heard the cooing of doves and ran round the banyan tree.

Entry into the Fair

The parents and the child entered the fair after passing through the mustard fields. In the fair, the child heard the sweetmeat seller selling sweets like *gulab jamuns*, *rasgulla*, *burfi*, *jalebi*, etc.

The child was attracted towards burfi that was his favourite sweet and wanted to eat it. However, he knew that if he asked for it, his parents would call him greedy. So without waiting for their answer, he moved on. Then, the child was attracted towards the garlands of gulmohar and wanted a garland. This time also, he knew that his parents would call it cheap and would refuse to buy it. So, he moved on.

Further, the child saw a balloon seller and desired to buy all the colourful balloons. However, he knew that his parents would call him too old to play with them so he walked away.

The Child is Lost

As the child walked, he saw a snake charmer. He was playing a flute to the snake. He went towards it but then remembered that his parents had told him not to hear such music. So, he moved away. Then, he saw a roundabout. He requested his parents to ride the roundabout. However, there was no reply. The child looked back around to search for his parents but couldn't find them. He, then, realised that he was separated from his parents and was lost.

The Child was in Trouble

As the child realised that he was lost, he started crying. He was filled with panic and called out for his parents. He looked around in all directions with the hope of finding them. However, he could not see them. His clothes were now muddy and his yellow turban was untied. He ran quickly to a shrine which was crowded by the people.

The Kind Man helps the Child

There was a huge rush of people near the temple. The child struggled to search his parents in the crowd but he was pushed back.

A man picked up the child in his arms when he heard his cry in the crowd. He asked the child about his parents and how he reached there. However, the child only said that he wanted his mother and father. The man took the child to the roundabout. He asked him to have a ride but the child continued crying for his parents.

The man offered many things to the child to divert his attention. The man took him to the place where snake-charmer was playing the flute and asked the child to listen to the music. The man also took him near the balloons and offered him a balloon.

He took him to the flower seller and offered the child a garland to put round his neck. He further took the child to the sweet shop and offered him sweets. However, the child had no fascination for all these things anymore. He only wanted his parents and kept crying for them.

Word Meaning

Word	Meaning
lingering on	to stay at a place longer than necessary because of reluctance to leave
receding	moving away
red-eyed	with eyes red with anger
tyrant's way	strict and harsh manner
melted	to become softer or less strong (in feeling)
free spirit	happy mood
melting gold	the colour of gold
gaudy	bright
intercepting	interfering with
still its wings	stop flying
teeming out	coming out in large numbers
wild capers	uncontrolled running
throngs	large number of people
converging	coming together
whirlpool	centre of attraction

Word	Meaning
half knew	thought that he knew
hawked	tried to sell by calling out
stole into	passed into
gentle rippling	soft rushing sound
roundabout	merry-go-round with animals and seats to ride on
flushed	excited
convulsed	to shake violently
hither and thither	this way and that
rage of running	running due to panic
filmy eyes	film of tears on the eyes
flashing, murderous	full of anger
trampled underfoot	walked over
stooping	bending
steered clear	moved away
soothe	pacify/calm down

NCERT FOLDER

NCERT Intext and Exercise Questions

THINK ABOUT IT (NCERT PAGE 6)

Q.1 What are the things the child sees on his way to the fair? Why does he lag behind?

Ans. On his way to the fair, the child sees many things like toys, the flowering golden mustard fields, the purple dragon flies, a black bee, butterfly, small insects and worms. Along the way, the child also hears the cooing of doves.

The child always lags behind his parents because of his attraction towards the beauty of nature and the things he sees on his way.

Q.2 In the fair he wants many things. What are they? Why does he move on without waiting for an answer?

Ans. As the child enters the fair, he desires to possess many things. These things include *burfi* at the sweetmeat seller, the garland of gulmohar and colourful balloons. He also wanted to ride the roundabout. He moved on without waiting for an answer because he knew that his requests would be refused every time.

Q.3 When does the child realise that he has lost his way? How have his anxiety and insecurity been described?

Ans. When the child asked his parents to get a ride on the roundabout, he got no reply. So, the child turned around and looked in all the directions to see his parents.

However, they were not present behind him. It was then that the child realised that he was lost and had gotten separated from his parents.

The anxiety and insecurity is described by the way the child reacted to the situation. As soon as the child realised that he was lost, he started crying. He ran here and there to look for his parents. He even entered the huge crowd of people gathered near the shrine.

Even when the man tried to console him, he refused to accept anything and called for his mother and father.

Q.4 Why does the lost child lose interest in the things that he had wanted earlier?

Ans. The lost child loses interest in the things that he wanted earlier because he was panic-stricken on being separated from his parents. All the things that attracted him in the fair no longer fascinated him and the only thing he wanted was his parents.

Q.5 What do you think happens in the end? Does the child find his parents?

Ans. The end is not mentioned in the story. It can be assumed that in the end, the parents, who continuously kept checking that their child was with them, may have suddenly realised that he was missing and came looking for him. The kind and understanding man who tried to console the little boy by offering him various things at the fair may have also asked him for some description of his parents and helped him find them.

It can be said that the child might have found his parents.

REVIEW EXERCISE

Including Competency Based Questions

Part - I

Multiple Choice Questions

1. Name the things that the child saw on his way to the fair.

(a) Toys
(b) Sweets and garlands
(c) Balloons
(d) All of these

Ans. (d) All of these

2. Why did the child lag behind his parents?

(a) Because of the stops he took to look closely at his favourite things
(b) Because he was walking slow
(c) Because he was crying
(d) All of the above

Ans. (a) Because of the stops he took to look closely at his favourite things

3. Why did the child keep moving without getting any answers?

(a) Because of distractions
(b) Because of too many attractions
(c) Because he knew his parents
(d) None of the above

Ans. (c) Because he knew his parents

4. What did the child want to eat at the fair?

(a) Burfi
(b) Pastry
(c) Ladoo
(d) Jalebi

Ans. (a) Burfi

5. When did the child realise that he had lost his way?

(a) While running around the playground
(b) When he asked them to buy him ice cream
(c) When he turned to ask his parents about the roundabout
(d) None of the above

Ans. (c) When he turned to ask his parents about the roundabout

6. What did the child do when he realised that he had lost his way?

(a) Cried and panicked
(b) Felt happy
(c) Reported to the office
(d) None of the above

Ans. (a) Cried and panicked

7. Why did the child lose his interest in all the things he was interested in earlier?

(a) Because of separation from his parents
(b) Because of no response from his parents
(c) Because his interest was changed
(d) Because he had a fickle mind

Ans. (a) Because of separation from his parents

8. What did the child say repeatedly after losing his parents?

(a) I want my father, I want my mother
(b) I want to ride on the roundabout
(c) I want toys that run on battery
(d) I want to see the snake dancing

Ans. (a) I want my father, I want my mother

9. How did the generous man try to calm down the child?

(a) By showing him different toys
(b) By taking him to rides
(c) By offering him sweets
(d) All of the above

Ans. (d) All of the above

10. Which of the following statements is false?

(a) The child got attracted by the butterfly
(b) The child was in a very happy mood
(c) The child could not succeed in catching the dragon fly
(d) The little insects and worms wanted to enjoy the sunshine

Ans. (c) The child could not succeed in catching the dragon fly

11. How did the child feel when he was about to enter the fair?

(a) Angry
(b) Confused
(c) Fascinated
(d) Both fascinated and confused

Ans. (c) Fascinated

12. The child ran here and there to find his parents. In the process,

(a) he fell down
(b) his clothes become dirty
(c) his turban got untied
(d) Both (b) and (c)

Ans. (d) Both (b) and (c)

Extract Based Questions

1. Read the following extract carefully and answer the questions that follow.

As he came to where they had stopped to wait for him, he could not suppress the desire of his heart, even though he well knew the old, cold stare of refusal in their eyes.

(i) Complete the analogy by selecting a suitable word from the text.

Known: Grown :: Care : ....

Ans. Stare

(ii) What can be said about the father from the child's description of 'old, cold stare of refusal'?

Ans. It can be deduced that the father of the child was a miser who habitually refused to buy any toys for his son.

(iii) Which word in the extract is an antonym of 'encourage'?

Ans. Suppress

(iv) Select the option that correctly captures the usage of the word 'cold' from the last line of the extract.

(a) She was cold, and I put some more wood on the fire.
(b) They went into the examination cold.
(c) How cold and calculating he was!
(d) They had some junk food with cold drinks.

Ans. (c) How cold and calculating he was!

2. Read the following extract carefully and answer the questions that follow.

His father looked at him red-eyed, in his familiar tyrant's way.
His mother, melted by the free spirit of the day was tender and,
giving him her finger to hold, said, "Look, child, what is before you!"
It was a flowering mustard-field, pale like melting gold as it swept across miles and miles of even land.

(i) How have the two parents been contrasted?

Ans. While his father looked at him angrily, his mother tenderly held his hand.

(ii) Complete the sentence appropriately.
Here the phrase 'the free spirit of the day' means ....

Ans. it signifies the festive mood of the day

(iii) Mention a few qualities of the mother based on the extract.

Ans. The mother of the child was kind, empathetic, loving and understanding. She recognised the hurt feelings of her child and tried her best to brighten his mood by distracting him with the beautiful sight of the flowering mustard fields.

(iv) What was before him?

(a) man selling balloons
(b) a flowering mustard field
(c) a snake charmer
(d) a roundabout

Ans. (b) a flowering mustard field

3. Read the following extract carefully and answer the questions that follow.

A sweetmeat seller hawked, "gulab-jamun, rasgulla, burfi, jalebi," at the corner of the entrance and a crowd pressed round his counter at the foot of an architecture of many coloured sweets, decorated with leaves of silver and gold. The child stared open-eyed and his mouth watered for the burfi that was his favourite sweet. "I want that burfi," he slowly murmured.

(i) Fill in the blanks appropriately.

The boy's shows ....

Ans. desire to eat a sweet

(ii) Read the following reasons and identify which one states the reason for the child's staring at the sweets.

1. **The child stared at the sweets because he wanted all of them.**
2. **The child stared at the sweet-burfi as it was his favourite.**
3. **The child stared at the sweets as he was attracted to their colours.**
4. **The child stared at the sweets as he wanted all of them.**
5. **The child stared at the sweets to just have a look.**

Select the correct option.

(a) Only 1 (b) 1 and 3
(c) Only 2 (d) 1, 4 and 3

Ans. (c) Only 2

(iii) Why did the boy walk ahead without waiting for an answer?

Ans. The boy walked ahead without waiting for an answer because he knew his plea would not be heeded.

(iv) The crowd was gathered around whom?

Ans. The crowd was gathered around the decorated shop of the sweetmeat seller in the corner.

4. Read the following extract carefully and answer the questions that follow.

The poor child struggled to thrust a way between their feet but, knocked to and fro by their brutal movements, he might have been trampled underfoot, had he not shrieked at the highest pitch of his voice, "Father, Mother!" A man in the surging crowd heard his cry and, stooping with great difficulty, lifted him up in his arms.

(i) Why did the child shriek?

Ans. The child shrieked because he was lost.

(ii) Complete the sentence appropriately.
When the writer says that, "child struggled to thrust a way between", he means that ....

Ans. the child was trying to find a way in the crowd

(iii) The statement that is true about the feelings of the lost child is

(a) he was feeling satisfied
(b) he was feeling anxious
(c) he was feeling terrified
(d) Both (b) and (c)

Ans. (d) Both (b) and (c)

(iv) Had the child not shrieked and been lifted up by a man, what would have happened to him?

Ans. If the child had not shrieked and been lifted up by a man, then he would have been trampled and crushed had he not called for help.

Part - II

Short Answer Type Questions

1. How did the mother distract the child's mind from the toy seller?

Ans. The child's mother distracted the mind of the child from the toy seller by pointing towards a flowering golden mustard field. It was pale like melting gold as it spread across a large area of flat land.

2. What happened when the 'lost child' entered the grove and how did he enjoy there?

Ans. When the lost child entered the grove a shower of flowers fell upon him. He forgot all about his parents and began to gather the petals. Then, he heard the cooing of doves and he ran excitedly to his parents, dropping the flowers that he had gathered.

3. What were the things which fascinated the child as he entered the fair?

Ans. As the child entered the fair, he was fascinated by the sweetmeat seller selling burfi, the flower seller selling garlands of gulmohar, a balloon seller, snake- charmer's enchanting music and people riding on the roundabout.

4. What did the child know when he wanted garland and *burfi* and why did he make no request for the balloons?

Ans. When the child wanted garland and burfi, he knew that his parents would refuse to buy them for him.

For the garland, he would be told by his parents that it was a cheap thing and he would be called greedy if he asked for *burfi*. The child made no request for balloons as he knew that his parents would say that he was too old to play with balloons.

5. How can you say that the child was scared of his father?

Ans. The child was tempted by many things but he asked for them only in slow murmurs. He also described his father in the following way – "His father looked at him red-eyed, in his familiar tyrant's way." This shows that he was scared of his father and could not express his demands as rightfully as some other children do.

6. What was the condition of the child when he lost his parents?

Ans. When the child realised that he had lost his parents, he ran here and there to search for his parents.
He had lost all his happiness and excitement. He was filled with panic and fear and started crying.
He wanted nothing but his parents.

7. What happened when the lost child reached the shrine?

Ans. When the lost child reached the shrine, men were pushing each other. The child struggled to make his way through but was knocked down. He might have been injured if he had not shouted loud for his parents.

8. Who rescued the lost child?

Ans. A kind-hearted man in the shrine rescued the lost child. He lifted him up in his arms and tried to comfort him. He offered to take him to the roundabout and also offered to buy him flowers, balloons and sweets. He did his best to make the child happy but the child was refusing all those things.

9. Why did the child reject all of the man's attempts to distract him with various attractions?

Ans. The child rejected all of the man's attempts to distract him with various attractions because he was overwhelmed with fear and longing for his parents. His emotional stress was so intense that no sweets, toys or entertainment could comfort him; he only wanted to be reunited with his mother and father.

10. The theme of Mulk Raj Anand's 'The Lost Child' centres on innocence and dependence during childhood. Substantiate. Competency Based

Ans. The theme of Mulk Raj Anand's 'The Lost Child' centres on innocence and dependence during childhood. The story highlights how children are naturally curious and easily distracted by the wonders around them. However, their sense of security and happiness is deeply tied to their parents' presence. When the boy loses his parents at the festival, his initial excitement and desires for toys and sweets vanish, replaced by fear and longing for them. The story emphasises the emotional bond between children and parents, showing that material attractions cannot replace the love and comfort of family.

11. What role does the setting play in intensifying the child's isolation and vulnerability? Competency Based

Ans. The setting in 'The Lost Child' heightens the child's sense of isolation and vulnerability in several ways. First, the fairground's crowded pathways and chaotic atmosphere contrast with the child's initial sense of security with his family. As he navigates through the crowds of unfamiliar surroundings and faces, the vastness of the fair becomes overwhelming, increasing his feelings of being lost and alone.

Long Answer Type Questions

1. What things did the child get attracted to and wanted to possess when he entered the fair? Was he able to get all the things he desired? Was his love for his parents affected in any way?

Ans. When the child entered the fair, he got attracted to many things and desired to possess all of them. He wanted the *burfi*. Next, he was attracted towards a garland of gulmohar flower and wanted a garland. He was also fascinated by the rainbow glory of coloured balloons and wanted all of them.

He was even attracted to the snake charmer's flute. The child knew that if he asked for these things, his parents will refuse, so he did not ask for any one of them. Thus, he was not able to get anything that he desired.

Although, he was denied everything that he asked for, his love for his parents was not affected in any way. His love for them did not lessen and he followed them obediently.

The child's love for his parents can be seen when he gets separated from them. As soon as he realises that he is lost, he gets panic-stricken. He starts crying for his parents. All the things he had wanted earlier had lost their significance and his only concern was to get his parents back.

2. How do you know that the 'lost child' was a nature lover?

Ans. In the story, the lost child was a nature lover as can be seen in his fascination and attraction towards all aspects of nature. On the way to the spring fair, when his mother diverted his attention towards the golden mustard fields, he was immediately fascinated by the young flowers in the field.

Then, he saw a group of dragon flies interfering in the flight of a butterfly or lone black bee. The child wanted to catch it but couldn't. He was also attracted to the insects and worms that were coming out to enjoy the sunshine.

Later, when he entered the grove, a shower of flowers fell on him and he forgot about his parents. He had begun collecting the raining petals when he heard the cooing of doves and he immediately ran towards them.

In his innocence, he was so engaged in the beauty of nature that he always lagged behind his parents.

3. The man who had rescued the child was compassionate and kind. Discuss.

Ans. The man who had rescued the child was compassionate and a kind hearted man. He had a heart full of goodness which could not ignore the painful cries of the boy who was shouting, screaming and crying for his parents. As soon as he heard the cry of the child, he picked up the child in his arms and saved him from getting walked over by the people. He risked his own safety to make sure that the child was safe. He forgot his own purpose of visiting the shrine and did his best to comfort the scared and anxious child. He very kindly inquired about his parents. Even when the boy did not reply he did not lose his patience. Instead, he tried to make him feel better by offering him things that children generally love and desire.

The strange man also tried to distract the child so that he could help him find his parents. The strange man showed that he loved children and handled the boy with love and care which reflects his compassion and kindness.

4. Compare the attitude of the child before and after his separation from his parents.

Or **"A child longs for toys, sweets and other things but not at the cost of his parents." Comment.**

Ans. Before separation from his parents, the child was happy and excited. On the way to the fair, he was attracted to and enjoyed the beauties of nature. In the fair, he was fascinated by the sweets, the colourful balloons and the garland of gulmohar among many things.

While moving in the fair, the presence of parents made him feel secure and he does not even wait for them when he demands those things.

However, all his cheerful and playful mood was converted to anxiety and fear as soon as he realised that he got separated from his father and mother. He started crying continuously and got lost in the large crowd gathering near the shrine to search for his parents. When a kind man rescued him and tried to comfort him, his only concern was his parents.

All the things such as sweets, toys, balloons and flowers lost their value in his eyes in the absence of his parents. He refused all those things that he wanted earlier and wanted only his parents.

5. The story uses various similes to indicate the beauty of the natural landscape and the industrial setting. Comment. **Competency Based**

Ans. The story uses various similes to indicate the beauty of the natural landscape and the industrial setting. Some of the similes used are

(i) **"It was a flowering mustard field, pale like melting gold as it swept across miles and miles of even land."** This simile compares the appearance of the flowering mustard field to melting gold. The use of 'pale like melting gold' suggests the golden-yellow colour of the mustard flowers under the sunlight. It produces a sense of beauty and richness that extends over a vast area. It enhances the visual imagery, making the field appear enchanting and precious.

(ii) **"...its head raised in a graceful bend like the neck of a swan....."** The simile compares the snake's raised head and the graceful curve of its neck to that of a swan.
It emphasises the elegance and fluidity of the snake's movements, making the potentially frightening creature appear beautiful and serene.

(iii) **"...the music stole into its invisible ears like the gentle rippling of an invisible waterfall..."** The simile compares the way the snake hears the music to a waterfall's gentle, soothing sound. It suggests a soft, calming effect that the music has on the snake, enhancing the mystical and enchanting atmosphere of the scene.

ASSESSMENT EXERCISE

Extract Based Questions

1. Read the following extract carefully and answer the questions that follow.

He hurried towards his parents, his feet obedient to their call, his eyes still lingering on the receding toys. As he came to where they had stopped to wait for him, he could not suppress the desire of his heart, even though he well knew the old, cold stare of refusal in their eyes.

(i) Complete the sentence appropriately.
When the writer says 'suppress the desire of his heart', he means ....

(ii) The statement that is true according to the extract is
(a) 'he' is a teenage boy
(b) 'he' is easily distracted by natural beauty
(c) 'he' knew that his parents would buy him the things he wanted
(d) 'he' wasn't sacred of his father

(iii) The phrase 'Feet obedient to their call' highlights that ....

(iv) What was the child aware of?

Short Answer (SA) Type Questions

1. What was the usual reaction of the father to the child's demands?
2. What kind of a person was the child's mother?
3. Where did the parents stop and why?
4. Why was the child forbidden to hear the music being played by the snake-charmer?
5. What did the child do in the grove?
6. How can you say that the child was obedient?
7. Where and how did the child meet the kind-hearted person?

Long Answer (LA) Type Questions

1. When did the child realise he was separated from his parents, what was his reaction?
2. "The company of parents is more important than the things of pleasure." Do you agree?
3. The reactions of the child at the shop of the sweetmeat seller, the flower seller and the balloon seller–were they natural reactions? From his reactions can we conclude that he was a realistic child?

The Adventures of Toto

by Ruskin Bond

CHAPTER 2

CHAPTER SUMMARY

'The Adventures of Toto' is an interesting tale written by Ruskin Bond. The story is about a mischievous baby monkey named Toto. The narrator's grandfather bought Toto from a tonga-driver for five rupees. He decided to add him to his private zoo. The grandfather tried to tame Toto but could not do so as he was a naughty monkey. He made many mischiefs and frequently got into trouble with his adventures. Finally, the grandfather realised that he could not keep Toto at home any longer. So, Toto was sold to the same tonga-driver for three rupees.

Grandfather Bought a Monkey

The narrator's grandfather was very fond of animals. Once, he bought a little red baby monkey from a tonga-driver for five rupees and named him Toto. He decided to add Toto in his private zoo.

Toto was a pretty monkey with bright eyes which sparkled with mischief. He had pearly white teeth which scared elderly Anglo-Indian ladies. His hands were very dry as if they had been pickled in the Sun for many years. However, his fingers were quick and his tail, while adding to his good looks, served as a third hand. Toto could use his tail to hang from a branch and scoop up any delicacy that might be out of reach of his hands.

Toto's First Mischief

The narrator's grandmother did not like animals. So, the narrator and his grandfather decided that Toto's presence should be kept as a secret. They put Toto in a little closet opening in the narrator's bedroom and tied him up to a peg in the wall.

When they returned, they saw that Toto had removed the decorative paper from the walls. He had also pulled out the peg attached to the wall and had torn the narrator's school blazer into shreds (pieces). Toto's mischief delighted the grandfather. He found Toto to be a clever monkey who would have converted the narrator's torn blazer into a rope and escaped from the window.

Toto Transferred in Servant's Quarters

Toto was transferred into a big cage after this incident. The cage was kept in the servant quarters where all the other animals lived together. The animals included a tortoise, a pair of rabbits, a domesticated squirrel and a pet goat. Even here, Toto proved to be a naughty monkey. He would not let any other animal sleep at night. So, the grandfather, who had to go to Saharanpur to get his pension next morning, decided to take Toto along with him.

Toto's Journey to Saharanpur

A black canvas kit bag was arranged for Toto. He was put in this bag. As the bag was closed, Toto could neither escape nor cause any mischief.

Toto was in the bag throughout his journey but when grandfather was showing his ticket to the ticket collector, Toto bought his head out of the bag and grinned at the ticket collector. This sudden appearance of an animal scared the ticket collector. He cleverly classified Toto to be a dog and charged three rupees for carrying Toto with him. This irritated the grandfather who decided to outwit the ticket collector. He pulled his pet tortoise out of his pocket and asked the ticket collector to charge money for it as well. The ticket collector said that it was not a dog and didn't collect any money for it.

Toto Accepted by Grandmother

Toto was accepted by the narrator's grandmother and was transferred into the stable with Nana, the family's female donkey. From his first night, Toto started teasing Nana. When grandfather came to see if Toto was comfortable, he found that Toto had bitten Nana's long ears. As a result, Toto and Nana could never become friends.

Toto's Bathing Routine

On winter evenings, grandmother gave Toto a large bowl of warm water for his bath. First, Toto would check the temperature of the water. Then, he would enter the bath until the water reached his neck. After this, he would take the soap and rub it all over his body.

When Toto would come out of his bath he would run to the kitchen fire to dry himself. If anyone happened to laugh at him, his feelings would be hurt and he would stop bathing.

Accident while Bathing

One day, Toto almost boiled himself alive while bathing. When he saw a large kitchen kettle with warm water, he got into the kettle. He started jumping up and down when the water came to boil. However, he didn't come out of the kettle because it was cold outside. It was grandmother who found him and took him out of the kettle.

Toto's Mischief Continues

Toto's mischief still continued. He was always damaging things. One day, as the narrator's family entered the dining room, they saw Toto eating the pullao made for lunch.

When his grandmother screamed at Toto, he threw a plate at her. Further, when one of the narrator's aunts came forward, Toto threw water on her face.

Later, when the narrator's grandfather came, Toto took the dish, ran outside and sat on the branches of the jack fruit tree. He sat there for the whole day. As soon as the pullao was finished, Toto threw the dish down and broke it into pieces because grandmother had screamed at him.

Toto is Sold

Toto's mischief caused much loss to the family. The narrator's family could not afford the loss of dishes, clothes, curtains and wallpapers. So, grandfather sold Toto to the same Tonga driver for three rupees.

Word Meaning

Word	Meaning
feeding-trough	a container containing food for the animal
pickled	dried
wicked	could create mischief
scooping	picking
fussed	feeling concern or annoyance
fastened	close or fix/hold in place.
wrenched	pull out with force
shreds	pieces torn apart
servants' quarters	living place given to servants

Word	Meaning
very sociably	in a friendly manner
tame	not dangerous
abode	a house or home
turnstile	exit gate
poked	stand out and be visible
taken aback	shocked
in vain	without success
quadruped	any four footed animal
prodded	push with a finger
triumphant	victorious/successful

Word	Meaning
halter	rope/strap placed around the head for tying the animal
haunches	one of the back legs of a four legged animal
fastened on to	bit into
cunningly test	cleverly feel
hauled	pull out with effort or force
spite grandmother	make grandmother miserable

NCERT FOLDER

NCERT Intext and Exercise Questions

THINK ABOUT IT (NCERT PAGE 11)

Q.1 How does Toto come to grandfather's private zoo?

or Why did the narrator's grandfather decide to buy Toto?

or Why did grandfather decide to add Toto to his private zoo?

Ans. The narrator's grandfather was fond of animals. He had seen a little red monkey tied to a feeding trough with a tonga-driver. He felt that the monkey looked out of place there. So, he decided to buy him to add him to his private zoo.

Q.2 "Toto was a pretty monkey." In what sense is Toto pretty?

or Why does the narrator call Toto 'a pretty monkey'?

Ans. According to the narrator, Toto was a pretty monkey. He had bright eyes that sparkled with mischief. He had white pearly teeth which could scare elderly Anglo-Indian ladies. His hands were dried up but his fingers were quick.

The unique feature possessed by Toto was his tail that served as his third hand. He would use it to hang from branches and to pick up any dish that he was unable to reach by his hands.

Q.3 Why does grandfather take Toto to Saharanpur and how? Why does the ticket collector insist on calling Toto a dog?

Ans. After Toto was shifted to the servant quarters with all other pets, he proved to be a problem for them. He would not let any animal sleep at night. So when the grandfather was going to Saharanpur to get his pension, he decided to take Toto along with him. He thought that Toto's absence would provide some relief to all other animals.

To take Toto along with him, a black canvas kit bag was filled with straw. Toto was put in it and the bag was closed so that Toto could neither escape nor cause any mischief.

When the Ticket collector saw Toto, he was shocked and unable to find any rule that fixed a monkey's fare. So, the ticket collector cleverly equated Toto with a dog and charged rupee three as his fare.

Q.4 How does Toto take a bath? Where has he learnt to do this? How does Toto almost boil himself alive?

or How did Toto take a bath during winter evenings?

Ans. On the winter evenings, Toto would take a bath in a bowl of warm water given to him by narrator's grandmother. First, he would check the temperature and then, he would put his feet one by one in the water. When the water reached his neck, he would take the soap and rub it all over his body. As soon as the water became cold, Toto would run to the kitchen fire to dry himself.

Toto had learnt bathing in this way by watching the narrator do the same.

Toto was fond of bathing in warm water due to which he once almost boiled himself. One day, water was boiling in the kettle for tea. Finding the water warm enough, Toto got into the kettle. When the water came to boil, Toto would lift himself from the heat but would sit down again since it was cold outside. He continued jumping up and down till grandmother found him and took him out of the kettle.

Q.5 Why does the author say, "Toto was not the sort of pet we could keep for long"?

Ans. Toto was not the sort of pet anyone could keep for long because Toto was a very naughty animal. He damaged a lot of things in the house. He tore wallpapers, curtains and dresses. He broke utensils and also scared the guests. He also did not get along with other animals in the house.

Therefore, grandfather decided to sell Toto back to the tonga-driver.

REVIEW EXERCISE

Including Competency Based Questions

Part – I

Multiple Choice Questions

1. Why did the little red monkey look out of place?

(a) As he was kept in a cage.
(b) As he was tied to the tonga.
(c) As he was kept with camels.
(d) As he was tied to the feeding trough.

Ans. (d) As he was tied to the feeding trough.

2. Toto had brightly sparkled eyes, ... eyebrows and .... teeth.

(a) brown, yellow
(b) deep-set, pearly white
(c) big, small
(d) deep black, bright white

Ans. (b) deep-set, pearly white

3. From where did grandfather buy the monkey?

(a) From the market
(b) From a pet shop
(c) From the jungle
(d) From a tonga-driver

Ans. (d) From a tonga-driver

4. Why did grandfather buy the monkey?

(a) To have a companion
(b) Because he was being abused
(c) To add to the collection of animals in zoo at his home
(d) None of the above

Ans. (c) To add to the collection of animals in zoo at his home

5. Why was Toto kept secretly?

(a) To save him from other animals
(b) Because grandmother disliked animals
(c) Because he was naughty
(d) None of the above

Ans. (b) Because grandmother disliked animals

6. Where was Toto initially kept?

(a) In a cupboard
(b) In the zoo
(c) In the field
(d) In the garden

Ans. (a) In a cupboard

7. Why did grandfather sell Toto back to its first owner?

(a) Because he was missing him
(b) They were unable to afford mischievous Toto
(c) Because he didn't like him
(d) None of the above

Ans. (b) They were unable to afford mischievous Toto

8. At what price did grandfather sell Toto back to its first owner?

(a) Ten rupees
(b) Nine rupees
(c) Seven rupees
(d) Three rupees

Ans. (d) Three rupees

9. Why was Grandfather pleased when Toto damaged things in narrator's bedroom?

(a) Because it showed Toto's cleverness.
(b) Because grandfather also wanted to damage narrator's bedroom.
(c) Because the bedroom was looking more attractive than before.
(d) None of the above

Ans. (a) Because it showed Toto's cleverness.

10. What became Toto's new abode on the train journey?

(a) A big black suitcase
(b) A big basket
(c) A big black canvas kit-bag
(d) A big black carry bag

Ans. (c) A big black canvas kit-bag

11. 'A great treat for Toto ......' The 'treat' in the line refers to

(a) the pullao eaten by Toto.
(b) Toto's visit to Saharanpur.
(c) a large bowl of warm water given to Toto by Grandfather in winter months.
(d) a large bowl of warm water given to the narrator by Grandmother in summer months.

Ans. (c) a large bowl of warm water given to Toto by Grandfather in winter months.

12. Why was Toto not a pet to keep for long?

A. He used to damage things.
B. He used to tear dresses of narrator's aunts.
C. He was not obedient.
D. He was a mischievous monkey.

(a) Only B
(b) C and D
(c) A and B
(d) All of the above

Ans. (d) All of the above

Extract Based Questions

1. Read the following extract carefully and answer the questions that follow.

He could use it to hang from a branch; and it was capable of scooping up any delicacy that might be out of reach of his hands.

(i) Who is 'he' in the given extract?

(a) A bear (b) A monkey
(c) A parrot (d) A cat

Ans. (b) A monkey

(ii) 'It' refer to .... (tail/teeth)

Ans. tail

(iii) How is it useful for him?

Ans. It helped Toto to hang from the branches and to pick up any dish that his hands couldn't reach. Further, it added to his looks.

(iv) What can we understand about him in the given lines?

Ans. Through the given lines, it can be understood that he was naughty.

2. Read the following extract carefully and answer the questions that follow.

We found him in the branches of the jackfruit tree, the dish still in his arms. He remained there all afternoon, eating slowly through the rice, determined on finishing each grain.

(i) Where was Toto found?

Ans. Toto was found in the jackfruit tree with a dish in his arms.

(ii) What does the pullao incident demonstrate about Toto's nature?

Ans. The pullao incident demonstrates that Toto was mischievous but he also held grudges. When the Grandmother screamed at him for stealing the pullao, Toto got offended. He took his revenge from the Grandmother by finishing every grain of rice in the pullao and then, also breaking the empty dish by smashing it on the floor.

(iii) Why was Toto eating slowly?

Ans. Toto was eating slowly because the dish of 'Pullao' that he had stolen was too much for him. Therefore, he couldn't finish his stolen food quickly.

(iv) The given extract shows that Toto was

(a) hungry (b) naughty
(c) plartfu (d) greedy

Ans. (b) naughty

3. Read the following extract carefully and answer the questions that follow.

When Toto was finally accepted by Grandmother he was given a comfortable home in the stable, where he had for a companion the family donkey, Nana. On Toto's first night in the stable, Grandfather paid him a visit to see if he was comfortable. To his surprise he found Nana, without apparent cause, pulling at her halter and trying to keep her head as far as possible from a bundle of hay.

(i) Why was Toto not accepted by the Grandmother before?

Ans. Toto was not accepted by the narrator's Grand–mother before because she didn't want another pet.

(ii) Choose the statements that are not true according to the given extract.

1. Toto was a mischievous pet.
2. Toto and Nana became friends.
3. Toto and Nana shared the same stable for a night.
4. Grandmother liked Toto's mischiefs.
5. Grandmother protected Toto in every incidence.
6. Toto was loved by every pet in the zoo.

Ans. 2, 4, 5, 6

(iii) When was Toto sent to the stable?

(a) When Toto was accepted by Grandmother
(b) When Toto was not feeling well
(c) When it was late at night and he had nowhere to go
(d) When other animals needed company

Ans. (a) When Toto was accepted by grandmother

(iv) Complete the analogy by selecting a suitable word from the text.
Continuous: Uninterrupted:: Clear ....

Ans. Apparent

4. Read the following extract carefully and answer the questions that follow.

This, with some straw at the bottom, became his new abode. When the bag was closed, there was no escape. Toto could not get his hands through the opening, and the canvas was too strong for him to bite his way through. His efforts to get out only had the effect of making the bag roll about on the floor or occassionally jump into the air — an exhibition that attracted a curious crowd of onlookers on the Dehradun railway platform.

(i) Why was Toto given a new abode?

(a) He was going to Saharanpur with Grandfather.
(b) Because he irritated all other animals

(c) Because he was to be trained
(d) Both (a) and (b)

Ans. (a) He was going to Saharanpur with Grandfather.

(ii) What does it say about Toto and the Grandfather that he decided to lock Toto in a bag to travel with him?

Ans. Grandfather could have put Toto on a leash to ensure safe travel. But he chose to lock him in a canvas bag because he was well aware of the mischief that Toto was capable of, if he was set loose in the train. Thus, Toto's mischievous nature is predictable and the Grandfather is very smart to think around it.

(iii) How did Toto's behaviour cause a commotion at the Dehradun railway platform?

Ans. At the Dehradun railway platform, Toto poked his head out of his canvas bag just as Grandfather presented his ticket. Mistaking Toto for a dog, the ticket collector insisted on charging a fare. Despite Grandfather's protests, Toto's unexpected appearance amused and confused onlookers, causing a humorous commotion.

(iv) The phrase "an exhibition that attracted a curious crowd of onlookers" refers to the ....

Ans. closed bag jumping and rolling

Part – II

Short Answer Type Questions

1. Why was Toto's presence kept a secret from Grandmother?

or **Where was Toto kept immediately after Grandfather got him? Why?**

Ans. Toto's presence was kept a secret from the Grandmother because she did not like animals.

She always got annoyed when Grandfather got some new bird or animals. So, Toto was kept hidden in a closet in the narrator's bedroom.

2. What did Toto do in the narrator's room?

or **What destruction was caused by Toto to the narrator's room?**

Ans. Toto had caused a lot of destruction in the narrator's room. He had torn off the decorative wall paper that covered the narrator's room. He had pulled off the peg, to which he was tied, from its socket. He had also completely torn the narrator's school blazer into shreds.

3. How many pets did the narrator's Grandfather have and where were they kept?

or **Give the names of Grandfather's pets. Where did they live?**

Ans. The narrator's Grandfather was fond of keeping pets. He had his own small private zoo where he kept his pets. In his zoo, he had a tortoise, a pair of rabbits, a domesticated squirrel and a pet goat.

Grandfather also had a female donkey called Nana who lived in a stable. Toto, a little red monkey was a new addition to his zoo.

4. How does Toto become a problem to grandfather while going to Saharanpur?

Ans. While Grandfather was going to Saharanpur, Toto became a problem for him. All through the journey, Toto was in the canvas kit-bag. However, when the grandfather was showing his ticket to the ticket collector, Toto brought his head out of the bag and grinned. The ticket collector got scared by seeing him and charged rupees three as a fare for carrying Toto.

5. Did Toto enjoy taking a bath? Justify your answer.

Ans. Yes, Toto enjoyed taking a bath. It was a treat for him to bath in the warm water given by Grandmother.
His love for taking a bath is evident in his act of getting into the kitchen kettle when the water was boiling for tea.
His fondness for bathing almost led him to being boiled alive.

6. What incident led to Grandfather's decision of not keeping Toto as a pet?

Ans. Grandfather had accepted Toto's naughty mischiefs but an incident led Grandfather to decide against keeping Toto as a pet. One day, Toto was caught eating the pullao made for lunch.

On being screamed upon, he threw a plate and a glass of water at the narrator's Grandmother and aunt. Later, he took the pullao outside and sat on the jack fruit tree. When he had finished the pullao, he threw down the plate, breaking it into pieces. This made Grandfather realise that Toto could not be kept as a pet.

7. Why was Toto sold back to the tonga-driver?

or **Why did the Grandfather sell Toto back to the tonga-driver?**

Ans. Toto's naughty acts and adventures troubled everyone in the house, including the pet animals. He caused loss to the family as he broke dishes, tore clothes, curtains and wallpaper. So, Grandfather decided to sell Toto back to the tonga-driver.

8. How was Toto a nuisance in the house?

Ans. Toto was a pretty, naughty and a clever monkey. He was always upto some mischief. He had damaged utensils, wallpapers, clothes and also annoyed Grandfather's other pets.
Toto enjoyed all his mischievous acts and thus was a nuisance in the house.

9. How did Toto behave when he was in the company of other pets?

Ans. Toto ill-treated the other animals in the house while other pets lived together very socially. He would create problems for them. He would not let them sleep at night. He teased Nana, the family donkey, continuously and even bit her long ears with his sharp teeth.

10. Describe Toto's relationship with Nana, the donkey in the stable.

Ans. Toto and Nana, the donkey, did not get along well in the stable. Toto's mischievous nature led him to bite and cling to Nana's ears, causing discomfort and tension between them. Their relationship was marked by conflict rather than companionship, reflecting Toto's disruptive presence in the stable environment.

11. How did Toto demonstrate his intelligence during his time with Grandfather? **Competency Based**

Ans. Toto demonstrated intelligence through various behaviours during his time with Grandfather. He showed problem-solving skills by escaping from his cage and adapting to his environment, such as testing bathwater temperature before entering. His ability to cause mischief also showcased his cunning and quick thinking.

12. What role does Toto's tail play in his daily antics? **Competency Based**

Ans. Toto's tail is crucial in daily antics, serving almost like an extra hand. According to the story, Grandfather believes a tail adds to anyone's good looks but for Toto, it's not just about appearance. His tail helps him in various practical ways- he can hang from branches using it, reach for food out of his immediate grasp and even scoop up delicacies otherwise inaccessible to his hands. This additional appendage enhances his mischief, making it easier for him to explore and cause trouble around the house. Despite its functional use, Toto's tail also adds to his charm and playful behaviour, making him both lovable and handful for the family to manage.

Long Answer Type Questions

1. Toto was a sharp and active monkey. Discuss.

Ans. Toto, the little red monkey was brought by the Grandfather as a new addition to his private zoo. He was a pretty monkey with bright eyes, white pearly teeth, dried fingers and a long tail. Along with being pretty, Toto was also a clever and an intelligent animal. He was so sharp that on the first day itself, he broke free from the peg attached to the wall.

According to the Grandfather, with his smartness Toto could have easily escaped the house. Toto was a playful pet who was never low on energy. He was keenly observant and swift in his actions.
His observation skills were so good that he could imitate (copy) the narrator's bathing style. In addition, Toto constantly performed mischiefs and tricks. He not only troubled the other pet animals in the house but also destroyed the walls, clothes and dishes. All these prove that Toto was a sharp and an active monkey.

2. Give a character sketch of the narrator's Grandfather.

Ans. The narrator's Grandfather is a lover of animals. He loves animals so much that he has his own private zoo. He does not mind spending money in order to get animals and birds even though this practice involves the risk of annoying his wife. He has an appreciative eye towards animals and that is why he believes that a tail adds to anyone's good looks.

He is a smart man as he devises various ways of hiding Toto. He is annoyed with foolish behaviour, like that of the ticket collector who calls Toto a dog and charges fare for it. He is both witty and sarcastic because he asks the ticket collector to charge him even for a tortoise that he had carried in his pocket.

3. Toto's mischiefs are beyond imagination. Support your answer.

or **"Toto was not the sort of pet we could keep for long." Explain, giving examples from the text.**

Ans. Toto's mischiefs are beyond imagination and he could not be kept for long due to three main reasons, i.e., he destroyed the family's possessions at home, annoyed the animals by teasing them and got into unnecessary trouble. His mischiefs included

(a) Damaging the wall when he wrenched out the peg to which he was tied.
(b) Tearing the author's school blazer into pieces.
(c) Not allowing the other pets to sleep at night.
(d) Teasing the family donkey Nana by biting her long ears.
(e) Throwing plates and water on the family and running out onto a tree to escape from them.
(f) Tearing the curtains and other clothes of the family, besides damaging other stuff belonging to the family.

4. How does Toto's personality contradict Grandmother's expectations and reactions?

Competency Based

Ans. Toto's personality contrasts sharply with Grandmother's expectations and reactions throughout the story. Grandmother is depicted as a figure who values order, decorum and peace in the household. She expresses her anger over new animals brought home by Grandfather, preferring a serene environment. In contrast, Toto is lively, mischievous and disruptive. His antics, such as tearing clothes, throwing dishes and causing general chaos, directly oppose Grandmother's desire for calmness.

When Toto acts out, Grandmother reacts with shock and frustration, often screaming or becoming angry. Her reactions highlight her preference for a well-mannered and predictable household, which Toto continuously challenges with his unpredictable behaviour. This stark contrast between Toto's naughty behaviour and Grandmother's expectations creates tension and humour in the narrative, highlighting the clash between an orderly household and a wild monkey.

ASSESSMENT EXERCISE

Extract Based Questions

Read the following extract carefully and answer the questions that follow.

To his surprise he found Nana, without apparent cause, pulling at her halter and trying to keep her head as far as possible from a bundle of hay.

(i) Who is 'his' in the given lines?
  (a) The narrator
  (b) The narrator's father
  (c) Toto
  (d) The narrator's Grandfather

(ii) Who is Nana? What do you think about her nature?

(iii) Why was he pulling her halter?

(iv) Did Nana ever become a friend of Toto?

Short Answer (SA) Type Questions

1. Initially, Toto was hidden in a cupboard, away from everybody's eyes. Why?
2. How was the author's Grandmother different from his Grandfather?
3. Was the Grandfather's decision to take Toto with him to Saharanpur correct or not? Justify.
4. Why did the ticket collector not charge for the tortoise?
5. How was Toto's mischief with the family donkey discovered?
6. Why did Toto enter the large kitchen kettle?
7. Why was the decision to sell Toto back taken?

Long Answer (LA) Type Questions

1. How can you say that Toto was an extraordinary animal? Give instances from the text to prove your point.
2. Justify whether it is advisable to keep a monkey like Toto as a pet in the house.
3. Describe Toto's bath in the kitchen kettle which almost killed him.
4. How was Toto an expensive deal for the Grandfather? Do you think it was a lesson for him?

Iswaran the Storyteller

CHAPTER 3

by RK Laxman

CHAPTER SUMMARY The following chapter 'Iswaran the storyteller' has been written by RK Laxman. The story revolves around a junior construction supervisor, Mahendra and his cook Iswaran. Iswaran was fond of telling stories to Mahendra so he would narrate a story every evening.

His stories were influenced by the popular Tamil thrillers that he read everyday. He would get inspired by reading these stories. One of his stories about a female ghost combined with his own haunted experience disturbed Mahendra so much that he decided to leave that place immediately.

Mahendra : A Junior Supervisor

The story was narrated to Ganesh by a man named Mahendra. Mahendra was a junior supervisor in a firm. The firm offered various construction sites including factories, bridges, dams, etc to supervisors on hire. His job was to keep an eye on the activities at the work site. Due to his job, he had to move from one place to another. Mahendra was a bachelor who led a simple life. His requirements were less, so he could adjust to all conditions.

Iswaran, Mahendra's Cook

Mahendra had a cook named Iswaran. Iswaran did all of the household works for Mahendra. He would cook, wash his clothes and entertain him with his stories. Iswaran also had an amazing capacity to produce vegetables and cooking ingredients which were not found anywhere.

Iswaran's Daily Routine

Mahendra would leave for work early in the morning after eating breakfast and taking some packed food. After Mahendra left for work, Iswaran would clean the shed, wash the clothes and would take a bath while praying. After eating his lunch, he used to read some popular Tamil thriller and then, he would go off to sleep.

Iswaran : A Great Storyteller

Iswaran was greatly influenced by the Tamil thrillers that he used to read. This influence was visible in his methods of story telling. He would narrate even the smallest incidents with suspense and surprise. For example, he described an uprooted tree as a bushy beast (wild animal) by using dramatic expressions and movements. Iswaran's imaginative stories entertained Mahendra who would listen to him without any judgement.

Iswaran's Story of a Tusker

Iswaran narrated an incident about a mad tusker (elephant) to Mahendra. He narrated that one day, a mad elephant escaped from the timber yard in his home town and destroyed everything that came in his way. It tore up the creepers and broke the branches.

After sometime, the elephant reached the outskirts of town. It came to the main road and smashed the stalls selling fruits, mud pots and clothes.

Then, the elephant entered the school ground and destroyed everything in it. During this incident, all the boys of school had locked themselves in their classrooms and the teachers climbed to the terrace.

Suddenly, Iswaran, a young schoolboy, took a cane (stick) from one of his teachers. He ran to the ground and hit the third toenail of the elephant, and it unexpectedly fell down. At this point, Iswaran left the story unfinished.

Iswaran's Concludes the Tusker Story

After sometime, Iswaran concluded the story and told Mahendra that an animal doctor was called to examine the elephant. After two days, the elephant was taken to the jungle by his mahout. When Mahendra asked Iswaran how he had controlled the elephant, Iswaran replied that it was either the Japanese Ju-jitsu or karate which had temporarily paralysed his nervous system.

Story of a Female Ghost

One day, Iswaran prepared a delicious dinner because it was the auspicious day of feeding the spirits of the ancestors. While Mahendra had his dinner, Iswaran told Mahendra about the factory where they were staying.

He informed Mahendra that this factory area was initially a burial ground. He himself had come across skulls and bones on the path and saw ghosts at night. He further told Mahendra about an ugly female ghost who would roam around at midnight during full moon. She would appear to be a skeleton carrying a foetus in her arms.

Mahendra's Reaction

Iswaran's ghost story disturbed Mahendra a lot. He immediately called the story to be imaginative and went to sleep. However, the story had greatly affected Mahendra. From that day, Mahendra would look outside the window every night to make sure that there was no movement outside. Earlier, Mahendra used to admire the landscape on full moon nights but now he avoided looking outside.

Mahendra Sees the Ghost

One night, Mahendra woke up when he heard a low moan or sound close to his window. At first, he decided not to look out but the sound became louder so, he looked out. He saw a dark cloudy figure holding a bundle. Mahendra was terrified by seeing it. Later, he thought that it might have been some trick of his subconscious mind.

Mahendra's Decision to Leave the Place

The next morning, Mahendra was ready to go to his office. He had completely forgotten his experience. However, Iswaran reminded him about the ghost. He told Mahendra that he had heard the sound coming from Mahendra's room and had come to see him. Mahendra was horrified at this reminder. He decided to leave the place next day and handed over his papers.

Word Meaning

Word	Meaning
keep an eye on	look after
coming up	being constructed
ill-equipped	not having proper facilities
makeshift	temporary
quarry	a place or deep pit from which stones are extract
uncomplainingly	without any protest
anecdotes	a real story about an incident or person
desolate	uninhabited or isolated
conjure up	make
dozing	sleeping
thriller	novel with an exciting plot
running to	consisting of
hold in thrall	captivate attention
sprawled	lie, spread out

Word	Meaning
hauled	pull or drag with effort
mahout	person who controls an elephant
prologue	introduction
tusker	elephant with big tusks
emulation	imitation
smash	break something noisily
depredations	destruction/damage
menacingly	frighteningly
red eyed	angrily
trumpeted	cried loudly (for elephant)
mustering	to collect or gain
whacked	strike forcefully
revive	bring back to consciousness
shrug casually	raise shoulders uncaringly
credible	something that can be believed

Word	Meaning
inimitable	typical
more than make up for	replace with ease
culinary skills	cooking ability
garish	detailed and showy
reverie	daydreaming
matted	tangled in a thick mass
shrivelled	wrinkled and shrunken
figment of imagination	something that can be mape up, invented or imagined
figment	made up
retired	went to sleep
sulk	be silent out of disappointment.
unease	anxiety
vicinity	the area near or surrounding a particular place.

Word	Meaning
sea of darkness	total darkness
moan	a low sound made by a person expressing suffering.
prowling	move in a quiet manner
guttural	sound produced from back of throat
lest	to avoid any risk
behold	see or observe
wailing	crying
feline	like a cat
panting	breathing with short quick breaths
ghastly	causing horror or fear
subconscious	part of mind which he was unaware of

NCERT FOLDER

NCERT Intext and Exercise Questions

THINKING ABOUT IT (NCERT PAGE 18)

Q.1 In what way is Iswaran an asset to Mahendra?

Or Mention any two qualities of Iswaran which made him an asset to Mahendra.

Ans. Iswaran was called Mahendra's asset because of his complete dedication towards his master. He cooked for him, washed his clothes and chatted with him at night. He was also a great storyteller and entertained Mahendra with his stories. Thus, he was a hard-working and loyal servant.

Q.2 How does Iswaran describe the uprooted tree on the highway? What effect does he want to create in his listeners?

Or How did Iswaran the storyteller describe the uprooted tree?

Ans. Iswaran describes the uprooted tree on the highway in a very dramatic way. He begins by saying that the road was empty and he was all alone. Suddenly, he spotted something that looked like a large bushy beast lying across the road.

As he came closer, he saw that it was a fallen tree, with its dry branches spread out. He wanted to create a long-lasting effect on the listener. He used suspense and a surprise ending to narrate every small incident to make it effective.

Q.3 How does he narrate the story of the tusker? Does it appear to be plausible?

or How did Iswaran make himself the hero in the elephant story?

or How did Iswaran manage to bring down the mad elephant?

or According to Iswaran how did he tackle the elephant in the school building?

Ans. One day, Iswaran narrated the story of a mad elephant or tusker to Mahendra. The mad elephant had escaped the timber yard and entered the town. It was destroying every thing that came in its path. The elephant, then, entered the school ground.

Seeing the wild elephant, the boys of the school locked themselves in classrooms and the teachers ran to the terrace.

Iswaran informed Mahendra that he was in junior class at that time. He took a cane from one of his teachers and ran to the ground. Then, he hit the elephant on its third toenail. As a result, the elephant fell onto the ground.

This incident does not appear to be sensible or real as it is difficult to believe that a child could control a wild and aggressive elephant.

Q.4 Why does the author say that Iswaran seemed to more than make up for the absence of a TV in Mahendra's living quarters?

Ans. The author says so because Iswaran provided a great company to Mahendra. He would chat with Mahendra at night, when he returned from his work. Iswaran would also entertain Mahendra by telling stories. Thus, with Iswaran around, Mahendra never felt bored and never felt the necessity of having a TV for entertainment.

Q.5 Mahendra calls ghosts or spirits a figment of the imagination. What happens to him on a full moon night?

Ans. Mahendra calls ghosts and spirits a figment of imagination when Iswaran told him that the place at which they were living was a burial ground and he had seen ghosts at night. However, Mahendra was frightened and disturbed when he encountered the ghost himself.

On one full moon night, Mahendra woke up when he heard a low moan close to his window but he did not look outside. When the sound became louder he looked out. He saw a dark cloudy figure holding a bundle. This sight terrified him. He broke into cold sweat and fell back on the pillow.

Q.6 Can you think of some other ending for the story?

Ans. The story could have ended on a more positive note. Instead of leaving the place, Mahendra could have been shown to be a courageous man who proved the ghost theory wrong.

Another ending can be of both Mahendra and Iswaran continuing to live in that place out of necessity and later, realising that the scary figure was not a ghost but some other person.

TALK ABOUT IT (NCERT PAGE 18)

Q.1 Is Iswaran a fascinating storyteller? Discuss with your friends the qualities of a good storyteller. Try to use these qualities and tell a story.

Ans. Yes, Iswaran is a fascinating storyteller. He knows how to build up suspense in his stories. He uses dramatic gestures to make his stories realistic.

A good storyteller should have the following qualities.

(*i*) He should have good oratorical skills, acting out what he is telling.

(*ii*) He should be able to vary the tone of his voice according to the situation.

(*iii*) He should be able to create and maintain the interest of the listeners through the use of suspense.

(*iv*) He should have a vivid imagination to think up interesting stories.

(*v*) He should have a sense of humour which he should use effectively for making his stories enjoyable.

Ans. Tell a story: Do it yourself

REVIEW EXERCISE

Including Competency Based Questions

Part–I

Multiple Choice Questions

1. According to Iswaran, earlier the factory site was a

(a) market place
(b) dumping ground
(c) burial ground
(d) citadel

Ans. (c) burial ground

2. How did Iswaran make the elephant unconscious?

(a) Using a gun
(b) Shooting at him
(c) Giving him injection
(d) Using Japanese Martial Art Karate (Jiu-Jitsu)

Ans. (d) Using Japanese Martial Art Karate (Jiu-Jitsu)

3. What did Mahendra tell Iswaran after hearing the ghosts' story?

(a) He was lying
(b) It was horrible
(c) Ghosts do not exist in reality
(d) All of the above

Ans. (d) All of the above

4. Why did Mahendra want to shift from his workplace?

(a) He didn't like the place
(b) Weather didn't suit him
(c) Because of the fear of ghosts
(d) All of the above

Ans. (c) Because of the fear of ghosts

5. Why does Iswaran use dramatic suspense and surprise in his story narration?

(a) To catch the attention of the listeners
(b) To boast
(c) To fake
(d) To befool others

Ans. (a) To catch the attention of the listeners

6. How did Iswaran describe the uprooted tree?

(a) Adding suspense and surprise
(b) Using hands and eyes dramatically
(c) Catching the attention
(d) All of the above

Ans. (d) All of the above

7. What influenced Iswaran's style of narration?

(a) Tamil Thrillers (b) His father
(c) His grandmother (d) None of these

Ans. (a) Tamil Thrillers

8. According to Iswaran, what made the story interesting and enjoyable?

(a) Elaborated descriptions
(b) Suspense and surprise
(c) Dramatic sense
(d) All of the above

Ans. (d) All of the above

9. What kind of a person did Mahendra claim himself to be?

(a) Intelligent (b) Well read
(c) Brave and rational (d) All of these

Ans. (c) Brave and rational

10. What did Mahendra see from the window?

(a) A cat running after a mouse
(b) Dark cloud like form holding a bundle
(c) A mouse
(d) A friend

Ans. (b) Dark cloud like form holding a bundle

11. How did Iswaran entertain Mahendra?

(a) Telling him stories just like a television
(b) By scaring him like ghosts
(c) By telling him jokes
(d) None of the above

Ans. (a) Telling him stories just like a television

12. What kind of person was Iswaran?

(a) Curious learner
(b) Dedicated, loyal and obedient worker
(c) Multitalented full of positive traits
(d) All of the above

Ans. (d) All of the above

Extract Based Questions

1. Read the given extract carefully and answer the questions that follow.

Mahendra's job was to keep an eye on the activities at the work site. He had to keep moving from place to place every now and then as ordered by his head office: from a coal mining area to a railway bridge construction site, from there after a few months to a chemical plant which was coming up somewhere.

(i) What kind of job did Mahendra have, and what did it entail?

Ans. Mahendra was a junior supervisor who worked at various construction sites. His job involved overseeing activities at factories, bridges and dams. He frequently moved from one site to another, ensuring everything ran smoothly and according to plan.

(ii) The statement that is true about Mahendra, according to the extract is

(a) Mahendra was a constructor.
(b) Mahendra loved his work of travelling.
(c) Mahendra was a young supervisor.
(d) Mahendra lived all alone.

Ans. (c) Mahendra was a young supervisor.

(iii) Complete the sentence appropriately.
From the given extract, we can infer that Mahendra ....

Ans. did not have a stable home

(iv) Complete the sentence appropriately.
When the writer says 'to keep an eye on', he means

Ans. to supervise

2. Read the given extract carefully and answer the questions that follow.

"The road was deserted and I was all alone. Suddenly I spotted something that looked like an enormous bushy beast lying sprawled across the road. I was half inclined to turn and go back. But I came closer I saw that it was a fallen tree, with its dry branches spread out."

(i) The given lines are said by .... (Mahendra/Iswaran)

Ans. Iswaran

(ii) What can be deduced about the speaker as a storyteller from the given passage?

Ans. It can be deduced that the speaker is an imaginative storyteller who is able to capture the attention of his audience with his words. He is able to take the most common occurences and narrate them in a way that the most boring things like a felled tree could be turned into a thrilling monstrous creature.

(iii) Is the given statement True or False?

'The speaker came upon a huge, monstrous beast and overcame it.'

Ans. False

(iv) The fallen tree is described as

(a) a beast (b) an alien

(c) a pipe (d) a snake

Ans. (a) a beast

3. Read the given extract carefully and answer the questions that follow.

"There is a richly wooded forest all around. The logs are hauled on to the lorries by elephants. They are huge well-fed beasts. When they turn wild even the most experienced mahout is not able to control them." After this prologue Iswaran would launch into an elaborate anecdote involving an elephant.

(i) 'There' as mentioned in the given lines refer to ……… .

Ans. Iswaran's village.

(ii) What can be said about Iswaran from the given extract?

1. Iswaran was a lazy person.

2. Iswaran was an amazing storyteller.

3. Iswaran had trouble talking to others.

4. Iswaran had a poor memory.

5. Iswaran was not interested in telling stories.

Select the correct option.

(a) 1 and 5 (b) Only 2

(c) 3 and 4 (d) Only 4

Ans. (b) Only 2

(iii) Complete the sentence appropriately.

When the writer says, 'after this prologue', he means ……… .

Ans. after giving an introduction.

(iv) How did Iswaran narrate his stories, and how did they affect Mahendra?

Ans. Iswaran narrated his stories with great drama, using suspense and surprise endings. He often included exaggerated details and vivid descriptions. Mahendra enjoyed these stories, finding them entertaining and engaging, even though they sometimes left him uneasy or spooked.

4. Read the given extract carefully and answer the questions that follow.

Mahendra who had been listening with rapt attention would be left hanging. When he returned, Iswaran would not pick up the thread of the story right away. Mahendra would have to remind him that the conclusion was pending. "Well, a veterinary doctor was summoned to revive the animal."

(i) The animal referred to in the given extract is ……… .

Ans. a wild elephant

(ii) Choose the options that lists the set of statements that are not true according to the given extract.

1. Iswaran was an amazing storyteller.

2. Mahendra loved listening to Iswaran's stories.

3. Iswaran was Mahendra's roommate.

4. Iswaran would always complete the story properly.

5. Mahendra would wait for Iswaran to complete the story.

(a) 1, 2, 3 (b) 3, 4 (c) 1, 3, 5 (d) 2, 4

Ans. (b) 3, 4

(iii) What could be Iswaran's intention behind leaving the story unfinished?

Ans. Iswaran's intention behind leaving the story unfinished was to arouse interest and anticipation in Mahendra.

(iv) The phrase 'Thread of the story' means ……………. .

Ans. storyline

Short Answer Type Questions

1. Why did Mahendra have to keep moving from one place to another?

Ans. Mahendra was a junior supervisor in a firm which provided supervisors for various types of construction sites. His job was to keep an eye on the activities at the work site.

As one site's work was over, he would have to move to another site. Thus, he had to keep moving from place to place.

2. What were Iswaran's duties in Mahendra's house?

***or* Who was Iswaran? What all he did for his master?**

Ans. Iswaran was Mahendra's cook who used to carry out all domestic works for him. He cooked delicious dishes for him, washed his clothes and kept his house clean. Besides, he would entertain Mahendra with his endless stories.

3. How did Iswaran show his usefulness to the narrator?

Ans. Iswaran showed his usefulness to the narrator by somehow getting vegetables and cooking ingredients even when no shops were there for miles around.

He could also prepare the most delicious dishes with fresh vegetables.

4. What made Iswaran so imaginative and a good narrator? Competency Based

Ans. Imagination is an outcome of deep thinking, sharp insight and extensive reading. Iswaran loved to read. In his free time, he would read popular Tamil thrillers that ran upto hundreds of pages. The imaginative descriptions and its narratives influenced him so much that he would use the same methods in his storytelling.

5. Why did Mahendra become fond of Iswaran?

Ans. Mahendra became fond of Iswaran because Iswaran was not only his domestic helper but also a good storyteller.

Iswaran's style of storytelling entertained Mahendra. He would add elements of suspense, thriller, horror and adventure which replaced the absence of a television in his quarters.

6. What destruction did the elephant cause in the town?

Ans. The elephant caused major destruction in the town by breaking tree branches and fences, smashing fruit stalls, and entering the school playground by breaking a brick wall. In the school, he destroyed a football goal post, tore down the volleyball net and crushed the water drum.

7. Why did Mahendra listen to Iswaran's stories without interrupting him?

Ans. Mahendra listened to Iswaran's stories without interrupting him because of the interesting and special way in which the stories were narrated.

Iswaran had replaced the entertainment value of a TV in Mahendra's living quarters. Because of Iswaran's stories, the absence of a source of entertainment was never felt in the house.

8. Why did Iswaran want to cook something special for dinner?

Ans. Iswaran wanted to make something special for dinner because that day was an auspicious day to feed the spirits of the ancestors. So, special delicacies were prepared by Iswaran.

9. When did Mahendra expect Iswaran to be bad-tempered? Did it really happen?

Ans. Mahendra expected Iswaran to be bad-tempered after Mahendra had scolded him for believing in ghosts and spirits. However, next morning, Mahendra found Iswaran as cheerful and talkative as ever. Iswaran never minded the rebukes of his master and remained devoted to him.

10. What impact did Iswaran's story of a female ghost have on Mahendra?

Ans. Iswaran's story of a female ghost disturbed Mahendra a lot. After hearing it, he would always look outside through his window to make sure that there was no movement. Before hearing the story, Mahendra loved to look at the landscape on full moon nights. Now, he completely avoided looking outside.

11. Do you think the ghost Mahendra saw on the night of the full moon was a real ghost?

Ans. No, the ghost that Mahendra saw on the night of the full moon was not a real ghost. It was a creation of his affected mind. Iswaran had affected Mahendra's thinking by telling him the ghost story.

When Mahendra rebuked him for believing in ghosts, he felt offended. To prove that he was right, he probably posed as a ghost. That was how he could later say that Mahendra had seen a ghost at night.

12. What did Mahendra decide after he had seen the ghost? Why?

Ans. After Mahendra saw a dark cloudy figure outside his window, he became very terrified. He was scared at the thought of the presence of ghosts in the location. So, Mahendra decided to leave the place the next day.

13. How did the factory's location play a role in Iswaran's ghost story?

Ans. The factory's location played a role in Iswaran's ghost story because it was built on an old burial ground. Iswaran claimed to have found human skulls and said he sometimes saw ghosts at night, adding to the eerie atmosphere and Mahendra's growing fear.

14. Analyse the story's conclusion. How does Mahendra's reaction to the supposed ghost sighting highlight his character development and the story's theme? Competency Based

Ans. The story's conclusion shows Mahendra's significant character development and reinforces the theme of fear and belief. Initially, Mahendra dismisses Iswaran's ghost stories as nonsense. However, after experiencing a supposed ghost sighting, his attitude changes. Seeing the dark, ghostly figure outside his window frightens him deeply. This reaction highlights Mahendra's vulnerability and the power of fear, even in a rational person. His decision to leave the site immediately shows that, despite his doubt, he is greatly affected by the supernatural possibility. The conclusion emphasises how deeply stories and imagination can influence perception and behaviour.

Long Answer Type Questions

1. Iswaran was a fascinating storyteller. How was he an asset to Mahendra? What skills did he have?

or **"Iswaran was a good cook as well as story teller". Elaborate with the help of examples.**

or **Give a character sketch of Iswaran.**

Ans. Iswaran was Mahendra's cook. He was an asset to Mahendra. He would follow his master wherever he went without any complaints. Not only did he cook delicious food for Mahendra but also clean his house and wash his clothes.

Iswaran's resourcefulness as a person did not end with him being a domestic help. He was also a great storyteller and entertainer. Due to this love for reading popular Tamil thrillers, he had all those qualities that are required for story telling.

Even while narrating the smallest of incidents, he would add suspense and surprise to make the story thrilling. He would use his voice and body movements to capture the attention of his listeners.

His style of storytelling was so interesting that Mahendra would sit every evening to listen to Iswaran's stories. Iswaran's presence, thus, made up for the absence of a television or source of entertainment in Mahendra's house.

2. What qualities of Iswaran make him a fascinating storyteller?

Ans. The qualities of Iswaran that make him a fascinating storyteller are as follows:

(i) He gives an imaginative descriptions of events.

(ii) He uses dramatic language and gestures to describe any situation.

(iii) He changes a simple event into a story full of suspense.

(iv) He creates surprising endings or unexpected twists and turns in his narration.

(v) All his stories have some elements of adventure, horror and suspense in them.

3. Examine the significance of the supernatural elements in the story. How do Iswaran's ghost stories influence Mahendra's perception of reality and his actions?

Ans. The supernatural elements in the story add intrigue and suspense. Iswaran's ghost stories significantly impact Mahendra's perception of reality and actions. Initially, Mahendra dismisses the stories as nonsense. However, the vivid and eerie details of Iswaran's tales gradually make Mahendra uneasy.

After hearing about the ghostly woman, Mahendra feels scared, particularly during full Moons. He avoids looking out his window and becomes more alert to strange sounds or movements. One night, he sees a ghostly figure outside his window, which terrifies him. This experience makes him believe that the place is haunted. Ultimately, the influence of Iswaran's ghost stories leads Mahendra to leave the construction site, showing how deeply the supernatural tales affected him.

4. Discuss the role of humour in the story, particularly in Iswaran's anecdotes. How does R.K. Laxman use humour to enhance the narrative and develop the characters?

Ans. Humour is key in the story, especially in Iswaran's anecdotes. Iswaran often adds exaggerated details and dramatic gestures to his stories, making them amusing and entertaining. For example, he describes an uprooted tree as a 'bushy beast' and mimics a mad elephant's behaviour, which adds a comedic touch.

R.K. Laxman uses humour to make the story more engaging and lively. Humour also helps to develop Iswaran's character, showing him as a creative person who enjoys entertaining others. It contrasts with Mahendra's more serious and practical nature. The humour enhances the story by providing lighthearted moments and showing the bond between Mahendra and Iswaran through shared laughter and enjoyment.

5. How does Iswaran's storytelling ability impact Mahendra's experience at various construction sites, and what does this reveal about their relationship? **Competency Based**

Ans. Iswaran's storytelling ability significantly impacts Mahendra's experience at various construction sites by providing entertainment and companionship. Mahendra often worked in remote and sometimes harsh locations, which could be lonely and boring. Iswaran's engaging and dramatic stories brought excitement and distraction.

Iswaran's storytelling also revealed the close relationship between Mahendra and Iswaran. Mahendra uncritically listened to Iswaran's tales, indicating his trust and fondness for his cook. Even though the stories Iswaran told were hard to believe, Mahendra appreciated having Iswaran around and listening to his stories. Their relationship showed that Iswaran was not just a servant but an important part of Mahendra's life, giving him emotional support and companionship.

ASSESSMENT EXERCISE

Extract Based Questions

Read the following extract carefully and answer the questions that follow.

Mahendra was jerked out of the pleasant reverie he had drifted into after the satisfying meal.

'I knew on the first day itself when I saw a human skull lying on the path. Even now I come across a number of skulls and bones,' Iswaran murmured.

(i) Why did Mahendra jerk out of his pleasant reverie?

(ii) Choose the options that lists the set of statements that are not true according to the given extract.

1. Mahendra already knew about the place being a burial ground.
2. Mahendra did not believe in Iswaran.
3. Iswaran was pranking Mahendra.
4. Mahendra does not like what Iswaran had told him.

(a) 1 and 3
(b) 1 and 2
(c) 3 and 4
(d) 2 and 4

(iii) How did Iswaran get to know that the place was a burial ground?

(iv) The phrase 'jerked out' means ....

Short Answer (SA) Type Questions

1. Describe Iswaran's daily routine.
2. How does Iswaran's description of the uprooted tree on the highway affect his listeners?
3. How did Iswaran control the wild elephant?
4. Do you think the ghost seen by Mahendra was only a trick played by his cook Iswaran? Elaborate.
5. Why did Mahendra expect that Iswaran will sulk?
6. How did Iswaran's reading of Tamil thrillers affect his behaviour?
7. Was Iswaran's story of how he tackled the wild elephant real? Why or why not?
8. How did Iswaran's story of the female ghost affect Mahendra's behaviour?

Long Answer (LA) Type Questions

1. How can you explain the female ghost that Mahendra thought he saw? Suggest two alternatives.
2. Could the story have ended differently after Mahendra thought that he 'saw' a female ghost? Give details of how you would have ended the story.

In the Kingdom of Fools

CHAPTER 4

by AK Ramanujan

CHAPTER SUMMARY The story 'In the Kingdom of Fools' has been written by AK Ramanujan. It is a story about a kingdom ruled by a foolish king and his foolish minister. They pass a strange order that is to be followed by the people. The story focuses on the death of a thief and how it leads the Guru to save the kingdom from the stupidity of the king and his minister. It highlights the dangers posed by the foolish people. It also emphasises the view that foolish people like the king and his minister can be very difficult to manage. Fools live in their own paradise and cannot be easily impressed by others. They can only be handled by wise people like the Guru.

The Strange Kingdom of Fools

Once there was a kingdom of fools where both the king and the minister were idiots. They wanted to do something different from the other kings so they decided to reverse everything. They ordered everyone to sleep in the day and work at night. If anybody in the kingdom disobeyed this, they would be punished with death.

Arrival of Guru and his Disciple

One day, a Guru and his disciple arrived in this kingdom. They were surprised to find that everyone in the kingdom was sleeping during the day. Even the animals had been taught to sleep during the day.

As soon as it was night, everyone woke up and started doing their work. By this time, the Guru and disciple had become very hungry so they went to buy groceries in a shop. It was surprising for them that everything had the same cost, a single *duddu*.

Decision of Guru to Leave the City

Initially, the Guru and his disciple were happy as they could buy all the food in a *duddu*. However, the Guru soon realised that it was the kingdom of fools and he decided to leave the place. He told his disciple that the behaviour of the fools cannot be predicted and it was not safe to stay there. However, the disciple was not ready, as he loved to eat and the food was cheap in the kingdom. Finally, the Guru left the kingdom alone. Everyday the disciple ate the cheap food and became fat.

Incident of Theft in a Merchant's House

One day, a thief broke into a rich merchant's house by making a hole in the wall. When the thief was carrying out stolen goods, the wall of the old house fell on his head and he died on the spot.

The thief's brother went to the king and complained that the owner of the house i.e. merchant should be punished for his brother's death.

The Owner of the House was Summoned

The king called the merchant in his court and told him that due to the weak wall of his house, the thief had died and now, he would be punished. However, the merchant claimed that the wall was built in his father's time and it was the fault of the bricklayer who built the wall.

Bricklayer and Dancing Girl were Summoned

The bricklayer was brought into the court. He said that when he was building the wall, his mind was distracted towards the jingling sound of the dancing girl's anklets. So, she should be punished instead of him.

The king was satisfied with the bricklayer's explanation and the dancing girl was brought into the court. She shifted the blame to the goldsmith. She said that she had to walk up and down the street many times because the goldsmith had delayed her order.

Goldsmith and Rich Merchant were Summoned

The goldsmith was brought into the court. He defended himself by saying that he could not complete the dancing girl's order in time because he had to finish a rich merchant's order. This rich merchant was the father of the merchant whose house's wall had fallen. So, the merchant was summoned again.

The merchant now stated that the jewellery had been ordered by his father but he was dead now.

So, the king decided that the merchant had inherited his father's riches as well as sins. Therefore, he should be punished in place of his dead father.

The Disciple in Trouble

A new stake was ordered for the execution but the merchant was too thin to fit the stake. So, it was decided that a person who could fit into the stake should be found. The disciple was found fat enough to fit the stake so he was brought into the court for the punishment. The disciple remembered his Guru's words that it was a city of fools and they could harm him. He, thus, prayed to his Guru.

The Guru saw everything by his magical powers and arrived to save his disciple. He explained a plan to the disciple in his ear to escape the execution.

Guru Fools the King

The Guru tried to trap the king in his words. The Guru and his disciple started fighting to decide who should be executed first. The king was confused by their behaviour. He asked the Guru why both of them wanted to die first. The Guru replied that it was the stake of God. Whoever died first would become the king in the next birth and the person who died next would become the minister.

Decision of Foolish King

After listening to the Guru, the king and his minister decided that they will die in place of the Guru and his disciple. They did not want to lose their kingdom in their next life.

So, they secretly went to the prison and released the Guru and the disciple. They disguised themselves to look like the Guru and the disciple. Then, they put themselves in their places and were executed the next morning.

New King and Minister

After the death of the king and minister, the people of the kingdom requested the Guru and his disciple to be their new king and the minister. The Guru and his disciple agreed to the proposal on one condition that the old laws must be changed. Now, the kingdom became just like any other kingdom where day was day and nothing could be bought for a single *duddu*.

Word Meaning

Word	Meaning
astonishment	surprise
duddu	unit of money
sneak	move secretly
collapsed	fell down
pursuing his ancient trade	doing his traditional work
blame	to charge of
compensate	to make good for the losses
summoned	called
sacred	holy
such and such	(imaginary name)
burgled	robbed
accused	convict
tied hand and foot	completely
execution	punishment by death
pleaded	argued
case deepens	matter is complicated
goldsmith	person who makes gold jewellery
scoundrel	dishonest person
damned	used to show anger

Word	Meaning
culprit	person responsible for a misdeed
bailiffs	officers enforcing the law
accusation	a claim about something wrong
impatient	not willing to wait
made a mess	in trouble
consulted	took the advice of
ruled decisively	gave his final decision
inherited	received as an heir
stake	a wooden post on which criminals are tied for being executed
final impaling	execution, pierce with a sharpened stake
sanyasi	a religious person (in Hindi)
decree	command
scrape	difficult situation
clamour	strongly protest
earshot	hearing distance
ascetic	a person who is free of worldly pleasures
executioners	persons who carry out executions
disguised themselves	changed their appearance
mourned	felt sad at the death

NCERT FOLDER

NCERT Intext and Exercise Questions

THINK ABOUT IT (NCERT PAGE 27)

Q.1 What are the two strange things the guru and his disciple find in the Kingdom of Fools?

Or **What did the Guru and the disciple find in the city of fools?**

Or **Which two things amazed the guru and his disciple when they arrived in the Kingdom of Fools?**

Ans. The first strange thing observed by the Guru and his disciple in the kingdom of Fools is that people and even animals slept throughout the day. All work was done during the night.

The second strange thing observed by them was that everything in the kingdom had the same cost, i.e., one *duddu*. Whether it was gold or a bunch of bananas, everything had the same value or cost.

Q.2 Why does the disciple decide to stay in the Kingdom of Fools? Was it a good idea?

Or **Why does the disciple not want to leave the Kingdom of Fools?**

Or **Why was the disciple not interested in leaving the Kingdom of Fools?**

Ans. The disciple decided to stay in the Kingdom of Fools because all the food available in the kingdom cost the same price and was very cheap.

According to the Guru, staying there was not a good idea as they were all fools and he was not sure about what they would do in the future.

Q.3 Name all the people who are tried in the king's court and give the reasons for their trial.

Ans. The following people were tried in the king's court

(i) **The Merchant** He was accused of murder because the wall which killed the thief belonged to him.

(ii) **The Bricklayer** He was accused of murder because he had built the wall.

(iii) **The Dancing Girl** She was accused because her jingling anklets had distracted the bricklayer.

(iv) **The Goldsmith** He was accused because he didn't complete the dancing girl's order on time.

(v) **the Merchant (Second Time)** He was accused because his father forced the goldsmith to finish his job first and thus, delayed the dancing girl's order.

Q.4 Who is the real culprit according to the king? Why does he escape punishment?

Ans. According to the king, the real culprit was the rich merchant. The king believed that the merchant had inherited his father's sins and crimes. Therefore, he decided to punish the merchant.

The merchant escaped punishment because he was too thin to fit on the new stake made for him.

Q.5 What are the Guru's words of wisdom? When does the disciple remember them?

Ans. The Guru's words of wisdom were that it was the Kingdom of Fools and nothing could be predicted about the behaviour of foolish people.

The disciple remembered this when he was going to be executed.

Q.6 How does the guru manage to save his disciple's life?

Or **How did the guru make the king change his mind about the execution?**

Or **What did the guru do to save his disciple's life? Was he successful in doing so?**

Ans. The guru tried to confuse the king by telling him that whoever is executed first will become the king in the next birth. The king believed him and later on, offered himself to be executed first so that he may remain king in the next birth. In this way, the guru was successful in saving his disciple's life.

REVIEW EXERCISE

Including Competency Based Questions

Part - I

Multiple Choice Questions

1. What kind of story is this?

(a) A folktale (b) A mocktale

(c) A humorous story (d) A serious story

Ans. (a) A folktale

2. What does this story throw light upon?

(a) Foolish people and the dangers they pose

(b) Kings and their ministers

(c) The virtue of being happy

(d) Wise people and their merits

Ans. (a) Foolish people and the dangers they pose

3. Why did the king and the minister decide to change night into day and day into night?

(a) They didn't want to rule the kingdom like other kings

(b) They were idiots

(c) Both (a) and (b)

(d) None of the above

Ans. (c) Both (a) and (b)

4. Why are the people in the kingdom called foolish?

(a) Because they follow all the ridiculous orders passed by their king

(b) Because they listen to their king

(c) Because they do silly things

(d) Because they are foolish

Ans. (a) Because they follow all the ridiculous orders passed by their king

5. Which of the following events made the Guru realise that it was a Kingdom of Fools?

(a) When everyone was asleep during the day.

(b) When everyone was working at the night.

(c) When everything cost the same-a single duddu.

(d) All of the above

Ans. (d) All of the above

6. Why did the guru decide to leave the place?

(a) Because of some urgent work
(b) He had a message to leave the place
(c) King ordered to leave the place
(d) Because he thought that it was not safe to be with fools for a long time

Ans. (d) Because he thought that it was not safe to be with fools for a long time

7. Which 'ancient trade' is being talked about by the thief's brother?

(a) Goldsmith (b) Robbery
(c) Bricklaying (d) Dancing

Ans. (b) Robbery

8. Who among the following was summoned to the court twice?

(a) The goldsmith (b) The bricklayer
(c) The dancing girl (d) The rich merchant

Ans. (d) The rich merchant

9. Which of the following statements is False?

(a) The disciple grew fat like a street-side sacred bull.
(b) The thief's brother complained to the king.
(c) The dancing girl put the blame on the bricklayer.
(d) The rich merchant was too thin to be properly executed on the stake.

Ans. (c) The dancing girl put the blame on the bricklayer.

10. According to the king, the merchant deserved the punishment because ....

(a) the man who ordered the jewellery was the rich merchant's father.
(b) the goldsmith put the blame on the rich merchant.
(c) he had inherited everything from his father, his riches and his sins.
(d) None of the above

Ans. (c) he had inherited everything from his father, his riches and his sins.

11. What do you understand by the term 'a street-side sacred bull'?

(a) The disciple started lookin like a bull.
(b) The disciple was considered sacred.
(c) He became overweight like a bull.
(d) He started living on street-side.

Ans. (c) He became overweight like a bull.

12. Why was the disciple being executed?

(a) He burgled the rich merchant's house.
(b) He was fat enough to fit into the stake.
(c) He was living illegally in the kingdom.
(d) He killed the thief.

Ans. (b) He was fat enough to fit into the stake.

13. Why were the guru and his disciple arguing among themselves?

(a) To fool the king and the minster.
(b) Both of them wanted to be the king in next life by getting executed first on the new stake.
(c) Both of them wanted to annoy the king and the minister.
(d) Both of them were quarrelsome.

Ans. (a) To fool the king and the minster.

14. "Do you know why we want to die right now, the two of us?"— Who are the 'two of us' in the given line?

(a) The king and the minister
(b) The guru and the disciple
(c) The bricklayer and the rich merchant
(d) The goldsmith and the dancing girl

Ans. (b) The guru and the disciple

15. How did the Guru save the people of the kingdom?

(a) By flattering the king
(b) Making the king believe that the new stake will bring fortune
(c) By helping the kingdom get rid of the foolish king and his silly minister
(d) All of the above

Ans. (d) All of the above

16. The guru said that it was the stake of ....

(a) God of wealth (b) God of justice
(c) God of execution (d) None of these

Ans. (b) God of justice

17. Why did the king and his minister decide to go for the stake themselves?

(a) Because of Guru's words and their greed to take the benefit themselves
(b) People's words
(c) Guru's cunning words
(d) Man's plight

Ans. (a) Because of Guru's words and their greed to take the benefit themselves

18. What message does the story convey?

1. One should stay away from the foolish people, else one is bound to suffer.

2. One should use wisdom rather than logic to tackle foolish people.

3. Fools can be beneficial for sometime but they are very dangerous.

(a) 1 and 2 (b) Only 1
(c) Only 3 (d) All of these

Ans. (d) All of these

Extract Based Questions

1. Read the following extract carefully and answer the questions that follow.

The two strangers were amazed by what they saw around them and wandered around town till evening, when suddenly the whole town woke up and went about its nightly business.

(i) Who are the two strangers in the given extract?

Ans. The two strangers in the given extract are a guru and his disciple

(ii) Why were they amazed?

Ans. They were amazed because during the day no one did anything. There was no one in the town. However, at night, people started coming out of their houses and started working.

(iii) What was the nightly business?

(a) Sleeping (b) Constructing
(c) Day-to-day activities (d) Robbery

Ans. (c) Day-to-day activities

(iv) Complete the analogy by selecting a suitable word from the text.

Friends : Foes :: Acquaintances : ....

Ans. Strangers

2. Read the following extract carefully and answer the questions that follow.

His brother ran to the king and complained, "Your Highness, when my brother was pursuing his ancient trade, a wall fell on him and killed him."

(i) Who is 'his' in the given lines?

(a) The rich merchant (b) The thief
(c) The bricklayer (d) The jeweller

Ans. (b) The thief

(ii) What is the ancient trade being referred to by the speaker?

Ans. The ancient trade being referred to by the speaker is theft.

(iii) The brother was .... when the incident happened.

Ans. stealing

(iv) Which 'wall' fell on him?

Ans. The wall of the rich merchant's house fell on him.

3. Read the following extract carefully and answer the questions that follow.

The king was now thrown into deep thought. He didn't want to lose the Kingdom to someone else in the next round of life. He needed time. So he ordered the execution postponed to the next day and talked in secret with his Minister. "It is not right for us to give over the Kingdom to others in the next life. Let's go on to stake ourselves and we'll be reborn as king and Minister again. Holy men do not tell lies", he said, and the Minister agreed.

(i) Why was the King thrown into deep thought?

Ans. The king was thrown into deep thought because he was in a dilemma as to keep his word or lose his kingdom.

(ii) Why did the King postpone the execution for the next day? Did he keep his promise to the holy man?

Ans. The King postponed the execution for the next day because he didn't want to give his kingdom to others in the next life. No, the king did not keep his promise to the holy man.

(iii) Which characteristic is displayed by the King in the above extract?

(a) Greed (b) Ambition
(c) Foolishness (d) Desperation

Ans. (a) Greed

(iv) Why did the king need time?

Ans. The king needed some time to find the solution to the threat of losing his kingdom in his next birth.

4. Read the following extract carefully and answer the questions that follow.

That was when this bricklayer saw me. It's not my fault. My Lord, it's the damned goldsmith's fault. "Poor thing, she's absolutely right," thought the king, weighing the evidence. We've got the real culprit at last.

(i) Who is the 'poor thing' in these lines?

Ans. The dancing girl is the 'poor thing' in the given lines.

(ii) Select the option that correctly captures the usage of the word 'fault' from the extract.

(a) A landscape broken by numerous faults will result in devastation.
(b) A fire was caused by an electrical fault.
(c) It was Ramya's fault that she trusted a stranger.
(d) Federer took advantage of his opponent's fault and gained a point.

Ans. (c) It was Ramya's fault that she trusted a stranger.

(iii) Complete the sentence appropriately.
The fault referred to in the extract is ....

Ans. the death of the thief

(iv) Complete the analogy by selecting a suitable word from the text.

Admire : Detest :: Innocent : ....

Ans. Culprit

5. Read the following extract carefully and answer the questions that follow.

The two men were hungry. Now that the shops were open, they went to buy some groceries. To their astonishment, they found that everything cost the same, a single duddu- whether they bought a measure of rice or bunch of bananas, it cost a duddu. The guru and his disciple were delighted. They had never heard of anything like this. They could buy all the food they wanted for a rupee.

(i) Why was the Guru and his disciple delighted?

Ans. The guru and his disciple were delighted because everything cost the same i.e. a single duddu.

(ii) Choose the option that lists the statements that are not true according to the given extract.

1. The Guru and his disciple were hungry.

2. The Guru and his disciple found the Kingdom strange.

3. The disciple wanted to leave the kingdom.

4. The Guru had recognised the Kingdom of Fools.

5. The Guru wanted to have cheap food and decided to settle in the Kingdom itself.

6. The King and the Minister of the Kingdom were wise people.

(a) 1, 2 and 3 (b) 2, 3 and 6

(c) 3, 5 and 6 (d) 4, 5 and 6

Ans. (c) 3, 5 and 6

(iii) What did they do after the shops were opened?

Ans. They went to buy groceries after all shops were opened.

(iv) Why were the shops closed in the Kingdom earlier?

Ans. The shops in the kingdom were closed because everyone had been asleep during day time by the order of the king.

Part-II

Short Answer Type Questions

1. What did the king and the minister do to change night into day and day into night?

Ans. To change night into day and day into night, the King and the minister ordered everyone to work at night and sleep in the day as soon as the Sun rises.

2. Why were the guru and his disciple surprised?

Ans. The guru and his disciple were surprised when they went to buy some grocery in the Kingdom of Fools. They found that everything cost the same i.e. a single *duddu* whether it was a measure of rice or a bunch of bananas.

3. What advice did the guru give to the disciple before going out of the city?

Ans. The advice that the guru gave to the disciple before going out of the city was that it was dangerous to stay in a Kingdom of Fools as their behaviour is unpredictable.

4. Why was the dancing girl walking up and down that street?

Ans. The dancing girl was walking up and down that street because she had given gold to the goldsmith to make some jewellery.

However, the goldsmith was busy with the order of the merchant's father and kept on promising her to give it soon, thus making her walk up and down his house a dozen times.

5. What was foolish about the king's trial of the merchant?

Or **Why did the king want to punish the merchant?**

Ans. A thief who had broken the wall of the merchant's house was killed due to the weak wall of the merchant's house collasping on his head. So, the king ordered that the merchant should be punished for the thief's death. This was a foolish judgement.

6. Why did the king order for the execution to be postponed?

Or **Why did the king decide to postpone the execution of the guru and his disciple?**

Ans. The guru made a fool of the king by telling him that the first person executed would be the king in his next birth and the second person executed would be the minister in the next birth.

As the king did not want to lose his kingdom even in his next birth, he postponed the execution so that he had time to think and take the advice of his minister.

7. What magical powers did the guru have?

Ans. The guru saw everything in a vision; he could see far, he could see the future just as the present and the past. Furthermore, he could appear anywhere at any time, just like the situation when the disciple remembered him and he appeared to save him from the stake.

8. What reason did the guru give to the king for dying first?

Ans. The guru told the king that whoever died first on that stake would be reborn as the king in his next birth and whoever died next would be reborn as the minister. That is why, the guru wanted to die first.

9. Who became the king and the minister of the kingdom?

Ans. The guru and his disciple became the king and the minister of the kingdom. When the kingdom was without a king after the death of the king, the people requested the guru to become the king and his disciple to become the minister. The guru, agreed on the condition that they could change the earlier laws.

Long Answer Type Questions

1. What values made the guru different from his disciple?

Ans. The values of farsightedness, wisdom, calmness and rationality made the guru different from his disciple. Although the guru and his disciple were both ascetics, it was the guru who made good use of the knowledge that he had accumulated over the years.

The danger of staying in the Kingdom of Fools was realised very quickly by the guru, while the disciple was easily attracted to the temptation of food and its cheap prices in the kingdom.

The values of calmness and rationality possessed by the guru, stood in a good way whereas anxiety and greed of the disciple put him in the difficult situation. Thus, the positive values of the guru not only made him different from his disciple but also helped in saving the disciple's life.

2. Give examples to prove that the king and the minister both were idiots.

Ans. The king and the minister both were idiots. Some examples that prove it are given below

- They ordered the night to be treated as day and day as night, so that everybody slept during the day and worked at night.
- They called the disciple for execution even though he was not involved in the case of robbery.
- Both the king and the minister did not understand the guru's plan and foolishly accepted his arguments.

3. How was the Kingdom of Fools different from other places?

Or **In the Kingdom of Fools, life was different. How was it different from common life? Explain.**

Ans. The Kingdom of Fools was different from other places because of a strange policy introduced by the king and the minister.

According to this new policy, everyone must work at night, ploughing their fields and running their businessess. They would sleep in the day. Anybody who disobeyed this order would be executed.

In addition, the price of everything was the same, that is one *duddu*. So, whether it was measure of rice or a bunch of bananas, everything cost the same.

Apart from these, the Kingdom also lacked justice. One could be executed for deeds that one had not even done. As seen in the story, the king and the minister both were foolish and did not understand the actual meaning of justice.

Consequently, the kingdom was in complete chaos. The complete lack of justice, the foolish authorities of king and minister, and the reverse order of the day makes the kingdom of fools different from other places.

4. Sometimes wisdom lies in being tactful. It was the guru's wisdom and knowledge that led him to become the king of the kingdom. Elaborate with reference to 'In the Kingdom of Fools'.

Ans. It is often said that wise people are sincere and believe in being honest and truthful. However, there are circumstances when even the wise may tell a lie for a positive end. In the lesson 'In the Kingdom of Fools', such a wise man is the guru, who at once realised that the place he and his disciple were in was the Kingdom of Fools. Upon the realisation, he decided to leave the place as he knew nothing good would happen in that kingdom.

However, the guru returned to save his disciple and lied for the same cause. He recognised the greed of the idiot king and his minister, and played a tactful trick on them. As a consequence of his lie, not just the disciple but the people of the kingdom were also saved.

Realising the wisdom and intelligence possessed by the guru, the people of the kingdom requested the guru to become their king. Therefore, it can be rightly said that "sometimes wisdom lies in being tactful." It was the guru's wisdom and intelligence that led him to become the king.

6. 'Greed is a deadly vice'. Elaborate with reference to 'In the Kingdom of Fools.'

Ans. Greed is a deadly vice. A greedy person can never be happy and constantly suffers. In the chapter, 'In the Kingdom of Fools', greed brought trouble to many people.

The disciple suffered because of his greed of food. Even though his guru advised him to not stay in the strange kingdom, the disciple prefered to stay there because of its cheap food. Consequently, he grew fat and was found to be a perfect fit for the new stake.

Apart from the disciple, the king and the minister also met their ends because of their greed. Both of them wanted power and luxury in their next birth. Hence, they believed the lie told by the Guru who played upon their weakness, i.e., greed. As a result, both of them decided to die to become the king and minister in their next birth as well. Therefore, it can be justified that greed brings problems and should be avoided.

ASSESSMENT EXERCISE

Extract Based Questions

Read the following extract carefully and answer the questions that follow.

"My Lord, this wall was built in my father's time. I know the man. He's an old man now. He lives nearby." The king sent out messengers to bring in the bricklayer who had built the wall. They bought him, tied hand and foot.

(i) Who is the speaker of the line 'My Lord, this wall'?
- (a) The poor man
- (b) The rich merchant
- (c) The disciple
- (d) The guru

(ii) Why did the king send the messengers to get the bricklayer?

(iii) How was the bricklayer brought before the king?

(iv) When was the wall built?

Short Answer (SA) Type Questions

1. Describe the daily routine of the people living in the Kingdom of Fools.
2. How did the disciple get fat?
3. How did the bricklayer defend himself?
4. How did the dancing girl defend herself?
5. How did the goldsmith defend himself?
6. How did the disciple defend himself?
7. Who saved the merchant from being executed when he was found guilty the second time?

Long Answer (LA) Type Questions

1. Give instances from the story to justify the title of the story.
2. Fools cannot continue with their follies for long. Justify.
3. The disciple was sentenced due to his greed. The king and his minister also died because of their greed. Explain.

The Happy Prince

by Oscar Wilde

CHAPTER 5

CHAPTER SUMMARY The story 'Happy Prince' has been written by Oscar Wilde. It is a story of a Prince and a little swallow.

The story highlights that love and sacrifice are important aspects in human life. Hence, disparity and sorrow in society can be overcome by compassion, generosity and sharing. The generous Prince and the gentle swallow sacrificed themselves to bring happiness to the poor and needy people.

The Statue of Happy Prince

A beautiful statue was installed on a tall column (Pillar) high above the city. It was the statue of the Happy Prince. The statue was covered with thin layers of gold. It had two bright sapphires fixed in the eyes. A bright ruby stone was placed in the hilt (handle) of his sword.

The Swallow Arrives

One night, a little swallow, who was going to Egypt, arrived in the city. He was tired, so he decided to spend the night at the feet of the statue. He was going to sleep but got disturbed by a large drop of water that fell on him. The swallow was amazed as the sky was clear. When the second drop fell, he decided to fly away. However, when the third drop fell, he looked at the statue. He found that it wasn't raining; instead the statue was crying.

The Happy Life of Prince

The swallow asked the statue the reason behind his tears. The statue of Happy Prince told the swallow that when he was alive, he did not know about miseries and sorrows. He lived a happy life in the Palace, where the sorrow was not visible to him. So, his courtiers called him the Happy Prince. However, now after his death, his statue was set up very high and he could see the misery, poverty and all the sadness that people face.

The Prince Wants to Help the Poor People

The Prince told the swallow that he wanted to help the poor people but he couldn't move. So, he requested the swallow to stay with him and help him to do so. The swallow agreed to help the Prince.

Helping the Seamstress and Her Ill Child

The Prince told the swallow that a poor seamstress lived in the city. She was embroidering flowers on a gown for the Queen's loveliest maid of honour. By her side, her little boy was lying ill and he was asking for oranges. However, the poor woman did not have money and she could only give him water.

So, the Prince requested the swallow to pick out the ruby from his sword and give it to the seamstress. The swallow replied that his friends were waiting for him in Egypt. The Prince asked the swallow to stay for just one night, and remarked that the boy was very thirsty and his mother was very sad. So, the swallow agreed and flew off with the ruby.

On the way he saw a cathedral tower with marble angles. He heard the sound of dancing and saw a beautiful girl on the balcony with her lover. She remarked that the seamstresses she had told to embroider flowers on her dress were very lazy and wondered if her dress would be ready on time. He passed over ships in the river and reached his destination. The woman had fallen asleep so he put the ruby beside her thimble (a small tube to protect the finger and push the needle in sewing).
He also fanned the sick boy's forehead with its wings and left.

Helping the Playwright

After coming back to the Happy Prince, the swallow remarked that even though the night was cold, he was feeling warm. The Happy Prince told him that it was because he had done something good. The swallow wanted to go Egypt but the Prince requested him to stay for another night. The Prince requested the swallow to help the playwright with brown hair, red lips and large and dreamy eyes.

The young playwright was trying to finish his play for the Director of the threatre but he couldn't do so. It was very cold to write anything and he was hungry which had made him faint.

The Prince said that the sapphires of his eyes had been brought from India a thousand years ago. He told the swallow to take one sapphire and give it to the playwright so that he would sell it and buy firewood. The swallow refused initially but he followed the Prince's command. He left the sapphire on the withered violets kept beside the young playwright. As a result, the playwright was very happy upon seeing the sapphire.

Helping the Poor Matchstick Girl

Next day, the swallow came to the Prince to say good bye but the Prince again requested him to stay. The Prince told the swallow that a little matchstick girl was standing and crying in the square. Her matchsticks had fallen in the drain and were all spoiled. Her father would beat her if she failed to take home some money. She had no shoes, stockings or even a hat.

The Happy Prince commanded the swallow to take another sapphire from his eye and give it to the poor girl. The swallow was not ready to do so because that would make the Prince completely blind, but the Prince forced him. The swallow put the sapphire into the little girl's hand. When the little girl got the sapphire, she felt very happy. The Prince became blind now. So, the swallow decided to stay with the Prince.

Swallow Reports the Matter

The Prince asked the swallow to fly over his city and tell him what he saw there. The swallow informed the Prince that the poor were leading a miserable life. He saw starving children taking shelter under a bridge to stay warm. He saw as the watchman drove them out into the rain.

The Prince requested the swallow to take the gold leaf by leaf from his statue and give it to the poor. The swallow took off leaf after leaf as per the request and made people happy. As the people grew happy and laughed, the Happy Prince became dull and grey.

Swallow Died

Now, the weather had become extremely cold. The swallow could not tolerate the cold weather. Yet, the swallow didn't leave the Prince. He tried to keep himself warm but was not able to do so.

He soon realised that he was going to die. He said goodbye and requested to kiss the Prince on his hand, but the Prince told the swallow to kiss on his lips. The Prince asked whether he was going to Egypt but the swallow replied that he was going to the house of death who was the brother of sleep. After kissing the Prince's lips, the swallow fell down and died. When the swallow died, the statue's leaden heart broke into two pieces.

The Statue is Removed

The Mayor of the city along with the town councillors visited the place. They found the statue to be ugly and useless as it was no longer beautiful. At the sight of the dead bird, the Mayor decided to issue a proclamation stating that birds were not allowed to die there as their dead bodies looked ugly. Hence, the statue was removed and sent to be melted. However, the broken lead heart couldn't be melted so the workmen at the foundry thought that it was strange. Since it was useless, they threw the heart away into the same dust heap where the swallow was lying dead.

God Sends the Angel

God sent one of his angels to bring him the two most precious things from the city. The Angel brought the leaden heart of the Happy Prince along with the dead swallow.

The God praised the angel. He also stated that the swallow would sing forever in his garden of paradise and the Happy Prince would praise him forever in his City of Gold.

Word Meaning

Word	Meaning
column	pillar
gilded	thinly covered
sapphires	transparent blue precious stones
hilt	handle
alighted	flew down to
putting his head under his wing	preparing to sleep
pity	sympathy
drenched	made completely wet
misery	unhappiness
worn	old and wrinkled
coarse	rough
pricked	punctured/damaged
seamstress	female tailor
pedestal	platform
cathedral	main church
marble angels	marble statues of God's messengers
sculptured	made
state ball	government dance programme
tossing feverishly	unsteady with fever
mast	a tall pole of ship
thimble	cap worn on finger for protection
delicious slumber	peaceful sleep
prospect	possibility
steeple	top of a church
commissions	work
garret	small room on roof
withered violets	dried up blue-purple flowers

Word	Meaning
grate	metal frame of fireplace
playwright	person who writes dramas
flutter	flap wings quickly
harbour	place where ships are kept in a port
vessel	ship
square	open area in a town
spoiled	not usable
bare	without any cap or hat
swooped	flied down fast
misery	hardships
listlessly	as if without life
fine	thin layer of
scarlet	bright red
skated	moved on skates
the brother of	something like
fell down dead	died
curious crack sounded	strange cracking sound
leaden heart	heart made of lead
snapped	broken
mayor	head of the municipal council
councillors	members of the municipal council
shabby	worn out and dirty
proclamation	government order
town clerk	municipal council secretary
foundry	furnace where metal is melted
garden of Paradise	heaven
city of gold	heavenly city

NCERT FOLDER

NCERT Intext and Exercise Questions

THINK ABOUT IT (NCERT PAGE 36)

Q.1 Why do the courtiers call the Prince 'The Happy Prince'? Is he really happy? What does he see all around him?

Or Why was the prince called the 'Happy Prince' by the courtiers?

Ans. The courtiers called the Prince 'The Happy Prince' because he was always happy when he was alive. He did not know what sadness was because he lived in a palace where sorrow was not allowed to enter.

When the Prince died and his statue was installed on a tall column overlooking the city, he could see the sorrow and poverty in many homes.

Thus, he was not happy as he could see all the misery and ugliness of the city around him.

Q.2 Why does the Happy Prince send a ruby for the seamstress? What does the swallow do in the seamstress' house?

Ans. The Happy Prince sent a ruby for the seamstress as she was extremely poor and could not feed her child who was suffering from fever. The swallow, on being persuaded by the prince, went to the seamstress' house.

He kept the ruby beside the seamstress on the table. The swallow, then, flew around the bed and fanned the boy's forehead with his wings.

Q.3 For whom does the Prince send the sapphires and why?

Ans. The Prince sends the sapphires for two people, the young playwright across the city and the poor girl selling matches, who had lost all the matches she had.

The young playwright was trying to finish a play for the Director of the Theatre. However, the young man became too cold as there was no firewood in his fireplace and hunger made him faint. The sapphire was sent to the young playwright so that he could sell it to the jeweller, and buy firewood and finish his play. On seeing the sapphire, the young man felt appreciated and believed that he could finally finish his play.

The Happy Prince, then, saw a poor little girl selling matches, who was standing in the square just below him.

Her matches fell in the gutter because of which they were all spoiled. The Prince knew that her father would beat her if she did not bring home some money. So, the other sapphire was sent to the little girl so that she could sell it to go home with some money.

Q.4 What does the swallow see when it flies over the city?

Ans. When the swallow flew over the city he saw a great difference between the rich and poor. He saw rich people enjoying life, unaware of the condition of the poor nearby. The swallow notices rich people living in beautiful houses, enjoying themselves, while many poor people struggle.
The swallow sees beggars sitting at the gates and hungry children with pale faces looking out at the dark streets.
It also sees two little boys huddled under a bridge, trying to stay warm because they have no home.

The swallow saw the worst conditions of the life of the poor when they were denied even proper sleep by police walking around the street.

Q.5 Why did the swallow not leave the Prince and go to Egypt?

Or Why did the swallow decide not to leave the Prince?

Or Why did the swallow decide to stay with Happy Prince?

Ans. As the Prince had given both of the two sapphires of his eyes to help the poor and needy, he had become blind. Therefore, the swallow decided to stay forever with the Prince and not go to Egypt.

Q.6 What were the two precious things brought to God by the angels?

Or What are the precious things mentioned in the story and why are they precious?

Ans. The two precious things mentioned in the story are the heart of the Prince which was made of lead and the dead swallow.

They are precious because both the Prince and the swallow were very kind, generous and selfless. The Prince could not bear to see the ugliness, misery and suffering in his city, and gave away all his precious stones and gold to make his people happy.

Similarly, the swallow sacrificed going to Egypt and acted as the Prince's messenger, carrying the precious stones and gold to the needy and spreading happiness all around.

TALK ABOUT IT (NCERT PAGE 36)

Q.1 The little swallow says, "It is curious, but I feel quite warm now, although it is so cold." Have you ever had such a feeling? Share your experience with your friends.

Ans. Whenever we help others, we get a feeling of satisfaction. Here the swallow feels good, i.e., warm, despite the cold, because he has helped others in their time of need. He did these acts of selfless service with devotion. Thus, he does not feel the cold, instead he feels good.

(Students can share their personal experiences here.)

REVIEW EXERCISE

Including Competency Based Questions

Part–I

Multiple Choice Questions

1. Complete the following sentence by choosing the correct word.

The friends of the swallow had gone away to Egypt .... before.

(a) two weeks (b) five months
(c) six months (d) six weeks

Ans. (d) six weeks

2. Why was the Prince called happy?

(a) Because he never cried
(b) Because he was very lucky
(c) Because he had everything
(d) Because he was living in the palace of happiness

Ans. (d) Because he was living in the palace of happiness

3. Whom did the Happy Prince send the Ruby to?

(a) Seamstress (b) A man (c) A beggar (d) Swallow

Ans. (a) Seamstress

4. Why did Happy Prince send the sapphire to a young writer and the matchgirl?

(a) To send hope and make them happy
(b) To show them power
(c) To surprise them
(d) To help them

Ans. (a) To send hope and make them happy

5. 'He sank into a delicious slumber' what does the line mean?

(a) The little boy got into deep sleep when the swallow fanned over him.
(b) The little boy got drowned into the river water.
(c) The swallow slept on his way to the seamstress.
(d) The statue slept after sending ruby to the seamstress.

Ans. (a) The little boy got into deep sleep when the swallow fanned over him.

6. Why was the statue of Happy Prince weeping?

(a) Seeing the miseries of its people.
(b) Seeing people cry for their poverty.
(c) Seeing the ugliness of his city.
(d) All of the above

Ans. (d) All of the above

7. Why did the swallow want to go to Egypt?

(i) It was winter in the city which he could not bear.

(ii) In Egypt, the Sun was warm on the green palm trees.

(a) Only (i) is correct
(b) Both (i) and (ii) are correct
(c) Only (ii) is correct
(d) Neither (i) nor (ii) is correct

Ans. (b) Both (i) and (ii) are correct

8. What moved swallow's heart?

(a) Happy Prince's tale
(b) Happy Prince's kindness
(c) Happy Prince's assets
(d) All of these

Ans. (b) Happy Prince's kindness

9. Why did the Happy Prince give away all his assets?

(a) To eradicate misery and sorrow from his city
(b) To show his power to the poor people
(c) To show his wealth to the citizens
(d) None of the above

Ans. (a) To eradicate misery and sorrow from his city

10. Name the most precious things in the story that the angel took to give to God.

(a) Leaden heart of Happy Prince and the dead swallow
(b) The Happy Prince and his assets
(c) Ruby, sword and sapphire
(d) All of the above

Ans. (a) Leaden heart of Happy Prince and the dead swallow

11. Why were Prince and the swallow so precious?

(a) Because of their kindness and selflessness
(b) Because of their services to God
(c) Because they had many possessions
(d) They were rich and cruel

Ans. (a) Because of their kindness and selflessness

12. Which of the following statements is False?

(a) Initially, the swallow found the statue of the Happy Prince useless.
(b) The statue looked beautiful in the moonlight.
(c) A large yellow ruby glowed on the sword hilt.
(d) The statue had leaves on it.

Ans. (a) Initially, the swallow found the statue of the Happy Prince useless.

13. 'And a red ruby glowed on his sword hilt' which of the following gives the correct meaning of the underlined word in the given phrase?

(a) The weakest part of the sword
(b) The strongest part of the sword
(c) The handle of a sword
(d) A cover for the blade of a sword

Ans. (c) The handle of a sword

14. Which of the following statements is true?

(a) The ruby was given to the playwright.
(b) The swallow felt warm because of doing a good deed.
(c) The playwright was trying to finish a play for the Secretary of the Theatre.
(d) The hair of the playwright was brown and crisp.

Ans. (b) The swallow felt warm because of doing a good deed.

15. What did the Happy Prince say about the sapphires in his eyes?

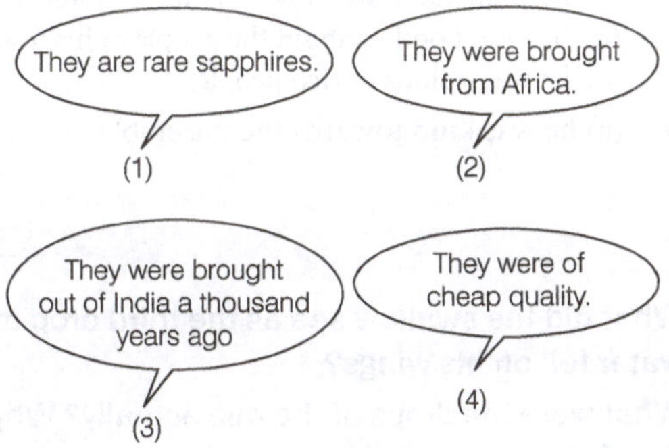

(a) Only (3)
(b) Both (1) and (3)
(c) Both (2) and (4)
(d) Only (1)

Ans. (b) Both (1) and (3)

16. How did the swallow survive the cold weather?

(a) By eating the crumbs outside the baker's door when he was not looking.
(b) By keeping himself warm by flapping his wings.
(c) By resting at the feet of the Happy Prince.
(d) Both (a) and (b)

Ans. (d) Both (a) and (b)

Extract Based Questions

1. Read the following extract carefully and answer the questions that follow.

"Where shall I put up?" he said. "I hope the town has made preparations."

(i) Who is the speaker of the lines in the given extract?

(a) A saint
(b) A tourist
(c) A swallow
(d) A rich boy

Ans. (c) A swallow

(ii) What did the swallow do in the town?

Ans. The swallow helped the statue.

(iii) Where was the speaker going?

Ans. The speaker was going to Egypt.

(iv) Where did he put up?

Ans. He put up at the foot of a statue.

2. Read the following extract carefully and answer the questions that follow.

He is leaning over a desk covered with paper, and in the glass by his side there is a bunch of withered violets. His hair is brown and crisp, and his lips are red as a pomegranate and he has large and dreamy eyes. He is trying to finish a play for the Director of the Theatre, but he is too cold to write any more. There is no fire in the grate, and hunger has made him faint.

(i) Who is 'he'? Describe his condition.

Ans. He is a young playwright. He is in a miserable condition as he has to give his play for the Director of the Theatre. However, he couldn't write anymore as he was cold and hungry.

(ii) Who spoke the words in the given extract and to whom?

Ans. The given words were spoken by the Happy Prince to the swallow.

(iii) Which word does 'withered' not correspond to?

(a) Diminish
(b) Disappear
(c) Flourish
(d) Dwindle

Ans. (c) Flourish

(iv) Complete the analogy by selecting a suitable word from the text.

Orange : Carrot : : Red : ....

Ans. Pomegranate

3. Read the following extract carefully and answer the questions that follow.

"We must really issue a proclamation that birds are not to be allowed to die here." And the town clerk made a note of the suggestion.
So they pulled down the statue of the Happy Prince. "As he is no longer beautiful he is no longer useful, "said the Art Professor at the University.

(i) Who spoke the words in the first line of the above extract?

(a) The Mayor (b) A rich man
(c) The seamstress (d) The playwright

Ans. (a) The Mayor

(ii) Who pulled down the statue of Happy Prince and why?

Ans. The town authorities pulled it down due to the order given by the Mayor.

(iii) Was the Arts Professor right to call the statue of the Happy Prince 'no longer beautiful' and 'no longer useful'?

Ans. No, the Arts Professor was not right to say that the Happy Prince's statue was no longer beautiful or useful.

Beauty should not be judged by outer appearance; it's the values of the person that matters. In my opinion, the Happy Prince became even more beautiful after giving all of his jewels. His outer 'ugliness' was proof that he had the most beautiful heart in the world.

(iv) The phrase 'pulled down' means ....

Ans. to destroy

4. Read the following extract carefully and answer the questions that follow.

"I will stay with you one night longer," said the swallow, "but I cannot pluck out your eye. You would be quite blind then."
"Swallow, Swallow, little Swallow," said the Prince, "do as I command you."

(i) What made the swallow say these lines?

Ans. The swallow says the given lines because the Prince requested it to pluck another sapphire from his eye.

(ii) Read statements 1-5 and select the option that correctly answers the question. Why does the Prince say, "Swallow, Swallow, little Swallow"?

1. Because he wanted the swallow to follow his command.
2. Because he wanted the swallow to forget about his eyes.
3. Because he wanted the swallow to understand the urgency of the situation.
4. Because he was not impressed with the swallow.
5. Because he felt threatened by the swallow.

(a) Only 3 (b) 1 and 2
(c) 4 and 5 (d) Only 5

Ans. (a) Only 3

(iii) Complete the analogy by selecting a suitable word from the text.

Cowardice : Bravery :: Request : ....

Ans. Command

(iv) The statement that is true regarding the Happy Prince statue is

(a) he was kind towards the miserable.
(b) he wanted the swallow to be stayed forever.
(c) he didn't bother about the people of his town.
(d) he was jealous of rich people.

Ans. (a) he was kind towards the miserable.

Part – II

Short Answer Type Questions

1. Give a brief description of the statue of the Happy Prince.

Or **Describe the statue of the Happy Prince as described in the beginning of the story.**

Ans. The statue of the Happy Prince is installed on a tall column in the city from where it could oversee the city. This statue was covered with thin leaves of gold.

He had two bright sapphires fixed in his eyes and a large red ruby on the handle of his sword.

2. What did the swallow see as the third drop of water fell on his wings?

Or **What were the drops of the rain actually? Why did they fall?**

Ans. When the third drop of water fell on his wings, the swallow looked upwards and saw that the eyes of the statue of the Happy Prince were filled with tears, which were running down his golden cheeks. He was weeping on seeing the misery and suffering of the people.

3. What filled the Happy Prince's eyes with tears?

***Or* Why was the 'Happy Prince' not really happy?**

Ans. When the Prince was alive, he never had any tears in his eyes because he lived in a palace far from where he could not see the misery of the people.

After his death, his courtiers set his statue on a high column from where he could see all the ugliness and the misery of his city. This made the Happy Prince's eyes fill with tears and the Happy Prince was not really happy.

4. Why was the seamstress distressed?

Ans. The seamstress was distressed because she had to complete a gown for Queen's Maid of Honour and her son was sick. Her son was asking for oranges but she had no money to buy food.

5. How did the Happy Prince help the seamstress?

Ans. The Happy Prince asked the swallow to take the ruby out of the handle of his sword and give it to the poor seamstress whose son was lying in bed with high fever. Thus, she could sell the jewel and buy food for her son. In this way, the Prince helped the seamstress.

6. What did the Prince request the swallow to do with the first sapphire from his eye?

Ans. The Prince requested the swallow to give the sapphire to the young man who had become too cold to write further and had fainted due to hunger. By selling the sapphire to the jeweller, he would buy firewood to warm himself and complete his play.

7. Why did the little matchstick girl go home laughing?

Ans. The little matchstick girl was sad because all the matchsticks fell into the gutter making them useless. She feared that her father would beat her if she did not bring home some money. In addition, she was barefoot and bareheaded. This made the Prince ask the swallow to give the last sapphire to her. So, the little girl became happy and went home laughing when she got the sapphire.

8. How did the Happy Prince help the poor children in the city?

Ans. The Happy Prince asked the swallow to distribute the gold leaves from his body to the poor people in the city and helped the children. Everybody was happy on getting the leaves of gold, which they could sell. In this way, the Prince helped the poor children in the city.

9. "The Swallow and the Prince were alike in many ways." Justify.

Ans. Both the swallow and the Prince were alike in many ways. They were very kind and full of sympathy for the poor and suffering people. Both of them gave everything they had, the swallow sacrificed his own life and the Prince gave all his valuable parts to help the needy people.

10. 'Good deeds always make one happy.' Explain with reference to the lesson 'The Happy Prince'.

Ans. Good deeds always make one happy. They give a sense of satisfaction and peace of mind. The good deeds of the Prince were that he sacrificed everything, including his eyes (sapphires), the ruby in his sword and the gold leaves covering his body to make others happy. These good deeds made the Prince very happy.

11. What is the moral of the story 'The Happy Prince'?

Ans. The moral of the story, 'The Happy Prince' is that we must help the poor and the needy. The Prince set an example by giving away his jewels and gold cover to the poor, while the swallow helped him in his task, also sacrificing his life in the process.

12. Why do the city officials think the Happy Prince's statue is no longer useful? **Competency Based**

Ans. The city officials think the Happy Prince's statue is useless because it has lost its beauty. The gold and jewels are gone so they see it as dull and ugly. They value the statue only for its appearance, not understanding its true worth or the kindness it showed.

13. How does the story show the theme of compassion?

Ans. The story shows compassion through the Happy Prince and the swallow. The prince gives his gold and jewels to help the poor and suffering people in the city. The swallow stays with the prince, giving up his journey to Egypt to help others, showing kindness and self-sacrifice.

14. Why does God choose the swallow and the lead heart as the most precious things in the city?

Ans. God chooses the swallow and the lead heart because they represent true love and kindness. The swallow sacrificed his life to help others and the lead heart shows the prince's generosity. They are precious because they cared for the poor and brought happiness, showing the true value of compassion.

15. What do you think the lead heart and the dead swallow symbolize in the story? **Competency Based**

Ans. The lead heart and the dead swallow symbolise genuine compassion and self-sacrifice. They show true value comes from helping others and showing love rather than wealth or appearance. The Happy Prince and the swallow's actions teach that kindness and giving are the most important qualities.

Long Answer Type Questions

1. How did the swallow prove to be the Happy Prince's true friend?

Or **How did the little swallow carry out the wishes of the Happy Prince?**

Ans. The little swallow was a true friend of the Happy Prince, a statue which he came across while flying to Egypt.

The swallow not only helped the Prince in helping the poor but also stayed back with him inspite of knowing that he may not survive the bitter cold.

The swallow became the prince's messenger and helped the prince in all the ways he could. The swallow did not leave the prince alone when the prince went blind. In the process, he also became a good doer.

As the winter started, the swallow tried all ways to be warm but he couldn't do that. By sacrificing his life, the swallow proved to be the true friend of the Happy Prince.

2. When and how did the Happy Prince realise the true meaning of life? What did this realisation prompt him to do?

Ans. The Happy Prince had lived a very comfortable life and had not known any sorrow when he was alive. Infact, sorrow was not allowed to enter the place where he lived. Thus, he was called the 'Happy Prince' by his courtiers. However, after his death, his gold and jewel-studded statue was placed on a high column in the city.

From there, the Happy Prince got to see the pain and miseries of the people. He, then, realised that ugliness and sufferings are the true faces of life. The Happy Prince felt that the misery suffered by the humans was the greatest mystery, and the condition of rural people was worse than the rich people. He, then started giving away his jewel to the needy and tried to relieve them of the pain of poverty.

3. "The two most precious things in the city" were the Happy Prince and the swallow. Do you agree? Illustrate.

Ans. The two most precious things in the city were the leaden heart of the Happy Prince and the dead swallow. Both these figures essentially lost their valuables for the cause of misery. The Happy Prince gave away all of his jewels to serve the suffering and help the poor. He sacrificed all the things that made people in the city happy.

In the cause, the Happy Prince was helped by the swallow who fulfilled the wishes of the prince. He not only sacrificed his self-interest of going to Egypt but also carried all of the statue's gold and jewels to the needy.

He even sacrificed his life to help the prince.

Hence, the Angel's decision to take these two kind and worthy souls to God was right.

4. "The statue of the Happy Prince and the name given to him is also ironical." Elaborate all the ironies in the lesson 'The Happy Prince'.

Ans. Irony is a literary device to bring out the difference between reality (what is) and what should be. The lesson 'The Happy Prince' is a story full of ironies.

The title of the statue, the Happy Prince is itself ironical. The statue seemed to be happy as he lived a happy life but in reality, it is full of grief and sorrow. The statue of the Prince is deeply disturbed by the poverty, misery and helplessness of the people.

Another instance of irony, is the profession of the seamstress.

She is working day and night to do embroidery on a beautiful satin gown for the Queen's maid of honour. However, her own life lacks beauty. Her life is full of suffering. Her son is ill and is crying for food but she cannot give him anything. Also, the Mayor and the town councillors order the statue to be removed and melted but the leaden heart of the prince does not melt. Ironically, it is the lead heart of the statue that weeps for the miseries of others and not the human heart.

Hence, by using irony, the author presents that one should do good deeds to become truly happy.

ASSESSMENT EXERCISE

Extract Based Questions

Read the following extract carefully and answer the questions that follow.

"So the swallow plucked out the Prince's eye and flew away to the young man's garret. It was easy enough to get in, as there was a hole in the roof. Through this he darted, and came into the room. The young man had his head buried in his hands, so he did not hear the flutter of the bird's wings and when he looked up he found the beautiful sapphire lying on the withered violets."

(i) Why did the swallow take out the sapphire from the Prince's eye?

(ii) The 'young man' was a ....
(a) chemist (b) dentist (c) playwright (d) prince

(iii) Why did the young man not hear the flutter of the bird's wings?

(iv) 'Withered' in the extract means ....

Short Answer (SA) Type Questions

1. Where was the swallow going? Why did he stop at the Prince's statue?
2. Why was the swallow always in high spirits when he used to tell the prince, "Tonight I go to Egypt"?
3. Why was the swallow hesitant to pluck out the sapphires from the Prince's statue?
4. What did the swallow do at the harbour?
5. How did the Prince's statue look after its gold leaf was removed? What was its fate?
6. Why did God approve of the angel's choices for the two most precious things in the city?

Long Answer (LA) Type Questions

1. Why could the Happy Prince not see the misery and ugliness of his city when he was alive? What does this show about his character at that time?
2. How did the swallow come to know that the Prince had compassion for the poor and needy?
3. 'Goodness can never be destroyed'. Justify this statement with reference to this lesson.
4. List all the people who were helped by the Prince and the swallow and what problems of the people were solved in each case.

The Last Leaf

CHAPTER 6

by O Henry

CHAPTER SUMMARY The story 'The Last Leaf' has been written by O Henry. It highlights the importance of hope and sacrifice in one's life. In the story, two friends Sue and Johnsy live together. Once Johnsy gets ill, she loses all hope and willingness to live. She develops a strange belief that she would die as soon as the last leaf on the ivy creeper outside her window falls.

It is their neighbour-Behrman, an artist by profession, who brings back hope in Johnsy's life. He paints a realistic leaf on the ivy creeper and in doing so sacrifices his own life.

Sue and Johnsy

Sue and Johnsy were two young artists who lived together in a small flat. It was located on the third storey of an old house.

Johnsy fell ill in November due to pneumonia. In her illness, Johnsy would lie on the bed without moving and looked out of the window. Johnsy's behaviour worried Sue so she called the doctor.

The Doctor's Visit

The doctor came everyday but there was no improvement in Johnsy's health. One day, the doctor informed Sue that Johnsy had lost her will/desire to live. Therefore, without hope and will, no medicine would cure her.

Since then, Sue tried to make Johnsy take interest in things. She would talk about clothes and fashion but nothing interested Johnsy. Sue even brought her drawing board into Johnsy's room to complete her work and whistled while painting.

Johnsy's Strange Belief

Suddenly, Sue noticed that Johnsy was looking out of the window and counting backwards.

Sue saw that Johnsy was looking at an old ivy creeper that was climbing the brick wall opposite to their window. The creeper was shedding its leaves due to the strong winds. Sue was shocked when she came to know that Johnsy believed that she would die when the last leaf of the creeper would fall. Johnsy had known it for the last three days.

Sue disregarded Johnsy's belief. She told Johnsy to think positively and also requested her to not look at the ivy creeper. When she tried to give Johnsy some soup, it was rejected as Johnsy said that the last four leaves would fall before night and Johnsy would die. Sue became sad. However, she tried her best to distract Johnsy. She told her ill friend that she could not close the curtain as she needed the light to paint. To this, Johnsy asked her to let her die peacefully.

The Old Behrman

Sue told Johnsy that she had to paint an old miner, so she called Behrman to be her model. Behrman was a sixty year old painter who lived on the ground floor of the same house.

Behrman was also an artist. He always had a dream of painting a masterpiece but was not successful in doing so.

Sue told Behrman about Johnsy's condition and belief. He called Johnsy stupid and foolish.

Later, Sue and Behrman went to Johnsy's room and saw that only one last leaf remained on the creeper.
Then, Behrman left the flat quietly.

The Leaf does not Fall

Next morning, Johnsy saw that the last leaf was still hanging on the ivy creeper. She was surprised to see that even after the strong winds and storm, the leaf had not fallen. In fact, it looked green and healthy. Johnsy stated that the last leaf would fall by the end of the day and then, she would die. She kept waiting but the leaf didn't fall. Even the storm that evening couldn't move the last leaf.

Looking at the leaf, Johnsy realised her mistake. She called Sue and apologised to her for losing hope. Sue hugged her and gave her lots of soup and a mirror to comb her hair.

Even the doctor now told Sue that Johnsy had the will to live so she would get cured soon. He also informed Sue that Behrman was suffering from pneumonia and would die soon.

Behrman's Masterpiece and Sacrifice

Next morning, Sue informed Johnsy that Behrman had died of pneumonia and he had been ill only for two days.

The Janitor (a person who is a caretaker or doorkeeper of a building) found Behrman on his bed and his clothes and shoes were wet. They found a ladder and a lantern near his bed as well as paint brushes and green and yellow paints.

Sue had realised what happened to Behrman and told Johnsy that the last leaf was infact a painted leaf. It was painted by Behrman in the stormy night when the real leaf had fell. He had painted his masterpiece and had sacrificed his own life to save Johnsy.

Word Meaning

Word	Meaning
masterpiece	a great book, painting, music, movie, etc
tiptoed	walked slowly
feeble	very weak
reluctantly	hesitantly

Word	Meaning
fierce	very violent
clinging	to hold onto someone or something very tightly
wicked	morally bad
flutter	to move with quick, light movements

NCERT FOLDER

NCERT Intext and Exercise Questions

THINK ABOUT IT (NCERT PAGE 48)

Q.1 What is Johnsy's illness? What can cure her, the medicine or the willingness to live?

Ans. Johnsy is suffering from pneumonia but her illness does not end here. She is also suffering psychologically (mentally). Johnsy, in her illness, had lost all her hope and will to live. She had started to believe that she would die when the last leaf on the ivy creeper outside her window would fall.

Johnsy can be cured by her willingness to live. Her medicines would start to cure her if she gains back her hope to live.

Q.2 Do you think the feeling of depression that Johnsy has is common among teenagers?

Ans. Yes, the feeling of depression that Johnsy has is quite common among teenagers.
Teenagers may undergo depression due to various reasons like stress, peer pressure, conflict with parents, academic pressure, etc.

Q.3 Behrman has a dream. What is it? Does it come true?

Ans. Behrman has a dream of painting a masterpiece. It does come true when he paints a leaf that looks similar to the leaf on the creeper. Johnsy survives because of this masterpiece.

Q.4 What is Behrman's masterpiece? What makes Sue say so?

Ans. The leaf painted on the creeper by Behrman is his masterpiece.

Sue said so as it was successful in saving the life of her friend, Johnsy.

REVIEW EXERCISE

Including Competency Based Questions

Part – I

Multiple Choice Questions

1. What misconception had Johnsy developed in her mind?

(a) She was great and indomitable
(b) She can't be cured of her illness
(c) She would die with the fall of the last leaf
(d) All of the above

Ans. (c) She would die with the fall of the last leaf

2. Sue was worried for Johnsy because ....

(a) she was not listening to Sue
(b) she was not taking proper rest
(c) she was not eating or drinking anything
(d) she was not completing her painting

Ans. (c) she was not eating or drinking anything

3. Who said the following line to whom?

"It seems, has made up her mind that she is not going to get well."

(a) Sue to Behrman
(b) Behrman to Sue
(c) Sue to doctor
(d) Doctor to Sue

Ans. (d) Doctor to Sue

4. What was Johnsy looking at out of the window?

(a) The ivy creeper climbing the brick wall
(b) The falling leaves of ivy creeper
(c) Behrman's masterpiece
(d) Sue completing her drawing

Ans. (b) The falling leaves of ivy creeper

5. Which of the following describes Johnsy?

(i) Compassionate	**(ii) Hopeless**
(iii) Ill	**(iv) Soft-hearted**
(v) Gloomy	**(vi) Depressed**

(a) (i), (ii), (iv) and (vi)
(b) (ii), (iii), (v) and (vi)
(c) (iii), (iv), (v) and (vi)
(d) (i), (ii), (iii) and (v)

Ans. (b) (ii), (iii), (v) and (vi).

6. What was Behrman's dream?

(a) To travel the world
(b) To paint a masterpiece
(c) To make a colourful painting
(d) To make a poster

Ans. (b) To paint a masterpiece

7. When was Behrman able to make his dream true?

(a) When he painted the last leaf
(b) When he died of illness
(c) When he thought of Johnsy
(d) None of the above

Ans. (a) When he painted the last leaf

8. What promise did Sue take from Johnsy?

(a) She would not look out of the window till Sue was painting.
(b) She would not die till they were friends.
(c) She would not draw curtains as Sue had to complete her drawing.
(d) She would not disturb Sue while she was painting.

Ans. (a) She would not look out of the window till Sue was painting.

9. What did Behrman's wet clothes and shoes tell?

(a) He was out in the stormy night
(b) He was shivering with cold
(c) He was suffering from pneumonia
(d) He washed them for the next day

Ans. (a) He was out in the stormy night

10. Why was Sue reluctant to draw the curtains next morning?

(a) She did not want light in the room
(b) She did not want Johnsy to look out of the window

(c) She was afraid that the last leaf must have fallen off
(d) None of the above

Ans. (c) She was afraid that the last leaf must have fallen off.

11. Why was the ivy leaf painting a masterpiece?

(a) Because it saved a life
(b) Because it was very beautiful
(c) Because it's colours were very bright
(d) None of the above

Ans. (a) Because it saved a life

12. What happened to Behrman after he painted his masterpiece?

(a) He died of pneumonia
(b) He felt proud and happy
(c) He was honoured
(d) None of the above

Ans. (a) He died of pneumonia

13. What happened to Johnsy when she saw Behrman's masterpiece painting?

(a) She became confident that she could be cured
(b) She felt delighted and clapped her hands
(c) She jumped out of bed and sang
(d) None of the above

Ans. (a) She became confident that she could be cured

14. The line "The last leaf has shown me how wicked I have been" suggests that

(a) Johnsy realised that one should not leave hope of living
(b) The last leaf showed Johnsy nothing is impossible if determined
(c) Both (a) and (b)
(d) Johnsy realised she was a bad girl

Ans. (c) Both (a) and (b)

15. What was found near Behrman's bed?

(a) Ladder and lantern
(b) Brushes and yellow and green paint
(c) Wet clothes and shoes
(d) All of the above

Ans. (d) All of the above

16. Choose the correct option for (i) and (ii).

(i) Behrman died of pneumonia.

(ii) Behrman went out in storm and icy cold wind to glue the last leaf on ivy.

(a) (i) is true (ii) is false
(b) (i) is the reason for (ii)
(c) (ii) is the cause for (i)
(d) (i) is independent of (ii)

Ans. (a) (i) is true (ii) is false

Extract Based Questions

1. Read the following extract carefully and answer the questions that follow.

She talked about clothes and fashions but Johnsy did not respond. Johnsy continued to lie still in her bed. Sue brought her drawing board to Johnsy's room and started painting. To take Johnsy's mind off her illness, she whistled while working.
Suddenly she heard Johnsy whispering.

(i) What was Johnsy whispering?

Ans. Johnsy was counting the leaves of the ivy creeper.

(ii) What did Sue try to talk about with Johnsy?

Ans. Sue tried to talk about clothes and fashion with Johnsy.

(iii) The statement that is true about Johnsy, according to the extract is

(a) she has no will to live.
(b) she needs love and care.
(c) she is suffering from Pneumonia.
(d) All of the above

Ans. (d) All of the above

(iv) What can be said about the relationship shared by the girls as given in the extract?

Ans. According to the extract, the girls are best friends and roommates.

2. Read the following extract carefully and answer the questions that follow.

She quickly rushed to the bed and heard Johnsy counting backwards. She was looking out of the window and was saying, "Twelve!" After sometime she whispered "eleven", then "ten", then "nine", "eight", "seven."

(i) What misconception had Johnsy developed in her mind? What does it indicate about her mindset?

Ans. The misconception that Johnsy had developed in her mind was that she would die with the fall of the last leaf on the creeper. Her misconception indicates that she had given up on life and adopted a defeatist attitude.

(ii) What was Johnsy counting?

Ans. Johnsy was counting the number of leaves.

(iii) How does Sue feel in the extract?

(a) Gloomy
(b) Sad
(c) Worried
(d) Disappointed

Ans. (c) Worried

(iv) Why was she counting in reverse?

Ans. She was counting in reverse because the number of leaves on the Ivy creeper were reducing.

3. Read the following extract carefully and answer the questions that follow.

In the evening there was another storm but the leaf did not fall. Johnsy lay for a long time looking at the leaf. Then she called out to Sue.

"I have been a bad girl. You have looked after me so lovingly and I have not cooperated with you. I have been depressed and gloomy. The last leaf has shown me how wicked I have been. I have realised that it is a sin to want to die."

(i) For what reason was Johnsy gloomy?

Ans. Johnsy was gloomy because she was suffering from pneumonia.

(ii) The word 'sin' means ....

Ans. a criminal and disgraceful act.

(iii) How does Johnsy relate the last leaf to herself?

Ans. Johnsy relates the last leaf to herself in two ways– Initially, she observes the shedding leaves in her depressed state of mind and decides that just like the brown leaves, she was also going 'fall' and die soon. Later on, as she observes the perseverance of the last leaf that survives the storm, she too decides to brave her illness and become healthy again.

(iv) Complete the analogy by selecting a suitable word from the text.

Ridiculous : Absurd :: Affectionately : ....

(a) Lovingly (b) Wicked

(c) Gloormy (d) Depressed

Ans. (a) Lovingly

4. Read the following extract carefully and answer the questions that follow.

"The next morning Sue came and sat on Johnsy's bed. Taking Johnsy's hand in her and she said, "I have something to tell you. Mr. Behrman died of pneumonia this morning. He was ill for only two days. The first day the Janitor found him on his bed. His clothes and shoes were wet and he was shivering. He had been out in that stormy night."

(i) Mr. Behrman died of ....

Ans. Pneumonia

(ii) Who found Mr. Behrman the first day?

(a) Sue (b) The Janitor

(c) Johnsy (d) None of these

Ans. (b) The Janitor

(iii) State True or False.

The given statements are True about Mr. Behrman according to the extract.

1. He was a 60 years painter.

2. He died due to pneumonia.

3. He was a careful fellow.

Ans. 2. True

(iv) How did Sue and Johnsy feel about Mr. Behrman's death?

Ans. Sue and Johnsy felt sad and depressed at Mr. Behrman's death.

Part – II

Short Answer Type Questions

1. What did the two friends in the story 'The Last Leaf' do? Where did they live?

Ans. The two friends in the story 'The Last Leaf', Sue and Johnsy, were artists. They used to paint and earn for their living. They lived in a small flat on the third floor of an old building.

2. Describe the things Sue did to make Johnsy interested.

Ans. Sue tried her best to make Johnsy take an interest in things. She talked about clothes and fashions. She started painting in Johnsy's room so that she would notice her and even whistled while painting to divert her mind from illness.

3. Name the creeper that Johnsy continuously looked at. Why was it shedding its leaves?

Ans. The name of the creeper that Johnsy continuously looked at was ivy creeper. The ivy creeper was climbing on the wall, opposite to their window. It was shedding leaves because it was autumn season and a storm with heavy rainfall and strong winds had come.

4. How did Johnsy spend her day?

Ans. Johnsy spent her day lying on her bed. She kept looking out of the window and counted the leaves that were remaining on the ivy creeper. At times, she also slept.

5. Describe the strange belief of Johnsy. Did it come out to be true?

Ans. The strange belief of Johnsy was that she would die once the last leaf on the creeper would fall. Johnsy kept on counting the remaining leaves on the Ivy creeper outside her window. No, her strange belief did not come true as the last painted leaf did not fall from the ivy creeper.

6. Who was Behrman? Why did he come to Sue's flat?

Ans. Behrman was Sue and Johnsy's neighbour. He was a sixty years old painter who lived on the ground floor of the old building. He came to Sue's flat to look at Johnsy's condition.

7. What made Johnsy change her mind?

Ans. Johnsy changed her mind when she saw that even after strong winds and heavy rainfall, the leaf was still hanging on the creeper.

She was filled with hope. She also wanted to get cured soon and live just like the leaf which looked green and healthy.

8. How did Behrman save Johnsy's life?

Ans. Behrman saved Johnsy's life by painting a leaf that looked similar to the last leaf on the Ivy creeper.

The leaf staying intact on the creeper inspite of the strong winds and storm led Johnsy to change her mind and save herself.

Long Answer Type Questions

1. "Behrman's visit to Sue's flat was a blessing in disguise for Johnsy."Justify the above statement.

Ans. It is true that 'Behrman's visit to Sue's flat was a blessing in disguise for Johnsy. Johnsy was suffering from pneumonia and had lost her will to live. She had also developed a strange belief that she would die as soon as the last leaf of the ivy creeper would fall. Her friend, Sue, had tried hard to make Johnsy positive but nothing worked. Sue needed to complete a painting project and earn money for Johnsy's treatment. She had to paint an old miner and called her sixty-year-old neighbour Behrman.

She told him all about Johnsy's condition and belief. Behrman saw the creeper. He knew that the last leaf would fall soon. So, he quietly left the room. Without telling anyone, he went out in the stormy night and painted a leaf to bring back hope in Johnsy's life and it worked. The healthy and green leaf made Johnsy realise her mistake. She gained hope and willingness to live. Consequently, her recovery was fast and she was well.

Therefore, Behrmans's visit to Sue's flat was a blessing in disguise for Johnsy.

2. What lessons do you learn from the story 'The Last Leaf'?

Ans. The story 'The Last Leaf' teaches us to be positive in life and to never believe in superstitions. When there is nothing left in your life then the excitement to live gets lost. However, an inspiration is always there to keep you going ahead in the life. A thought which is positive keeps you well on the path of life. The story teaches us not to lose hope in difficult circumstances and help others.

Johnsy, an artist in the story, falls ill and loses hope of living. She could not get well despite the best efforts of her roommate, Sue and her doctor. She even develops a strange belief. Later on, she realises that her superstition was stupid and nonsensical. She also learnt that life is precious and it is a sin to want to die.

This realisation in Johnsy came because of a sixty year old painter, Behrman. After realising Johnsy's ailment, he painted a realistic leaf on the creeper. In the process of doing so, the old man caught pneumonia and eventually died. He sacrificed his life to help his neighbours, Sue and Johnsy. This selfless act of Behrman teaches us to be compassionate and helpful towards others.

3. Give a character sketch of Behrman.

Ans Behrman was a sixty-year-old painter who lived just below Sue's apartment. He was a poor alcoholic who earned some money by working as a model to other painters.

Although he had a rough exterior look, he was a very kind man with lots of affection for Sue and Johnsy.
He was also very intelligent and thoughtful. He somehow wanted to boost Johnsy's confidence to improve her health. Johnsy was very depressed due to her sickness from pneumonia. She believed that she would die when the last leaf from the ivy tree outside their window would fall. So, Behrman bravely withstood the cold outside and painted an ivy leaf on the window. He painted the leaf for Johnsy to believe that the leaf did not fall and hence, she would also live long like the leaf. This also made Johnsy realise her mistake and she decided to live. However, unfortunately, Behrman contracted pneumonia and died. This reveals his self-sacrificing character.

ASSESSMENT EXERCISE

Extract Based Questions

Read the following extract carefully and answer the questions that follow.

Then they found a ladder and a lantern still lighted lying near his bed. There were also some brushes and green and yellow paints on the floor near the ladder. "Johnsy dear", said Sue, "look out of the window. Look at that ivy leaf. Haven't you wondered why it doesn't flutter when the wind blows? That's Behrman's masterpiece. He painted it the night the last leaf fell."

(i) Who are 'they' in the given lines?

(a) Behrman's family

(b) Johnsy and Sue

(c) The doctor and Sue

(d) Sue and Behrman's family

(ii) Why was there a ladder and lantern near his bed?

(iii) What was Behrman's masterpiece?

(iv) What made Behrman paint his masterpiece?

Short Answer (SA) Type Questions

1. What did the doctor tell Sue?
2. Why didn't Johnsy eat anything?
3. Where did Behrman go after leaving Sue's flat? What did he do?
4. Why did Johnsy curse herself?
5. How did Behrman fall ill? How long was he ill?
6. Draw a character sketch of Sue.

Long Answer (LA) Type Questions

1. Describe the incidents that led Johnsy to change her mind?
2. Draw a character sketch of Sue in your own words.
3. "A patient should never lose hope of getting well". Justify the statement with reference to the story 'The Last Leaf'.

A House is Not a Home

by Zan Gaudioso

CHAPTER 7

CHAPTER SUMMARY The story 'A House is Not a Home' has been written by Zan Gaudioso. It depicts the importance of love, care and affection in one's life. The author, a high school student feels strange in his new school. The situation becomes worse when his house catches fire and his cat is lost. Then, it is his schoolmates' love and care that supports him. His feelings of loneliness and loss disappear with them slowly and the author comes back to normal life again.

Author's Love for the Old School

After leaving junior high school, the author had shifted to the new high school. He felt lonely among new teachers and students. His new school was twice as big as the old school. His old friends were sent to another high school. He missed his old teachers and he often went to meet them. They encouraged him to get involved in new school activities. The author's old teachers also told him to come and meet whenever he wanted.

Author's House Caught Fire

One Sunday afternoon, the author was sitting on his dining-room table and doing his homework while his favourite red cat was lying on top of all his papers. The author had rescued the red cat when she was a kitten. It seemed like she knew that the author was responsible for giving her 'the good life'. It was cold and the fire was burning in the fireplace. The author's mother was stoking (adding fuel to) the fire to keep the house warm. Suddenly, the author noticed that the room was filled with smoke as the roof had caught fire. As the smoke increased, the author and his mother ran out into the front yard. Soon, the fire spread through the whole house.

When the author ran to the neighbours to call the fire department, he saw that his mother ran back into the house. She wanted to save some important documents. Soon, she came out with a small metal box which was full of important documents.

The author's mother again ran into the house to get some pictures and letters from her husband. As her husband was dead, she did not want to let his pictures and letters burn in the fire. The author was also about to run after his mother but he was caught by a fireman.

Arrival of Firemen

After the arrival of firemen, one of them went inside the burning house and saved the author's mother. The author ran to his mother and hugged her. He took author's mother to the truck and put an oxygen mask on her mouth. The author was also wrapped in a blanket and seated down in the car.

Author Lost His Cat

After five hours, the fire was put out but the author's house was completely burned down. Suddenly, the author remembered his cat which could not be found anywhere. The author started crying while thinking that his cat was also burnt in the fire. The author and his mother went to the author's grandparent's house to spend the night.

Going to School

On the next day i.e., Monday, the author went to the school. He was wearing the dress he had worn to church. He had no shoes, books or backpack. He had borrowed some tennis shoes from his aunt. In such a situation, he did not want to grow up and felt like dying. In school, he felt strange and embarrassed. One day, while the author was returning from school, he saw his burnt house. He was shocked to see the damage. He also cried for his missing cat.

The Author Moves on

The author and his mother had to start their life again. They borrowed money from author's grandparents because all of their cash and their credit cards were burned. So, they couldn't withdraw any money from their account. After a week, the rubble (remains) of the house was cleared. The author used to think about his cat, and how she would climb up his robe and get into his pocket to sleep.

Schoolmates Help the Author

Next day, when people in the author's new school got to know about his situation, they all started behaving more friendly. They took the author to the gym and gifted him different things that he would require in his daily life like notebooks, school supplies, jeans, tops, sweatsuits, etc. People who had never spoken to the author came up to him to introduce themselves and invited him to their house. His schoolmate's concern made him realise that everything would go back to normal again.

Life Back to Normal Again

A month later, when he visited his house, it was being rebuilt. His two new friends also visited with him. The fire had changed the life of the author. He stopped focussing on his feeling of insecurity and started to mix-up with the people around him.

The Author Got his Cat Back

When the author was talking to his friends and planning his new bedroom, a lady came up with a cat. The author immediately recognised that it was his cat. The author took the cat in his hands and started crying out of happiness. The author realised that his cat had run away during the fire. Their phone number was written on the collar of the cat but people could not contact them as their phones were destroyed in the fire. The lady who brought the cat searched for the author and finally found him. Now the author was happy again and he was getting back to his normal life.

Word Meaning

Word	Meaning
freshman	a student in the first year of high school or college
nonetheless	inspite of what has just been said
tabby	a domestic cat with a striped and mottled coat.
swat	to hit someone or something with a quick motion
stoke	to stir or add fuel to something that is burning
seam	a line where two pieces of wood, metal, etc. are joined together
groping	to move forward carefully by putting your hands in front of you so that you can feel anything that blocks you.
yard	ground
engulfed	to flow over and enclose
crazed	insane
yelling	to say something very loudly especially because you are angry, surprised or trying to get someone's attention
tow	accompanying someone
dazed	(especially of an emotional or physical shock) make someone unable to think or react properly
outcast	a person who has been rejected by their society or group.
geek	a person who is socially awkward and unpopular

Word	Meaning
surreal	very strange or unusual
ripped	torn or destroyed
grieve	feel intense sorrow
ache	feel intense sadness or compassion
rubble	waste or rough fragments of stone, brick, concrete, etc.
tag along	a person or animal who follows a person
robe	a long, loose outer garment reaching to the ankles
plight	a dangerous, difficult or otherwise unfortunate situation
milling	to move in a confused or disorderly manner within a limited area.
shove	push someone or something roughly
outpouring	an outburst of strong emotion
sigh	make a long, deep audible breath expressing sadness, relief, tiredness, etc.
curb	a short border along the edge of a street that is usually made of stone or concrete
leapt	move quickly and suddenly
freaked	terrified
sorely	to a very high degree or level of intensity

NCERT FOLDER

NCERT Intext and Exercise Questions

THINK ABOUT IT (NCERT PG 54-55)

Q.1 What does the author notice one Sunday afternoon? What is his mother's reaction? What does she do?

Ans. The author noticed smoke coming from the ceiling of his house on a Sunday afternoon. The author and his mother ran out of the house. The author's mother was worried she immediately ran back into the house to save important documents, photographs and letters of his father.

Q.2 Why does he break down in tears after the fire?

Ans. The author broke down in tears after the fire as he was unable to find his pet cat. He was already sad as he missed his old school and now, his house got burned while his pet cat was missing.

Q.3 Why is the author deeply embarrassed the next day in school? Which words show his fear and insecurity?

Ans. The author was deeply embarrassed the next day in school as his clothes looked weird, he had no books or homework and his backpack was destroyed in the fire. The words 'outcast', 'geek' and 'zombie' show his fear and insecurity.

Q.4 The cat and the author are very fond of each other. How has this been shown in the story? Where was the cat after the fire? Who brings it back and how?

Ans. It is true to say that the cat and the author were very fond of each other. This is shown through the author's constant remembering of the cat. The author missed the cat badly when she got lost. Many times he would go to his damaged house to search for the cat. He would also remember the time that he spent with the cat.

The cat used to climb on him and crawl into his pocket to sleep when it was a kitten. She would also follow him. All this shows that the author and the cat were very fond of each other.

The cat was terrified when the author's house caught fire so she had run away.

A lady brought the cat back by holding it in her arms.

Q.5 What actions of the schoolmates change the author's understanding of life and people and comfort him emotionally? How does his loneliness vanish and how does he start participating in life?

Ans. The author's schoolmates gave him school supplies, notebooks and clothes as his house had been completely destroyed by the fire. They also introduced themselves to him and invited him to their house. All these things comforted the author emotionally and changed his understanding of life and people. This incident made the author think for the first time that things are going to be normal in the future. It made his loneliness vanish and led him to make new friends.

Q.6 What is the meaning of "My cat was back and so was I"? Had the author gone anywhere? Why does he say that he is also back?

Ans. The sentence "My cat was back and so was I" means that the author is back to normal life after finding his cat. The author had not gone anywhere. He says this sentence because finding his cat gives him new hope that replaced the feelings of loss and tragedy. His beloved cat rescued his interest in life and he came back to a positive state of mind.

REVIEW EXERCISE

Including Competency Based Questions

Part–I

Multiple Choice Questions

1. What is most precious according to this lesson?

(a) A well furnished house
(b) Bond of love and care amongst the members of a family
(c) A house filled with material possessions
(d) None of the above

Ans. (b) Bond of love and care amongst the members of a family

2. Why did the narrator feel strange in high school?

(a) Because he was a freshman
(b) All his friends went to other places
(c) Because he was all alone
(d) All of the above

Ans. (d) All of the above

3. What was the narrator doing when the fire broke out?

(a) He was playing with his dog
(b) He was in the neighbour's house
(c) He was sleeping
(d) He was doing his homework

Ans. (d) He was doing his homework

4. What did the author notice while doing his homework?

(a) That his cat was jumping
(b) That his cat was sleeping
(c) That smoke was coming through the ceiling
(d) None of the above

Ans. (c) That smoke was coming through the ceiling

6. What changed the author's perception of life and made him accept his new life?

(a) His new friends' compassionate behaviour
(b) Arrangement of all basic necessities by his classmates
(c) When his new friends started inviting him to their place
(d) All of the above

Ans. (d) All of the above

7. Why did the author feel isolated in his new school?

(a) His closest friends were sent to a different high school.
(b) Nobody talked to him.
(c) He found everybody strange in the new school.
(d) All of the above

Ans. (a) His closest friends were sent to a different high school.

8. How did author's old teachers encourage him for his new school?

(a) By motivating him to talk to his classmates.
(b) By asking him to talk to his teachers.
(c) By asking him to participate in school activities.
(d) By suggesting him to talk to his seniors.

Ans. (c) By asking him to participate in school activities.

9. The author was responsible for giving his cat 'the good life'. Here 'the good life' means

(a) loving and caring family
(b) a happy and enjoyable life
(c) Both (a) and (b)
(d) None of these

Ans. (c) Both (a) and (b)

10. Why was author's mother stoking the fire?

(a) It was the chilling day of December.
(b) It was a cold and windy fall day.
(c) The author was feeling cold.
(d) The author's mother was feeling cold.

Ans. (b) It was a cold and windy fall day.

11. A fireman brought author's mother <u>in tow</u>. What does the underlined phrase mean?

(a) The fireman accompanied the author's mother.
(b) The fireman followed the author's mother.
(c) The fireman brought his vehicle to tow.
(d) None of the above.

Ans. (a) The fireman accompanied the author's mother.

12. How did the author feel when he saw his mother lying in the truck with oxygen mask?

(a) He was afraid of losing her.
(b) He forgot about the time he argued and hated her.
(c) He felt relieved.
(d) He felt ashamed of himself for letting his mother go into the fire.

Ans. (b) He forgot about the time he argued and hated her.

13. When did the thought of the cat strike the author?

(a) When he was at his grandparents' house.
(b) When he was at the school.
(c) After five hours when the fire was put out.
(d) When he was watching his house burning.

Ans. (c) After five hours when the fire was put out.

14. Why was the author embarrassed to go to school the next day?

1. He did not have school uniform.

2. He did not have his school books, homework and school bag.

3. He was looking weird.

4. He did not have shoes.

(a) 1, 2 and 3 (b) 1 and 2
(c) 3 and 4 (d) 1, 2, 3 and 4

Ans. (d) 1, 2, 3 and 4

15. How did the author feel on walking by his old house from school?

(a) He was happy about the incident.
(b) He was not feeling well.
(c) He did not want to see his old house.
(d) He was shocked on seeing the damage.

Ans. (d) He was shocked on seeing the damage.

16. Why did the author say "This was not the kind of attention I was looking for"?

(a) Everyone at his school got to know about his plight.
(b) Everybody in school was looking at him with pity.
(c) Everybody in the school got to know him.
(d) Everyone in the school wanted to help him.

Ans. (b) Everybody in school was looking at him with pity.

17. Select the correct option for (1) and (2).

1. Everybody was trying to push the author in the school gym.

2. There was a big table set-up with all kinds of stuff on it, just for the author.

(a) (1) is the result of (2) (b) (2) is the result of (1)
(c) (1) is true (2) is false (d) (1) is independent of (2)

Ans. (a) (1) is the result of (2)

Extract Based Questions

1. Read the following extract carefully and answer the questions that follow.

"The firemen wouldn't let us go back into the house that night. It was still too dangerous. Dead or alive, I couldn't imagine leaving without knowing about my cat. Regardless, I had to go. We piled into the car with just the clothes on our backs and a few of the firemen's blankets, and made our way to our grandparents house to spend the night."

(i) Where did the narrator and his mother stay that night?

Ans. The narrator and his mother stayed at their grandparents' house.

(ii) Why did the firemen refuse to let the narrator and his mother into the house?

Ans. The firemen refused to let the narrator or his mother go back into the house because the house was burning.

(iii) Choose the options that list the set of statements that are not true according to the given extract.

1. The narrator's cat was killed in the house fire.

2. The narrator was very much attached to his cat.

3. Both the narrator and his mother spent the night in the park.

4. The narrator felt that he was responsible for the accident.

5. The firemen provided narrator and his mother with few blankets.

6. The firemen didn't allow the narrator and his mother to go back in the house.

(a) 1, 3 and 4 (b) 2, 5 and 6
(c) 4, 5 and 6 (d) 2, 3 and 6

Ans. (a) 1, 3 and 4

(iv) Find a word in the extract which means the same as 'despite everything'.

Ans. Regardless

2. Read the following extract carefully and answer the questions that follow.

In the early morning when I would disturb her and get out of bed, she would tag along after me, climb up my robe and crawl into my pocket to fall asleep. I was missing her terribly.

(i) Who is 'her' in the given lines?

Ans. 'Her' in the given lines is the author's pet cat.

(ii) Why was the narrator missing her?

Ans. The narrator was missing her because she had got lost after the fire.

(iii) What does the given line tell us about the author?

(a) He loved his pet
(b) He was very friendly
(c) He was very irritating
(d) He loved disturbing animals

Ans. (a) He loved his pet

(iv) What did she do when the author disturbed her?

Ans. When the author disturbed her, she crawled into his pocket.

3. Read the following extract carefully and answer the questions that follow.

A month later, I was at my house watching them rebuild it. But this time it was different — I wasn't alone. I was with two of my new friends from school. It took a fire for me to stop focusing on my feelings of insecurity and open up to all the wonderful people around me. Now I was sitting there watching my house being rebuilt when I realised my life was doing the same thing.

(i) Why was the author's house being rebuilt?

(a) Because it was in a bad condition.
(b) Because it was destroyed in a storm.
(c) Because it was destroyed in fire.
(d) Because of an infestation.

Ans. (c) Because it was destroyed in fire.

(ii) Why was it different this time?

Ans. It was different this time because the author had friends to help him. He had his cat and had become confident.

(iii) Complete the sentence appropriately. 'Them' here represents

Ans. The people rebuilding the author's house.

(iv) How did the destruction of the house help the author?

1. Removed his insecurity
2. Made him courageous
3. Allowed him to open up
4. Gave him confidence
5. Help him win friends

Select the correct option.

(a) 1 and 3 (b) 2 and 4 (c) Only 1 (d) Only 5

Ans. (a) 1 and 3

Short Answer Type Questions

1. Why was the author's first year of high school awkward?

Ans. The first year of the author's high school was awkward as he had joined a new school and his old friends were in a different school. He felt alone among new teachers and students. The unfamiliarity of the place made it awkward for him.

2. What were the author and his cat doing when the fire broke out?

Ans. The author was sitting on his dining-room table doing his homework when the fire broke out. His cat was lying on top of his papers, purring loudly and playing with his pen.

3. What two things were rescued by the author's mother and why?

Ans. The author's mother rescued a small metal box and the pictures and letters of author's father. The metal box was rescued as it contained important documents, and the pictures and letters were rescued as they were the only memories of his father.

4. 'I just wanted to curl up and die'. When and why did the author say these words?

Ans. The author said these words when he had to go to school after his house was destroyed by fire.
He said this as all his belongings had been destroyed, and he had to go to school wearing borrowed shoes and without a bag and homework.

5. Why did the author get attention in his new school?

Ans. The author got a lot of attention in his new school when everyone, including the teachers, came to know that his house had been completely destroyed in the fire.

6. Describe the author's pet cat. When was she rescued?

Ans. The author's pet was a red tabby cat. It was rescued by the author when she was a kitten and somehow she knew that the author was responsible for giving her a good life. The cat was loved by the author very much.

7. Why was the author overcome by emotions when he got help from his schoolmates?

Ans. The author was overcome by emotions when he got help from his schoolmates because they had gone out of their way to bring him things that he needed. He was touched by their genuine concern.

8. What was the author doing when he got his cat back? Who was with him?

Ans. The author was watching his house being rebuilt and planning his new bedroom when he got his cat back. The author's two friends from his new school were with him when a lady approached him with his pet cat and asked if the cat belonged to him.

9. Whom all did the author feel grateful to after getting his cat?

Ans. After getting his cat, the author felt grateful to his life, his new friends, the kindness of the stranger and his beloved pet cat. He was back to normal life. He was grateful for everything now and very happy as his cat was back.

Long Answer Type Questions

1. Compare and contrast the author's life before and after the fire incident.

Ans. The author was leading a peaceful life before the fire broke out in his house. The author had joined a new high school. It felt strange to him to start all over as a fresher. The author felt very lonely as his closest friends were sent to a different high school. He was a little disappointed for he was missing his old school, friends and teachers. He used to meet his teachers regularly. He was trying to be normal with everything in his life.

After the fire incident, the author was completely devastated. The loss of all his belongings and his pet cat added to the misery of joining a new school.

He did not want to go to his new school and at one point of time even wanted to die. He missed his pet cat very much and used to go to the place where his house once stood to search for her.

2. Describe the hardships faced by the author and his family in the story 'A House is Not a Home'.

Ans. The author and his family faced a lot of hardships in the story 'A House is Not a Home'. The author's house was completely destroyed in the fire.

As a result, he lost all his belongings and his pet cat. He and his mother had to stay at his grandparents' home. His mother had to borrow money from his grandparents as her money, credit cards and identification proofs were lost in the fire.

The author had to face a lot of mental stress as he had to go to school without his school bag, notebooks and homework. He even had to borrow shoes from his aunt in order to attend the school. He felt like an outcast going to the school like this and at one point of time, he even wanted to die. He also missed his pet cat badly and kept looking for her everywhere.

3. Justify the title of the story 'A House is not a Home'.

Ans. The title 'A House is Not a Home' is justified in relation to the story. In the story, the author's house gets completely destroyed in a fire.

Due to this, he and his mother had to take refuge at his grandparents' home and later, in a rented apartment. The places where the author lived after the fire incident cannot be called a home.

A home is the place where one gets comfort, the joy of belongingness and freedom of doing whatever one wishes. On the other hand, a house is without these sentiments and emotions. House is just a confined place made up of the four walls.

The grandparents' house and the rented apartment were merely places where he took shelter. Moreover, these places were without the belongings and things which the author loved. As one has a sense of belonging while at home, it cannot be fulfilled by a place where one takes temporary shelter. Hence, the title of the story is justified.

ASSESSMENT EXERCISE

Extract Based Questions

Read the following extract carefully and answer the questions that follow.

Everyone in the High school, including my teachers, was aware of my plight. I was embarrassed as if somehow I were responsible. What a way to start off a new school! This was not the kind of attention I was looking for.

(i) What was the plight of the speaker in the above extract?

(ii) Which word from the extract does not signify the narrator's suffering?
- (a) Plight
- (b) Embarrassed
- (c) Attention
- (d) Responsible

(iii) Choose the option that list the set of statements that are not true according to the given extract.
1. He was new in town.
2. He missed his father very much.
3. He had changed his clothes after the incident.
4. His new schoolmates helped him get through those hard times.
5. The incident was a new start for him.
6. His only comfort during those times was his cat.

(a) 1, 2 and 3 (b) 4, 5 and 6
(c) 2, 3 and 6 (d) 1, 4 and 5

(iv) From the given lines, what can we gather about the speaker?

Short Answer (SA) Type Questions

1. What did the teachers advise the author?
2. How did the firemen help the author and his mother?
3. Describe an incident from the story which shows that the author is kind towards animals.
4. Describe the author's first day in school after the fire destroyed his house.
5. How were the author's father's photographs saved? Why were they saved?

Long Answer (LA) Type Questions

1. What disturbed the author in the story 'A House is Not a Home'? How did he come to a state of normalcy?
2. Describe the author's attachment to his pet cat in your own words based on the story 'A House is Not a Home'.

The Beggar

CHAPTER 8

by Anton Chekhov

CHAPTER SUMMARY The following story 'The Beggar' has been written by Anton Chekhov. This story highlights how kindness and compassion can bring about a change in anyone. In the story, Lushkoff, a beggar is caught in a lie and later, given work by Sergei, an advocate. Lushkoff agrees to do the work but the work given to him is done by an old woman Olga (Sergei's cook). Her kindness and compassion bring a change in Lushkoff's way of life. Because of Olga's selfless help, Lushkoff starts living a respectable life and becomes a responsible man.

Sergei Stopped by a Beggar

One day Sergei, an advocate, was stopped by a beggar. The beggar requested Sergei to have pity on him. The beggar also said that he had eaten nothing for the last three days since he didn't even have five copecks for accommodation. The beggar told Sergei that he had been a school teacher for eight years but had lost his job about a year ago.

Sergei looked at the beggar. He was wearing a ragged, fawn (light yellowish) coloured overcoat. He had dull drunken eyes and a red spot on either cheek. The beggar told Sergei that he had found a job in the province of Kaluga and needed money to go there.

Sergei Recognises the Beggar

While talking to the beggar, Sergei recognised him by his shoes. One of the beggar's shoes was high and other was low. Sergei told the beggar that he had met him earlier on Sadovya Street and at that time, he told him that he was a student. Sergei threatened the beggar that he would call the police for swindling (cheating).

The Beggar Tells the Truth

After Sergei's threat, the beggar said that he had lied to him for money. He told Sergei that he was in a Russian singing group, but he was thrown out because of his drinking habits. Now, he couldn't find work anywhere and did not have any other option rather than to beg. So, he lied to get money.

Sergei Offers Work to the Beggar

After listening to the beggar's truth, Sergei offered him the work of chopping wood. The beggar had not wanted to work, but he agreed because of shame. So, Sergei took the beggar to his home. He called his cook, Olga and told her to take the beggar into the wood-shed. Sergei hurried to a window in the dining room from which he could see everything happening in the shed. It looked like Olga was scolding the beggar. Olga gave the beggar an axe to chop the wood. The beggar tried to chop the wood but couldn't do so. Sergei realised that he kept a drunken man who was too weak to work in cold.

Different Types of Work for the Beggar

The wood was chopped after an hour. The beggar was given money (half a rouble) and informed that he could come to Sergei's house in the starting of the month to get work.

The beggar was given various kinds of work. He would remove the snow, cut wood, clean the rugs and mattresses, etc. When Sergei was shifting into a new house, the beggar was called to help in packing and carrying the furniture. The beggar looked weak and unhealthy. He hardly helped porters (people who transport things) in carrying the furniture and in shifting. Sergei thought that he should not give him hard work and decided to send him to his friend for a job of copying. After shifting, Sergei called the beggar and got to know that his name was Lushkoff. Sergei gave Lushkoff a letter and told him to go to his friend, who would give him a new job.

Sergei Meets Lushkoff after Two Years

After two years, on one evening, Sergei met Lushkoff at the theatre near the ticket window. He was wearing a coat collar of curly fur and a sealskin cap. Lushkoff informed Sergei that he had become a notary and was now earning 35 roubles a month. Lushkoff thanked Sergei for his help and guidance. He also thanked Sergei's cook Olga who (according to him) actually changed him.

Lushkoff's Confession

Lushkoff confessed to Sergei that Olga's kindness had changed him. It was Olga who would scold him and cry for him. Lushkoff told Sergei that he did not cut any wood for him. It was Olga who cut the wood. Olga's caring actions changed his heart, stopped him from drinking and helped him become a responsible person.

Word Meaning

Word	Meaning
swear	a solemn declaration by some sacred being or object
lodging	temporary accommodation
copeck	a monetary unit of Russia equal to one-hundredth of a rouble
intrigues	secret plans made to harm someone
calumny	defamation of character
advocate	lawyer
ragged	(of clothes) old and torn
suppliant	a person making a humble plea to someone in power or authority.
province	district; region
mendicant	a beggar
obliged	bound to do something
overshoes	a shoe worn over a normal shoe, typically made of rubber to protect the normal shoe
expelled	removed
mumble	murmur
flushed	(of a person's skin) red and hot, typically as the result of illness or strong emotions.
disgust	a feeling of dislike for something or someone.
swindling	cheating
damn	an expression highlighting anger or frustration.
formerly	in the past
choir	an organised group of singers
drunkenness	intoxication
chop	to cut
skilled	experienced

Word	Meaning
hasten	to move or act quickly
scarecrow	a person who is very badly dressed, odd-looking, or thin
shrugged	raise shoulders slightly to express doubt
perplexity	confusion
irresolute	hesitant
gait	a person's manner of walking
undermined	lessen the effectiveness, power or ability of someone.
inclination	a tendency
toil	hard work
glared	stare in an angry way
wrathfully	in an extremely angry manner
shoved	push roughly
banged	strike or put down forcefully
pseudo	not genuine
spat (past tense of spit)	eject saliva from one's mouth, sometimes as a gesture of contempt or anger
billet	(here) a thick piece of wood.
feebly	lacking in force
waver	move back and forth
menial	(of work) not requiring much skill and lacking prestige.
rouble	Russian currency
waif	a homeless, neglected or abandoned person
shovel	move something with a shovel (Shovel is a tool with a long handle used for lifting and throwing dirt, sand, snow, etc.

Word	Meaning
rug	mat
hauling	pulling or dragging
sober	serious, sensible and dignified
gloomy	sad or depressed
pretence	acting
wagon	a vehicle used for transporting goods
carter	a person who transports goods by a vehicle
jeer	make rude and mocking remarks, typically in a loud voice
tattered	old and torn; in poor condition
parting	leaving
timidly	unconfidently
notary	a person authorised to perform certain legal formalities

Word	Meaning
delighted	very happy
roasting	severe criticism
grateful	thankful
dragged	pulled
pit	a large hole
noble	having or showing fine personal qualities or high moral principles.
indebted	owing something (such as money or thanks) to someone
sot	a habitual drunkard
miserable	being in a pitiable state of distress or unhappiness
strain	an outburst filled with emotional speech
owing to	due to
bow	to bend the head or body in respect to someone or something

NCERT FOLDER

NCERT Intext and Exercise Questions

THINK ABOUT IT [NCERT PAGE 61-62]

Q.1 Has Lushkoff become a beggar by circumstance or choice?

Ans. Lushkoff became a beggar by choice as he did not want to work. He was a drunkard and was thrown out of the singing group in which he sang, due to his drinking habits.

Q.2 What reasons does he give to Sergei for his telling lies?

Ans. Lushkoff told Sergei that nobody would take pity on him. He also told that nobody would give him anything if he told the truth. So, he had to lie to earn money.

Q.3 Is Lushkoff a willing worker? Why, then, does he agree to chop wood for Sergei?

Ans. No, Lushkoff was not a willing worker. He agreed to chop wood for Sergei because of shame and guilt. He was trapped in his own words. He had told Sergei that he had to beg because he could not find any work.

Q.4 Sergei says, "I am happy that my words have taken effect." Why does he say so? Is he right in saying this?

Ans. Sergei says the given statement on seeing Lushkoff coming to his house regularly for work. By this, Sergei meant that he had encouraged Lushkoff to leave begging and start working.

No, he is not right in saying so as Lushkoff did not change his ways because of him. He became a better person because of the empathy that Olga showed when she cried for him.

Q.5 Lushkoff is earning thirty five roubles a month. How is he obliged to Sergei for this?

Ans. Lushkoff is obliged to Sergei for his respectable life. Before meeting Sergei, Lushkoff was a beggar who lied to get money. Sergei offered him work. It was at Sergei's house where Lushkoff met Olga, a kind old lady who led him to change his life. When Sergei was confident that Lushkoff was ready for a proper job, he sent Lushkoff to his friend's house for a new job. Due to this, he became a notary who earned 35 roubles a month.

Q.6 During their conversation Lushkoff reveals that Sergei's cook, Olga, is responsible for the positive change in him. How has Olga saved Lushkoff?

Ans. During his conversation with Sergei, Lushkoff revealed that it was Sergei's cook, a kind and compassionate old lady named Olga, who was responsible for a positive change in him. When Lushkoff met Olga, she called him by various names and even shouted at him.

She would, then, weep for his miserable condition and life. Olga would also cut the wood that Lushkoff had to cut. Her selfless acts gradually made Lushkoff quit drinking. He, thus, started working diligently and was now a respectable man.

REVIEW EXERCISE

Including Competency Based Questions

Multiple Choice Questions

1. What forced Lushkoff to be a beggar?

(a) Choir group (b) His circumstances
(c) His employer (d) His drunkenness

Ans. (d) His drunkenness

2. How was the beggar earning money?

(a) By singing
(b) By telling lies
(c) By rousing sympathy in the listeners
(d) Both (b) and (c)

Ans. (d) Both (b) and (c)

3. What is the theme of the lesson?

(a) Be kind
(b) Don't be kind
(c) Kindness can transform anyone
(d) All of the above

Ans. (c) Kindness can transform anyone

4. Who made the beggar lead a good life?

(a) Olga, the cook (b) Sergei
(c) A music teacher (d) None of these

Ans. (a) Olga, the cook

5. How much money did Sergei pay to the beggar for cutting wood?

(a) Half a rouble (b) 40 Copecks
(c) 35 Copecks (d) 25 Copecks

Ans. (a) Half a rouble

6. How much money was Lushkoff earning as a notary?

(a) 25 roubles a month (b) 35 roubles a month
(c) 45 roubles a month (d) 20 roubles a month

Ans. (b) 35 roubles a month

7. How did Olga help the beggar?

(a) By giving him food
(b) Giving him medicine
(c) By chopping wood for him
(d) None of the above

Ans. (c) By chopping wood for him

8. What lies did the beggar tell Sergei?

(a) He was a village school teacher and fell victim to conspiracy.
(b) He had an offer of a position in the province of Kaluga but didn't have money to go.
(c) He was a student and was expelled.
(d) All of the above

Ans. (d) All of the above

9. Why did Sergei threaten to call the police?

(a) Because the beggar stole money from Sergei
(b) Because the beggar was asking money by telling lies to people
(c) Because the beggar was drinking alcohol on the road
(d) Because the beggar was threatening Sergei

Ans. (b) Because the beggar was asking money by telling lies to people

10. How did the beggar get trapped in his own words?

(a) By asking for work even though he didn't want to
(b) By asking for money.
(c) He was hungry and had to do some work to get money to eat.
(d) All of the above

Ans. (a) By asking for work even though he didn't want to

11. Why did the beggar agree to chop wood for Sergei?

(a) Because he was hungry
(b) Because he was poor
(c) Because he wanted to work
(d) Because of his pride and shame

Ans. (d) Because of his pride and shame

12. What showed Sergei that the beggar was unwilling to work?

(a) His appearance
(b) His way of talking
(c) His way of walking towards the wood-shed
(d) His way or chopping

Ans. (c) His way of walking towards the wood-shed

13. Why was the beggar not willing to work?

(a) Because of poor health
(b) Because of his drunkenness
(c) Because he was hungry and weak
(d) All of the above

Ans. (d) All of the above

14. Which of the following works did the beggar used to do for Sergei?

1. Wood cutting

2. Shovel snow

3. Putting wood-shed in order
4. Beating dust out of rugs and mattresses

(a) 1 and 2 (b) 2, 3 and 4
(c) 1, 2, 3 and 4 (d) 3 and 4

Ans. (c) 1, 2, 3 and 4

Extract Based Questions

1. Read the following extract carefully and answer the questions that follow.

"Kind sir, have pity; turn your attention to a poor, hungry man! For three days I have had nothing to eat; I haven't five copecks for a lodging, I swear it before God. For eight years I was a village school teacher and then I lost my place through intrigues. I fell a victim to calumny. It is a year now since I have had anything to do."

(i) Who was 'I' in the given extract?

Ans. 'I' in the given extract is Lushkoff.

(ii) What was he doing?

1. Asking for work
2. Begging
3. Requesting for help
4. Acting
5. Creating trouble for others

(a) 1 and 3 (b) Only 2
(c) 4 and 5 (d) Only 5

Ans. (b) Only 2

(iii) What was his condition? Answer in one word.

Ans. Poverty stricken

(iv) Complete the analogy by selecting a suitable word from the text.

Meagre : Small :: Bad-mouthing : ....

Ans. Calumny

2. Read the following extract carefully and answer the questions that follow.

"Thank you for your kind words and deeds.
I am very grateful to you and your cook. God bless that good and noble woman! You spoke finely then, and I shall be indebted to you to my dying day; but strictly speaking, it was your cook, Olga, who saved me."

(i) Who is the speaker of the given lines?

Ans. Lushkoff is the speaker of the given lines.

(ii) Who is he grateful towards?

Ans. He is grateful towards both sergei and Olga for encouraging him to lead a respectable life.

(iii) The phrase 'dying day' refers to

1. career
2. the day he dies
3. the day of the festival
4. till he is working
5. till he is living

(a) 1 and 3 (b) Only 2
(c) 3, 4 and 5 (d) 1, 2, 3, 4 and 5

Ans. (b) Only 2

(iv) Complete the analogy by selecting a suitable word from the text.

Crops : Farmer :: Cooking : ....

Ans. Cook

3. Read the following extract carefully and answer the questions that follow.

The scarecrow of a beggar shrugged his shoulders, as if in perplexity and went irresolutely after the cook. It was obvious from his gait that he had not consented to go and chop wood because he was hungry and wanted work, but simply from pride and shame and because he had been trapped by his own words.

(i) Why was the beggar working even though he did not want to?

Ans. The beggar was working out of pride and shame. He was ashamed because Sergei had caught him in a lie. If he did not do as Sergei said then his pride would have been hurt even more.

(ii) When the writer says, 'scarecrow of a beggar', he means to ....

Ans. describe the beggar as thin.

(iii) Which of the following statements is true about the beggar?

(a) He was a lazy drunkard.
(b) He was a school teacher.
(c) He was in need of work.
(d) He faced the threat of imprisonment.

Ans. (a) He was a lazy drunkard.

(iv) Who was the beggar going to work for?

Ans. The beggar was going to work for Sergei.

4. Read the following extract carefully and answer the questions that follow.

Next he saw the pseudo-teacher seat himself on a log and become lost in thought with his red cheeks resting on his fists. The woman flung down an axe at his feet, spat angrily and judging from the expression of her lips, began to scold him.
The beggar irresolutely pulled a billet of wood

towards him, set it up between his feet, and tapped it feebly with the axe. The billet wavered and fell down.

(i) **Why is the beggar called a pseudo teacher?**

Ans. The beggar is called a pseudo teacher because he had posed as a teacher to beg.

(ii) **Choose the options that lists the set of statements that are not true according to the given extract.**

1. **The beggar was not a teacher.**
2. **The beggar was thin and weak.**
3. **The beggar seemed interested in his work.**
4. **The beggar did not know how to chop wood.**
5. **The beggar was being supervised by a woman.**
6. **The beggar was affected by the kindness of the woman.**

(a) 1, 2 and 3 (b) 4, 5 and 6
(c) 3, 4 and 6 (d) 1, 2 and 5

Ans. (c) 3, 4 and 6

(iii) **Complete the sentence appropriately. From the given extract, it can be said that the woman ....**

Ans. dislikes the beggar

(iv) **What happened to the billet?**

Ans. The billet wavered from between the beggar's feet and fell down.

5. Read the following extract carefully and answer the questions that follow.

This time the waif was sober, gloomy and silent. He hardly touched the furniture and walked behind the wagons hanging his head, not even making a pretence of appearing busy. He only shivered in the cold and became embarrassed when the carters jeered at him for his idleness, his feebleness, and his tattered, fancy overcoat.

(i) **The 'waif' here refers to ....**

Ans. the beggar

(ii) **'This time' in the given extract refers to**

1. **another time when the beggar met Sergei.**
2. **a winter morning.**
3. **the day when Sergei was moving to a new place.**
4. **another task given to the beggar.**
5. **the only time that was suitable.**

(a) 1 and 5 (b) Only 3
(c) 2 and 3 (d) Only 5

Ans. (b) Only 3

(iii) **What could be the possible reasons behind the low mood of 'the waif'?**

Ans. 'The waif' could be in a low mood because he was expected to work hard at shifting the furniture. He could also be gloomy because Sergei moving to a new house meant that he could no longer be able to meet Olga.

(iv) **Complete the analogy by selecting a suitable word from the text.**

Sweating : Hot :: Shivering : ....

Ans. Cold

Short Answer Type Questions

1. Describe the appearance of the beggar.

Ans. The beggar was wearing an old torn fawn coloured overcoat. He had dull, drunken looking eyes and also had a red spot on either cheek. One of his overshoes was higher and the other was lower.

2. What request did the beggar make before Sergei?

Ans. The beggar requested Sergei to have pity on him as he was poor and hungry.

He also said that he was jobless and had nothing to eat for three days. He also didn't have money for lodging.

3. How did Sergei recognise the beggar?

Ans. When Sergei saw the beggar's shoes and noticed that his one shoe was high and the other was low, he recognised the beggar. He had seen him begging in the Sadovya street.

4. Why did Sergei threaten to call the police?

Ans. Sergei threatened to call the police as the beggar, Lushkoff, was lying. He was posing as a student and a jobless school teacher at different times in order to get money from people. Since he was cheating, Sergei threatened him.

5. Describe the initial behaviour of Olga towards the beggar.

Ans. Olga looked angrily at the beggar and moved him aside with her elbow. Then, she threw down an axe at Lushkoff's feet and shouted angrily at him. She scolded him for his drinking habit.

6. What different kinds of work did Lushkoff do at Sergei's house?

Ans. At Sergei's house, Lushkoff cut wood, removed snow, put the wood-shed in order, removed the dust out of rugs and mattresses, etc. He also helped in the packing and moving of the furniture when Sergei was shifting.

7. Why did Sergei send Lushkoff to his friend? What advice did he give to him?

Ans. Sergei sent Lushkoff to his friend so that he could get some employment and didn't have to be a manual labour. Sergei advised him to work hard and not to drink. He wanted Lushkoff to be successful at his work.

8. Who saved the beggar? How?

Ans. Both Sergei and Olga saved Lushkoff. Sergei guided Lushkoff in taking a respectable path whereas Olga's kindness and compassion saved the beggar emotionally and mentally. Olga not only criticised him but also used to cut the woods for him. She would also call him by different names and cried for his miserable condition. Seeing all this led the beggar to stop drinking and start working.

Long Answer Type Questions

1. Describe Sergei's meeting with the beggar.

Ans. Sergei met Lushkoff (the beggar) on a street. Lushkoff was acting as a village school teacher and requested Sergei to show pity on him. Sergei looked at him. When he saw his shoes, one of which was high and the other low, he recognised that he had met him earlier on Sadovya Street. Sergei told Lushkoff that when he had met Lushkoff earlier, he was acting as a student. Lushkoff was shocked and said that it was not him.

Sergei called him a liar and a dishonest person, and threatened to call the police. This made Lushkoff admit that he was lying. He told him that he was neither a school teacher nor a student. He told that he sang in a Russian singing group and was thrown out due to his drinking habits. Lushkoff also explained that if he told the truth no one would give him anything. When Sergei asked Lushkoff about work, he told that he could not find any work. So, Sergei offered him the work of cutting wood at his house. Although, he did not want to work, he accepted his offer because of shame and went with Sergei to his house.

2. Give a character sketch of Lushkoff.

Ans. Lushkoff was a poor drunken beggar with dull drunken eyes. He had a red spot on either cheek and was wearing an old and torn coat. As a beggar, Lushkoff cleverly told lies to people so that they would take pity on him and give him money. He did not want to work and thus resorted to begging. Initially, Lushkoff was in a Russian singing group.

However, because of his drinking habits, he was thrown out of it.

When Sergei offered him a job, he agreed just because of his shame and guilt. Physically, Lushkoff was a weak man who was not able to cut the wood. Lushkoff, essentially was a stubborn man who was not affected by any insults, care or taunts. Sergei's care and taunts did not change him.

However, Olga's kindness and compassion affected him deeply. Not only did he quit drinking for her but also started working hard.

As a notary, he was a great person with a strong willpower. He knew he was indebted to Sergei and Olga for helping him. Both of them took the difficult task of changing his lifestyle.

3. "You can lead a horse to water, but you can't make it drink." Justify the above proverb with reference to the story 'The Beggar'.

Ans. The story 'The Beggar' justifies the proverb "You can lead a horse to water, but you can't make it drink."

Lushkoff, the beggar, was a drunkard. He had to beg as he was not willing to work. Sergei helped him by giving him the job of cutting wood at his house and thought that he would change his thinking.

However, Lushkoff had no intention to change and did no work. All his work was done by Olga, Sergei's cook. He would come to Sergei's house so that he could get money without doing any work. When Lushkoff saw Olga's concern for him and her unconditional help, he changed his thinking.

He stopped drinking and started working hard. It was due to his own willpower that he quit drinking and became a better person and not because of the request or force of someone else.

ASSESSMENT EXERCISE

Extract Based Questions

Read the following extract carefully and answer the questions that follow.

"This is dishonesty, my dear sir!" he cried angrily. "This is swindling—I shall send the police for you, damn you!"

"Sir!" he said, laying his hand on his heart, "the fact is I was lying! I am neither a student nor a school teacher. All that was fiction. Formerly I sang in a Russian choir and was sent away for drunkenness. But what else can I do? I can't get along without lying. No one will give me anything when I tell the truth, what can I do?"

(i) Why did Sergei threaten to call the police?

(ii) What truth did the beggar reveal?

(a) He was a school master.
(b) He was in a choir.
(c) He was a student.
(d) He was uneducated.

(iii) Why did the beggar lose his job?

(iv) Which word in the extract means the same as 'to obtain something falsely'?

Short Answer (SA) Type Questions

1. Who was Sergei? Why did he help the beggar?

2. The beggar was a liar. What two lies did he tell to get money?

3. Give a character sketch of Sergei.

4. Why did the other carters make fun of Lushkoff?

5. Why did Sergei call Lushkoff his godson?

Long Answer (LA) Type Questions

1. Give a character sketch of Olga.

2. Sergei's sympathy was as important as Olga's noble deeds that reformed Lushkoff. Discuss.

ASL

Assessment of Speaking and Listening Skills

CBSE has clearly outlined the significance of Speaking and Listening Skills as a part of co-scholastic areas of achievement by every learner and also stressed the clear integration of Assessment of Speaking and Listening Skills as a part of the curriculum.

As good communication skills raise the self-esteem of a student, CBSE essentially desires that the students acquire proficiency in it by the time they leave school. In the present day global markets, speaking and listening are considered to be the essential skills of real life. So it has been felt for a long time that CBSE must focus on assessing speaking and listening skills for qualification in examination.

Considering this, CBSE has proposed to give 5% weightage to the Assessment of Speaking and Listening Skills from 2017-18 onwards. Therefore, the Assessment of Speaking and Listening Skills will be done formally at the term-end examination. Schools may conduct ASL themselves as per the guidelines provided by the CBSE.

The overall purpose of the test is to help improve and standardise student's communicative skills. Thus, in keeping with the international standards, the CBSE has put this assessment in place.

Listening Skills

The **Listening Comprehension** section tests the student's ability to listen for basic interpersonal, instructional and academic purposes. A number of sub-skills need to be developed in the everyday classroom transaction. Given below are some of the sub-skills of listening which need to be assessed.

(i) Listening for specific information
(ii) Listening for general understanding
(iii) Predictive listening
(iv) Inferential listening
(v) Listening for pleasure
(vi) Intensive listening
(vii) Evaluative listening

Role of Examiner

Here the Examiner is assigned the job of assessing a student's performance in any of the skills that is to be assessed.

It is extremely important to keep in mind the factors listed below as they can significantly influence the expected outcome of the Listening Test.

- Size of the room
- Seating arrangement
- Acoustics of the room
- Equipment used
- Quality of the recording of the listening input
- Quality of the oral rendering of the listening input (in case it is to be read aloud by the Examiner), in terms of volume, clarity, enunciation, intonation, pace, etc.

Test Administration : For the Examiner (Teacher)

- Select the time and date of the assessment.
- Plan the seating arrangement in advance.
- Decide exactly how much time is to be reserved for instructions or any possible interaction regarding clarifications etc and for the actual test.
- Make the announcement giving general instructions directed to the students before the recording is played or before the reading of the text.
- Adhere strictly to the time specified for each of the three phases of the Test (Pre-listening, While listening and Post-listening)

The Listening Assessment

The Listening Assessment comprises a variety of tasks. These tasks are graded according to the length of the task and the difficulty level. Schools may download the sample tasks and reorganise them into two parts - transcripts and the marking scheme for the examiner and the worksheets for the students on which students will write answers.

General Instructions for Students

- You are not allowed to ask questions or interrupt the Examiner at any point.
- You are being tested on your Listening Skills.
- You will hear a set of recordings of the Listening Input or listen to a reading of the Listening Input.
- Each of the recordings will be played twice. In case there is an oral rendering of the Listening Input, it shall take place twice.
- You are required to answer a set of questions based on each of the Listening Inputs.
- The assessment consists of 4 sections. You are required to attempt all 4 sections (tasks) of the assessment.
- Familiarise yourself with the questions on the worksheet. It will help you to answer them later on.
- After you have listened to the input, you will be given specified minutes to answer the questions on your worksheet.
- You may answer the questions on your worksheet while listening.
- Do not interact/comment until you have moved out of the examination room.

PRACTICE ASSIGNMENT

Instructions

The test comprises four tasks which have been divided into twenty questions.

Each question carries 1 mark.

Each of the tasks is based on a transcript which may be in the form of a speech, conversation, or a short extract conveying some useful information.

Answer the questions as you listen to the transcripts.

TASK 1

Through the given QR code or link, you will hear Roshan Taneja, head of the Literary Club of your school, talking about the importance of reading as a skill. Read the questions below, then listen to the extract and choose four of the options A to G which are correct. You will hear the recording twice.

DOWNLOAD LINK OR QR CODE FOR TRANSCRIPT

Link https://goo.gl/LjTTWx OR **Scan the Code**

Transcript

Good morning friends! Today I wish to talk to you about the importance of reading as a skill. I strongly believe that reading is the master key to success.

Today you have many opportunities to gather information. You can practise reading from books, electronic tablets, smart phones or on computers.

Reading is a vital skill in finding a job. Many well-paying jobs require reading as a part of job performance. There are reports and memos which must be read and responded to.

Good readers develop their ability to concentrate. They read and comprehend the main message easily. Reading helps people focus on what someone else is communicating.

Reading also helps us discover new things. We live in an age where there is an overflow of information, but reading is the main way to take advantage of it.

Last but not the least; let's not forget that reading is fundamental in developing a good self-image.

So what are you waiting for? You should come and join our literary club, see the wonders and start your new journey on the road to success today.

Questions

Which FOUR of the following statements does the speaker believe to be true?

- **A.** Reading is a guarantee for success as a student.
- **B.** Many students like to read books and magazines these days.
- **C.** These days there are many sources of reading to get information.
- **D.** Reading increases focus on the message.
- **E.** For getting jobs reading skill is not required these days.
- **F.** Reading is required in the discovery of new things.
- **G.** Good readers are isolated from society.

TASK 2

Through the given QR code or link, you will listen to two students, a boy and a girl, debate on the topic 'Technology makes us alone'. Read the sentences below, then listen to the conversation and complete the sentences with one or two words only. You will hear the recording twice.

DOWNLOAD LINK OR QR CODE FOR TRANSCRIPT

Link https://goo.gl/GXAgVu OR **Scan the Code**

Transcript

Sohan Hi! Why are you not using your mobile phone?

Sheetal Well. I've accepted the challenge to live without my mobile for a week.

Sohan Wow. That's some challenge, but why? Who convinced you to do something like that?

Sheetal My mother of course! She feels that I am becoming lonely because I'm too much on the phone.

Sohan Hmm. There is some truth in the statement.

Sheetal What do you mean? I have three thousand friends on Facebook.

Sohan Exactly because you have three thousand friends on Facebook you have no time to say hello to your real friends who are around you. Because of excessive use of mobile phones, nowdays you see so many talking fingers and silent mouths.

Sheetal Don't get carried away. There is another side to the argument. I think technology and social media are really good. They help us do things faster and in a more effective way.

Sohan There may be some truth in what you are saying.

Sheetal There is a lot of truth in what I am saying. Technology has enabled us to strengthen relationships by keeping in contact with old friends, colleagues and co-workers.

Sohan Ugh…h…don't get angry, all that I am saying is don't forget your real friends in real world chasing virtual friends in virtual world.

Sheetal Okay, I will not. Happy now!

Questions

1. The girl is becoming .... because she is too much on phone.
2. The girl thinks that we cannot .... technology for our laziness.
3. Technology has created people with .... fingers and .... mouths.
4. Technology helps us do things .... and more efficiently.
5. According to the boy, we forget our .... in keeping track of virtual friends.

TASK 3

Through the given QR code or link, you will listen to some tips for maintaining healthy skin. Read the notes given in your worksheet, then listen to the tips and complete the notes with one or two words only. You will listen to the recording twice.

DOWNLOAD LINK OR QR CODE FOR TRANSCRIPT

Link https://goo.gl/5nhhGg OR **Scan the Code**

Transcript

Here are simple tips that can help you prevent various skin problems. Hot water baths remove oils from your skin. So limit your bathing time and use warm rather than hot water. Avoid strong soaps and detergents as they can also strip oil from your skin. Instead choose mild cleansers for bathing and washing. After bathing, gently pat or blot your skin dry with a towel so that some moisture remains on your skin. Eat plenty of fruits, vegetables, whole grains and proteins to look and feel your best. Stress can make your skin more sensitive and trigger various skin problems. So take steps to manage your stress and make time to do the things you enjoy having healthy skin.

Questions

Tips for Healthy Skin

1. You are advised against using hot water for bathing to avoid losing .... from your skin.
2. You should .... your skin for drying after taking a bath.
3. A well balanced diet is essential to .... your finest.
4. You need to control the .... in your life as it causes many skin problems.

TASK 4

Through the given QR code or link, you will listen to a girl and her friend having a conversation about benefits of travelling. Read the statements below, then listen to the conversation and choose five of the options A-H which are correct.

DOWNLOAD LINK OR QR CODE FOR TRANSCRIPT

Link https://goo.gl/syW3U5 OR **Scan the Code**

Transcript

Girl Hi, how's life? I didn't see you in the holidays. Where have you been?

Boy I had gone with my family on a trip to the North East.

Girl You and your family seem to love travelling.

Boy Yes, we do. Travelling has many benefits.

Girl I know....such as having fun and getting to spend time with our family. It also provides us an opportunity to relax.

Boy Well, yes. It is said travelling refreshes our mind and clears off stress and so improves our overall health. But travelling also helps us broaden our mind.

Girl What do you mean by that?

Boy I feel travelling is a fun way to learn not only about new places but meet different people and develop an understanding about their culture.

Girl Umm … I never thought of it, but you are correct. Travelling helps us discover the similarities we have with other people as well as the differences between us.

Boy Quite correct. You know in addition to gaining knowledge of History and Geography, travelling also helps us to learn important life skills.

Girl You mean … we become more independent.

Boy Yes, we also learn to find our way in an unknown place amongst unknown people who may speak a different language. Nothing can replace the unique experiences that travelling offers.

Girl Yes and now I too feel inspired to plan a trip in the autumn break. I'll take some suggestions from you since you travel so much.

Boy Sure, any time. Travel the world – learn, see, absorb and enjoy. All the best!

Questions

A. The boy and his family enjoy travelling.
B. Travelling provides a refreshing change from our daily routine.
C. Meeting new people and understanding their culture makes us more tolerant.
D. Travelling boosts our creativity and imagination.
E. Our knowledge of History and Geography increases through travelling.
F. We pick up new languages when we travel to new places.
G. Travelling offers us unique experiences like none other.
H. One must read books on travelling.

☑ TASK 5

Through the given QR code or link, your School Counsellor has been asked to address the students in the school assembly and share some tips for getting over the fear of exams. You will now hear the speech given by the Counsellor. Read the questions given in your worksheet, then listen to the extract and choose a, b or c for each question. You will hear the recording twice.

DOWNLOAD LINK OR QR CODE FOR TRANSCRIPT

Link https://goo.gl/JrBnP3 OR **Scan the Code**

Transcript

Good morning, dear students. My regular interaction with many students has shown that many of you feel scared of exams. Actually many students don't know how to study and prepare properly for exams. So today I'm here to share with you some tips that I'm sure will benefit you.

First while in class, it is important to listen attentively to the teacher. Also take notes for taking notes will help you comprehend and recall information that you have learned. You must not hesitate from asking questions to clarify your doubts.

Doing homework regularly is of great help. Next, while doing self-study, you should always start with studying the easiest topic first. Develop the habit of skimming or quickly glancing through whatever it is that you have to read, before you actually read it.

Reread notes that you have taken down in class. If you don't remember the answer to a question, all you would have to generally do is to quickly check your notes. Next, I would say there is no getting away from hard work.

Finally, I would suggest that you form or join study groups. A study group is an excellent way to share and clarify information. Don't be shy in asking your friends or siblings for help.

I do hope you will use these tips and be more confident.

Questions

1. Many students are afraid of exams because they

(a) feel confused. (b) lack knowledge.
(c) are unprepared.

2. Taking notes helps you to

(a) break down content into small points. (b) better understand and remember things.
(c) be more focused while studying.

3. Asking questions is helpful for

(a) expressing your doubts. (b) understanding main ideas.
(c) overcoming your hesitation.

4. To improve reading comprehension

(a) study the easiest topic first. (b) glance through what you have to read.
(c) reread the text carefully.

5. You have to study hard, but

(a) regular practice helps in memorisation.
(b) understanding is more important than memorisation.
(c) making acronyms and songs help in memorisation.

6. Joining a study group is a good way of

(a) not feeling shy in asking for help. (b) getting your work reviewed.
(c) sharing information and removing doubts.

Answers

Task 1

A, C, D, F

Task 2

1. lonely **2.** blame **3.** talking, silent **4.** faster **5.** real friends/ friends

Task 3

1. oils **2.** gently pat **3.** look **4.** stress

Task 4

A, B, C, D, E

Task 5

1. c **2.** b **3.** b **4.** b **5.** c **6.** c

Speaking Skills

Speaking skill has acquired a very important place as a communication skill. Like listening skill, a number of sub-skills of speaking need to be consciously developed among students. Some of the sub-skills which can be assessed are as follows

- Speaking intelligibly using appropriate word stress, sentence stress and intonation patterns.
- Narrating incidents and events, real or imaginary in a logical sequence.
- Presenting oral reports or summaries; making announcements clearly and confidently.
- Expressing and arguing a point of view clearly and effectively.
- Taking active part in group discussions, showing ability to express agreement or disagreement, summarising ideas, eliciting the views of others and presenting own ideas.
- Expressing and responding to personal feelings, opinions and attitudes.
- Participating in spontaneous spoken discourse in familiar social situations.

General Instructions

1. The total administration time for the speaking assessment is approximately 10-12 min.
2. The speaking assessment will be conducted for two students at a time.
3. There will be a single teacher to function as the Examiner.
4. The Examiner should be a qualified English teacher.

Role of Examiner

- The Examiner should ensure that the room is quiet and has good acoustics.
- The tone, manner and body language of the Examiner should be relaxed, encouraging and pleasant. Care should be taken to make the candidates feel at ease.
- Students must not be discouraged from making a fresh start in case they are unable to do so at the first attempt.
- The Examiner needs to be flexible, sympathetic and reassuring in her/his demeanour.
- The Examiner should also be a proficient user of the language in order to conduct the Speaking Assessment successfully. For example, the Examiner should be skilled in elicitation techniques, so that questions such as... "Explain how"/"Why"..."Tell me what you think of" .... may be asked. "Yes/ No" questions should generally be avoided.
- Ideally, the Examiner should award marks after the candidates have left the examination room. If necessary, notes can be made discreetly to be used later in the scoring, so that it does not make the candidates unduly tense and self-conscious.

The Speaking Assessment is divided into three stages

Stage 1 General Introduction

The aim of this introductory task is to put the candidate at ease through some general, open-ended questions, thereby creating a space for the candidate to respond with personal feelings and opinions. Simple warm up questions based on the candidate's name, place of residence, leisure preference etc are asked.

Stage 2 Topic Presentation

This can take the form of PowerPoint/OHP presentations, book reviews, debates, speech etc. The focus of this task is to assess a candidate's ability to sustain a straightforward, subjectwise description, mapped out in a fluent and cohesive style.

In this section, the Examiner gives each candidate the choice to pick up a Role Card or a Cue Card with a topic written on it. The candidates are given 1 minute to prepare. The examiner should be ready with sheets of paper and a pencil. Candidates may organise their thoughts and ideas. Prior to the day of the Speaking Assessment, as an assistance to students to prepare for the presentations, the teacher can give a choice of 20 to 30 topics in class to students so that they can prepare presentations based on the topics and organise their ideas. Similar topics can be given in the actual assessment.

Students are not allowed to write full length answers. They may jot down points only in the sheets given by the Examiner. Therefore, a pencil and sheet of paper should be provided on the table. Students are not allowed to carry pen, paper or mobile phone to the examination room. After a minute for making notes, each student will be given 2 minutes to present his/her ideas. In case a student is unable to speak during/for the allotted time, the Examiner may ask some rounding off questions.

Stage 3 Problem Solving (Pair Interaction)

The third section of the test is for 3 minutes. Both students are given a verbal or visual stimulus and asked to respond to it. Both the students are given a total of 3 minutes to interact. Both of them will talk together. After 2 minutes, the Examiner can ask questions based on their discussion.

Closing

The closing is for 1 minute duration only. In case a student has not been able to speak or has been unable to speak owing to nervousness, the dominance of the second candidate or any other factor, then the Examiner may use the 1 minute to give a fresh opportunity to that student.

CBSE Assessment of Speaking and Listening (ASL) Descriptors for Assessment of Speaking

Interactive Competence	5	4	3	2	1
Task Management	Contributions are highly effective and fulfil the task. Can fulfil the communicative functions of the level with spontaneity.	Contributions are effective and fulfil the task. Can fulfil the communicative functions of the level.	Contributions are adequate and fulfil the task. Can fulfil functions of the level but may not do so consistently.	Contributions are limited and there is some attempt at the task which is not fulfilled and/or may be repetitive.	There is almost no contribution and/or contributions may not be related to the task.
Initiation and Turn-taking	Is prompt to initiate discussions on the themes/ functions at the given level appropriately. Contributes spontaneously to keep the interaction going; takes turns appropriately.	Is easily able to initiate discussions on the themes/ functions at the given level appropriately. Contributes effectively to keep the interaction going and takes turn appropriately.	Is able to initiate discussions on the themes/ functions at the given level. Makes an effort to keep the interaction going; takes turns.	Struggles to initiate discussions on the themes/functions at the given level. Makes little effort to keep the interaction going.	Does not initiate discussions. Makes no effort to keep the interaction going.
Appropriacy and Relevance	Speaks with a clear sense of purpose and audience in both formal and informal situations. Contributions are always appropriate to the context/ situation.	Speaks with a fair sense of purpose and audience in both formal and informal situations. May be less confident in normal situations	Speaks with an awareness of purpose and audience may not adapt/register effectively. Contributions are appropriate to the context/ situation.	Has unclear sense of purpose and may be unable to adapt/ register. Contributions may be unconnected to the context/ situation.	Has hardly any sense of purpose and cannot adapt to register.

Fluency	5	4	3	2	1
Cohesion and Coherence, Speed of Delivery	Presents information in a logical sequence of linked utterances with a clear connection between ideas, arguments and statements. Uses a range of cohesive devices. Speaks fluently with minimal hesitation. Intelligible speed of delivery.	Presents information in a logical sequence of linked utterances with a connection between ideas, arguments and statements. Uses with ease some cohesive devices. Speaks fluently with some hesitation. Intelligible speed of delivery.	Presents information generally in a logical order but overall progression may not always be clear. Uses a range of cohesive devices but some over/under use. Coherence may be affected by hesitancy or rephrasing. Intelligible speed of delivery.	Presents information but without clear progression. Uses limited cohesive devices repetitively. Severe hesitation may impede communication. Speed of delivery impedes understanding.	Presents information with no progression and/or little control of organisational features. May use only isolated words and phrases.
Pronunciation	**5**	**4**	**3**	**2**	**1**
Pronunciation, Stress and Intonation	Has clear, natural pronunciation that can be easily understood by the listener. Varies stress and intonation in keeping with the task, content and meaning.	Has pronunciation that can be easily understood by the listener. Varies stress and intonation in keeping with the task, content and meaning.	Is intelligible though there are examples of some mispronunciation. Tries to speak, varying stress and intonation according to task, content and meaning.	Is not always intelligible and the listener may have to ask for repetition from time to time. Flat intonation and/or inappropriate stress for the task, content or meaning.	Is not intelligible.
Language	**5**	**4**	**3**	**2**	**1**
Accuracy	Uses a range of grammatical patterns with accuracy, including some complex forms. Makes only negligible errors.	Uses a range of grammatical patterns with accuracy, including few complex forms and makes only noticeable errors.	There may be some mistakes which affect meaning but there is an attempt to correct most of these mistakes.	There are mistakes which affect meaning but there is hardly an attempt to correct these mistakes.	Communicates with fragments of words and structures but does not manage to bridge the gaps or correct his/her mistakes.
Range	Uses an expressive and appropriate range of structures, words and phrases on topics appropriate to the level and to deliver an effective message.	Uses an expressive and appropriate range of words and phrases on topics appropriate to the level. These may be repetitive.	Can use the language of the level but is repetitive. May search for words with the risk of the message becoming weaker.	Uses basic, simple words and phrases for the level. There may be an effort to find suitable words, which may hamper the message.	Uses simple, isolated words for the level. There is little effort to find words.

AN OVERVIEW OF SPEAKING TEST

STAGE 1

1. Introduction (1 min)

Section Time	Procedure
10 secs	Examiner Hello, please sit down. My name is X. What's your name? *(to Candidate A)* And what's your name? *(to Candidate B)* So your names are *(name and serial number A)* and *(name and serial number B).*
25 secs	*(Candidate A), tell me something about (e.g. where you live).* Candidate A responds.
25 secs	*(Candidate B), tell me something about (e.g. your school).* Candidate B responds.

STAGE 2

2. Topic Presentation (4 mins)

Section Time	Procedure
5 secs	Examiner Now *(Candidate A)*, you are going to tell us about your topic. When you have finished, *(Candidate B)* will ask you a question and then I will ask you some more questions. Would you like to begin please?
1 min	Candidate A speaks
15 secs	Examiner Thank you. *(Candidate B)* can you ask *(Candidate A)* a question please? Candidate B asks question; Candidate A responds.
40 secs	The Examiner asks 2 or 3 follow-up questions as appropriate from the topic prompt list. *Stage 2 example follow-up questions* How often do you .... ? Why? When you .... do you .... ? Why do you think .... is important?
5 secs	Examiner Thank you. Now *(Candidate B)*, you are going to tell us about your topic. When you have finished, *(Candidate A)* will ask you a question and then I will ask you some more questions. Would you like to begin please?
1 min	Candidate B speaks.
15 secs	Examiner Thank you. *(Candidate A)* can you ask *(Candidate B)* a question please? Candidate A asks a question; Candidate B responds.
40 secs	The examiner asks 2 or 3 follow-up questions as appropriate from the topic prompt list.

☑ STAGE 3

3. Problem Solving (3 mins)

Section Time	Procedure
25 secs	Examiner Thank you. Now let's go to the next task. I'm going to give you a card which has information about a problem. I'd like you to read the information and then discuss together how you are going to solve the problem. You have 2 mins to do this. Here is your problem. *Stage 3 sample problem solving card* Your classmates have not been keeping the school tidy. After lessons, there is litter in the classrooms and in the halls. With your partner, discuss this problem and decide what you can do to make the school a nicer, cleaner place for everyone. Candidates read the given card (20 secs) and then the examiner asks to start speaking.
2 mins	Candidates discuss the problem and a solution.
35 secs	Examiner OK, can you stop now please. Option A (for candidates who have not reached a solution): Thank you. *(Move straight on to a question)* Option B (for candidates who have not reached a solution): *Can you agree on a solution? What is it?* Candidates explain Then the examiner asks 1 or 2 follow-up questions as appropriate from the list of problem solving prompts. *Stage 3 example follow-up questions* • Do you think your solution will be effective enough? Why?/Why not? • What role do you think ………… plays in this problem? Why? • ……… sounds interesting. Could you tell me more about that/this? Please stop there. That's the end of the test. Thank you and go.

PRACTICE ASSIGNMENT

Instructions

The speaking assessment will be conducted for two students at a time.
Students should not carry pen, paper, mobile phone etc.
The teacher will be both the Examiner and Assessor who will also give marks to the candidates.

STAGE 1

1. General Introduction (1 min)

The Examiner makes the students feel comfortable.

Examiner Good morning, I am …… . Hope you are looking forward to this brief interaction.
Student A Yes …………………./I am ………………………….
Examiner And what about you? *(Looking at Student B)*
Student B ……………………………………………………….
Examiner What do you do in your spare time? *(To Student B)*
Student B ……………………………………………………….
Examiner And how about you? *(To Student A)*
Student A ……………………………………………………….
Examiner What makes you special? *(To Student A)*
Student A ……………………………………………………….
Examiner What about you? *(To Student B)*
Student B ……………………………………………………….
Examiner What do you admire in other people? *(To Student A)*
Student A ……………………………………………………….
Examiner How about you? *(To Student B)*
Student B ……………………………………………………….
Examiner Thank you. This is the end of the first part of the test.

STAGE 2

2. Mini Presentation (1 min Preparation + 2 mins each for the students = 5 mins)
Now, in this part of the test, candidates are given a topic with some points. They have a minute to prepare on the given topic and two minutes for the presentation.

Students are given the following sets of inputs on cards or sheets of paper. Three options are given. Only one option has to be used at a time.

Examiner *(To both A and B)* Here is your topic. Both of you prepare your presentation on it. You are given one minute for preparation. Please use the pencil and paper for writing points. After one minute, I will ask you to present your views on the topic. I can ask either one of you first. So be prepared and get ready. *(Examiner hands over one card with clues to both A and B)*

Mobile phones in school

- Security
- Multiple uses
- Distraction

If the student is not able to speak at length, the teacher could ask rounding off questions.

- Do you think mobile phones should be allowed in school?
- Give two advantages of carrying a mobile phone to school.
- Do you think advantages outweigh the disadvantages?

2. Changing concepts and methodologies of teaching-learning in India
   - Examination pattern
   - Variety of subjects
   - Assessment parameters

If the student is not able to speak at length, the teacher could ask rounding off questions.

- Do you like this present system of evaluation?
- Do you learn better when you are stress free?
- Do you think some students take this system very casually?

3. An incident/person/book that changed my life.
   - Name of Book/Person or Incidents.
   - What is it about?
   - How has it affected you?

If the student is not able to speak at length, the teacher could ask rounding off questions.

- What was that specific quality that remained with you?
- What did you learn?
- How would you like to be now?

STAGE 3

3. Pair Interaction (3 mins)

Examiner In this part of the test, the candidates A and B will discuss the given topic together. The examiner can refer to the assessment scale while the candidates are discussing together.

Students respond to visual/verbal stimulus.

1. **Changing roles of women— a multi-tasker, works in office, answers phone calls and is always under pressure of work. Working at home is additional.**

2. **Growing Pollution—all kinds of pollution, water, air and tourism pollution.**

3. **Discipline issues in schools are now becoming a serious concern. As responsible citizens discuss**
   (i) Kinds of indiscipline issues
   (ii) Reasons for growing indiscipline
   (iii) Advice/solutions for your fellow students.

4. **Closing (1 min)**
   Thank you very much. That was the end of your test. The Examiner retrieves the pencil and paper.

Suggested Topics for Presentation

1. Women Empowerment
2. Child Abuse in India
3. Speaking English is the ladder to success
4. Does Science hold the key to the future?
5. Corruption cannot be eradicated from India
6. Crime against women
7. Biodiversity
8. Effects of pollution on historical monuments
9. Social networking has made us antisocial
10. Is Delhi a home away from home for North-Eastern students?
11. Female Foeticide
12. Effects of Advertisement on children
13. Keeping pets is a violation of animal rights
14. Science is a threat to humanity
15. Parents should let teens make their own decisions
16. Reality Television does more harm than good
17. Juveniles should be tried as adults
18. Mercy Killing
19. Value-based politics is the need of the hour
20. Global climate change is man-made

Suggested Questions for Problem Solving Task

1. Some of your classmates are under-confident in speaking English. They are also a little shy and do not know how to get help. They simply do not know how to improve their spoken English. With your partner, discuss what could be done to help them.
2. Your school's basket ball team has been performing badly for a few months and has not won any matches. The morale of the team is also very low. With your partner, discuss how the situation could be handled, and the performance of the team could be improved.
3. You have a friend in your class who wants to learn swimming, but also confesses that he/she is scared of water. With your partner, discuss how this fear can be overcome.

Sample Question Paper 1 (Solved)

A Highly Simulated Sample Question Paper for CBSE Class IX

English Language and Literature

Time : 3 hrs	M.M. : 80

General Instructions

1. This question paper is divided into three sections.
2. All questions are compulsory.
3. Separate instructions are given with each section and question, wherever necessary. Read these instructions very carefully and follow them.
4. Do not exceed the prescribed word limit while answering the questions.

Section-A (Reading Skills) (20 Marks)

1. Read the passage given below carefully. **(10)**

1. The three major effects of viewing TV violence are: children may become less sensitive to the pain and suffering of others, they may be more fearful of the world around them and they may be more likely to behave in aggressive or harmful ways towards others. Parents can limit the effects of violence by viewing TV together with the child and discussing the violence with the child. Talk about why the violence happened and how painful it is. They may ask the child how conflicts can be 'solved' without violence and explain to the child how violence on an entertainment programme is actually 'fake'. Parents must restrict violent videos. Encourage your child to watch programmes with characters that cooperate, help and care for one another. These programmes have been shown to have a positive influence on children.
2. Television programming currently is all about showing reality without censorship, meaning that children are inundated with shows depicting physical and sexual violence, as well as the use of illegal substances and harsh language. According to the American Academy of Pediatrics, "Extensive research evidence indicates that media violence can contribute to aggressive behaviour, desensitisation to violence, nightmares and fear of being harmed." Statistics say that some cartoons average twenty acts of violence in one hour and that by the age of eighteen children will have seen 16,000 simulated murders and 200,000 acts of violence on television. Young people are especially in jeopardy of the negative effects of television violence because "many younger children cannot discriminate between what they see and what is real".
3. Read to your child rather than watch television. Children's stories, written by thoughtful authors, portray conflict in a more realistic and constructive manner. The best TV teachers are entertaining as well as informative and they are also child-centred, so that they expand the horizons of the young minds.
4. Watching these programmes provides children with the right stimulus to acquire knowledge through an indirect play-way methodology. Absorption of such knowledge and the love for learning are stirred and the child begins to understand the explorative thrills of the knowledge track, where he becomes the racing car driver speeding the knowledge vehicle through his own speedometer of knowledge acquisition.

Answer the following questions on the basis of the passage you have read.

(i) How can parents limit the effects of violence on their children? **(1)**

(ii) Complete the sentence appropriately. **(1)**

The methodology suggested by the author for effective learning is ....

(a) hit and trial (b) play way

(iii) State drawbacks of viewing TV violence. **(2)**

(iv) The passage includes some words that are opposites. Identify the antonyms. **(1)**

(a) aggressive – violent (b) reality – videos
(c) conflict – cooperate (d) expand – limit
(e) speeding – aquisition

(v) State whether the given statement is true or false. **(1)**

TV time and programme should be scrutinised.

(vi) Which among the following will help to have a positive influence on children? **(1)**

(a) Watch programmes which encourage positivity.
(b) Watch programmes which are showing reality with harsh language.
(c) Watch programmes with characters that cooperate, help and care for each other.
(d) Watch programmes which boost up your morale.

(vii) Suggest an appropriate title for the passage. Give reason for your answer. **(2)**

(viii) Choose the option that best captures the central idea of the passage. **(1)**

(a) TV is not the only source of entertainment. (b) TV affects the young children.
(c) Effects of violence by viewing TV. (d) Sensitive approach towards television programmes.

2. Read the passage given below carefully. **(10)**

The Amazon River Basin is home to the largest rainforest on Earth. The basin — roughly the size of the forty-eight contiguous United States — covers some 40 percent of the South American continent and includes parts of eight South American countries: Brazil, Bolivia, Peru, Ecuador, Colombia, Venezuela, Guyana, and Suriname, as well as French Guiana, a department of France.

Reflecting environmental conditions as well as past human influence, the Amazon is made up of a mosaic of ecosystems and vegetation types including rainforests, seasonal forests, deciduous forests, flooded forests, and savannas.

The basin is drained by the Amazon River, the world's largest river in terms of discharge, and the second longest river in the world after the Nile. The river is made up of over 1,100 tributaries, 17 of which are longer than 1000 miles and two of which are larger, in terms of volume, than the Congo river. The river system is the lifeline of the forest.

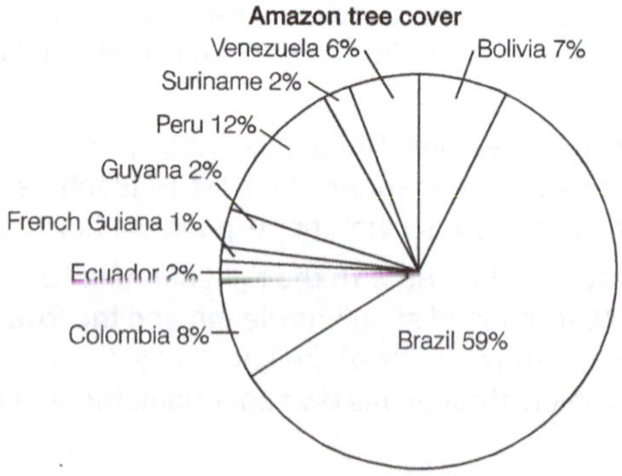

The extent of the Amazon depends on the definition. The biogeographic Amazon ranges from 7.76-8.24 million sq km (3-3.2 million sq mi), of which just over 80 percent is forested. Today the Amazon River is the most voluminous river on Earth, carrying more than five times the volume of the Congo or twelve times that of the Mississippi, draining an area nearly the size of the forty-eight contiguous United States.

The Amazon has a long history of human settlement, but in recent decades the pace of change has accelerated due to an increase in human population, the introduction of mechanised agriculture and integration of the Amazon region into the global economy. Vast quantities of commodities produced in the Amazon — cattle beef and leather, timber, soy, oil and gas and minerals, to name a few — are exported today to China, Europe, the U.S. Russia, and other countries. This shift has had substantial negative impacts on the Amazon.

Answer the following questions on the basis of the passage you have read.

(i) Based on your understanding of the passage, choose the option that lists the types of vegetation not found in the Amazon rainforests. **(1)**

1. Seasonal forests | **2. Deciduous forests**

3. Flooded forests | **4. Savannas**

5. Tropical evergreen forests | **6. Mangrove forests**

(a) 1 and 2 (b) 3 and 4 (c) 5 and 6 (d) 2 and 6

(ii) Select the option that is true for the Assertion (A) and Reason (R) given below. **(1)**

Assertion (A) The Amazon rainforest is larger than the USA.

Reason (R) The rainforest is home to many endangered species.

(a) Both the (A) and (R) are true, and (R) is the correct explanation of (A).
(b) Both the (A) and (R) are true, but (R) is not the correct explanation of (A).
(c) (A) is true, but (R) is false.
(d) (A) is false, but (R) is true.

(iii) Identify the word from the passage which means the same as 'joining'. **(1)**

(iv) Which region contains the largest forest cover of the Amazon? **(1)**

(v) Select the correct option to complete the following sentence. **(1)**

About .... (80%/85%/95%) of the land covering the Amazon is forested.

(vi) What are the features of the Amazon? **(2)**

(vii) Complete the following sentence. **(1)**

To show the vastness of the Amazonian river basin, the writer compares it to ....

(viii) What can the vastness of the Amazonian land be credited to? What is the development of the Amazon rainforests dependent on? **(2)**

Section-B (Grammar) (10 Marks)

3. Attempt ANY TEN of the following questions.

(i) Fill in the blank by choosing the correct option to complete the following sentence. **(1)**

A theory .... only when a hypothesis .... by consistent results from many observations or experiments.

(a) may have been developed, was being supported (b) can be developed, has been supported
(c) will be developed, was supported (d) has been developed, had been supported

(ii) Identify the error in the given sentence. **(1)**

It has taking almost a year for India to let its pessimism translate into fewer jobs.

Use the given format for your response.

Error	Correction

(iii) Write the correct indirect speech of the following sentence. **(1)**

Rajan said to Urvashi, "I'm going to Kashmir tomorrow."

(iv) Select the correct option to fill in the blank for the given line. **(1)**

I've seen .... of his work to know that he's ready for a promotion.

(a) both (b) a few (c) several (d) enough

(v) Complete the sentence keeping the meaning of the statement intact. **(1)**

'Turn around.' he told her.

He ....

(vi) Select the option that identifies the error and supplies the correction for the following line. **(1)**

Millions of Jews lost their kith and kin in Hitler concentration camps.

Options	Error	Correction
(a)	of	In
(b)	their	Its
(c)	Hitler	Hitler's
(d)	camps	camp

(vii) Complete the given sentence from a report, by filling in the blank with the correct option. **(1)**

Helen .... her driving test five times so far without success.

(a) takes (b) has taken (c) was taking (d) is taking

(viii) Identify the error in the given sentence. **(1)**

Police reports claim that substantial seizure of cocaine have been made in the last two months.

Use the given format for your response.

Error	Correction

(ix) Select the correct option to complete the narration of the dialogue between Sameera and her brother. **(1)**

Brother : Gaaaaahhhh!

Sameera : Yeah, so I decided to try something different with my hair.

When Sameera came back from the hair salon, her brother was waiting for her. He was shocked to see his sister. She told him ....

(x) Fill in the blank by choosing the correct option. **(1)**

When the river was flooded, the farmhouse was surrounded by water on .... sides.

(a) every (b) either (c) all (d) each

(xi) Fill in the blank by using the correct form of the word. **(1)**

An elephant .... other animals in intelligence.

(a) excelled (b) excels (c) excel (d) will excel

(xii) Report the given statement. **(1)**

I said to my friend, "Can you pick me up after work?"

I asked my friend ....

Error	Correction

Section-B (Writing Skills) (10 Marks)

4. **Last summer vacation you went to your friend's village. His grandmother looked after you as if you were her grandchild. Describe her in 100-120 words.** **(5)**

Or

Describe the Annual Day celebrations in your school in about 150 words. Use the following hints.

Date and Time - 22nd April, 2020 at 6:00 pm Place - School Auditorium

Chief Guest - Mr Ravindra Gupta, District Magistrate

Activities - Annual Report Presentation, Prize Distribution, Cultural Programmes, Speech by the Chief Guest, Vote of Thanks

5. **You are Naresh/Naina. You happened to go to your friend's place in a crowded bus today. Record your experience in 100-120 words in the form of a diary entry.** **(5)**

Bad experience – board the bus – so hot – pushing each other – thirty hours – sigh of relief

Or

Complete the story in 100-120 words which begins as follows

There was a storm brewing outside and my brother and I were all alone at home. Suddenly the lights went out..........

Section-C (Literature) (40 Marks)

Reference to the context **(5 + 5 = 10)**

6. The game's up as far as I'm concerned. Things went wrong with me. I said it with bullets and got away. Unfortunately they got one of my men and found things the fool should have burnt. Tonight I'm expecting trouble. My bag's packed ready to clear off. There it is. *(If I were you)* **(5)**

(i) What is the purpose of the given lines?

(a) To convince the intruder to not to kill me
(b) To distract the intruder
(c) To join the intruder
(d) Both (a) and (b)

(ii) What does he pose himself to be? Why?

(iii) Fill in the blank appropriately.

He had committed .... (a theft/a murder)

(iv) What is the 'game' here? Is it true? If not why?

Or

"As he is no longer beautiful, he is no longer useful." said the Art Professor at the University. Then they melted the statue in a furnace. "What a strange thing?" said the overseer of the workmen at the foundry. *(The Happy Prince)*

(i) Read the sentence and choose the option that complete it. The Beauty of 'he' is connected with

(a) Its size
(b) Jewels
(c) Facial expression
(d) Position

(ii) What is being talked about in the given extract?

(iii) "He is no longer beautiful, he is no longer useful."

These lines show the immense inclinations towards .... (creativity/beauty)

(iv) What strange thing was observed by the overseer?

7. Or pulled out entirely,
Out from the earth-cave,
And the strength of the tree exposed
The source, white and wet,
The most sensitive, hidden
For years inside the earth. *(On Killing a Tree)* **(5)**

(i) What does 'Earth-cave' in the extract refer to?

(ii) Complete the sentence appropriately.

Strength of the tree is in ....

(iii) Do you think the tree is a metaphor? If yes, of what?

(iv) What is the rhyme scheme of the given extract?

(a) abcdef (b) aabbcc (c) ababcc (d) aaabbb

Or

Away, away in the Northland,
Where the hours of the day are few,
And the nights so long in winter
That they cannot sleep them through *(A Legend of the Northland)*

(i) Where do you think Northland is located?

(ii) Who are 'they' in the above lines?

They are ....

(iii) Why do you think 'they' cannot sleep through the night?

(iv) Why do you think nights are long and days are shorter in the region?

1. Location of the place makes a difference.

2. The region does not receive much sunlight through the winters.

3. The region receives maximum sunlight during winters.

(a) Only 3 is correct (b) 1 and 3 are correct
(c) 1 and 2 are correct (d) 2 and 3 are correct

Short and Long Answer Questions

8. Answer ANY FOUR of the following questions in 40-50 words each. **($3 \times 4 = 12$)**

(i) What kind of book did Tommy show to Margie?

(ii) Describe in brief the efforts made by Einstein after he realised how atomic bombs will be used as a weapon of destruction.

(iii) What did Saint Peter ask the old lady for? What was the lady's response?

(iv) In 'The Rain on the Roof' how does the poet describe the rainy night?

(v) After the encounter with the snake, why did the narrator want to remove his things from his room? Why did he find that he had little to carry?

9. Answer ANY TWO of the following questions in 40-50 words each. **($3 \times 2 = 6$)**

(i) How did the author of 'A House is Not a Home' regain a sense of security and life?

(ii) Why was Grandfather pleased even though Toto had escaped from the closet? What does this tell us about his character? (The Adventure of Toto)

(iii) Why was the bird unable to sleep peacefully the first night? (The Happy Prince)

10. Answer ANY ONE of the following questions in 100-120 words. **(6)**

"The only woman in the world who has scaled Mt Everest twice was born in a society where the birth of a son was regarded as blessing and a daughter, though not considered a curse, was not generally welcome."

Based on the above lines describe what qualities in Santosh Yadav helped her get into the record books both times she conquered Mt Everest? Do you think, Evelyn Glennie shows the same characteristics? Justify your stance.

Or

"Our life is often governed by the choices we make." Do you agree with this statement? Justify your answer with reference to the poem 'The Road Not Taken'.

11. Answer ANY ONE of the following questions in 100-120 words. **(6)**

You are the narrator of the 'The Adventures of Toto'. You have written a letter to your friend telling him about your grandfather. What would you tell him about your grandfather?

You may start like this

Grandfather is a lover of animals. He loves ....

Or

By nature and from childhood itself' human beings have dual or ambiguous attitude to react differently in different situations. Keeping in mind the lesson 'The Lost Child', support the given statement in the form of a diary entry.

Answers

1. (i) Parents can limit the effects of violence on their children by discussing violent scenes to guide them better about how to resolve conflict.

(ii) (b) play-way

(iii) The drawbacks of viewing TV violence are that it promotes aggressive behaviour and harmful practices among children. They becomes less sensitive to pain and suffering of others. Further, they may become more fearful of the world around them.

(iv) (c) and (d)

(v) True

(vi) (c) Watch programmes with characters that cooperate, help and care for each other.

(vii) The most appropriate title of the passage will be 'TV and Violence'. This is so becuase the passage talks about how violence present in television programmes impacts the young minds. It also presents various ways on replacing/negating the impacts of TV violence in children.

(viii) (a) TV is not the only source of entertainment.

2. (i) (c) 5 and 6

(ii) (c) (A) is true, but (R) is false.

(iii) integration

(iv) Brazil contains the largest forest cover of the Amazon.

(v) 80%

(vi) A large drainage, largest rainforest cover and being the second longest river are features of the Amazon.

(vii) the rivers Congo and Mississippi along with the 48 states of USA.

(viii) The vastness of the Amazonian land can be credited to environmental conditions and post human influence. The development of the Amazonian rainforest depends on the Amazon river.

3. (i) (b) can be developed, has been supported

(ii)

Error	Correction
taking	taken

(iii) Rajan told Urvarshi that he was going to Kashmir the next day.

(iv) (d) enough

(v) asked her to turn around.

(vi) (c)

Error	Correction
Hitler	Hitler's

(vii) (b) has taken

(viii)

Error	Correction
have	has

(ix) that she decided to try something new with her hair

(x) (c) all

(xi) (b) excels

(xii) If I can pick her after work.

4. In every summer vacation, I visit some hill station, but last time I visited my friend's grandmother's village due to her repeated invitations. She gave me a warm welcome. She cared a lot, especially for me as I was her guest. Her sweet and soft speaking nature really impressed me. The breakfast, lunch and dinner prepared by her were not only tasty but full of love. She took care of every small need of mine. I felt as if I were in grandmother's paradise. She showed many photographs from her album. She also told me that she was a champion in swimming. She had won many gold medals in swimming competition. She showed me all the prizes she had achieved in her life. I was very excited.

Or

Our school Annual Day function was celebrated on 22nd April, 2020. Great preparations were made for it. Invitations were extended to the students and the parents. Our Chief Guest was Mr. Ravindra Gupta, the District Magistrate. The function began at 6:00 pm with lighting of the lamp followed by a prayer dance. The Head Girl delivered a short welcome speech. The Principal introduced the Chief Guest and presented the Annual Report. Various other dances, musical programmes and cultural events were performed. The Chief Guest, then, gave away the prizes to the winners of the competitions that were held throughout the year. The programme concluded with a vote of thanks by the Principal followed by the National Anthem. It was a well organised show and was admired by everybody present there.

5. Sunday, 10th August, 20XX 10:00 pm

Dear Diary

Today, I had a very bad experience. I wanted to go to Patel Nagar to meet my best friend, Naaz. So, I went to the bus stand to board the bus. I had to wait for a long time before the bus came. It was so hot and I was sweating profusely. Finally, the bus arrived after waiting for over half an hour.

The bus was jam-packed. I somehow managed to get into it. People were pushing each other to get some space to stand. With great difficulty, I secured a place in the corner and purchased the ticket. I held the railing with one of my hands and used the other to take care of my belongings. Thirty minutes in the bus seemed like thirty hours to me! When my stand came, I alighted the bus and heaved a sigh of relief!

Naina

Or

One Stormy Day

There was a storm brewing outside and my brother and I were all alone at home. Suddenly, the lights went out and there was total darkness. As we sat up, there was a strange sound from the front door which scared me terribly. I told my brother, "Vicky, go and see what is there." Vicky himself had jumped in fright at the sound and did not move. Finally, I plucked up the courage to go and open the door. I screamed in horror at what I saw! There was a ghostly apparition standing there which was shaking from side to side. I shut the door and ran back to my room.

For some time, only the howling of the storm was heard. Then, to my relief, the electricity came back. I opened my room door and switched on the porch light. When I looked again, I saw my father standing there in a white *kurta pyjama* with a white cap. He was totally wet from head to toe and could not speak as he had a very sore throat. I said sorry to him for not recognising him. He forgave me and I hugged my father.

6. (i) (d) Both (a) and (b)

(ii) He, i.e. Gerrard poses himself to be a criminal. He does so to save himself from being killed at the hands of the intruder.

(iii) a murder

(iv) The game here refers to Gerrard being perceived as a common man and not a criminal. No the game is not true. It is just a ploy to distract the intruder from his plan.

Or

(i) (b) Jewels

(ii) The given extract talks about current condition of the statue of the happy prince wherein he is stripped of all the precious metals, it was adorned with. Now, it is just a lead statue which looks ugly.

(iii) beauty

(iv) That the statue's broken lead heart will not melt was the strange thing observed by the overseer.

7. (i) (a) 'Earth-cave' refers to a space created in the Earth by uprooting a tree.

(ii) its roots

(iii) Yes, the tree can be a metaphor representing something deeply rooted and difficult to eliminate such as strong emotions, deeply ingrained beliefs, traditions or even oppression.

(iv) (a) The poem do not follow a rhyme scheme. It is written in free verse.

Or

(i) According to me, Northland is not a real place. However, if it did exist, it would be somewhere near the North Pole.

(ii) people of Northland region

(iii) They cannot sleep through the night because the nights are very long, probably more than 12 hours.

(iv) (c) 1 and 2 are correct

8. (i) The book that Tommy found and showed to Margie was an old, real book which belonged to his grandfather's grandfather. It had crinkly yellow pages in which all the stories were printed on paper and the words stood still.

(ii) Einstein wrote a long letter to the United Nations in which he proposed the formation of a world government, but to no avail. He continued to work for world peace and democracy and involved himself more in politics for years to come. He campaigned to end the arms build up.

(iii) Saint Peter asked the old lady to give one of her baked cakes to him so that he could satisfy his hunger. The lady tried to bake smaller and smaller cake for him but finally did not give him anything.

(iv) The poet, in 'The Rain on the Roof' describes how the stars in the sky are not visible as they are covered by the dark rainy clouds. The sky looks sad and the rain looks as if tears are falling from human eyes.

(v) After the encounter with the snake, the narrator was afraid of the snake coming there again. So he wanted to remove his things from his room to shift to some other place. He found that he had little to carry because a thief had stolen most of his things in the night when he ran away to the house of his friend.

9. (i) The author regained a sense of security and life when his schoolmates gifted him school supplies like notebooks and all kinds of clothes like jeans, tops, sweatsuits, etc. The author was greatly moved at this love shown by his schoolmates.

(ii) The narrator's grandfather was pleased at Toto's intelligence as how he had managed to get free from the peg he had been tied to. This reveals the fact that the narrator's grandfather was a true animal lover and enjoyed the antics of the monkey.

(iii) When the bird was about to sleep during the first night, he was disturbed by the three drops that fell from the eyes of the statue. The bird was filled with pity and could not sleep when he saw the tears running down the cheeks of the statue.

10. Santosh yadav displays many qualities which that helped her get into the records book both times she conquered Mt. Everest. Santosh Yadav was born in an orthodox society in Haryana where a girl child was not welcomed. From her early childhood, she showed the qualities of a rebel. She went to pursue her higher studies out of her village despite her parents' unwillingness, as they wanted her to get married at the age of sixteen. She also enrolled to pursue mountaineering which requires a lot of hard work, dedication and determination.

Hard-working with an Iron-will Santosh showed qualities in her training like physical endurance, iron will, mental toughness and resistance to cold at high altitude. These qualities helped her to scale Mt Everest twice and get her name into the record books. She is an inspiration for all of us, especially for girls.

Yes, we can find some similar characteristics in Evelyn Glennie. She is courageous and persistent in her attempt to go over her disability. Her sincerity and dedication made her a successful musicians who became an inspiration for millions of people.

Or

In our lives, we often come across situations which present us options and we are required to make a choice. It is often difficult to choose amongst the multiple options that are available before us. Still, we have to take a decision, as we cannot avoid or escape from the truths or realities of life.

Making a choice depends upon several factors like circumstances, needs, family members, friends, etc. As we are guided by so many aspects which may sometimes even mislead us, we must be very sensible and careful about making the right decisions, because our life depends upon the choices we make. Besides, once we make a choice, we cannot go back, as one decision leads to another. The poem 'The Road Not Taken' presents this fact with the poet who takes a path which had led to him to become a poet. His one decision paved the way for his other decisions which define our lives.

11. Grandfather is a lover of animals. He loves animals so much that he has his own private zoo. He does not mind spending money in order to get animals and birds even though this practice involves the risk of annoying his wife. He has an appreciative eye towards animals, that is why he believes that a tail adds to anyone's good looks.

He is a smart man, as he devises various ways of hiding Toto. He is annoyed with foolish behaviour, like that of the ticket collector who calls Toto a dog and charges fare for it. He is both witty and sarcastic because he asks the ticket collector to charge him even for a tortoise that he had carried in his pocket.

Or

Wednesday, 10th March, 20XX 10:00 pm

Dear Diary

Human beings are born and brought up in such an atmosphere that they learn to react differently over the same things in different circumstances. In a way, nothing is perfectly right and nothing is absolutely wrong. It is the situation that turns the same thing sometimes right while at another moment wrong.

In the lesson 'The Lost Child' the child is the perfect example of these attributes. While being at the fair, he had demanded so many things to be bought by his parents. When they refused to get him any of these, he had reacted as if all those things meant a lot to him. Later, he gets separated from his parents and is found by a kind and noble stranger. At this point, he does not want any of those things despite repeated offers being made by the stranger but he reacts as if they mean nothing to him now. Now, he is longing for his parents only and nothing else. It clearly reveals that we have a dual or an ambiguous attitude to react differently at the same thing in different situations. Our attitude and priorities keeps changing from time to time.

Raghav

Sample Question Paper 2 (Solved)

A Highly Simulated Sample Question Paper for CBSE Class IX

English Language and Literature

Time : 3 hrs	M.M. : 80

General Instructions

1. This question paper is divided into three sections.
2. All questions are compulsory.
3. Separate instructions are given with each section and question, wherever necessary. Read these instructions very carefully and follow them.
4. Do not exceed the prescribed word limit while answering the questions.

Section-A (Reading Skills) (20 Marks)

1. Read the passage given below carefully. **(10)**

1. It is common knowledge that school children are under great pressure to perform well in all fields, study ten subjects, play games and develop an impressive image. How do they manage? The skills, techniques and principles which they pick up while still young help them cope.
2. Two of twentieth century's finest minds have lamented that schools are not teaching the basics of personal excellence or the science of success. "Almost all of what a child learns at school after the age often is totally irrelevant to his need in later life. Most schools do not teach thinking at all." We need to understand that management must be taught as a school subject. The weightiest argument is that children are managers.
3. Many of the children are called upon to play directly three of the interpersonal roles: 'Figurehead', 'Leader' and 'Liaison Officer'. They do this while assisting teachers as monitors or group leaders, while captaining teams on playgrounds and while leading teams in competitions. Many more play these roles as surrogates.
4. The decision role of 'Entrepreneur' and 'Resource Allocator' may only occasionally be assigned to children. However, it is worth noting that, according to a recent survey in Delhi, a monthly allocation of up to ₹ 1000 is available as pocket money to school children. Therefore, they too need to have control over money and to develop a sense of budget. If we add to these financial resources to the resources of time, information and intellect available to children, we find that the decision making roles are not irrelevant to them. Children play the other two decision roles: 'Disturbance Handler' and 'Negotiator' more often.
5. Children are managers in the making: Many of the management habits (e.g., using a to-do list), management skills (e.g. sensitive listening), management attitudes and values are formed early in life. Personality theorists believe that it is extremely difficult to change personality traits, styles of thinking and habits of behavior once they are formed.
6. As in language learning, where basic and abstract aspects of language like pronunciation and rhythm are extremely resistant to learning after puberty, good management habits, attitudes and values are difficult to acquire in adulthood. Computer skills, lateral thinking and swimming, often felt to be forbidden by adults are easily learnt by children. In fact, both research evidence and specialists strongly support the view that children's ability to learn skills like swimming and creative thinking is much more developed than adults. Equally important, complex organisms (a) learn what is necessary or pleasurable and (b) adapt themselves in ways that will serve their needs and interests with amazing enthusiasm, ease and effectiveness.

Answer the following questions on the basis of the passage you have read.

(i) Complete the following sentence appropriately. **(1)**

Management skills, habits, attitudes and values are formed ....

(ii) Complete the sentence appropriately.

The reason of pressure on children is .... **(1)**

(iii) According to the passage, why can children easily learn good management habits, attitudes and values? **(2)**

(iv) What according to few educationists, is lacking in school teaching? **(1)**

(a) Basics of personal excellence
(b) Science of success
(c) Thinking
(d) All of these

(v) Supply the purpose of the author behind the passage. **(1)**

(vi) Which of the following will be the most appropriate title for the passage? **(1)**

(a) Skills for Life
(b) Going Beyond Books
(c) Management Education
(d) Learning Differences

(vii) Children are managers in the making. Justify. **(2)**

(viii) What is the tone of the author regarding the education system? **(1)**

(a) Matter-of-fact
(b) Critical
(c) Wonder
(d) Doubtful

2. Read the passage given below carefully. **(10)**

India is home to 18 per cent of the global population but has only 4 per cent of the global water resources. Its per capita water availability is around 1,100 cubic meter (m^3), well below the internationally recognised threshold of water stress of 1,700 m^3 per person, and dangerously close to the threshold for water scarcity of 1,000 m^3 per person.

Paradoxically, India is also the largest net exporter of virtual water (the amount of water required to produce the products that India exports) and has one of the most water-intense economies. Despite looming water scarcity, India is one of the largest water users per unit of GDP suggesting that the way in which India manages its water resources accounts for much of its water woes. The problem lies with the government capacities which are lacking in improving water management, while policies and incentives favour inefficient and unproductive use of water. This coupled with weak or absent institutions (e.g. for water regulation) and poor data collection and assessment results in the increasing state of water woes in the country.

When it comes to improving water service delivery, India can learn from Brazil, Colombia, Mozambique and New South Wales (Australia). We don't even have to go overseas to see good examples of water resources management. The Maharashtra Water Resources Regulatory Authority, established under a World Bank project, is putting in place policies, regulations, institutions and incentives that promote more efficient and more productive use of water. Efforts to establish effective authorities are also underway in other states, and Maharashtra is disseminating the lessons learned from its experience.

Further, the World Bank's Country Partnership Framework for India recognises the importance of the efficient use of natural resources, including water, in support of the country's ambitious growth targets. Several World Bank projects support India's efforts in the water sector; Through the National Mission for Clean Ganga, the World Bank is helping the Government of India build institutional capacity for the management and clean-up of the Ganga and investing to reduce pollution.

Another World Bank project, the Dam Rehabilitation and Improvement Project, has improved the safety and performance of 223 dams in the country. The National Hydrology Project is providing significant support to strengthen capacities, improve data monitoring and analysis, and laying the foundations for benchmarking and performance-based water management. There are many more such projects that aid an efficient water management system.

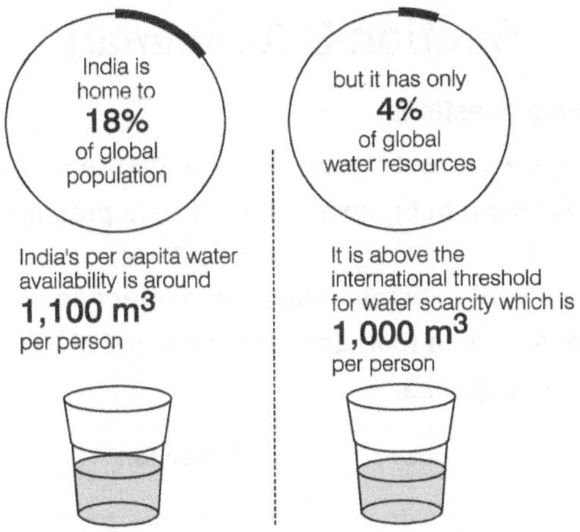

Answer the following questions on the basis of the passage you have read.

(i) What is the National Mission for Clean Ganga? **(1)**

(a) A mission by the World Bank for the management of the river Ganga.
(b) A mission of the Government of India in building institutional capacity for the management of the river Ganga.
(c) A mission to build institutional capacity for the management and clean-up of the Ganga and investing to reduce pollution.
(d) A mission for cleaning the river Ganga while reducing the pollution causing elements.

(ii) Select the option that is true for the Assertion (A) and Reason (R) given below. **(1)**

Assertion (A) India is one of the water intense countries in the world.

Reason (R) India is the largest net exporter of virtual water.

(a) Both the (A) and (R) are true, and (R) is the correct explanation of (A).
(b) Both the (A) and (R) are true, but (R) is not the correct explanation of (A).
(c) (A) is true, but (R) is false.
(d) (A) is false, but (R) is true.

(iii) State one example which proves the statement. **(1)**

The way in which India manages its water resources accounts for much of its water woes.

(iv) Why are the water woes in the country ever on rise? **(2)**

(v) How does the Maharashtra Water Resources Regulatory Authority serve as an example for the nation? **(1)**

(a) By putting in place policies, regulations, institutions and incentives that promote more efficient use of water.
(b) By limiting the use of water to certain hours of the day.
(c) By putting strict enforcement of laws against those who pollute or waste potable water.
(d) All of the above

(vi) What does the author mean by 'water-intense economies'? **(2)**

(vii) Complete the following correctly with a word/phrase from the passage. **(1)**

The writer of the given passage blames .... for the country's water woes.

(viii) Complete the sentence appropriately. **(1)**

.... recognises the importance of water to meet India's growth targets.

Section-B (Grammar)

(10 Marks)

3. Attempt ANY TEN of the following questions. **(1×10 = 10)**

(i) Fill in the blank by choosing the correct option to complete the following sentence. **(1)**

I .... basketball quite well, but I haven't had time to practice it since I came to Mumbai.

(a) will play (b) play (c) am playing (d) have played

(ii) Identify the error in the given sentence and supply the correction. **(1)**

I study Agriculture and Economics. In fact, Economics are my favourite.

Use the given format for your response.

Error	Correction

(iii) Shreya asked for some information from the shopkeeper about the bike's price. Report her question. **(1)**

Shreya said to the shopkeeper, "What is the price of this bike?"

(iv) Fill in the blank by using the correct form of the word in the bracket for the given portion of the letter. **(1)**

Subject Complaint about a damaged product received

Sir/Ma'am,

I purchased a black top from your online store. I ....(receive) the product today, and I tried filing a return request as the size is smaller than the one I had ordered and the cloth is torn on the left side.

(v) Read the conversation between Dilip and Rohan. Complete the sentence by reporting Rohan's reply correctly. **(1)**

Dilip Why do you ask me to keep quiet whenever I say something?

Rohan Have you ever said anything sensible?

Dilip angrily asked Rohan why he asked him to keep quiet whenever he said something to which Rohan asked ....

(vi) Select the option that identifies the error and supplies the correction for the following line.

The princely states of Jammu and Kashmir triggers the first undeclared war with Pakistan. **(1)**

Option	Error	Correction
(a)	triggers	triggered
(b)	states	state
(c)	the first	first
(d)	Pakistan	the Pakistan

(vii) Complete the given narrative by filling in the blank with the correct option.

She .... (look) very worried for the past few days but when I asked what the matter was she said that it was nothing. **(1)**

(a) looked (b) had been looking (c) had looked (d) looks

(viii) Identify the error in an online advertisement. **(1)**

Gerber Foods	Shimla
We knows the value of fruits and veggies.	

Use the given format for your response.

Error	Correction

(ix) There................. something wrong with the cooker today. **(1)**

(a) must be (b) should have been

(c) must have been (d) could have been

(x) Fill in the blanks by choosing the correct option to complete the given statement. **(1)**

He went there so that he .... borrow money.

(a) may (b) can (c) might (d) should

(xi) Select the correct option to complete the narration of the dialogue. **(1)**

Prakash said, "I will not stop until this factory is shut down."

Prakash promised that .... until that factory was shut down.

(a) he will not stop (b) he would not stop (c) he should not stop (d) he could not stop

(xii) Report the dialogue between Dilip and Rohan to complete the following sentence. **(1)**

Dilip I have been watching the sea and there hasn't been any trace of a ship.

Rohan I told you yesterday too that we'll be rescued, so have patience.

Dilip said that he had been watching the sea and that there had not been any trace of a ship. Rohan replied that .... that they would be rescued and asked him to have patience.

Section-B (Writing Skills) **(10 Marks)**

4. Write a descriptive paragraph in 100-120 words based on the visual given below. **(5)**

Or

A free health camp was organised by your school during autumn break. Well known health specialists were invited on this occasion. Write a description of the event.

The date - the venue - number of students and people who benefitted from this camp - purpose - Chief Guest

5. A week ago you were travelling to Kolkata and you met a celebrity who was travelling on the same flight. Write a diary entry about your experience. You are Akash/Reena. (100-120 words) **(5)**

Or

• Sachin Tendulkar	• Felt lucky
• Took autograph	• Clicked pictures
• Talked about cricket	• Very simple and humble

Complete the story in 100-120 words which begins as follows. **(5)**

'Long ago a man was alone in the wilderness. All around him were wild beasts, thick forests, black night and from time to time there were howling storms. He felt very strange and very alone ....

Section-C (Literature) **(40 Marks)**

Reference to the context **(5 + 5 = 10)**

6. Within twelve months, Santosh found herself a member of an Indo-Nepalese Women's Expedition that invited her to join them. She then scaled the Everest a second time, thus setting a record as the only woman to have scaled the Everest twice, and securing for herself and India a unique place in the annals of mountaineering. *(Reach for the Top)* **(5)**

(i) When did Santosh conquer Mount Everest the second time?

(ii) What made Santosh scale Mt. Everest the second time?

(iii) Fill in the blank with ONE WORD only.

The word 'scaled' in the extract means ....

(iv) Choose the option that lists the set of statements that are NOT TRUE according to the given extract.

(a) Santosh's parents wanted her to become a sportsperson since her childhood.
(b) Santosh was always supported by her family to pursue her studies.
(c) Santosh was never pressurised for early marriage.
(d) All of the above

Or

Everyone in the High school, including my teachers, was aware of my plight. I was embarrassed as if somehow I were responsible. What a way to start off a new school! This was not the kind of attention I was looking for. *(A House is not a Home)*

(i) Which word from the extract does not signify the narrator's suffering?

(a) Plight (b) Embarrassed (c) Attention (d) Responsible

(ii) Why was he embarrassed?

(iii) Fill in the blank appropriately.

From the given lines, we can gather that the speaker was .... (social/shy)

(iv) What was the plight of the speaker in the above extract?

7. Remember they have eyes like ours that wake
Or sleep, and strength that can be won
By love. In every land is common life
That all can recognise and understand *(No Men Are Foreign)* **(5)**

(i) 'They' in the extract refers to

(a) the rich people (b) the poor people (c) the poet's countrymen (d) the people from other countries

(ii) Complete the sentence appropriately.

.... can be recognised or understood.

(iii) What is the poet's message in this stanza?

(iv) State whether the following statement is TRUE or FALSE.

We all are the same.

Or

Wind, come softly.
Don't break the shutters of the windows.
Don't scatter the papers.
Don't throw down the books on the shelf.
There, look what you did–
you threw them all down.

You tore the pages of the books.
You brought rain again.
You're very clever at poking fun at weaklings.
Frail crumbling houses, crumbling doors,
crumbling rafters, crumbling wood,
crumbling bodies, crumbling lives,
crumbling hearts
- the wind god winnows and crushes them all. *(Wind)*

(i) What is the tone of the poet in the line "There, look what you did — you threw them all down"?

(a) Requesting (b) Angry (c) Pleading (d) Threatening

(ii) What is the rhyming scheme of the above extract?

(iii) What do you mean by the line "You're very clever at poking fun at weaklings"?

(iv) Complete the sentence appropriately.

"The wind god winnows and crushes them all" indicates that ....

Short and Long Answer Questions

8. Answer ANY FOUR of the following questions in 40-50 words each. **(3 × 4 = 12)**

(i) How did Kezia's grandmother encourage her to get to know her father better? (The Little Girl)

(ii) What does each sound on the shingle create? (Rain on the Roof)

(iii) Who was Saint Peter? How did he reach the little woman's cottage?

(iv) Describe the evolution of Shehnai from Pungi. (The Sound of Music)

(v) What things were there to gain as far as the intruder was concerned? (If I Were You)

9. Answer ANY TWO of the following questions in 40-50 words each. **(3 × 2 = 6)**

(i) What superstition had Johnsy developed? (The Last Leaf)

(ii) How did Toto behave with Nana, the pet donkey? (The Adventure of Toto)

(iii) Why did the king want to punish the merchant? (In the Kingdom of Fools)

10. Answer ANY ONE of the following questions in 100-120 words. **(6)**

Then good Saint Peter grew angry,
For he was hungry and faint;
And surely such a woman
Was enough to provoke a saint.
And he said, "You are far too selfish
To dwell in a human form,
To have both food and shelter,
And fire to keep you warm.

The quoted lines have been taken from which poem? What events are being described in the stanza.

Or

How would you react to your school being replaced by a computer operated system and a mechanical teacher replacing your present teacher, keeping in mind the lesson 'The Fun They Had'?

11. Answer ANY ONE of the following questions in 100-120 words. **(6)**

Do you think it is advisable to keep a monkey like Toto as part of pets in the house? Why/Why not?

(The Adventures of Toto)

Or

Justify the title of the story 'A House is Not a Home'.

Answers

1. (i) early in life

(ii) absence of skills

(iii) According to the passage, children can easily learn good management habits, attitudes and values because they are complex organisms who learn what is necessary for them and adapt themselves in ways that will serve their needs with amazing enthusiasm, ease and effectiveness.

(iv) (a) Basics of personal excellence

(v) The author has written the given passage to highlight that certain skills needs to be taught to children from childhood as children are more open-minded, sincere and dedicated.

(vi) (a) Skills for Life

(vii) The given statement is true because many of the management habits (e.g. using a to-do list), management skills (e.g. sensitive listening), management attitudes and values are formed during the various activities one performs during childhood.

(viii) (b) Critical

2. (i) (c) A mission to build institutional capacity for the management and clean-up of the Ganga and investing to reduce pollution.

(ii) (b) Both the (A) and (R) are true, but (R) is not the correct explanation of (A).

(iii) The given statement can be proved by the fact that India is lacking in improving water management, while policies and incentives often favour inefficient and unproductive use of water.

(iv) The water woes of the country are ever on rise because of the following reasons

(a) Lacking in the improvement of water management.

(b) Policies and incentives favouring inefficient and unproductive use of water.

(c) Poor data collection and assessment.

(v) (a) By putting in place policies, regulations, institutions and incentives that promote more efficient use of water.

(vi) Water-intense economies are economies where water is a major component of production.

(vii) government

(viii) World Bank's Country Partnership Framework

3. (i) (b) play

(ii)

Error	Correction
are	is

(iii) Shreya asked the shopkeeper what the price of that bike was.

(iv) received

(v) if he had ever said anything sensible

(vi) (a)

Error	Correction
triggers	triggered

(vii) (b) had been looking

(viii)

Error	Correction
knows	know

(ix) (a) must be

(x) (c) might

(xi) (b) he would not stop

(xii) he had told him the day before too

4. Mother Teresa had an impressive personality. She was born on 26th August, 1910, in Skopje, the current capital of the Republic of Macedonia. She always wore a smile on her face and had immense sympathy for the poor people. She was very dedicated and generous in doing her work. She served the people of the slums in whatever way she could. She opened a dispensary and a home for the dying destitutes lying unclaimed on the roadsides. She gave love and care to the hungry, the naked, the homeless, the crippled, the blind, the lepers, and all those people who felt unwanted in the society. Mother Teresa received a number of honours, including the 1962 Ramon Magsaysay Peace Prize and 1979 Nobel Peace Prize. After several years of deteriorating health, including heart, lung and kidney problems, Mother Teresa died on 5th September, 1997 at the age of 87. She was canonised (recognised by the church as a saint) on 4th September, 2016.

Or

During the autumn break, a free health check-up camp was organised by our school in the school playground. The camp was organised for three days and various specialist doctors were called from different cities for this purpose. The free check-up for diabetes, blood pressure, obesity, joint pains, etc. was provided to the residents of neighbouring areas.

Around 150 students and 200 people were benefitted from this camp. The purpose of the camp was to spread awareness regarding the increasing health problems among growing children and middle aged people due to eating unhealthy food and leading an inactive lifestyle. Pamphlets containing diet charts for the patients of diabetes and blood pressure were distributed.

The closing ceremony was graced by Mr. Pitambar Singh, the MLA of the area. He appreciated the efforts of the school and the doctors who gave their valuable time to make the camp a grand success.

5. Monday, 13th October, 20XX 9:30 pm

Dear Diary

I'm feeling on the top of the world right now. Yesterday, I met the 'Little Master' Sachin Tendulkar while travelling to Kolkata by flight. I was so excited because he was sitting just one row ahead of me in the flight. Thus, I was able to talk freely with him. I was luckier than many others because the great man not only gave me his autograph but also clicked selfies and spent a lot of time talking to me. The ease and openness with which he meets people, the joy he expresses while mingling with normal people and his humble nature is indeed touching. He talked about many glorious moments in his cricketing career. I listened to him with a lot of interest.

He is known as the God of Cricket but his humility and simplicity is astonishing. I feel so amazed to have met him.

Reena

Or

Long ago, a man was alone in the wilderness. All around him were wild beasts, thick forests, black night and from time to time there were howling storms. He felt very strange and very alone in the wilderness. He could not speak to anyone because the animals did not understand the language of human beings. So, he learnt to speak the language of the animals and talked to them in their own language for as long as he lived with them.
He also had no opportunity to eat proper food meant for humans. He depended on what the animals ate in order to survive. Thus, he learnt to eat roots, various kinds of wild fruits and many kinds of nuts. One night he saw that a safari had come to that forest for hunting. He was happy to see human beings after a long time. He met the hunters and narrated his story about how he had got lost in the forest. Finally, with their help he got back home. He was very happy to be with his family and narrated the experience to them.

6. (i) Santosh conquered Mt. Everest for the second time in 1993.

(ii) Santosh was invited by an Indo-Nepalese Women's Expedition to scale Mt. Everest again.

(iii) climbed (iv) (d) All of the above

Or

(i) (d) Responsible

(ii) He was embarassed because he held himself responsible for his shabby appearance at the school.

(iii) shy

(iv) That his house and belongings were burnt down was the plight of the narrator.

7. (i) (d) the people from other countries.

(ii) That life is common everywhere

(iii) Through the given stanza, it can be learnt that physical strength can be won by love.

(iv) True

Or

(i) (b) Angry

(ii) There is no rhyme scheme in the given extract.

(iii) Through the given phrase, the poet means that the wind is making fun of weak people by throwing and breaking weak things.

(iv) the wind tests the courage of the people and leaves only the strong people to survive

8. (i) Kezia's grandmother encouraged her to get to known her father better by sending her on Sunday afternoons to talk to her parents who used to sit in the drawing room. She also suggested Kezia to make a pin-cushion as a birthday present for her father with a piece of yellow silk she gave to Kezia.

(ii) Every raindrop on the tiles of the roof created a rythm with the poet's heartbeat. This evoked thousands of dreams which made his thoughts busy. While he focused on listening to the pitter-patter on the roof, his mind started to weave recollections of fond memories of his childhood.

(iii) Saint Peter was an apostle (follower) of Christ. He travelled from place to place while preaching. He reached the little woman's cottage at the end of a tiring day during one of his travels.

(iv) A barber decided to improve the tonal quality of the pungi. When it was played by closing and opening some of the holes, soft and melodious sounds were produced. It was also played in temples which is why it is now considered auspicious.

(v) There were some important things for the intruder to gain. If he could take on the identity of Gerrard, then he would be free to go anywhere he liked. He would lead a very peaceful life in the name of Gerrard.

9. (i) Johnsy was seriously ill and had got pneumonia. She would keep on lying on her bed and stare out of the window at the Ivy creeper. Being mentally upset, she developed the superstition that she would die as soon as the last leaf of the ivy creeper would fall.

(ii) Once Toto was kept in the stable where his companion was Nana, the family donkey. On Toto's first night with Nana, he hung himself on to Nana's long ears with his sharp teeth. Nana pulled at her halter to keep his head away as far as possible from Toto.

(iii) The King wanted to punish the merchant because the wall of his house had fallen on the thief and killed him. The wall was built by the merchant's father. According to the king, since the merchant had inherited his father's wealth, he inherited his sins too. Therefore, he should be punished.

10. The quoted lines have been taken from the poem 'The Legend of the Northland'. Here, the selfish behaviour of the woman made Saint Peter angry. He was very weak and hungry. It is not easy for a compassionate and kind saint like Saint Peter to become angry but the actions of the woman had made him so. Hence, Saint Peter tells her that she is very selfish and curses her to become a woodpecker since she did not deserve to be a human being and live a comfortable life with good food to eat and a house to live in with fire to keep her warm.

Or

It is true that it is the era of technological advancement. Technology has certainly made our lives easy and full of comfort. For sure, machines are replacing manual work to save time, labour and probably the cost to a certain extent. However, when it comes to replacing a school and its teachers with a machine operated system, I can't even think of it, forget endorsing it. After all, it is the human beings, both man and woman who as teachers have either directly developed or have at least helped a number of aspiring technocrats to create this wonderful world of technology.

In the chapter, 'The Fun They Had', the mechanical teacher at the most can feed you with factual details. How would it recreate the fun, the emotions, fruitful discussion, feeling of togetherness, team spirit and the bond of love in students. The pious objective of a school to develop human beings with versatile personalities to handle adverse circumstances will be at stake if this happens.

11. No, it is not advisable to have a pet like Toto. Toto was a naughty monkey. Such an animal may harm the children at home and may damage the things around him. It may hurt the guests too. Moreover, animals remain happy in their natural surroundings. The wilds are always beautiful in the lap of the wild as they are born free and brought up in that environment.

In the context of the story, Toto was devoted to mischief's due to its instincts. It was impossible for the family to afford the frequent loss caused by Toto. Moreover, he kept disturbing other pets in the house. Should he be freed, he would be happy in the forest. So, it is inhumane to keep them captive. They are happy to be free. We must not hunt or catch animals for our selfish motives. Some animals may prove dangerous too.

Or

The title 'A House is Not a Home' is justified in relation to the story. In the story, the author's house got completely destroyed in a fire. Due to this, he and his mother had to take refuge at his grandparents' home and later in a rented apartment. The places where the author lived after the fire incident could not be called a home. A home is the place where one gets comfort, the joy of belonging and freedom of doing whatever one wishes. On the other hand, a house is devoid of these sentiments and emotions. The grandparents' house and the rented apartment were merely places where the author and his mother took shelter. Moreover, these places were without the belongings and things which they loved. Hence, the title of the story is justified.

Sample Question Paper 3 (Unsolved)

A Highly Simulated Sample Question Paper for CBSE Class IX

English Language and Literature

Time : 3 hrs	M.M. : 80

General Instructions

1. This question paper is divided into three sections.
2. All questions are compulsory.
3. Separate instructions are given with each section and question, wherever necessary. Read these instructions very carefully and follow them.
4. Do not exceed the prescribed word limit while answering the questions.

Section-A (Reading Skills) **(20 Marks)**

1. Read the passage given below carefully. **(10)**

1. An escalating epidemic of overweight and obesity is affecting many countries in the world; more than 300 million people are overweight or obese. Obesity could be region specific. In India, some people tend to be overweight because of their high calorie diet and lack of physical activities. In the United States, obesity is more prevalent in lower economic groups. Obesity is now well recognised as a disease in its own right. Though obesity commonly means very overweight, it is defined as an excess amount of body weight that includes muscles bone, fat and water. 'Obesity' specifically refers to an excess amount of body fat. Some people, such as body builders or other athletes with a lot of muscle can be overweight without being obese.
2. One of the causes of obesity is psychological. Negative emotions such as boredom, sadness or anger, respond to people who overeat. There is also 'binge eating', when people eat large amounts of food thinking that they cannot control how much they are eating. Those with the most severe binge eating problems are also likely to have symptoms of depression and low self-esteem. These people may have more difficulty in losing weight and keeping it off than people without binge eating problems.
3. Obesity is more than a cosmetic problem; it is a health hazard. Several serious medical conditions have been linked to obesity, including type-2 diabetes, heart disease, high blood pressure and stroke. Obesity is also linked to higher rates of certain types of cancer. Other diseases and health problems linked to obesity include gall bladder disease and gallstones, liver disease, osteoarthritis which leads to deterioration of joints, gout which also affects the joints and reproductive problems in women.
4. As the trend is to equate attractiveness with slimness, especially for women, obesity makes people feel unattractive. There are many methods of treatment but the benefits of exercise are much more than any other way of losing weight. Not only does exercise help you to lose weight but it also improves your fitness and flexibility and improves skin texture. Exercises are also free from the harmful side effects of crash dieting, slimming capsules and the heat treatment used by slimming centres.

Answer the following questions on the basis of the passage you have read. **(10)**

(i) **What is one of the major cause of obesity?** **(1)**

(ii) **Complete the sentence appropriately.** **(1)**

Exercise had been suggested as it ....

(iii) **Obesity is related to lack of attractiveness for woman. Do you agree? Give reasons for your answer.** (1)

(iv) **The word 'deterioration' means ....** (2)

(a) modification (b) exponential (c) decline (d) revitalisation

(v) **Justify the following statement.** (1)

Obesity could be region specific.

(vi) **Choose the option that best captures the central idea of the passage.** (1)

(a) Obesity is a disease.
(b) Obesity leads to depression.
(c) Effects of obesity on health.
(d) Obesity is more than a cosmetic problem.

(vii) **What connect does the writer draw out between obesity and attractiveness?** (2)

(viii) **Which of the following justify the purpose of the passage as implied by the author?** (1)

1. Suggestive 2. Advisory 3. Neutral
4. Informative 5. Opinionated 6. Factual

(a) 1, 2, 3 and 4 (b) 3, 4, 5 and 6 (c) 1, 2, 4 and 6 (d) 2, 4, 5 and 6

2. Read the passage given below carefully. (10)

It is globally acknowledged that 'gender equality and women's empowerment' are at the core of achieving development objectives, fundamental for the realisation of human rights, and key to effective and sustainable development outcomes. However, on the contrary, despite their "proven abilities as leaders and agents of change", from the local to the global level, women's leadership and political participation is restricted.

The 2011 UN General Assembly resolution on women's political participation reiterated that "women in every part of the world continue to be largely marginalised from the political sphere, often as a result of discriminatory laws, practices, attitudes and gender stereotypes, low levels of education, lack of access to health care, and the disproportionate effect of poverty on women." Therefore, to eliminate the multi-faceted problem like gender inequality, a multi-pronged approach must be adopted; and among the various initiatives, political empowerment of women could act as a catalyst. Political empowerment could lead to opening more opportunities for women and as a result, create a level playing field for them.

Over the past two decades, gender gaps have narrowed in various areas, viz., education, health, employment, legal rights of women, participation in governance, and so on. But, despite the improvement, substantial inequalities with varying degrees still persist across all the areas across countries. It would be noteworthy to mention that India is a signatory to all the international commitments. However, India is far behind in achieving gender equality, especially in terms of representation of women in political decision making, among others.

Representation of women in executive government and parliament is extremely low in India, both in absolute numbers as well as globally. Only a miniscule progress is observed in the entire post-independence era. In the cabinet, formed after the general election in 2014, there were only 5 women ministers out of total 27 ministers. India's global rank is 88 in this regard as per the 'Women in Politics Map 2017', published by the Inter-Parliamentary Union (IPU) and UN Women.

Between the First Lok Sabha (1952) and the Sixteenth Lok Sabha (2014) women's representation has increased from 4.4 per cent to 11.9 per cent. Women's representation in Rajya Sabha has increased from 6.9 per cent in 1952 to 11.4 per cent in 2014 . Considering the share of women (49.5%) in the total population of India, their representation in Parliament represents a skewed statistic which does not befit the world's largest democracy.

Thus, it is evident that despite our constitutional commitment and several global commitments, India's performance in political empowerment of women is dismal. Therefore, it is imperative that the government takes legislative and constitutional reforms to ensure women's fair access to political spheres, especially in the Lok Sabha (Lower House) and Rajya Sabha (Upper House). There is an urgent need to bring back to the table the Women's Reservation Bill guaranteeing 33 per cent reservation to women. An intense parliamentary discussion is necessary to bring the issue to the fore and greater political commitment is the prerequisite for achieving the objective of political empowerment of women.

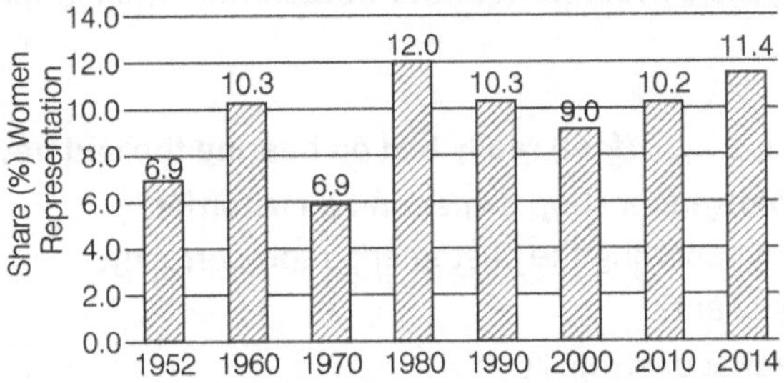

Answer the following questions on the basis of the passage you have read.

(i) Based on your understanding of the passage, choose the option that does not list the ways of marginalisation faced by women. **(1)**

1. Discriminatory laws **2. Gender stereotypes**

3. Low levels of education **4. Lack of access to health care**

5. Poverty **6. Violence**

(a) 1 and 4 (b) 5 and 6 (c) 2 and 3 (d) 1 and 6

(ii) Gender equality and women empowerment are important. Justify. **(1)**

(iii) According to the writer of the given passage who can aid women's upliftment as leaders? **(2)**

(iv) Fill in the blank with one of the options given in bracket. **(1)**

Between 1953 and 2014, the women representation at .... (Lok Sabha/ Rajya Sabha) has increased.

(v) The given passage especially points out India to highlight what? **(1)**

(vi) Complete the sentence appropriately. **(1)**

Women Representation was highest in the year .... in Rajya Sabha.

(vii) Complete the sentence appropriately. **(1)**

The author of the given passage shows India's bad condition through the example of ....

(viii) How is the progress that India has shown as far as gender equality is considered? **(2)**

Section-B (Grammar) (10 Marks)

3. Attempt ANY TEN of the following questions. **(10)**

(i) Fill in the blank by choosing the correct option to complete the sentence. **(1)**

Peehu .... her mother. Doesn't she?

(a) taken after (b) takes after (c) tooks after (d) takes upon

(ii) Identify the error in the given sentence. **(1)**

I did not know how to play a piano. Can you please teach me?

Use the given format for your response.

Error	Correction

(iii) Samarth shared some information with Sameer. Report Sameer's question. **(1)**

Do you like to play tennis?

(iv) Fill in the blank by using the correct form of the word in the bracket, for the given portion of diary entry. **(1)**

Dear Diary,

I want to tell you that I .... (feel) really bad on hearing the sad news.

(v) Read the conversation between a shop owner and a customer. **(1)**

Complete the sentence by reporting the customer's reply correctly.

Shop Owner What do you want?

Customer I need a packet of strepsils.

The shop owner asked the customer what he wanted.

The customer replied that ....

(vi) Select the option that identifies the error and supplies the correction for the following line. **(1)**

Tendulkar would play cricket when he was three.

Options	Error	Correction
(a)	would	could
(b)	play	plays
(c)	when	while
(d)	he	his

(vii) Select the correct option to fill in the blank for the given line, from a school notice board. **(1)**

All students .... bring their writing pads and stationery for writing the exam.

(a) could (b) would (c) must (d) will

(viii) Identify the error on the given advertisement. **(1)**

XYZ Company
We need boys/girls who speak fluently English and are willing to travel.

Use the given format for your response.

Error	Correction

(ix) Report the dialogue between a grandson and a grandmother by completing the sentence. **(1)**

Grandson : Who is your favourite actor?

Grandmother : I do not watch movies.

In reply to the question about favourite actor, grandmother said that ....

(x) Complete the given sentence by filling the blank with the correct option. **(1)**

I .... this work since ten o'clock today.

(a) had been doing (b) have been doing (c) have done (d) did

(xi) Fill in the blank by choosing the correct form of the word given in bracket. **(1)**

Did you .... (give) a copy of this letter to the MD?

(xii) Fill in the blank by choosing the correct option.

.... you need any help, please contact the undersigned. **(1)**

(a) Will (b) May (c) Can (d) Should

Section-B (Writing Skills) (10 Marks)

4. Write a descriptive paragraph on the personality shown in the picture below in 100-120 words. **(5)**

Or

In spite of preparing well for the Maths Olympiad, you were not able to clear it. Write a paragraph in 100-120 words describing how you dealt with the failure to live upto your expectations.

5. You have had a student from a school in Australia living with you as part of a student exchange programme and he/she has just returned to his/her own country. Write a diary entry in 100-120 words about his/her stay at your home and how you have benefitted from the experience based on the verbal clues given below and your own ideas. You are Madhav/Madhavi. **(5)**

Student from Australia – living together – wonderful time - learn new things - family was impressed - memories shared - missing.

Or

Write a story in 100-120 words with the help of the following outline.

Farmer has hen – lays a golden egg every day – farmer collects ten eggs in ten days – happy at his sudden fortune – hopes to become rich soon – then he gets impatient – wants to become rich overnight – kills the hen – moral

Section-C (Literature) (40 Marks)

Reference to the Context. **(5 + 5 = 10)**

6. However, the rapid ascent in a fiercely competitive world began nine years before with a level of sacrifice few children would be prepared to endure. Little Maria had not yet celebrated her tenth birthday when she was packed off to train in the United States. That trip to Florida with her father Yuri launched her on the path to success and stardom. But it also required a heart-wrenching two-year separation from her mother Yelena. The latter was compelled to stay back in Siberia.

(Reach for the Top) **(5)**

(i) Choose the option that lists the set of statements that are NOT TRUE according to the given extract.

1. Maria was born in the USA.

2. Maria belongs to a poor family.

3. Maria had to sacrifice her childhood to achieve her success.

4. Maria was loved by her batchmates.

5. Maria had strength and courage to go through her intense training.

6. Maria played for Russia.

(a) 2, 3 and 4 (b) 1, 4 and 6 (c) 1, 2 and 3 (d) 4, 5 and 6

(ii) How did staying in the USA changed her life?

(iii) What sacrifice did Maria make?

(iv) Fill in the blank with ONE WORD only.

Maria had to stay away from Yelena for .... years.

Or A sweetmeat seller hawked, "gulab-jamun, rasgulla, burfi, jalebi," at the corner of the entrance and a crowd pressed round his counter at the foot of an architecture of many coloured sweets, decorated with leaves of silver and gold. The child stared open-eyed and his mouth watered for the burfi that was his favourite sweet. "I want that burfi," he slowly murmured. *(The Lost Child)*

(i) What was the sweetmeat seller selling?

(ii) Select the option that correctly captures the usage of the word 'murmured'.

(a) The murmured sky was overcast.

(b) After hearing the news, he murmured something to himself.

(c) The murmured way did not make any sense to me.

(d) He started to murmured when I asked his name.

(iii) Why did the boy walk ahead without waiting for an answer?

(iv) Complete the analogy by selecting the suitable word from the text.

Shouted : Hawked : : Collected : ....

7. The wind blows out weak fires
He makes strong fires roar and flourish
His friendship is good
We praise him everyday *(Wind)* **(5)**

(i) Complete the sentence appropriately.

It is clear that Personification is the poetic device used in the extract because ....

(ii) What does 'He' do to weak fires?

(a) It makes them burn brightly. (b) It extinguishes them.

(c) It helps them. (d) It teases them.

(iii) Complete the sentence appropriately.

"The wind blows out weak fires/he makes strong fires roar and flourish" indicates which qualities of wind?

(iv) What is the rhyme scheme of the given extract?

Or Let us remember, whenever we are told
To hate our brothers, it is ourselves
That we shall dispossess, betray, condemn
Remember, we who take arms against each other
It is the human earth that we defile.
Our hells of fire and dust outrage the innocence
Of air that is everywhere our own,
Remember no men are foreign, and no countries strange. *(No Men are Foreign)*

(i) In the given lines, the poet argues against

(a) the concept of borders. (b) the concept of difference based on nationalities.

(c) the concept of wars. (d) Both (b) and (c)

(ii) The poet says "Whenever we are told to hate our brothers". Who do you think tells us to do so?

(iii) Complete the analogy by choosing the appropriate word from the extract.

Forget : Remember : : Praise : ....

(iv) **How do we defile the Earth, according to the poet?**

8. Answer ANY FOUR of the following questions in 40-50 words each. **$(3 \times 4 = 12)$**

(i) What things are common between all human beings? (No Men are Foreign)

(ii) Why was the lady cursed to become a woodpecker? (A Legend of the Northland)

(iii) Why did Aurangzeb ban the playing of the 'pungi'? (Sound of Music)

(iv) Why was Kezia dragged to the hall by her parents? (The Little Girl)

(v) What 'fun' did Margie think about and wished for? (The Fun They Had)

9. Answer ANY TWO of the following questions in 40-50 words each. **$(3 \times 2 = 6)$**

(i) Was the long cherished ambition of Behrman fulfilled? How? (The Last Leaf)

(ii) Describe all the attractions that the child is drawn to till he gets lost in the fair. (The Lost Child)

(iii) What made the sick boy fall into a deep, restful sleep? (The Happy Prince)

10. Answer ANY ONE of the following questions in 100-120 words. **(6)**

Albert Einstein was an unusual child. How? He was different from others in many ways. Do you think that those who think differently succeed in their life like Einstein? Comment.

Or Kathmandu and Innisfree are places with two very different natures. Elucidate with reference from the chapters.

11. Answer ANY ONE of the following questions in 100-120 words. **(6)**

Willingness to live is more important than medication. Do you agree? Discuss with reference to the story 'Last Leaf'.

Or Taking clues from the lesson 'In the Kingdom of Fools', throw light on the importance of wisdom even at the cost of sacrificing comfort and luxuries for negligible payment.

Sample Question Paper 4 (Unsolved)

A Highly Simulated Sample Question Paper for CBSE Class IX

English Language and Literature

Time : 3 hrs	M.M. : 80

General Instructions

1. This question paper is divided into three sections.
2. All questions are compulsory.
3. Separate instructions are given with each section and question, wherever necessary. Read these instructions very carefully and follow them.
4. Do not exceed the prescribed word limit while answering the questions.

Section–A (Reading Skills) (20 Marks)

1. Read the passage given below carefully. (10)

1. A youngster quit Facebook in December after spending over three years on the social networking site. With that one act, he bid a silent adieu to more than 300 contacts that he had added to his account during the period. Last week a new feature on Facebook called timeline forced him to reconsider the pros and cons of being on the networking site.
2. Everyone has some skeletons in their closet and I am just not comfortable with Facebook digging out and displaying all the facts of my life on a bulletin board, says this youngster who joined the network in July 2013.
3. Facebook, you see, had compressed the time he spent on the site and arranged it in chronological order. And while he initially liked the new neatly organised scrapbook like feature, he wasn't happy to reveal posts from the past, those that, until recently, were hidden under layers and layers of recent updates. Just clicking on a date on the timeline could transport his friends back in time and enable them to view every embarrassing comment, link or photo he had posted on his profile.
4. I think it's a recipe for disaster, he says. In 2013, I had some wall posts which seemed appropriate at a time but now after a lapse of our years, I have moved on and don't want them to be openly displayed for all to see.
5. And he is not alone. Many users, worried about how Facebook activity could possibly effect their offline lives, are choosing to commit Facebook Suicide. While some have privacy concerns, others feel that the site that was meant to bring them closer to their friends actually does the opposite - it reduces their friendship to something superficial.
6. Poking and liking are not enough to keep a friendship going, says a business analyst. Having quit Facebook three years ago, she prefers meeting her friends face to face, instead of reading their trite posts online. On Facebook, people hype everyday issues including what they ate and where they went on a daily basis, says this analyst who continues to use Twitter.
7. Facebook has become a time sink and it could not justify the time I spent on it, he says. I spend more time calling up friends or relatives over the phone now......I also go out and meet people whenever possible and have a good offline life. I do not regret the change. Today, Facebook has 800 million users of which 37 million are Indians. The site has become an online identity for most, and many of those who decided to quit cannot overcome the withdrawal symptoms and return.

Facebook, fully aware of its addictive powers, facilitates this return by allowing users to deactivate their accounts but continues to store information on its servers so that they can return from their break, whenever they wish.

Answer the following questions on the basis of the passage you have read. **(1 × 10 = 10)**

(i) Why are people generally not comfortable with the new feature? How does it work? **(2)**

(ii) For what reason did the business analyst quit Facebook? **(1)**

(iii) Supply points to justify the following. **(1)**

Facebook is aware of its addictive power.

(iv) Choose the option that correctly states the meanings of 'digging out', as used in the passage. **(1)**

1. To get something out of something
2. To accelerate any act or event
3. To find out a secret
4. To look for something old
5. To find something that you have not used or seen for a long time
6. To present an embarrassing information or photo

(a) 2 and 3 (b) Only 4 (c) 1 and 6 (d) Only 5

(v) Complete the following. **(1)**

Opinion	Reason
Facebook is called a recipe for disaster	....

(vi) What did the youngster do with his Facebook account? **(1)**

(a) He updated it. (b) He deleted it. (c) He deactivated it. (d) He made it private.

(vii) What are the concerns regarding Facebook? **(2)**

(viii) Which of the characteristics can be apt for the lives of the people who had quit Facebook? **(1)**

1. Embarrassing **2. Peaceful** **3. Real**
4. Nostalgic **5. Social** **6. Addictive**

(a) 2 and 4 (b) 3 and 5 (c) 3 and 6 (d) 1 and 5

2. Read the passage given below carefully. **(10)**

The Municipal Corporation of Gurgaon recently admitted that untreated sewage from the city mixes with treated wastewater in the drains into the Yamuna. The putrid river that flows through New Delhi is only one of the severely polluted surface water bodies in the country. Today, government agencies estimate that as much as 80% of India's surface water is contaminated and most of it comes from sewage.

The effects of this contamination are immediately felt with the onset of the monsoons. No sooner had the rains begun, the reports of water-borne diseases like diarrhea and cholera breakouts trickled in from Delhi, Pune, Varanasi and Chennai as broken water pipes and flooding allowed faecal sludge mix into potable water.

The Central Pollution Control Board in 2009 calculated that major cities and towns together generate more than 38 billion litres of sewage everyday, of which only 30% is collected. Less than 20% of this is treated because that's the treatment capacity available. The rest is just emptied into rivers, lakes, seas and ponds.

A report by Water Aid India on faecal sludge management documents the chinks in India's sewage system. 17 million, or roughly 20% of urban households lack sanitation facilities, the report says. Among those that have access to sanitation only 32% are connected to a sewage network, the rest depending on septic tanks and pit latrines. There are more numbers to raise a stink about. More than 5 lakh pit latrines are unsanitary, being nothing more than open pits. More than 9 lakh toilets empty directly into drains. Among the 18% of urban households that don't have access to individual toilets, more than 12% resort to open defecation.

The story gets murkier beyond the numbers. Where sewers exist, they often leak or overflow. Instead of being cleaned every few years, septic tanks are left to accumulate faecal sludge that percolates into ground water. When the tanks are cleaned the black water is disposed off in fields and water bodies, once again contaminating open fresh water.

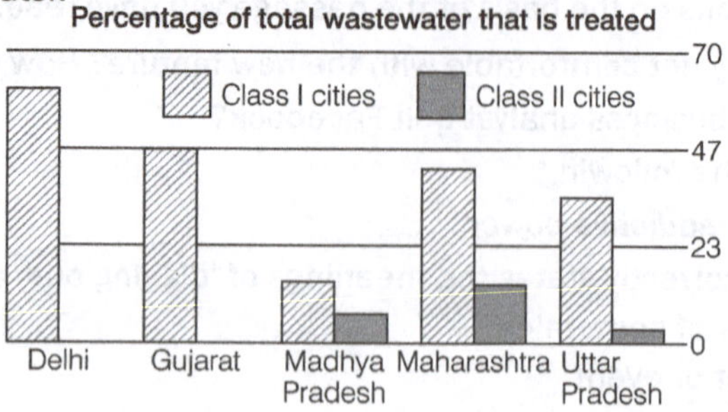

The Water Aid Report looks at sanitation systems in six states litres and offers a snapshot of how much wastewater is dumped untreated. Delhi, for instance, uses 4,346 million liters of water per day of which 87% returns as waste. However, Delhi has the capacity to treat only 61% of the total wastewater it generates. The 51 Class I cities in Maharashtra together consume three times as much as Delhi does, turn 80% of that into sewage and treat less than half of their total wastewater. The statistics are far worse for Class II cities.

Even with the creation of the National Urban Sanitation Policy in 2008 and several thousands of crores being spent by states on sewage networks, the problem has grown worse in the last five years.

The Water Aid Report recommends enforcing a national building code, public promotion campaigns and decentralising sewage treatment plants as remedies to the sewage problem. Water experts, for years have been calling for freeing up the flow of rivers to allow them to rejuvenate.

Answer the following questions on the basis of the passage you have read. **$(1 \times 10 = 10)$**

(i) What is true regarding the contaminated water? **(1)**

(a) Only 20% of the contaminated water is treated.
(b) Most of the contaminated water is dumped into the water bodies.
(c) Contaminated water is the reason for the lack of potable water.
(d) Both (a) and (b)

(ii) Select the option that is true for the Assertion (A) and Reason (R) given below. **(1)**

Assertion (A) Gurugram Municipal Corporation agreed to have a part in pollution of Yamuna.

Reason (R) Untreated sewage is mixed with treated water in Yamuna.

(a) Both the (A) and (R) are true, and (R) is the correct explanation of (A).
(b) Both the (A) and (R) are true, but (R) is not the correct explanation of (A).
(c) (A) is true, but (R) is false.
(d) (A) is false, but (R) is true.

(iii) Which of the following facts can be inferred from the given graph? **(1)**

(a) The sewage treatment capacity of the country needs to be increased.
(b) The condition of treatment of sewage is still better in Class II cities.
(c) The maximum contamination of water takes place in Delhi.
(d) The class I cities are the reason for contamination of water bodies.

(iv) What is the reason for Yamuna being the most polluted river in the country? **(2)**

(v) List reasons for a severe contamination of water in spite of available treatment facilities. **(1)**

(vi) Why is the freeing of water bodies necessary today? **(1)**

(vii) Complete the sentence appropriately.

According to the passage, less than 50% of water used is treated in .... **(1)**

(viii) Why does the presence of Septic Tanks result in contamination of groundwater? **(2)**

Section–B (Grammar)

(10 Marks)

3. Attempt ANY TEN of the following questions.

(i) Fill in the blank by choosing the correct option.

Amit is going to .... the company after the retirement of his father. **(1)**

(a) take on (b) take over (c) takes upon (d) shake on

(ii) Identify the error in the given sentence from a school notice board and supply the correction. **(1)**

All the students are request to assemble in the playground by 9 am.

Use the given format for your response.

Error	Correction

(iii) Ajit shared same information with Navin regarding a cricket match. Report Navin's question.

How many runs did Virat score? **(1)**

(iv) Fill in the blank by using the correct form of the word in the bracket for the given paragraph.

Many people .... (take) to drinking due to stressful situation at home. **(1)**

(v) Read the conversation between two friends. Complete the sentence by reporting the other friend's reply correctly. **(1)**

Nitin How are you feeling today?

Jatin I am feeling better than yesterday.

Nitin asked Jatin how he was feeling that day. Jatin replied that ....

(vi) Select the option that identifies the error and supplies the correction for the following line. **(1)**

They checked his bag thoroughly and than allowed him to enter the hall.

Options	Error	Correction
(a)	his	him
(b)	thoroughly	thorough
(c)	than	then
(d)	enter	enters

(vii) Select the correct option to fill in the blank for the given line. **(1)**

If you come late, you .... be allowed to enter the hall.

(a) could not (b) would not (c) will not (d) cannot

(viii) Identify the error on a shop's hoarding and supply the correction. **(1)**

SANJAY STORES NANGAL RAYA

MASSIVELY DISCOUNT ON PURCHASE OF GROCERY ITEMS.

Use the given format for your response.

Error	Correction

(ix) Select the correct option to complete the narration of the dialogue between Priyanka and her father.

Father Are you preparing for the exam? **(1)**

Priyanka Yes, father. I am devoting 4 hours every day to prepare for it.

Father asked Priyanka if she was preparing for the exam. Priyanka replied in the affirmative and said that .... everyday to prepare for it.

(x) **Complete the narrative by filling the blank with the correct option.** **(1)**

As I was standing at the shore, I felt that I .... away by the coming waves.

(a) will being swept (b) would be swept (c) swept (d) can be sweeped

(xi) **Fill in the blank by choosing the correct option.** **(1)**

.... I leave early today, ma'am?

(a) Would (b) Must (c) May (d) Might

(xii) **Report the dialogue between a son and a father by completing the sentence.** **(1)**

Son Why did you join the army?

Father I wanted to serve the nation.

In response to the questions about joining the army, father said that he did so as ....

Section-B (Writing Skills) **(10 Marks)**

4. Write a descriptive paragraph in 100-120 words based on the personality shown in the visual clue below. **(5)**

Or **You recently went bungee jumping. Write a brief description of the event on the basis of the following points. (100-120 words)**

Venue for the sport - description of the surrounding - enquiry that occurred - weight and height measurement- protection measures - the exhilarating experience

5. After the recent terrorist attacks in Hyderabad, you are in a state of shock and at the end of the day you express your feelings of fear, shock and concern about the people whose dear ones died in the blast. Write a diary entry in 100-120 words based on the visual given below and your own ideas. You are Janvi/Kapil. **(5)**

Or **Here is a story that is to be published in the school magazine. Unfortunately, it has been left unfinished. Complete the story by adding a few points of your own.**

"Pooja was coming out of her history class. She saw Ms. Mary, her English teacher, waiting in the corridor. Suddenly, two boys came running and pushed Ms. Mary ....".

Section–C (Literature)

(40 Marks)

Reference to the context. **(5 + 5 = 10)**

6. The Macdonalds lived next door. They had five children. Looking through a gap in the fence the little girl saw them playing 'tag' in the evening. The father with the baby, Mao, on his shoulders, two little girls hanging on his coat pockets ran around the flower-beds, shaking with laughter. Once she saw the boys turn the hose on him-and he tried to catch them laughing all the time. Then it was she decided there were different sorts of fathers. *(The Little Girl)* **(5)**

(i) What sort of difference the little girl noticed after watching Macdonalds with their children?

(ii) What is the purpose of the extract in the context of the entire story?

(iii) Choose the statements that are NOT TRUE according to the given extract.

1. Little girl was afraid of her father.

2. Little girl didn't want to stay with her father.

3. Little girl always admired her father for his good behaviour.

4. Little girl wanted her father to be like Macdonald's father.

5. Her Father was a fun-loving person.

6. Both father and daughter had a strong bond as they share everything.

(iv) Complete the analogy by selecting the suitable word from the text.

Stayed : Lived :: Hole : ....

Or

When Toto was finally accepted by grandmother he was given a comfortable home in the stable, where he had for a companion the family donkey, Nana. On Toto's first night in the stable, grandfather paid him a visit to see if he was comfortable. To his surprise he found Nana, without apparent cause, pulling at her halter and trying to keep her head as far as possible from a bundle of hay. *(The Adventure of Toto)*

(i) Choose the option that lists the set of statements that are NOT TRUE according to the given extract.

1. Toto was a mischievous pet.

2. Toto and Nana became friends.

3. Toto and Nana shared the same stable for a night.

4. Grandmother liked Toto's mischief.

5. Grandmother protected Toto in every incidence.

6. Toto was loved by every pet in the zoo.

(a) 1, 2 and 3 (b) 2, 4, 5 and 6 (c) 3, 4 and 6 (d) 2, 3 and 6

(ii) Why was Toto sent to the stable?

(iii) Fill in the blank with ONE WORD only.

Grandfather went to the stable at night to see if .... was comfortable there.

(iv) Why was Toto not accepted by the grandmother before?

7. "When the humid shadows hover
Over all the starry spheres
And the melancholy darkness
Gently weeps in rainy tears,
What a bliss to press the pillow
Of a cottage-chamber bed
And lie listening to the patter of the soft rain overhead." *(Rain on the Roof)* **(5)**

(i) Identify the dominant tone present in the lines and explain how you came to the conclusion.

(ii) Complete the sentence appropriately.

The word 'starry' in the extract describes ....

(iii) How is the poet feeling in the given extract?

1. Happy 2. Pitiful 3. Desperate 4. Excited 5. Sad

Select the appropriate option.

(a) 1 and 4 (b) 2 and 3 (c) 2 and 5 (d) Only 5

(v) Which figure of speech has been used to describe the rain in the given extract?

Or

It takes much time to kill a tree,
Not a simple jab of the knife
Will do it. It has grown
slowly consuming the earth
Rising out of it, feeding
Upon its crust, absorbing
Years of sunlight, air, water,
And out if its leprous hide
Sprouting leaves.

(On Killing a Tree)

(i) Complete the sentence appropriately.

The poet is taking the tree to be symbolic of ....

(ii) State whether the following statement is TRUE or FALSE.

'hide' in the extract refers to the bark of the tree.

(iii) The tone used by the poet in the given lines is

(a) amusing (b) regretful (c) nostalgic (d) sarcastic

(iv) The poet says 'It has grown slowly consuming the Earth' to indicate what?

8. Answer ANY FOUR of the following questions in 40-50 words each. **$(3 \times 4 = 12)$**

(i) What is the meaning of Santosh's name? Was she according to her name? (Reach for the Top)

(ii) Mention some of the achievements of Evelyn Glennie. (The Sound of Music)

(iii) Give the reason why the doctor uttered the following words "Death lurked four inches away". (The Snake and The Mirror)

(iv) What did the narrator hope that he would do one day? Was he sure? (The Road Not Taken)

(v) What is the significance of 'strong fires' near the end of the poem? (Wind)

9. Answer ANY TWO of the following questions in 40-50 words each. **$(3 \times 2 = 6)$**

(i) What used to happen when Grandfather gave Toto a large bowl of warm water in winter evenings? (The Adventure of Toto)

(ii) How do we know that Lushkoff had no previous experience of cutting wood? (The Beggar)

(iii) Why did the Guru want that he and his disciple should die first? (In the Kingdom of Fools)

10. Answer ANY ONE of the following questions in 100-120 words. **(6)**

In what ways was Albert Einstein an unusual child. How was he different from others in many ways? Do you think that those who think differently succeed in their lives like Einstein? Comment. (A Truly Beautiful Mind)

Or

How does Yeats create the atmosphere of the island and its sights and sounds in 'The Lake Isle of Innisfree'? Refer closely to the use of language in the first two stanzas.

11. Answer ANY ONE of the following questions in 100-120 words. **(6)**

Kindness is an agent of change. Discuss with reference to 'The Beggar' and 'The Last Leaf'.

Or

What are the two most precious things that the Angels find in the city? Why according to you are they precious? (The Happy Prince)

Sample Question Paper 5 (Unsolved)

A Highly Simulated Sample Question Paper for CBSE Class IX

English Language and Literature

Time : 3 hrs	M.M. : 80

General Instructions

1. This question paper is divided into three sections.
2. All questions are compulsory.
3. Separate instructions are given with each section and question, wherever necessary. Read these instructions very carefully and follow them.
4. Do not exceed the prescribed word limit while answering the questions.

Section–A (Reading Skills) (20 Marks)

1. Read the passage given below carefully. **(10)**

1. Evolution is a word that is often on our lips. We speak of the evolution of the railway engine, the evolution of the aeroplane, and even of the evolution of man's character. What we mean is that since they were invented, the railway engine and the aeroplane have changed a great deal. They have changed their shape and size, they have become faster and more powerful, and so on. In the same way, as a man grows older his character may change. Ill health may make him bad-tempered, poverty may turn him into a miser, too much success may lead him to be careless and boastful, and so we say that with the passing year his character has evolved from one kind to another. This idea of evolution is an old one but it was Darwin who first showed beyond doubt that it was the way in which species of living things change. As the centuries went by, he taught species of animals and plants change very slowly. During thousands of years, the horse has evolved from a small, clumsy and hairy animal to the splendid animal that we know. Every species of living creatures has changed and is changing. Some species, such as the pre-historic sabre-toothed tiger, have died but some are slowly dying out, and sometimes new species appear. The dog is a species which man has caused to evolve from the wolf.
2. How do some species survive and how do others become extinct? How have species changed? These were the other questions that Darwin had set himself to answer. The answer he gave us was that in the world of nature there is ceaseless struggle for life. One wild animal preys on another, and all living things compete for food, water and shelter. It is the strongest, fastest and hardiest creature or plant that survives. The weak perish. Species which are able to conquer their rivals and fit or adapt themselves to the climate and the country in which they live, outlive those which are weaker and less adaptable. For example, the giraffe with the longest neck could get more food than the shorter necked ones, and so the latter disappeared from the Earth.
3. Darwin planned to write a book describing his discoveries. He spent nearly 20 years collecting the matter for this book, which was to deal with every known fact concerning the problem of the species. Unluckily for Darwin, a naturalist named Wallace had been thinking over the same problems and had reached the same solution. He sent Darwin an essay which almost word for word repeated Darwin's own ideas. Yet Wallace, who was an explorer, had been working far away in the Malay Archipelago, whilst Darwin had not left England for several years. The two naturalists decided not to quarrel for the first place and their discovery was published under both their names. Afterwards, Wallace yielded the leadership to Darwin, in whom he recognised a greater naturalist than himself. In 1859, Darwin published the book he had planned for so many years. It was called 'The Origin of the Species'.

On the basis of your reading of the passage, answer any ten of the following questions.

(i) Based on your reading of the text, list the reason why Wallace surrendered the leadership of the theory to Darwin. (1)

(ii) Complete the sentence appropriately.

According to the given passage, evolution is .... (1)

(iii) Which characteristics are not apt about the naturalists as per the given passage? (2)

(iv) Select the option that displays what the writer projects, with reference to the following. (1)

In the natural world, there is an endless struggle for survival.

(a) Conviction (b) Caution (c) Denial (d) Doubt

(v) What connect does the writer draw out between 'struggle' and 'survival'? (1)

(vi) Choose the option that incorrectly states the meanings of 'ceaseless', as used in the passage. (1)

1. Constant 2. Brief 3. Dogged
4. Endless 5. Alternate 6. Eternal

(a) 1, 2 and 3 (b) 4, 5 and 6 (c) 2, 3 and 5 (d) 1, 4 and 6

(vii) Supply examples to justify the following. (2)

Every species of living creature has changed or is changing.

(viii) Which of the following is True according to the passage? (1)

(a) Because of evolution, our ecosystem is imbalanced. (b) Because of evolution many species are extinct.
(c) Evolution results in changes of fortune. (d) Because of evolution, no man is stable.

2. Read the passage given below carefully. (10)

A new survey by the Ministry of Health has found distressingly high levels of malnutrition among Indian children and adolescents. Only 6.4% of children surveyed under the age of 2 had received a minimum acceptable diet. One in five children between the ages of 5 and 9 was stunted, which means that they were at a low height for their age. One in four adolescents between the ages of 10 and 19 was thin for their age.

Conducted between 2016 and 2018, the Comprehensive National Nutrition Survey collected data on the nutritional status of a representative sample of 1.1 lakh children and adolescents from the ages of 0 to 19 years from 29 states and Delhi.

The study measures the nutritional status of children in three age groups: 0-4, 5-9 and 10-19 using different techniques. For children under 2 years of age, the parameter measured was 'minimum acceptable diet', a WHO standard that is a composite of two indicators: Dietary diversity or whether the child ate foods from four of seven food groups in the past day and Meal frequency or how often the child was fed in a day. While for adolescents, Body Mass Index was used.

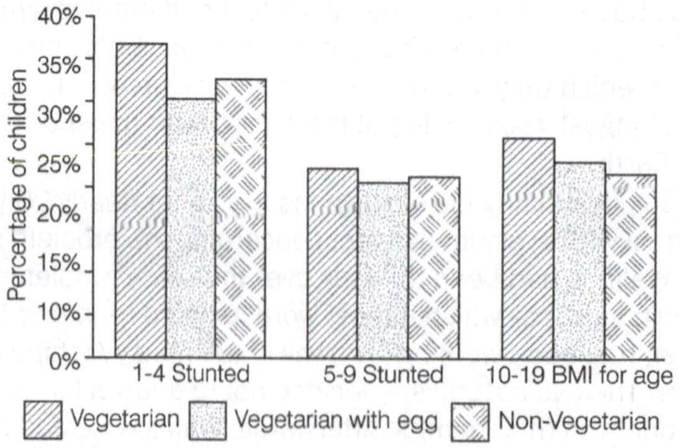

Correlating both sets of data, it found better nutritional outcomes among those consuming non-vegetarian diets. More significantly, there is a strong correlation between the consumption of eggs and better nutritional status in most states, particularly among younger children.

These findings are significant in light of the debate over whether eggs should be served in lunches in government schools and *anganwadis*. Several studies have shown consumption of eggs turns children healthier. Children whose mothers were vegetarian were more likely to be stunted than children whose mothers consumed eggs or meat, in all three age groups.

It must be noted, however, that there are several other factors at play in determining rates of stunting, including the child's area or residence, sanitation practices, the mother's education, and the wealth of the child's family. Taken together, malnutrition appears highly correlated with lack of consumption of eggs and meat across age groups. There are several anomalies, as would be expected, given that this is state-level data and nutrition and dietary habits vary from district to district, these merit closer study.

Answer the following questions on the basis of the passage you have read.

(i) Based on your understanding of the passage, choose the option that lists the factors that affect stunting. **(1)**

1. Diet	**2. Sanitation**	**3. Residence**
4. Education	**5. Financial status**	**6. Meal frequency**

(a) 1 and 2 (b) 3 and 6 (c) 4 and 5 (d) All of these

(ii) Select the option that is true for the Assertion (A) and Reason (R) given below. **(1)**

Assertion (A) The condition of malnutrition has not improved in the country.

Reason (R) The BMI of the children surveyed was found to be appropriate.

(a) Both the (A) and (R) are true, and (R) is the correct explanation of (A).
(b) Both the (A) and (R) are true, but (R) is not the correct explanation of (A).
(c) (A) is true, but (R) is false.
(d) (A) is false, but (R) is true.

(iii) How can we define Dietary diversity? **(2)**

(iv) According to the passage, what are the anomalies of the study? **(1)**

(v) What is the most effective conclusion of the passage? **(1)**

(vi) Fill in the blanks appropriately. **(1)**

From Paragraph 5, we can infer that the consumption of .... makes children ....

(vii) Complete the sentence appropriately. **(1)**

.... showed better nutritional outcomes.

(viii) What does the given passage highlight? **(2)**

Section–B (Grammar) (10 Marks)

3. Attempt ANY TEN of the following questions.

(i) Is it true that the students from NASA .... this afternoon? **(1)**

(a) was arriving (b) are arriving (c) is arriving (d) were arriving

(ii) Identify the error in the given sentence and provide the correction. **(1)**

At least half an hour of exercise a day did wonders to one's health.

Use the given format for your response.

Error	Correction

(iii) Report the given sentence. **(1)**

My friend said to Divya, "Have you ever been to Mumbai?"

(iv) Fill in the blank by using the correct form of the word in the bracket for the given portion of the letter. **(1)**

Subject : Job Application for Assistant Manager

Sir/Ma'am

I write to apply for the position of Assistant Manager - Supply Chain at your esteemed firm.

I .... (possess) the requisite qualification and find myself suitable for the post.

(v) The teacher asked some question from the boys about the assignment. Report the teacher's question. **(1)**

The teacher said to the boys, "Have you done your homework?"

(vi) Select the option that identifies the error and supplies the correction for the following line. **(1)**

The receptionist gave us much of the informations we needed.

Options	Error	Correction
(a)	gave	give
(b)	of	to
(c)	informations	information
(d)	needed	need

(vii) .... of the peach trees in their garden bear fruit twice a year. **(1)**

(a) A little (b) Much (c) More (d) Some

(viii) Identify the error in an online advertisement. **(1)**

Apex Classes Chander Nagar, Lucknow

Education is not only learning facts but train the mind to think.

Use the given format for your response.

Error	Correction

(ix) Report the following sentence said by Garima. **(1)**

Garima said, "I am sorry but I am not making a new file for you."

Garima told me that she was sorry but she ....

(x) Complete the given narrative by filling in the blank with the correct option. **(1)**

They .... in an old house right now because they can't find a decent house.

(a) have been living (b) are living (c) had been living (d) were living

(xi) Fill in the blanks by choosing the correct option to complete the given statement. **(1)**

He went there so that he .... lead the team.

(a) may (b) can (c) might (d) should

(xii) Select the correct option to complete the narration of the dialogue. **(1)**

Kanak I saw Jyoti in the market.

Karan What was she doing there? Isn't she ill?

Kanak told Karan that she saw Jyoti in the market. Shocked Karan asked her ....

Section-B (Writing Skills)

(10 Marks)

4. Write a descriptive paragraph in 100-120 words based on the visual clue given below. (5)

Or

After giving your Class X board exams, you are in a dilemma regarding which stream to choose in Class XI. Write a descriptive paragraph based on it in about 100-120 words.

5. You visited a hill station in your summer vacations. Write a diary entry in about 100-120 words describing the place you visited using the given clues and your own ideas. (5)

• Place Visited	• Weather	• Tourist Place
• Food	• Culture	• Your Experience

Or

Complete the story in 100-120 words which begins as follows.

When Karan reached near his house from the school, he saw a crowd gathered there. Shocked ....

Section-C (Literature)

(40 Marks)

Reference to the context. (5 + 5 = 10)

6. Within 12 months, Santosh found herself a member of an Indo-Nepalese Women's Expedition that invited her to join them. She then scaled the Everest a second time, thus setting a record as the only woman to have scaled the Everest twice, and securing for herself and India a unique place in the annals of mountaineering. *(Reach for the Top)* **(5)**

(i) Choose the option that lists the set of statements that are NOT TRUE according to the given extract.

1. Santosh was a member of an Indo-Nepalese Women's Expedition.

2. Santosh's parents were affluent landowners.

3. Santosh's parents wanted her to become a sportsperson since her childhood.

4. Santosh was always supported by her family to pursue her studies.

5. Santosh was never pressurised for early marriage.

6. Santosh was honoured with the Padmashri by the Government of India.

Comment on the tone of the extract and how it impacts us.

(a) 1, 2 and 3 (b) 3, 4 and 5 (c) 4, 5 and 6 (d) 1, 5 and 6

(ii) Why was the second expedition to Mt. Everest crucial for Santosh Yadav?

(iii) Fill in the blank with ONE WORD only.

Santosh Yadav scaled Mt. Everest for the .... time in the year 1992.

Comment on the tone of the extract and how it impacts us.

Or The two men were hungry. Now that the shops were open, they went to buy some groceries. To their astonishment, they found that everything cost the same, a single duddu- whether they bought a measure of rice or bunch of bananas, it cost a duddu. The guru and his disciple were delighted. They had never heard of anything like this. They could buy all the food they wanted for a rupee.

(In the Kingdom of Fools)

(i) Choose the statements that are NOT TRUE according to the given extract.

1. The Guru and his disciple were hungry.

2. The Guru and his disciple found the Kingdom strange.

3. The disciple wanted to leave the kingdom.

4. The Guru had recognised the Kingdom of Fools.

5. The Guru wanted to have A cheap food and decided to settle in the Kingdom itself.

6. The King and the Minister of the Kingdom were wise people.

(ii) The given information is bound to humour the reader. Do you agree?

(iii) Complete the analogy by selecting the suitable word from the extract.

Close : Open : : Sad : ....

(iv) 'They had never heard of anything like this.' What does this tell you about the place they were at?

7. And both that morning equally lay
In leaves, no step had trodden black.
Oh, I kept the first for another day!
Yet knowing how way leads on to way,
I doubted if I should ever come back.

(The Road Not Taken) **(5)**

(i) The poetic device used in the third line of the extract is ....

(ii) What did the poet choose?

(iii) What does "no step had trodden black" indicate?

(iv) What is the rhyme scheme of the given extract?

(a) aabbc (b) abaab (c) abcab (d) ababcc

Or

The wind god winnows and crushes them all.
He won't do what you tell him.
So, come, let's build strong homes,
Let's joint the doors firmly,
Practice to firm the body.
Make the heart steadfast.
Do this, and the wind will be friends with us.

(Wind)

(i) What do you understand by the term 'winnow' in context of the above extract?

(ii) The poetic device used in the second line of the extract is

(a) hyperbole (b) personification (c) simile (d) apostrophe

(iii) Complete the analogy about the 'heart' mentioned in the extract.

Body : Firm : : Heart : ....

(iv) What does the wind poke fun at?

8. Answer ANY FOUR of the following questions in 40-50 words each. **(3 × 4 = 12)**

(i) Why was the performance of Margie deteriorating day by day? (The Fun They Had)

(ii) How was Bismillah a perfect example of India's Cultural Heritage? (The Sound of Music)

(iii) What did Kezia make as a birthday gift for her father? How did she prepare it? (The Little Girl)

(iv) How can the tree get back to its former size? (On Killing a Tree)

(v) What is the central idea of the poem 'Wind'?

9. Answer ANY TWO of the following questions in 40-50 words each. **(3 × 2 = 6)**

(i) Why did the swallow cry when the Happy Prince asked him to pluck out one of the sapphires? (The Happy Prince)

(ii) Describe the character of Olga in 'The Beggar'.

(iii) How did Iswaran manage to make even the simplest incident interesting? Give an example. (Ishwaran the Storyteller)

10. Answer ANY ONE of the following questions in 100-120 words. **(6)**

Presence of mind and patience are the two values that help a person at the time of adversity and danger. How did these two attributes of Gerrard help him get rid of the Intruder? (If I Were You)

Or

Strong determination, motivation and right direction helped Bismillah Khan in being what he was. Do you agree? How important are these characteristic traits in our lives? (The Sound of Music)

11. Answer ANY ONE of the following questions in 100-120 words. **(6)**

The Swallow in the story 'The Happy Prince' played a crucial role in making the Prince happy. What traits does the bird possess which makes it fulfil its tasks?

Or

Do you really find a house different from a home. Explain with reference to 'A House is Not a Home'.